The Making of the British Isles

The Library at Queen's
College Park
Queen's University Belfast
www.qub.ac.uk/lib
tel: 028 9097 6135
email: library@qub.ac.uk

7 NIGHT

Loan period
One full week

Fine rate: 50p per day

For due dates, renewals,
charges, loans and reservations
see *My Account*

BRITISH ISLES SERIES

The Making of the United Kingdom
1660–1800
Jim Smyth

THE MAKING OF THE BRITISH ISLES

The State of Britain and Ireland, 1450–1660

Steven G. Ellis
with Christopher Maginn

Harlow, England • London • New York • Boston • San Francisco • Toronto
Sydney • Tokyo • Singapore • Hong Kong • Seoul • Taipei • New Delhi
Cape Town • Madrid • Mexico City • Amsterdam • Munich • Paris • Milan

PEARSON EDUCATION LIMITED

Edinburgh Gate
Harlow CM20 2JE
United Kingdom
Tel: +44 (0)1279 623623
Fax: +44 (0)1279 431059
Website: www.pearsoned.co.uk

_____

First published in Great Britain in 2007

© Pearson Education Limited 2007

The right of Steven G. Ellis to be identiÞed as author
of this work has been asserted by him in accordance
with the Copyright, Designs and Patents Act 1988.

ISBN: 978-0-582-04003-8

British Library Cataloguing in Publication Data
A CIP catalogue record for this book can be obtained from the British Library

10   9   8   7   6   5   4   3   2   1
11   10   09   08   07

Set in 11/13.5pt Columbus by 35
Printed and bound in Malaysia (CTP-VVP)

The PublisherÕs policy is to use paper manufactured from sustainable forests.

CONTENTS

SERIES EDITOR'S PREFACE (2001)

The last few years have witnessed an explosion of interest in what is now generally known as 'the New British history'. By this is meant a holistic approach to the history of the British Isles, in which the familiar story of the rise of an English, later British, nation is replaced by a more comparative account focusing on interaction between the archipelago's different peoples, countries and cultures, particularly in the context of state formation. If we look for the reasons behind this change of emphasis, they apparently have most to do with very modern developments, reflecting changed political circumstances. In particular, the recent readjustments in internal relations between the constituent parts of the British Isles and also parallel changes in relations with continental Europe have reminded both historians and the general public of different, less familiar aspects of their past. Most obviously, Britain's retreat from empire in the two decades after World War II inaugurated a period of introspection and a reconsideration of traditional imperial perspectives in which the United Kingdom appeared as the civilising centre of a large and successful empire. Where previously there had been a remarkably unanimous belief in the homogeneity of the British political system, following the collapse of the imperial mission, the 'home nations' began to rediscover their differences. Thus, the last thirty years have seen a marked growth of separatist parties, the Scottish National Party and Plaid Cymru, and most recently the establishment of Scottish and Welsh assemblies. In the case of Ireland, separatism has had a rather longer history, but the Northern troubles since 1969 and the chequered history of the Stormont regime also underline the recent tensions in the union. And alongside this partial reversal of earlier centralising initiatives within the archipelago, the period has also witnessed successive moves at European level in the direction of integration into an embryonic, quasifederal superstate, the European Union, with a consequent loss of national sovereignty.

There have of course been earlier attempts to look at particular aspects of British history from this kind of state-centred, archipelagic perspective. For instance, the origins of the various unions (1536, 1707, 1801) which marked the development of the modern British state have long attracted the historian's attention, and more recently the implications of an archipelagic approach have been discussed in essays of a more theoretical, historiographical bent. Yet only in the past decade has the New British history attracted the kind of attention associated with a major departure in history writing. In essence, this has involved a distinct shift in focus from nation-building to state formation as an interpretative principle of British historiography. It is reflected both in the growing number of scholars writing from this perspective and also in the increased numbers of historical conferences given over to discussion of the subject. Among members of the general public and in the media, moreover, suggestions that modern nations are themselves a product of state formation have recently sparked a debate about other fundamental questions like the characteristics of Englishness or Britishness, and the differences between them – matters that had previously been considered so self-evident as to occasion scarcely any debate.

Recent indications of instability in the modern British state have perhaps served as a reminder about its composite, multinational character and the problematic nature of British identity; but until very recently the historiography of the British Isles had in practice remained resolutely nation-based in character. Following Leopold von Ranke in the nineteenth century, historans were long content to chart the origins of the modern nations within the archipelago, dividing the British Isles into separate national territories, England, Ireland, Scotland and Wales. Thus, for instance, English history charted the growth of the modern English nation, in England, ignoring for the most part those English communities established in medieval Ireland or Wales which – above all because they were not destined to remain English – were the preserve of Irish or Welsh historians. Similarly, Scottish historians focused on those *Gaedhil* and *Gaill* living in Scotland, as Scots in the making, but the similar process of interaction between those *Gaedhil* and *Gaill* living in the Gaelic parts of Ireland and the Englishries there supplied a quite separate story of national development told by Irish historians. Paradoxically, only when the union in its post-1920 form seemed in danger of collapse did British historians begin seriously to address the question of how it had been established and how it actually operated in the first place.

Perhaps a more deep-seated reason for the emergence of the New British history has to do with the phenomenon known as Revisionism. Revisionism first emerged in the 1970s, at a time when debates about the concepts of modernity and modernisation in the scientific community were beginning to influence the writing of history. As faith was eroded in such ideas as scientific progress, social and technological development, and civilisation by education, so the notion of history as grand narrative was increasingly challenged. Revisionism marked a reaction to what has been described as 'present-centred' history and a refocusing of the historical agenda on contemporary problems and concerns – history 'as it actually was', so Leopold von Ranke most famously described it. Von Ranke, however, was ultimately responsible for another extremely tenacious assumption of which revisionism was critical, the idea of the rise of the nation and the growth of the nation-state. This idea reflected his belief that nations were the divinely appointed unit at work in history and that each nation had its own appointed moment of destiny. Thus the initial impact of revisionism was to challenge traditional perspectives on the rise of four modern nations in the archipelago.

In this context, the crucial revisions were to English history, since England was the dominant and historically best-documented of the four nations. In particular, English revisionism sought to challenge the grand narrative known as Whig history, viz. an interpretation of the English past which served to validate a set of present-day political beliefs and goals, notably a belief in England's natural progress towards liberty and prosperity, together with the assumption that English history was quite unique, its main patterns of development owing nothing to outside influences. Contemporary developments, particularly Britain's membership of the European Union and EU initiatives towards closer economic and political integration, have also seemed to undermine this English grand narrative, transposing England from its dominant position in the British Isles to the periphery of an expanding Europe. Moreover, the revisionist shift from vertical to horizontal presentations of history has meant that critiques of exceptionalism (and a renewed interest in comparative history) have also been a feature of revisionist-style writings in the other national historical accounts. Yet English revisionism was also critical of the formerly dominant social interpretaion of the English Civil War as a proto-modern event, one of the bourgeois revolutions that, by overthrowing feudalism and advancing socialism, ushered in the modern world. Again, events in eastern Europe since the mid-1980s have likewise seemed to discredit these Marxist perspectives.

For all these reasons, traditional nation-centred perspectives on the British past have no longer seemed quite so convincing in recent years. Yet the step from nation-based history to an alternative view based on New British perspectives was by no means obvious. Once again, European developments have been influential in pointing the way. Partly this reflects the decline of the nation-state, at least in western Europe, even though in eastern Europe the disintegration of the Soviet Union and Yugoslavia have seemed to reverse this trend. Perhaps more important historiographically, however, has been the influence of continental European historians, particularly given the renewed interest in comparative history which followed the revisionist emphasis on problems and perspectives as they appeared to contemporaries. Although, allegedly, the nation achieved modernity in the nation-state, the typical political entity of the pre-modern period was in fact the composite monarchy, viz. monarchies ruling territories with more than one people and culture, and originally distinct kingdoms and principalities with a common king. In other European historiographies a state-centred approach had in practice long been common currency, despite the continued preoccupation here with nations rising. For instance, the work of British-based continental specialists on European composite states and multiple monarchies offered convenient models with which the Anglo-Norman empire or the Tudor–Stuart kingdoms might be compared. The problems surrounding the Habsburg monarchy, Denmark–Norway, or the Polish–Lithuanian commonwealth might not exactly match the British kingdoms, but they underlined the point that pre-modern states were frequently composite and multinational. Thus, for instance, once revisionism had undermined social-change explanations of the English Civil War, a European-style three-kingdom approach supplied an obvious alternative, and in point of fact royal authority did collapse first in the Scottish and Irish kingdoms of the British multiple monarchy. Moreover, English revisionists soon discovered that, besides offering a new perspective on the Civil War, analyses of the British kingdoms as a multiple monarchy had other applications, notably in terms of charting both the origins of empire and also of the modern British state.

The discovery of the New British history thus promised a quite radical revision of the historical agenda, particularly in terms of periodisation, which is only now being gradually worked out. For instance, in a British context, 1066 was chiefly important because it inaugurated a period of expansion which saw the transformation of the Anglo-Saxon kingdom over the following 250 years into a multinational entity covering large parts of Ireland, Scotland and Wales and in which the English kingdom was also closely linked to French territories, latterly as a dual monarchy. In this context, too, the collapse of the Anglo-French dual monarchy (1449–53) seems more of a watershed than the advent of the Tudor dynasty in 1485. The Anglo-Scottish diplomatic realignments of 1558–60 created for the first time a British state system: even though 1603 remains important, this was more for the Anglo-Scottish dynastic union heralded by these realignments, together with the completion of the Tudor conquest of Ireland, than for the replacement of a Tudor by a Stuart on the English throne. Similarly, the high points in the Stuart century were not so much the successive political crises between king and parliament as the various union projects and proposals that prefigured 1707, notably the 1652 Cromwellian union. And in the last century, earlier moves towards the consolidation of a multinational British state have seemed to unravel, first in Ireland and more recently in other Celtic countries. In short, grand narrative has reappeared after a decent interval, but this time the organising principle is state formation rather than nation building. Admittedly, in some respects the New British history appears to mark a retreat from postmodernism, but more by way of highlighting inconvenient facts about the present (partition in Ireland, for instance, and the problematic character of the present United Kingdom of Great Britain and Northern Ireland – to give it its full, but revealingly awkward title) than as a simple reinstatement of modernisation theories. Particularly for the early modern period, the focus on interaction between four nations and three kingdoms also includes a strong, characteristically revisionist, comparative dimension. In any event, the new synthesis does, at least, have the merit of explaining how people in Ireland, Scotland and Wales also happen to be part of the modern British state.

The *Longman History of the British Isles* is a series of volumes written by leading British historians, which has been devised with this new perspective in mind. The series will offer a substantial grounding in the subject, an overall interpretation of the period covered, and an assessment of the latest historiographical developments. Yet, beyond the requirement that each volume should offer an expose of the period's main developments in a transnational, archipelagic context, no attempt has been made to impose a 'house style'. The New British History has an obvious political dimension to it, and we are so far at present from achieving a consensus among historians about its strengths and weaknesses that even key terms like 'the British Isles' are contested. Broadly, the aim has been to offer an interpretative survey focusing on those areas in which the new approach provides a more obvious departure from traditional histories, rather than to provide a comprehensive account intended to supplant the national histories. Each volume, however, develops its own range of topics as determined by the author.

PREFACE

I have struggled with this book for longer than I care to remember. The initial stimulus for writing it came from teaching an undergraduate survey course on British history in Galway in 1987 and then an invitation from Brendan Bradshaw and John Morrill to contribute guest lectures to a similar course they were teaching when I was on leave in Cambridge in 1988. These early initiatives led to a conference on what came to be called 'the New British history', and a volume of essays; but by then I was more conscious of the difficulties involved in trying to write British history. I tried instead to write a history of the early Tudor state as seen from the peripheries, and I also became more aware of the potential for British history of some of the big collaborative projects on European state formation which were undertaken in the 1990s.

The need for the kind of British history explored here is, I think, clear enough. The modern British state is not simply England writ large: to understand the untidy processes by which particular territories have been added to or subtracted from what became the British monarchy requires a broader canvass extending well beyond the state's core territory. Besides asking how successive monarchs were able to consolidate their authority over countries and peoples outside Lowland England, we also need to look at those attempts which ended in failure. British government was ultimately unsuccessful in the west of Ireland, for instance, but Galway's political ties with London stretched over some seven centuries. And even within the narrower compass of 'English history', it is surely legitimate to include the history of those English communities in France, Ireland, or Wales which were not destined to remain English. Similarly, events in Tudor Ireland are also part of the story of the Tudor state: it is hard to imagine that Tudor monarchs and their officials would have been satisfied with historical accounts which abstract Irish developments from the genesis and implementation of Tudor policy more generally and discuss them only in terms of the making of an Irish nation-state. Readers well versed in the history of England may thus find somewhat surprising the book's structure and content – more on state formation, less on nation building – particularly the short measure given to important aspects of its domestic history. My explanation is that there are many fine surveys of early modern England, written from various perspectives; and in recent years some of these perspectives have been adapted and extended to British history. What I was hoping to do in this survey, however, was to explore other, perhaps less familiar, perspectives; and hard choices had to be made if the book were to be kept to a manageable length.

A major problem in the writing of British history is the uneven nature of the sources. The records are, naturally, much more plentiful for the more intensely-governed parts of the Tudor state, in Lowland England; and to a lesser extent the same is true of the Stewart monarchy's core region of Lowland Scotland. The modern historiography of these regions is likewise much richer than for the so-called 'Celtic fringe'. In offering a survey of early modern British history there is thus a temptation to draw more heavily on the many fine studies of these intensively-governed regions on the assumption that what these detailed studies have revealed would have been replicated elsewhere if only the surviving documentation had been of the same quality. This assumption is unsafe, however. It is not just a question of accidents of survival. The character of the surviving documentation is also in part a measure of the government's success and efficiency. Over-reliance on the historiography and richer sources for these Lowland regions skews the perceived pattern of state formation in favour of those parts in which government was more successful. And as is argued below, the geography, patterns of landholding and social structures in these core territories were uniquely favourable to the untrammelled exercise of royal authority. So it is scarcely surprising that royal government should be more successful here.

The real test of government, however, was the monarch's ability to shape and influence developments elsewhere where conditions were less favourable – either because of geographical remoteness, unfavourable terrain, marcher conditions, or in some cases external challenges to royal authority. Both monarchies struggled to vindicate their authority in these more peripheral territories. They also faced the rather different problem in 1603 of how to reorganise channels of authority when traditional power structures were disrupted by one of the dynastic unions which were a typical product of the political diplomacy of early modern Europe, that which created the British multiple monarchy, or dynastic agglomerate.[1] At the start of the period, moreover, the basic character of the southern monarchy was also transformed by the loss of territories in France which had long been associated with English kings. Historians tend to write these failures out of the script, as if they were somehow inevitable, or even 'a good thing'. But this is not how English monarchs, or many of their subjects, saw things. We need to beware the conceptual trap of projecting modern attitudes and ideas about the composition of nations and the geography of their national territories back into the past and then painting a picture of triumphant progress towards the present. Even the book's subject area, the British Isles, is a product of the untidy pattern of success and failure which was the normal product of these early modern processes of state formation. By accident or design, it came to mark the normal geographical limits of what became the British monarchy's core territory for three centuries or so from 1603. As for the preceding 150 years, it can at least be said that this British context is no more anachronistic than traditional depictions of an autonomous English realm and nation-state still with approximately the same geographical boundaries as had existed in Anglo-Saxon times.

---

1   Cf. John Morrill, *'Uneasy lies the head that wears a crown': dynastic crises in Tudor and Stewart Britain 1504–1746* (Reading, 2005), p. 11.

The book's unorthodox structure and menu thus reflect my attempts to get beyond a version of British history which is essentially English history with Celtic bits tacked on. In my efforts to make British history interesting and 'relevant' for students, I have also learned much from their responses and reactions (conscious and unconscious). These have ranged from NUI Galway students – undergraduates who did my seminar or British surveys, postgraduates in my research seminar – to students from other universities (the many visiting American and continental European students who come to Galway each year), and also the students who took my courses during two – for me, highly stimulating – spells as visiting professor at Gießen and Potsdam in Germany. Intriguingly, their responses to problems of historiography, and issues of state formation and national identity have varied quite considerably, and this is itself revealing. Yet, without considerable external support, I should never have finished this book. My university generously gave me two periods of sabbatical leave, in 1993–4 (when I escaped to Cambridge) and again in 2002, during which I did much of the writing. Progress slowed again when I became head of department, but I was then extremely fortunate that my former student, Dr. Christopher Maginn, now Assistant Professor of History at Fordham University, was both willing and able to research and write the last three narrative chapters (1584–1603; 1603–37; 1637–60) for me – in between revising his doctorate for publication and starting at Fordham. I am very grateful to him for taking on this arduous task. He has had a free hand in this, with little input from me, but by a happy coincidence our styles of writing are, I think, quite similar. In the event, even Chris found that the writing dragged on, but we did at least spend two pleasant summers together discussing problems of British history and writing these chapters.

Steven G. Ellis

INTRODUCTION
The making of British history

The British Isles is the name most commonly given to a group of islands off the north-west coast of Europe. By 1603 the whole group was governed from London by a Scottish king, James VI and I, who united the three kingdoms of England and Wales, Scotland, and Ireland in a dynastic union. Over the next two centuries successive governments at Westminster attempted to integrate these three kingdoms and the four nations which inhabited them into a new, consolidated nation-state, Britain,[1] with a common sense of nationality as Britons. The distinctly-qualified success which attended these efforts is underlined by the rather awkward title applied to this developing British state, the United Kingdom of Great Britain and Ireland. Indeed the process has over the last century seemed to go into reverse, with the secession from the Union in 1922 of the Irish Free State, the rise in the 1970s of separatist political parties like the Scottish National Party and Plaid Cymru in Wales, and most recently the (re-)establishment of regional representative institutions, the Northern Ireland assembly, the Scottish parliament, and the Welsh assembly. At present, the only major population grouping which actively proclaims its British identity is the unionist community of Northern Ireland, the region which is least well integrated into the United Kingdom as presently constituted.

British history focused, traditionally, on the role of the United Kingdom in the administration of a large and successful empire. It also investigated the origins and growth of those institutions and values which distinguished the United Kingdom from continental Europe and which, allegedly, were later to establish Britain's pre-eminence on the world stage – freedom, civilisation and democracy. And from early modern times onwards, it treated of the dissemination of this British heritage among what were seen as the less fortunate peoples of the Empire. Thus traditional British history stressed the common traditions and civilisation of the peoples of the United Kingdom *vis-à-vis* Europe and the wider world. Even so, those institutions which were singled out by historians as epitomising British culture – parliament, the common law and the English

---

1   I take it that 'Britain', rather than 'the British Isles' would have been the preferred geographical term for the archipelago as the national territory, if this political process had enjoyed wider success. It is of course implied by the development of subcategories (which have had a chequered history) like 'Great Britain', 'North Britain' (for Scotland), 'the British mainland' (with reference to Northern Ireland), and 'West Briton' (now a term of abuse for an Irish person who apes British customs), as also by the earliest (Greek) usage which styled as British both the island of Albion and that of Ierna.

language – were usually ones which were more closely identified with England. And this in turn helps to explain the pronounced anglocentricity of traditional British history. What was then called 'British history' often amounted to little more than the history of England and of English interventions in Wales, Scotland and Ireland.

With the professionalisation of history as an academic discipline in the late nineteenth century, however, came a renewed stress on the emergence and growth of the nation as the proper focus and organising principle of historical study. To some extent, this development prompted a search for the supposed characteristics of a British national identity, especially in relation to continental Europe and the wider world. More often it led to a shift of focus, from the rise of the modern state, to the emergence of the modern nations which inhabit the British Isles, and in particular to the study of England as the dominant nation within the archipelago. At the time, there was much to be said for the study of national history, since the wider British perspective tended to deflect historical attention from vital differences between the separate nations and kingdoms of these islands. Indeed the value of a nation-based approach to the history of Ireland, Scotland and Wales was explicitly endorsed in many of the new universities established from the mid-nineteenth century onwards by the practice of studying 'the home nations' apart from other branches of history in a separate department of national history.[2] This was particularly necessary for Ireland, where the creation of two new states after 1920 imposed on historians the duty of investigating the origins of their separate existence. In the case of Northern Ireland, political developments were accommodated without too much difficulty, since those in charge of the new state stressed its continuity with a British past. The Irish Free State (officially renamed *Éire*, or Ireland, in 1937; and since 1948 commonly known as the Republic of Ireland) consciously rejected this British heritage, choosing instead to emphasize differences of culture, language, religion and national identity, although in practice it retained much in common with the United Kingdom.

Nation-centred approaches also had considerable shortcomings, however, for a number of reasons. Focus on the nation naturally tended to point up what was unique to each nation. But this tendency was artificially accentuated by the way in which the archipelago was divided up, for the purposes of teaching history at the universities, into separate sections or departments, each charged with courses in a particular national history. For the most part, these divisions reflected modern ideas of nationhood and modern national (*v.* state) boundaries. Thus English history focused on the English people inhabiting that part of Britain now called England which had been settled by the Anglo-Saxons before 1066, disregarding the Englishries which were established in Ireland and Wales under the Norman kings. Irish history, by contrast, treated of all those peoples who had inhabited the island of Ireland at different times – but most especially the *Gaedhil* (the native, Gaelic-speaking peoples) and those settlers of medieval English

---

2 A study of this process is much to be desired. Also relevant here is the comparatively recent date at which some of the academic journals which underpinned this development of national history first appeared – *English Historical Review* (1885), *Scottish Historical Review* (1903), *Irish Historical Studies* (1938), and *Welsh History Review* (1962).

descent – who collectively helped to shape the modern Irish nation; but it excluded the [x v i i]
indigenous Gaelic peoples who happened to live across the North Channel in what is
now Scotland. They, in turn, were the focus of a second 'grand narrative' of interaction
between *Gaedhil* and *Gaill* which supplied the story of Scotland; and a similar story of
interaction between native and settler constituted the history of Wales.[3]

Likewise, the research training of historians was geared to the source material relating
to a particular national territory, as presently defined, rather than to the archipelago as
a whole. Thus the evidence concerning the broad pattern of interaction between
Germanic and Celtic peoples and cultures, which is the essence of the British experience,
was divided up between four groups of historians, each familiar with that relating to the
home territory, but seldom equipped – in terms of linguistic competence, for instance –
to develop comparisons based on the primary sources relating to another national
territory. Finally, the concepts of the nation and of national territory developed by
nation-centred approaches were of little help in assessing either the origins of the modern state or the present relationship between nation and state in each territory.

There is, thus, clearly a need for a history of the British Isles which examines the relations between the different peoples of the archipelago and the process of state formation
which created the modern states there – what is now generally called 'the New British
history'. But this is much easier said than done: even the terminology is problematic.
The very concept of 'the British Isles', and of New British history, is rejected by some
Irish historians.[4] In part this reflects the different nuances of the term within the two
islands: in nationalist Ireland, 'British' is the antithesis of 'Irish', is frequently synonymous with 'English', and refers to the modern British state; whereas in Britain it is also
frequently used as an 'umbrella' term to describe the peoples of the British Isles collectively without respect to their nationality. There is, however, clearly a need for a term to
denote the modern mix of Celtic, Germanic and Romance cultures and peoples and the
Anglo-Norman administrative structures which are common to Britain and Ireland, and
in default of a convenient, neutral and readily recognisable alternative, the traditional
usage must be allowed to stand. Nonetheless, the very fact that no single word, analog-
ous to Japan or Indonesia, was coined to describe the group of islands dominated by
Britain and Ireland is itself significant: the very phrase 'the British Isles' also draws attention to an arrested process of state formation.

Particularly since the collapse of the Union of Soviet Socialist Republics, the United
Kingdom of Great Britain and Northern Ireland has enjoyed the unusual distinction of

---

3   S.G. Ellis, 'Writing Irish history: revisionism, colonialism, and the British Isles' in *The Irish Review*, xix (1996), pp. 3–6; idem, 'Tudor Northumberland: British history in an English county' in *Kingdoms United? Great Britain and Ireland since 1500: integration and diversity* (Dublin, 1999), pp. 29–30.

4   See, for instance, Nicholas Canny, 'The attempted anglicization of Ireland in the seventeenth century: an exemplar of "British history"' in R.G. Asch (ed.), *Three Nations – a common history? England, Scotland, Ireland and British history c.1600–1920* (Bochum, 1993), pp. 49–50; Hiram Morgan, 'Acknowledgements' in idem (ed.), *Political ideology in Ireland 1541–1641* (Dublin, 1999), p. 7.

being one of the very few modern states which actually refuses nationality in its official title.[5] It is, nonetheless, like many modern states, a multi-national one. For much of its history, successive governments of what was to become the United Kingdom have attempted, with only partial success, to integrate its constituent nations and territories into a collective British nation whose national territory was co-extensive with the British Isles. The high points in this process were the various 'unions' and 'united king-doms' which attempted to regulate relations between the different peoples of these islands. Among the more successful were the so-called Act of Union with Wales (1536), the Kingdom of Ireland (1541), and the Anglo-Scottish Act of Union (1707), all of which were important stages in the building of the modern states. By contrast, the respective terms of the Union of the Crowns of 1603, the Cromwellian Union of 1652–4, and the 1801 Act of Union with Ireland generated deep-seated hostility from powerful élite groups within the countries affected, and eventually had to be modified or abandoned.

British history, then, ought properly to refer to the whole process of state building in the archipelago. This wider perspective is important, if a more balanced assessment of the British experience of state formation, its strengths and weaknesses, is to be made. Admittedly, nation-centred approaches treat of aspects of this process, in particular the role of the state as an external force in the shaping of the nation. Yet since so many of its categories are present-centred, it is hardly surprising that much nationalist history reads like triumphant progress towards the present. In this respect, traditional anglocentric presentations of British history are particularly misleading: concentration on the domi-nant nation in the archipelago skews the perceived pattern of development in favour of the area in which the process was most successful, since the eventual terms of the Union reflected English sensibilities more than any other. The real pattern of state formation, however, was more of a continuum of success and failure, ranging from southern England, through northern England and Wales, to Scotland, Northern Ireland, and at the opposite extreme the present Republic of Ireland.

The apparent exception to this pattern, Ireland, does indeed prove the rule. Uniquely in the case of Ireland, the terms of all of the successive strategies to integrate the island into a wider British state and to regulate relations between the different peoples of the archipelago proved so unacceptable to powerful interest groups there as to lead eventually to the establishment of a separate state. This pattern of rejection is indeed very well described in traditional accounts of the making of modern Ireland.[6] Yet nationalist approaches are much less useful in explaining why Northern Ireland remained part of the United Kingdom and why, for all its political independence, the Irish Republic actually remains quite British in terms of its cultural, administrative and legal traditions. The British perspective neatly accounts for this paradox of modern Irish

---

5   Benedict Anderson, *Imagined communities: reflections on the origin and spread of nationalism* (2nd ed., London, 1991), p. 2.
6   For instance, T.W. Moody and F.X. Martin (eds), *The course of Irish history* (Dublin, 1967), or the earlier M. Hayden and G.A. Moonan, *A short history of the Irish people from the earliest times to 1920* (Dublin, 1921).

history. The Irish Republic is no less a product of the British process of state formation than is Wales: the actual instruments of British integration were broadly acceptable in Ireland, but the terms of Union were not.

The period covered by this volume witnessed both the gradual accumulation of power and authority into a single imperium which by 1603 covered the whole of the British Isles, and also the earliest phases of the attempt to integrate its disparate territories into a centralised British nation-state. The volume attempts to address some of the major questions which surround the New British history. To what extent did a British monarchy, aristocracy, institutions or culture develop in the sixteenth and seventeenth centuries? How far was the British experience of state formation a response to a perceived need to integrate the three kingdoms of England, Ireland and Scotland into an United Kingdom, and with what results? The agenda reflects my experiences of teaching undergraduate courses in British history and the complaints of students that the existing nation-centred historiography had comparatively little to say in regard to some aspects of the process of state formation in the Atlantic archipelago. The overall aim was to produce a survey which could be used by undergraduates in conjunction with the existing nationalist historiography and which would open up comparative themes and problems.

These remarks may help to clarify the differences between British history as a process of state formation and nationalist history as the making of the nation. Ideally, British history should complement nationalist history – the former focussing on common traditions and experiences and the process of state-building, the latter on the individual characteristics of the four nations of the British Isles. The growing popularity of British history, however, requires a different explanation. The last few years have seen an upsurge of interest in what one recent Irish *taoiseach* (prime minister) described as 'the totality of the relationships between the peoples of these islands'.[7] To some extent this may be a response to contemporary problems of European integration, exemplified by the recent difficulties over the Single European Act. Historiographically, it is manifested in such programmes as the European Science Foundation's collaborative project on 'The Origins of the Modern State in Europe, 13th–18th Centuries'.[8] A more important stimulus, however, is surely a growing popular awareness of political tensions within the modern British state. This reflects a new political agenda as, following the retreat from empire, public attention has shifted from the United Kingdom's role as a world power to a much more internalised perspective on relations between the British state's constituent parts. The revival of separatist sentiments in the 1970s indicates, at the least, a more critical attitude in some quarters to England's traditional dominance within the Union. Even more clearly, the instability of the Union in its present form is highlighted by the recent troubles in Northern Ireland, which have also drawn attention to the ambiguity of the United Kingdom's relationship with the Republic of Ireland. At the time of writing,

---

7   Martin Mansergh (ed.), *The Spirit of the Nation: the speeches and statements of Charles J. Haughey (1957–1986)* (Cork, 1986), p. 476, echoing the phraseology of an intergovernmental communique (cf. ibid., p. 406).

8   The proceedings of this programme appeared in seven volumes. The English version was published by Oxford University Press, 1997.

[x x] whether recent political trends in these islands, or in Europe more generally, will lead eventually to a Yugoslavian-style disintegration of the Union into smaller national units remains unclear. Even if it does, however, the distinctively British pattern of state formation which first emerged in the period covered by this volume will leave certainly its mark on the British successor states, as it continues to do on the Republic of Ireland.

ACKNOWLEDGEMENTS

We are grateful to the following for permission to reproduce copyright material:

Map 1 is adapted from: *The Wars of the Roses: military activity and English society, 1452–97*, Anthony Goodman, Copyright 1981, Routledge. Reproduced by permission of Taylor & Francis Books UK; Map 2 from *The Oxford illustrated history of Tudor and Stuart Britain* (OUP, 1996), (after S.G. Ellis and S. Barber (eds), *Conquest and Union: Fashioning a British state, 1485–1725* (Longman, 1995)) with permission from Pearson Education; Map 3 from John Morrill (ed.), *The Oxford illustrated history of Tudor and Stuart Britain* (OUP, 1996), (after S.G. Ellis and S. Barber (eds), *Conquest and Union: Fashioning a British state, 1485–1725* (Longman, 1995)) with permission from Pearson Education; Map 4 from S.G. Ellis and S. Barber (eds), *Conquest and Union: Fashioning a British state, 1485–1725* (Longman, 1995), (after S.G. Ellis, *Tudor Ireland: crown, community and the conflict of cultures 1470–1603* (Longman, 1985)) with permission from Pearson Education; Map 5 from S.G. Ellis and S. Barber (eds), *Conquest and Union: Fashioning a British state, 1485–1725* (Longman, 1995) (after A.G.R. Smith, *The emergence of a nation-state: the commonwealth of England 1529–1660* (Longman, 1984)) with permission from Pearson Education; Map 6 from John Kenyon with Jane Ohlmeyer (eds), *The Civil Wars: a military history of England, Scotland and Ireland, 1638–1660* (OUP, 1998) by permission of Oxford University Press; Map 7 from John Morrill (ed.), *The Oxford illustrated history of Tudor and Stuart Britain* (OUP, 1996) with permission from Oxford University Press; Map 8 from John Morrill (ed.), *The Oxford illustrated history of Tudor and Stuart Britain* (OUP, 1996) by permission of Oxford University Press; family tree illustration adapted from John Morrill (ed.), *The Oxford illustrated history of Tudor and Stuart Britain* (OUP, 1996) by permission of Oxford University Press.

In some instances we have been unable to trace the owners of copyright material, and we would appreciate any information that would enable us to do so.

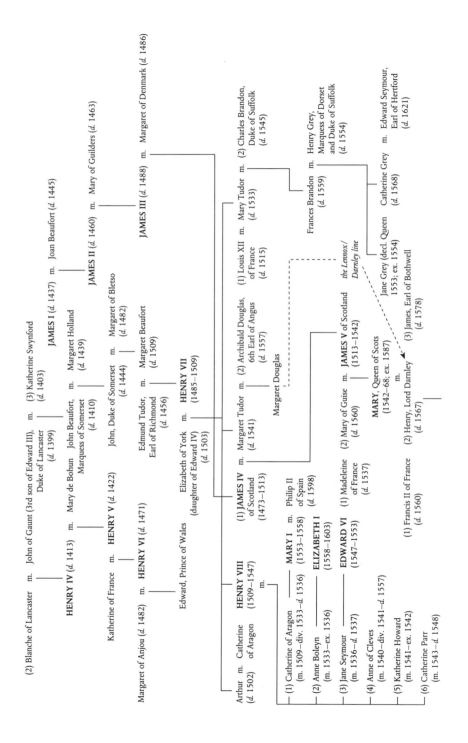

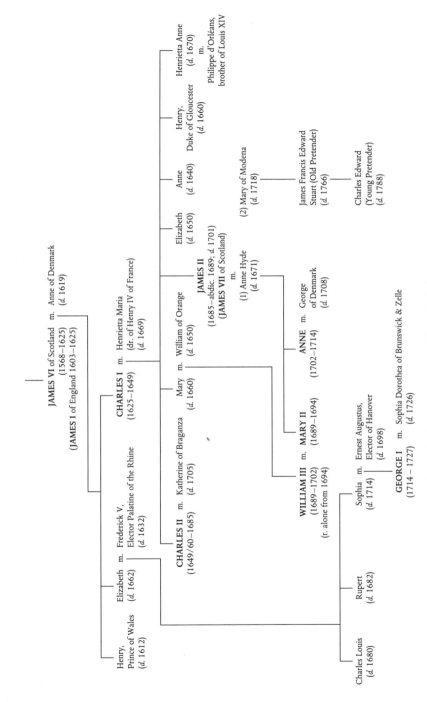

The Royal Houses of England (1422–1603), Scotland (1437–1603) and Great Britain (1603–1727)

Note: The Royal House of Scotland and its offshoots were almost always spelt 'Stewart' in the fifteenth and sixteenth centuries, and 'Stuart' (as an anglicising affectation) only after 1603.

JAMES VI of Scotland   m.   Anne of Denmark
(1568–1625)   (d. 1619)
(JAMES I of England 1603–1625)

Henry,   Elizabeth   m.   Frederick V,   CHARLES I   m.   Henrietta Maria
Prince of Wales (d. 1662)   Elector Palatine   (1625–1649)   (dr. of Henry IV of France)
(d. 1612)   of the Rhine   (d. 1669)
                                   (d. 1632)

Charles Louis   CHARLES II   m.   Katherine of Braganza   Mary   m.   William of Orange
(d. 1680)   (1649/60–1685)   (d. 1705)   (d. 1660)   (d. 1650)

Rupert   Sophia   m.   Ernest Augustus,
(d. 1682)   (d. 1714)   Elector of Hanover
                                                (d. 1698)

Elizabeth   Anne   Henry,   Henrietta Anne
(d. 1650)   (d. 1640)   Duke of Gloucester (d. 1670)
                                 (d. 1660)   m.
                                                     Philippe d'Orléans,
                                                     brother of Louis XIV

JAMES II
(1685–abdic. 1689; d. 1701)
(JAMES VII of Scotland)
m.
(1) Anne Hyde   (2) Mary of Modena
    (d. 1671)   (d. 1718)

ANNE   m.   George
(1702–1714) of Denmark
             (d. 1708)

WILLIAM III   m.   MARY II
(1689–1702)   (1689–1694)
(r. alone from 1694)

GEORGE I   m.   Sophia Dorothea of Brunswick & Zelle
(1714–1727)   (d. 1726)

James Francis Edward
Stuart (Old Pretender)
(d. 1766)

Charles Edward
(Young Pretender)
(d. 1788)

MAPS

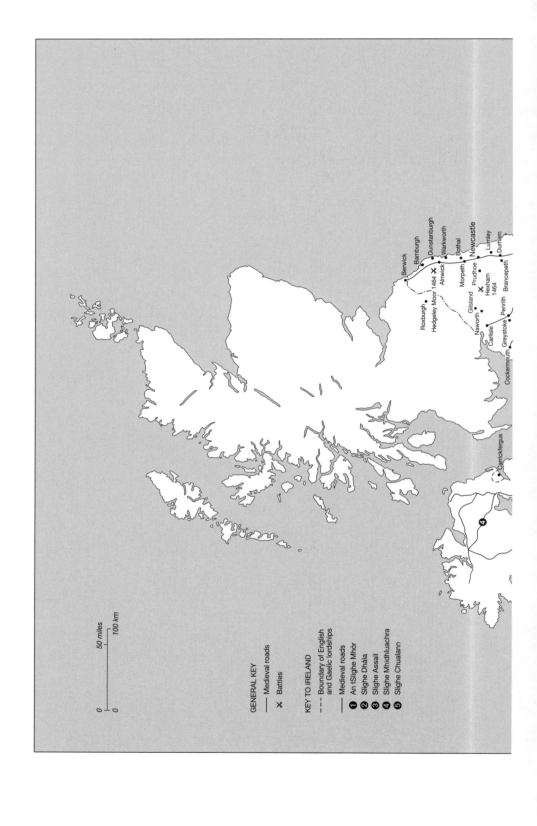

GENERAL KEY

—— Medieval roads

✗ Battles

KEY TO IRELAND

– – Boundary of English
and Gaelic lordships

—— Medieval roads

❶ An tSlighe Mhór
❷ Slighe Dhála
❸ Slighe Assail
❹ Slighe Mhidhluachra
❺ Slighe Chualann

0 ____ 50 miles
0 ____ 100 km

Berwick

Roxburgh

Bamburgh
Dunstanburgh
Hedgeley Moor 1464 ✗
Warkworth
Alnwick
Bothal
Morpeth
Newcastle
Prudhoe
Lumley
Durham
Gilsland
Hexham 1464 ✗
Branceporth
Naworth
Penrith
Brancepeth
Carlisle
Greystoke
Cockermouth

Carrickfergus

❹

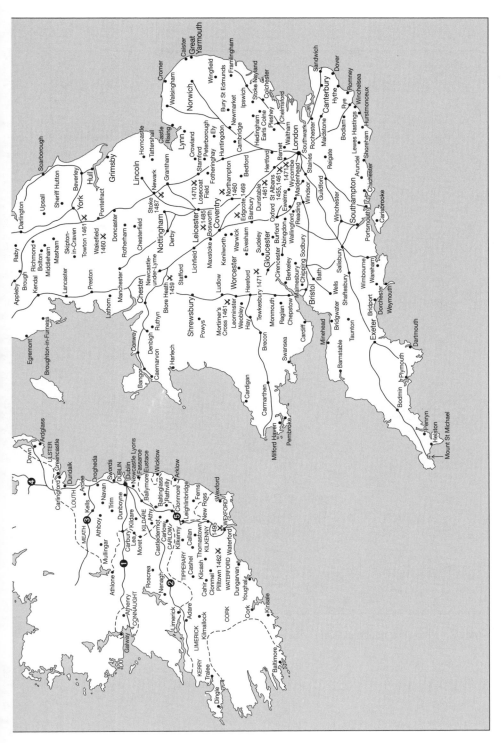

Map 1   Battle sites during the Wars of the Roses, 1455–87

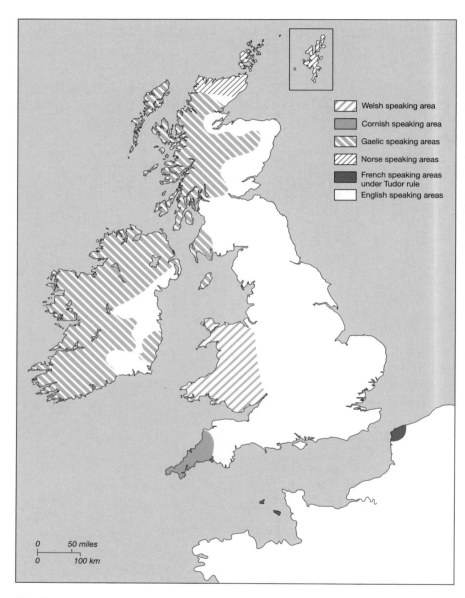

Welsh speaking area

Cornish speaking area

Gaelic speaking areas

Norse speaking areas

French speaking areas
under Tudor rule

English speaking areas

0   50 miles

0   100 km

Map 2   Linguistic boundaries of the British Isles *c.*1500

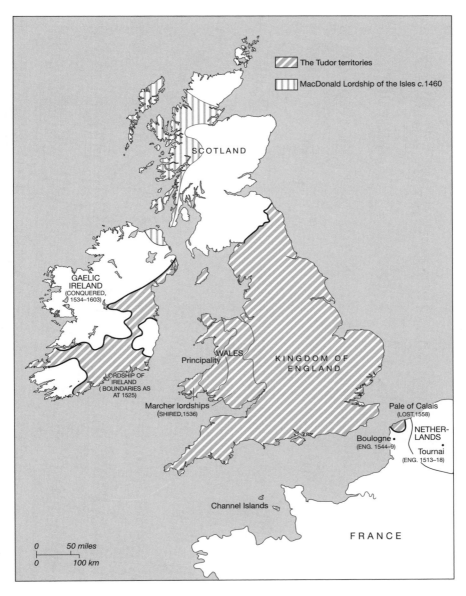

The Tudor territories

MacDonald Lordship of the Isles c.1460

SCOTLAND

GAELIC
IRELAND
(CONQUERED,
1534–1603)

LORDSHIP OF
IRELAND
(BOUNDARIES AS
AT 1525)

WALES
Principality

KINGDOM OF
ENGLAND

Marcher lordships
(SHIRED,1536)

Pale of Calais
(LOST,1558)

NETHER-
LANDS

Boulogne
(ENG. 1544–9)

Tournai
(ENG. 1513–18)

Channel Islands

FRANCE

0   50 miles

0   100 km

Map 3   The Tudor territories c.1525

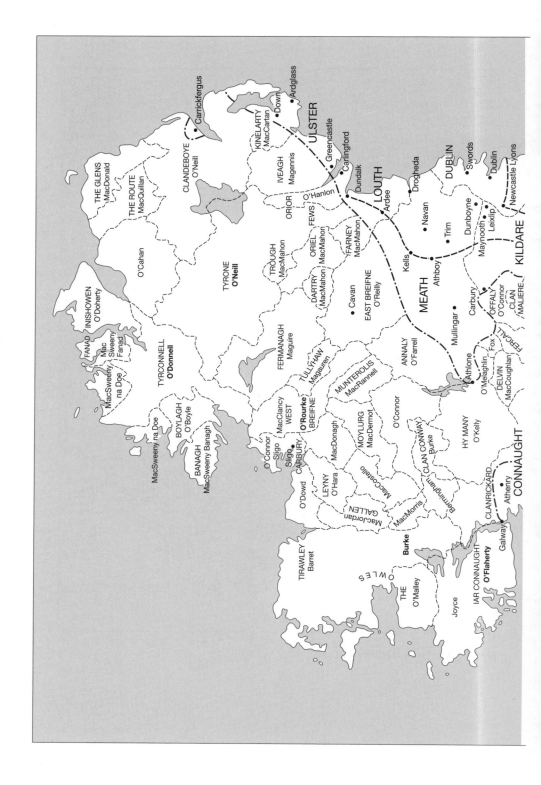

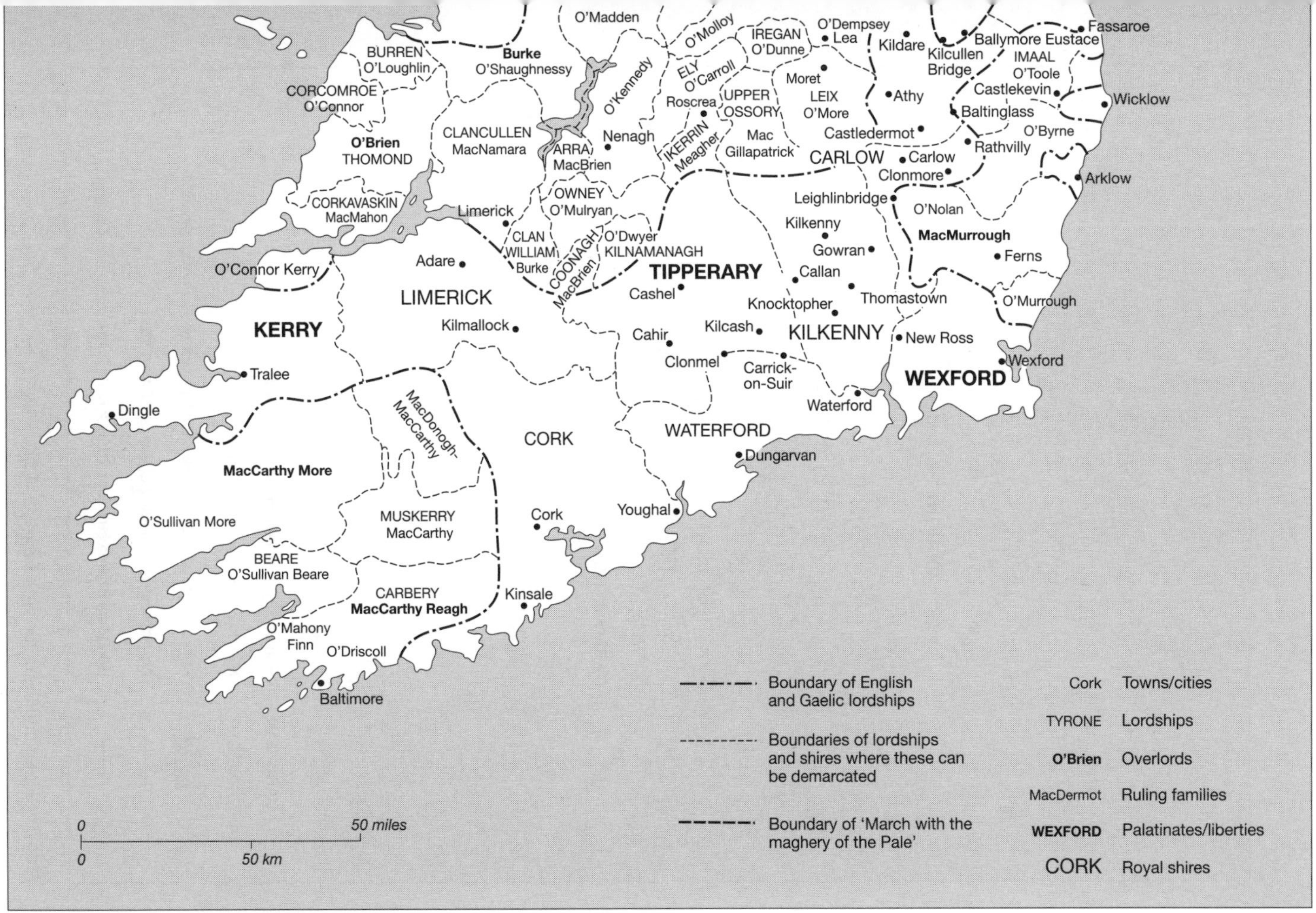
O'Madden
O'Dempsey
Lea
Kildare
Fassaroe
Ballymore Eustace
Kilcullen Bridge
IMAAL
O'Toole
BURREN
O'Loughlin
Burke
O'Shaughnessy
O'Molloy
IREGAN
O'Dunne
ELY
O'Carroll
Moret
Athy
Castlekevin
Wicklow
CORCOMROE
O'Connor
O'Kennedy
Roscrea
UPPER OSSORY
LEIX
O'More
Baltinglass
O'Brien
THOMOND
CLANCULLEN
MacNamara
Nenagh
IKERRIN
Meagher
Mac Gillapatrick
Castledermot
O'Byrne
Rathvilly
ARRA
MacBrien
CARLOW
Carlow
Clonmore
Arklow
OWNEY
O'Mulryan
Leighlinbridge
CORKAVASKIN
MacMahon
Limerick
O'Nolan
CLAN WILLIAM
Burke
COONAGH
MacBrien
O'Dwyer
KILNAMANAGH
Kilkenny
MacMurrough
Adare
Gowran
Ferns
O'Connor Kerry
TIPPERARY
Callan
LIMERICK
Cashel
Thomastown
O'Murrough
Knocktopher
KERRY
Kilmallock
Cahir
Kilcash
KILKENNY
New Ross
Clonmel
Carrick-on-Suir
Wexford
Tralee
WEXFORD
Waterford
Dingle
MacDonogh-MacCarthy
CORK
WATERFORD
Dungarvan
MacCarthy More
O'Sullivan More
MUSKERRY
MacCarthy
Cork
Youghal
BEARE
O'Sullivan Beare
CARBERY
MacCarthy Reagh
Kinsale
O'Mahony
Finn
O'Driscoll
Baltimore
Boundary of English and Gaelic lordships
Boundaries of lordships and shires where these can be demarcated
Boundary of 'March with the maghery of the Pale'
Cork Towns/cities
TYRONE Lordships
O'Brien Overlords
MacDermot Ruling families
WEXFORD Palatinates/liberties
CORK Royal shires
0 50 miles
0 50 km

Map 4 Ireland *c.*1534, showing the English lordship and the Gaelic lordships

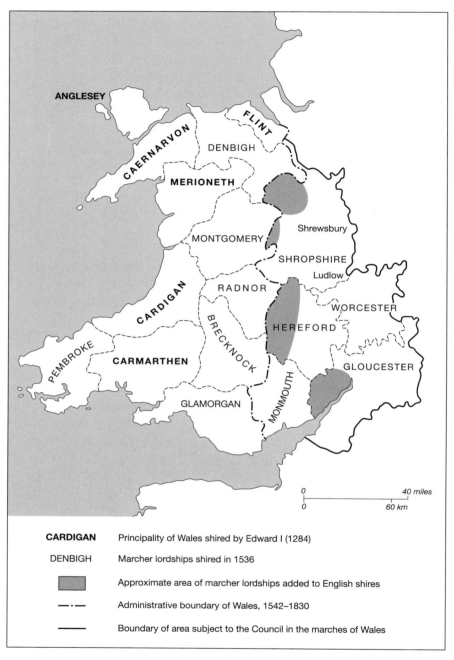

ANGLESEY

CAERNARVON

FLINT

DENBIGH

MERIONETH

Shrewsbury

MONTGOMERY

SHROPSHIRE

Ludlow

RADNOR

CARDIGAN

WORCESTER

BRECKNOCK

HEREFORD

PEMBROKE

CARMARTHEN

GLOUCESTER

GLAMORGAN

MONMOUTH

0   40 miles

0   60 km

CARDIGAN	Principality of Wales shired by Edward I (1284)
DENBIGH	Marcher lordships shired in 1536
▨	Approximate area of marcher lordships added to English shires
—·—	Administrative boundary of Wales, 1542–1830
——	Boundary of area subject to the Council in the marches of Wales

Map 5   Wales and the union with England, 1536–43

Map 6 The War of the Three Kingdoms, 1638–52

Scottish Counties

1	Aberdeen
2	Argyll
3	Ayr
4	Banff
5	Berwick
6	Bute
6a	Caithness
7	Clackmannan
7a	Kinross
8	Cromarty
8a	Nairn
9	Dumbarton
10	Dumfries
11	Edinburgh
12	Elgin
13	Fife
14	Forfar
15	Haddington
16	Inverness
17	Kincardine
18	Kirkcudbright
19	Lanark
20	Linlithgow
21	Orkneys & Shetlands
22	Peebles
23	Perth
24	Renfrew
25	Ross
26	Roxburgh
27	Selkirk
28	Stirling
29	Sutherland
30	Wigtown

English Counties

1	Bedford	21	Lincoln
2	Berkshire	22	Middlesex
3	Buckingham	23	Monmouth
4	Cambridge	24	Norfolk
5	Cheshire	25	Northampton
6	Cornwall	26	Northumberland
7	Cumberland	27	Nottingham
8	Derby	28	Oxford
9	Devon	29	Rutland
10	Dorset	30	Shropshire
11	Durham	31	Somerset
12	Essex	32	Stafford
13	Gloucester	33	Suffolk
14	Hampshire	34	Surrey
15	Hereford	35	Sussex
16	Hertford	36	Warwick
17	Huntingdon	37	Westmorland
18	Kent	38	Wiltshire
19	Lancashire	39	Worcester
20	Leicester	40	Yorkshire

Welsh Counties

41	Anglesey	47	Flint
42	Brecknock	48	Glamorgan
43	Cardigan	49	Merioneth
44	Carmarthen	50	Montgomery
45	Caernarvon	51	Pembroke
46	Denbigh	52	Radnor

SCOTLAND

IRELAND

St Andrews
Edinburgh
Berwick
Newcastle
Stirling
Glasgow
Inverness
Londonderry

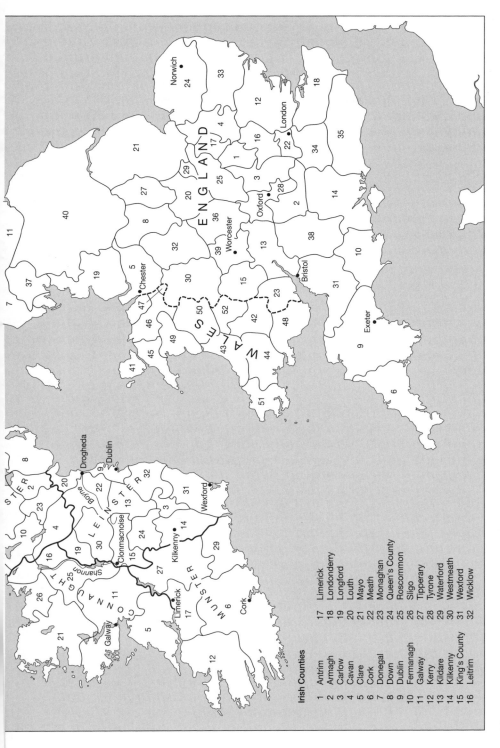

Map 7   The counties of England, Scotland, and (from the 1540s) Wales and Ireland

Irish Counties

1	Antrim	17	Limerick
2	Armagh	18	Londonderry
3	Carlow	19	Longford
4	Cavan	20	Louth
5	Clare	21	Mayo
6	Cork	22	Meath
7	Donegal	23	Monaghan
8	Down	24	Queen's County
9	Dublin	25	Roscommon
10	Fermanagh	26	Sligo
11	Galway	27	Tipperary
12	Kerry	28	Tyrone
13	Kildare	29	Waterford
14	Kilkenny	30	Westmeath
15	King's County	31	Wexford
16	Leitrim	32	Wicklow

CAITHNESS

ROSS

MORAY

ABERDEEN

BRECHIN

DUNKELD

DUNBLANE

ST ANDREWS

GLASGOW

DURHAM

CARLISLE

GALLOWAY

ARGYLL

THE ISLES

CONNOR &

DERRY

RAPHOE

50 miles

100 km

0

0

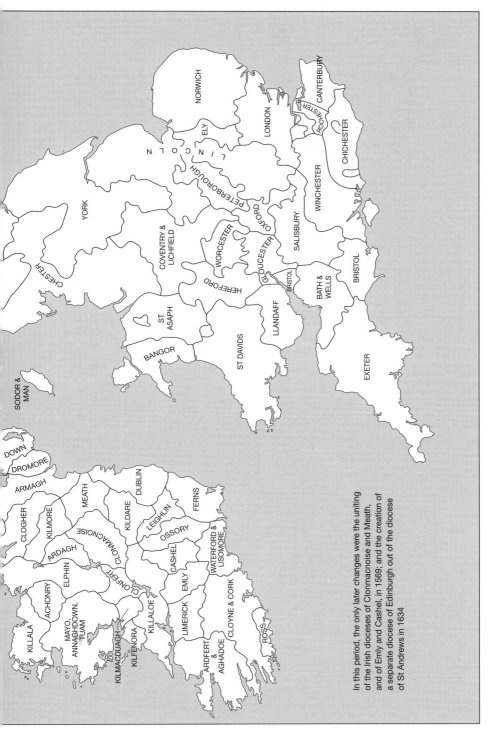

Map 8   The dioceses of the churches of England, Scotland and Ireland, as confirmed in 1559–60

In this period, the only later changes were the uniting
of the Irish dioceses of Clonmacnoise and Meath,
and of Emly and Cashel, in 1569; and the creation of
a separate diocese of Edinburgh out of the diocese
of St Andrews in 1634

GEOGRAPHY, SOCIETY AND GOVERNMENT
The structures of power

The British Isles in the later middle ages was not much more than a geographic entity, culturally divided and politically fragmented. The most powerful monarchy in the archipelago was the crown of England. To the north of England lay the smaller and less powerful kingdom of the Scots, while in a wide arc from the Scottish highlands and islands to south-west Ireland lay numerous but tiny Gaelic lordships which were in practice more or less independent. In 1450, the concept of a centralised British state could not have been foreseen. The traditional diplomatic alliances of the two major monarchies cut across ties based on geography and instead connected the islands firmly into an emerging west European state system which included the Low Countries and the Iberian peninsula (England's traditional allies) and France (which enjoyed close ties with Scotland). Thus, even the traditional English ambition of political unification under an English monarch was little more than a dream: no one would have imagined that within 150 years unification might be accomplished by a Scottish king. In practice, politics within the archipelago had since 1296 revolved around an Anglo-Scottish rivalry, precipitated initially by English attempts to conquer its northern neighbour. During the ensuing Scottish Wars of Independence these efforts were finally rebuffed. The last two strongholds of the English Pale established in southern Scotland in the fourteenth century were finally recaptured in 1460–1, so restoring the Anglo-Scottish border to the Tweed-Solway line agreed by the treaty of York between the two kingdoms in 1237. Roxburgh held out as an English enclave in Scotland until 1460, when it was razed to the ground, but Berwick-on-Tweed, formerly Scotland's chief port, was recovered by the English in 1482, this time permanently.

State formation: unions and conquests

In many ways the modern British state had its origins in the Anglo-Scottish dynastic union of 1603 and the later parliamentary union of 1707. The

[2] acquisition of territory by dynastic inheritance was a common aspect of Renaissance monarchy, and the British multiple monarchy was a typical product of the dynastic marriages between Europe's ruling houses. The later medieval English monarchy, however, was much more the product of a different process of territorial aggrandisement – by conquest. The kingdom of England was indeed a conquest lordship *par excellence*; and to the crown of England were later annexed Wales (divided between a western principality finally conquered in 1283, and the Welsh marches in the east), the lordship of Ireland (those parts conquered and brought under English rule from 1169 onwards), and some other smaller scraps of territory like Calais, the Isle of Man, and parts of England's northern borderland with Scotland. The English monarchy was, however, also inextricably linked to the politics of continental Europe. English armies of 'bills and bows' had established it as a major European power which, for much of the later middle ages, controlled large stretches of France. English kings indeed claimed to be kings of France and the territories they ruled there, principally the duchies of Normandy and Gascony, were held of their crown of France. The constitutional status of the English king's continental possessions varied, but the most recent recension of English claims was contained in the treaty of Troyes (1420). In accordance with its terms, the infant Prince Henry succeeded as Henry VI to the crown of England on the death of his father, Henry V, in August 1422 and to the crown of France on the death of his maternal grandfather, Charles VI, two months later, thus creating an Anglo-French dual monarchy. Subsequently, Henry VI was crowned king of England at Westminster in 1429 and king of France in Paris in 1431.[1]

This distinction within the late medieval English monarchy between the conquest lordships held of the English crown and the continental dynastic inheritance held of the French crown was a fundamental one, introducing a further distinction in terms of law and administration which was to have unforeseen consequences after 1603. Broadly, England itself was governed by a comparatively centralised and uniform administrative system, based on counties and sheriffs, with a uniform legal code, English common law, as modified by statute enacted in parliament, all supervised by the king's council and the central law courts at Westminster. The system had been extended to Ireland, Wales and the English far north. Outside the core region of

---

1 S.G. Ellis, 'From dual monarchy to multiple kingdoms: unions and the English state, 1422–1607' in A.I. Macinnes and Jane Ohlmeyer (eds), *The Stuart kingdoms in the seventeenth century: awkward neighbours* (Dublin, 2002), pp. 37–48 for this and the following two paragraphs.

Lowland England, however, the needs of defence ensured that the system was supplemented by a quasi-military system, based on feudal liberties and different systems of march law, and medieval settlement in these conquest territories had introduced English customs and culture alongside the indigenous customs of the surviving native populations. By contrast, the continental territories were more 'core' than 'periphery': each was governed by its own law and customs, in which English statutes and common law had no place and the English courts no jurisdiction. The years after Normandy's recovery in 1417 had witnessed substantial settlement from England in a bid to underpin the English occupation (or to vindicate the hereditary rights of English kings), but no attempt was made to 'anglicise' its administration or centralise royal authority in accordance with English practice. Paradoxically, the inhabitants of these territories were not even English subjects. In 1455, for instance, the Irish parliament enacted that merchants of Bordeaux – subjects of Henry VI as of his crown of France – who had fled to Ireland on the collapse of English Gascony should be made English subjects and pay customs 'as Englishmen born in England or Ireland'.[2]

The territories ruled by English kings thus included a wide variety of customs, laws and peoples. It would be a mistake, however, to view this dual monarchy as the artificial creation of English imperialism and 'dynastic roulette', despite its sudden collapse. By the standards of the time it had at least as much in common as the later Anglo-Scottish union, let alone such artificial constructs as the unwieldy empire inherited by Charles V in the early sixteenth century. English kings, for instance, were – and long remained – far more interested in their rich and cultivated French inheritance than in the acquisition of remote and barren territories in the north-western periphery. As capital of this medieval monarchy, their chief city, London, was ideally situated – which is more than can be said of its later status as a capital of the British multiple monarchy. And French remained a familiar language of the English court, albeit spoken with an accent which Parisians found hard to understand. Legal proceedings and parliament rolls were still written in an archaic language known as law French. And if the dual monarchy had survived, it would in all probability have been forced to modernise along the same lines as continental monarchies – developing a standing army, a professional bureaucracy, and an effective system of taxation – in order to defend these valuable but vulnerable territories. Conceivably, royal officials and

---

2   H.F. Berry (ed.), *Statute rolls of the parliament of Ireland, reign of King Henry VI* (Dublin, 1910), p. 386.

[4] pamphleteers might then have defended the dual monarchy on grounds of common bonds – geographical proximity, language, Anglo-Norman feudalism – in much the same way as they were to do its British successor following Anglo-Scottish union in 1603.

The loss of the French territories – in the longer term, only the Channel Islands remained – was to relieve English kings of one set of problems associated with centralising monarchy. The status of English law and culture within the English territories now became unassailable. In the British Isles as a whole, however, the balance of law and culture was rather different. Most of England and also Scotland south of the Forth was a strongly feudalised region, where dialects of English and Scots were spoken and Anglo-Norman administrative structures and law were strongly entrenched. The archipelago was still predominantly Celtic-speaking – at least when measured in terms of geographical area, although not of population. Much of Ireland, Wales, and the Scottish highlands and Western Isles also had lineage- or clan-based societies and native legal systems which were much less influenced by feudalism. This 'Celtic fringe' was itself divided between an area of Gaelic supremacy, the *Gaedhealtacht*, in Ireland and Scotland and perhaps the Isle of Man; and a region of Brittonic language and custom which included most of Wales, a few adjacent districts of what is now England, and western Cornwall. In 1450 the balance between these regions of English and Celtic culture was finely poised: the anglophone areas were more heavily populated, but particularly in Ireland and Wales English had been in decline for at least a century.

In other respects, however, it was possible to glimpse the beginnings of a greater Britain. The great wave of Anglo-Norman expansion in the two centuries or so down to *c.*1300 had seen a comparatively uniform system of administration, law and feudalism extended from England to gain a secure hold in parts of Ireland, Scotland and Wales. Until 1603 this area of 'writ culture' was divided politically between the English and Scottish monarchies, but the basic governmental structures for a centralised British state already existed and might serve as a focus for greater unity. And for all its political rivalries, the British Isles was by 1450 increasingly under the control of native dynasties. In 1468 the king of Scots secured possession of the Northern Isles from the king of Denmark and Norway, and also a favourable resolution of a 200-year-old dispute over payment of an annual tribute by the Scots for the Western Isles.[3] Thus the boundaries of the kingdom of

3 Michael Lynch, *Scotland: a new history* (London, 1991), pp. 90, 155–6.

the Scots had, in theory at least, reached their fullest extent, and the last of [5]
those links which since the eighth century had tied the British Isles to the
Scandinavian kingdoms was finally broken.

There remained, however, major obstacles to the creation of a united
Britain. In the north-west Scottish sovereignty was only intermittently
recognised by Clan Donald, whose lordship of the Isles was the most powerful of the Gaelic lordships, and in Ireland the independence of the Gaelic
chiefs had long been a reality. The mid-fifteenth century was to mark the
peak of the Gaelic Revival which had begun two centuries earlier. Profiting
from Anglo-Scottish rivalry, the movement had witnessed a cultural resurg-
ence and political revival within medieval Gaeldom's fragmented, clan-
based society. In Scotland this manifested itself by the expansion of the
aggressively Gaelic Clan Donald. Indeed the lordship of the Isles, the political manifestation of Clan Donald power, now spanned the North Channel,
stretching from the earldom of Ross in the far north to the Glens of Antrim
in the south-west. Much later, in 1617, when most of the lordship had since
been absorbed into the Scottish kingdom, a celebrated court case was heard
to decide to which kingdom Rathlin belonged, since this small island, now
part of Ireland, had been part of the lordship. The lordship of the Isles thus
offered a potential focus for political unity within the *Gaedhealtacht*, in the
form of a third maritime kingdom in the north-west, building on Gaeldom's
cultural unity in opposition to the area of foreign rule, the *Galltacht*.[4] In
Ireland the Gaelic revival likewise saw the political restoration of provincial
overlordships by major chiefs like O'Neill and MacMurrough-Kavanagh and
a recovery of land once settled by the English. For all its political fragmentation, moreover, the Gaelic world boasted an apparently uniform legal system,
known as Brehon Law. Each chief appointed a professional judge (or
brehon, from the Gaelic *breitheamh*) mainly to try cases affecting himself or
matters of public concern. The brehon's decision was an arbitration to
which, at least in theory, both parties had given prior consent. There was no
criminal law as such, and what common law deemed capital offences were
simple torts resolved by payment of compensation, a proportion of the fines
going to the chief. The standard *eraic* (the blood-price for homicide) for a
man of good family was 105 cows, half that if the killing were unintended.
A thief was obliged to restore twice the value of the goods stolen, and the

---

4   Lynch, *Scotland*, pp. 64–70; Julian Goodare, *State and society in early modern Scotland* (Oxford,
    1999), p. 214; S.G. Ellis, 'The collapse of the Gaelic world, 1450–1650' in *Irish Historical
    Studies*, xxxi (1998–9), pp. 449–69. See now also, Simon Kingston, *Ulster and the Isles in the
    fifteenth century: the lordship of Clann Domhnaill of Antrim* (Dublin, 2004).

[6] cost of tracking the stolen goods (the same amounts, interestingly, as on the Anglo-Scottish borders), plus a fine levied by the lord. In accordance with the principle of *cinn comhfhocuis* (also adopted by common law in its dealings with the Irishry and some English marchers), the corporate family or clan was responsible for the acts of its members, and so for any compensation. The brehons also preserved ancient law texts in connection with their professional activities: these could be consulted and quarried for legal maxims to be quoted in pleadings, but the fact was that this was little more than 'antiquarian windowdressing'. Even in Ireland, late Gaelic law was in reality strongly influenced by Roman law and by common law concepts and institutions like the jury. In Scotland, moreover, aspects of Gaelic law had long been absorbed into Scots law, and there Brehon law was in any case heavily overlaid by feudalism.[5]

If the 1450s onwards marked a period of expansion for the Scottish monarchy, it also marked a nadir in English monarchical power. Paradoxically, the decisive campaigns for the future of the British Isles were in 1450 being fought on the fields of France, where the Hundred Years War (1337–1453) between England and France had entered its final phase. Although the wars along the Anglo-Scottish border and in Ireland were also going badly for the English, successive English kings were far more concerned about events across the English Channel than the relatively minor threat presented by the Scots and the Irish. Between 1449 and 1453, the French completed the reconquest of Normandy and then annexed English Gascony, leaving the military outpost of Calais as the only English bridgehead on the European mainland. The collapse of Lancastrian France had little impact in the short term on traditional diplomatic alliances in western Europe, or on English political ambitions which remained firmly fixed on the continent. The French monarchy likewise continued to cultivate 'the auld alliance' with the Scots as an insurance against renewed English aggression. In the 1420s a Scottish expeditionary army had even fought alongside the French in Europe against 'the auld inemie', the English,[6] and until 1560 French troops were periodically sent to Scotland to stiffen resistance against the English. In the longer term, however, English interests became more insular. The

---

5 K.W. Nicholls, *Gaelic and gaelicized Ireland in the middle ages* (rev. ed., Dublin, 2003), ch. 3; Katharine Simms, *From kings to warlords: the changing political structure of Gaelic Ireland in the later middle ages* (Woodbridge, 1987), chs 4–5; A.I. Macinnes, *Clanship, commerce and the house of Stuart, 1603–1788* (East Linton, 1996), ch. 3; Michael Newton, *A handbook of the Scottish Gaelic world* (Dublin, 2000), pp. 57, 142–8.

6 Ranald Nicholson, *Scotland: the later middle ages* (Edinburgh, 1974), pp. 250–2, 258, 260, 288–9.

Lancastrian collapse in France was followed by a period of civil war in [7] England; and by the time English kings were again strong enough to contemplate sustained continental adventures, notably in Henry VIII's reign, a resurgent French monarchy had consolidated its control of the continental coastline opposite England and now proved more than capable of resisting English aggression. To match the loss of 'core' regions in France, the English were left to strengthen their control over the British Isles; but the monarchy's only significant acquisition to 1603, the conquest of 'peripheral' lands in Gaelic Ireland (which were simply added to the existing English dominion there), proved very poor compensation.

Geography, power and society

In 1450, the relationship between power and society in the British Isles still reflected in many ways basic geographical differences within the archipelago, in terms of relief, climate and soil. In broad terms, England south-east of a line running from Teesmouth in the north-east to Weymouth in the south was the only really extensive Lowland region which, by reason of a coincidence of suitable soils and a favourable climate, could almost everywhere support arable farming. This absence of major river barriers or extensive forests, fens or bogs meant that Lowland England was also a region which was uniquely favourable to the exercise of strong centralised monarchy. The boundaries of the region coincided quite neatly with those of the old Anglo-Saxon monarchy, and provided a firm base from which English kings could, from Norman times, dominate the larger upland zone to the north and west, annexing Wales and parts of Ireland. Within this upland region pastoral farming predominated, although there were smaller but still substantial regions suitable for agriculture in Scotland, in parts of the eastern Lowlands and Galloway, and in Ireland along the eastern coastal plain and the Barrow-Nore-Suir valley basin. Almost everywhere lay small pockets of land where some crops could be grown, if only oats, but the prevailing westerly winds made for a wetter colder climate: grain crops failed to ripen, and even in the Lowland region of the Irish midlands the poor, acid soils discouraged cultivation.[7]

---

7   For this paragraph, see especially Joan Thirsk (ed.), *The agrarian history of England and Wales, IV 1500–1640* (Cambridge, 1967); *Atlas of Ireland* (Royal Irish Academy, Dublin, 1979), map 28; Alexander Grant, *Independence and nationhood: Scotland 1306–1469* (London, 1984), chs 3, 8.

For reasons of geography, therefore, the British Isles was predominantly a marcher region where power was much more fragmented than in Lowland England. In medieval times, a frontier or border was typically a march – a whole borderland often with its own peculiar characteristics which marked it off from other territories away from the exposed periphery. There were four main borders within the British Isles. The Anglo-Scottish border and the Anglo-Gaelic frontier in Ireland formed the boundary between the area inhabited by subjects of the English crown and independent peoples of pre-dominantly Celtic culture to the north and west of the English state. Until the completion of the English conquest of Wales in 1283, the Anglo-Welsh marches had formed a third such border, while the fourth was the highland-Lowland divide in Scotland. One of the most salient characteristics of these marches was the coincidence within each of them of different kinds of borders – political, geographical, social, administrative and cultural. This coincidence of borders was particularly striking in parts of Ireland where the arable Lowlands of the east and south constituted the heart of the Englishry and of England's medieval lordship, whereas English settlement had not normally occurred above the 400-foot contour line, or in boggy Lowlands. Stretching to the west and north were the numerous independent Gaelic lordships which constituted the Irishry, none of them larger than an English shire and most much smaller; but even within the main English districts there were pockets of higher ground, notably the Leinster mountains, which had remained under Gaelic rule. Within the space of a few short miles south of Dublin, the medieval traveller would have crossed all five of these borders in journeying from the English lordship's administrative capital into the Irishry of the Leinster mountains. The fertile plain between Dublin and Carlingford was a well-populated, heavily-manorialised region of mixed farming, whose nucleated villages and numerous market towns imparted a strongly English character to it. This, 'the English Pale' of Tudor times, was inhabited by 'the king's loyal English lieges', who were predominantly English-speaking, dressed after the English manner, and were governed by English administrative structures and common law. To the south lay Gaelic Leinster, a much more sparsely-populated region of pastoral uplands, inhabited by 'the king's Irish enemies', a clan-based people with their own very distinct system of Gaelic law and administration, customs and language, which was quite different. Sandwiched precariously in between, in some of the more exposed parts of the south Dublin borderland, lived semi-autonomous, upland marcher lineages of English descent, the Harolds, Archbolds and Walshmen, who straddled the cultural divide between the

'civil English' of the Lowlands and the 'wild Irish' of the mountains.[8] These
divisions between Englishry and Irishry were replicated in many other parts
of Ireland's fragmented and fluid frontier.

In the case of the other borders, the pattern was a little less complicated
and the contrasts were not quite so stark. The area of Gaelic law and custom,
late medieval Gaeldom, extended in a great arc from south-west Ireland
across the North Channel to the highlands and islands of Scotland. Here,
within Scotland, they formed an internal linguistic and cultural boundary
within the Scottish kingdom which also coincided with the highland line.
Thus in many ways, the division between English-speaking Lowlands and
Gaelic-speaking highlands was characteristic of Scotland too. It appears, for
instance, in John of Fordun's memorable description of 'the manners and
customs of the Scots':

> For two languages are spoken amongst them, the Scottish [= Gaelic] and the
> Teutonic [= English], the latter of which is the language of those who occupy
> the coastal and low-lying regions, while the race of Scottish speech inhabits the
> mountains and outlying islands. The people of the coast are of domestic and
> civilized habits, trustworthy, patient and urbane, decent in their attire, law-
> abiding and peaceful, devout in religious observance, but always ready to resist a
> wrong at the hand of their enemies. The highlanders and people of the islands,
> on the other hand, are a wild and untamed nation, rude and independent, given
> to robbery, ease-loving, of artful and impressionable temperament, comely in
> person but unsightly in dress, hostile to the English people and language and,
> owing to diversity of speech, even to their own nation, and exceedingly cruel.[9]

Yet in Scotland, the Lowland zone stretching from the English border to the
Forth was too small, and the highland zone too extensive, to permit the same
kind of domination of the highlands by Lowland culture as the English
monarchy exercised over its frontier regions to the north and west. The
Scottish Lowlands south of Edinburgh also lay within striking distance of
English raids. The military character of the Anglo-Scottish frontier was, if
anything, even more pronounced than the Anglo-Gaelic frontier in Ireland,
because the Scottish monarchy was a far more formidable adversary than any
Gaelic chief.

8   See especially, Robin Frame, *English lordship in Ireland 1318–1361* (Oxford, 1982), pp. 27–46;
    Christopher Maginn, 'English marcher lineages in south Dublin in the late middle ages' in
    Irish Historical Studies, xxxiv (2004–5), pp. 113–36; S.G. Ellis, *The Pale and the Far North:
    government and society in two early Tudor borderlands* (Galway, 1988), pp. 28–30; D.B. Quinn and
    K.W. Nicholls, 'Ireland in 1534' in T.W. Moody, F.X. Martin, and F.J. Byrne (eds), *A new
    history of Ireland. III Early Modern Ireland, 1534–1691* (Oxford, 1976), pp. 6–7.
9   *J. de Fordun, Cronica Gentis Scotorum*, ed. W.F. Skene (1871–2), i, 24.

[10]   By contrast, the political and military importance of the Welsh marches had declined sharply after 1283, since they no longer had to be defended from independent Welsh princes beyond. The marches of Wales had now become a closed frontier, a closely defined geographical area, separate both from the realm of England and the principality of Wales, with its own particular customs and institutions, such as the officially-sanctioned law of the march. Yet, despite the gradual attenuation of its frontier character, the Welsh marches for long retained many of the characteristic features of a march. The frontier survived in terms of law and administration at least until 1536, when the so-called Welsh Act of Union abolished Welsh law and incorporated Wales and the marches into the English kingdom, and until much later in terms of culture and society. In much of the Welsh marches, for instance, English settlement in the more fertile Lowlands (again, generally below the 400-foot contour line) had only partially displaced the native Welsh who had clung on stubbornly to their estates in the neighbouring uplands. Thus, for instance, the lordships of Pembroke and Glamorgan were divided into Welshries and Englishries, and the region exhibited a similar coincidence of geographical, cultural and administrative frontiers. Within many marcher lordships, the 'mere Welsh' of the *blaenau*, or upland areas, retained their own traditional agricultural methods, native laws and local officials, while in the Englishries of the Lowlands ('*bro-*' in Welsh place-names) the influence of Anglo-Norman feudalism, English common law, and administrative structures was much stronger.[10]

Patterns of settlement and social structures also reflected these divisions between highland and Lowland zones. Broadly, in Lowland England, those areas of Ireland and Wales which had experienced heavy Anglo-Norman settlement, and on the Scottish east coast and around Lothian, good land, comparative peace and peasants of English stock had provided the conditions and expertise needed for the introduction of a more intensive and efficient system of cereal production than was obtained by the native practices of Celtic Britain. These regions were heavily manorialised, with large open fields, relatively high levels of population, and settlement in nucleated

10   See especially the works by Rees Davies, *Lordship and society in the March of Wales 1282–1400* (Oxford, 1978); 'Frontier arrangements in fragmented societies: Ireland and Wales' in Robert Bartlett and Angus MacKay (eds), *Medieval frontier societies* (Oxford, 1989), pp. 77–100; 'The twilight of Welsh law, 1284–1536' in *History*, li (1966), pp. 143–64. Glanmor Williams, *Recovery, reorientation and Reformation: Wales c.1415–1642* (Oxford, 1987), pp. 35–9, 58–65.

villages around a church, castle or manor house. Almost all the major towns [1 1] were located in these regions too. And with the advent of Anglo-Norman feudalism, the land had been divided into comparatively small manors (baronies in Scotland), which usually corresponded ecclesiastically with the parish. Among the manorial tenants who worked the common fields, there were many gradations, ranging from substantial freeholders – yeomen and husbandmen – with hereditary tenures and owing low levels of rent and service to their feudal lords, to cottars with smallholdings and short leases, and landless labourers. Thus, society was quite diversified, with many rungs on 'the great chain of being' occupied by those prosperous peasants, artisans and small merchants of the towns, who comprised a substantial 'middling sort' between the nobility and landless labourers.

By contrast, the upland zone was more sparsely inhabited, and the population was generally much poorer, with dispersed patterns of settlement in isolated hamlets surrounded by moors, bogs and mountains, and quite different patterns of land usage. In the predominantly lineage- or clan-based societies of upland Britain feudalism had, at best, secured a much more tenuous hold and manors and parishes, where they existed, were much larger. A leading Scottish historian has argued, with reference to the highland-Lowland division in that kingdom, that 'Highland society was based on kinship modified by feudalism, Lowland society on feudalism tempered by kinship'.[11] This statement was true also of many other parts of upland Britain, where bonds of kinship were frequently more important than feudal ties. Society was more sharply divided between landowners and smallholders and the landless, so that social and political structures were quite different from those in the Lowlands. In general, the nobles had compact holdings of land rather than the dispersed estates scattered across several shires which were characteristic of Lowland England. This, and the absence of a substantial middle class, meant that noble power was potentially much stronger, even though, paradoxically, tenants enjoyed great personal freedom by comparison with smallholders in heavily manorialised regions. The most extreme illustration of this paradox was Gaelic Ireland, where the land was cultivated by share-cropping labourers who were legally free but in practice had no rights in the land, security of tenure, nor access to law against their landlords.[12]

---

11   T.C. Smout, *A history of the Scottish people 1560–1830* (London, 1972), p. 43.
12   K.W. Nicholls, *Gaelic and gaelicized Ireland in the middle ages* (rev. ed., Dublin, 2003), pp. 77–81.

[1 2]   In principle, the nucleated manorial villages of the arable Lowlands were much easier to govern than the dispersed settlements of the pastoral uplands, particularly if the lord of the manor were resident. Manorial courts provided an effective means by which the lord could both enforce seigneurial rights, including the conditions of leases, entry fines and labour services, and generally also regulate the economic life of the village; while the spiritual welfare of the community was regulated by the parish priest and churchwardens. The central government thus had access, when necessary, to the local community through the parish gentry or priest. By contrast, among the less feudalised lineage societies of the pastoral uplands, manors and parishes were less easy to control on account of their size. Parishes might have one or two dependent chapels; and manors were more of a legal entity than a self-sufficient unit of production. Fewer gentry (lairds in Scotland) lived in these poor and remote communities, and those who did were more usually humble parish gentry than wealthy squires.

Frontiers and defence

These divisions between land capability and the structures of power and society were also reflected in the character of the British archipelago's political frontiers. At a practical level, and especially in the immediate frontier districts, security was an overriding consideration. In those parts of the border where the quality of the land permitted agriculture, the population could be concentrated in nucleated villages in accordance with the English system of manorialism, thus facilitating defence. The cottages of the manorial tenants were clustered around the church and the principal dwelling of the lord of the manor – usually a towerhouse in the marches. In the English Pale in Ireland, for instance, this was the case with the chain of manorial villages along the southern marches to the south-west of Dublin – Tallaght, Saggart, Rathcoole and Newcastle Lyons.[13] Exceptionally, and thanks to the conservative estate-management policies of the archbishops of Dublin, tenants of their manor of Tallaght in 1528–9 even included villeins, as did

13   See, for instance, the manorial extents printed in Gearóid Mac Niocaill (ed.), *Crown surveys of lands 1540–41 with the Kildare rental begun in 1518* (Dublin, 1992); Charles McNeill (ed.), *Calendar of Archbishop Alen's register, c.1172–1534* (Dublin, 1950); N.B. White (ed.), *Extents of Irish monastic possessions, 1540–41* (Dublin, 1943).

the manors of Finglas and Swords to the north of Dublin city. Serfdom in Tudor England was by then largely confined to small pockets of the English Lowlands, however.[14] This system of defence also operated in other parts of English Ireland, most notably along sections of the Pale's northern frontier in Co. Louth, from Carlingford to Dundalk and Louth itself. It prevailed too in the English east marches towards Scotland along the coastal plain and the lower Tweed between Berwick and Norham and south along the Till valley to Etal, Ford and Wooler in Glendale. Significantly, the west bank of the River Till towards the Cheviot Hills was more vulnerable to Scottish raids. The 1541 border survey noted that it was 'a very good plenteous and fertile country' with 'a very fertile soil' which could 'sustain a great number of men with living able to maintain horse & harness for defence of the borders there'. Yet there were not 'towers and fortresses sufficient to relieve all the inhabitants thereof with their horses' as most of them were situated on the east bank. Thus in wartime the inhabitants were mostly forced to withdraw inland, so leaving the border 'almost desolate & waste'. In 1519, a lease of half the manor of Wooler specified a rent of £14 a year, but only half that in time of war between England and Scotland.[15]

Even so, Tudor officials spoke approvingly of these English villages with their yeomen and husbandmen well armed and organised for war. The English peasantry were accustomed to bearing arms and were generally obliged, as an incident of tenure, to perform military service with weapons, horse and harness appropriate to their status and the size of their holding. In the Scottish Lowlands the more prosperous peasants were likewise expected to fight under their lord – along with his kin, friends and servants. Yet the poorer peasants with few weapons – cottars, for instance – fought only locally for their laird, but did not serve in the king's wars, while no military service at all was expected of those 'boys and young men' without weapon who comprised in practice over 40 per cent of the musters. In the highlands 'them that labours the ground are commanded to remain at home'; and in Gaelic Ireland likewise the peasantry traditionally did not bear arms. Thus, individually, these English manorial villages had no difficulty in repelling

---

14   McNeill (ed.), *Archbishop Alen's register*, p. 279. Cf. Diarmaid MacCulloch, 'Bondmen under the Tudors' in Claire Cross, David Loades and J.J. Scarisbrick (eds), *Law and government under the Tudors: essays presented to Sir Geoffrey Elton on his retirement* (Cambridge, 1988), pp. 91–109.

15   Survey of the border by Sir Robert Bowes and Sir Ralph Ellerker, 1542, printed in John Hodgson, *A history of Northumberland* (3 pts in 7 vols, Newcastle, 1820–25), III, ii, 186–8; Northumberland County History Committee (ed.), *A history of Northumberland*, (15 vols, 1905–40), xi, 316.

THE MAKING OF THE BRITISH ISLES

[1 4] casual raiders and reivers; and clusters of manorial villages organised by resident lords and gentry (with hue and cry, and a system of beacons to warn of approaching enemies) also proved able to defend themselves against the larger raiding parties and even small armies which were the common coin of march warfare.[16] In these areas, the actual march, or frontier region, might be quite narrow and the frontier was likely to be comparatively stable. For instance, the English Pale briefly established in fourteenth century Scotland was soon reconquered, so restoring the frontier to the Tweed–Solway line. In Ireland, and despite the Gaelic Revival, the limits of the English marches south of Dublin did not change very much after 1400. And unlike its continental counterparts, the English monarchy did not after 1450 acquire large stretches of territory from neighbouring rival states whose subjects and administrative institutions needed to be homogenised, only minor clans in Ireland.[17]

More normally, the quality of the land and the prevailing patterns of settlement precluded the maintenance of any kind of self-sufficient defensive system. For much of its course, the mutually-agreed 'border line' of the Anglo-Scottish frontier followed the watershed of the Cheviot Hills, a major geographical obstacle which presented a 'natural frontier' long before the doctrine of continuous linear frontiers emerged in the seventeenth century.[18] This region of high pasture and moorland waste divided the more concentrated settlement areas of southern Scotland and northern England. Cross-border holdings had been broken up in the fourteenth century. There were a few small debatable lands on the border itself, notably one to the north of Carlisle: but in general, there was an absence of feudal enclaves of conflicting jurisdiction such as those that existed along the frontier between French Picardy and Habsburg Flanders.[19] In contrast, Ireland had no agreed frontier

16   S.G. Ellis, *Reform and revival: English government in Ireland 1470–1534* (London, 1986), ch. 2; Goodare, *State and society in early modern Scotland*, pp. 136–40; Nicholls, *Gaelic and gaelicized Ireland*, pp. 77–81.

17   Ellis, *Tudor frontiers and noble power: the making of the British state* (Oxford, 1995), pp. 22–3. Cf. for instance, Harald Gustafsson, 'The conglomerate state: a perspective on state formation in early modern Europe' in *Scandinavian Journal of History*, xxiii (2002), pp. 189–213; S.G. Ellis, 'Integration, identities and frontiers in the British Isles: a European perspective' in Harald Gustafsson and Hanne Sanders (eds), *Vid gränsen: Integration och identitet i det förnationella Norden* (Gothenburg, 2005), pp. 19–45.

18   P.T.J. Morgan, 'The government of Calais 1485–1558' (unpublished D.Phil. thesis, Oxford University, 1966), p. 252; Ellis, *Tudor frontiers*, pp. 24–5.

19   Ellis, *Tudor frontiers*, p. 25. Cf. David Potter, *War and government in the French provinces: Picardy 1470–1560* (Cambridge, 1993), ch. 8.

and was indeed 'a land of many marches'. Medieval English settlement had focused on the arable Lowlands, especially the eastern coastal plain of the English Pale and the Barrow-Nore-Suir river valleys in the south. In these regions, the native Irish were displaced into the surrounding uplands and less profitable boglands, leaving a series of marches that frequently followed the contours of the land or intersections between areas of different land capability.[20] Unlike the Pale's truncated northern and southern frontiers, however, no major mountain range enclosed its long meandering western marches. The Dublin administration divided the Pale administratively into the 'maghery', a Gaelic term (from *machaire*, meaning champaign ground) which, revealingly, was borrowed by the Palesmen to denote the English heartland; the 'marches', which constituted the inhabited frontier district of the Englishry; and the uninhabited waste or 'fasagh land' beyond (*fásach*, another Gaelic word, meant 'waste' or 'wilderness'). Geographically, the champaign ground of the eastern coastal plain simply faded imperceptibly into the bogs of the Midlands. The western end of the Anglo-Scottish frontier, marked by streams which flowed into the Solway Firth, likewise presented no major geographical obstacle. In the Pale marches, even where nucleated villages and cereal-based agriculture had been established on marginal land, the late medieval population decline and increased border raids subsequently undermined their economic viability, thus prompting a reversion to pastoralism and leading to the phenomenon of scores of deserted villages. Elsewhere, in the lordship's less densely-settled west and north, the Gaelic Revival had led to entire regions being wiped out, thus leaving seaports like Galway and Carrickfergus as isolated English outposts.[21]

Pasture farming was the principal economic activity in these border regions, although the defence of pastoral communities was much more difficult to organise due to their more dispersed patterns of settlement. By and large, the Tudor state could not afford to support standing armies (much less its Scottish counterpart), nor to provide the lavish expenditure needed to maintain England's sole continental outpost, the elaborately-fortified and strongly-garrisoned Pale of Calais. Even in peacetime, Calais was a serious drain on royal finances: in addition to maintaining the peacetime garrison of 600 men, military works there cost at least £8,000 per annum under Henry VIII, thus necessitating regular subventions of at least £10,000 a year and

20   Robin Frame, 'Power and society in the lordship of Ireland, 1272–1377' in *Past and Present*,
       no. 76 (Aug. 1977), pp. 3–33 (esp. pp. 7, 32).
21   Ellis, *Tudor frontiers*, pp. 19–20, 23–5.

[1 6]   swallowing up some 10 per cent of the crown's ordinary income.[22] Small permanent garrisons were maintained at Berwick-on-Tweed and Carlisle, the two major military outposts at either end of the Anglo-Scottish frontier, and also in Ireland, while Scottish kings had professional garrisons at the major royal castles of Edinburgh and Stirling. At the outbreak of actual war with Scotland, the English marches were heavily reinforced by 'inlandmen' from Yorkshire or the Midlands. In Ireland the Dublin government could also call on English reinforcements in the event of a crisis. Castles such as Rockcliffe in the west marches towards Scotland and Lea in the Irish Midlands were specially built to house these additional wartime garrisons.[23]

In the 1560s, the regular establishment for wardens and troops along the Scottish frontier cost almost £4,900 a year, including a garrison of 357 in Berwick and 28 in Carlisle. The Irish garrison also approached the size of a small army, particularly from 1547 when it usually numbered at least 1,500 men.[24]

For the most part, however, the protection of long stretches of thinly-populated marchland relied on defence in depth. This was a true march, with an extended but fluctuating wasteland (or 'no-man's-land') beyond the so-called 'plenished ground'; a chain of strong points – peles, towerhouses and fortified bridges – between major castles; and where possible a system of earthworks ('dikes and ditches') constructed between the wasteland and the march proper to inhibit cattle rustling. Moreover, the earlier feudal settle-ment of these regions had included a series of compact lordships created for defence purposes. Thus, society was everywhere dominated by marcher lords rather than the pool of wealthy gentry responsible for the shires in Lowland England where a more dispersed pattern of landholding was the norm.[25] In early Tudor Cumberland, for instance, there were only two prominent tenants-in-chief: an inquisition of 1429 revealed that, of the other crown tenants, only two held as much as half a knight's fee.[26] In these circumstances, the

---

22   Morgan, 'Government of Calais', pp. 133, 149–50, 178–84; Charles Cruickshank, *Henry VIII and the invasion of France* (Stroud, 1990), ch. 2.

23   Ellis, *Tudor frontiers*, pp. 94, 120, 152, 160–61, 248; idem, *Ireland in the age of the Tudors 1447–1603: English expansion and the end of Gaelic rule* (London, 1998), pp. 164, 186; Goodare, *State and society in early modern Scotland*, pp. 144–9.

24   Samuel Haynes (ed.), *A collection of state papers relating to affairs in the reigns of King Henry VIII . . . Queen Elizabeth from the year 1542 to 1570* (London, 1740), pp. 397–8; Ellis, *Ireland in the age of the Tudors*, pp. 164, 186.

25   Ellis, *Tudor frontiers*, pp. 20, 23–32, 69–73.

26   *Inquisitions and assessments relating to feudal aids . . . 1284–1431* (4 vols, London, 1899–1906), i, 244–5.

obvious and most militarily effective means of defending these marches [17] was the traditional one of concentrating power in the hands of a great regional magnate, such as the Fitzgerald earls of Kildare in Ireland or the Percy earls of Northumberland in the north of England. The Percy estates in Northumberland were worth around £900 a year and also provided the earl with an army of almost 2,000 tenants, of whom 850 were horsemen. In 1528, when the sixth earl was appointed warden of the east and middle marches (i.e. Northumberland plus adjacent liberties), 69 of the 118 resident gentry were retained to assist the warden, thus ensuring that most of the shire's 6,375 able-bodied men were immediately available to the warden.[27] A similar situation existed in Co. Kildare, a smaller shire, where the estates of the Fitzgerald earl, then the crown's normal choice as governor of Ireland, were worth over IR£700 a year. In Co. Kildare, however, the military situation in the early 1530s represented a marked improvement on the situation 80 years earlier when, in the absence of a recognised earl, the Irish had reoccupied a series of border manors and destroyed others in less exposed locations. Recovering their ancestral estates and securing the county against Gaelic raids had taken almost 50 years of effort on the part of the seventh and eighth earls – in military campaigning, building towerhouses and strengthening major castles, fortifying key bridges, cutting passages, erecting dikes and ditches, and rebuilding and retenanting villages. Developing and maintaining the power of the Fitzgerald dynasty also required consistent royal support through successive grants of land, favourable marriages and, above all, the authority which accompanied the governorship.[28]

Military forces and the border surnames

The effects of this combination of accumulated noble power and delegated royal authority were starkly evident in England's west marches towards Scotland. The key to its defence was the large barony of Gilsland held by Thomas, third Lord Dacre of Gilsland, a poor border baron whose landed inheritance was worth only £320 a year. Gilsland was a compact block

---

27 Mervyn James, *Society, politics and culture: studies in early modern England* (Cambridge, 1986), pp. 60, 76; J.M.W. Bean, *The estates of the Percy family, 1416–1537* (Oxford, 1958), passim; S.G. Ellis, 'Civilizing Northumberland: representations of Englishness in the Tudor state' in *Journal of Historical Sociology*, xii (1999), pp. 103–27.

28 Ellis, *Tudor frontiers*, ch. 4.

of 15 manors with a perimeter of over 80 miles extending from the Northumberland county boundary high in the Cheviot Hills to the coastal plain a few miles short of Carlisle. By the late fifteenth century, Scottish military pressure had long since destroyed the English settlements north of Carlisle, leaving an extended no-man's-land, and throwing the burden of defence on Gilsland. In the winter of 1485–6 the barony was almost waste as a result of increasing Scottish raids, and Dacre's income there had been reduced to a mere £18 per annum. Most tenants had abandoned their holdings in fear of the Scots, thus leaving a gaping hole into the heart of the county, but Dacre simply lacked the resources to defend Gilsland properly. Thereafter, however, a favourable marriage with the heiress of the much richer Greystoke baronial family, together with a 40-year tenure of the wardenship (1485–1525) transformed Dacre into a major regional magnate. By 1525, Dacre's estates in Cumberland alone were worth over £600 a year, of which Gilsland contributed almost £140. The 1534 muster roll for this small, mainly pastoral border shire lists 6,502 able-bodied men, armed almost exclusively with the traditional English 'bills and bows', of whom 1,974 were mounted. Yet, by close attention to his *manraed* (the tenants, friends and followers available to the lord for military service) Dacre also was able to raise 434 horsemen and nagmen, plus 196 footmen from among his own tenants in Gilsland alone. The barony thus provided around 22 per cent of the county's mounted troops at military musters, even though it constituted less than 10 per cent of the county's available manpower.[29]

In Scotland, the balance between noble power and delegated royal authority was tilted even more firmly in favour of the nobility. The power of the nobles derived chiefly from their ties of kinship, together with relatively compact landed holdings and their hereditary sheriffships and regalities. These kinship ties were reinforced by the Scottish custom of giving bonds of manrent. Throughout Scotland, men bound themselves to serve their lords for life and to give counsel and military service in return for a promise of maintenance and protection. The earls of Huntly and Errol in the north-east, of Argyll in the west, and Lord Maxwell or the earl of Angus on the borders accumulated these bonds in much the same way as William Lord Hastings accumulated indentured retainers in England. Some 800 of these contracts survive, made between 1442 and 1603, thus ensuring that the lords could

---

29 Ellis, *Tudor frontiers*, ch. 3; idem, 'Collapse of the Gaelic world', p. 459; Public Record Office, Kew, C 54/394, m. 7, E 150/112 (*Calendar of inquisitions post mortem, Henry VII* (3 vols, London, 1898–1955), I, no. 157).

continue to deploy sizeable armies of their tenants, servants and followers.
In the 1560s, for instance, magnates like the earls of Arran, Huntly and
Crawford readily agreed to provide 1,000 men for a campaign, and the earl
of Argyll could raise 5,000. Alongside them were bonds of friendship, made
for the same purpose of assistance and protection but between lords and
lairds of roughly equal status. One reason for these bonds of manrent and
friendship was the more institutionalised survival in Scotland of the bloodfeud. Most commonly feuding persisted at a local level, usually involving
barons, clan chiefs, and lairds, plus their tenants and servants, but sometimes
with peers involved. Occasionally feuds achieved a regional importance,
such as the Caithness-Sutherland feud in the far north, or the Maxwell-
Johnstone feud in the south-west which lasted for 50 years from 1573. More
often, a feud might last for five years until composed by the king, the church,
or the nobility. In periods of weak government, such as the later sixteenth
century, the incidence of feuding escalated: Keith Brown has identified 365
feuds in Scotland between 1573 and 1625, mainly before 1610.[30]

At least until 1603, however, Scottish kings lacked the patronage and
resources to challenge the magnates in their local spheres of influence, and
so had no alternative but to accept noble rule in local government, and to
focus instead on encouraging them to maintain good rule within their
spheres of influence. During the sixteenth century, however, the English
monarchy became increasingly reluctant to delegate authority to marcher
lords who were seen as unreliable. In May 1534, when Henry VIII's suspicions were aroused as to the conduct of Lord Dacre and the earl of Kildare,
they were suddenly arrested and dismissed from office. Thereafter, no Irish
peer was ever appointed governor of Tudor Ireland. Dacre recovered the
wardenship after Henry VIII's death and was later joined by the restored earl
of Northumberland, but Elizabeth I in particular distrusted the northern
nobles who were solidly Catholic, and she opted to pack the wardenries with
southerners and lesser men. This strategy thus ensured that the wardenries
were in reliable hands, but the borders themselves suffered because the
wardens lacked sufficient *manraed* to govern. Elizabeth was less concerned
about defence because after 1560 there was no further war between England

---

30 Jenny Wormald, *Lords and men in Scotland: bonds of manrent, 1442–1603* (Edinburgh, 1985);
idem, *Court, kirk, and community: Scotland 1470–1625* (London, 1981), chs 1–2; K.M. Brown,
Bloodfeud in Scotland 1573–1625 (Edinburgh, 1986); J.E.A. Dawson, *The politics of religion in the
age of Mary, queen of Scots: the earl of Argyll and the struggle for Britain and Ireland* (Cambridge,
2002), pp. 51–4; Goodare, *State and society in early modern Scotland*, pp. 136–40, 287–9.

[2 0]   and Scotland and relations between the two governments were generally good.[31]

Alongside the organisation of defence through manorial tenants in predominantly arable regions, and the role of marcher lords in pastoral uplands and boglands, a third kind of frontier had developed in those areas without resident lords. For instance, almost the entire length of the northern boundary of the English middle marches was formed by Tynedale and Redesdale. Feudally, Tynedale and Redesdale comprised the two enormous manors of Wark and Harbottle respectively. Harbottle was not a manor in any real sense of the word, but a wild stretch of territory some 18 miles long by 10 miles wide and covering almost 88,000 acres in a land of constant war. (In contrast, the manor of Etal in the nearby Lowlands covered less than 4,900 acres.) Yet Harbottle was worth only £13 a year: Sir Robert Tailboys was its absentee lord and large parts of the manor were waste. In the 1540s, the crown acquired it through an exchange with the Tailboys' heiress, although this hardly made much difference. The adjoining manor of Wark, measuring 27 miles by 17 miles and covering a whopping 183,000 acres, had long been in the hands of the crown, but it was in no better condition.[32] Conditions in the middle march, and also in parts of Ireland, thus promoted a third variation in regard to the impact of the frontier on social structures, the phenomenon of the border surnames, or lineages in Ireland. These extended family groupings (also called clans and kindreds) were peculiar to the frontier regions of the English state, although they were of course indigenous to Gaelic and Welsh society. The surnames (often castigated as 'thieves') inhabited parts of the actual frontier districts, particularly the poorer upland areas of the west and middle marches, on both sides of the border line. In default of a resident lord to defend them against the Scots, the surnames appointed their own captains and headsmen to organise defence and negotiate with the warden of the marches and other royal officials. Tenurially, their feudal obligations were minimal, apart from military service under their keeper to guard the valley from wolves and thieves. Yet the government could only control them, with great difficulty, by

31   Ellis, *Tudor frontiers*, pp. 173–5, 248–9; Christopher Haigh, *Elizabeth I* (London, 1988), pp. 52–4.
32   Sanderson (ed.), *Survey of the Debateable and Border Lands*, pp. 53, 85, 128; Public Record Office, C 142/10, no. 6 (*Cal. inq. p.m. Hen. VII*, I, no. 971); Ellis, 'Civilizing Northumberland', pp. 113–14, 117–19.

appointing special keepers for Tynedale and Redesdale and imprisoning leading members of the surnames as pledges for the conduct of others. In the marches of Scotland too, there were other surnames who operated equally independently of royal authority. They were kinship groups acting together in all things. They collectively sought vengeance when one of their number was attacked or injured ('the deadly feud') and they often accepted joint responsibility for the conduct of individual members. In Ireland, too, English officials sought to apply joint responsibility (*cinn comhfhocuis*, a basic principle of Gaelic law) in their dealings with Gaelic clans. Their main livelihood consisted of raising cattle, sheep and horses, but this was supplemented by the profits of warfare, reiving and robbery.

Although the first reference to surnames does not appear until 1498, they clearly developed in response to the endemic insecurity of the Anglo-Scottish Marches from 1296 onwards; the period between 1333 and 1502 being marked by periodic truces and temporary abstinences of war, with no formal peace. In the west march the leading English border lineages were the Routledges and Nixons of Bewcastle, with Storeys and Forsters in Eskdale; in north Tynedale in the middle march the Charltons predominated, followed by Robsons, Dodds and Milburns; and in Redesdale the Halls were the leading clan, with Hedleys, Redes and Potts. Across the border there were similar surnames, notably the Armstrongs and Elliots of Liddesdale, and the Grahams from around Gretna. The indigenous English surnames intermarried not only with each other but with the Scottish clans, so that in the early sixteenth century there were English branches of the Armstrongs and Grahams established in Bewcastledale and Eskdale respectively. The clansmen had in turn allies and sympathisers among some of the less law-abiding border gentry, and even among local magnates like Lord Dacre. Royal control of the marches, therefore, normally depended on inducing the local nobles and gentry to exert their influence with the border surnames in approved ways, and if necessary, reinforcing this persuasion with the threat of force. Yet the surnames constituted a formidable force in their own right. When 'booked' by the Tudor government in 1528, the Tynedale and Redesdale surnames alone numbered 403 and 445 respectively; and when mustered with the rest of the shire in 1538, all the 391 from Tynedale and 185 Redesdale surnames were equipped with horse and harness. Given that the muster returns for the whole shire totalled 6,375 able men, of whom 2,913 were equipped with horse and harness, the Tynedale and Redesdale surnames supplied about 13 per cent of Northumberland's available manpower and almost 20 per cent of the most highly prized troops in border warfare, the mounted spearmen.[33]

We may set the size of these forces in context. Dumfriesshire could apparently raise 5,970 fighting men in 1547. Although there were perhaps 100,000 able-bodied men in the whole of Scotland, most had few or no arms: the Scottish host summoned from the entire kingdom normally produced around 20,000 fighting men. (In the Pinkie campaign of 1547, around 22,500 men served – the largest Scottish army actually assembled in this period.) A significant proportion of this military manpower came from Scottish Gaeldom: the earls of Argyll normally supplied around a quarter of the Scottish host, and the fifth earl commanded the largest independent military force in the British Isles, with his own fleet and artillery train. In 1545, the last serious MacDonald pretender, Donald Dubh, brought 4,000 redshanks (Gaelic mercenaries) in 180 galleys with him to Ireland. At that date, Scottish Gaeldom was probably more militarised than Irish Gaeldom, and also had a tradition of exporting its surplus manpower to Ireland for service as galloglass and redshanks. For Ireland, an English 'description of the power of Irishmen' dating from c.1490 lists 88 Gaelic chieftaincies whose combined military power amounted to 3,089 horse, 41 battalions of galloglass (armoured mercenary footsoldiers, around 3,000 men) and 15,744 kerne (footsoldiers). The size of these forces undoubtedly increased in the later sixteenth century as major Irish chiefs militarised in response to Tudor expansion: O'Donnell hired 500 of Argyll's mercenaries in 1555, for instance. Militarily, however, 70 per cent of Irish forces were unarmoured kerne, whose combat value was decidedly limited, particularly in pitched battles. Henry Tudor's army took a fearful toll of the Gaelic kerne deployed at the battle of Stoke in 1487: when they again saw service in Henry VIII's armies in France and Scotland in 1544–5, English officials accounted them good for burning, foraging and looting, but for little else. Yet it was unusual for more than two or three Irish chiefs to combine, and the forces of individual chiefs were quite small – three battle of galloglass, 200 horse and 300 kerne in the case of O'Neill of Tyrone, a major provincial chief, but just 24 horse and 80 kerne for O'Toole, a weak border chief.[34]

In wartime the surnames thus provided an important addition to military might, but frequently they preyed on the surrounding Lowland communities,

33   Ellis, *Tudor frontiers*, pp. 59–76; idem, 'Civilizing Northumberland', pp. 114, 120–21; Nicholls, *Gaelic and gaelicized Ireland*, pp. 63–4.

34   Dawson, *The politics of religion in the age of Mary, queen of Scots*, pp. 51–6; Goodare, *State and society in early modern Scotland*, pp. 136–40; Ellis, 'Collapse of the Gaelic world', pp. 458–61.

or extorted blackmail from them. In the sixteenth century, when the population increased and 'the long peace' meant a reduction of more legitimate
targets, the English surnames became virtually uncontrollable. The crown
appointed special keepers for Tynedale and Redesdale and took pledges
from the surnames for good behaviour. Occasionally, the king's officers were
reduced to mounting military campaigns against them, but even this was not
the deterrent it seemed. For instance, in 1525, officials predicted (accurately)
that 'when so ever we begin our war with Tynedale, the thieves shall avoid
and flee the country', disappearing into the woods or mountains, or into
Scotland, 'and more than to dispoil the country and burn their houses we
cannot do'. Some parts of their valleys were almost inaccessible to horsemen
lacking local knowledge; the headsmen living in houses of oak strongly
bound with earth or turf roofs which were well hidden and difficult to break
or burn. The thatched cottages of their followers, though easily burned,
could be rebuilt within three or four hours. Moreover, the surnames would
'immediately after our departing . . . invade the good countries', so that garrisons would have to be laid for their defence.[35] By 1542 there was only one
towerhouse left standing in north Tynedale, and the border commissioners
recommended that two old fortresses should be rebuilt and 'plenished with
some true & honest defencible men' so as to restrain the passage of thieves
thereabouts. No amount of persuasion or threats could curb their activities
for very long, however. In Ireland, there were likewise the English lineages
in the more exposed parts of the Dublin marches, and also the Dillons,
Daltons and Delamares in south-west Meath.[36] And in Wales there were
thieves and robber bands operating out of the marcher lordships.

Nation, culture and identity

How far and in what ways did the rule of frontiers and marcher societies
help to reshape senses of national identity during this period? Scottish
identity had been forged during the long, increasingly bitter Wars of
Independence of the fourteenth century, when the 'community of the realm'

35   British Library, Caligula B. I, f. 47v (*L. & P. Hen. VIII*, iv (i), no. 1289); Survey by Bowes and
       Ellerker, 1542: Hodgson, *Northumberland*, III, ii, 201, 231–3; R.T. Spence, 'The pacification
       of the Cumberland borders, 1593–1628' in *Northern History*, xiii (1977), p. 62.
36   Bowes and Ellerker's survey, 1542 in Hodgson, *Northumberland*, III, ii, 228–9, 231; Ellis,
       Tudor frontiers, pp. 71–4.

[2 4] under a patriot king and backed by the Scottish church had resisted English aggression and claims of overlordship. The most famous document in Scottish history, the Declaration of Arbroath (1320) included a mythology of the nation's past, a vision of the relationship of the kings of Scots and the Scottish people, and a summary of the opening stage of the Wars. The Wars also gave the Scots a popular martyr in the form of William Wallace; a new national saint with the reconsecration of St Andrews Cathedral in 1318; and a new official history written between 1375 and 1450 culminating in Walter Bower's *Scotichronicon*, followed later by a populist version, *The Wallace*, which denounced the Anglo-Scottish treaty of 1474.[37] English identity was likewise forged in a national struggle, the Hundred Years War against the French. At least in outlying parts of the monarchy, however, English nationality and identity had traditionally coincided with a strong sense of regional identity among 'the northern men' and 'the English of Ireland' respectively.[38] Yet the situation in these two regions was also some-what different. In the Anglo-Scottish marches, Scottish Armstrongs and English Charltons were culturally indistinguishable, speaking the same lan-guage, practising the same customs as border surnames, and enjoying the same lifestyle, in despite of the border. In large measure, the lords and lairds of southern Scotland and the nobles and gentry of northern England were also culturally homogeneous, despite the emergence of separate English and Scottish senses of identity. What legally determined nationality was place of birth: Tudor officials doggedly classified the border surnames as English or Scots depending on which side of the border line they resided (residence being a presumption of birth), even though this did not make the surnames act any differently. At the battle of Flodden in 1513, for instance, the English surnames waited until the two armies dismounted to fight, and then plundered both sides indiscriminately, making off with the English horse and baggage.[39] In Ireland, however, the cultural gap between the two nations was much more deep-seated and clear-cut while, at the same time, the frontier between English and Gaelic parts was indistinct and ill-defined. In principle, the legal criteria of nationality were the same in both marches: the English were those of free birth born in territories under the allegiance of the English crown. Just as Scots were aliens who were denied the rights and privileges of the king's subjects, so likewise legislation in Ireland excluded

---

37 Grant, *Independence and nationhood*, pp. 7–9, 14–15, 29–35, 54–7; Lynch, *Scotland*, pp. 111–14, 132–5.
38 Ellis, 'Crown, community and government', pp. 187–204.
39 *L. & P. Hen. VIII*, i (2nd ed.), nos. 2246, 2283.

the king's Irish enemies from English law, or from holding office, land or [25]
ecclesiastical benefices within the Englishry.[40]

Yet where 'the English ground' ended was far less clear in Ireland than
Britain, and Gaelic labourers could also move easily into the English districts
– indeed, the late medieval labour shortage encouraged them to do so. Thus,
in Ireland, culture was a more important determinant of nationality: later
fifteenth-century legislation, for instance, insisted that the English of the
marches should dress like Englishmen and shave their upper lip, and that
Irishmen living in the English Pale should likewise wear English dress,
adopt English surnames, and be sworn the king's lieges. Long residence
within the Englishry combined with English customs seemingly made a man
English: conversely English marchers who adopted Irish habits and dress
could also be treated by the English as Irish (although never so accepted by
the Irish themselves).[41] The effect of this legislation is unclear: probably it
had little impact on the lower social orders. Yet among those with land and
property, the distinction between English marchers and Irish enemies was
fundamental. Irish clansmen stood outside the king's protection, their land
and property was liable to forfeiture. Not surprisingly, many of the Irish
nation chose to purchase what was revealingly described as a 'charter of
English liberty and freedom from Irish servitude': like Scots living in the
English marches, they took the oath of allegiance and were, in the telling
phrase, 'sworn English'.[42]

Thus, English identity was not without its attractions in the Anglo-Gaelic
marches, even during the period of the Gaelic Revival. Acculturation was of
the essence of marcher society, and there were long-standing complaints
by Tudor officials about the widespread adoption by English marchers of
Gaelic customs and language. Yet the distinction between English lieges and
Irish enemies was not just a legal technicality upheld by English officials. To
be English was to be free and civilised; Irishness was synonymous with
servitude and savagery. English subjects also looked to the king and council
for favour and protection. For instance, 'the king's poor subjects of this city
of Cork, Kinsale and Youghal' in Munster petitioned the king's council to
send 'two good justices . . . and some captain with twenty Englishmen' to

40 Griffith, 'The English realm and dominions', pp. 83–105; Ellis, 'Crown, community and
   government', pp. 187–204.
41 Parliament rolls, 25 Henry VI c. 20, 5 Edward IV cc. 12–17, 16 & 17 Edward IV c. 10 (*Stat.
   Ire.*, *Hen. VI*, p. 88, *Edw. IV*, i, 288–92, ii, 528–32).
42 Ellis, *Reform and revival*, pp. 129–31; idem, 'An English gentleman', p. 36; idem, *Ireland in the
   age of the Tudors*, p. 54 (quotation).

[26] resist the Irish thereabouts; 'and if you do not, then we are all cast away, and then farewell Munster for ever'.[43] Similarly, a Meath marcher petitioning the earl of Ormond for a lease of land lamented the prevalence of Irish horsemen and galloglass in the marches thereabouts, complaining that very few now 'rideth in a saddle daily' or 'weareth gown and doublet' in the English fashion, and reminding the earl that 'I, my lord, I am an Englishman'.[44] Thus, as Peter Sahlins has argued with regard to the Franco-Spanish frontier, defensive needs also stimulated a rhetoric of patriotism among the marchers, helping to strengthen ties between centre and periphery.[45]

Overall, therefore, the rule and defence of long landed frontiers posed a series of intractable problems to monarchical government. These were tackled in a number of ways – through the delegation of power to marcher lords, by the development of permanent garrisons, by the appointment of reliable outsiders. These different strategies for rule and defence had a major impact on border society, but none of them provided an effective solution to the problem of the marches. This only came in 1603, when the Union of the Crowns and the completion of the Tudor conquest of Ireland led to the dismantling of the two remaining military frontiers. For the first time, the whole of the British Isles was now governed from London by the same king, King James VI and I, and the erstwhile frontiers simply disappeared. Even so, the Union had no impact on traditional problems of geography and communication within the archipelago, and 'civil society' did not automatically oust the more turbulent forms of marcher society just because the frontiers themselves, with military institutions and border tenures, had been abolished.

43 A.J. Otway-Ruthven, *A history of medieval Ireland* (2nd ed., London, 1980), p. 381 (quotation); Ellis, 'An English gentleman', p. 36.
44 Edmund Curtis (ed.), *Calendar of Ormond deeds, 1172–1350* [etc.] (6 vols, Dublin, 1932–43, iv [1509–47], app. 76.
45 Peter Sahlins, *Boundaries: the making of France and Spain in the Pyrenees* (Berkeley, 1989), pp. 112–23.

POLITICS, WAR AND DIPLOMACY, 1450–1502

The period 1450–1502 saw the beginnings of a fundamental realign- ment of politics in the British Isles, which was to lead by 1560 to the emergence of a more self-contained British political system. In 1450 insular politics were still dominated by the traditional west European alliances and rivalries which had first emerged around 1300. Chief among these was Anglo-French rivalry, manifested in the Hundred Years War (1337–1453). In the late middle ages, England was a major European power, with signi- ficant possessions in France, as well as conquest lordships in Ireland and Wales. The English monarchy had traditionally enjoyed good relations both with the kingdoms of the Iberian peninsula, which were important for the defence of English Gascony, and also with other territories on the margins of the French kingdom, particularly Flanders and Burgundy. Conversely, Scotland's 'auld alliance' with France forced the English monarchy to fight a war on two fronts. French kings prompted and encouraged Scottish attacks on England by making subsidies available; French troops occasionally served in Scotland, and likewise a large Scottish army served in France in 1424. The final phase of the Anglo-French War had begun in 1415 with striking successes for the English in Normandy, and then the treaty of Troyes in 1420 by which Henry V of England was recognised as heir to Charles VI of France. The establishment of a Lancastrian dual monarchy with the acces- sion of Henry VI to the crowns of England and France in 1422 thus marked the summit of English ambitions on the continent.[1]

---

1 For this and the next paragraph, see for instance, Nigel Saul (ed.), *England in Europe 1066–1453* (London, 1994), chs 9–10, 12–14.

[28] English defeat, Scottish monarchy and Gaelic revival

The English occupation of Normandy and other parts of northern France was underpinned by relatively dense English settlement in parts of the region. Between 1435 and 1441, moreover, the Lancastrian regime also came close to establishing a professional standing army for the defence of its French possessions against the Valois king, Charles VII.[2] Had things turned out otherwise in 1449–53, the relationship between the British Isles and continental Europe might well have been very different, precipitating the development of a far more powerful, aggressive and absolute Tudor monarchy than eventually materialised. Yet after 1436, when the English lost Paris, the Lancastrian regime in northern France was gradually confined to the duchy of Normandy. The government found it increasingly difficult to harness English resources for an unsuccessful French war; and then, between March 1449 and August 1450, the English position in Normandy collapsed, as military defeat followed financial exhaustion.

The English were defeated in France chiefly because of the Lancastrian regime's growing financial weakness. In the later fourteenth century, English successes in France had reflected in large measure the financial superiority of her rulers: kings of England could spend double that of their adversaries on warfare, and so recruit and maintain larger armies. In the fifteenth century, however, the Valois kings redressed the balance by imposing taxation without consent on their subjects, at a time when, by contrast, Henry VI's government was increasingly unable to tax effectively the growing wealth of his subjects. The well-known financial estimates of the English crown's revenues, produced by Ralph Lord Cromwell when he was treasurer in 1433, revealed that ordinary income (£58,794) just about sufficed for the government's normal domestic needs (£59,605), but that permanent commitments to the defence of Gascony, Ireland, and particularly Calais created a chronic deficit of £15,892.[3] And when the English garrisons in Normandy

---

2   Anne Curry, 'The first English standing army? Military organisation in Lancastrian Normandy, 1420–1450' in Charles Ross (ed.), *Patronage pedigree and power in later medieval England* (Gloucester, 1979), pp. 193–214; Robert Massey, 'The land settlement in Lancastrian Normandy' in A.J. Pollard (ed.), *Property and politics: essays in later medieval English history* (Gloucester, 1984), pp. 76–96.
3   R.A. Griffiths, *The reign of Henry VI* (London, 1981), pp. 107–8; N. Saul (ed.), *England in Europe*, pp. 16, 151–4.

were left without food and pay, they preyed on the local population, arousing deep popular resentment. In the final campaign, the majority of the beleaguered garrisons were bribed to surrender by the French, so that by August 1450, as John Paston was informed, 'we have not now a foot of land in Normandy'. There followed two final campaigns (1451, 1452–3) in the duchy of Gascony, where Gascon resistance to the French proved more spirited than that of the Normans, and which, unlike the recently-conquered duchy of Normandy, had been held continuously by the English crown since 1152. Yet, when the English expeditionary force under John Talbot, earl of Shrewsbury, was defeated at Castillon in 1453, the garrison at Calais (conquered and colonised by the English in 1347) became the sole remaining outpost of Lancastrian power in continental Europe.[4]

The collapse of Lancastrian France inevitably made a deep impression on the crown's English subjects. The loss of prestige suffered by Henry VI's government was a major cause of the dynastic struggle between Lancaster and York (1455–87). Later kings maintained the traditional English claim to the crown of France, and Edward IV and Henry VIII in particular mounted campaigns in the hope of recovering the lost territories, but the odds were now heavily stacked against the English. Initially, internal dissensions interspersed with recurrences of civil war distracted successive kings from this traditional goal of English foreign policy. Concurrently, however, French kings were annexing and absorbing into the kingdom the remaining quasi-independent fiefs which had offered England intermittent support during the Hundred Years War, notably, the duchy of Burgundy in 1477, and Brittany in 1491. Thus between 1450 and 1491 the French monarchy secured control of the whole coastline opposite England between the Iberian peninsula and the single surviving English military outpost at Calais.[5] By the time Henry VIII attempted to recommence the Hundred Years War in 1512, the French monarchy greatly outstripped its English counterpart in financial and military resources. Such successes as the English subsequently enjoyed in France owed more to French ambitions in Italy than England's ability to match French military might.[6]

Yet of more immediate concern to the balance of power in the British Isles was the impact of this Lancastrian collapse on Anglo-Scottish relations. The

4   Saul (ed.), *England in Europe*, ch. 14 (quotation, p. 151).
5   Denys Hay, *Europe in the fourteenth and fifteenth centuries* (London, 1966), pp. 138–45.
6   David Potter, 'Foreign policy' in Diarmaid MacCulloch (ed.), *The reign of Henry VIII: politics, policy and piety* (Basingstoke, 1995), pp. 111–14.

central fact of Scottish foreign policy in the late middle ages had been generally bad relations with England. Between 1332 and 1502, there was no formal peace between England and Scotland, only periodic war interspersed with a series of shaky truces and even more fragile temporary abstinences of war. The military and financial weakness of the Lancastrian regime, and then the Wars of the Roses, effectively ended any serious English claim to overlordship over Scotland. For almost the first time since the start of the Scottish Wars of Independence in 1296, the Scottish crown enjoyed an extended respite from constant English military pressure in the south. In the short term, Scottish kings profited from this interlude to recover the last remaining parcels of land under English occupation since the fourteenth century, the erstwhile English Pale in southern Scotland. James II (1437–60) was killed at the siege of Roxburgh, when one of his siege guns 'brake in the firing', but his army went on to capture the castle, so ending the English occupation of Teviotdale. The following year the defeated Lancastrians ceded Berwick-on-Tweed in return for Scottish support against the Yorkists.[7] Berwick-on-Tweed would remain a bone of contention in Anglo-Scottish relations throughout the 1480s, and it was not until 1552 that the Debateable Land, north of Carlisle, was finally partitioned between the two kingdoms. Yet the Anglo-Scottish frontier was now much more clearly delineated than the English state's fragmented and fluid frontier with Gaelic Ireland.[8]

In other ways too, the position of Scottish kings within the geographical boundaries of Scotland was becoming easier. The Western Isles had been annexed from Norway in 1266, but it was not until 1468 that Orkney and Shetland were acquired, initially as pledge for payment of a dowry (which remained unpaid) for the marriage of James III (1460–88) to Margaret, daughter of Christian I of Denmark, and at the same time a dispute was settled over payment of an annual tribute for the Western Isles.[9] Moreover, throughout the later middle ages Scottish kings had had to cope with a succession of powerful magnates with extended landed possessions whose loyalty was sometimes suspect and who exercised a disruptive influence on politics. Eventually, in 1452, when the king had stabbed to death with his knife William eighth earl of Douglas, the new earl had turned for support to

7 Ranald Nicholson, *Scotland: the later middle ages* (Edinburgh, 1974), pp. 396–400 (quotation, p. 396); Michael Lynch, *Scotland, a new history* (London, 1991), chs 8–10.
8 S.G. Ellis, 'The English state and its frontiers in the British Isles, 1300–1600' in Daniel Power and Naomi Standen (ed.), *Frontiers in question: Eurasian borderlands, 700–1700* (Basingstoke, 1999), pp. 153–81.
9 Lynch, *Scotland*, pp. 155–6.

Henry VI of England. He was joined in rebellion by John of Islay, the powerful earl of Ross and lord of the Isles, who seized the castles of Inverness,
Urquhart and Ruthven. In the ensuing struggle, the king canvassed the support of the lesser nobility, creating three new earldoms and seven lords. The
Black Douglas family estates were eventually forfeited in 1455, swelling
the crown's income by SC£2,000.[10] After this, however, those who now
appeared at the head of Scottish political society were, individually, men
with whom the king could cope more easily: Gordon of Huntly, Hamilton,
Erskine of Dun, and Campbell (created earl of Argyll c.1458) all belonged to
old substantial baronial families, but they had a smaller territorial base and
income, so that their power and influence depended more on government
service. Institutionally too, this change was recognised by the development
c.1450 of the peerage rank of 'lord of parliament'.[11]

A more intractable problem from a Scottish Lowland perspective were
developments within the traditional Gaelic world spanning the North
Channel between Ireland and Scotland, where c.1450 the MacDonald maritime lordship was showing distinct signs of developing into an autonomous
Gaelic kingdom in the far north west of the British Isles. With its power base
in the Western Isles, Clan Donald had exploited the weakness of Scottish
kings in this recently-acquired territory to build up an aggressive lordship
which championed Gaelic values, culture, and even independence against
the increasingly Lowland values of the Scottish crown and the *Gaill*
(English-speakers) there. By the 1350s, John MacDonald possessed all the
Hebrides, except Skye, and most of the Scottish west coast from Glenelg to
Kintyre. He was also expanding into the Glens of Antrim at the expense of
the earldom of Ulster. He and his successors styled themselves lords of the
Isles (*dominus Insularum*); but perhaps more significantly, they retained in
their Gaelic style (*Rí Innsí Gall*) the traditional title of *Rí* (king), at a time
when Gaelic chiefs in Ireland were abandoning it in favour of the title *tig-
hearna* (lord) which English and Scottish kings found less offensive to their
own pretensions.[12] In the early fifteenth century, Clan Donald had expanded
into Ross where Donald, the second lord, had married the earl of Ross's
heiress. MacDonald pretensions were checked at the battle of Harlaw, fought
near Aberdeen in 1411, at which the lord of the Isles reputedly deployed

10 Nicholson, *Scotland*, pp. 355–78.
11 Nicholson, *Scotland*, pp. 376–7; Alexander Grant, *Independence and nationhood: Scotland
    1306–1469* (London, 1984), pp. 195–6.
12 Cf. Katharine Simms, *From kings to warlords: the changing political structure of Gaelic Ireland in the
    later middle ages* (Woodbridge, 1987), ch. 3.

[3 2]   10,000 men against a royal army; but at Inverlochy in 1431, a royal force was actually defeated by the lordship's army. Eventually in 1437, the Lord's feudal claim to the earldom of Ross through his mother (inadmissible in Gaelic law) was recognised by the crown; and through this combination of a west-coast lordship with an east-coast earldom, the MacDonalds became the dominant force in the Highlands.[13]

The ambiguity of the Lord's position is perhaps the key to Clan Donald success. His willingness to adopt feudalised concepts as circumstances dictated, for instance by accepting royal charters and issuing his own, helped to introduce greater cohesion into the lordship and also to tie it more closely into the Scottish realm. At the same time, however, successive lords intrigued with the English crown – the nominal overlord of their possessions in Antrim – and were claimed by the English as allies in fifteenth-century Anglo-Scottish truces. Alexander, third lord (1423–49) may also have tried to get the Danish king to reassert Norwegian suzerainty over the Western Isles. In 1462, John, fourth lord (1449–93) concluded a secret tripartite treaty with Edward IV of England and the exiled earl of Douglas, whereby MacDonald and Douglas agreed to become Edward's subjects, to conquer Scotland with English assistance, dividing the region north of the Forth between them, and holding it of the English king.[14] Scottish nationalist accounts of Clan Donald fortunes stress how much the clan was part of 'the national community'; and of course the language and terminology of Scottish royal government naturally stressed this perspective on clan and lordship. A more accurate (but neglected) indicator of MacDonald pretensions, however, was the Gaelic verse composed for the fourth lord by his hereditary bard, in which Scottish and Irish themes are interwoven to stress the Lord's over-arching position throughout late medieval Gaeldom:

> Pride of the *Gaedhil*, the champion of Ulster . . .
> His prime purpose is to come to Tara,
> putting Meath in commotion, the leopard of Islay.[15]

13   Grant, *Independence and nationhood*, pp. 210–18; Nicholson, *Scotland*, pp. 234–7, 316–17.
14   Nicholson, *Scotland*, pp. 315, 401–2. The latest account of the rise of Clan Donald is marred by the author's failure to examine the Gaelic sources: Alexander Grant, 'Scotland's "Celtic fringe" in the late middle ages: the MacDonald lords of the Isles and the kingdom of Scotland' in R.R. Davies (ed.), *The British Isles 1100–1500: comparisons, contrasts and connections* (Edinburgh, 1988), pp. 118–41.
15   Guaire Gaoidheal, aoinfher uladh . . . /a bhert bunaidh techt go temhair/measgadh midhe onchu íle: 'The book of Clanranald', in Alexander Cameron, *Reliquiae Celticae: texts, papers, and studies in Gaelic literature and philosophy*. Eds Alexander MacBain and John Kennedy (2 vols, Inverness, 1892–4), p. 260.

Traditionally, high kings of Ireland had been inaugurated at Tara, but as is [3 3]
clear from an elegy of John of Islay, composed by an Irish bard, the fourth
lord claimed all that and more:

> The sovereignty of the *Gaedhil* to Clann Colla.
> It is right to proclaim it.
> They were again in the same battalions, the heroes of *Fodla* [Ireland].
> The sovereignty of Ireland and Scotland of the sunny lands was had by the
> bloody sharp-bladed tribes, the fighting champions.
> The sovereignty of the entire tribes was obtained, by John of Islay.[16]

In sum, the lords of the Isles presented an increasingly dangerous challenge to fifteenth-century Scottish kings. Their maritime traditions and their
more thoroughgoing acceptance of feudalised concepts set them apart
from the comparatively weak and land-based chieftaincies of Gaelic Ireland,
enabling them to deploy both a powerful fleet of galleys and a far larger
army than chiefs of Irish lordships, where the lower orders did not bear
arms.[17] At the same time, however, their conquest lordship in Ulster, under
the nominal overlordship of the English crown as residual earl of Ulster, gave
them a secure base against the Scottish monarchy. The lordship's authent-
ically Gaelic values also secured for Clan Donald a following in Gaelic Ulster,
where traditional concepts focusing on the island of Ireland as the Gaelic
national territory were increasingly rivalled by newer, ethnic senses of Gaelic
identity which straddled the North Channel. Thus, while John of Islay laid
claim to the conventional Gaelic title of 'ardrígh na hÉireann' (high king of
Ireland), his description in a prose account as 'áird rígh . . . Gaoidheal' (the
high king of the *Gaedhil*) constituted a wider claim to leadership of Gaeldom
as a whole.[18] At bottom, however, Clan Donald power reflected their peripheral location on the margins of the English and Scottish monarchies, and the
vindication of MacDonald pretensions depended on continued animosity
between these two kings.

In the century to *c.*1450, the growing strength of the lordship of the Isles
was simply the most striking manifestation of a wider political and cultural

16 Ceñus Ghaoidheal do chlann cholla, coir a fhógra/síad arís na gcathibh cétna, flatha fodla
    ceñus eireñ 7 albuin an fhuiñ ghríanaigh/ata ag an dréim fhuilidh fhaobhraigh cuiridh
    cliaruidh/Fuair ceñus na haicme uile, Eoin a híle: ibid., pp. 208–10; A.M. MacDonald (ed.),
    The MacDonald collection of Gaelic poetry (Inverness, 1911), pp. vi, 6.
17 S.G. Ellis, 'The collapse of the Gaelic world, 1450–1650' in *Irish Historical Studies*, xxxi
    (1998–9), pp. 449–69, for this and the following account of the Gaelic Revival in Ireland.
18 'Book of Clanranald', p. 264.

[3 4] movement affecting the whole of late medieval Gaeldom. This was the Gaelic Revival which from the later thirteenth century had spread throughout Gaelic Ireland and Scotland. In Ireland, the Gaelic chiefs had gradually acquired some of the military technology which had underpinned the earlier Anglo-Norman advance there. In particular, they were able to blunt the English advantage in heavy cavalry by importing from Scotland armoured mercenary footsoldiers, the famous galloglass, and then equipping their light horsemen with armour. They had also learned many of the principles of siege-warfare, and by 1400 Irish chiefs were also building their own stone castles. Thus, whereas Gaelic chiefs had generally once accepted the overlordship of neighbouring English magnates (and so, indirectly, the authority of the English crown), during the Gaelic Revival they broke away and very often reconquered adjacent borderlands from English settlers. At the same time, English Ireland was much more seriously disrupted by the late medieval demographic decline. The consequent labour shortages and the collapse of food prices undermined the manorial system, and ultimately defence, in outlying parts of the English lordship. Thus, whereas c.1300 the English lordship had extended over about two-thirds of the island, in large parts of Ireland which had not been intensively colonised by English settlers, notably the de Burgo earldom of Ulster and lordship of Connaught, the authority of the Dublin administration collapsed in the face of this Gaelic Revival. By 1450, the area of English rule had been reduced to around a third of the island, in two contracted areas – 'the four obedient shires' around Dublin in the east, and another region centred on the Barrow-Nore-Suir river system in the south – plus a few outlying towns like Galway and Carrickfergus.

This changing political and military balance precipitated a remarkable efflorescence of Gaelic culture, attesting to the growing confidence of native society in this period. It was reflected in such areas as architecture, the foundation of friaries, and in the making of the so-called Great Books like 'An Leabhar Breac' ('The Speckled Book'), the 'Yellow Book of Lecan', and prose compositions such as 'Caithréim Thoirdhealbhaigh' ('The Triumphs of Turlough'), all written in the standard literary language, classical common Gaelic. There was also a heightened sense of national consciousness among the *Gaedhil*. This renaissance of Gaelic literature, culture, and identity was also a feature of fifteenth-century Scotland (particularly under the patronage of the lords of the Isles), though perhaps getting under way a little later than in Ireland. During this period, entries in the Irish annals underscored the pan-Gaelic context in which leading members of the Gaelic learned classes were again operating, noting for instance the death of 'the head of the schools of Ireland and Scotland', or of 'the professor of music for Ireland and Scotland'. Similarly, the recent compilation should be noted of most poems by Scottish-based poets included in the early sixteenth-century Book of the Dean of Lismore, the first of the Great Books to survive from a Scottish provenance. At the same time, the Gaelic language's geographical retreat in Scotland had been halted: the linguistic boundary established in the four-teenth century, with Gaelic the language of the Highlanders and English the language of the Lowlanders, lasted for over four centuries. In the 1520s, John Major thought that 'half of Scotland' spoke Gaelic.[19] In Ireland, Gaelic's retreat was actually reversed after 1300, and by 1450 English was the predominant language only in the future English Pale, parts of Cos. Wexford, Kilkenny and Tipperary, and the towns and cities elsewhere. In other parts of the English lordship Gaelic predominated, although the nobles and gentry could normally speak English. In Gaelic Ireland very few understood English.[20]

The evidence from the Gaelic side is mirrored by the atmosphere of crisis among officials in the English lordship, as the fourteenth-century 'land of peace' seemed to contract into a small English Pale. Reports to the king described how in outlying parts nobles and gentry of English descent had gone over almost totally to the Gaelic way of life.[21] In contemporary ter-minology, they had 'degenerated', a word which derived from the Latin gens, meaning a people descended from a single founding father or progenitor, with a sense of its own historical identity: they had mingled with another people and lost their identity.[22] In turn, this process of acculturation in the marches prompted a series of vain attempts by the Dublin administration – notably through the law code known as the Statutes of Kilkenny, passed by the Irish parliament in 1366 and periodically confirmed by later parliaments – to proscribe the use of Gaelic law, customs and culture among the English. Thus, by 1450 English rule in Ireland was in serious difficulties. Mindful of

19   Grant, *Independence and nationhood*, p. 202.

20   S.G. Ellis, *Ireland in the age of the Tudors 1447–1603: English expansion and the end of Gaelic rule* (London, 1998), p. 33.

21   For instance, Lambeth Palace Library, Carew MS 635, ff 188–8v. See S.G. Ellis, 'An English gentleman and his community: Sir William Darcy of Platten' in V.P. Carey and Ute Lotz-Heumann (eds), *Taking sides? Colonial and confessional mentalités in early modern Ireland* (Dublin, 2003), pp. 19–41.

22   R.R. Davies, 'The peoples of Britain and Ireland 1100–1400. I. Identities' in *Transactions of the Royal Historical Society*, 6th ser., iv (1994), pp. 1–20.

[3 6] the collapse of Lancastrian Normandy, the king's lieutenant, Richard duke of York, who had twice served as lieutenant in France, wrote that failure to pay his salary threatened the lordship's collapse. Rather than preside over this, he would return home: 'for it shall never be chronicled nor remain in scripture, by the grace of God, that Ireland was lost by my negligence'.[23]

Yet the problems of English rule in the two territories were in fact essentially different. In Normandy, English rule was by the 1440s predominantly a military occupation with little local support: it was overthrown by a resurgent French monarchy whose financial and military resources increasingly outstripped the English crown's. By contrast, English rule in the lordship of Ireland commanded widespread support among a population which was predominantly English by culture and descent. Admittedly, the period of the Gaelic Revival had witnessed a grave weakening of English power in Ireland; but this had much less to do with Gaelic military might than with the problems and priorities of the English monarchy – in particular, that Ireland came a poor third, after France and Scotland, in the allocation of money and men for war and defence. And despite the diffusion in Gaelic Ireland of armour, siege engines and castle-building skills, techniques of warfare there languished far behind contemporary European norms. Gaelic *ceithirn* (anglicised as 'caterans' and 'kerne' respectively in Scottish and Irish historiography), or footsoldiers, who comprised over 70 per cent of Gaelic armies in Ireland, were still 'naked men', without armour; Irish horsemen still rode without stirrups; and Irish bows were half the length of English longbows and correspondingly less penetrative. Moreover, the armies of even the strongest of the Irish chiefs seldom exceeded 1,000 men: in the 1490s, MacMurrough, prince of Leinster, could make '200 horse well harnessed, a battle of galloglass [100 galloglass, each with manservant and boy] & 300 kerne', while O'Neill of Tyrone disposed '3 b[attle of galloglass], 200 h[orse, and] 300 k[erne]'. By 1562 the English government estimated that O'Neill could raise around 1,200 troops.[24] Thus there was little likelihood that Gaelic chiefs would, as the bards cynically prophesied, rout the English across the sea. Although the administration of English Ireland presented additional problems associated with the control of a remote frontier region inhabited in part by non-English peoples, these problems were not, for the most part, peculiar to Ireland but common to the English monarchy as a

---

23 Quoted, A.J. Otway-Ruthven, *A history of medieval Ireland* (2nd ed., London, 1980), p. 382.
24 Ellis, 'Collapse of the Gaelic world', pp. 457–61; Dawson, *The politics of religion in the age of Mary, queen of Scots*, p. 53.

whole; and their solution lay rather in the restoration of royal authority and [3 7] the reform of crown government.

Both Wales and the English far north were likewise remote from the centre of power, with turbulent, lineage-based societies which offered a ready supply of semi-professional soldiers in wartime but were difficult to discipline in peacetime. In Wales, the chief obstacle to good rule was the fragmentation of authority. Wales was divided into the six shires of the principality – three in the north-west, Flint in the north-east, and two in the south – which were governed by English officials and English criminal law; and around 130 marcher lordships mainly in the east, in each of which the king's writ did not run and the lord was responsible for law and order. Many of these lords were English absentees, most notably the king himself, and government was entrusted to local gentry who acted as constables, stewards and receivers. By statutes enacted by the English parliament in 1401–2, a series of restrictions (the so-called 'Lancastrian penal code') was imposed on the 'mere Welsh', who were excluded from these principal posts, or from acquiring land, goods or offices in English border towns or English towns in Wales. Yet increasingly in the late fifteenth century these statutes were disregarded, as Welsh gentry assumed responsibility for local government under absentee English lords.[25]

As in Gaelic society, in which the clan had important legal and judicial functions, particularly in regard to land, so in native Welsh society the *gwely* or *gafael* (the lineage or descent-group) remained important. Title to land was vested in the *gwely* and kin-responsibility also operated in the event of homicide.[26] In both principality and marches, moreover, Welsh law and customs survived, albeit in increasingly attenuated form. Welsh land law was frequently used among the Welsh in the principality; and most marcher lordships were divided into two parts, the more fertile, low-lying area of the Englishry, and the upland region of the Welshry. Although English and Welsh parts had their own separate courts and officials, the tendency was for march law to develop as an amalgam of English and Welsh law and custom, as both lord and tenants saw financial or procedural advantages in preserving or adapting different usages. For instance, despite Edward I's prohibition on the use of Welsh criminal law, the practice of *galanas*, the redeeming of a homicide by a money payment (equivalent to a Gaelic *eraic*), still survived in

---

25   Glanmor Williams, *Recovery reorientation and Reformation: Wales c.1415–1642* (Oxford, 1987), ch. 2.

26   R.R. Davies, *The age of conquest: Wales 1063–1415* (Oxford, 1991), pp. 122–7.

some lordships. This and two other Welsh customs, *arddel* and *cymhorthau*, were felt by English officials to encourage the prevalence of theft and violence for which Wales was notorious. Offenders who fled from one lordship to another in order to escape justice could pay the *arddel* or avowry fine to place themselves under the lord's protection or be harboured by the lord's officers. Thus marcher lordships became refuges for outlaws, and men from the march committed offences in England and escaped unpunished. Similarly, gentry who compounded with a lord's officers for murder or theft could levy *cymhorthau* from the inhabitants in order to pay their fine.[27]

In the English far north, the underlying problem was not the proliferation of feudal franchises or two nations and cultures – although both were complicating factors – but rather the difficulties created by the defence of a remote frontier against a Scottish monarchy which was far more formidable than even the most powerful Gaelic chief. Since the crown could not afford the cost of a large permanent garrison, it was forced to delegate authority to local magnates who were entrusted with the coordination of defence and good rule as wardens of the marches. In these marcher conditions, a lord's *manraed* was much more important than mere rents, and the magnates consolidated their landed holdings and the military service of their tenants and retainers so as to build up private armies for defence. Accordingly, marcher lords like the Percies acquired a virtual stranglehold on power and could, in other circumstances, deploy their armies against the crown. Elsewhere, absentee lordship undermined the defence of whole marches – the English middle marches, in particular – leading either to the appearance of large stretches of wasteland or to the emergence of heavily militarised communities such as the border surnames or clans. The surnames were not indigenous, as in Gaelic or Welsh society, but developed in response to the endemic insecurity of the marches from 1296 onwards. They pursued their own interests in collaboration with other clans, English or Scottish. They were kinship groups who acted together, collectively seeking vengeance when a clansman was harmed and (in a manner redolent of the Gaelic principle of *cinn comhfhocuis*) often accepting joint responsibility for offences with which individual clansmen were charged. Culturally, the English and Scottish clans were virtually indistinguishable, and generally ignored the respective governments' efforts to classify them as English or Scots according to place of birth. Although military needs provided a ready outlet for their energies in

---

27 Williams, *Recovery reorientation and Reformation*, ch. 2.

wartime, their activities proved much less acceptable to the two governments
during extended periods of truce. The barren uplands where the surnames
resided were unable to sustain even the scanty population which lived there,
so that the surnames frequently survived by preying on the surrounding
Lowlands. Reiving (cattle rustling) and robbery were thus endemic in the
marches, regardless of the actual state of Anglo-Scottish relations.[28]

Centre and periphery in the Wars of the Roses

Within the English monarchy, however, the problems of royal government
tended in the short term to deteriorate further, due almost entirely to the in-
competence of Henry VI. This was very much an age of personal monarchy,
in which kings were expected to rule as well as reign. The king aimed to
impress both subjects and foreigners alike by the magnificence and display
of his court. He took all important decisions himself and intervened personally to compose the countless disputes among his nobles and wealthy gentry.
The ability to do justice impartially was a vital task of monarchy: faction and
feud among the magnates threatened the peace and stability of the kingdom
since, in reality, 'good rule' – as it was described by contemporaries – chiefly
depended on the king harnessing the cooperation and support of the leading landowners there. In general, this was an easier task in those parts which
were closer to the usual location of the king's court in the Home Counties, or
those regions which were at least periodically visited during royal progresses. Further afield, in north Wales or the far north of England which the
king rarely visited except in an emergency, good rule depended even more
heavily on resident lords and gentry, while in Ireland the lack of a resident
court proved a major weakness of English rule. The devolved administration
based in Dublin and headed by a governor and council proved a poor sub-
stitute in an age of personal monarchy.

Even in Lowland England, however, there were recognised procedures for
government by the king's council during his absence, or if he were a minor
(as Henry VI was until 1437). Indeed in Scotland, government remained
effective despite three minorities lasting altogether 39 years in the period

---

28   R.L. Storey, *The end of the house of Lancaster* (2nd ed., Gloucester, 1986), ch. 7; Ellis, *Tudor frontiers*, chs 1–2.

1406–69.[29] Yet no provision could be made for what happened after Henry VI came of age. He alienated crown lands and rights on an unprecedented scale to his favourites, so that royal revenues declined alarmingly. For most of the time, he was easily led, especially by the duke of Suffolk (murdered in 1450) and the duke of Somerset (killed in 1455 at St Albans in the opening battle of the civil war). This meant that a small clique around the king dominated government and royal patronage, at the expense of other magnates, notably the duke of York, whom Henry VI feared, and who was his heir apparent until 1453. Yet Henry was also capable of unpredictable bouts of wilfulness, when he would intervene inexplicably in minor matters. His choice of ministers was frequently poor and he failed to do justice impartially. Finally, in 1453 and again in 1455 he became temporarily insane, but unfortunately he recovered his sanity on both occasions before the kingdom had had a chance to recover from his misrule.[30]

The result was that the nobles increasingly took the law into their own hands, built up private armies, and eventually took to deciding disputes on the battlefield. In the lead-up to the civil war, the rule of the provinces was increasingly disrupted by noble feuds, notably between Courtenay and Bonville in the south-west, Neville and Percy in the north, and Butler and Fitzgerald in Ireland. These feuds, and disputes among leading landowners elsewhere, gradually acquired a national dimension as the conflict at regional level became aligned to conflict at court, where the faction led by the duke of York attempted to break the stranglehold on royal patronage established by the clique of courtiers around the duke of Somerset. Ultimately, the only solution was to depose the king (as had happened to Edward II in 1327 and Richard II in 1399), but this was a drastic and dangerous remedy which everyone was anxious to avoid. Some of York's supporters eventually and reluctantly acquiesced in this course of action, while others led by Henry VI's queen, Margaret of Anjou (who gradually emerged as the power behind the throne after Somerset's death in 1455), held out for the Lancastrian king.[31]

29   Jenny Wormald, 'The house of Stewart and its realm' in Jenny Wormald (ed.), *Scotland revisited* (London, 1991), pp. 18–21.

30   B.P. Wolffe, 'The personal rule of Henry VI' in S.B. Chrimes, C.D. Ross and R.A. Griffiths (eds), *Fifteenth-century England 1399–1509* (Manchester, 1972), pp. 29–48. The standard account of the reign is Griffiths, *Reign of King Henry VI*. See also, John Watts, *Henry VI and the politics of kingship* (Cambridge, 1996).

31   Storey, *End of the house of Lancaster*, chs. 5–15; M.C. Griffith, 'The Talbot-Ormond struggle for control of the Anglo-Irish government' in *Irish Historical Studies*, ii (1940–1), pp. 376–97; Ellis, *Ireland in the age of the Tudors*, pp. 28, 57–64.

Historians have labelled the ensuing period of dynastic struggle between
Lancaster and York (1459–71), and later of York against Tudor (1483–7) as
the Wars of the Roses. This period of political instability, disturbances and
dynastic rivalry saw the deposition of five English kings in 25 years. It is
commonly argued that the Wars began in 1455 with the first battle of
St Albans (really a skirmish and a slaughter) and eventually petered out after
the battle of Stoke in 1487 which followed Lambert Simnel's invasion from
Ireland. Yet these dates are fairly arbitrary: Henry VI's authority was feeble
before 1455, Henry VII's remained weak after 1487; and this was not one
long period of civil war but a period which witnessed many years of tran-
quillity, and even comparatively strong government, interspersed with brief
bouts of campaigning. In fact, the periods of actual campaigning amounted
to somewhere between 14 and 28 months in 32 years.[32] The two Roses
referred to the red rose of Lancaster and the white rose of York, but much of
this symbolism was later, Tudor propaganda, based on the fact that Henry
Tudor, the last and doubtful heir of the Lancastrian kings (Henry IV, Henry
V and Henry VI), married Elizabeth of York (daughter of Edward IV, niece of
Richard III) in 1486 and allegedly brought peace.

It is impossible, in a short survey like the present volume, to offer a
comprehensive account of the complex and fluctuating politics of the civil
war. What follows focuses on the wider aspects of the struggle, which have
been rather neglected in traditional surveys. Briefly, there were three main
phases of the war – from the first military engagements in autumn 1459
(Blore Heath and Ludlow) to the final defeat of the Lancastrians in the far
north of England in summer 1464; the events surrounding the Readeption
(i.e. reattainment of the throne) of Henry VI (1469–71); and the gradual
collapse of the Yorkist cause after the death of Edward IV (1483–7).[33] The
causes of the war centred on events at court; but what is most striking in
a British context is the extent to which its course was dictated by events
in the more remote parts of the English monarchy. In many ways, this was a
contest between centre and periphery. The English borderlands – the north,
Wales and Ireland, together with Calais – offered a ready supply of experienced troops, but were less easily controlled from London. The far north
of England was a war zone: its inhabitants were inured to defending the
marches against the Scots, and there were permanent garrisons stationed at

32   A.J. Pollard, *The Wars of the Roses* (London, 1988), pp. 13–19, 74–5.
33   Pollard, *Wars of the Roses*, ch. 2 offers a convenient summary of these three phases of the
      struggle.

[42]   Carlisle and (until their capture by the Scots) Berwick-on-Tweed and
Roxburgh. English Ireland had also to be defended from the 'wild Irish'; and
in Wales too, society was more militarised because of political disturbances
and the fragmentation of power between dozens of marcher lordships.
Lastly, Calais was a military outpost, and its garrison, usually numbering
1,000 men, was the largest standing force in the English territories.[34] Very
often, control of these recruiting bases determined the outcome of different
phases of the war.

Initially, the factional struggle focused on attempts to dominate the court
and manipulate the king, not to depose him. By 1459, however, events were
moving towards a showdown, and over the summer both sides prepared for
battle. Queen Margaret enjoyed overwhelming support among the nobles
and gentry, but the Yorkists' control of key outposts meant that militarily the
two sides were more evenly matched than a roll-call of the nobility might
suggest. York himself was in a particularly strong position because he held
a solid block of marcher lordships in Wales, from Caerleon and Usk in the
south to Denbigh in the north, worth almost £3,500 per annum. Since 1447
he had also been the king's lieutenant of Ireland. Besides exploiting this
office to build up a powerful affinity, which included Ireland's two resident
earls (Desmond and Kildare), he was also a leading landowner there, being
earl of Ulster, lord of Connaught, and lord of Trim. The two other leading
Yorkists, the earls of Warwick (the Kingmaker) and Salisbury, were respectively captain of Calais and warden of the west marches towards Scotland.
Even so, they were heavily outnumbered by the royal army mustered against
them, and after retreating from a Yorkist rendezvous at Worcester to Ludlow,
they fled on the eve of battle.[35]

York took refuge in Ireland, while the two earls withdrew to Calais, along
with York's son, the earl of March, the future Edward IV. They were attainted
of treason by the Coventry parliament in October and their lands forfeited.
During March, however, Salisbury and Warwick visited York in Waterford to
agree plans for a coordinated invasion the following summer. York delayed
in Ireland, but the three earls invaded south-east England and defeated the
royal army at Northampton in July, capturing the king. And after York had
landed at Chester, he displayed the royal banner (as the king's Irish viceroy
customarily did, but only in Ireland) and claimed the throne. Eventually,

---

34   John Gillingham, *The Wars of the Roses* (London, 1981), pp. 29–30, 137–40.
35   Williams, *Recovery, reorientation and Reformation*, p. 178; Otway-Ruthven, *Medieval Ireland*,
      pp. 377–81, 386–7; Ellis, *Ireland in the age of the Tudors*, p. 59.

however, a fundamentally unworkable compromise was confirmed by parlia- [4 3]
ment in October whereby Henry would remain king for life and would then
be succeeded by York, so excluding Henry's son, Edward, prince of Wales.[36]

Not surprisingly, Queen Margaret refused to accept the disinheritance of
her son. She retired north to raise troops while the Yorkist lords were still
busy in parliament. Reinforced by the duke of Somerset and northern nobles
led by the Percy earl of Northumberland, warden of the east marches towards
Scotland, her army then surprised the Yorkist lords near Wakefield as they
moved north to confront her. York was killed on the battlefield, Salisbury
soon after. Queen Margaret pushed on towards London with a large, indis-
ciplined army which pillaged and plundered, harrying the duke's estates in
particular. The army's approach spread terror in the south. At St Albans, she
defeated Warwick, who had marched out from London to confront her, and
freed Henry VI, but with the capital now in reach, she hesitated and then
retired northwards. Fearful of pillage by northern soldiers, the Londoners
shut and barred the gates against the Lancastrians, in the hope of relief from
Edward of March. Edward was then approaching from the west, where he
had secured the Welsh marches against Jasper Tudor and the earl of Wiltshire.
Having lost control of the king, Edward had little alternative but to seize
the throne himself. Joined by the defeated Warwick, he entered London,
and within a fortnight he was proclaimed king, raised reinforcements, and
departed northwards to encounter the Lancastrians. The largest battle of the
civil war was fought at Towton in Yorkshire on 29 March, and the Yorkist
victory left Edward IV in control of England.[37]

One of the major long-term consequences of the Wars of the Roses was
the way in which it exacerbated inter-provincial antagonisms. As early as
1460–1, the troubles appeared to many as a war between a Lancastrian
north and a Yorkist south. Whipped up by Yorkist propaganda about the
activities of Queen Margaret's northern levies, southerners feared that 'the
people in the north rob and steal and been appointed to pill all this country,
and give away men's lifeloads in all the south country'. Thus, the commons
there could hardly be restrained, 'for they would be up on the men in
north, for it is for the weal of all the south'.[38] In the final phase of the War,
however, these roles were reversed, after Edward's brother, Richard duke of
Gloucester, took up residence there in the 1470s. The north became solidly

---

36 Gillingham, *Wars of the Roses*, ch. 8; Ellis, *Ireland in the age of the Tudors*, pp. 58–64.
37 Gillingham, *Wars of the Roses*, ch. 8.
38 James Gairdner (ed.), *Paston letters*, I (London, 1872), p. 541. See in general, Anthony
     Goodman, *The Wars of the Roses* (London, 1981), pp. 224–6.

[4 4]   Yorkist, and in the period following his usurpation of the throne in 1483, Richard became increasingly reliant on this northern support. For long after Henry Tudor's accession in 1485, his position in the north remained weak. There were disturbances in Yorkshire in 1486 – 'a sedition set on foot by those ingrates in the north, whence every evil takes its rise', as the Croyland Chronicler Continuator put it. The pretender Lambert Simnel won considerable support there in 1487. And when in 1489 another revolt began in Yorkshire, Henry Tudor sought to exploit regional animosities by having it proclaimed throughout the south that the rebels intended 'to rob, despoil, and destroy all the south parts of this . . . realm'.[39] It was only in the 1490s, as another pretender, Perkin Warbeck, ill-advisedly attempted to invade with the assistance of the north's traditional enemy, the Scots, that the region's loyalty to the Tudor regime was finally secured.

In large measure, the Yorkist victory in 1460–61 had stemmed from their ability to exploit the strategic and military value of England's military outposts. It was a lesson which was not lost on the Lancastrians: the next three years saw a series of attempts to employ this strategy in reverse. Henry VI, his queen and Prince Edward had evaded capture after Towton, but their decision to seek Scottish assistance for a descent on Lowland England from the north tended to erode northern support for the Lancastrians. Specifically, the surrender of Berwick to the Scots in return for their support, and the unsuccessful siege of Carlisle by a combined Lancastrian-Scottish force with the same intention, were very damaging to Henry VI's reputation. Yet, with Scotland providing a safe refuge and the Percies unreconciled, a long drawn-out struggle ensued for control of the Percy heartland of Northumberland, with the castles of Alnwick, Bamburgh and Dunstanburgh changing hands several times. It was not until 1464 that Lancastrian resistance there was finally crushed.[40]

In Wales, Harlech castle held out even longer as a centre of Lancastrian resistance, until 1468; but the other significant campaign of these years was in Ireland where in the 1450s rivalry between the lordship's two leading lineages, the Butlers and Fitzgeralds, had similarly become aligned with the dynastic struggle. Lancastrian risings in Meath and Kilkenny in 1462 coincided with an invasion of the lordship by English Lancastrians, led by John Butler, brother and heir of the Lancastrian earl of Wiltshire (fifth earl of

39   N.T. Ridley (ed.), *Ingulph's Chronicles* (London, 1854), p. 509; W. Campbell, *Materials for a history of the reign of Henry VII* (2 vols, London, 1873), ii, 447; M.A. Hicks, 'The Yorkshire rebellion of 1489 reconsidered' in *Northern History*, xxii (1986), pp. 39–62.

40   Gillingham, *Wars of the Roses*, ch. 9; Goodman, *Wars of the Roses*, pp. 55–60.

Ormond in Ireland), who was attainted and executed after Towton. In the name of Henry VI, and styling himself earl of Ormond, Butler recovered control of the family estates in Kilkenny and Tipperary and captured Waterford city. Lancastrian resistance there collapsed, however, after the Butler defeat by Thomas Fitzgerald, earl of Desmond, at the battle of Pilltown. John Butler fled to Portugal.[41]

After 1464, when Lancastrian resistance in the far north was finally crushed at the battles of Hedgeley Moor and Hexham, Edward IV was very much in control of his kingdom. In 1465 Henry VI was finally captured and lodged in the Tower. Yet a rift then developed between king and kingmaker: Edward remained very dependant on Neville support, but his marriage to Elizabeth Wydeville inevitably set up an alternative focal point to Warwick at court led by the queen's father, Earl Rivers, and William Herbert, earl of Pembroke. Besides faction, however, a more tangible difference between the two emerged over foreign policy: Warwick favoured a pro-French line over the intense rivalry which had developed between Burgundy and France, but in 1468 Edward concluded terms for the marriage of his sister with Charles duke of Burgundy, even while the earl was negotiating for an alternative French match. Warwick's response was, first, to try to force his way back into favour at court, and then to set up an alternative king, thus repeating the pattern of events from the 1450s.[42]

From late 1468, the discovery of Lancastrian plots coincided with a series of northern risings led by 'Robin of Redesdale' which, it was revealed, were instigated by Warwick's northern affinity. Warwick himself sailed to Calais where, despite the king's earlier veto, his daughter married Edward's unstable younger brother, George duke of Clarence. Warwick and Clarence then mounted an invasion and sent forces to join Robin of Redesdale who had marched south. In an account of the rebel victory over the king's forces at Edgecote near Banbury (July 1469), *Warkworth's Chronicle* highlighted the regionalised nature of the conflict and the tensions which this created:

> against [the northerners] arose by the king's commandment Lord Herbert earl
> of Pembroke, with 43,000 of Welshmen, the best in Wales, and Humphrey
> Stafford, with 7,000 of archers of the West Country. And as they went together

---

41   Williams, *Recovery, reorientation and Reformation*, pp. 200–2; S.G. Ellis, 'Butler, John, sixth earl
      of Ormond (*d.* 1476/7), magnate' in H.G.C. Matthew and Brian Harrison (eds), *Oxford
      Dictionary of National Biography* (Oxford, 2004), ix, 169–70; S.G. Ellis, 'Fitzgerald, Thomas,
      seventh earl of Desmond (1426?–1468), administrator' ibid., xix, 846–7.

42   Pollard, *Wars of the Roses*, pp. 28–9.

to meet the Northern men at a town, there fell in a variance for their lodging, and so the earl of Devonshire departed from the earl of Pembroke with all his men.[43]

In the aftermath, Earl Rivers and the earls of Devon and Pembroke were executed and the king taken prisoner. In Wales, the bards saw the earl of Devon's conduct as a typically English act of treachery and betrayal: Pembroke's death at the hands of English Lollards and traitors was a national disaster.[44]

Like York before him, however, Warwick soon found that ruling through a captive king was almost impossible. Edward was released in September, and apparently decided to overlook Warwick's conduct. Yet when Warwick then fomented further northern risings in March 1470, in a new plan to put Clarence on the throne, Edward took swift and decisive action. Warwick and Clarence fled to France. Warwick now had little choice but to do a deal with Margaret of Anjou and the Lancastrian exiles there. There followed a public reconciliation and marriage alliance between Warwick's younger daughter and Prince Edward, after which Warwick prepared to invade England with French help in the name of Henry VI. King Edward was expecting invasion, but Warwick once again drew him away by fomenting another northern rising through his retainers there. Clarence and Warwick thus landed un-opposed near Exeter in September, with Edward still in Yorkshire. Six months earlier, Edward had restored Henry Percy as earl of Northumberland in place of Warwick's brother, John Neville, Lord Montagu, in a bid to strengthen his influence in the north. Neville was compensated with lands and titles else-where, but apparently not enough. He now defected with his northern levies to Henry VI, and Edward was forced to flee to avoid the two Neville armies. He escaped to his brother-in-law, Charles the Bold, in the Netherlands, while Henry VI was released from the Tower and restored to the throne (3 September).[45]

By this time, however, Henry VI was a broken man of 50 and the Readeption, as contemporary legal documents called it, was fatally weakened by the mistrust between Warwick and Queen Margaret, who delayed in France with Prince Edward until it was too late. With Burgundian support, Edward lost no time in preparing a challenge to this unstable Neville–Lancastrian coalition before it could consolidate its position, landing with a

---

43 *Warkworth's Chronicle* (ed. J.O. Halliwell, Camden Soc., London, 1839), p. 6; Gillingham, *Wars of the Roses*, ch. 10.

44 Williams, *Recovery, reorientation and Reformation*, pp. 204–7.

45 Gillingham, *Wars of the Roses*, chs 11–12.

small force at Ravenspur in mid-March. There was little enthusiasm for Edward's cause in Yorkshire, but with the Percy earl unwilling to confront him and Lord Montagu unsure of his ability to do so, he was able to advance south and raise troops from his supporters in the Midlands. Awaiting reinforcements, Warwick refused Edward's challenge to battle outside Coventry, but Clarence then changed sides and joined his brother with 4,000 men. The Yorkists marched on to London, which opened its gates, and took Henry VI prisoner. Bringing the old king with him, Edward then doubled back northwards to encounter Warwick, who was following him, at Barnet. In a confused battle fought in thick mist on Easter Sunday, Warwick and Montagu were both killed. Edward had no time to enjoy his victory, however. Within hours of the battle, Queen Margaret and Prince Edward had landed at Weymouth. By a forced march, King Edward intercepted them at Tewkesbury before they could cross the Severn to raise troops among the Lancastrians in Wales. Edward was again victorious in the ensuing battle. Prince Edward was killed, and Margaret of Anjou was taken prisoner. Edward returned to London on 21 May, following the suppression of Lancastrian risings both in the north and Kent. Henry VI was put to death that night, and after this, all but a handful of Lancastrian die-hards such as Henry Tudor, duke of Richmond, submitted. Edward remained secure on his throne until his death in 1483.[46]

The final phase of the Wars was precipitated by rivalries which broke out in the Yorkist camp after Edward's death, notably between his queen and his younger brother, Richard, duke of Gloucester. Richard had been Edward's lieutenant in the north since 1471 and, according to precedent, was made lord protector of Edward's twelve-year-old son, now King Edward V. In a *coup d'état*, Richard seized the king, then arrested some influential councillors, and finally claimed the throne on the grounds that Edward IV's two sons were illegitimate. They disappeared into the Tower and Richard III was crowned on 6 July. The Wydevilles and Edward IV's household men had been caught off guard by Richard's usurpation. Yet in October, they raised most of southern England for Edward V's restoration. Inexplicably, they were joined in the *coup d'état* by the duke of Buckingham, Richard's key supporter. By then, it had become clear to the rebels that the two princes were dead, and they turned instead to the Lancastrian exile, Henry Tudor, whose prospects were now transformed. Before he could reach England, however,

46   Gillingham, *Wars of the Roses*, pp. 179–216.

the risings were crushed and Buckingham executed. So Henry sailed back to Brittany, to be joined in exile by a group of Edward IV's courtiers who had fled after the risings.[47]

Although Richard had probably half-expected trouble from disappointed servants of Edward IV, Buckingham's defection was a shattering blow to his confidence. He became even more reliant on his predominantly northern, ducal following. Unsurprisingly, northerners had been intruded into key positions following Richard's *coup d'état*, as the king displaced the politically suspect and rewarded old friends; but after Buckingham's revolt, the king's basic insecurity was registered in a sweeping act of attainder passed by parliament against 103 leading rebels (nearly half of them servants of Edward IV), and the wholesale redistribution of lands and offices in the south among members of his northern affinity. For instance, in 1484 most of the new sheriffs appointed for counties in the deep south were northerners.[48] It was an unwritten convention of English local government that the king should entrust the rule of the provinces to its local élite: 'self-government at the king's command' was the hallmark of the English tradition. Yet during the Wars of the Roses, English kings were sometimes forced by the narrow base of support they enjoyed to override this principle by appointing outsiders. The periodic intrusion into local government of courtiers and household men occasionally led to friction, sometimes between northerners and southerners, or between 'the English of England' and 'the English of Ireland', or in Wales between natives and Saxons. Yet Richard III was driven not only to break this principle, but also to challenge the further convention that Lowland England was the core region of the English state.

The *Crowland Chronicler Continuator* thought that Richard III's reign was remarkable in that 'so many great lords, nobles, magnates and commoners, and even three bishops were attainted', whereby 'great numbers of estates and inheritances' were forfeit. King Richard 'distributed all these amongst his northerners whom he planted in every part of his dominions, to the shame of all the southern people who murmured ceaselessly and longed more each day for the return of their old lords in place of the tyranny of the present ones'. At a time when royal grants of land were normally confined to members of the royal family, Richard rewarded over 150 nobles and gentry with grants of land during his reign, including grants in the south to around

47   Gillingham, *Wars of the Roses*, pp. 217–33; Pollard, *Wars of the Roses*, pp. 35–7.
48   Rosemary Horrox, *Richard III: a study of service* (Cambridge, 1989), chs 4–5.

36 northerners. At its crudest, in Kent, three northerners were given one [49] manor each there and included on the commission of the peace.[49]

Even so, this northern plantation alienated those whom the king needed to win over to broaden his support, and it also created a group of influential royal servants with a strong vested interest in the land settlement. Traditionally, much confiscated land was kept in crown hands and was therefore available for restoration to the families of attainted rebels who made their peace with the king. In the case of these northern retainers (as, later, with New English adventurers in Elizabethan Ireland), restoration would have undone them. Thus, there was a steady trickle of defections by old Yorkists to Richard's enemies abroad, which Henry Tudor encouraged by promising to marry Edward IV's daughter, Princess Elizabeth, and to rule jointly with her. Once again, foreign support was instrumental in allowing a pretender to mount a challenge for the throne. Henry Tudor landed at Milford Haven in early August 1485, and taking a circuitous route through Wales in order to raise support, he confronted Richard near Market Bosworth on 22 August. Although Richard had much the larger army, it proved unreliable: the earl of Northumberland, who commanded the northern levies, sat idly by and watched the battle, as did Lord Stanley, while Stanley's brother, Sir William, deployed his men against Richard at a crucial moment. Richard was hacked to pieces.[50]

Initially, Henry Tudor's victory at Bosworth left the crown in the same weak state as it had been after Edward IV's victory at Towton. The north was equally resentful of this new, southern-dominated regime. And if in Wales, the accession of a Welsh king was greeted with enthusiasm, he had far less support than Edward among the English of Ireland, where events on the mainland were viewed with dismay. In the north, Henry VII had little choice but to appoint Northumberland as his lieutenant to control the region against Richard III's resentful northern retainers. The first revolt there, led by Lord Lovell in spring 1486, soon fizzled out. Yet the following year, a much more serious challenge was mounted from Ireland. Lambert Simnel, claiming to be Edward earl of Warwick, then a prisoner in the Tower, landed in Ireland with John de la Pole, earl of Lincoln, who was Richard's heir, plus Lord Lovell and 2,000 German mercenaries supplied by Margaret of Burgundy. His title to the throne was accepted by the governor of Ireland,

49   Nicholas Pronay and John Cox (eds), *The Crowland Chronicle Continuations 1459–1486* (London, 1986), p. 171; Horrox, *Richard III*, chs 4–5.
50   Horrox, *Richard III*, chs 4–6; Charles Ross, *Richard III* (London, 1981), pt. III.

[5 0] Gerald Fitzgerald, earl of Kildare, and he was crowned King Edward VI in Christ Church Cathedral, Dublin. With a mixed army of Germans, Gaelic kerne, and English bills and bows, the Yorkists then invaded England, landing at Furness in Lancashire. Gathering support in Cumbria and north Yorkshire, they marched down the east side of the Pennines to confront Henry's much larger army at Stoke-by-Newark, where the unarmoured kerne were slaughtered in the unequal battle. Stoke was the last military campaign of the Wars of the Roses, and even though some Yorkists still held out, the Wars were now fought chiefly by diplomatic rather than military means. The earl of Northumberland was murdered in a tax riot in Yorkshire, being blamed for betraying Richard III; and in the 1490s another pretender, Perkin Warbeck, mounted a series of unsuccessful invasions, landing twice in Ireland (1491, 1495), in Kent (1495), from Scotland (1496), and was finally captured in Cornwall (1497). Yet these challenges became less and less serious as Henry VII consolidated his position and English politics became more stable.[51]

The Scottish monarchy and Anglo-Scottish relations

Taken together, the collapse of Lancastrian France and the Wars of the Roses brought about a significant and long-term weakening of English royal power, both in the British Isles and also in Europe. In Britain, the chief beneficiary of this was the Scottish monarchy. Despite the successive minorities of the 1406–69 period, the Scottish monarchy had remained comparatively stable by European standards. In part, of course, this reflected its weakness in an impoverished and remote kingdom. James III's annual income of £5,000 was, at best, a tenth of the English king's. The comparatively compact landholdings of the Scottish nobility also left the monarchy even more dependent on the nobles in local government and unable to exercise more than a general oversight over everyday life in the provinces.[52] Yet, if only because the king generally represented no threat to the magnates' local authority, the kinds of tensions between crown and magnates which

51 Ellis, *Ireland in the age of the Tudors*, pp. 83–97; A.J. Pollard, *North-eastern England during the Wars of the Roses* (Oxford, 1990), pp. 375–7; Gillingham, *Wars of the Roses*, pp. 247–53.
52 Jenny Wormald, *Court, kirk, and community: Scotland 1470–1625* (London, 1981), pp. 12–14.

had brought about the Wars of the Roses in England were far less pronounced in Scotland. Scottish kings could thus exploit this English weakness to extend their control over territories on the margins of the Scottish kingdom; and in the later fifteenth century they even found themselves with the luxury, for the first time, of having one or two options in terms of foreign policy.

The increasing confidence of Scottish kings in the diplomatic theatre was reflected in James III's masterminding of an alliance between his father-in-law, Christian I of Denmark, and Louis XI of France. The young James III also planned military campaigns on the continent to vindicate his slender claims either to the duchy of Brittany, the county of Saintonge, or the duchy of Guelders. He was, however, deflected in all this by parliament.[53] Of more significance in the longer term was the advent of intermittently better relations with the 'auld inemeis' (as the English were called), culminating in the Treaty of Perpetual Peace (1502). Hitherto, Anglo-Scottish relations had been very poor, the legacy of the failed fourteenth-century English conquest of Scotland. Following the recovery of Berwick in 1461, Scottish hopes of acquiring additional territory by supporting Henry VI had gradually subsided as the Yorkists slowly got the upper hand in Northumberland. Accordingly, a 15-year truce with Edward IV was signed in June 1464, optimistically extended to 1519 in December 1465 after Henry VI's capture had removed a major source of friction between the two realms. In 1474 this led, unusually, to a marriage agreement, 'forasmuch as this noble isle called Great Britain cannot be kept and maintained better in wealth and prosperity'. Accordingly, it was agreed that James III's son, James, should marry Edward IV's daughter, Cecilia, when they grew up, and meanwhile that James should receive an annual pension of 2,000 merks (£445) as advance payment of the dowry.[54]

From an English perspective, the agreement neutralised the Scottish threat in preparation for Edward IV's invasion of France in 1475. Yet, after extorting an annual pension of 50,000 crowns from the French at Picquigny, Edward was less enthusiastic about James's further proposals for marriage alliances. Renewed advances from Louis XI secured a ratification of the auld alliance in 1479, and by 1480 had precipitated another war with England, resulting in the loss of Berwick in the brief campaign of 1482, before

53 Nicholson, *Scotland*, pp. 472–5; Wormald, *Court, kirk, and community*, pp. 5–6.
54 Nicholson, *Scotland*, pp. 400–6, 475–9 (quotation, p. 478).

another truce was agreed which was successively renewed, and a further breach avoided, until 1492.[55]

Yet traditional Anglo-Scottish antagonisms remained strong in both kingdoms. James III, in particular, incurred popular hostility for his tenacious policy of peace and alliance with England which, to the Scottish borderers, meant an end to border warfare and its profits and also increased royal interference in the marches. James's conduct in his dealings with his nobility was also arbitrary and unpredictable. He was acutely mistrustful of his younger brothers, Albany and Mar, and this undermined his resistance to renewed English aggression. The ambitious duke of Albany took revenge by offering to cede Berwick in return for English support for a bid for the throne. Although Richard of Gloucester's army encamped outside Edinburgh in 1482, there was no support for Alexander IV as an English vassal-king. And after his *coup d'état* in 1483, Richard could not afford Scottish adventures. He dropped Albany, and sought to improve relations with James III. Not surprisingly, however, James welcomed Henry Tudor's accession. Relations between the two kings became quite cordial as Henry struggled to consolidate his authority in a hostile north of England. Neither king could afford to move too far ahead of public opinion, however, and negotiations in 1487 to strengthen the existing truce foundered on the opposition of the Scottish parliament to a marriage alliance which made no provision for Berwick's return to Scotland. Nonetheless, by this time, James had by his conduct alienated a large number of his leading subjects. Very few supported him in the ensuing rebellion in 1488, leading to his defeat and murder by dissident nobles at the battle of Sauchieburn. He was seen as an aloof, overbearing and vindictive king who did not administer firm justice but rather took gifts and granted remissions for serious crimes. In later years, he also debased the currency and hoarded money. Thus, it was his personality, rather than his pro-English policies, which brought about his downfall.[56]

The young James IV, although he renewed the truce, followed a more traditional line in Anglo-Scottish relations, and was soon involved in Yorkist intrigues. Even though he continued some of his father's dubious money-raising strategies, he was, according to the Spanish ambassador, Don Pedro de Ayala, 'as handsome in complexion and shape as a man can be', and his firm administration of justice and magnificent court quickly won the respect

55 Nicholson, *Scotland*, pp. 480, 487–97, 505–7; Wormald, *Court, kirk, and community*, p. 6.
56 Nicholson, *Scotland*, pp. 496–7, 505–14; Norman MacDougall, *James III, a political study* (Edinburgh, 1982), ch. 12; S.B. Chrimes, *Henry VII* (London, 1972), pp. 70, 86–7.

of his nobles. Ayala remarked that he 'executes the law without respect to [5 3] rich and poor' – unlike James III. The ambassador was also impressed with his command of languages – Latin, French, German, Flemish, Italian and Spanish, also 'the language of the savages who live in some parts of Scotland and the islands'. Yet he also loved war, and soon took his opportunity against the English. In 1495 Perkin Warbeck arrived in Scotland, where he was acknowledged as Richard duke of York and married to the king's kinswoman, Catherine Gordon. Henry VII responded by wooing the Scots with proposals for a marriage alliance between James and his elder daughter, Margaret, but he also prepared to resist invasion. Again Berwick proved a sticking point. Having secured a promise from Warbeck to cede Berwick and pay the Scots 50,000 marks, James crossed the Tweed in support of Richard IV in September 1496. Yet Northumberland refused to rise: after capturing two border towers and advancing four miles into England, the Scottish army retreated after a few days. The following year saw further border raids by both sides. Revolt in Cornwall prevented Henry from concentrating the full weight of English preparations against the Scots, but equally James counted the cost of his support for Warbeck. Accordingly, Warbeck was encouraged to leave in July, sailing from Ayr to Cork and then on to Cornwall, where he was captured after a second small-scale rising, and in September a seven-year truce was finally agreed at Ayton. This truce was renewed in 1499, and further negotiations then led to the treaty of Ayton in January 1502. This comprised a marriage treaty, whereby James was to marry Margaret Tudor, and a treaty of perpetual peace, the first full peace between the two realms since 1328. The marriage was eventually solemnised in Holyrood abbey in August 1503, and celebrated in William Dunbar's poem 'The Thrissil and the Rose': Queen Margaret received a dower of lands in Scotland worth £2,000 and James received a dowry of £10,000 from Henry VII. Subsequently, James indulged his love of war in tournaments and jousting, taking an active part in tournaments as 'the wild knicht' in 1507 and 1508. Yet he also 'daunted' the Western Isles, and in the raid of Eskdale, also in 1504, he spent a few weeks in the company of the English warden of the west marches, Lord Dacre, in arresting, trying and hanging border thieves.[57]

The 'perpetual peace' of 1502 was not destined to last more than eleven years, but this was a long time in the shifting sands of European diplomacy, and it did bring friendship and cooperation between the two courts. That, a

57   Chrimes, *Henry VII*, pp. 88–91; Norman MacDougall, *James IV* (Edinburgh, 1989), pp. 282–312 (quotations, pp. 283, 287, 294); Nicholson, *Scotland*, pp. 550–5.

[5 4] century later, it was also to bring about a union of the crowns was thought an unlikely possibility which, however, Henry had considered. He informed his councillors presciently that even if a Scottish king succeeded to the English throne, the greater would draw the less, with England inevitably becoming the dominant partner in a greater Britain. Already by the time of the marriage, however, that possibility had come a small step closer, following the death in April 1502 of Henry's son and heir, Arthur, so that only his younger son, Henry, stood against that eventuality.[58] Particularly during the reign of the second Tudor, Henry VIII, relations between the two kingdoms sometimes seemed as bad as ever, but the kinship between the two dynasties which was established by the birth and later the accession of James V, son of James and Margaret, nephew of Henry VIII, intruded a new element into Anglo-Scottish diplomacy which both sides tried periodically to exploit.

58   Chrimes, *Henry VII*, pp. 88–91; Nicholson, *Scotland*, pp. 550–5.

THE REVIVAL OF CROWN GOVERNMENT

G overnments in Renaissance Europe were overwhelmingly monarchical. The British Isles proved no exception to this pattern. Government revolved around the person of the monarch, the king of England, the king of Scots, or a petty Gaelic chieftain: the court was the political centre of the kingdom. The English monarchy was the most centralised in late medieval Europe, but it still had much more in common administratively with the Scottish monarchy, or even one of the more powerful Gaelic lordships, than with a modern centralised state. From the Renaissance onwards, the English and Scottish monarchies increasingly lagged behind developments in continental Europe where in the more powerful monarchies the increased costs of government – especially military costs – fostered the growth of royal absolutism and the decline of representative institutions. In effect, the development of standing armies to wage war and protect extended frontiers required both higher levels of taxation and larger bureaucracies to collect the taxes and pay the troops. Yet in the British Isles, the facts of geography and England's dominant position there meant that English kings did not face quite the same problems in organising the defence of long landed frontiers against powerful neighbours. Scottish kings lacked the resources to emulate their continental counterparts, and the resources available to even the most powerful Gaelic chief were in no way comparable to those of English or Scottish kings. Thus the administrative methods of the British monarchies were more conservative: levels of taxation were lower, parliaments remained important, and particularly away from the centre, bureaucracies were less developed.

Even so, the half century from *c.*1470 was one of reconstruction and consolidation for monarchical power in the British Isles. James III's acquisition of Shetland as a dowry from Denmark in 1469 (and Orkney the previous year) brought the kingdom of Scotland to its fullest extent and the whole of the British Isles under native princes. Equally important in the longer term was the 1493 forfeiture of the lordship of the Isles: six major risings followed over the next half-century (the last in 1545), but the destruction of this

[5 6]   autonomous power centre with the potential to resist territorial integration into the Scottish kingdom opened the way to the extension of royal authority in the Highlands and Isles.[1] The revival of English royal power in the same period was perhaps less spectacular but equally sustained. It was also more focused on the monarchy's core territory. In particular, Henry Tudor, by assiduous attention to the details of administration, came close to maximising the potential of English medieval monarchy in regard to internal control.[2]

Behind the differing priorities of the two monarchies lay basic differences in their financial and administrative resources. Essentially, English administrative practices assumed a more formalised, bureaucratic character. Professor J.R. Lander has estimated that by the later fifteenth century the total bureaucracy of royal government in England was around 1,500 officers. Of these, the politically significant section of the royal household comprised 250–300 knights, esquires, yeomen and pages; with around 400 officers of the central courts, the exchequer, chancery, king's bench and common pleas; 30–40 auditors and receivers of crown lands, 80–90 customs officials; and in the provinces 700–800 other officers, mainly keepers of forests and castles or stewards of manors. Since the formal institutions of government were almost exclusively financial and legal, its officers were likewise predominantly employed in doing justice and levying the king's revenues.[3] England had long had a recognised administrative capital, London. Even so, when Henry VIII went on progress, as he regularly did from June until October, politics moved with him: courtiers and leading officials accompanied the king and he regularly stayed at episcopal residences, monasteries, or with leading nobles, or courtiers. Government in Scotland was even more peripatetic: Scottish kings divided their time between Edinburgh, Perth or Stirling, but James III was in fact seen to spend too much time in Edinburgh, which finally emerged as the administrative capital during his reign, and not enough on progresses around his kingdom. Dublin was likewise consolidating its status during this period as the administrative capital of the English

1   Lynch, *Scotland*, pp. 167–8.
2   The standard biography of Henry Tudor remains S.B. Chrimes, *Henry VII* (London, 1972), but R.L. Storey, *The reign of Henry VII* (London, 1968) is in many ways more in tune with the perspectives developed in this survey. See also, Margaret Condon, 'Ruling elites in the reign of Henry VII' in Charles Ross (ed.), *Patronage, pedigree and power in later medieval England* (Gloucester, 1979), pp. 109–42.
3   J.R. Lander, *Government and community: England 1450–1509* (London, 1980), pp. 84–5.

lordship of Ireland: in the later fourteenth century Carlow had briefly played
this role.[4]

By 1483, the English ordinary revenues had recovered to just over
£90,000 per annum in cash, which was far more than the moneys available
to late fifteenth-century Scottish kings. The Scottish revenues were estimated c.1486 at only SC£16,380 (£5,460) per annum, a figure which was
rather more comparable with the IR£1,600 (£1,067) per annum then available to English kings as lords of Ireland. Yet personal supervision by an adult
king was able to drive up receipts to much higher levels: James IV probably
received SC£44,500 (£14,833) annually in his last years, and James V's
ordinary revenues had risen to SC£46,000 by 1539–40, although the
devaluation of the Scottish pound meant that this was then worth only
£11,500 sterling. The central bureaucracy of the Scottish monarchy was
much more comparable with the Irish lordship's tiny central administration
of 34 based in Dublin.[5]

All this meant that, even in England, the potential of Renaissance monarchy was strictly limited. In theory, the powers of monarchy were sweeping,
but in practice the king was heavily dependent for government on the good
offices of leading landowners – the nobles and gentry (or lairds in Scotland).
Individual ruling magnates or coalitions of lesser nobles and leading gentry
assumed responsibility, under the king, for the maintenance of 'good rule'
in different parts of the kingdom in accordance with a basic principle of
English local government, characterised by modern historians as 'self-
government at the king's command', whereby the crown appointed as
sheriffs and justices of the peace (JPs) the leading landowners of each shire.
Reliance on the magnates was even more pronounced in Scotland where
their landed influence was reinforced by the proliferation of regalities –
feudal franchises in which particular lords had quasi-royal powers of justice.
Thus, despite the formal machinery of government, much still depended on
informal contacts, especially at court. It was said of Edward IV, for instance,

---

4   Neil Samman, 'The progresses of Henry VIII, 1509–1529' in Diarmaid MacCulloch (ed.), *The
    reign of Henry VIII: politics, policy and piety* (Basingstoke, 1995), ch. 3; Wormald, *Court, kirk,
    and community*, p. 14; MacDougall, *James III*, pp. 304–5; Ellis, *Ireland in the age of the Tudors*,
    pp. 20–1, 166, 172.
5   Lander, *Government and community*, pp. 34–5, 101; John Guy, *Tudor England* (Oxford, 1988),
    pp. 9–10, 69; Grant, *Independence and nationhood*, ch. 6; Nicholson, *Scotland*, pp. 20–3, 454;
    James Cameron, *James V: the personal rule, 1528–1542* (East Linton, 1998), pp. 257–8; Marcus
    Merriman, *The rough wooings, Mary queen of Scots, 1542–1551* (East Linton, 2000), p. 95; Ellis,
    Ireland in the age of the Tudors, pp. 178–9.

that the names and estates of the gentry 'scattered over the counties of the kingdom, were known to him just as if they were daily within his sight'.[6]

In these circumstances, kings were bound to tailor their policies to the interests of 'the political nation' – the top two per cent of the population in England who had a say in the political process, a smaller percentage still in Scotland. Serious divisions among the magnates could easily spell disaster for the monarchy, as in the Wars of the Roses. Similarly in Scotland, James III was defeated and killed in 1488 by a rebel army led by the earls of Argyll and Angus. And in Ireland in 1487, the earl of Kildare's support for the pretender, Lambert Simnel, was decisive in his coronation in Dublin as 'Edward VI'.[7] Throughout the British Isles, the nobility were powerful men in their own localities without whose *collective* support the king could not govern. Kings thus had to earn the respect of their magnates.

Yet the accepted duties of Renaissance monarchy were still very limited, essentially to organise defence, do justice, and maintain law and order. Kings were expected to defend the realm from foreign invasion, and for this purpose could expect taxation from their subjects to supplement their ordinary revenues. In Scotland grants of taxation were extremely sporadic and might raise SC£5,000: James III incurred considerable unpopularity by his repeated but largely unsuccessful attempts to levy extraordinary taxation in parliament. During his personal rule, however, James V was more successful in securing taxation.[8] Direct taxation was levied more regularly in England, where a traditional subsidy of tenths and fifteenths was generally worth £29,500, and almost annually in early Tudor Ireland, where a parliamentary subsidy eventually yielded over IR£600 per levy.[9]

Closely related to defence was the maintenance of law and order. Society in late medieval Britain remained very militarised. The magnates remained a military elite, except perhaps in sheltered parts of Lowland England. Apart from Gaelic Ireland, even the peasantry was accustomed to bear arms.[10] Thus, military leadership was also an attribute of successful monarchy: Edward IV won and kept his throne partly because he was a better general than his rivals. Three successive Scottish kings (James II, III and IV) were all killed in

---

6 Nicholas Pronay and John Cox (eds), *The Crowland chronicle continuations: 1459–1486* (London, 1986), pp. 152–3 (quotation); Grant, *Independence and nationhood*, pp. 150–3.

7 Ellis, *Ireland in the age of the Tudors*, pp. 84–5; Nicholson, *Scotland*, pp. 527–30; T.B. Pugh, 'The magnates, knights and gentry' in S.B. Chrimes, C.D. Ross and R.A. Griffiths (eds), *Fifteenth-century England: studies in politics and society* (Manchester, 1972), pp. 86–128.

8 MacDougall, *James III*, p. 301; Cameron, *James V*, pp. 259–61.

9 Lander, *Government and community*, p. 80; Ellis, *Ireland in the age of the Tudors*, pp. 75–6, 95.

10 Kenneth Nicholls, *Gaelic and gaelicised Ireland in the middle ages* (Dublin, 1972), p. 71.

battle.[11] Yet, even though high levels of violence were endemic in society, governments were concerned lest riots and disorders spilled over into more serious disturbances and threatened royal security. Without a standing army, kings remained extremely vulnerable to rebellion. The king's third, closely-linked duty was to do justice – indirectly through the royal law courts in most cases, but if necessary by personal arbitration in the disputes of the nobility. The failure of Henry VI to do justice impartially was a major underlying cause of the Wars of the Roses: when magnates despaired of 'indifferent justice' at the king's hands, they took to settling disputes themselves.[12]

Restoring royal finances

Traditional accounts of the revival of English royal government under the Yorkists and Tudors devote much space to developments in Lowland England, but do rather less than justice to the more remote English territories. Given that Lowland England was the political centre of the English monarchy, this focus on events as seen from Westminster is scarcely surprising: it reflects both the official perception of what was happening and also the bias of the surviving evidence. Yet conditions in this region were much more favourable to the exercise of royal authority than in outlying parts, and so give an exaggerated impression of the vigour and effectiveness of monarchical government. Particularly in a British context, there is a need to give closer consideration to developments in other parts where the impact of royal government was less immediate and the pattern of change slower.

A basic reason for the revival of English royal government in the later fifteenth century was that Edward IV and Henry VII simply did right what Henry VI had got wrong – in terms of leadership, relations with the magnates, justice and financial administration. Edward was a competent rather than a great king. His main achievement was perhaps to restore crown finances, so that in this sphere Henry VII built on solid foundations. In other respects, Edward succeeded as much by good luck as good management. He was prepared to take risks, proved a vigorous and effective military commander, but politically he also made some serious mistakes. He was outmanoeuvred by the wily Louis XI of France in terms of foreign policy, so that by 1480

11   Lynch, *Scotland*, pp. 151–3; Goodman, *Wars of the Roses*, pp. 84–5, 174.
12   Watts, *Henry VI*, pp. 176–9, 261–4, 298–323.

[6 0] England was (temporarily) isolated. He was also the first English king since 1066 to marry one of his own subjects, Elizabeth Wydeville, who had two children by her previous husband. The marriage was clearly impulsive and was seen by contemporaries as unsuitable, and Edward also allowed her large family to dominate the marriage market, so alienating leading magnates like the earl of Warwick. He governed too much by faction, which he failed adequately to control. Warwick suborned his brother, the duke of Clarence, in 1469 and brought him down; while after his death in 1483 rivalry between the Wydevilles and his other brother, Richard duke of Gloucester, led to the *coup d'état* by which his young son, Edward V, was deposed. Edward IV was also extremely fortunate that rivalry within the Lancastrian alliance of 1470–1 allowed him to defeat Warwick's larger army at Barnet before Queen Margaret's return. Nonetheless, he also made progress in restoring political stability and law and order.[13]

Edward's son-in-law, Henry VII, was a very different kind of personality. He had spent much of his life in exile, living on his wits, and this had clearly affected him. He was cautious and calculating, but a shrewd judge of character. He had little or no experience of government, and was very suspicious of baronial autonomy. He relied instead on councillors whose authority and influence derived from the crown rather than on extensive lands and ancient title. Contemporaries remarked on how very few people had any real influence over the king – no more than five or six ministers, plus his mother, Lady Margaret Beaufort. He was a reluctant general, and had little interest in continental adventures. Yet through his focus on administration, by his exploitation of a number of favourable circumstances, and by building on the Yorkist achievement in terms of finance and justice, he came close to maximising the English medieval monarchy's potential in regard to internal control of the country.[14]

One indication of the consolidation of royal control in this period was the increase in the king's revenues. For both English and Scottish kings, the two main sources of revenue were crown lands and the customs, although Renaissance monarchs also attempted to raise more money from the crown's feudal rights and from taxation. The English royal demesne was heavily concentrated in Lowland England: traditionally, the king had little more than IR£100-worth of land and a few fee-farm rents in Ireland, and not

13 The standard biography is Charles Ross, *Edward IV* (London, 1974). On the crisis of 1469–71, see esp., M.A. Hicks, *False, fleeting perjur'd Clarence: George duke of Clarence, 1449–78* (Gloucester, 1980), ch. 2.
14 On Henry VII, see the works cited in footnote 2, above.

much more in the far north of England. In Wales the crown controlled the principality and a few marcher lordships.[15] This imbalance constituted a serious weakness in the English crown's position in outlying parts because it left the king without the *manraed* or effective control of local offices which were associated with landed income. Nonetheless, net income from crown lands in England and Wales was gradually raised from c.£8,250 per annum under Henry VI (Lord Treasurer Cromwell's estimate of 1433) to £22,000 from 1483 and over £40,000 by 1502. Circumstances in Henry VII's later years were nonetheless unusual: Henry VIII's reversal of his father's attainders and the necessary provision for his queen reduced his landed income considerably. Even income from the crown's minuscule Irish estates more than doubled between 1460 and 1495. Crown lands in Scotland were likewise increased significantly by forfeitures of leading magnates, and were estimated at SC£10,600 in 1486. The English customs revenue showed a more modest increase, rising from an estimated £30,722 per annum in 1433 to average over £40,000 by 1500; and in Ireland from IR£175 in 1465 to IR£450 by 1497. Yet about half this revenue came from the port of London, with very little from outlying parts; and from the 1520s, when the average for the decade was £35,000 a year, the overall trend was downwards as exports of cloth, on which less duty was payable, outstripped exports of raw wool. Customs supplied a proportionately smaller part of royal revenue in Scotland, varying from SC£2,500 to SC£4,000 in the late fifteenth century, but SC£5,300 in 1542.[16]

The crown was much less successful in its efforts to increase revenue from taxation and feudal incidents. Although parliamentary taxation could, in theory, raise considerable sums, it was an unreliable source and might also generate considerable popular resentment which an insecure dynasty could ill-afford. In addressing parliament in 1467 Edward IV felt obliged to confirm the commons' traditional perception of the role of taxation: 'I purpose to live upon mine own, and not to charge my subjects but in great and urgent causes, concerning more the weal of themselves, and also the defence of them and of this my realm, rather than mine own pleasure.'[17] Yet popular

15   Ellis, *Ireland in the age of the Tudors*, p. 180; Chrimes, *Henry VII*, pp. 246–8; A.J. Pollard, *Northeastern England during the Wars of the Roses* (Oxford, 1990), pp. 99–100.
16   B.P. Wolffe, *The crown lands 1461–1536* (London, 1970), pp. 38, 49, 64, 69; Chrimes, *Henry VII*, pp. 196, 212; Richard Hoyle, 'War and public finance' in MacCulloch (ed.), *Reign of Henry VIII*, pp. 76–7; Ross, *Edward IV*, p. 381; Ellis, *Ireland in the age of the Tudors*, p. 180; Nicholson, *Scotland*, pp. 454–6, 565–70; Merriman, *Rough wooings*, p. 95.
17   Printed, Wolffe, *Crown lands*, doc. 8.

[6 2]   resentment against taxation was exploited by political opponents of the regime, notably in 1469–70 and again in 1489.[18] Edward IV in 1472 and Henry VII in 1489 demanded an income tax instead of the traditional parliamentary subsidy (theoretically of tenths and fifteenths), but both kings were thwarted by passive resistance. Cardinal Wolsey was much more successful in this respect, reflecting Henry VIII's stronger position, and a new method of taxation was successfully introduced in the parliaments of 1512–14 and 1515. This was a tax on lands, goods and wages, which could be varied to tax only the wealthier sections of the community or to bring more people into the net, as circumstances dictated. The new Tudor subsidy was much more efficient (and progressive) in terms of assessment and collection than the traditional quotas of tenths and fifteenths. In 1513–16 it was worth around £43,000 per levy, and even more in the early 1520s after an enhanced rate and valuation had been introduced.

In practice, therefore, the total yield of parliamentary lay taxation under Edward IV amounted to £186,000, and from the clergy £140,000, a combined average of only £15,500 per annum: almost all of it was spent on war, particularly the invasion of France in 1475. Henry VII did slightly better, raising £305,000 from lay taxation (including the subsidy granted in lieu of feudal aids in 1504) and perhaps £216,000 from the clergy, an average of £21,700 per annum. Henry VIII did significantly better, raising over £1m. in parliamentary lay taxation (excluding loans and benevolences, see below), and around £370,000 from the clergy, an average of about £37,700 a year.[19] In Ireland, marcher conditions justified more regular taxation, and reforms of 1477 and 1494–5 converted the parliamentary subsidy from an occasional grant of IR£325 to the governor into a regular royal tax worth over IR£600 per annum, and up to IR£1,500 annually in the years 1495–9.[20]

Efforts to raise money in other ways were less successful. A devaluation of the coinage raised at least £17,500 in two years (1464–6) and smaller

18   Workworth's *Chronicle*, s.a. 1469, in Keith Dockray (ed.), *Three chronicles of the reign of Edward IV* (Gloucester, 1988), pp. 3, 7–8, 12; Pollard, *North-eastern England*, pp. 304–15, 379–83.
19   Ross, *Edward IV*, pp. 214–17, 371–2, 385; Lander, *Government and community*, pp. 80–81, 97–9; Chrimes, *Henry VII*, pp. 195–202; Roger Schofield, 'Taxation and the political limits of the Tudor state' in Claire Cross, David Loades and J.J. Scarisbrick (eds), *Law and government under the Tudors* (Cambridge, 1988), pp. 228–32; G.W. Bernard, *War, taxation and rebellion in early Tudor England* (Brighton, 1986), pp. 119–22; Hoyle, 'War and public finance', pp. 85–91; W.G. Hoskins, *The age of plunder: the England of Henry VIII* (London, 1976), pp. 19–21, 214–16.
20   S.G. Ellis, *Reform and revival: English government in Ireland, 1470–1534* (London, 1986), pp. 67–72. There was also a tradition of granting local subsidies, and scutages (worth c.IR£250) were still occasionally levied until 1531.

amounts thereafter. Edward IV made some money by personal trading ventures, and from 1475 to 1482 he received a French pension of £10,000 a year. The pension was restored in 1492 following Henry VII's invasion. Under Henry VIII its value increased, so that after 1525 it was worth £21,316 a year. Scottish kings secured significant windfalls by way of dowries: the dowry of Cecily, daughter of Edward IV, was set at 20,000 marks sterling in 1474; James IV received SC£35,000 for his marriage to Margaret Tudor; and the dowries of James V's two French queens amounted to SC£168,750. Edward IV also initiated the policies developed by Henry VII of exploiting the crown's feudal rights more intensively, issuing numerous commissions of inquiry into concealed lands, viz. lands legally held of the king but on which payments for reliefs, licences or other feudal incidents had been evaded. Yet even by 1504 Henry was only receiving £6,200 per annum from wardships, the most lucrative feudal incident. Episcopal temporalities during vacancies after the death of bishops raised a similar sum. Henry VII also revived the ancient feudal practice of distraint of knighthood, but in one year these fines added only £1,125 to the king's revenues.

Much the most successful of these money-making devices was Henry VIII's attempt to institute a system of extra-parliamentary taxation, by way of loans and benevolences. In 1522, the government launched an unparalleled survey throughout England into individual wealth and military preparedness, which then formed the basis for its demand for a loan from those worth £20 or more in lands or goods. The following spring another survey preceded a demand for a loan from those worth £5 or more in goods. Altogether £212,000 from the laity and £62,000 from the clergy was collected within a year, which was far more than could be raised annually by parliamentary taxation. The failure of the Amicable Grant precluded the further development of this initiative; but the loan was never repaid, being cancelled by act of parliament in 1529, and from 1542 Henry VIII again collected £245,000 or more by way of loan, benevolence, or contribution.[21]

If we turn to the means by which these increases in revenue were effected, the main reason for the increase in customs revenue was probably the

21 Ross, *Edward IV*, pp. 351–2, 378, 380–83; Chrimes, *Henry VII*, pp. 129, 204; Lander, *Government and community*, pp. 76–7, 89; R.L. Storey, *The reign of Henry VII* (London, 1968), pp. 105–7; Wolffe, *Crown lands*, p. 145; David Potter, 'Foreign policy' in MacCulloch (ed.), *Reign of Henry VIII*, pp. 125–6, Hoyle, 'War and public finance', pp. 78, 86–95; G.W. Bernard, *War, taxation and rebellion in early Tudor England* (Brighton, 1986), pp. 117–30; Jamie Cameron, *James V: the personal rule, 1528–1542* (East Linton, 1998), p. 261; Nicholson, *Scotland*, p. 479.

upswing in trade. Beginning in 1473 Edward IV issued a series of commissions to inquire into customs evasion. From 1481 he also appointed special surveyers for twelve of the chief ports, and the law was tightened by a statute of 1472 which confiscated smuggled goods. These initiatives were continued by Henry VII.[22] With regard to crown lands, the main reform was the gradual introduction of chamber administration beginning in 1461. This extended to the crown lands the more efficient techniques of private estate management which were already in use on the duchy of Lancaster lands, and which were familiar to Yorkist kings from their own duchy of York and the earldom of March. Remote supervision exercised by exchequer officials based in Westminster was replaced by a corps of professionally-educated, highly-skilled and well-paid officers (headed by a surveyor, receiver-general and auditor) with good local knowledge of the estates in question. The receiver paid over the profits directly to the king's chamber and a greatly simplified method of accounting was employed. Moreover, close royal control not only ensured that the king now had a good idea of his receipts and expenditure, but also that the money was immediately available to him. Although exchequer control was temporarily restored from 1485 due to Henry VII's financial inexperience, by the early 1490s the chamber was handling most of the customs income and eventually over 90 per cent of the king's revenues.[23]

Besides employing a more efficient system of administration, the Yorkist kings and Henry VII also had a larger pool of land available to them. In part, this was because the crown acquired substantial additional estates, either through inheritance (notably the duchy of York and earldom of March in 1461; the Neville of Middleham patrimony and the earldom of Richmond in 1483–4) or forfeiture. Altogether, 397 people (excluding members of the houses of Lancaster and York) were attainted of treason by English parliaments during the Wars of the Roses, 1453–1504. Yet 256 of them ultimately had their attainders reversed, and of the leading landowners, attainders went unreversed for only 5 peers out of 34 and 72 knights and squires out of 254. Initially, of course, some of the attainders swelled the king's revenues quite considerably. It has been estimated that the 1461 attainders against 113 people, plus the Yorkist inheritance and various wardships, raised £30,000 a year for the crown, but the long-term effect on the crown's landed endowment was much smaller.[24] In addition, a series of parliamentary acts of resumption (eleven passed by the English parliament, 1450–95, seven by the Irish parliament, 1460–95) reversed previous royal grants (mainly of land) by which the king's revenues had been diminished. Finally, in regard to the Tudor subsidy and Henry VIII's loans, the major development was to abandon static rates of tax and stereotyped assessments of wealth in favour of a graduated income tax, whereby individual taxpayers were assessed individually by royal commissioners. In this way, the country's real wealth could be taxed more efficiently, and the proportion of the subsidy, or 'loan', which was paid by the rich also increased considerably.[25]

Overall, crown revenues had fallen sharply under Henry VI, to perhaps a mere £24,000 a year in the later 1450s, and current charges and outstanding debts had gradually mounted, reaching £372,000 by 1450. Thus on Edward IV's accession the restoration of the crown's financial stability was an urgent necessity. Edward IV and Henry VII succeeded in this, but chiefly by increasing existing sources of landed and customs revenue rather than by harnessing new sources. Already by 1466–7 Edward's treasurer of the household recorded a surplus of £650 for that year, and subsequently the king gradually paid off all his debts, making him the first English king to die solvent since Henry II. Like Edward IV, Henry VII also started in financial difficulties: both had supporters to reward. Towards the end of his reign, however, Henry VII was receiving £105,000 a year in cash in his chamber, plus £12,600 in cash and assignments through the exchequer. On his death in 1509, he reputedly left a treasure hoard worth £300,000 in jewels and plate, equivalent to three years' unspent revenues. Henry VIII's first French war (1512–14) certainly accounted for any outstanding surplus, and until the early 1530s his ordinary revenue was probably less than £90,000 a year, but as we have seen, Henry was also much more successful in raising money by way of extraordinary taxation and loans.[26]

24 J.R. Lander, *Crown and nobility 1450–1509* (London, 1976), ch. 5; C.D. Ross, 'The reign of Edward IV' in S.B. Chrimes, C.D. Ross and R.A. Griffiths (eds), *Fifteenth-century England 1399–1509* (Manchester, 1972), p. 55; Pollard, *North-eastern England*, p. 100.
25 Wolffe, *Crown lands*, pp. 53–4, docs 3, 9; Lander, *Government and community*, pp. 68–9; Ellis, *Ireland in the age of the Tudors*, pp. 55, 60, 66, 79, 95, 181; Schofield, 'Taxation and the political limits of the Tudor state', pp. 227–55; John Guy, 'Thomas Wolsey, Thomas Cromwell and the reform of Henrician government' in MacCulloch (ed.), *Reign of Henry VIII*, p. 44.
26 B.P. Wolffe, 'Henry VII's land revenues and chamber finance' in *English Historical Review*, lxxix (1964), p. 217; Lander, *Government and community*, pp. 82–5, 101–2; Ross, *Edward IV*, pp. 371–3, 385–6; Storey, *Reign of Henry VII*, p. 104; Hoyle, 'War and public finance', pp. 75–99.

This recovery in royal finances was, however, less impressive than it appears at first sight. By continental standards, for instance, these revenues placed English kings very much in the second division of European princes: they compared poorly with the £350,000 annually available c.1520 to French kings (double this, with taxation) or the £560,000 which the Emperor Charles V disposed in the 1540s.[27] Moreover, crown revenues were still less than they had been a century and a half earlier. For instance, Edward III had received £157,000 per annum, albeit briefly in the 1350s, and earlier kings had also levied more by way of taxation.[28] Essentially, the crown's renewed solvency rested less on a sizeable revenue than on the absence of heavy expenditure, notably for foreign war. Henry VIII's decision to fight the French very quickly exposed the inadequacy of his financial resources. Moreover, the main sources of income were still heavily concentrated on Lowland England. Landed income from Wales had by then almost doubled to c. £6,000 and now included significant receipts from the Welsh marches, but income from Ireland and the north hardly covered the costs of their defence.[29] And despite further attainders, the growth in the value and extent of crown lands in Henry VII's later years chiefly reflected the reversion of lands previously allocated to the support of other members of the royal family (Henry VII's queen and Princes Arthur and Henry, for instance). Henry VIII recycled these to provide for Catherine of Aragon and also, in 1525, his illegitimate son, the duke of Richmond.[30] It is thus hard to avoid the conclusion that the English monarchy was falling behind the leading continental monarchies during the Renaissance period, at least in terms of its revenue-gathering capacity.

English provincial administration

The restoration of royal finances was only a part of the wider campaign initiated by Edward IV and Henry VII to strengthen crown influence in the

---

27 Potter, 'Foreign policy', pp. 111–12.
28 G.W. Bernard, *War, taxation and rebellion in early Tudor England* (Brighton, 1986), pp. 125–8; Lander, *Government and community*, pp. 79–81, 101–2.
29 Hoyle, 'War and public finance', ch. 4; Wolffe, *Crown lands*, doc. 16.
30 Lander, *Government and community*, pp. 79–81, 101–2; Ross, *Edward IV*, pp. 215–16, 381, 387; Hoyle, 'War and public finance', pp. 76–7. The lands previously held by Queen Elizabeth and Princes Arthur and Henry apparently swelled the crown lands by c.£12,800 per annum: Wolffe, *Crown lands*, pp. 45–6, 72, doc. 16.

provinces and so restore the political stability which had been disrupted by civil war. The thrust of crown policy was conservative: both kings focused their attention on reestablishing royal authority in the traditional heartland of monarchical power, Lowland England, but without addressing the underlying weaknesses of English royal government elsewhere. Until *c.*1525, for instance, Henry VIII did little more than continue the policies of his father for the rule of the borderlands. In order to understand the overall impact of this campaign, we need to survey the inherited structure of English administration in the provinces.[31]

By continental standards, English government was unusually centralised and uniform. England was divided into counties, for each of which the king appointed the same combination of local officials, headed by sheriffs, JPs, escheators and coroners. Throughout the realm, the king's subjects were governed by the same uniform code of law, English common law, which was enforced through grand and trial juries of local men empanelled by the sheriff for each district. In theory, the king could appoint to local office whoever he wished. Yet, since office in local government was unpaid, the crown relied on the leading gentry, nobles and wealthy burgesses to supervise the rule of the provinces and to discharge the most important duties themselves. There were, in theory, clear bureaucratic channels of command from the king and the central courts to local officials, but in practice the enforcement of law and order in the provinces depended as much on cooperation between members of the local elite as on orders sent down from London. Equally important was the maintenance of effective lines of communication between the province and the centre, so that the views and grievances of the locality could be represented to the centre and vice versa. Twice a year the king's judges of the central courts came on circuit, visiting each shire to hold assizes at which civil suits and the most serious crimes were determined through the jury system. Four times a year other major crimes were likewise tried before the JPs at their quarter sessions. The assizes presented the king and council with an opportunity to inform the nobles and gentry of each shire (the county community) of its policies and to secure their cooperation, while the system of grand juries allowed the community to bring local grievances to the notice of the king and leading crown servants. In this way, the necessary political consensus, fundamental to the effective operation

31   For the following, see G.R. Elton, *The Tudor constitution* (2nd ed., Cambridge, 1982), chs 5, 10; Williams, *Tudor regime*, ch. 12; Griffiths, 'English realm and dominions', pp. 83–105; Ellis, 'Crown, community and government', pp. 187–204; Ellis, *Tudor frontiers*, ch. 2.

[6 8] of the system, could be maintained between the crown and the leading magnates and gentry. These links between crown and community were also strengthened by the institution of parliament and by the work of special royal commissions. Each shire and corporate borough sent two elected representatives to parliament, and these sat in the lower house separately from the lords spiritual (the bishops and greater abbots) and temporal (the lay peers) in the upper house. The consent of parliament was necessary for law-making and for grants of national taxation. Special commissioners were often appointed by the king to carry out other duties in the provinces, particularly matters of a difficult or delicate nature.

There were also other, less familiar, prerequisites for the effective operation of English administrative structures. The English system of government had developed most fully in the original area of monarchical power, the former Anglo-Saxon kingdom. It reflected particular assumptions about settlement patterns, social structures and geography which broadly accorded with conditions on the ground in southern and central England – but not, however, those elsewhere. Southern and central England was a predominantly Lowland region with a climate and fertile soils which were better suited to agriculture than elsewhere and where there were no major obstacles to the untramelled exercise of royal authority. Accordingly, this well-populated landscape of market towns and nucleated villages had been heavily manorialised. Dispersed patterns of landholding in an area of small parishes and manors both fostered the growth of an ordered society and also assisted the emergence of a numerous and vigorous group of lesser land-owners, the gentry, to rule the commons on the king's behalf.

Within this region, vigorous action by the monarchy soon curbed the worst excesses of aristocratic violence. In regard to law enforcement, Chief Justice Hussey remarked at a meeting of justices in 1485 that:

> the law would never be carried out properly until the lords spiritual and temporal are of one mind, for the love and fear they have of God or the king, or both, to carry [the laws] out effectively. Thus when the king on his side and the lords on theirs will do this every one else will quickly do it.[32]

Edward IV announced in the first parliament of the reign his intention to take vigorous action against magnate lawlessness, and he exerted himself immediately against the worst disorders. In East Anglia, a series of

---

32 Printed, C.H. Williams (ed.), *English Historical Documents, V: 1485–1558* (London, 1967), p. 533.

outrages in the 1450s culminated in 1461 in the seizure of Caister castle from Sir John Paston by the duke of Norfolk after a five-week siege. Edward responded by committing both Paston and Sir John Howard, sheriff of Norfolk, to the Fleet prison and appointing as sheriff Sir Thomas Montgomery, a trusted servant whom he could ill spare from court, and sending him down with a leading judge, William Yelverton, J.K.B., to hold sessions. They were commanded to 'set a rule' in the country and 'let the people understand that the king would have his laws kept'. Even so, Edward's accession made little immediate difference in terms of law and order. The king gave another indication of his concern for justice when in Michaelmas term 1462 he personally sat for three days in the court of king's bench.[33] Especially in the 1460s, Edward was also extremely active in royal progresses throughout Lowland England, and was very often accompanied by his judges so as to hold sessions. For instance, he toured the West Country and Welsh borders in 1461, the east midlands in 1462, and early in 1464 he visited Gloucester, Cambridge, and Dartford, Kent, within a matter of weeks.[34]

The chief judicial instrument for dealing with treason, riots and other disturbances under Edward IV was the commission of oyer et terminer. The commissioners normally included at least one justice of king's bench or common pleas, but those who sat in judgement were otherwise reliable councillors or Yorkist nobles and gentry, with an important magnate in overall charge – the king's brothers, Clarence and Gloucester, or Lord Hastings or the earl of Warwick. In this way, pressure could, if necessary, be placed on juries to secure a conviction. Alongside these commissions, Edward also made use of trial by the law of arms or martial law for those Lancastrians actually caught in arms against him, but these extraordinary procedures, plus Edward's known interest in justice, soon prompted charges of tyranny under the guise of justice.

In fact, such open violence was exceptional, and from the 1470s things settled down somewhat. Under Henry VII, the emphasis shifted more to close supervision by the king's council of the work of JPs in their quarter sessions. The reason for this was that with the death throes of the Wars of the Roses the worst excesses were becoming fewer, although cases of treason

33 Thomas Playter to John Paston, December 1461, in Norman Davis (ed.), *Paston letters and papers of the fifteenth century*, ii (Oxford, 1976), 262–3; Ross, *Edward IV*, pp. 134, 399–400; B. Wilkinson, *Constitutional history of England in the fifteenth century* (London, 1964), p. 358; Lander, *Government and community*, p. 232.
34 Ross, *Edward IV*, pp. 400–01.

still necessitated a special commission of oyer et terminer, or trial in king's bench. Instead, the emphasis was now on curbing unlawful assemblies, livery and maintenance which could be tried by the JPs or the council itself. From c.1490, Henry VII was particularly interested in the question of retaining (the practice of attaching men to the service of a lord by annuity or indenture): on average two cases per term came before king's bench, referred by assize judges and JPs. Most ended in pardon or dismissal, but the king secured significant sums in fines for pardon from offenders.[35]

The rule of the English marches

Even in Lowland England, progress towards a more peaceful, 'civil' society was only gradual, following the personal efforts of successive monarchs down to Elizabeth's reign. To the north and west, however, lay a predominantly upland zone which medieval English kings had traditionally dominated from their base in Lowland England but where the problems of royal government were more intractable. Historians have traditionally stressed the extent to which an ordered, relatively peaceful society, governed through centralised administrative structures, had already emerged in England by the thirteenth century. Surveys of early Tudor government and society likewise focus on the operation of these supposedly standard administrative structures in Lowland England.

In over half the early-Tudor state, however, society and patterns of settlement diverged quite sharply from the norms of Lowland England. The far north of England, the principality and marches of Wales, and the lordship of Ireland formed a second, distinctly different, region of the English monarchy. This was a predominantly marcher region of conquest lordships which had been added piecemeal to the realm of England in the high middle ages. It also had a very different landscape, including great stretches of pastoral upland and boggy Lowland, with fewer towns or prosperous gentry. Ties of lineage were stronger among its more scattered, frequently Celtic-speaking population, and society was frequently dominated by great magnates with compact holdings and a warlike tenantry. The full system of English common law operated only in parts of the north and Ireland. There it was supplemented by different systems of march law, which also operated in parts of

---

35   Ross, *Edward IV*, ch. 17; John Bellamy, *Crime and public order in England in the later middle ages* (London, 1973), pp. 9, 12; Lander, *Government and community*, pp. 36–8, 232, 333–8.

Wales. Many areas were not shired but were administered as great feudal franchises from which royal officials were excluded. Links with the centre were attenuated. Neither Wales (until 1542) nor Ireland were represented in the English parliament, and the north, with large counties and few towns, was greatly underrepresented. In sum, this was a more militarised region with a predominantly military system of administration, and with significant cultural and legal differences between the king's English subjects and the Welsh, the Irish, or the Scots respectively.[36]

The result was that royal government was much less effective in the borderlands and the structures of power there developed differently. In the English Lowlands, the extension of royal government in the thirteenth century had established a new, direct political relationship between the crown and the lesser landowners who administered this system, thus, potentially at least, threatening the regional influence of the magnates. The Tudor achievement, so it has been argued, was 'to make a reality of that direct relationship' between crown and subject 'which the earlier growth of royal authority had made latent'.[37] In the borderlands, however, royal government was less developed. More importantly, the defence of the marches was most conveniently organised by a resident lord through his tenantry and political affinity. This in turn heightened the importance of the lord's *manraed* and seigneurial power over tenants, while cutting across royal authority over the subject. Thus changed circumstances created countervailing pressures which actually strengthened noble power and influence *vis-à-vis* the crown.

Moreover, English kings and their officials had long held a low opinion of the inhabitants of the upland zone. Giraldus Cambrensis had dismissed the Welsh as an untamed and undisciplined people, living like animals. Though now partially anglicised, they remained light-headed and liable to rebel. The Irish were 'a barbarous people' with 'primitive habits'[38] and were likewise relegated to the nether links of the great chain of being: Polydore Vergil saw them as 'wild men of the woods', 'savage, rude and uncouth'.[39] Many of them had also migrated to Scotland, another savage land, particularly the Highlands. The people of the Scottish Lowlands were perhaps more civil,

---

36 On all this, see, in general, Ellis, *Tudor frontiers*, pp. 46–8; idem, 'Crown, community and government in the English territories, 1450–1575' in *History*, lxxi (1986), pp. 187–204.

37 P.R. Coss, 'Bastard feudalism revised' in *Past and Present*, 125 (Nov. 1989), pp. 27–64 (quotation, p. 62).

38 Andrew Hadfield and John McVeagh (eds), *Strangers to that land: British perceptions of Ireland from the Reformation to the Famine* (Gerrards Cross, Bucks., 1994), p. 27 (quotation); Ellis, *Tudor frontiers*, p. 60.

39 *Anglica Historia*, ed. D. Hay (London, 1950), p. 79.

but those Scots who infiltrated northern England were beggarly rogues, thieves and reivers, who undermined border defence. In all three regions, the king had some loyal English lieges of course, but their relations with the natives raised suspicions in London of degeneracy and corruption by the natives' evil ways and beastly habits.[40]

These English perceptions of the peoples of 'the Celtic fringe' as intrinsically evil and savage can be traced back to William of Malmesbury in the twelfth century. During the fourteenth century, moreover, the English also discovered that God was an Englishman (which explained recent English successes in the Anglo-French wars). And both ideas continued in Tudor times to exercise a powerful influence on English policy towards the benighted natives of the British Isles. Since God was an Englishman, 'civility' (as the manifestation of English culture) was self-evidently closest to godliness; and to the extent that other peoples fell short of English norms, they were less civil. Thus, the classification of the archipelago's inhabitants in terms of civility and savagery supplied the Tudors with a deceptively simple model for the extension of royal authority. Not only was this task a Christian duty, representing the triumph of civilisation over savagery, but it was thought that simply imposing the cultural and administrative norms of Lowland England on these remote and savage parts would turn them into little Englands, reducing them to peace and civility. Even so, while the Tudors were conscious of their divine mission to civilise, they were in no great hurry to discharge these duties, since they also had other, more urgent responsibilities. Accordingly, for almost the first 50 years of Tudor rule, until the developing crisis over Henry VIII's divorce and the Reformation prompted the monarchy to tighten royal control there, Tudor intervention in the upland zone was generally sporadic and piecemeal.[41]

In reality, the problems of Tudor government in the borderlands were far more intractable than contemporary Tudor analysis implied, but the Tudors only gradually became aware of these difficulties from the 1530s, when the

40   Ellis, *Tudor frontiers*, ch. 2; John Scattergood (ed.), *John Skelton: the complete English poems* (London, 1983), poems 11–12, 14, 23; John Gillingham, 'Foundations of a disunited kingdom' in Alexander Grant and Keith Stringer (eds), *Uniting the Kingdom? The making of British history* (London, 1995), pp. 48–64.

41   John Gillingham, 'Foundations of a disunited kingdom' in Alexander Grant and Keith Stringer (eds), *Uniting the Kingdom? The making of British history* (London, 1995), pp. 48–64; J.W. McKenna, 'How God became an Englishman' in D.J. Guth and J.W. McKenna (eds), *Tudor rule and revolution* (Cambridge, 1982), pp. 25–43; S.G. Ellis, 'The limits of power: the English crown and the British Isles' in Patrick Collinson (ed.), *The short Oxford history of the British Isles: the sixteenth century* (Oxford, 2002), pp. 51–2.

suggested remedies failed to achieve the expected results. Henry VII was more concerned to secure the new dynasty against internal and external enemies. His policies in the borderlands were essentially conservative, although his Welsh birth and descent were an advantage in his dealings with Wales. Indeed, while Wales seemed to present a similar range of problems to Ireland and the far north of England, the basic problem there was the fragmentation of power and authority. There was no single territorial entity called Wales, but rather about 130 marcher lordships in the east, and the six counties of the principality in the west. This fragmentation was the product of an earlier military frontier between the original areas of English settlement in Wales and those parts still controlled by native Welsh princes before the Edwardian conquest. The lordships, moreover, were divided between enclaves of Englishries ruled by march law, and Welshries where native customs prevailed; and the population was similarly divided between English and Welsh. Violence and lawlessness in the region were further fuelled by the practice of buying off the sessions in return for money and by two Welsh customs which were increasingly abused: *arddel* (avowry) effectively allowed marcher lords to harbour criminals; and criminals were then often given pardons for felonies in return for a fine which might then be met by extorting *comhorthau* (subsidies) from the local community.[42]

These divisions between natives and settlers were replicated elsewhere, notably in parts of Ireland. In part, the reasons for this had to do with concepts of nationality, the determinants of which were not just place of birth, but chiefly law, language and culture. The English nation *c.*1500 comprised all those of free birth, English blood and condition, born in territories under the allegiance of the English king: thus, English nationality was in the first instance a legal status, and included the English of Calais, Ireland and Wales, not just those born in England. Traditionally, only freeborn Englishmen had access to the king's courts: the mere Irish living in the Englishry and the mere Welsh were treated like serfs and were legally disabled from holding many royal offices. The Irish living in Gaelic parts and the Scots were aliens, and frequently enemies to the crown. Henry VII's belated sale of charters (1504–8), granting whole communities in north Wales the status of freeborn Englishmen, anticipated the more general emancipation of the Welsh in 1536. Yet charters had long been sold to individuals: Scots or 'wild Irish' living among the English could also purchase their freedom. Henry VII also

42 Glanmore Williams, *Wales and the Act of Union* (Bangor, 1992), pp. 10–14, 37.

[7 4] continued Edward IV's device of establishing regional councils to supervise local government, but the decisive factor in the rule of the early Tudor borderlands was the king's handling of the great territorial magnates there.[43]

In Wales, starting in 1490, the king exacted from marcher lords an 'indenture for the marches', requiring each lord to take surety from his men for good behaviour, due appearance in court, and to surrender suspects on request for trial elsewhere. Given that king's personal application to the minutiae of government, this no doubt had some impact in curbing the country's lawlessness. His son, Henry VIII, had little interest in this work, however. Thus, more important in the longer term was the fact that many of the larger lordships came into crown hands by inheritance or forfeiture. Twenty-two comprised the earldom of March and passed to the crown in 1461; the attainder of Sir William Stanley in 1495 brought in four more; and the attainder in 1521 of the third duke of Buckingham, lord of Brecon, Caurs and Newport, removed the last of the great marcher lords capable of challenging royal power. With landed influence now increasingly concentrated in crown hands, the council had greater scope in maintaining law and order. After Prince Arthur's death, the council continued to operate (1502–4) under a president, Bishop Smyth of Lincoln, as likewise after 1509, albeit ineffectually, when it became the king's council.[44]

By contrast, the Tudors had no natural ties with Ireland and the English north where good rule and good lordship were seen to depend far more heavily on effective arrangements for defence. In the far north, for instance, large tracts of marchland lay waste in 1485, following the recent Scottish war. Yet Henry VII's main priority was to stifle any challenge to his position from disaffected nobles in regions which were solidly Yorkist. The king deliberately excluded the Nevilles and the Percies, the ruling magnates, from offices which were traditionally theirs, notably the wardenships, diffusing power instead among lesser landowners, and also reducing the crown's usual financial and military subventions for the defence of the borders. For instance, separate royal constables were appointed for the chief royal castles of Berwick-on-Tweed and Carlisle, with their garrisons.[45]

43   R.A. Griffiths, 'The English realm and dominions and the king's subjects in the later middle ages' in John Rowe (ed.), *Aspects of government and society in later medieval England: essays in honour of J.R. Lander* (Toronto, 1986), pp. 83–105; Ellis, *Tudor frontiers*, pp. 74–5; Ellis, 'Tudor state formation and the shaping of the British Isles' in idem et Sarah Barber (eds), *Conquest and Union: fashioning a British state, 1485–1725* (London, 1995), pp. 46–8.
44   Williams, *Recovery, reorientation and Reformation*, chs 8–1.
45   Ellis, 'Tudor state formation', pp. 48–50; Ellis, *Tudor frontiers*, ch. 2.

Initially, however, Henry could only reappoint as king's lieutenant and [7 5]
warden-general Henry Percy, earl of Northumberland, whose failure to
support Richard III at Bosworth had been crucial in the Tudor victory. In
Ireland, likewise, there was no obvious alternative as deputy-lieutenant to
the ruling magnate, Gerald Fitzgerald, earl of Kildare. Thomas Butler, earl of
Ormond, clearly preferred life at court to service in Ireland; and despite an
ominous delay, Kildare eventually recognised Henry, following the example
of the nominal lieutenant, John de la Pole, earl of Lincoln. In spring 1486,
Northumberland apparently foiled a plot by Francis Viscount Lovell to seize
the king at York, and the following year Northumberland's speedy response
to Lambert Simnel's landing at Furness again steadied York and the north-
east. In 1489, however, further disturbances occurred in Yorkshire following
new tax demands there despite an exemption previously negotiated by
Richard in 1474 in return for service against the Scots. The collector,
Northumberland, was murdered, a full-scale rebellion began, and York was
again besieged. The king was forced to raise another army to crush the
revolt. In the aftermath, he replaced Northumberland with a rank outsider,
Thomas Howard, earl of Surrey. And whereas Northumberland had contracted to defend the marches in wartime in return for £3,000 a year,
Surrey's salary as lieutenant was only £1,000, with his troops in wages. This
change was an extension of Yorkist policy, both in Ireland and in the west
marches, where a minor peer, Thomas Lord Dacre, was appointed lieutenant.
It reduced both costs and the political influence of the ruling magnates:
Northumberland, for instance, had on his death been retaining 84 lords,
knights and squires costing over £1,700.[46]

In Ireland, relations with Kildare remained strained, despite a royal pardon concerning Simnel, but when the earl reacted equivocally to another
Yorkist pretender, Perkin Warbeck, he was finally dismissed from office
(1492). Disorders ensued, as the king attempted to balance Kildare influence
by building up the Butlers, in the form of Lord Ormond's illegitimate elder
brother, Sir James Ormond, appointed joint-governor with the archbishop
of Dublin. Yet unlike the north, where the fifth earl of Northumberland was

46   A.J. Pollard, *North-eastern England during the Wars of the Roses* (Oxford, 1990), pp. 125,
      367–96; S.G. Ellis, 'Civilizing Northumberland: representations of Englishness in the Tudor
      state' in *Journal of Historical Sociology*, xii (1999), pp. 108–15; Ellis, *Tudor frontiers*, pp. 41–2,
      148; Ellis, *Ireland in the age of the Tudors*, pp. 83–9; Michael Bennett, 'Henry VII and the
      Northern Rising of 1489' in *English Historical Review*, cv (1990), pp. 38–55; Michael Bennett,
      Lambert Simnel and the battle of Stoke (Gloucester, 1987); M.A. Hicks, 'The Yorkshire rebellion
      of 1489 reconsidered' in *Northern History*, xxii (1986), pp. 39–62.

under age, Kildare was well able to protect his local standing, and the ensuing feud with the Butlers threatened to attract Warbeck back. The king was eventually forced to despatch another expedition to Ireland, led by Sir Edward Poynings who, as deputy-lieutenant of Calais, had been counteracting Warbeck's intrigues in the Netherlands. In summer 1495, after port-towns and nobles in Munster had declared for him, Warbeck did indeed return, blockading Waterford (July–August); but Poynings broke the blockade with his artillery, after which Warbeck fled to Scotland.[47]

In large measure, the equivocal response to the new dynasty Tudor in Ireland and the north reflected local perceptions of serious shortcomings by the Tudors in the discharge of their basic duties of providing good rule and defence for their subjects. Good rule still depended far more on the region's resident ruling magnates, chosen instruments of the popular Yorkist kings, than on an unknown absentee king from a rival dynasty. By contrast, the most striking manifestations of Tudor authority were the intrusion of outsiders like Poynings and Surrey. It was perhaps only when opposition to the Tudors became increasingly identified with support for England's traditional enemies that the Yorkist loyalties of these regions finally evaporated. Within a few years, however, improved relations with Scotland also supplied Henry VII with a convenient solution to his northern problem. The truce of 1497, followed by the peace of 1502 allowed Henry to scale down arrangements for the defence of his northern frontier. Surrey returned south, being replaced initially by Archbishop Savage of York, appointed president of a restored northern council in 1501. The council's authority was restricted to Yorkshire, however, and it lapsed again on Henry's death in 1509.[48]

In the far north, however, the existence of extensive liberty jurisdictions, akin to the Welsh marcher lordships or Scottish regalities, continued to hamper the work of government. Border rule was now entrusted to local gentry and minor peers, notably Thomas Lord Dacre who had by 1511 amassed authority over all three marches. Yet, in the absence of the traditional ruling magnates to supervise border rule and defence, the region's precarious peace dissolved into feuds and reiving. The border surnames, in particular, became virtually uncontrollable: Bishop Fox was reduced to excommunicating them in a bid to maintain a semblance of order and secure restitution for robberies. Yet, once peace with Scotland had extinguished the main threat to Tudor

---

47   Ellis, *Ireland in the age of the Tudors*, pp. 85–97; Ian Arthurson, *The Perkin Warbeck conspiracy 1491–1499* (Stroud, 1994).

48   Pollard, *North-eastern England*, pp. 394–6; Storey, *Henry VII*, pp. 85–8, 148–9.

rule, Henry VII was prepared to tolerate such disorders as preferable both to renewed dependence on 'overmighty subjects' like the Percies and the high costs of a more effective system of border rule. The peace commissions of the three most northerly shires were both smaller and renewed less frequently under Henry VII than they had been under the Yorkists. Moreover, the combined salaries of the three wardens or lieutenants was now less than £400 per annum, and much of this was recouped by reviving the ancient practice of farming the shrievalties. For instance, from 1506 Nicholas Ridley of Willimoteswick, a lawless borderer, paid 100 marks a year for the privilege of serving as sheriff of Northumberland. Yet no sheriff or escheator of Northumberland accounted at the exchequer between 1461 and 1515, and by 1526 quarter sessions had not been held there for a long time.[49]

Affairs were marginally better in the west marches, even though financial compositions sometimes replaced trials for murder. Power was gradually concentrated in the hands of Lord Dacre, who controlled the wardenship, the captaincy of Carlisle and the shrievalty of Cumberland, as well as holding the strategically vital baronies of Burgh and Gilsland against the Scottish border. Dacre's ancestral possessions were extremely modest, but his wife was heiress to the wealthier Lord Greystoke. Henry VII exploited this, gradually allowing Dacre to acquire the Greystoke lands in return for loyal service. The Greystoke inheritance included estates throughout the north, so that by the time Dacre became warden-general in 1511, his standing had been transformed from that of a poor border baron to a major northern magnate. He continued to rule all three marches until a few months before his death in 1525.[50]

The revival of crown government allowed Henry VIII to pursue his penchant for war against France, and this soon had repercussions in the far north. Dacre needed all his increased landed endowment and *manraed*, since the young king's belligerent foreign policy breathed new life into the 'auld alliance' between France and Scotland, with James IV 'aboutward to have stolen the town of Berwick'.[51] In the west marches, following a programme of castle-building and military reorganisation on his estates, Dacre could raise 5,000 men from his battle-hardened tenantry to invade Scotland. Yet he was hard put to control the strategically more important east and middle

49 Ellis, *Tudor frontiers*, chs 2–3, 5; Ellis, 'Civilizing Northumberland', p. 115; *The register of Richard Fox, lord bishop of Durham, 1494–1501* (Surtees Soc., Durham, 1932), p. 110.
50 Ellis, *Tudor frontiers*, chs 2–3, 5.
51 British Library, Caligula B. II, f. 200 (*L. & P. Hen. VIII*, I, no. 2913).

marches from his modest territorial base around Morpeth. For major campaigns the king sent north a lieutenant with command of an army royal, but otherwise Dacre was expected to defend the marches with minimal assistance. He intrigued against the French party in Scotland and tried to make the Scottish marches ungovernable. Yet, if the king had exploited effectively the opportunity provided by the English victory at Flodden in 1513, all this should have been unnecessary.

Essentially, therefore, the limits of royal power and the limitations of Tudor policy were graphically exposed by conditions in the far north where the borders remained lawless and disturbed. After Dacre's dismissal in 1525, allegedly for maladministration, bands of up to 400 thieves roamed the marches, eventually necessitating a military campaign to subdue them. Attempts to curb noble power and the magnates' bastard feudal connexions had simply stoked disorders, leading to a virtual collapse of local government; and continued Tudor reliance on the Dacres as a more trustworthy alternative to the unreliable Percies had eventually created a new 'over-mighty subject'.[52]

Early Tudor rule in Ireland was equally reliant on noble power. Following Kildare's reappointment as deputy-lieutenant in 1496 – this time with full royal backing following the earl's marriage to Henry's kinswoman and guarantees for his conduct – Earl Gerald consolidated English influence in the Pale marches and even extended it further afield. As in the north, Henry VIII was long content to maintain the administrative arrangements devised for Ireland by his father; and in 1513 when the old earl finally died (of a gunshot wound sustained while watering his horse in the River Barrow), the king soon appointed as deputy, Gerald Fitzgerald, the young ninth earl of Kildare. The Kildares exploited the governorship to reconquer ancestral estates from the Gaelic Irish, constructing or enlarging castles and towers to protect their tenantry and strengthen the English marches, much as Dacre was doing in the north; and they expanded into Gaelic Leinster, the midlands, and east Ulster. Yet in Ireland, the marches were more fluid because there was no agreed border line, and because individual Gaelic chiefs were far weaker and more divided than the Scottish crown and community. Accordingly, Kildare wielded much more influence there, building up a Gaelic clientage network and cross-border alliances to protect the English marches in a way which was far less feasible for Dacre in the Scottish borders. Moreover, although the two magnates both had unusually compact

---

52   Ellis, *Tudor frontiers*, chs 3, 5; Ellis, 'Civilizing Northumberland', pp. 115–16.

lordships and very comparable landed incomes (over 2,000 marks a year), [79] in terms of wealth and landed influence Kildare stood head and shoulders above any other magnate in Ireland. From a Tudor perspective, however, Ireland was even less strategically important than the English north; and to divert scarce resources to rule and defend this remote outpost from a bunch of savages was – as Henry VIII phrased it, when surveying the dismal achievements of Surrey's expedition in 1520–2 – 'consumption of treasure in vain'.[53] Yet, with decisive interventions and other convincing demonstrations of royal power an even rarer occurrence in Ireland than the north, Tudor rule also remained more dependent on noble power. In both regions, long tenure of office helped to transform a local noble into a great regional magnate; but the personal system of defences and alliances built up by the two ruling magnates to offset the shortcomings of royal government made their replacement extremely difficult when circumstances dictated a change of Tudor policy in the later 1520s.

Overall, therefore, the early Tudor achievement in the borderlands was very undistinguished. Apart from extinguishing residual support for Yorkist pretenders, the Tudors failed to promote good rule, or even to defend them properly, so that the marches remained disturbed and faction-ridden at a time when Lowland England was becoming more peaceful and prosperous.

Royal government in Scotland: an alternative approach

If English government was comparatively centralised, with uniform structures, Scottish provincial administration was much more decentralised. This decentralisation reflected not only the scantier resources of Scottish kings but also the country's more pronounced geographical and cultural divisions. Scotland had a much larger proportion of less fertile upland, especially in the centre and west, with a mainly pastoral economy. The Forth-Clyde and eastern coastal plains were more suited to arable farming but much smaller than was Lowland England in relation to the English borderlands. The 'Highland Line' which separated the barren and mountainous centre and west from the more fertile Lowlands also formed a cultural and linguistic boundary

---

53 S.G. Ellis, 'Tudor policy and the Kildare ascendancy in the lordship of Ireland, 1496–1534' in *Irish Historical Studies*, xx (1976–77), p. 239 (quotation); Ellis, *Tudor frontiers*, ch. 4; Ellis, *Ireland in the age of the Tudors*, pp. 96–126.

between Scotland's two peoples and two different forms of life, the Gaelic-speaking Scots (*Gaedhil*) and those of English speech and culture (*Gaill*). Burghs, royal castles, monasteries, cathedrals and sheriffs' seats were concentrated in the Lowlands, with very few located beyond the Highland Line, a division which somewhat resembled that between English and Gaelic Ireland.[54] To some extent, the lowlander perception of Scottish Gaeldom as rude and savage also paralleled English attitudes to the 'wild Irish', but at this stage criticism of the 'wild Scots' was still good-humoured, and as the Spanish ambassador reported, James IV also spoke 'the language of the savages' – unlike his brother-in-law, Henry VIII. The utter contempt later shown by James VI for Gaelic society and culture, his attempt to plant lowlanders and royal burghs on Lewis, and the castigation by Scottish officials of Gaelic ('the Irish language') as 'one of the chief and principal causes of the continuance of barbarity and incivility amongst the inhabitants of the isles and highlands' lay very much in the future. There was at this stage no thought of emulating English efforts to 'spread civility' by imposing English law and local government on 'the Celtic fringe'. Norse law, for instance, was not abolished in Orkney and Shetland until 1611.[55]

Superficially, Scotland's administrative division into 30 counties and sheriffdoms, with baronies and parishes, resembled English practice, with sprawling upland counties and smaller Lowland ones. The 10 largest counties covered more than half the geographical area of Scotland. (A third of England's 39 shires were likewise disproportionately large.).In fact, almost all the institutional unity which Scotland possessed was supplied by the monarchy, the symbol of national integrity. The monarchy was indispensable in the system of land tenure, and it was also the source of patronage – of offices, lands and pensions. The king was also the fount of justice, but in fact large areas of the country were administered through heritable jurisdictions. The normal royal court in the localities was the sheriffship, but the sheriff was often a local magnate holding his office in heritage. There were also extensive regalities (akin to the much less numerous liberties palatine in England) where the lord could try all crimes except treason, receive forfeitures and escheats, and 'repledge' tenants from the courts of royal justiciars and sheriffs. Moreover, many branches of law – matrimony, proceedings for the fulfilment of obligations – were administered by ecclesiastical courts.

54 Donaldson, *Scotland*, pp. 3–4.
55 Gordon Donaldson (ed.), *Scottish historical documents* (Edinburgh, 1974), p. 178 (quotation); Wormald, *Court, kirk, and community*, pp. 39–40, 61–3 (quotation, p. 62); Donaldson, *Scotland*, pp. 228, 288.

Essentially, therefore, there was little tangible or visible in the localities to
remind people of the central government. The only officer to be seen permanently in the localities was the local magnate. Royal castles were likewise
in their custody. In practice, the magnates controlled local government. Thus,
despite some similarities, this was a different administrative system from the
classic English model where, in the Lowlands, the king was capable of vigorous (but often disruptive) interventions in local government and where, in
the marches, the king's failure to play his part in maintaining 'good rule' led
to disorders and administrative paralysis. In Scotland, the king might show
himself to his subjects on progress, hold justice ayres in person, or send out
justiciars, but lacking the powers and resources to dominate the great feuda-
tories, he could only maintain government by coming to terms with them.[56]

Paradoxically, this more *laissez-faire* style of government often made for
greater political stability in the provinces, because the crown did not seek to
alter the relationship between centre and locality. Magnates who failed to
maintain good rule might attract unwelcome royal interference, but by and
large the king needed to attract the nobles to his service, to persuade the
magnates to take part in central government so as to strengthen his influence
in the provinces. Royal patronage was one way, but the crown's ability to
reward service with land, pensions and local offices was much more limited
than in England. For those so inclined, service in the king's privy council
was another means, but most magnates had no appetite for the detailed
and sometimes trivial business of the council, which was left to the king's
professional administrators, the lawyers, and the clergy. Better was the king's
parliament, which was unicameral. Parliament allowed the magnates to represent the interests of the locality and even, if necessary, to criticise the direction of royal policy. The baronial estate of the Scottish parliament comprised
in theory all the king's tenants-in-chief, but in practice it was dominated
by the lords and earls. The other two estates were the prelates (abbots and
bishops) and burgesses. The latter were drawn almost entirely from the royal
burghs, of which there were around 40 in the early sixteenth century, but
only a handful of burghs were regularly represented. (There was no elected
shire representation until 1587, when two commissioners per shire from
among the freeholders were added.) The prelates attended more regularly,
playing an important role with the onset of the Reformation, but even so in

---

56   Wormald, *Court, kirk, and community*, pp. 12–17; Donaldson, *Scotland*, pp. 4–6. See also
       I.D. Whyte, *Scotland before the Industrial Revolution: an economic and social history c.1050–c.1750*
       (London, 1995), maps 3, 4.1, 10.1 (pp. 58, 180, 339).

[8 2] the average sixteenth-century parliament attended by some 60 members, almost half were normally nobles. The extended royal minorities of the period increased the attractiveness of parliament and privy council to the magnates, as they strove to limit the powers of the regent, but the most important means by which the king attracted the service of the nobles was the royal court. Here, Scottish kings avoided the quasi-religious propaganda of their English or French counterparts (touching for the King's Evil, for instance, or the personality cult and adulation encouraged by Henry VIII): they wished to attract, not overawe. They were anxious to be personally familiar and on easy terms with the magnates, since personal links with those who controlled local government enabled the crown to extend its influence at local level. Magnificent buildings, clothes, pageants and ceremonial were one way to impress subjects and visitors, but Scottish monarchs also concentrated on the familial nature of their kingship. This was best articulated by James VI's projection of himself as father of his children, but more generally the Stewart kings were stewards of their kingdom and kings of the Scots, not kings of Scotland. For their part, the magnates expected to counsel the king and to be rewarded for their service.[57] Overall, however, the Scottish example of a more devolved system of government reminds us that the Tudor drive towards centralised bureaucracy and administrative uniformity did not necessarily provide better rule and political stability in an age of personal monarchy.

57 Wormald, *Court, kirk, and community*, pp. 16–23, 27; Donaldson, *Scotland*, pp. 8–9, 276–89.

4
___

MACHINES BUILT FOR THE BATTLEFIELD
Renaissance monarchy, 1502–60

The opening years of the sixteenth century were ones of relative harmony in the generally troubled relations between the two British kingdoms. The peace allowed James IV more scope for manoeuvre in terms of his European diplomacy than Scottish kings had enjoyed for some considerable time. James used the opportunity to provide modest military support in the Baltic for his uncle, King Hans of Denmark, and also to bombard the European chanceries unavailingly for a crusade by Christendom against the Turks. At home, he indulged in extensive building work on both Edinburgh and Stirling castles, and he also built up the royal navy, spending at least SC£100,000 from 1505 to 1511 on his ships, notably his flagship, the 'great' *Michael*, completed in 1511, which was larger than Henry VIII's *Mary Rose* of 1509.[1]

For Henry VII, the Scottish peace greatly simplified the problems of administering the remote northern frontier, although it did little to curb the almost constant reiving and robbery by the marchers across the border line. The respective wardens generally cooperated to bring offenders to justice, but the murder by the Herons at a day of truce of the Scottish warden of the middle marches, Sir Robert Kerr, threatened a more serious breach, until Henry VII surrendered William Heron of Ford, keeper of Redesdale, as a hostage. Overall, the chief credit for this peaceful interlude in Anglo-Scottish relations apparently belonged to Henry VII, but the alliance was brittle and neither side thought in terms of union. Essentially, good relations rested on Henry Tudor's desire for general diplomatic recognition by the European courts and his particular preference for internal reconstruction over the hazards and expense of another war against France. Yet this was a passing phase.[2]

1 Michael Lynch, *Scotland, a new history* (London, 1991), p. 160; Nicholson, *Scotland*, pp. 555–6.
2 Ralph Robson, *The rise and fall of the English highland clans: Tudor responses to a mediaeval problem* (Edinburgh, 1989), p. 75; Lynch, *Scotland*, pp. 160–2; R.G. Eaves, *Henry VIII's Scottish diplomacy 1513–1524: England's relations with the regency government of James V* (New York, 1971), pp. 25–7.

[8 4]   It is a measure of Henry VII's achievements in restoring royal authority both at home and abroad that when he died in 1509, his son became the first king to succeed to the English crown unopposed since 1421. Henry VIII, however, was a very different kind of king from his father. He had a powerful, complex and, at times, contradictory personality. Moreover, his extremely elevated view of his monarchical authority was not unlike that of James III, although of course he had more ample resources with which to support it. Yet he was also, like his brother-in-law, James IV, in many ways a more conventional king, preferring hunting, jousting and, above all, war to his father's penchant for privacy, administration and quiet diplomacy.[3] These differences were very soon registered in the character of the royal court. Around 1495 Henry VII had reorganised the privy chamber (his private apartments), restricting access by providing it with its own staff (half a dozen grooms) and separating it from the great chamber and presence chamber in which the ceremonial and public aspects of monarchy were conducted. In this way, Henry VII shut himself off from outside influences. By contrast, Henry VIII wanted a public, participatory monarchy. He was insecure personally, and liked being surrounded by great men. The nobles he regarded as his friends – unlike his wary father – but he also had much higher expectations concerning their conduct.[4]

Henry VII had died on Saturday 21 April, but not even the young Henry VIII was informed until the following Monday. The involvement in this deception of Richard Empson and Edmund Dudley, leading ministers of the old king, led to their arrest and execution – the first of many by which the more ruthless Henry VIII commonly disposed of ministers and magnates who failed him.[5] In the ensuing reaction, a whole series of recognisances by which Henry VII had bound over individual nobles in large sums of money to be of good bearing were cancelled: 175 in all by 1515, and in 51 cases it was specifically stated that these bonds had been levied unjustly.[6]

---

3   The best full biography of Henry VIII remains J.J. Scarisbrick, *Henry VIII* (2nd ed., London, 1997), although now rather dated. David Starkey, *The reign of Henry VIII: personalities and politics* (London, 1985) is good on court politics; and M.A.R. Graves, *Henry VIII: a study of kingship* (London, 2003) offers a more rounded summary. Diarmaid MacCulloch (ed.), *The reign of Henry VIII: politics, policy and piety* (Basingstoke, 1995) is a good collection of essays.

4   David Starkey, 'Intimacy and innovation: the rise of the privy chamber, 1485–1547' in David Starkey *et al.* (ed.), *The English court from the Wars of the Roses to the Civil War* (London, 1987), pp. 73–82; Starkey, *Henry VIII*, pp. 40–57.

5   Steve Gunn, 'The accession of Henry VIII' in *Historical Research*, lxiv (1991), pp. 278–88.

6   Lander, *Crown and nobility*, pp. 297–9.

War, taxation and the rise of Wolsey [85]

Initially, government was run by a handful of aristocrats and other intimates of the old king led by the earls of Oxford and Surrey. Technically, Henry VIII was not yet 18: he 'was young and lusty, disposed all to mirth and pleasure and to follow his desire and appetite, nothing minding to travail in the busy affairs of this realm'.[7] Yet he very quickly made his preferences felt, particularly in terms of foreign policy, where he dreamed of emulating the great victories of Edward III and Henry V at Crécy and Agincourt, and so recovering England's medieval French territories. Essentially, early modern states were, in Perry Anderson's well-known phrase, 'machines built for the battlefield', and Henry's determination to display the monarchy's enhanced authority in warfare constituted a more conventional application of royal power than his father's defensive strategy.

Yet, to mount an effective challenge to the French king, Henry now needed the support of Spain and the Emperor Maximilian because, following the expulsion of the English from Normandy and Gascony at the end of the Hundred Years War (1337–1453), the French monarchy had further consolidated its position by absorbing the formerly independent duchies of Burgundy and Brittany, whose dukes had once offered the English intermittent support.[8] His first move was to marry Catherine of Aragon, widow of his elder brother, Arthur, who had died unexpectedly in 1503. This move had also been contemplated by Henry VII, but discarded, perhaps because Catherine was seven years older than Henry. The marriage was celebrated in June 1509, and in effect brought with it a dynastic alliance with Spain through Henry's new father-in-law, Ferdinand of Aragon. Yet not until late 1511, when Ferdinand decided on another contest with Louis XII of France over supremacy in Italy, was there any real prospect of war. Meanwhile, the impressionable young king could only indulge his love of chivalry by following the example of his brother-in-law, James IV, and appearing *incognito* at a tournament at Richmond in January 1510.[9] In 1512, however, an English army of 10,000 men under the marquis of Dorset was despatched to

---

7   George Cavendish, *The life and death of Cardinal Wolsey* (Early English Texts Society, 1959), p. 12 (quotation); Starkey, *Henry VIII*, pp. 40–60.
8   David Potter, 'Foreign policy', in MacCulloch (ed.), *Henry VIII*, pp. 101–33 (quotation, p. 112); Starkey, *Henry VIII*, pp. 48–60.
9   Virginia Murphy, 'The first divorce: literature and propaganda' in MacCulloch (ed.), *Henry VIII*, pp. 136–7; Scarisbrick, *Henry VIII*, pp. 7–13; Starkey, 'Intimacy and innovation', p. 77; Starkey, *Henry VIII*, pp. 47–9, 57–60; MacDougall, *James IV*, p. 295.

Spain, but Ferdinand simply used it to distract the French as he himself conquered the small Pyrenean kingdom of Navarre.[10]

In 1513, however, Henry prepared a major expeditionary force to invade northern France from his Calais bridgehead, while his allies Ferdinand and Maximilian were to dismember France from the south and north-east. Both Edward IV and Henry VII had invaded France to recover the lost territories, but it is hard to determine how serious they were. In 1475 Edward had marched into Picardy with an inexperienced, hastily-assembled force of perhaps 15,000 men, but he made peace readily enough when his chief ally, Charles the Bold, proved unreliable and Louis XI offered him an annual pension of £10,000 instead. Henry Tudor sent 6,000 men to Brittany in 1489 and then laid siege to Boulogne in 1492, but he was likewise bought off readily enough by the restoration of the French pension.[11] In 1513, however, Henry VIII assembled an army of 30,000 men. Henry's army greatly impressed foreign observers, in that the troops were experienced and well-armed, they were well supplied, and the force was also equipped with an impressive siege train. It was the largest and best-equipped force to leave England since 1415.

The army was of a multi-national character, and so the king also prudently gave orders that no man reproach another 'because of the country that he is of, that is to say, be he French, English, Northern, Welsh, or Irish'.[12] In early Tudor times, the more militarised borderlands were still highly prized as a source of experienced troops, and Henry's army royal included companies of northern men under Lord Darcy, Welshmen under the earl of Worcester, and 500 Irishmen. English armies had acquired a formidable reputation in Europe in the fourteenth century, but by 1,500 English longbowmen and billmen were beginning to look old-fashioned against the new handguns and pikes; and the exaggerated respect which the French accorded Henry VIII's armies when they invaded was largely unmerited. The king's original aim had been to capture Boulogne so as to extend the Calais bridgehead, but Henry allowed himself to be distracted by the Emperor Maximilian into attacking French enclaves in Burgundy. His army won a cavalry skirmish, grandiosely dubbed the Battle of the Spurs, rased the French fortress at Thérouanne, and then besieged the city of Tournai, which quickly

10 Scarisbrick, *Henry VIII*, pp. 28–31.
11 Ross, *Edward IV*, ch. 9; Lander, *Government and community*, pp. 287–92, 341–3; Storey, *Henry VII*, pp. 77–81.
12 C.G. Cruickshank, *Henry VIII and the invasion of France* (Stroud, 1990); A.J. Kempe (ed.), *The Losely manuscripts* (London, 1835), pp. 114–15 (quotation).

surrendered. The king then proceeded to garrison this remote outpost over 70 miles from Calais, and over the next 5 years he rebuilt its defences at a cost of £230,000. The doctrine of continuous linear ('natural') state frontiers did not develop until the late seventeenth century, but this was nonetheless an expensive English occupation, which was increasingly resented by the citizens of Tournai.[13]

The French war established Henry VIII's reputation as a powerful Renaissance prince. Much more decisive, however, was the English victory achieved far to the north, on the Anglo-Scottish frontier. In July, King James had sent the Scottish fleet, with the *Michael*, twelve other large ships and ten smaller vessels, to support his French ally, Louis XII. They sacked the chief English fortress in Ulster, Carrickfergus, en route and eventually reached Brest. On board were 3,000 experienced troops and choice artillery. King James himself then invaded England, capturing Norham, Etal, Ford and Wark castles, before waiting on high ground at Flodden to do battle with the English relief army commanded by the earl of Surrey. The two armies were of roughly equal size, about 20,000 men each. An artillery duel ensued, but in the prevailing bad weather the lighter, more manoeuvrable English guns soon dislodged the Scots, forcing them forward down the rain-soaked hill towards the English, where at close quarters on muddy ground their freshly-imported Swiss pikes proved no match for the shorter English bills. King James himself, 2 bishops, 11 earls, 15 lords, and reputedly 10,000 men were all killed, as against 1,500 English. Of the Scottish fleet, the *Michael* was sold to France and the rest disbanded.

The English commander, Thomas Howard, earl of Surrey, was subsequently rewarded by promotion to his father's old title of duke of Norfolk. In the short term, Surrey's northern levies could easily have occupied the Scottish Lowlands, but Queen Catherine as regent ordered the army disbanded to save money for the French campaign. Much more shortsighted was Henry's squandering of the promising diplomatic opportunities created by the accession to the Scottish throne of his young nephew, James V. Henry revived the old claim to overlordship over Scotland and tried to have his sister, Margaret, James's mother, reappointed regent. Margaret had initially assumed the regency, but she was soon forced to flee to England, together with her new husband, Archibald Douglas, sixth earl of Angus. Thereupon

---

13   C.G. Cruickshank, *The English occupation of Tournai* (Oxford, 1971); Cruickshank, *Henry VIII and the invasion of France*, passim; Scarisbrick, *Henry VIII*, pp. 21–40, 71–3; M.C. Fissel, *English warfare 1511–1642* (London, 2001), pp. 4–8; Potter, 'Foreign policy', pp. 112–15.

[8 8]   the council appointed as governor John Stewart, duke of Albany, the French-born heir presumptive. Yet for Henry the unlikely chance of realising his claim to the rich and sophisticated French kingdom just across the Channel was far more appealing than the much more realistic but far less glamorous strategy of consolidating Tudor influence, and thereby England's land frontier, in a poor, backward and remote kingdom far to the north.[14]

Altogether, the cost of war between 1512 and 1514 amounted to c.£1 million. Presumably, the campaigns were funded chiefly from a surplus built up by Henry VII towards the end of his reign (we do not know how much), since only around a third of this sum was eventually raised by taxation. Yet, with the introduction of the new Tudor subsidy in the parliaments of 1512–14 and 1515, a total of £170,000 was eventually collected in the four years 1512–17, plus £90,000 from three traditional subsidies, and £74,000 in clerical taxation.[15] Whatever about the campaign's cost and questionable achievements, however, its organisation had been an undoubted success, and the credit for this went to Thomas Wolsey, royal almoner and councillor since 1509. Not only did Wolsey show himself a tireless and talented administrator, but he also proved a much shrewder handler of the king than the more senior councillors. Despite realising that the king was 'more disposed to war than peace', Wolsey had initially tried, as his mentor Bishop Fox had wished, 'to suppress this appetite'; but he soon understood that, although Henry was often hesitant about his aims, sketchy about details, and quite indifferent about means, once the royal will was exerted, there was no denying it.[16] Wolsey rose, as his gentleman-usher, George Cavendish, later remembered, because 'he was most earnest and readiest among all the council to advance the king's only will and pleasure without any respect to the case'.[17]

Accordingly, in 1514 Wolsey became bishop of Lincoln, bishop of Tournai, and archbishop of York in quick succession. By then, he was outdistancing leading councillors of the previous reign. In December 1515, he was appointed lord chancellor, Archbishop Warham resigning in order to

14   Elizabeth Bonner, 'Scotland's "Auld Alliance" with France, 1295–1560' in *History*, lxxxiv (1999), pp. 22–3; Nicholson, *Scotland*, pp. 597–606; Lynch, *Scotland*, pp. 160–2; Elton, *Reform and Reformation*, pp. 39–40; Eaves, *Henry VIII's Scottish diplomacy*, ch. 1.

15   John Guy, 'Thomas Wolsey, Thomas Cromwell and the reform of Henrician government' in Diarmaid MacCulloch, *The reign of Henry VIII*, pp. 43–5; Richard Hoyle, 'War and public finance' ibid., pp. 85–6.

16   Starkey, *Reign of Henry VIII*, ch. 3 (quotation, p. 58).

17   Cavendish, *Life and death of Cardinal Wolsey*, pp. 11–12.

make way for him and, with Bishop Fox, retiring from politics. Wolsey had also been made a cardinal by the pope in September 1515, but this did not confer the power over the English church which Wolsey's ambition required, since Canterbury outranked York. Finally, in 1518, Wolsey managed to circumvent Warham's authority by persuading the pope to appoint him legate *a latere*, that is, special envoy sent from Rome with special powers, whatever the pope wished his legate to have. Unprecedentedly, however, Wolsey was appointed legate *a latere* on a permanent basis, with full papal authority over both English provinces, so subordinating Canterbury to York. In this way, Wolsey combined the leading offices in church and state in a manner which gave him almost unlimited power under the king, and was also to form an important precedent during the ensuing Reformation crisis.

Despite occasional aristocratic plots against him, Wolsey retained power until his fall in 1529. Yet, as he fully understood, this power depended on controlling the king, a difficult task when Wolsey had, as lord chancellor, to keep terms at Westminster, and when for much of the summer the king was usually far away from London on progresses or hunting. Wolsey therefore took great care to ensure that the people close to Henry at court were reliable, occasionally engineering changes to prevent the king's councillors from becoming too independent. In particular, the king's privy chamber was soon identified as a threat to Wolsey's position because, unlike his father, Henry wanted 'pastime with good company' rather than solitude to work. Gradually, the king introduced close companions like Francis Bryan (nicknamed his 'Vicar of Hell') or Henry Norris ('gentle Mr Norris') in place of the nonentities of his father's reign. The change was epitomised by the appointment of Henry's influential companion and favourite, William Compton, as his first groom of the stool and head of the privy chamber, in place of the colourless, hard-working Hugh Denys. By 1517, the activities of the king's 'minions', as they were known, were attracting the attention of foreign ambassadors and, eventually, of Wolsey.

Yet, until September 1518, when an important French embassy arrived in London, the 'minions' held no formal office in the privy chamber. The inclusion of Francis I's leading *gentilshommes de la chambre* in the embassy prompted the king to confer the same title on the 'minions', so that they could be paired off in processions with them: by 1520, the title had been anglicised as 'gentlemen of the privy chamber'. Formal office consolidated their position. Immediately afterwards, the leading minions paid a return visit to the French court. When they returned 'they were all French, in eating, drinking and apparel; yea in French vices and brags . . . so that nothing by them was

[9 0] praised but if it were after the French turn'. They also exercised a strongly pro-French influence on foreign policy.[18]

Faced with this threat to his influence with the king, Wolsey struck first. Hitherto, he had encouraged the king in his pleasures, but now he reversed his strategy, introducing wide-ranging proposals for reform so as to attract Henry's attention, including even the defence of the borders and the reduction of Ireland to good rule. With the king now attending to business, the minions could be denigrated as 'youths of evil counsel', whose conduct was unbecoming. In May 1519, most of them were expelled from court, and some despatched to Calais. Wolsey then secured the appointment to the privy chamber of older, more reliable men. Predictably, however, this attempt to pack the privy chamber failed because Henry soon tired of this selfless devotion to duty and invited the minions back from Calais. Yet, over the following five years, Wolsey could exploit the demands of diplomacy and war to send away on errands individual minions who threatened his influence with the king.

The French embassy of 1518 had arrived in connection with the treaty of London. This treaty ended a period of warfare by proxy with the French, following the accession in 1515 of the young and warlike Francis I, who rivalled Henry in athleticism and looks and outshone him by military successes in Italy. Attempts by Henry and Wolsey to persuade the Spaniards, the Emperor, and the Swiss to fight him came to nought. So, with the king running out of money, Wolsey attempted in 1518 to recapture the moral high ground by a treaty of universal peace, encompassing all the major European powers and several minor ones and intended as a prelude to a crusade against the Turks. The treaty did indeed look very splendid: Henry and Wolsey appeared as the arbiter of Europe and won fame and renown, particularly among humanists like Erasmus who had long campaigned for such an initiative (for instance, his *Querela Pacis*), while also allowing the king to sell Tournai back to the French for £130,000 without loss of face.

Yet the treaty of London began to unravel almost immediately, with the death of the Emperor Maximilian and the election of Charles V. This dynastic combination of Habsburg and the Empire with Burgundy and the Spanish kingdoms greatly upset the balance of power in Europe, and Francis and Charles soon squared up for war. Yet, with Henry pledged by the treaty

18 Starkey, *Reign of Henry VIII*, pp. 69–78 (quotations, 69, 70, 72, 77); idem, 'Intimacy and innovation', pp. 78–82, 103–4 (quotations, pp. 81, 82).

to side against either monarch who broke the peace, neither wished to begin hostilities until he was sure of English support. So appearances were maintained on all sides as Wolsey manoeuvred adroitly towards an alliance with Charles V under a veneer of English neutrality. The Emperor visited the English court briefly in May 1520. The following month the English and French courts met in all their splendour at the Field of the Cloth of Gold: Henry, Wolsey and the flower of the English nobility crossed to Calais for a long-planned meeting with Francis I, a magnificent, but quite insincere, proclamation of their friendship which cost Henry almost £15,000 to stage. In fact Henry was already negotiating with Charles V to betray the peace. The real business took place at Gravelines which Wolsey visited three weeks later. By August 1521, Henry and Charles had come to an agreement whereby the Emperor was to marry Henry's daughter, Princess Mary (previously promised to the French dauphin) and to support Wolsey's candidature for the papacy. (In practice, he supported the successful candidate, Adrian VI, when Leo X died in December.) In return Henry promised English support in men and money for a new war with France.[19]

Meanwhile, the earl of Surrey had in May 1520 been despatched to Ireland for a reconnaissance in force. At one level, this was an aspect of Wolsey's reform strategy: besides neutralising the minions, the expedition also aimed, together with other displays of royal power, to remind would-be contraveners of the treaty of London of the king's capacity for a spectacular military intervention in continental Europe. The strategy worked: the king was eagerly courted by both Charles and Francis, but at a cost of heavy expenditure. Surrey's force of 550 men (chiefly northern and Welsh light cavalry) cost the king around £10,000 a year, for instance, and this was now needed 'for the advancement of other higher enterprises', as was Surrey himself – he was Henry's best general. Thus, unlike 1512, when in 1522 war recommenced with France, there was no financial surplus available to finance the ensuing campaigns.[20]

The war of 1522–5 very rapidly exposed the inadequacy of Henry's financial resources and consequent military effort. Moreover, the king was soon reminded that, for Charles and Francis, the real contest was over Italy: the English campaigning was merely a sideshow which helped or hindered

19 Starkey, *Henry VIII*, pp. 73–84; Elton, *Reform and Reformation*, pp. 38–9, 69–74, 79–80, 83–6.

20 Ellis, *Ireland in the age of the Tudors*, pp. 119–26 (quotation, p. 125); Scarisbrick, *Henry VIII*, pp. 80–95.

this struggle. In summer 1522, Surrey led a powerful raiding force into northern France. In autumn 1523 the duke of Suffolk commanded another expeditionary force of 15,000 men. Henry's original aim of capturing Boulogne was abandoned in favour of a descent on Paris with the support of Burgundian auxiliaries and the duke of Bourbon. Despite the failure of Bourbon's rebellion, the Anglo-Burgundian force advanced to within 50 miles of Paris, which was hurriedly prepared to stand siege, but by then the cold weather was decimating the English, and when the unpaid Burgundians departed in mid-November, Suffolk's troops likewise refused to stay. At this stage, the king's coffers were empty. Henry blamed the Emperor for the Burgundians' shortcomings, and refused Charles's eager pleas for another English expedition in 1524, preferring to prepare a 'great enterprise' the following year. When he heard of the crushing imperial victory at Pavia (February 1525), and Francis I's capture, he immediately determined on a new invasion, but Charles had now achieved his objectives and was discouraging. Henry and Wolsey had, accordingly, little option but to revive earlier peace negotiations with France, and to conclude the treaty of the More in August 1525.[21]

In order to meet the costs of war, Henry and Wolsey had first initiated a forced loan. The assessment for this was completed by a ruse through which it was given out that the information was required for a survey of the nation's military preparedness. This was indeed one aim of the survey. There was an obligation, imposed by the Statute of Winchester (1286), on all able-bodied males between the ages of 16 and 60 throughout the king's dominions to serve in the defence of their country. Accordingly, the population was mustered by counties, and their names, skill, military equipment, and wealth in lands and goods were noted. The returns survive for 28 counties, disclosing that 128,250 able men were available for militia service. Yet Wolsey was less happy with the financial returns, and so ordered a repeat survey for a second loan in 1523, which gave the game away. Together the two loans raised £212,000, plus £62,000 from the clergy who were taxed at 5s. in the £1 (viz. 25 per cent). Yet in 1522 alone, the campaigning had cost £372,000.[22]

---

21 G.W. Bernard, *War, taxation and rebellion in early Tudor England: Henry VIII, Wolsey and the Amicable Grant of 1525* (Brighton, 1986), pp. 3–45, 156–7 (quotation, p. 19); Hoyle, 'War and public finance', pp. 86–91; R.J. Knecht, *Francis I* (Cambridge, 1982), chs 10–11; Fissel, *English warfare*, pp. 8–12.

22 Bernard, *War, taxation and rebellion*, ch. 2; Hoyle, 'War and public finance', pp. 86–91; Jeremy Goring, 'The general proscription of 1522' in *English Historical Review*, lxxxvi (1971), pp. 683–95; Fissel, *English warfare*, pp. 8–12.

Thus, in 1523, the king and Wolsey had no option but to call parliament. Wolsey asked for a tax of 4s. in the £1 (20 per cent) which, he claimed, would raise £800,000. After much opposition, he got a subsidy spread over two years of 2s. in the £1 (10 per cent) on those with lands, or goods worth £20; 1s. in the £1 (5 per cent) on those with goods worth between £2 and £20; and a poll tax of 8d. ($3^{1}/_{3}$ per cent) on those with wages of £1 or goods worth £2. In addition, a surcharge of 1s. in the £1 on lands worth £50 was payable in the third year, and in the fourth year a surcharge of 1s. in the £1 on goods worth £50. Concurrently, the clergy also granted taxation at the rate of 10s. in the £1 over five years for those worth £8 a year, with lower rates for those worth less: Wolsey calculated that the clerical grant would yield £120,000 overall.[23]

Contemporaries believed that this 'right large subsidy' was without precedent, although in fact the two loans had raised far more. Eventually, the first two instalments yielded £72,000 and £64,000 from the laity, the two surcharges only £15,000. Yet Wolsey's effort to secure part payment in 'anticipation' in autumn 1523 raised less than £45,000. All this was too little too late for the English war effort. Upon news of Pavia, the king attempted – despite growing murmurs against heavy taxation – to extort more by extra-parliamentary means, demanding what he called an Amicable Grant of 4s. in the £1. Essentially, this was an old-fashioned benevolence, declared illegal by statute in 1484. The Commons responded with what amounted to a taxpayers' strike. Parliamentary consent to taxation and legislation, so people felt, enshrined English liberties, by contrast with continental absolutism. When Wolsey persisted, disturbances occurred throughout the south-east and a small rising of 4,000 poor men occurred in south-west Suffolk around Lavenham. At this point, Henry intervened and the Grant was cancelled.

The Taxpayers' Strike of 1525 was an important episode which reflected the limits of English monarchical power. It was one of the few occasions when Henry misread public opinion and overstepped the mark. More normally, he had a keen appreciation of just how far he could push things. Yet, the financing of the Anglo-French war had also taught the king another lesson, that it was not possible to sustain a protracted campaign by taxation in parliament. Subsidies simply took too long to collect: 'loans' raised far more, and far more quickly. Thus, despite the failure of the Amicable Grant,

23   Bernard, *War, taxation and rebellion*, pp. 120–3.

renewed war in the 1540s again prompted Henry VIII to experiment with prerogative taxation.[24]

Tudor reform, rebellion and the royal divorce

The Anglo-French treaty of 1525, followed by peace with Scotland, brought to an end the first phase of Henry VIII's reign, during which foreign affairs, and particularly foreign war, had dominated the political agenda. For the next 15 years, until the fall of the king's second chief councillor, Thomas Cromwell, the developing crisis over the royal divorce and the Reformation meant a growing preoccupation with internal security. This prompted in turn a renewed drive to strengthen royal control and promote good rule in the Tudor borderlands. Yet, by comparison with previous kings, Henry VIII had little first-hand knowledge of these outlying territories or their problems. The Yorkist kings had known Wales and the north well (and may even have visited their father in Ireland). Henry's father had also known Wales, from his childhood there. Henry himself knew only Lowland England (although he paid a brief visit to York in 1541). On his death, he owned over 50 houses, more than any other English monarch before or since; but the half dozen or so large properties which could accommodate the full court between late autumn and early summer mostly lay near the Thames Valley, and the many smaller 'houses of abode' which the king used while hunting or when he went on progress between June and October were not that much further afield. No wonder, then, that he was even less tolerant than his predecessors of what was perceived as border lawlessness.[25]

Initially, the most striking manifestation of the king's new priorities was the revival – at the expense of ruling magnates – of the regional councils, now associated with a junior member of the royal family as figurehead, to supervise local government. Yet these quasi-bureaucratic initiatives were weakly supported; and in all three borderlands the chief result was to antagonise established local interests. In Wales, following the death in 1525 of

24 Bernard, *War, taxation and rebellion*, pp. 120–4, 136–48; Hoyle, 'War and public finance', pp. 87–99.
25 Eric Ives, 'Henry VIII: the political perspective' in MacCulloch (ed.), *Henry VIII*, pp. 20–1; Neil Samman, 'The progresses of Henry VIII' ibid., pp. 59–73; Ellis, 'The limits of power', p. 48.

Sir Rhys ap Thomas, effectively a Tudor viceroy there, a reconstructed council was set up under Princess Mary at Ludlow, with Bishop Vesey of Exeter appointed president and Walter Devereux, Lord Ferrers, receiving ap Thomas's old offices as justice and chamberlain of south Wales. The result was a feud between Ferrers and ap Thomas's disappointed grandson, Rhys ap Gruffydd.

For the north, the king's bastard son, Henry Fitzroy, was created duke of Richmond and despatched to Sheriff Hutton to head a new council. Initially, the council's authority was extended to the marches, where the earls of Westmorland and Cumberland served as Richmond's deputy-wardens. Yet, without financial and military assistance, neither proved able to rule effectively in opposition to the traditional ruling families, the Percies and Dacres. In 1527 the ensuing disorders forced the king to back down. The council's authority was again confined to Yorkshire, and William Lord Dacre secured his father's office of warden of the west marches and, after renewed feuding with Cumberland, also the captaincy of Carlisle in 1529. Across the Pennines, the young Percy earl of Northumberland was also appointed as warden, although his father, the fifth earl, whom the Tudors did not trust, had been excluded from the wardenship throughout his life. He was allowed £1,000 with 69 gentry retainers and other officials costing £486 a year to help him restore order. In effect, therefore, Henry had restored the ancien regime. Yet these changes strengthened the marches at a time when deteriorating relations with Scotland were again threatening war. Hostilities eventually began in 1532 over an 'ungracious doghole' in the west marches, called the Debateable Land, and continued half-heartedly for 18 months with the French offering to mediate. Yet as soon as peace was signed, Dacre was arrested for treasonable communications with Scots in wartime and replaced by his old adversary, the earl of Cumberland. Moreover, French mediation also stretched to eventually-successful negotiations with James V for a French bride to consolidate 'the auld alliance', so further undermining Tudor influence in Scotland.[26]

---

26 Williams, *Recovery, reorientation and Reformation*, ch. 10; idem, *Wales and the Act of Union* (Bangor, 1992), pp. 5–8; R.R. Reid, *The king's council in the north* (London, 1921), ch. 5; Ellis, *Tudor frontiers*, chs 5–6; Ellis, 'Tudor state formation', pp. 52–4; Jamie Cameron, *James V: the personal rule, 1528–1542* (East Linton, 1998), pp. 119–24, 131–3; C.P. Hotle, *Thorns and thistles: diplomacy between Henry VIII and James V 1528–1542* (Lanham, 1996), ch. 2; Mervyn James, *Society, politics and culture: studies in early modern England* (Cambridge, 1986), pp. 80–2, 95, 98–9; *L. & P. Hen. VIII*, iv (iii), nos. 5906(6), 5952; Ellis, 'Civilizing Northumberland', pp. 111–13.

[9 6]   Even less successful were Henry VIII's interventions in Ireland. They
began in 1520 with Surrey's reconnaissance in force which aimed to discover
'by which means and ways your grace might reduce this land to obedience
and good order'.[27] Surrey's report – that it could only be done by compul-
sion, with an army of 6,000 and colonists from England – proved remarkably prescient, but it was not what Henry wanted to hear. Rather than
lose face by reappointing Kildare, the king turned to his rival, the earl of
Ormond, so stoking the feud between the two families. In fact, Kildare soon
had to be allowed home to control his own kinsmen and defend his estates
from the border Irish; and Ormond proved no more able to defend the
English Pale from Kilkenny castle than could Cumberland control the west
marches from Skipton castle. Kildare was then reappointed deputy, but
the Kildare–Ormond feud continued virtually unabated, amidst mounting
violence and disorder, as both sides encouraged their Gaelic allies to raid
their rival's lands. 1528 marked a nadir when, following the summons of the
two earls to court in another bid to end the feud, Kildare's nominal deputy,
Lord Delvin, was kidnapped by O'Connor. The ensuing 'O'Connor's Wars'
prompted further royal initiatives; first, the duke of Richmond's appointment as absentee head of an executive 'secret council', in a weak imitation of
the northern conciliar experiment (1529–30); then the despatch of troops
(chiefly northern borderers, from the west marches) with an experienced
commander, Sir William Skeffington, to stabilise the military situation.
Kildare's obstructive attitude to these changes earned him lengthy periods of
detention in England (1519–23, 1526–30), interspersed with short spells as
deputy (1524–6, 1532–4). Yet, despite all these experiments, the king discovered no real alternative to continued reliance on an 'overmighty subject'
like Kildare as deputy, or the heavy cost of maintaining an outsider, such as
Poynings or Surrey. In practice, the Reformation crisis rapidly led to a breakdown in all three regions, forcing the king into administrative reform and a
more interventionist policy.[28]

By 1525, Henry was increasingly concerned about his lack of a son to
succeed him on the throne. Queen Catherine had borne him just the one
healthy daughter, Mary: otherwise, there had been a succession of miscar-
riages, stillbirths, or babies who had shortly died. Convincing himself that

27 Quoted, S.G. Ellis, 'Tudor policy and the Kildare ascendancy in the lordship of Ireland,
    1496–1534' in *Irish Historical Studies* xx (1976–77), p. 239.
28 Ellis, *Ireland in the age of the Tudors*, pp. 119–36; Ellis, *Tudor frontiers*, ch. 6. See also now,
    David Edwards, *The Ormond lordship in County Kilkenny 1515–1642. The rise and fall of Butler
    feudal power* (Dublin, 2003), pp. 150–63.

his marriage was invalid (on the grounds that Catherine had previously
been married to his elder brother, Arthur), the king attempted to repudiate
Catherine so as to marry a younger woman who would bear him a son.
'The king's great matter' dominated his affairs from 1527, as Henry tried to
pressurise Pope Clement VII into annulling the marriage, and by then he had
conceived a growing passion for a court lady, Anne Boleyn. Wolsey was
charged with procuring the pope's agreement. Yet, regardless of the legalities
of the suit, politically it stood little chance because, after the sack of Rome
in May 1527, the pope was a virtual prisoner of Charles V, whose aunt
Catherine was. Henry therefore encouraged Francis I in his Italian ambitions
in the hope that this would free the pope, who was indeed sufficiently
encouraged by French successes in 1528 to establish a commission under
Cardinals Campeggio and Wolsey to try the case in England, but in summer
1529 the commission was revoked. Thereupon, Wolsey was dismissed as
chancellor and charged with treason, as the king cast about for some other
means of achieving his ambitions. Eventually, after a series of false starts, the
king hit on the idea of using parliament to have the case tried in England.
In spring 1533, the Act in Restraint of Appeals to Rome allowed the new
archbishop of Canterbury, Thomas Cranmer, to determine the case: in May
Cranmer duly decided that Henry's marriage to Catherine had been invalid
and so upheld his union with Anne Boleyn (whom he had secretly married
in January, when it was known that she was pregnant). Anne was crowned
queen six days later, and in September was delivered of a daughter, Elizabeth.
And Henry, having broken with Rome on the issue of the divorce, then
pushed through parliament a series of important statutes in 1533–4 which
transformed the two provinces of Canterbury and York into a national
Church of England, of which the king was Supreme Head on earth.[29]

Having effected these revolutionary changes at the centre, the king
had then to ensure that they were accepted elsewhere. Accordingly, in 1534
the king began a major overhaul of provincial government which lasted
throughout the 1530s. Those charged with ruling the more remote
provinces were replaced by more trusted crown servants, and the king later
reorganised the councils and other institutions of regional government. In
Ireland, Skeffington was reappointed deputy in place of Kildare; in the
north, Cumberland again displaced Dacre as warden of the west marches;

29   Virginia Murphy, 'The literature and propaganda of Henry VIII's first divorce' in MacCulloch
      (ed.), *Henry VIII*, ch. 6; Elton, *Reform and Reformation*, chs 5–8; Scarisbrick, *Henry VIII*,
      chs 7–10.

[98] and in Wales Bishop Rowland Lee replaced Bishop Vesey as president —
all in the same month. The overall thrust of the changes was to centralise
control and bring marcher administration more into line with arrangements
for Lowland England. In each case, the changes strengthened central
authority and reduced aristocratic influence, but they also cost more, exacerbated political tensions there, and did not necessarily lead to stronger
government.[30]

In Ireland and the English north, the charges of treason levelled simul-
taneously (May 1534) against Kildare and Dacre, allegedly because of their
contacts with Irish and Scottish enemies, look like a pre-emptive strike
by Henry against potentially the most dangerous of the nobles suspected of
plotting against him. Dacre was disgraced and dismissed following his
arrest, fined £10,000 on a lesser charge, and forbidden to reside in the
marches; but his unexpected acquittal on the main charge of making private
treaties with Scots enemies in wartime left the king still dependent on his
cooperation to govern the west marches but unable to use him as warden.
By contrast, Kildare's resistance to his dismissal sparked a major rebellion
lasting 14 months and costing £40,000 to suppress. In June, the acting
governor, Kildare's son and heir, Lord Thomas Fitzgerald (tenth earl after his
father's death in the Tower in September), defied the king and denounced
his religious policies. From late July the rebels besieged Dublin castle (at one
stage with 15,000 men) and gradually consolidated their position throughout English Ireland. Lord Deputy Skeffington arrived with a relief army of
2,500 men in mid-October (most formidably, 450 mounted spearmen, veterans from the west marches released by the peace with Scotland), and some
powerful artillery. By then, loyalist resistance was largely confined to three
major towns, Kilkenny, Waterford and Dublin — the latter close to surrender.
The Pale gentry mostly rallied to Skeffington on his arrival, but he then fell
sick, and the army spent the winter uselessly garrisoning the main towns. Yet
even a small but ill-equipped royal army proved more than a match for the
rebels in the field: the one significant military event of the campaign was the
ten-day siege of Kildare's chief castle of Maynooth in March. The basecourt
was taken by artillery assault, the great castle tricked into surrender, and
the garrison executed. Thereafter, however, the earl retreated to the Irishry
and Skeffington's force was ill-suited to counter the series of raids on the
Pale which he mounted from the rough terrain of the Gaelic midlands.

30 Ellis, *Tudor frontiers*, pp. 174–5.

Eventually, he was persuaded to surrender on terms (which the king ignored), shipped to England, and after a lengthy spell in the Tower, was executed in February 1537.[31]

The attainder of the earl and his supporters also precipitated the collapse of the system of defences and alliances by which English rule had been consolidated during the Kildare ascendancy, and the dissolution of the monasteries further undermined traditional power structures there. Yet appointing an English-born deputy and other key officials to a remodelled council did nothing to address the resultant crisis of lordship, which Gaelic chiefs exploited to encroach on the English marches, and the king was forced to maintain a permanent garrison there. The king expected that the increased costs of the new governor and garrison would be met from his Irish revenues. Landed revenues did indeed climb spectacularly from IR£400 in 1533–4 to IR£3,100 by 1537, as a result of rebel forfeitures, monastic dissolutions and the confiscation of the lands of English absentees. By 1542, total Irish revenues were estimated at nearly IR£7,500, but in practice most of these new crown lands were marchlands which were difficult to defend, particularly after the garrison was reduced from 700 to only 340 men in 1537. In the following three years, actual revenues, averaging only IR£4,500 annually, barely covered the ordinary charges of government, let alone the inevitable 'extraordinary' expenses of defence. Thus, the lordship became an increasing drain on English finances, but the crown remained generally unwilling to accept this deficit as the price of increased control: hence the general neglect of Ireland, punctuated by the periodic volte-face and frenetic bouts of activity which characterised Tudor rule there after 1534.[32]

Northern developments broadly followed the same path, but with significant differences. In particular, the government's efforts to strengthen royal control in response to the Reformation crisis were further advanced when the Pilgrimage of Grace broke out. By 1536, the royal divorce and supremacy had been followed by new demands for taxation in peacetime, the suppression of feudal franchises and lesser monasteries in the region, and the crown's imminent acquisition of the Percy inheritance. Accordingly, the Pilgrimage attracted much stronger popular support than Kildare, and rebel demands were more specific, even though they reflected a similar combination of noble, regional and religious grievances. A major revolt

31 Ellis, *Ireland in the age of the Tudors*, pp. 136–41; Ellis, *Tudor frontiers*, chs 7–8.
32 Ellis, *Ireland in the age of the Tudors*, pp. 142–8; idem, 'Thomas Cromwell and Ireland, 1532–1540' in *Historical Journal*, xxiii (1980), pp. 497–519.

[1 0 0]   was mounted, organised through parishes and hundreds (the administrative sub-division of the shire), with the commons mustered into nine large rebel hosts. The Pilgrims demanded a parliament at York or Nottingham to redress grievances and repeal unpopular legislation. In the north-west, moreover, socio-economic grievances were prominent among the peasantry; and in Cumberland the rebel captains pointedly urged the commons to organise resistance 'when the thieves or Scots would rob or invade us', 'because the rulers of this country do not come among us and defend us'. Everywhere in fact, the great noble houses stood aside, and without active magnate support the northern council proved powerless to contain rebellion. Confronted by a rebel army of 30,000 men, the king's lieutenant, Norfolk, was forced to negotiate, and having been promised a pardon with assurances that their grievances would be redressed, the rebels dispersed. The king then seized on renewed disturbances in the north-west the following January as an excuse to repudiate the agreement. Norfolk's army returned and forcibly restored order, executing 74 Cumberland peasants by martial law. Significantly, on this occasion, the northern gentry, anxious to prove their loyalty after their equivocal conduct the previous autumn, provided Norfolk with enthusiastic support.[33] This pattern of noble-inspired revolt in defence of regional autonomy was to be a recurring feature of the border response to Tudor centralisation, presenting a most serious challenge to the regime. Yet, as in Ireland after the 1534 rebellion, the government was not even able to make an example of all the leading rebels because to have done so would have left the marches undefended and ungovernable. Altogether, about 75 executions followed the Kildare rebellion. This compares with around 153 executions after the Pilgrimage (and a further 46 for the related Lincolnshire rebellion).[34]

Henry VIII's record in ruling the borderlands was very undistinguished, and his handling of the ruling magnates there was particularly inept. Deprived of the king's confidence and support, they lacked the status and resources to maintain firm control, but understandably they resented the crown's intrusion of other nobles, weakly supported, to offices they saw as

33   Recent work on the Pilgrimage has greatly improved our understanding of this movement. See especially, R.W. Hoyle, *The Pilgrimage of Grace and the politics of the 1530s* (Oxford, 2001); Michael Bush, *The Pilgrimage of Grace: a study of the rebel armies of October 1536* (Manchester, 1996) (quotation, p. 335). A good summary of recent work on this subject is Anthony Fletcher and Diarmaid MacCulloch, *Tudor rebellions* (5th ed., London, 2004), ch. 4.
34   S.G. Ellis, 'Henry VIII, rebellion and the rule of law' in *Historical Journal*, xxiv (1981), pp. 513, 527–9; idem, *Ireland in the age of the Tudors*, pp. 141–2; Michael Bush and David Bownes, *The defeat of the Pilgrimage of Grace* (Hull, 1999), pp. 363–5 and app. 2.

rightfully theirs. Outside Lowland England, the one substantial achievement of Henry's reign was the union with Wales where, however, there was no frontier to defend. The fragmentation of power and authority in Wales had long been a serious hindrance to good rule.[35] The feud between Ferrers and ap Gruffydd finally erupted in riots between their respective retainers at the Carmarthen sessions in 1529. Ap Gruffydd was eventually tried and executed on a trumped-up charge of treason in 1531, but under the slack President Vesey disorders simply continued elsewhere. With the king and council increasingly concerned about the possibility of religious opposition, rebellion and invasion, disorders in Wales were now seen as part of a wider problem. Sir Edward Croft, vice-chamberlain of South Wales, urged the appointment of a president who would 'use the sword of justice': 'otherwise, the Welsh will wax so wild it will not be easy to bring them to order again.'[36] Finally, in 1534, the energetic Bishop Lee took charge, armed with instructions to restore order and five statutes to strengthen his authority. The old Welsh customs of *arddel* and *comhortha* (see above, p. 73) were forbidden; jurors returning false verdicts were to be punished; and English JPs were empowered to enter marcher lordships to arrest known offenders for trial and punishment in England. Boasting that he would 'make one thief hang another',[37] Lee scoured the marches for thieves and robbers, hanging even gentlemen.

More important in pacifying Wales, however, was the so-called Act of Union – the two statutes enacted and gradually promulgated, 1536–43. Effectively, they abolished the distinction between marches and principality by shiring the marcher lordships, imposing English law and administrative structures throughout Wales, and creating a new kingdom of England and Wales. Sheriffs, JPs and other English local officials were introduced, Welsh shires and ancient boroughs received representation in parliament (one member each, not the normal two, so as to reduce costs), Welsh law and custom were abolished, and the English practice of primogeniture in regard to inheriting land was to replace the Welsh custom of partible inheritance (*cyfran*, equal shares for all sons). The English language was also made compulsory for administrative and legal business. Administratively, therefore,

35 See esp., Williams, *Wales and the Act of Union*; Peter Roberts, 'The English crown, the principality of Wales and the council in the marches, 1534–1641' in Brendan Bradshaw and John Morrill (eds), *The British problem, c.1534–1707: state formation in the Atlantic Archipelago* (Basingstoke, 1996), pp. 118–47 for this and the next four paragraphs.

36 Quoted, Williams, *Wales and the Act of Union*, p. 11.

37 Quoted, Roberts, 'English crown, principality of Wales and the council', p. 122.

[1 0 2]   Wales was now assimilated to England; 'the mere Welsh' received the same rights and privileges as Englishmen; and within its newly defined boundaries a unity of jurisdiction and administration for Wales was established for the first time.

Lee opposed the changes, arguing that the natives were not ready for English-style self-government. 'There are very few Welsh in Wales above Brecknock who have £10 in land', he declared sternly, 'and their discretion is less than their land.' In fact, Wales had to be excluded from the requirement that JPs have an annual landed income of £20; but even then the clause in the Act of 1542/3 specifying that the lord chancellor should appoint just eight JPs and a *custos rotulorum* in each county underlined the difficulties of finding sufficient and substantial gentry in poor upland regions to serve on the English-style commissions. Others were equally mistrustful of the Welsh gentry as 'bearers of thieves and misruled persons'.[38] Yet in Wales, where native Welsh gentry had long served as deputies of the (mainly absentee) English marcher lords, the gentry were less dependent on the marcher lords because there was no frontier to defend. Whole communities had long petitioned for grants of English law and land tenure, finding the privileges of marcher lords, march law, *cyfran*, and the practice of redeeming the sessions, increasingly irksome and arbitrary. Thus the Union attracted considerable support in Wales, particularly since it ended the threat that the Lancastrian penal code might yet be enforced against the native Welsh gentry.

In other respects, however, the Union was far from being the unqualified blessing which Elizabethan apologists implied. A Shrewsbury chronicle praised Lee for having 'brought Wales into civility before he died', but his presidency was also long remembered for its draconian rule – reputedly 5,000 executions in 6 years.[39] Considerable areas of Welsh speech and custom were now included in England, notably Monmouthshire, as were several parishes belonging to Welsh dioceses. Initially too, the Union's language clause created tensions. The English bishop of St Davids, for instance, urged the establishment of grammar schools whereby 'Welsh rudeness would soon be framed to English civility'.[40] In the longer term, the Union did lead to a strengthening of law and order. William Gerard, vice-president of the council under Elizabeth, 'affirmed that in Wales universally are as civil people

---

38   Quoted, Williams, *Wales and the Act of Union*, p. 20.

39   Quoted, Williams, *Wales and the Act of Union*, p. 18.

40   Peter Roberts, 'Tudor Wales, national identity and the British inheritance' in Brendan Bradshaw and Peter Roberts (eds), *British consciousness and identity: the making of Britain, 1533–1707* (Cambridge, 1998), p. 14.

and obedient to law as are in England'. It is unclear, however, whether this statement really just reflected his familiarity with the increasingly English practice of law and government in Wales, as opposed to the strange customs of Gaelic Ireland (where he was lord chancellor, 1576–81). Yet the Welsh antiquarian, George Owen of Henllys (d. 1613) proclaimed ecstatically that 'no county in England so flourished in one hundred years as Wales hath done since the government of Henry VII'.[41] The Union also had a fundamental impact in shaping Welsh senses of identity, since it promoted the idea of a single territorial entity called Wales, in place of the region's late medieval fragmentation, even as it downgraded the status of the Welsh language, hitherto the most potent symbol of Welsh identity.

In the wider context too, the successful implementation of Tudor reform in Wales came to be seen as offering a blueprint for the reduction of other borderlands to peace and civility, despite the fundamental differences between these marchlands. Success in Wales strengthened official convictions that the mere extension of standard English administrative structures to other outlying parts would automatically promote good rule there. Thus later on, when reform initiatives in Ireland ran into trouble, leading officials with experience in both countries, notably Sir Henry Sidney and William Gerard, urged the application to Ireland of 'the Welsh policy'.[42]

In the short term too, experience in Wales was seen as offering lessons for Ireland. After the Kildare rebellion, and in spite of the lordship's continuing military weakness, Skeffington's successor as deputy, Lord Leonard Grey, had made a series of progresses through Gaelic Ireland in a bid to extend royal authority. Making skilful use of the king's artillery in difficult terrain, he destroyed O'Connor's new castle at Dangan in Offaly in 1537 and recovered Athlone castle. In 1538 he attacked the MacMahons in Farney and made a longer progress to Galway; and in 1539 he journeyed to Armagh and through Munster. In February 1540 he even reached Dungannon, plundering the heart of O'Neill's lordship. In response, mounting mistrust in Gaelic Ireland about the government's real intentions prompted a number of leading chiefs to band together in the so-called Geraldine League whose nominal aim was the restoration of Gerald Fitzgerald, heir to the earldom of Kildare. In particular, the Ulster chiefs intrigued with James V, reportedly their 'special comforter and abettor', offering him the crown of Ireland, and they sent envoys to Rome via Scotland. In 1539, O'Neill and O'Donnell led

---

41 Quotations, Williams, *Wales and the Act of Union*, pp. 39–40.
42 Brady, 'Comparable histories?', pp. 77–86.

[1 0 4]   an unprecedented joint invasion of the Pale. They sacked Ardee and Navan and drove off large numbers of cattle. Lord Deputy Grey pursued them with half the garrison and Pale levies, surprised them at dawn at Bellahoe, south of Carrickmacross, and routed them.[43]

Yet the so-called Geraldine League did not then collapse, as experienced observers predicted; and Henry was forced to despatch reinforcements and to mount a new initiative. What followed, the strategy devised by the incoming deputy, Sir Anthony St Leger, which is now known as 'surrender and regrant', bore some striking similarities to, as well as profound differences from, 'the Welsh policy'. As with Wales, Tudor reform addressed Ireland's political fragmentation by attempting to incorporate the Gaelic chieftaincies with the English lordship into a single political entity, with the Gaelic peoples accorded the same status as freeborn Englishmen. Yet, rather than union with England, the erection of Ireland into a separate Tudor kingdom would be the means whereby the island's medieval partition between Englishry and Irishry would be abolished and English government extended throughout. This involved Gaelic chiefs recognising English sovereignty in return for feudal charters confirming the lands they occupied. Thus, the Gaelic lordships would be shired as English counties, and 'the mere Irish' would become English subjects rather than Irish enemies, with protection at common law for their lands and goods.

This was an extremely ambitious undertaking: Ireland was four times the size of Wales, which had taken seven years to assimilate administratively to England. Moreover, the strategy also entailed the break-up of the old Gaelic world extending into Scotland, the assimilation of the Gaelic peoples into separate 'foreign' kingdoms of Ireland and Scotland, and a parallel acceptance by those *Gaedhil* living in Ireland of the Tudors with whom, unlike the Welsh, they had no natural ties. Yet, of all the Tudor initiatives for Ireland, 'surrender and regrant' most nearly matched ultimate aims with available resources, providing for a gradual extension of English rule with Gaelic cooperation. Initially, moreover, a promising start was made, with the creation of O'Neill and O'Brien as earls of Tyrone and Thomond respectively, the rehabilitation of the earl of Desmond, and other peerages for MacGillapatrick (Lord Fitzpatrick of Upper Ossory) and for one of the 'degenerate English', Burke of Clanrickard (earl of Clanrickard). For the local English, the initiative promised lucrative leases of ex-monastic land, as

---

43   Ellis, *Ireland in the age of the Tudors*, pp. 148–9; Marcus Merriman, *The rough wooings: Mary queen of Scots, 1542–1551* (East Linton, 2000), p. 71 (quotation); Lynch, *Scotland*, p. 161.

prospects for peace improved, and provincial office in an extended administration. By 1544–5, moreover, the consequent reduction in racial tensions
even permitted an unprecedented deployment of Irish troops in France and
Scotland.

Conversely, some destabilising pressures were slower to manifest themselves. Tudor reform held fewer attractions for the local elite than in Wales
because the Pale gentry were already English subjects, not 'mere Irish'. Yet
initially, Ireland's new status as a separate kingdom had seemed to represent
a reassuring statement against further Tudor centralisation, so allaying
tensions which had emerged in the Dublin administration between local
English and newcomers from England. Moreover, while he lived, the old
king's refusal to countenance any increase in the administration's annual
shortfall of c.£4,000 made good from England ensured continued reliance
on the Englishry as the mainstay of Tudor rule there.

In practice, however, Ireland's new status had little impact on Anglo-Irish
constitutional relations. Although now styled a kingdom, Ireland remained
an English dependency, not a sovereign kingdom. Policy for Ireland, and
much other legal and governmental business was still determined by king
and council in England; Irish lawsuits were tried on appeal by the English
king's bench; Irish officials were appointed under the great seal of England,
and without a licence so warranted, the Irish parliament could not meet nor
enact legislation. The English parliament, moreover, still legislated occasionally for Ireland, for instance the Edwardian reform legislation, even though
Ireland was not accorded representation there. Thus in practice, this alleged
'constitutional revolution' simply supplied a mechanism for incorporating
Gaelic Ireland into the Tudor state, broadly along Welsh lines. As power was
concentrated in the hands of king and privy council, the local Englishry
found itself increasingly excluded from the making of policy, with disastrous
results in the longer term.[44]

The king had also at this time to develop new structures for the rule of the
Tudor north, again in the aftermath of a major rebellion. The northern council was remodelled, and proved fairly successful in containing simmering

44 Ellis, *Ireland in the age of the Tudors*, chs 6, 10; Ciaran Brady, 'The decline of the Irish kingdom', in Mark Greengrass (ed.), *Conquest and coalescence: the shaping of the state in early modern
Europe* (London, 1991), ch. 6; idem, 'Comparable histories?: Tudor reform in Wales and
Ireland' in Ellis and Barber (eds), *Conquest and union*, ch. 3; Brendan Bradshaw, *The Irish constitutional revolution of the sixteenth century* (Cambridge, 1979), pt. 3 (which, however, offers a
different interpretation).

[1 0 6]   discontent in Yorkshire. In the marches, Henry nominated himself warden-general, in a grandiose but empty gesture, appointing gentlemen deputy-wardens to replace the ineffectual Cumberland and the recently-deceased Northumberland. The king's acquisition of the Percy and monastic estates, and then Hexhamshire and Redesdale by 'exchange', established the crown for the first time as a major landowner there, while concurrently the 1536 statute strengthened royal control over the region's extensive feudal franchises. Militarily, however, the changes weakened the marches by undermining established structures of lordship, even though the king fee'd 66 local gentry in a bid to strengthen the *manraed* at the wardens' disposal. The new arrangements cost the king over £2,600 a year in fees, but this was far less than the crown's additional landed income there. In other words, this apparent extension of royal power was really only a redistribution in the crown's favour of the region's existing financial and military resources, public and private.

Initially, however, the deputy-wardens had only to contend with the activities of the border surnames, since the 1534 peace with Scotland still held and James V too was keen to maintain good rule on the borders. Yet once war recommenced in 1542, they were soon in difficulties, lacking tenants to defend the borders. The great landowners, since they were no longer entrusted with the wardenship, had less need of border service from their tenants, and so raised rents and entry-fines in response to inflation. For instance, where the fourth earl of Northumberland had raised 1,000 spearmen from his tenants in Northumberland, the sixth earl only had 100. By 1543 the whole shire could only raise 300 horsemen, and the great Percy castles there, now in crown hands, were in decay for want of reparations. Northumberland was no longer able to defend itself in wartime: in 1544 the king even deployed 400 Irish kerne on the borders, part of a garrison of *c*.2,500 men, with a southern noble as warden, and he abandoned conciliar supervision of the wardenries. Overall, therefore, the impact of the northern reforms was very uneven: Tudor power and influence was consolidated in more sheltered parts like Yorkshire, but the marches weak and the border surnames uncontrollable. After Henry's death, the Somerset regime soon moved to strengthen the borders by rehabilitating the Percies and reappointing Dacre as warden.[45]

---

45   Michael Bush, 'The problem of the far north: a study of the crisis of 1537 and its consequences' in *Northern History*, vi (1971), pp. 40–63; Ellis, 'Civilizing Northumberland', pp. 116–20; idem, *Ireland in the age of the Tudors*, p. 156.

Anglo-Scottish relations and the renewal of war [107]

The basic reason for this failure was continued poor relations with Scotland. In the aftermath of Flodden, the Scottish privy council, acting on James IV's will, had appointed Queen Margaret guardian of the infant James V and regent of the realm. Henry VIII thus had a golden opportunity to reshape Scottish politics in the English interest, through his sister acting for his nephew. Within a year, however, Margaret had fled to England with her new husband, Archibald Douglas, sixth earl of Angus: Henry's clumsy diplomacy, notably his claim to be 'protector and governor of Scotland', drove the Scots back into the arms of the French. The 'auld alliance' was ratified in January 1515 and in May the duke of Albany returned from France as governor and protector. Thereafter, Albany showed great skill in maintaining his position, amidst the usual factional feuds which disrupted royal minorities, and despite English efforts to dislodge him. Margaret returned to Scotland in 1517, just as Albany departed to negotiate a treaty with Francis I. This confirmed the 'auld alliance', conferred trading privileges on Scottish merchants, and agreed that James V should marry a daughter of Francis. The Scottish lords wanted a treaty of reciprocal defence between the three countries, without prejudice to the Franco-Scottish alliance, but they easily saw through Henry's efforts to exclude Albany, foster civil strife, and 'compel a peace which will give England control'. Then, as the treaty of London began to unravel, Francis distributed money to members of the Scottish parliament and sent back Albany.

Henry's response was a high-handed warning to the Scottish estates not to support Albany, 'a stranger of inferior repute', who 'intended to sever the queen [Margaret] from her husband and marry her himself, to the great danger of the king [James V], the ruin of the queen, and Henry's honour'. Margaret, however, supported Albany. In September 1522, he led a Scottish army to the west marches to invade England, but no doubt with Flodden in mind, the Scots refused to cross the border. Thereupon, Henry tried again over the winter, offering a long truce and the marriage of Mary to James V, in return for Albany's removal from the regency, but again he was outmanoeuvred. Francis sent Albany back with 4,000 men and munitions, including powerful artillery, and with these Albany attempted another invasion, unsuccessfully attacking Wark in October 1523, but again the Scots nobles refused to invade. Albany's regency was eventually ended in mid-1524, when the queen mother arranged for the 'erection' of the 12-year-old James, but the return and rehabilitation of Angus in 1525 soon led to *de facto* rule by the Douglases, with the young king virtually a captive. James finally escaped in May 1528, and by December he held the reins of power. Essentially, Henry's efforts to control Scotland by exploiting the position of his sister as queen mother proved a failure because the northern kingdom was not, for Henry, a consistent priority of Tudor foreign policy, more a pawn in the wider Anglo-French struggle. His French rival valued the 'auld alliance' more highly.[46]

Once in control, James was eagerly courted by the leading European princes for his marriage, being offered his niece, Catherine de Medici; Mary of Hungary, Charles V's sister; Danish and Portuguese princesses; Mary Tudor; and finally Marie de Bourbon. He eventually signed a marriage contract for the latter in May 1536, but he was bitterly disappointed when he met her in France in September, and requested instead Francis's daughter, Madeleine de Valois. This marriage, celebrated in Paris on 1 January 1537, accorded well enough with the prevailing Anglo-French entente of the period from 1525 onwards, but she died soon after. Thereupon, negotiations began for another French bride, Mary of Guise. Henry also courted her, following the death of his third wife, Jane Seymour, but embarrassingly for him, she declared that her neck was too small, and in 1538 married his nephew instead.

By the late 1530s, Anglo-Scottish relations were again coming under strain over Scotland's adherence to the Catholic church, redress for border offences, and the harbouring of rebels. English embassies to Scotland pointed to the financial advantages of dissolving the monasteries, and urged a meeting with Henry 'in some commodious part northwards'. James, however, preferred the French faction headed by David Beaton, cardinal archbishop of St Andrews, and refused Henry's increasingly insistent invitations to conclude an English alliance which the latter desired as a prelude to another invasion of France. In September 1541, war became almost inevitable when James, afraid of kidnapping, refused to come, as expected, to an interview at York with his imperious uncle. Eventually, as Henry's army launched a border raid, the king's printer issued a *Declaration* in late 1542 which formally reasserted Henry's 'true and right title . . . to the sovereignty of Scotland' as part of the king's 'imperial' authority and jurisdiction throughout the British Isles. Henry even contemplated advancing the border

46 Bonner, 'Scotland's "Auld Alliance" ', pp. 23–8; Eaves, *Henry VIII's Scottish diplomacy*, passim; Hotle, *Thorns and thistles*, ch. 1.

to the Forth, with cooperative Scottish lords swearing allegiance to him as [109] supreme lord of Scotland, as the earl of Angus had done in 1532.

Yet what followed owed little to Tudor policy. A Scottish army of around 15,000, attempting a surprise raid, advanced through the Debateable Land and crossed the River Esk, but then got itself trapped by the rising tide and was forced to surrender to a far smaller, but more-disciplined English force. Very few were killed at Solway Moss, but around 500 Scottish landowners were taken prisoner. Three weeks later James V suddenly died, leaving his ministers to face the worst of all situations – a kingdom at war, divided between English and French factions, and the accession of a minor, a queen regnant, his week-old daughter, Mary.[47] This time, unlike Flodden, Henry did at least appreciate the extent of his opportunity. Yet because his main priority remained France, he tried to exploit it indirectly. If the king had simply unleashed his army to occupy Scotland, he would probably have succeeded in his aim of controlling Scotland by marrying his son, Prince Edward, to Queen Mary and so procuring a dynastic union, despite the poor state of Anglo-Scottish relations. Yet far less realistic was his ostensibly statesmanlike attempt to procure it by consent (so avoiding the cost of conquest). The Solway Moss prisoners were entertained at court, sworn to the project as 'assured lords' and meanwhile to Mary's upbringing in England, and sent home to work as an English party in Scotland. The shrewd and devious James Hamilton, earl of Arran, Mary's heir presumptive and now governor, used the opportunity to have Beaton arrested. He negotiated the treaties of Greenwich (July 1543) with Henry, including provision for the marriage, but not for Mary's English upbringing, and talked about reforming the church. By then, moreover, Henry had – after two years of hard bargaining and double-dealing – signed in February 1543 the Treaty of Mutual Aid with Charles V (war had recommenced between Habsburg and Valois in July 1541), so ending 18 years of alliance (now close, now strained) with France and disengagement from Europe.

Accordingly, in June 1544 a massive English army of over 40,000 men crossed to Calais. A joint attack on Paris had once again been intended, but this time Henry VIII refused to be distracted from capturing Boulogne. He came in person to lay siege to the town, which fell in September – just as the emperor deserted the king to conclude the peace of Crépy with France. This

47 Merriman, *Rough wooings*, ch. 3 (quotation, p. 62); Bonner, 'Scotland's "Auld Alliance"', pp. 23–8 (quotations, pp. 23, 25, 26, 28); Cameron, *James V*, chs 12–13; Gordon Donaldson, *Scotland, James V–James VII* (Edinburgh, 1965), pp. 48–62; Hotle, *Thorns and thistles*, ch. 6.

left Henry to face alone a war on two fronts, because in autumn 1543 Arran, aware that Scottish opinion was shifting, had been reconciled with Beaton, had defected to the French party and had repudiated the English marriage. Arran probably hoped to have the queen married to his son. Henry's response was to unleash the earl of Hertford on some deliberately brutal raids: a seaborne invasion to sack Edinburgh in May 1544 and an effective border raid in September 1545 established Hertford's reputation as Henry's best general. Moreover, hoping to capture Dumbarton cheaply, the king also exploited a rising of Clan Donald in the Western Isles, led by Donald Dubh, claimant to the lordship of the Isles. Donald Dubh brought 4,000 redshanks in 180 galleys with him to Carrickfergus in summer 1545, with the aim of combining with the earl of Lennox and an English fleet to attack Dumbarton. Yet Donald Dubh then died at Drogheda, and by the time the Dublin government had scraped together a reduced force of 2,000 kerne, the season was too advanced and the attack was repulsed.

By devastating Lowland Scotland, Henry had hoped to eliminate any threat from that quarter, not to coerce the Scots into accepting the English marriage, as was believed in Scotland. Yet the result was to drive the Scots into the arms of the French who, in 1545, sent 2,500 troops to support their allies. A more cautious king might have cut his losses in September 1544, but Henry clung on at Boulogne, spending over £1m on its capture and fortification. By summer 1545 England was threatened with invasion as the French raided Portsmouth and the Isle of Wight. Finally, in June 1546, the king reluctantly accepted the inevitable and concluded a French peace which, while it provided for the eventual return of Boulogne, allowed the English to retain possession until 1554 as a kind of surety for the payment of still outstanding amounts of the French pension. Anglo-Scottish hostilities also petered out with Scotland's comprehension in the French peace – just after anglophile Scots, with English encouragement, had seized St Andrews castle and murdered Cardinal Beaton – but the legacy of Henry VIII's 'great enterprise' was hostile neighbours.[48]

48 Potter, 'Foreign policy', pp. 106–8, 127–8, 132–3; Richard Hoyle, 'War and public finance', p. 91; Merriman, *Rough wooings*, chs 5–8; Elizabeth Bonner, 'The genesis of Henry VIII's "rough wooing" of the Scots' in *Northern History*, xxxiii (1997), pp. 36–53; idem, 'The recovery of St Andrews castle in 1547: French naval policy and diplomacy in the British Isles' in *English Historical Review*, cxi (1996), pp. 578–98; Knecht, *Francis I*, pp. 366–75; Ellis, *Ireland in the age of the Tudors*, pp. 156, 245–51; Simon Adams, 'Britain, Europe and the world' in Patrick Collinson (ed.), *The short Oxford history of the British Isles: the sixteenth century* (Oxford, 2002), pp. 194–5; Elton, *Reform and Reformation*, pp. 307–10; Guy, *Tudor England*, pp. 190–2; Fissel, *English warfare*, pp. 13–10.

In other respects too, the cost to both monarchy and realm of this vindication of Henry's 'honour' was extremely high. Altogether, Henry's Scottish and French wars cost well over £2.1m, with a further £1.3m spent under Edward VI down to 1550 as the new government struggled with Henry VIII's legacy. To meet these charges, Henry had demanded a loan as early as 1542, although the subsidy of 1540 was still being collected: this raised over £112,000 and, predictably, was later converted into a grant. In 1543, parliament granted a subsidy, payable in three instalments in early 1544, 1545, and 1546: these raised £79,000, £59,000 and £56,000 respectively. Then in 1545, there was a demand for an emergency grant, which was this time called a Benevolence rather than an Amicable Grant, and was collected at the rate of 8d. in the £1 (3⅓ per cent) from those worth £2 in lands or £3 6s. 8d. (£3.33) in goods, and 1s. in the £1 (5 per cent) from those worth £20 a more. That raised £120,000. The 1545 parliament also granted another (heavier) subsidy payable over two years (these raised £114,000 and £100,000 respectively), plus two old-fashioned fifteenths (usually worth £59,000). Then, in summer 1546, taxpayers worth £2 in lands or £15 in goods were required to pay a Contribution, of which the overall yield is unknown. Finally, the clergy also granted a subsidy at 6s. in the £1 (30 per cent) in 1543 and 1545 (worth perhaps £42,000 per levy), and were also included in the Benevolence and Contribution.

Altogether, this mixture of prerogative and parliamentary taxation raised around £888,000 in six years, which was probably the heaviest in England since the fourteenth century. Yet it came nowhere near to meeting the costs of the war. From the outset, sales of crown land had been planned, but despite modifying the terms of sales in 1545, the government only managed to raise £799,000. The king also borrowed on the Antwerp money market, but probably no more than £100,000. Even more disastrous was the decision to debase the coinage – following a small-scale but successful experiment in Ireland with 'harp groats' to pay the troops there in 1536. This eventually raised around £1.27m between 1544 and 1551. It was not that ministers were oblivious to the damage which these short-term measures were causing. In 1545 Lord Chancellor Wriothesley wrote despairingly,

> As to money, I trust you will consider what is done already. This year and last the king has spent about £1.3m, his subsidy and benevolence ministering scant £300,000 and the lands consumed and the plate of the realm melted and coined. I lament the danger of the time to come . . . and yet you write me still, pay, pay, prepare for this and that.

Moreover, the manipulation of the currency (by 1546 English silver coins were only 4oz. fine) fuelled inflation and also destroyed the country's good reputation for coinage. Yet the king's will could not be gainsaid. The warrior-prince was a very important image during the sixteenth century, and Henry VIII made a powerful impression on subjects and foreigners alike: according to William Camden, 'great virtues he had, and no lesse vices'. Yet the financial burdens of Henry's military greatness were very high. When he died in January 1547, his kingdom lay in a parlous condition, with an empty treasury, large debts, an economic crisis, an unstable peace and a boy-king.[49]

Following Henry's death, Edward Seymour, earl of Hertford, quickly secured control of his nephew, the young Edward VI, and was then named lord protector. In the political manoeuvrings of Henry's final months, the reformist faction had succeeded in excluding from influence leading conservatives such as Bishop Gardiner (who was excluded from the regency council), the duke of Norfolk (under sentence of death in the Tower), and his heir, the earl of Surrey (executed for treason). Councillors were now informed of the late king's alleged intention to reward certain of them by grants of land and advancement in the peerage, so enabling Hertford to consolidate his position and promote himself duke of Somerset. Subsequently, the remaining conservatives, led by Lord Chancellor Wriothesley, were edged out of power.[50]

Somerset's policy until his fall in October 1549 revolved around the Scottish problem, the attempt to coerce the Scots into sanctioning the dynastic marriage between Queen Mary and Edward VI. In the short term, this marked a reversal of the normal priorities of Tudor foreign policy, but only in the circumstances of a royal minority where, by convention, ministers focused on the resolution of inherited problems rather than pursuing new policy initiatives. Chief among these unresolved problems of the old king's reign was his design of annexing Scotland. Unfortunately for Somerset, the new French king, Henri II (Francis had died in March) had the same idea, and hoped to use the queen mother, Mary of Guise, to effect a marriage between the Scottish queen and his son and heir, Francis, thus bringing about a dynastic union between Scotland and France. A preliminary

49   Hoyle, 'War and public finance', pp. 90–9 (quotation, p. 92); Graves, *Henry VIII*, pp. 25–8, 187–91 (quotation, p. 26); Ellis, *Ireland in the age of the Tudors*, p. 145; Elton, *Reform and Reformation*, pp. 310–32; Guy, *Tudor England*, pp. 191–2; C.E. Challis, *The Tudor coinage* (Manchester, 1978), p. 254.

50   Elton, *Reform and Reformation*, pp. 328–34; Penry Williams, *The later Tudors: England 1547–1603* (Oxford, 1995), pp. 31–9; Guy, *Tudor England*, ch. 7.

step was the restoration of stable government in Scotland. Henri took a small step towards this by mounting a surprise naval raid in July to capture St Andrews castle and restore it to the Scottish government. The murderers and rebels who held it were imprisoned in France, and John Knox who had recently arrived was consigned to the galleys.

Relations with France thus remained difficult. Somerset ignored successive French provocations, notably the non-payment of the pension and military aid for the Scots, in order to focus on Scotland and avoid open war over Boulogne; but since French priorities had likewise shifted northwards English initiatives were matched by the French. In September 1547, Somerset invaded East Lothian with a well-equipped army of 15,000 men. At Pinkie, a large and experienced Scottish army awaited him behind well-prepared trenchworks, but the English advantage in artillery and heavy cavalry proved decisive: 10,000 Scots were killed. Yet instead of mounting periodic invasions with armies royal, Somerset now planned to secure English influence by means of garrisons. He neglected the opportunity to assault Edinburgh, or later to capture Dunbar, but forts were built or repaired to house permanent English garrisons, initially at seven locations in the Scottish borders and up the east coast. More followed over the next two years. Their main purpose was to protect the 'assured Scots' and chastise others, and at first they achieved spectacular results as the Scots of Lothian, the Merse, Teviotdale and the south-west rushed to assure.

Force was also backed by propaganda. As early as 1513, Henry VIII had declared himself overlord of Scotland; and in 1542, when Norfolk invaded, the king had a *Declaration* printed invoking the familiar legend of Brutus and his supposed grant of superiority throughout Britain to the eldest of his three sons who ruled England. Naturally, the Scots preferred alternative origin myths, but in 1521 the eminent Scottish theologian, John Major, had for the first time sparked a debate in Scotland over union with England by publishing his *Historia Maioris Brittanniae tam Angliae*, a strongly pro-unionist tract which also attacked both sets of origin myths. Henry now attracted the services of Scottish Protestants like the cleric John Elder and the merchant James Henrisoun who both wrote unionist propaganda. Elder's tract, which remained unpublished, dismissed Scotland's Gaelic traditions at one point, affirming that it was 'part of your Highness's empire of England': it had once been inhabited by 'giants and wild people', 'as we read in ancient Irish stories', but Brutus's second son, Albanactus, 'reduc[ed] them to order and civility', changing its name 'Eyryn veagg' (*Éirinn bheag*, little Ireland), and calling them 'Albonyghe' (*Albanaigh*, Scots). Much more important

[1 1 4]   was Henrisoun's *Exhortacion*, printed in summer 1547 just before before Somerset's invasion. Henrisoun asserted that Britain had once been united: war was an 'unnatural division' between countries 'of one native tongue and bred in one isle compassed with the see'. He urged the abandonment of those 'hateful terms of Scots and Englishmen' in favour of 'Briton', believing also that union would lead to 'the concord & unity of one religion', the 'pure, sincere & incorrupt religion of Christ'. Henrisoun's *Exhortacion* was followed by Somerset's *Proclamation* of September, which said nothing about English overlordship but asserted that the English marriage would unite the subjects of the two realms 'being both of one descent of blood, and of one language' 'by the name of Britons', that it would advance God's word and that it would abolish the bishop of Rome's usurped jurisdiction. Somerset followed it, in February 1548, by a moderately-stated *Epistle*, observing that the Scots had consented to the marriage, which would 'make of one isle one realm' and was clearly God's will, since the two nations dwelt on one island and spoke the same language. Essentially, however, these arguments were convincing only to assured Scots with Protestant leanings. Later propaganda was directed chiefly to English audiences and revived earlier arguments in favour of English overlordship.[51]

The propaganda campaign certainly helped to familiarise both English and Scots with the concept of Great Britain and to introduce the idea of Anglo-Scottish union to Englishmen, but the issue was decided militarily. In June 1548 the French landed 10,000 men in the Firth of Forth, so negating the protection afforded by the garrisons to the assured Scots. In fact, many of the English garrisons were poorly sited, notably the major fortress at Haddington, 18 miles from Edinburgh. The French proceeded to establish their own garrisons, often at places coveted by the English, and they besieged Haddington which now had to be relieved and provisioned by relief armies from England. When in August Queen Mary was shipped back to France and then betrothed to the Dauphin, the whole strategy was rendered unworkable. Yet Somerset's increasing obsession with using garrisons instead of armies precluded resort to a naval blockade and army royal to flush the French out; lack of adequate manpower and the miserable conditions in the garrisons enjoined reliance on expensive foreign mercenaries; and because of the French threat, the garrisons were also larger and more costly

---

51   Merriman, *Rough wooings*, pp. 11–12, 42–6, 265–91 (quotations, pp. 44, 272, 275, 276); Bonner, 'Recovery of St Andrews Castle', pp. 578–98; Bush, *Government policy of Protector Somerset*, ch. 1; Jennifer Loach, *Edward VI* (New Haven, 1999), ch. 5.

than originally intended. In August 1549, when Henri II finally declared [1 1 5] war, Somerset even offered to return Boulogne immediately instead of waiting until 1554. Initial negotiations collapsed after Henri demanded Calais as well, but the government simply lacked the resources to fight a war on two fronts and also, over summer 1549, to repress peasant risings in large parts of England. Following the protector's overthrow in October 1549, the new government headed by the duke of Northumberland ended the French war in March, surrendering Boulogne in return for £133,000. In August it reluctantly abandoned the remaining garrisons because of the difficulties and expense of maintaining them; and in the following year peace was finally signed with Scotland, leaving that kingdom within the French orbit. Overall, military expenditure under Edward VI amounted to £1.39m, financed chiefly by further coinage debasements, together with more land sales, parliamentary taxation and borrowing. Indeed, Somerset had spent £580,000 overall on his Scottish ambitions, which was far more and over a shorter period than under Henry VIII.[52]

'The monstrous regiment of women'

In one sense, however, the question of an Anglo-Scottish dynastic union was soon rendered academic: King Edward's health collapsed in spring 1553, and he died of pulmonary tuberculosis in July, aged 15. Northumberland's attempt to alter the succession in favour of Lady Jane Grey, whom he then married to his son, was frustrated by a legitimist rising in favour of Henry VIII's elder daughter, Mary, cousin of the Emperor. Thus Mary's accession strengthened England's traditional alliance with the Habsburgs just as the French victory in the struggle for Scotland had confirmed the 'auld alliance'. And as suitable husbands were proposed for the two unmarried Queen Marys, the fate of both kingdoms now seemed to hang on traditional dynastic marriages. The Scottish queen was declared of 'perfect age' in 1554, when 12 years old, but this was merely a device to consolidate French influence by ousting Arran from the regency in favour of the queen mother, Mary of Guise: negotiations for her marriage to the dauphin would not commence for another three years. While the English regime was Protestant, a moderate line had been followed with the more anglophile and Protestant

---

52 M.L. Bush, *The government policy of Protector Somerset* (London, 1975), ch. 2; Guy, *Tudor England*, pp. 202–3, 218–19; Merriman, *Rough wooings*, chs 12–13.

[1 1 6] nobles (bought off with French pensions in 1550) so as to discourage appeals to England. Yet with the accession of a Catholic, pro-Habsburg queen in England, the possibility of English support for Scottish Protestants disappeared. The new regent pursued a much more determinedly pro-French policy. French troops, albeit in far smaller numbers, continued to garrison Scotland, fuelling anti-French feeling; Frenchmen were infiltrated into the household and even upper echelons of government; and regular taxation was exacted to help pay for the French troops.[53]

The marriage question was far more pressing in the case of England, because the new English queen was already 37 and almost past child-bearing age. Yet Mary could at least choose her own consort, though she deferred to the Emperor. Her ministers wished her to marry an Englishman (Edward Courtenay, earl of Devon, was the only real option) so as to protect English independence, but Mary overruled them in order to marry Charles's son, Philip, regent of Spain. The terms were, in the circumstances, very favourable: Charles was keen to secure English support against France and to build up Philip's influence against his nephew Ferdinand, king of the Romans. Any child born to Mary and Philip would inherit England and the Netherlands, but Philip's son by his previous marriage would inherit the main Spanish Habsburg territories. If they had no children, then the English throne would pass to the next heir by English law – in fact Mary's half-sister, Elizabeth (though Mary disapproved, and this was not spelled out). Meanwhile, Philip was merely styled king during Mary's lifetime, without executive authority in his own right; no foreigners should receive offices, and England was not to be involved in the Habsburg–Valois struggle – terms which Philip found highly insulting and repudiated in a secret declaration. The marriage was highly unpopular in England, too: even before the treaty was ratified (in April 1554) or celebrated (in July), a revolt planned by supporters of Somerset and Northumberland had very nearly succeeded.[54]

The terms of the Scottish queen's marriage were distinctly less generous. In a secret clause to the treaty just before her marriage in April 1558, Mary agreed that the French king should inherit both Scotland and her claim to England should she die without issue; she accepted liability for the cost to France of defending Scotland and her upbringing; and she negated in advance any agreement she might make with the Scottish estates which ran

53 Jenny Wormald, *Mary queen of Scots, a study in failure* (London, 1991), pp. 82–6; Donaldson, *Scotland*, pp. 80–4; Loach, *Edward VI*, chs 12–13.
54 D.M. Loades, *The reign of Mary Tudor: politics, government and religion in England, 1553–1558* (London, 1979), ch. 4; Williams, *The later Tudors*, pp. 86–102.

counter to French interests. This clause was widely known by November, when the Scottish parliament consented to 'the crown matrimonial', that is, that Francis should be king of Scots in right of his wife. Overall, these arrangements provided some safeguards for the protection of Scottish law and custom, but they appeared also to confirm French attempts since 1548 to incorporate Scotland as a province of the French crown.[55]

By then, the two kingdoms were already embroiled in another war, pressed into service at the behest of the major powers whose satellites they were. Despite undertakings in the marriage treaty, Philip returned to England in March 1557 to seek English assistance against France. It took Mary three months to move the privy council, but eventually war was declared in June, whereupon Scotland's pro-French regime dutifully declared war on England. Yet England was in no condition to fight another war. Financially, Mary had inherited debts of £185,000, and her re-endowment of the church had also reduced her income by £29,000 annually. Only renewed sales of crown land in 1554, a further debasement of the Irish coinage, peacetime taxation in 1555 (which raised £181,000), and a forced loan in 1556 helped to stave off insolvency. Expenses still exceeded income even before the outbreak of war, at which point the government initiated further land sales and a larger forced loan (this yielded £109,000, but £42,000 was used to repay the previous loan).[56]

The English military effort was spread over four theatres. A small but effective army of 7,000 under the earl of Pembroke served over the summer with King Philip at the siege and capture of St Quentin, but otherwise the main effort was defensive. Berwick and the borders were reinforced against invasion by a projected Franco-Scottish invasion: this collapsed in September when the Scots halted at the Tweed, saying 'that in no wise would they invade England'. Yet King Philip saw this northern theatre as a distraction and avoided declaring war on the Scots. With his encouragement, the English navy had been extensively rebuilt and now protected his supply lines to the Netherlands by clearing French shipping out of the Channel. Calais was also briefly reinforced, but when in January 1558 a French army of 27,000 was secretly redeployed for an assault on Calais, the English authorities were caught napping, and within three weeks the undermanned garrison of 2,000 had been forced to surrender. Although Philip offered his

55   On Mary Stewart, see now John Guy, 'My heart is my own': the life of Mary queen of Scots (London, 2004); Wormald, Mary queen of Scots; and on the marriage, Guy, ch. 6; Wormald, pp. 21, 85–6; Donaldson, Scotland, pp. 88–9.
56   Loades, Reign of Mary Tudor, chs 6, 9, 12; Wormald, Mary queen of Scots, p. 85 (quotation).

[1 1 8]   own field army in the Netherlands for a joint operation to recover Calais, the privy council costed at £170,000 a projected English expeditionary force of 20,000 men for 5 months and despondently declared that neither the troops nor the money could be raised. So fell England's last outpost in continental Europe, the last token of medieval greatness. Calais's loss was a stunning blow to the regime's prestige, even if to modern eyes the expense of its upkeep far outweighed its political and commercial value. The threat from Scotland, moreover, remained serious over the summer: 9,000 troops were held ready to resist, and Berwick's fortifications were reconstructed. Yet by now even the principal belligerents were exhausted, and peace negotiations began in September.[57]

By 1558, it was increasingly clear that Mary's eventual successor would be her half-sister Elizabeth: despite rumours of her pregnancy, Mary remained childless. Then over the summer her health declined alarmingly, and in November she died. In France, Mary and Francis assumed the arms and style of sovereigns of England, arguing that by canon law Elizabeth Tudor was illegitimate. Elizabeth's accession was unopposed, but in other respects she was in an extremely weak position. Her first priority was to settle religion, but in February when negotiations with France resumed, Philip's support was vital to conclude a satisfactory peace. The realm was exhausted, and there were neither the men nor the money to continue the war. Initially, Elizabeth had insisted on the return of Calais, but fearing that Philip might conclude a separate treaty, she eventually yielded. In the treaty of Câteau-Cambrésis, signed in April 1559, a face-saving formula allowed the French to retain Calais for 8 years, and then either to restore it or to pay an indemnity of 500,000 crowns.[58]

By then, too, the political situation in Scotland was changing. Hitherto, the regent had tolerated the Protestants, who could expect no support from a Catholic England, but she now feared Protestant intrigues with England and so acted to suppress the movement. In July, the death of Henry II in a jousting accident brought the accession of Mary's husband as Francis II. French policy now began to press Mary's claims more forcefully to the English throne, and in August reinforcements were sent to restore control in Scotland where Protestant-inspired disorders and insurrection were spreading. The English government responded by secretly assisting the Protestant Lords of

---

57 Loades, *Reign of Mary Tudor*, ch. 11; Guy, *Tudor England*, pp. 247–8.
58 Williams, *The later Tudors*, pp. 110–11, 229–33, 237–8; W.T. MacCaffrey, *The shaping of the Elizabethan regime: Elizabethan politics, 1558–1572* (Princeton, 1968), ch. 3; Guy, *Tudor England*, pp. 248–9, 264.

the Congregation with money. In October, the Lords declared the regent suspended, but Protestant volunteers were too weak to dislodge a regular French garrison of 4,000 men. Elizabeth was extremely reluctant to provide open assistance to Scottish rebels against their lawful queen, and she loathed John Knox, author of the famous *First blast on the trumpet against the monstrous regiment of women* (1558), but under Secretary Cecil the privy council finally persuaded her to authorise military support. Lord Grey entered Scotland with 5,000 men in March. Two months before, an English fleet had been 'accidentally' blown off course into the Firth of Forth, where it blocked French supply lines. English operations on land proved disastrous, the French garrison easily repulsing Grey's assault on Leith, but then the loss of the French fleet in a storm, religious tumults in France, and the death of Mary of Guise in June, all encouraged the French to negotiate. In the resultant treaty of Edinburgh, signed in July, all foreign troops were to be withdrawn from Scotland, and assurances were also given that Queen Mary would recognise Elizabeth's title, allow freedom of worship to Scottish Protestants, and summon parliament. In practice, the Lords of the Congregation acted as a provisional government, and when parliament met in August, instructions not to treat of religion were ignored: a reformed confession of faith was enacted, papal authority abrogated, and mass prohibited. By the end of the year too, Mary had ceased to be queen of France with the death of her husband, King Francis, so reducing considerably the chances of a French recovery in Scotland.[59]

It was to be some time before the new regime could consolidate its precarious hold on power, and in England too the outlook remained uncertain in regard to politics and religion. Yet in retrospect, the events of the years 1558–60 seemed to mark a distinct shift away from traditional political alignments and towards the development of a more self-contained British state system.[60] By the mid-1550s, in place of their long-standing alliances with the Habsburg and Valois monarchies respectively, England and Scotland had in effect been reduced to little more than satellite kingdoms of these rival monarchies. In 1560, however, the autonomy of both kingdoms was far more assured. English forces had entered Scotland in response to appeals for military assistance against a new threat to Scottish sovereignty

---

59 Donaldson, *Scotland*, pp. 100–7; Wormald, *Mary queen of Scots*, p. 102; Wallace MacCaffrey, *Elizabeth I* (London, 1993), ch. 6; MacCaffrey, *Shaping of the Elizabethan regime*, ch. 4; Williams, *The later Tudors*, pp. 238–40.

60 On this, see in particular, Jane Dawson, 'William Cecil and the British dimension of early Elizabethan foreign policy' in *History*, lxxiv (1989), pp. 196–216.

presented by the 'auld alliance', and having secured Scottish independence, they had then immediately withdrawn. The 'auld enemy' bent on imperial conquest had suddenly appeared in the guise of liberator. From 1560, moreover, the two regimes were both Protestant and, at a time when European politics were increasingly polarised along confessional lines, came to see each other as natural allies. By contrast, in the longer term Scotland's 'auld alliance' with France was fatally compromised by the latter's Catholicism; and ideological differences also gradually undermined England's traditional alliance with the Habsburgs. Indeed, against the emerging threat of a Habsburg universal monarchy, Anglo-French relations even improved to the extent of agreeing by the treaty of Blois (1570) a wary alliance across the confessional divide, once the problem of Calais had been resolved.

THE REFORMATION CRISIS
The origins of a Protestant state

R eligious beliefs were a central aspect of people's lives in early modern times. The ceremonies associated with the ritual year shaped work and holidays for rich and poor alike. People attended their parish churches regularly for mass, matins and evensong on Sundays and feastdays, less frequently for the ceremonies associated with births, marriages and deaths, annually at Easter for confession and communion. These activities were regulated by the church, but the secular authorities too had a particular interest in the practice of religion. They cooperated closely with the church hierarchy in the enforcement of traditional Christian norms and values. Specifically, princes were concerned with the enforcement of obedience to authority, since theories of political obligation were overwhelmingly religious in the Renaissance period. God had ordained princes to rule, and princes were answerable solely to God for their actions: therefore, disobedience to lawful authority was not only a secular offence, it was also a sin against God. In addition, princes depended heavily on the church for the enforcement of orders and statutes and to disseminate information, because announcements by the priest to parishioners at Sunday mass were the usual and easiest means of reaching ordinary subjects. Moreover, the clergy still provided the largest pool of trained lawyers and administrators; although levels of literacy were rising, so that merchants, nobles and gentry could now mostly read and write, and the royal bureaucracy included increasing numbers of laymen. Kings employed the leading clergy as crown servants, and they nominated their leading officials to bishoprics and other important positions in the church as a reward for crown service.[1]

1 On the ritual year, see esp. Ronald Hutton, *The rise and fall of merry England* (Oxford, 1994); idem, *The stations of the sun* (Oxford, 1996). The latter extends to Wales, Scotland and off-shore islands, but there is as yet no extended study relating to Ireland. More generally on the pre-Reformation church and church–state relations, see Eamon Duffy, *The stripping of the altars: traditional religion in England c.1400–c.1580* (New Haven, 1992), pt 1; J.J. Scarisbrick, *The Reformation and the English people* (Oxford, 1984), chs 1–3; Christopher Haigh, *English Reformations: religion, politics, and society under the Tudors* (Oxford, 1993), pt 1; and (with a broader compass) Felicity Heal, *Reformation in Britain and Ireland* (Oxford, 2003).

[1 2 2]   The Reformation, portending as it did the most revolutionary series of changes in the church since the first establishment of Christianity in the British Isles, immediately called in question these established relationships between church and state. Religion quickly became a central issue in terms of state formation and, more gradually, of national identity. Before the Reformation, a working compromise had been reached in terms of church-state relations. The Lollard movement still posed some kind of challenge to Catholic orthodoxy in parts of south-east England, but the combined resources of church and state had brought it very much under control. The Lollards, intellectual descendants of the followers of John Wycliffe, a fourteenth-century Oxford don, rejected some key doctrines of the late medieval church: they denied the real presence of Christ in the Eucharist, denounced the pope as Antichrist, rejected confession to a priest, and objected to images. Instead, they emphasised the authority of the Bible over the traditions of the church, and they secretly read English translations of the Bible which circulated illicitly in manuscript, or learned off by heart key chapters such as the Epistle of St James. In many ways, the teachings of the Lollards anticipated those of the early Protestants, and certainly in the mid-Tudor period there was a correlation between the major centres of Protestantism and the old Lollard districts. Yet these doctrinal and geographical connections only became important once the hold of Catholic orthodoxy had been broken. And in the years before the Reformation there was no sign of that. Heresy was deeply unpopular, and the faggot emblem which an abjured heretic was obliged to wear was very much felt as a badge of shame. Even in its traditional centres in south-east England, in London and Lincoln dioceses, Lollardy as an organised movement was very much on the defensive, and there were few Lollards in the west, the midlands or northern England, hardly any in Scotland or Wales, and none at all in Ireland.[2]

Elsewhere in the British Isles, there were no heretical movements, although manifestations of late medieval Christianity might vary quite considerably – from lay support for the Observant movement (the movement for stricter observance of rules in mendicant orders) in the predominantly pastoral Gaelic parts, for instance, to popular enthusiasm for religious confraternities in the towns.[3] Yet these movements were firmly under the

---

2   On Lollardy, see esp. J.A.F. Thompson, *The later Lollards, 1414–1520* (Oxford, 1965); M. Aston, *Lollards and reformers: images and literacy in late medieval religion* (London, 1984); A. Hudson, *The premature Reformation: Wycliffite texts and Lollard history* (Oxford, 1988); J.F. Davis, *Heresy and Reformation in the south-east of England 1520–1559* (London, 1983).

3   Heal, *Reformation in Britain and Ireland*, pp. 55–9, 89–93.

church's control. The onset of the Reformation raised a series of new questions. Princes could not avoid taking a stand on matters of religion, and
generally it was their preferences which determined whether the territories
they ruled remained Catholic or became Protestant. The two British monarchies eventually opted for Protestant settlements, with the further result
that Protestantism became an important element in both English and
Scottish identities, and eventually in senses of Britishness. Nonetheless, this
was a hard-fought issue, both because individual monarchs had different
preferences in regard to religious change, but also because their choices
were contested by many of their subjects, so giving rise to the problem of
religious minorities.

Even though the Tudor and Stewart monarchies both eventually accepted
and enforced broadly Calvinist forms of Protestantism within their territories, there were considerable differences in the methods by which these,
in many respects, very similar religious settlements were achieved. For one
thing, the onset of the Tudor Reformation occurred almost 30 years before
its Scottish equivalent, and central to its origins were Tudor dynastic needs.
But for Henry VIII's desire for a son and heir, it is doubtful whether this
'defender of the faith' and leading critic of Martin Luther would have broken
with Rome, particularly since for almost 20 years Henry's diplomatic ambitions had usually accorded with those of the papacy. Thereafter, for the rest
of Henry VIII's reign, the royal supremacy constituted one of the few fundamental departures from late medieval Christianity. And even with the introduction under Edward VI and Elizabeth I of a Protestant religious settlement
along continental European lines, the supremacy remained one of the most
distinctive features of what later came to be called Anglicanism.

The Henrician Reformation

In the first phase of the Tudor Reformation, to the accession of Queen
Elizabeth, the emphasis was firmly fixed on change at the centre, the statutory enactment of religious change. This phase of state-sponsored reform
reflected overwhelmingly the power of the Tudor state but it also saw a vast
extension of this power over the lives of ordinary subjects. Accordingly, the
first part of this chapter offers a sketch of the nature of these changes.
Broadly, the religious settlement under Henry VIII remained much closer to
traditional pre-Reformation Christianity than to the practices of the leading

[1 2 4] continental reformers. The initial steps towards Tudor reform were geared chiefly to bringing the church in England more securely under royal control for the purpose of securing the royal divorce.

In May 1532, the English clergy in Convocation (the church's parliament) finally submitted to the king's demand for the surrender of their legislative independence by agreeing that henceforth no Convocation should be convened except by royal writ, that no new canons should be enacted without the king's assent, to allow a royal commission to approve or disallow existing canons, and that those canons approved should henceforth stand by virtue of the royal assent.[4] The Act of Appeals passed in 1533 by the English Reformation Parliament (1529–36) ended the judicial links between England and Rome, so ensuring that the archbishop of Canterbury could finally determine Henry's divorce from Catherine of Aragon. In 1534 a series of statutes passed by the English parliament completed the changes. The Dispensations Act authorised Canterbury to issue all ecclesiastical licences and faculties. The Act in Restraint of Annates ended payments by bishops to Rome, and established a new method for the king to appoint new bishops at each vacancy. The Act for the Submission of the Clergy confirmed the 1532 submission and made it legally binding. The Successions Act vested the succession to the throne in the heirs of Henry VIII and his new queen, Anne Boleyn, and made it treason to slander the marriage. In the second session of parliament in 1534 the Act of Supremacy recognised the king's new title as Supreme Head of the Church of England and gave the king power to conduct visitations of the clergy. The Act for First Fruits and Tenths in effect transferred to the king the payments formerly made to the bishop of Rome, viz. the first year's income of the bishopric: these payments were extended to all benefices, and an additional, ongoing tax of 10 per cent of the annual value of each benefice was introduced. Finally, the Treasons Act extended the meaning of treason (as defined by the earlier, 1352 act) to include additional offences, notably treason by words, such as calling the king a heretic, tyrant or usurper, where previously an overt deed had been necessary.[5] These statutes were subsequently confirmed in regard to Ireland

4   Printed, Gerald Bray (ed.), *Documents of the English Reformation* (Cambridge, 1994), p. 71. See also, Scarisbrick, *Henry VIII*, pp. 297–301. The latest account of the Henrician Reformation is G.W. Bernard, *The King's Reformation: Henry VIII and the remaking of the English church* (New Haven, 2005) which offers a detailed reappraisal of the king's policies, arguing that Henry by and large shaped religious policy as he had planned it.

5   A.G. Dickens, *The English Reformation* (2nd ed., London, 1989), pp. 137–45. The more important acts are printed in Bray (ed.), *Documents of the English Reformation*, pp. 72–114.

by the Irish Reformation Parliament (1536–7) which in 1536 enacted *mutatis mutandis* the chief statutes of the English Reformation Parliament. In Ireland, however, the Act for First Fruits and Twentieths fixed the annual tax on benefices at 5 per cent on grounds of the poverty of the Irish church.[6]

Essentially, therefore, the Henrician Reformation involved a considerable extension in the powers of the state, epitomised by the 1533 Act of Appeals which, by declaring that 'this realm of England is an empire . . . governed by one Supreme Head and King', established the Tudor territories as a sovereign state free from all foreign authority.[7] The early Tudor church became a department of state, a sort of ministry of spiritual welfare, and the king as Supreme Head acquired important new revenues from the church. The new tax on benefices was initially worth c.£40,000 per annum (£20,000 annually from the 1540s, following the dissolution of the monasteries), and in order to collect it the government assessed the value of every living in England and Wales, throughout c.9,000 parishes altogether. The detailed assessments of clerical income entered in the *Valor Ecclesiasticus* provided a kind of *Domesday Book* of the Tudor church. Their Irish equivalent, the less informative *Valor Beneficiorum Ecclesiasticorum in Hibernia*, which initially included the net values of only 541 benefices within the Englishry, assessed c.1538–9 out of a total of c.2,400 parishes throughout Ireland; but as Tudor rule was extended, other dioceses lying in the Irishry were gradually added, down to 1629. Income from twentieths, while miniscule, rose from c.IR£300 per annum initially to just over IR£370 by 1553, despite the dissolutions.[8]

Theologically, the king, or Cromwell as his vicegerent in spirituals, issued a number of statements from 1536 onwards. The Ten Articles were influenced by recent negotiations in Germany between English envoys and prominent Lutherans: for instance, they ignored the four traditional sacraments denounced by Martin Luther – but otherwise they were closer to Rome than to Wittenberg. They were accompanied by a series of royal injunctions, issued by Cromwell, requiring Bibles in English and Latin to be provided in each church, and that children and servants be taught the Lord's Prayer, Creed, and Ten Commandments 'in their mother tongue'. No

6   Ellis, *Ireland in the age of the Tudors*, pp. 143–4, 205–7.
7   Bray (ed.), *Documents of the English Reformation*, pp. 78–83 (quotation, p. 78).
8   Dickens, *English Reformation*, pp. 144, 174–5; W.G. Hoskins, *The age of plunder: the England of Henry VIII 1500–1547* (London, 1976), pp. 123–5; S.G. Ellis, 'Economic problems of the church: why the Reformation failed in Ireland' in *Journal of Ecclesiastical History*, xli (1990), pp. 239–65.

approved vernacular Bible was yet available: two English versions had been published by 1539, but Welsh- and Gaelic-speaking parts had to wait until the final phase of the Tudor Reformation. In 1537, the king licensed for a trial three-year period a series of 'official' sermons or homilies. These were published in September and known as *The Bishop's Book*: they restored the four 'missing' sacraments, but were closer to the evangelical position on the key debates about biblical authority or tradition, and faith and good works in regard to justification. A second set of injunctions appeared in 1538: these required parish priests to provide quarterly sermons by licensed preachers; to keep a register of christenings, marriages and burials; and to ensure that their parishioners all knew the common prayers in English (again overlooking the fact that for many of the king's subjects this was not their 'mother tongue'). The injunctions also attacked much more trenchantly the abuse of pilgrimages, images and relics.[9]

For the English parts of Ireland, doctrinal pronouncements by Archbishop Browne of Dublin in 1538 mirrored the broad thrust of English statements. The clergy were to teach English versions of the common prayers to their congregations, and Browne also denounced indulgences and images and ordered the use of new bidding prayers, 'The form of the beads'. These instructed the clergy to pray for the Church of England and Ireland and for 'the King's Highness . . . Supreme Head in earth, immediate under God, of this Church of England and Ireland', to inveigh against the bishop of Rome's usurped authority, his bulls and pardons, and to urge their congregations instead to place their 'confidence and trust in our Saviour, Jesus Christ'. In autumn 1538, Cromwell issued a version of the 1538 injunctions for Ireland which, however, apparently omitted the requirement for English Bibles. Nonetheless, even though the Irish Act of Supremacy had declared the king Supreme Head of 'the whole Church of Ireland, called *Hibernica Ecclesia*', it is clear that at this date Browne and Cromwell regarded the Irish church as simply a part of the English church in the same way as the Welsh church.[10]

By 1539, however, the king was increasingly concerned about religious dissent, and determined to use parliament to establish unity in religion. The

9 Dickens, *English Reformation*, pp. 150–6, 200, 204. See esp., Bray (ed.), *Documents of the English Reformation*, pp. 162–83 (quotation, p. 177).
10 *S.P.Hen. VIII*, ii, 564–5; *Statutes at large, Ireland*, i, 90; Brendan Bradshaw, 'George Browne, first Reformation archbishop of Dublin' in *Journal of Ecclesiastical History*, xxi (1970), pp. 305–13; idem, *Irish constitutional revolution*, pp. 155–8; Williams, *Wales and the Reformation*, pp. 105, 114.

result was the Act of Six Articles, which upheld the conservative position [1 2 7]
on all the vexed issues, enjoining transubstantiation, lay communion in one
kind, clerical celibacy, vows of chastity, private masses and auricular confession. Denial of these articles was punishable by death by burning (without
exception in the case of transubstantiation; otherwise, for the first offence,
those who recanted would merely be imprisoned at the king's pleasure).
By 1543, too, *The Bishop's Book* had also been conservatively revised by the
bishops along the lines of the Six Articles: this revision was known as
The King's Book since its preface was specially written by the king himself.
By then, even the English Bible was incurring the king's suspicion: the Act
for the Advancement of True Religion condemned 'crafty false and untrue'
translations, and limited the reading of the Bible to nobles, gentry and rich
merchants. Yet change was not always in a conservative direction. The king
endorsed a *Litany* in English published in 1544, with a reduction in the
invocation of saints, and a new *Primer* in 1545, which also paid less attention
to saints.[11]

The only other major departure from the practice of the pre-Reformation
church under Henry VIII was the dissolution of the monasteries, beginning
in 1536 with an act to dissolve those with incomes of less than £200 a year
and a further act of 1539 to confirm the crown's title to 'greater' monasteries
which had since surrendered 'voluntarily'. Again, the crown was the major
beneficiary of the changes. This and the later attack on chantries (foundations supporting priests to pray for the dead) were chiefly financial measures:
they were not a principled attack on the doctrine of purgatory and the value
of endowed prayer, as Protestants hoped, although by the time of the king's
death his beliefs in this area were quite ambiguous. The crown's income
from monastic lands in England and Wales reached a peak of £126,296 in
1540–1, but subsequently most of these lands were sold on to the laity to
pay for the French war.[12] In Ireland, the dissolutions, sanctioned by parliamentary acts of 1537 and 1542, had reached 55 per cent of the island's
monasteries and 40 per cent of the mendicant communities by 1547, netting
the crown an additional IR£4,070 from lands according to the 1540–1
survey; but by contrast with the Tudor mainland, monastic lands in Ireland

---

11   Dickens, *English Reformation*, pp. 201, 207–9, 211–13 (quotation); Haigh, *English Reformations*,
     pp. 162–3. See Bray (ed.), *Documents of the English Reformation*, pp. 222–32.
12   J.A. Youings, *The dissolution of the monasteries* (London, 1971); S.J. Gunn, *Early Tudor
     government, 1485–1558* (Basingstoke, 1995), pp. 116–21; Dickens, *English Reformation*,
     pp. 169–86.

mostly remained in crown hands, so that the eventual impact of the dissolutions was rather different.[13]

For instance, the king's original plans for the dissolutions in England had included the creation of 13 new sees, based upon former monastic buildings and lands, to tackle the problem of overlarge dioceses, but only 6 of these eventually emerged – Bristol, Chester, Gloucester, Oxford, Peterborough and Westminster, the last surviving only until 1550. In Ireland, however, the problem was one of numerous small but wretchedly poor dioceses, 32 in all: yet nothing at all was done to tackle this problem. Similarly, initial hopes in Ireland for humanist-inspired reform through the establishment of secular colleges, new schools, and a university so as to create a more learned ministry gradually subsided as the crown retained all but a fraction of ecclesiastical wealth to finance royal government. The essential nature of Henry VIII's campaign was again underlined in 1546 when St Patrick's cathedral, Dublin, was downgraded to a parish church, so netting the crown an additional IR£1,432 per annum.[14] By the mid-1540s, however, the king was increasingly pressed for cash to sustain his French war. Piecemeal surrenders of individual chantries encouraged Henry to procure a more extensive (though still partial) suppression of chantries by an act of 1545, although this had not yet been implemented when the king died.[15] In Gaelic parts, much of the lands and wealth of the religious passed to the local chiefs as part of the political rapprochement between the crown and Gaelic Ireland from 1541 onwards known as surrender and regrant. In the late 1530s the political campaign of the Geraldine League (see pp. 103–4) had also inspired opposition to the king's religious policies, but by the time a Jesuit mission arrived in Ulster in 1542 to exploit this, the political climate had changed. The two Jesuits were cold-shouldered by O'Neill and O'Donnell and soon withdrew. Throughout the sixteenth century, the reaction to Tudor reform in Gaelic Ireland continued to turn, by and large, on the attitude of the local chief.[16]

13 Brendan Bradshaw, *The dissolution of the religious orders in Ireland under Henry VIII* (Cambridge, 1974); N.B. White (ed.), *Extents of Irish monastic possessions, 1540–1541* (Dublin, 1943).
14 Dickens, *English Reformation*, p. 176; Ellis, *Ireland in the age of the Tudors*, p. 216.
15 Dickens, *English Reformation*, p. 230; Haigh, *English Reformations*, pp. 163–4.
16 Bradshaw, *Dissolution of the religious orders*, pp. 197–8, 210–16; Ellis, *Ireland in the age of the Tudors*, pp. 212–17, 235–6, 241, 256–61.

Reform and reaction: the Tudor church militant

Overall, Henry VIII had apparently steered a middle course for the Tudor church between the rival conservative and evangelical versions of Christianity. In reality, the king's eclectic combination of traditional and reformed beliefs was to prove quite unstable. After his death, the Tudor state was ruled in turn by two rancorously partisan regimes which attempted, respectively, to impose an unambiguously Protestant religious settlement under Edward VI, and to restore a staunchly conservative one under Mary. By the time of Elizabeth's accession, the growing polarisation of religious opinion as medieval Christendom broke up into rival churches, the outbreak of confessional strife in Europe, and the erosion of the religious middle ground meant that the crown had little choice but to assume the leadership of one of these rival factions. And the circumstances of the queen's birth and upbringing virtually ensured that she would prefer a Protestant settlement.

The gradual introduction of a Protestant religious settlement under Edward VI cast a very different light on the reform movement. Hitherto, the changes had appeared to the more conservatively-minded as little more than the erection of individual provinces of the medieval church into a distinct national church, governed by the territorial ruler as Supreme Head, but still part of the universal catholic church. Conservative clergy who had accepted the royal supremacy as a means to the religious reform for which many leading churchmen had long campaigned now discovered that it might equally be used to promote protestantism. Protector Somerset was undoubtedly sympathetic to reform, but his regime tried to carry conservative opinion with it by constantly stressing the need for unity. Somerset was also anxious to stress the moderation of his religious beliefs for fear of alienating Charles V, England's only possible ally in the Scottish war. Even so, Edward VI's first parliament immediately repealed the old anti-Lollard statute, *De Haeretico Comburendo*, which enforced burnings for heresy; the Act of Six Articles; and the 1543 statute limiting the reading of the Bible. Other government initiatives carefully balanced traditional doctrines with more evangelical ideas. A new set of injunctions issued in July 1547 required the reading of the epistle and gospel at mass in English, and ordered the destruction of shrines, images and other 'monuments of superstition'. A parallel *Book of Homilies* tackled the problem of seditious or ignorant preaching, providing twelve stock sermons which clergy were to read Sunday by Sunday to their congregations unless they had a licence to preach, but it included a broadly Lutheran sermon by Archbishop Cranmer on justification. Other statutes prescribed lay communion in both kinds and extended Henry VIII's act of 1545 by abolishing chantries, confraternities and guilds, this time on the novel grounds that they had maintained the twin superstitions of purgatory and prayers for the dead.

During 1548, preparations were made for more sweeping changes, culminating in an English prayer book. Proclamations enjoined the use from Easter of the *Order of Communion*, which inserted English prayers of preparation for communion into the Latin mass, and also abolished all remaining images and a series of traditional ceremonies – candles at Candlemas, ashes on Ash Wednesday, palms on Palm Sunday, creeping to the cross on Good Friday, and holy bread and holy water. Finally, in December, parliament debated the new prayer book, and in January an Act of Uniformity authorised *The Book of Common Prayer* for use 'throughout England, Wales, Calais . . . and other the king's dominions' from Whit Sunday following. Essentially, the book was an English translation of the traditional Latin services, simplified and somewhat modified to make them more acceptable to Protestants but, as leading conservatives like Bishop Gardiner affirmed, still capable of construction in the traditional sense. Its ambiguities were neatly epitomised by the catch-all title accorded there to the Eucharist, 'The supper of the Lord and the holy communion, commonly called the mass'.[17]

By 1550, the failure of a conservative *coup d'état*, a shift in the religious balance of the episcopal bench, and the conclusion of the Scottish war, all allowed the government to accelerate the pace of reform. In March 1550, a new Ordinal was published which charged the new priest with 'authority to preach the word of God and to minister the holy sacraments' instead of the traditional charge to offer sacrifice and celebrate mass for the living and the dead. The significance of this change was underlined in November by the council's directive that stone altars be replaced by wooden communion tables. More importantly, a revised version of *The Book of Common Prayer* was authorised by the second Act of Uniformity: this aimed to prevent conservative priests from 'counterfeiting the mass' by mumbling the English text half audibly like the old Latin and illicitly retaining the traditional gestures

17 The most convincing treatment of the Edwardian Reformation is now Diarmaid MacCulloch, *Tudor church militant: Edward VI and the Protestant Reformation* (London, 1999). See also Bush, *Government policy of Protector Somerset*, pp. 119–23; Dickens, *English Reformation*, pp. 212, 222–55; Bray (ed.), *Documents of the English Reformation*, pp. 247–62, 266–71 (quotation, p. 267).

'in bowings and beckings, kneelings and knockings'. Accordingly, although the new prayer book made few changes to matins and evensong, it altered the structure of the Eucharist, now pointedly renamed 'The Lord's Supper or Holy Communion', splitting the Canon into three separate parts. Moreover, the medieval priestly vestments were explicitly forbidden, only a surplice being required; the communion table was repositioned with its ends east and west, the priest standing on the north side; new words of administration emphasised the commemorative nature of the sacrament; and a late addition by the council (the so-called Black Rubric) further explained that kneeling for communion did not imply adoration of the sacrament.

Finally, in Edward's last months, Archbishop Cranmer worked on a revision of canon law and a new doctrinal statement for the Church of England. Political infighting precluded the promulgation of his *Reformatio Legum Ecclesiasticarum*. The project was revived unofficially under Elizabeth, and in a bid to pressurise the queen into further reforms the *Reformatio* was published in 1571. Elizabeth opposed it, although the Church of Scotland gave it more sympathetic consideration. Just before Edward's death, however, the council issued The Forty-Two Articles of Religion, which offered an unambiguously Protestant interpretation of the Christian faith, and denounced the errors of Rome. This borrowed extensively from the (Lutheran) Augsburg confession, but its Eucharistic teaching reflected the recent agreement between the church leaders of Zürich and Geneva known as the *Consensus Tigurinus*, and the predominant influences in its statements about predestination and election were also what would shortly be described theologically as 'reformed'.[18]

The enactment of reform was one thing; but its imposition on an unwilling populace quite another. By 1553, the government's programme had run far ahead of public opinion. Reformed Christianity had then few committed supporters outside the more urbanised parts of Lowland England where conditions were uniquely favourable to its reception. As before, arrangements for Ireland give a clearer insight into the essential character of the reform campaign. There the government did not even trouble to convene a parliament in order to obtain formal assent to the changes. Relying on the English legislation, the deputy and council issued a series of proclamations, beginning in November 1548, to bring the Irish church into line. This included

18 MacCulloch, *Tudor church militant*, pp. 87–104, 154–5, 167–74, 195; Dickens, *English Reformation*, pp. 256–86 (quotation, p. 270); Bray (ed.), *Documents of the English Reformation*, pp. 281–311; John Bale, *The vocacyon of Johan Bale*, ed. Peter Happé and J.N. King (Binghamton, N.Y., 1990), p. 51 (quotation).

[1 3 2]   *The Book of Common Prayer*, promptly authorised for use from 9 June 1549, although the revised (1552) version had still not been generally implemented in Ireland when Edward died. In 1551 a printing press was also established in Ireland in response to complaints about a shortage of prayer books, but a more fundamental difficulty was that English was not widely understood in large parts of Ireland. Accordingly, the English council grudgingly authorised Gaelic services where 'a convenient number' could not understand English, and a Latin version of the prayer book was also introduced experimentally in Limerick; but it is unclear how widely these were used.[19]

Much the same problems were encountered in Wales where English was, if anything, even less widely spoken. English was confined to parts of the south Wales coast and the eastern borders, the market towns and plantation boroughs, although many of the gentry, lawyers and clerics were bilingual. When Bishop Ferrar preached in English in Carmarthen, his congregation apparently understood, but at Abergwili just outside the town only three or four in a congregation of around 140 could follow his sermon. In 1551 William Salesbury published *Kynniver Llith a Ban*, a Welsh translation of the epistles and gospels prescribed by the prayer book. Salesbury also published three other works at this time, two of them in Welsh: one argued in favour of a married ministry by invoking provisions of ancient Welsh laws; the other argued that the Bible had existed in Welsh in early Britain and should now be restored. The English work was a conventional Protestant attack on altars and the sacrifice of the mass. Yet enthusiastic Welsh Protestants were a tiny minority at this time. Even the bishops, with the exception of Ferrar, were cautious, conformist Henricians who enforced the changes with considerable reluctance, and their stance was emulated by other senior clergy. It is no wonder then that, for the most part, the authorities were able to secure no more than a sullen and unwilling conformity.[20]

At least in Ireland and Wales, there were no major rebellions against the religious changes, which is more than could be said of Tudor Cornwall. Among the grievances listed by the commons of Devon and Cornwall in the rebel articles of June 1549 was the following:

> Item, we will not receive the new service because it is but like a Christmas game, but we will have our old service of matins, mass, evensong and procession in Latin, not in English, as it was before. And so we, the Cornishmen (whereof certain of us understand no English) utterly refuse this new English.

19   Ellis, *Ireland in the age of the Tudors*, pp. 219–23 (quotation, p. 221).
20   Williams, *Wales and the Reformation*, pp. 171–3, 176–7, 183–4, 187.

One response to the articles by the evangelical Devon gentleman, Philip Nichols, taxed the rebels with their presumption: 'we Cornishmen utterly refuse this new English were too much for a parishioner to say to his curate', much more for subjects to their governors. 'If ye had understood no English' and had 'made humble request to the King's Majesty' for the prayer book's translation 'into our Cornish speech', a remedy might have been provided. In the event, the failure to provide for a Cornish liturgy led to a very rapid decline in the language under Elizabeth.[21]

Yet, linguistic incomprehension was more an excuse than a cause of the rising in Devon and Cornwall. Already in 1548 there had been a small rising around Helston against the religious changes, and in spring 1549 the announcement that the new prayer book must be used from Whit Sunday sparked new disorders, with rebels across Cornwall establishing a camp at Bodmin and, encouraged by local priests, drawing up articles of grievance to set before the government. Meanwhile, a separate rising in Devon began spontaneously on Whit Monday at Sampford Courtenay in response to the introduction of the English prayer book there the previous day. The two movements then coalesced and, led by a council of three Devon and three Cornish gentry, plus three commoners, besieged Exeter. New articles were drawn up which were overwhelmingly religious in content, in essence demanding a restoration of the religious settlement as it had been ten years before. These articles were heavily scripted by clerical interests, but there were also hints both here and elsewhere of social conflict and unrest at high food prices. Some at least of the gentry were plundered, imprisoned or humiliated, and subsequently a King's Bench indictment quoted a rebel manifesto with a very mixed message: 'Kill all the gentlemen and we will have the Act of Six Articles up again and ceremonies as were in King Henry the Eighth's time.' Initially, Somerset failed to appreciate the seriousness of the situation and the force he provided for Lord Russell, charged with restoring order, was entirely inadequate. Russell dared not advance to relieve Exeter, and reinforcements promised with Lord Grey had to be diverted to deal with a 'stir here in Bucks and Oxfordshire by instigation of sundry priests for these matters of religion'. Russell only felt strong enough to move on Exeter in late July, defeating the rebel army of 6,000 in engagements on 3–4 August just east of Exeter to lift the siege, with a final bloody battle at

---

21 Fletcher and MacCulloch, *Tudor rebellions*, pp. 60–3, 151–5 (quotations, pp. 62, 152); Mark Stoyle, *West Britons: Cornish identities and the early modern British state* (Exeter, 2002), pp. 45–9 (quotation, p. 46).

Sampford Courtenay on 16 August. Around 4,000 rebels were said to have died at the hands of the king's army, although the leaders were sent to London for trial and execution. Final proof is lacking, but what apparently had precipitated revolt in a badly-divided society was an uneasy alliance between conservative gentry and priests, and a commons seething with religious and socio-economic grievances.[22] Elsewhere, in the south-east, social conflict was to be a much more evident precipitant of rebellion in 1549 (discussed below, pp. 192–6) but there, intriguingly, social unrest combined with Protestantism as a means of legitimating popular socio-economic grievances.

The death of 'the virtuous imp', Edward VI, stopped the Reformation in its tracks. As quickly became apparent, the Edwardian reforms were chiefly the product of state power rather than of popular conviction. For this reason, the Marian regime had little difficulty in suppressing reform once the statutory instruments underpinning the settlement had been withdrawn. In autumn 1553, pending the repeal of the Acts of Uniformity, the Edwardian settlement remained officially in force, but Mary sanctioned Catholic worship alongside it, and indeed the mass had already been spontaneously restored in many parts. From December, the religious settlement reverted to that at the end of Henry VIII's reign, and finally in January 1555 the Second Statute of Repeal restored full communion with Rome.[23] In Ireland, Lord Deputy St Leger was simply instructed in October 1553 that religion should be that 'of old time used'; although a parliament eventually met in 1557 to repeal the Henrician legislation.[24]

The Elizabethan settlement

Mary's reign was to prove even shorter than that of her half-brother, however, and in 1559 the authorities moved once again to restore a national church. Queen Elizabeth apparently began by using the 1549 liturgy in the Chapel Royal, but she soon realised that this was no longer acceptable even

---

22 There is little recent work on the revolt in Devon and Cornwall, but see Joyce Youings, 'The south-western rebellion of 1549' in *Southern History*, i (1979), pp. 99–122; Helen Speright, 'Local government and the south-western rebellion of 1549' ibid., xviii (1996), pp. 1–23; Robert Whiting, *The blind devotion of the people: popular religion and the English Reformation* (Cambridge, 1989), passim. A useful summary is Fletcher and MacCulloch, *Tudor rebellions*, pp. 52–64, 151–5 (quotations, pp. 57, 60); and see also Andy Wood, *Riot, rebellion and popular politics in early modern England* (Basingstoke, 2002), pp. 54–9.

23 Dickens, *English Reformation*, pp. 287–315.

24 Ellis, *Ireland in the age of the Tudors*, pp. 223–5.

to moderate Protestants. Probably, when parliament met to discuss religion in January 1559, she aimed at restoring the 1552 prayer book, although the evidence is unclear. At any rate, the government's reform programme was blocked, apparently by conservative opposition in the Lords. Accordingly, Elizabeth decided on an additional parliamentary session after Easter. She introduced two new bills for Supremacy and Uniformity so as to divide the opposition, and some concessions were also made to conservative opinion: as a result, Supremacy passed comfortably, Uniformity very narrowly. The Act of Supremacy now declared Elizabeth Supreme Governor (rather than Supreme Head) of the church (but with the same powers), empowering her to visit and correct the church through commissioners; it repealed the heresy laws and provided that nothing was to be adjudged heresy except on the authority of the scriptures or the first four general councils of the church; it revived ten statutes of Henry VIII, including the Act of Appeals; and it imposed an Oath of Supremacy on office holders in church and state.

The Act of Uniformity imposed the 1552 prayer book but with crucial modifications designed to make it more acceptable to conservatives: offensive references to the pope disappeared, the omission of the Knoxian 'Black Rubric' and the combination of the 1549 and 1552 words of administration permitted belief in the real presence (albeit at the expense of an impossibly long sentence to be repeated by the minister), and a new Ornaments Rubric permitted the traditional vestments to be worn by the minister, who was also to stand in 'the accustomed place'. Even so, it would not have passed, but that the Marian episcopal bench was seriously depleted: four bishoprics had long been vacant, six more bishops died from May 1558 onwards, two were excluded from parliament, and two were under arrest. After parliament had been dissolved, Elizabeth issued injunctions which offered further concessions to conservative opinion: communion tables were to stand where the altar had stood, only images subject to superstitious abuse, not all images, were to be removed, and traditional wafers were to be used in communion rather than ordinary bread.[25]

---

25 Perhaps the most convincing account of the conflicting pressures, reformist and conservative, which shaped the Elizabethan Settlement is N.L. Jones, *Faith by statute: parliament and the settlement of religion* (London, 1982). See also W.S. Hudson, *The Cambridge connection and the Elizabethan settlement of 1559* (Durham, NC, 1980); J.E. Neale, *Elizabeth I and her parliaments* (2 vols, London, 1953–7), i, 33–84; MacCulloch, *Tudor church militant*, p. 219; Dickens, *English Reformation*, pp. 349–61; Haigh, *English Reformations*, pp. 235–42; Bray (ed.), *Documents of the English Reformation*, pp. 318–49. Figures concerning the Marian bishops in 1559 calculated from E.B. Fryde, D.E. Greenway, S. Porter, and I. Roy (eds), *Handbook of British chronology* (3rd ed., London, 1986), pp. 225–99.

In Ireland, perhaps because the government had prepared the ground more carefully after its experiences with opposition in the English parliament, the Acts of Supremacy and Uniformity were enacted promptly by parliament within four weeks in January 1560. A bill for communion in both kinds had also been sent over to allow the Dublin administration some freedom of manoeuvre, but it was not needed. The two acts followed their English counterparts, except that ministers who did not know English were permitted to use a Latin version of the prayer book. (No Gaelic version was published until 1608.) The absence of articles of religion in Ireland also allowed the clergy more latitude to interpret the prayer book as they wished. Thus, if in England a liturgical compromise had in 1559 allowed conservative priests to celebrate communion much as if it were a traditional mass, in Ireland the widespread retention of Latin probably rendered these differences obscure to all but the theologically educated.[26]

By the beginning of Elizabeth's reign, however, religious opinion in England was far more polarised than it had been 30 years before. Elizabeth had hoped, by concessions to the English conservatives in the new injunctions, to carry with her the more moderate bishops, particularly old Henrician servants like Heath, Thirlby and Tunstall who had previously accepted the 1549 prayer book. At the royal visitation which followed in summer 1559, however, none would subscribe the supremacy, the prayer book, or the injunctions: all had to be deprived. The queen also tried to preserve some semblance of a *via media* by appointing to leading positions Protestant conformists like Matthew Parker, her first Primate of All England, who had, like herself, stayed in England under Queen Mary; John Jewel, her bishop of Salisbury, who had initially conformed; or even William Downham, the new bishop of Chester, who had been her Catholic chaplain under Mary. Yet in 1553, the Protestant leadership had mostly either gone into exile or, like Cranmer, Hooper and Ridley, had later been burned for heresy. Thus, although her bishops were mostly these survivors of Edward's clerical leadership, experience of exile had also left them with fixed views of what constituted acceptable practice in the best reformed churches. Among these, she favoured men like Dr. Richard Cox who had demanded 'the face of an English church' at Frankfurt over those led by John Knox who had withdrawn to Geneva and replaced the 1552 prayer book with an English

---

26   Henry Jefferies, 'The Irish parliament of 1560: the Anglican reforms authorised' in *Irish Historical Studies*, xxvi (1988–9), pp. 128–41; Ellis, *Ireland in the age of the Tudors*, pp. 225–7, 236.

translation of the Geneva liturgy, *The Book of Common Order*. Yet Knox's [1 3 7]
particular fault was his disastrous and unfortunately-timed *The first blast on
the trumpet against the monstrous regiment of women* (1558) against the two Queen
Marys, appearing just before Elizabeth's accession with its uncompromising
opening that:

> To promote a woman to bear rule, superiority, dominion or empire above any
> realm, nation, or city is repugnant to nature, contumely to God, a thing most
> contrarious to His revealed will and approved ordinance, and finally it is the
> subversion of good order, of all equity and justice.

In Edinburgh, when he repeated these arguments in an audience with the
queen, Knox reduced Mary to tears. Elizabeth, however, was made of sterner
stuff. She refused to allow him back, never forgave him, and she excluded from
leading positions any cleric with the slightest hint of Genevan connections.

Despite all this, and against her wishes, Elizabeth's bishops then sought
in 1562–3 to use the convocation of Canterbury to implement sweeping
reforms; in 1566 they backed similar reform bills in parliament. For
Protestants generally, however, Elizabeth was an English Deborah who had
delivered her people from popery and Spanish tyranny. Only later did they
lose confidence in her desire for further reform. In the event, the most
Elizabeth would allow was a new statement defining belief, the Thirty-Nine
Articles: actually, they were the Edwardian Forty-Two Articles, slightly
revised in a conservative direction. These Articles were much more precise
(and contentious) than the brief and general Eleven Articles issued by the
bishops in 1561. They were approved by convocation in 1563 and eventually confirmed by statute, despite the queen's reluctance, in 1571.[27] In
Ireland, by contrast, religious opinion was as yet much less polarised: at least
six bishops, probably eight or more, had taken the Oath in 1560 and agreed
to serve in the Church of Ireland. In Wales, too, the three surviving bishops
also showed signs of flexibility: Bishop Kitchin of Llandaff eventually subscribed. And in yet another variation on English practice, the problem of the
different vernacular there was addressed by a private act of parliament in
1563 which permitted services in Welsh, not Latin as enacted for Gaelic
Ireland, and ordered Welsh translations of the prayer book and Bible accordingly: a Welsh prayer book and New Testament were published in 1567.

---

27 W.P. Haugaard, *Elizabeth and the English Reformation: the struggle for a stable settlement of religion*
    (Cambridge, 1968); Haigh, *English Reformations*, pp. 242–3; idem, *Reformation and resistance
    in Tudor Lancashire* (Cambridge, 1975), p. 210; Guy, *'My heart is my own': the life of Mary queen
    of Scots*, pp. 142–3, 176–7; MacCulloch, *Tudor church militant*, pp. 177–9, 184–6, 189–92
    (quotation, p. 186); Bray (ed.), *Documents of the English Reformation*, pp. 349–51.

Overall, therefore, the Elizabethan settlement of religion was not really one settlement at all, but three, and in the short term it settled nothing. From the outset, even its leaders were far from united as to the essential character of the Elizabethan church. The queen struggled to restrain the more zealous Protestants among her English bishops, while concurrently her Irish bishops included crypto-Catholics like Archbishop Bodkin of Cashel and Bishop Walsh of Waterford.[28] Moreover, it soon became apparent to the queen and her ministers that the enforcement of the settlement also presented very different problems in the different Tudor territories. Specifically, in large parts of Lowland England the Reformation in the parishes achieved a different momentum and threw up quite different problems from the Reformation in the various Tudor borderlands where the particular difficulties of enforcement were largely variations on the one theme.

These differences reflected the initial policy decisions taken by the queen in regard to religion and the uneven capacity of Tudor government to supervise and enforce change. In 1559, having so narrowly secured a settlement which was broadly acceptable to her, Elizabeth then did what almost no one had foreseen: she proceeded to a rapid and rigid enforcement of the settlement and refused all further changes. This sudden transition was in marked contrast to the pattern of piecemeal change under Henry VIII and Edward VI. Yet enactment was one thing, enforcement quite another: as we shall see, in those regions where the capacity of Tudor government was more limited, such as Ireland and Wales, change was perforce much more gradual. A third pattern of reform was presented by those parts of the British Isles which lay entirely beyond Tudor control. In Scotland the Lords of the Congregation faced a similar problem when they took power in 1560. Yet a sharp and rigid enforcement of religious change was so clearly beyond the Scottish government's slender resources that it was not even attempted there: in Scotland, two organisations continued side by side, both enjoying some legal status in the years 1560–7, with the result that the Reformation engendered far less contention and resistance than was the case in the Tudor state.

---

28 Ellis, *Ireland in the age of the Tudors*, pp. 228–30; Alan Ford, 'The Church of Ireland, 1558–1634: a puritan church?' in idem, J. McGuire, and K. Milne (eds), *As by law established: the Church of Ireland since the Reformation* (Dublin, 1995), pp. 56–8; Williams, *Wales and the Reformation*, pp. 216–21.

Scotland: an alternative pattern of reform

The Scottish Reformation was in many ways a quite different, more popular movement from its state-directed English counterpart. It occurred well after the main expansion of Protestantism in Europe, and this in turn shaped its character. There was little about doctrine, on which the Scottish kirk generally followed the dogmas laid down elsewhere. Very frequently, the lead here came from England, if only because Scottish reformers used English prayer books and Bibles in their worship, so that liturgical practices were heavily influenced by the English model. Yet a crucial difference was that Scotland lacked a godly prince like Edward or Elizabeth during the formative period of the Reformation. Mary queen of Scots was a minor, then an absentee in France, and finally a wicked idolatress, castigated by John Knox and deposed in 1567 in favour of her infant son, James VI. Thus the pressures which in England had produced the peculiarly Anglican concept of the royal supremacy were much less pronounced in Scotland: yet, particularly after James VI had reached his majority, the Scottish crown attempted to recover lost ground in this area. Overall, the distinctively Scottish feature of the Reformation concerned organisation and funding rather than doctrinal debate. Whereas in England, in theory at least, a Protestant organisation replaced a Catholic one almost overnight, and traditional church funding was likewise speedily transferred, in Scotland the transition from Catholic to Protestant was in many ways a more gradual, less violent affair, which, however, reflected the relative weakness there of central control over the provinces.[29]

As in England, Lutheran literature began to circulate in Scottish east-coast burghs in the 1520s. Lollard influence, moreover, had percolated into south-west Scotland with the appearance in the 1490s of a group later called the Lollards of Kyle. In 1528 Patrick Hamilton became the first Scottish Lutheran to be burned for heresy. Ten more burnings followed in the 1530s, and altogether 21 had been executed by 1558. When compared with the burning of the 300 or so Protestants by Mary Tudor, or the execution of 200 Catholics by Elizabeth, these were relatively small numbers, reflecting both the Scottish Reformation's relative lack of violence and the weakness of central authority in Scotland. From 1536 more Scottish Protestants fled abroad,

---

29   On the Scottish Reformation, see esp. Gordon Donaldson, *The Scottish Reformation* (Cambridge, 1960); I.B. Cowan, *The Scottish Reformation* (London, 1982); J. Kirk, *Patterns of reform: continuity and change in the Reformation kirk* (Edinburgh, 1989); and on church–state relations see Wormald, *Court, kirk, and community*, pt II.

in response to persecution, many of them to the court of Henry VIII initially, men like Alexander Alane (Alesius), John MacAlpine (Maccabeus), John Willock, George Wishart and Robert Richardson; but after Cromwell's fall they mostly moved on.[30] There was also some demand for religious literature in English, particularly Bibles. James V held up to the pope these reformist activities, and the implication that he might follow the example of his English uncle, so as to increase his control of church patronage and to levy regular taxation on the church. Yet in reality, the reformers were a tiny minority: as was the case in England, so long as church and state cooperated against them, they presented no real threat to the established order. Things only began to change after James V's death. The collapse of strong central control in the 1540s and the emergence of two warring factions of nobles and lairds gradually promoted an alignment between reformist sympathisers and the politically pro-English lairds of Fife, Lothian and the borders.

The old king's death released an immediate demand for vernacular works, which was encouraged by the first regent, James Hamilton, earl of Arran. Arran solicited Henry VIII's advice about reform and requested English books from his ambassador, Sir Ralph Sadler. An act of 1543 also made it lawful to read the Bible in English or Scots (just as, ironically, King Henry was limiting this practice). Arran's sympathies were widely thought to be Protestant. Yet, at most, his religious policy briefly attempted to mirror Henry VIII's most recent pronouncements. Even so, there were serious riots in Dundee and Perth. Dundee's two friaries were sacked by a mob, and in Fife too the abbey of Lindores was sacked and the monks expelled. Many of the 'assured Scots' were also sympathetic to reform: Alexander Crichton of Brunstane offered to assassinate Cardinal Beaton in 1544, and he and John Cockburn of Ormiston later harboured George Wishart, who had returned to Scotland two years previously and preached openly in Ayrshire, Fife, Lothian and Perth, apparently converting John Knox. Yet as French influence revived, so too did activity against the few Protestants. Beaton had Wishart burned for heresy in 1546, and in revenge Beaton was then assassinated in his castle of St Andrews by reformist sympathisers among the 'assured Scots'.[31]

30 Jenny Wormald, *Court, kirk, and community: Scotland 1470–1625* (London, 1981), pp. 92, 102–3; Michael Lynch, *Scotland a new history* (London, 1991), pp. 186–7; I.D. Whyte, *Scotland before the industrial revolution: an economic and social history c.1050–c.1750* (London, 1995), p. 104.

31 Merriman, *The rough wooings*, pp. 115–19, 154, 209–11; I.B. Cowan, *Regional aspects of the Scottish Reformation* (London, 1978), pp. 14–15; Wormald, *Court, kirk, and community*, pp. 104–7; Donaldson, *Scotland*, pp. 73–6.

Once the English had been ousted from southern Scotland, however, the [1 4 1] pro-French government avoided cracking down hard on heresy for fear of driving two groups of malcontents together – reformist sympathisers, and the politically pro-English lairds of Fife, east Lothian and the borders. Moreover, in 1553 the politico-religious balance also shifted with the collapse of Protestantism in England and the establishment of a Catholic regime there. There was now no possibility of English assistance for Scottish Protestants, and from 1554 the new Scottish regent, the indulgent Mary of Guise, tolerated discreet Protestant activity. Yet this French dominance came at a high price: the French troops in Scotland proved highly unpopular and whipped up nationalist sentiments. From 1555, moreover, a sustained Protestant effort commenced: preachers were allowed to work freely among the small groups of lairds, burgesses and occasional magnates sympathetic to reform in Angus and the Mearns, where matters were organised by John Erskine of Dun; in Kyle, influenced by the earl of Glencairn; and in Lothian. John Knox also paid a brief visit in 1555–6, as did John Willock. Emboldened by this preaching, the Protestant party's secular leaders issued in December 1557 the *First Band of the Lords of the Congregation*, pledging themselves to work for recognition of a reformed church. The making of bonds (or 'bands') for social and political purposes was a commonplace of Scottish society, but this was the first time it had been turned to religious use. It subsumed the Calvinist concept of a religious covenant, and the idea that secular authority should only be obeyed if it were godly. Given the Protestants' weakness at the time, the gesture seemed almost foolhardy: only five of the signatories could be described as influential (the earls of Glencairn, Morton and Argyll, Argyll's son, and the latter's cousin, John Lord Erskin); the rest were, at most, local lairds. The regent, however, was reluctant to take firm measures while negotiations for the royal marriage and the crown matrimonial were proceeding. Thus, regular Protestant congregations now began to meet for worship, using the English prayer book, and electing elders and deacons in the same way as English exiles on the continent.[32]

Meanwhile, the bishops had begun a series of reforming initiatives to try and set the church in Scotland in order. The long-heralded general council of the church had finally opened at Trent in late 1545: even though no Scottish bishop attended, the leader of the commission which drew up the

---

32 Donaldson, *Scotland*, pp. 86–90; J.E.A. Dawson, *The politics of religion in the age of Mary, queen of Scots: the earl of Argyll and the struggle for Britain and Ireland* (Cambridge, 2002), p. 24; Wormald, *Court, kirk, and community*, pp. 107, 111; Cowan, *Regional aspects of the Scottish Reformation*, p. 22.

[1 4 2] Tridentine decree on the vexed doctrine of justification was the Scottish churchman, Robert Wauchope, titular archbishop of Armagh. Through Wauchope, the Scottish bishops had an authenticated copy of the early decrees of Trent in time for the opening in 1549 of their provincial council under Archbishop Hamilton. Further councils followed in 1552 and 1559. Reforming statutes forbad concubinage, non-residence and pluralism, enjoined regular preaching and episcopal visitations, and made provision for the better education of priests and monks. Hamilton also issued a *Catechism* for the instruction of the people. Remarkably, the council of 1559 even introduced common prayers, litanies and evening prayer in the vernacular, and it issued a brief Exhortation on the Eucharist to be given before communion and known as the 'Twopenny Faith'.[33] Yet this Catholic Reformation had made little progress in the parishes when it was overtaken by the revolution of 1559–60. As fears grew that Scotland would be reduced to an appendage of France, more nobles and lairds aligned themselves with the reform party. In Edinburgh, rioting broke up the traditional procession of St Giles in September, at which the public recantation of heretics had been scheduled: the 'idol of Sanct Giles' was drowned in the loch nearby. Yet the major turning point in the Scottish Reformation occurred only in November 1558, and for two reasons. First, the Scottish parliament's consent to the crown matrimonial and the revelation of the secret clause in the marriage treaty seemed to undermine Scottish independence.[34] Second, also in November, Queen Mary of England died and was succeeded by Queen Elizabeth. This immediately altered the politico-religious balance in Scotland because the French monarchy, with its own Huguenot minority, had since 1553 seemed more sympathetic to Scottish reformers, whereas the restoration of a Protestant regime in England now seemed to open the possibility of English support for a Protestant nationalist alliance against French domination. Indeed, Elizabeth's secretary, William Cecil, soon appreciated the new opportunities afforded by these developments for recasting Tudor foreign policy along British lines: within a year, he was urging his mistress to respond to the appeals of the Protestant lords for English assistance, and he later treated with the earl of Argyll. Argyll undertook to bring over 3,000 redshanks, to use his connections with the MacDonalds of Antrim and Calvagh O'Donnell against Shane O'Neill, and to provide the English

33 Donaldson, *Scottish Reformation*, pp. 33–7, 45; Wormald, *Court, kirk, and community*, pp. 92–3.
34 Wormald, *Court, kirk, and community*, pp. 109–15; Donaldson, *Scotland*, pp. 88–95; Lynch, *Scotland*, p. 191 (quotation).

government with assistance from Scottish Gaeldom 'to reduce the north parts of Ireland to the perfect obedience of England'. Moreover, the Franco-Spanish truce of October 1558, which was to lead to the treaty of Câteau-Cambrésis (March 1559) boded ill for Scottish reformers: King Henri II of France wrote to the pope specifically about the need to deal with the heretics in Scotland, and the regent also initiated a new crackdown at a time when their hopes had been raised by religious change in England.[35]

These developments precipitated civil war during summer 1559. On 1 January, the 'Beggars' Summons', nailed to the doors of the friaries, had called on the friars to quit their houses in favour of the poor before 12 May. By May, when John Knox returned from exile, Perth and Dundee had publicly accepted the Reformation, and other towns followed soon after, notably Ayr, Perth and St Andrews. The regent's attempts to restore Catholic worship by using French troops sparked military resistance by the townsmen who, backed by nobles and lairds, combined together in the 'army of the Congregation'. Widespread disorders, iconoclasm and looting of friaries followed, although the lairds' principal purpose was to oppose French domination. Between June and November, Edinburgh was twice occupied and abandoned by the Lords of the Congregation: rival councils, Catholic and Protestant, struggled for control, until the Congregation again reoccupied the city five months later. By August, when French reinforcements arrived, this Protestant revolution against established authority was running into difficulties. Thereupon, the Protestant leaders changed tack, insisting that the essential issue was the restoration of Scottish independence, and appealing even to Catholic lords to fight for 'the liberty of this your native country'. In this way, they won renewed support against the French. The Congregation now formally appealed for English assistance, and in October they declared the regent suspended.[36] A stalemate followed. The Protestant Lords corresponded with Cecil, proposing a marriage between Queen Elizabeth and James Hamilton, earl of Arran. Their commissioners in London later told Elizabeth that this would create the basis for 'the union of these two kingdoms in one', asserting that Arran was 'no stranger, but in a manner

35   Dawson, *Politics of religion*, pp. 1–2, 104–10 (quotation, p. 2); idem, 'William Cecil and the British dimension of early Elizabethan foreign policy' in *History*, lxxiv (1989), pp. 196–216; idem, 'Two kingdoms or three?: Ireland in Anglo-Scottish relations in the middle of the sixteenth century' in R.A. Mason (ed.), *Scotland and England 1286–1815* (Edinburgh, 1987), pp. 113–38; Wormald, *Court, kirk, and community*, pp. 115–16.

36   Donaldson, *Scotland*, pp. 91–7; Dawson, *The politics of religion in the age of Mary, queen of Scots*, pp. 96–7; Wormald, *Court, kirk, and community*, pp. 115–17; M. Lynch, *Edinburgh and the Reformation* (Edinburgh, 1981); idem, *Scotland*, pp. 196–7 (quotation, p. 197).

your own country man, seeing the isle is a common country to us both, one that speaketh your own language, one of the same religion'. The proposal was later broadened into one for an extended monarchy of Scotland, England and Ireland 'by itself in the ocean divided from the rest of the world', whereby 'the queen of England should be the strongest princess of Christendom upon the seas'.[37]

Elizabeth politely rejected this marriage proposal, but she did reluctantly bow to the urgings of her ministers for military intervention in Scotland. An English army arrived in March and besieged the main French base at Leith. Although the siege was unsuccessful, the treaty of Edinburgh in July 1560 secured the withdrawal of both English and French troops from Scotland, leaving the Lords of the Congregation in control. They moved quickly to consolidate their position. When parliament met in August, political and religious issues were intertwined. Even the staunchly Catholic earl of Huntly supported the Lords of the Congregation against the threat of French domination. The Reformation parliament was also signally well attended: with no less than 101 lairds present, most of them Protestant (lairds had rarely attended in such numbers before), plus 6 bishops, 21 commendators, 14 earls, 19 lords and 23 burgh commissioners. Despite the prohibition by the king and queen on any discussion of religion there, parliament passed three major religious acts: the acceptance of a Reformed Confession of Faith, the abrogation of papal authority, and a prohibition on celebrating mass. The Reformed Confession was a clear and positive statement of faith of the new church. It reduced the sacraments to two, baptism and holy communion; it denied transubstantiation, but retained a belief in the real presence, and it ended with a firm statement about the elect and the reprobate which, however, fell somewhat short of the developed Calvinist doctrine of predestination. It also said surprisingly little about papistical errors or superstition.[38]

Yet the 1560 parliament did nothing to build a new church in accordance with these principles. It simply destroyed the old. In part, this was because of disagreements over the draft of a *Book of Reformation* which the Congregation had commissioned in April. What eventually emerged from the committee of ministers established to revise it is now known as the *First Book of Discipline*, which was approved by a convention of nobles and lairds in January 1561.

37 A.H. Williamson, 'Scotland, Antichrist and the invention of Great Britain' in J. Dwyer, R.A. Mason and A. Murdoch (eds), *New perspectives on the politics and culture of early modern Scotland* (Edinburgh, 1988), pp. 38–42 (quotations, p. 41); Dawson, *The politics of religion in the age of Mary, queen of Scots*, pp. 96–104.
38 Wormald, *Court, kirk, and community*, pp. 117–21; Lynch, *Scotland*, p. 197.

(A *Second Book* followed in 1578 which was much more precise in regard to [145] ecclesiastical organisation.) The *Book* claimed for the reformed kirk all the revenues which had previously been available to the pre-Reformation kirk, with the exception of monastic temporalities which had fallen into lay hands and which the laity now clung onto. The lay convention accepted this on condition that existing clergy should enjoy their livings for life in return for their formal acceptance of the Reformation. In practice, however, there was no way of compelling recalcitrant Catholic clergy to surrender their benefices. A further compromise (the Thirds of Benefices) was agreed with Queen Mary in 1562, whereby all benefice holders were required to surrender a third of their incomes which would be divided between the crown and the kirk for the support of its ministry. In 1573, there was a third attempt to solve the problem. In practice, however, the kirk only secured control of much church wealth as the old Catholic clergy died out.[39]

At parish level, the *Book of Discipline* prescribed that each congregation should have annually-elected lay elders, who would exercise fraternal discipline over the congregation and, if necessary, 'admonish' or 'correct' their minister. The parish ministry comprised ministers, who were qualified to preach and administer the sacraments, and readers who might read the 'common prayers' or homilies (from the English *Book of Homilies*). Initially, too, there were exhorters who were authorised to preach and so could conduct the whole of a normal Sunday service, but these disappeared in the early 1570s. Above this congregational level, however, the *Book of Discipline* was much vaguer about any supreme organ of government. In other circumstances, a godly prince might have exercised a royal supremacy as in the Church of England. In practice, there was initially a General Assembly, which began as a quasi-parliament of clergy and godly magnates, and which had oversight over the superintendents or bishops of the church. The bishops were themselves preachers with oversight over the clergy and congregations of their regions.

The reformers argued that there were three marks 'by which the true kirk is discerned from the false': the Word, the Sacraments and Discipline (its polity, or constitution, as described above). The Word (in particular, preaching) and the Sacraments formed the content of church services, which aimed to strike a balance between the two. The aim was to avoid the separation of

---

39   J.K. Cameron (ed.), *The first Book of Discipline* (Edinburgh, 1972); Donaldson, *Scotland*, pp. 102–6, 143–4; Heal, *Reformation in Britain and Ireland*, pp. 364–5, 369–72; Wormald, *Court, kirk, and community*, pp. 130–1.

preaching and the sacraments which had characterised the pre-Reformation church, and also to restore communion as a corporate action in which the whole congregation (not just the priest) participated. Ideally, these requirements suggested a regular Sunday Eucharist, with a sermon and the reading of common prayers. In practice, the reformers were unable to eradicate the medieval practice of infrequent lay communion, with the result that communion services were held quarterly or biennially, and the regular Sunday service consisted of a general confession, psalms, Bible readings, a sermon, followed by bidding prayers, and concluding with the Lord's Prayer and Apostles' Creed.[40] This form of service was in fact that laid down by the English prayer book, which was quite widely used in Scotland – initially, at least, because no other vernacular service book was available. In 1562 (and again in 1564), however, the General Assembly had authorised for use *The Book of Common Order* which had been devised by Knox and the English exiles in Geneva and which was now printed for the first time in Scotland. Essentially, *The Book of Common Order* retained the content of the English prayer book (which for some time continued in use alongside it), although the liturgy and form of words was much less rigid.

Overall, the Scottish Reformation developed in a very different manner from the predominantly state-sponsored reform movement of the Tudor territories. Essentially, it was the product of a nationalist revolt, a revolution, against growing French domination. Its success also represented a defeat for the monarchy and the power of the state. By contrast, the Tudor Reformation reflected both in its origins and development the growing power of the monarchy, notably in the royal supremacy. Despite these dissimilarities, however, the Reformation movement in the British Isles not only led by the 1560s to the establishment of two Protestant regimes; but at least in doctrine and liturgy, the reformed churches of the three kingdoms also exhibited a degree of unity or congruity which belied their different origins. The content of the two prayer books was similar; and the churches also shared a reformed theology. Even as regards discipline, the Scottish kirk had initially retained conforming bishops as superintendents, and some new bishops were subsequently appointed.[41] In part, of course, this congruity reflected an earlier Scottish dependence on English service books, and some interchange of personnel – Scots like John Knox and John Willock, who had served the

---

40 Donaldson, *Scottish Reformation*, chs 4–6 (quotation, p. 78); Kirk, *Patterns of reform*, pp. 334–49.
41 Donaldson, *Scottish Reformation*, pp. 49, 83–4, 89, 180–81; Kirk, *Patterns of reform*, pp. 75–6, 298–304, 332, 338.

English church under Edward VI, Englishmen like Christopher Goodman, [1 4 7] appointed minister of Ayr and then St Andrews.[42] Yet the essential difference was the royal supremacy of the Elizabethan church. Elizabeth used this to impose a degree of uniformity in accordance with her own preferences which was not found in the Scottish kirk. Thus, the Christian year and holy days (retained by Elizabeth) were officially disregarded by Scottish reformers; but even so the observance of Lent was enforced by law, kirk sessions frequently mentioned holy days by name, and the Kalendar was printed in successive editions of *The Book of Common Order*. The English prayer book was officially maintained in the Elizabethan church, but was not prohibited in Scotland. And there were certain ceremonial differences: kneeling for communion, wafer bread, and the priestly vestments, which were retained in England.

Even as regards the requirements imposed by the Elizabethan acts of supremacy and uniformity and the injunctions, however, the differences were initially *de jure* only and not necessarily observed in practice. As we shall see, in the parishes a wide variety of religious practices prevailed throughout the British Isles: it was only gradually that a measure of uniformity was imposed on the Elizabethan church. Moreover, it should be remembered that considerable variation in the performance of the prayer book services was legally permitted by the Elizabethan settlement, particularly in the Church of Ireland. Even the Welsh church had services in Welsh. It is also far from clear that, had Scotland had a godly prince, he would not have imposed similar requirements on the kirk in regard to *adiaphora* (things indifferent), citing similar considerations of public order.[43] Indeed, once he reached his majority, James VI soon tried to recover some lost ground in this sphere; but by then these differences had hardened, and the task was much more difficult.

Yet in 1560 the main issue still remained to be decided. The two Protestant regimes had only recently taken power, and neither the Scottish nor the Tudor Reformation was at that point secure. The struggle to consolidate control in the parishes and to build Protestant nations from the subjects of the Tudor and Stewart monarchies was only just beginning.

---

42   Kirk, *Patterns of reform*, pp. 91–3, 105–6; Donaldson, *Scottish Reformation*, pp. 155–75.
43   Kirk, *Patterns of reform*, pp. 334–41; Donaldson, *Scottish Reformation*, ch. 7.

THE REFORMATION CRISIS
Reform in the parishes

'The polities of the best reformed kirks': Scotland

Given the particular circumstances in which the Scottish Reformation had originated – quite different from the centralised campaign mounted by a Tudor, but owing much more to local initiative and more akin to the popular movements in some territories of the Holy Roman Empire – it is no surprise that the further development of reform in Scotland was on rather different lines from the Tudor experience. Despite these fundamental differences, however, Scottish and Tudor divines also faced a range of common problems in building their churches. Those of the royal supremacy and prescribed external forms of worship, for instance, were in the event tackled in different ways, but decisions taken in regard to the one kingdom also had a habit of intruding on the pattern of reform in the other. The legal basis of the Scottish reformed kirk was the three acts of the Reformation parliament together with the *Book of Discipline* as endorsed by the General Assembly and, in some sense, tolerated by Queen Mary. These appropriated for the reformed kirk the resources of the pre-Reformation church, providing the kirk with a body of doctrine, a ministry and constitution, and also financial resources. Yet, while a proclamation forbad 'any alteration or innovation in the state of religion . . . found public and universally standing at Her Majesty's arrival', Mary refused to ratify the acts of the 1560 parliament. Moreover, existing Catholic clergy retained their livings for life (minus the thirds of benefices) in return for a nominal acceptance of the Reformation; the religious houses continued until the monks died out in the 1570s; and initially too the queen's chapel at Holyrood also encouraged Catholic sympathies around Edinburgh.[1] Thus, even though the mass and papal authority

---

1 Donaldson, *Scottish Refomation*, ch. 3 (quotation, p. 67); Wormald, *Mary queen of Scots*, pp. 109, 112; Kirk, *Patterns of reform*, ch. 9 (quotation, p. 334).

were proscribed by law, in practice, two churches existed side by side [149] throughout the 1560s. It was only gradually, and thanks largely to local initiatives, that the reformers gained the upper hand.

Initially, the towns had played a key role as bastions of the reformed faith. In 1560, there was little by way of a regular ministry outside the towns, although the influence of local lairds was often vital in persuading towns to accept reform. During the next decade the reformed church developed an effective presence along the east coast south of Aberdeen, in the central Lowlands, and in more accessible parts of the south-west and the borders, but progress elsewhere was much slower. Nominally, the church had around 1,080 parishes: by late 1561 a resident ministry had been provided for just 240 parishes; by 1567 there were around 850 clergy; and by 1574 just over 1,000.[2] Yet these figures are not really comparable with those for the Tudor church. The Scottish church was initially crippled by a lack of money to support its ministers, and progress also depended on a series of local reformations. As we shall see, the Elizabethan authorities accepted almost anyone who would serve, in a bid to provide some kind of ministry no matter how unsatisfactory. The kirk was much more discriminating: over a quarter, and in some areas a half, of the pre-Reformation clergy agreed to serve in the reformed church, but only around half of these converts were found sufficiently qualified to be admitted as ministers, who might preach and minister the sacraments. The average Scottish minister was probably more committed and effective in advancing reform than his Tudor counterpart. Many of these converts were indeed senior clergy, including three bishops (who were allowed to continue as bishops) and many heads of religious houses. The rest were only accepted as readers, with strictly limited pastoral functions. The General Assembly viewed them with some suspicion. Some said mass in private while using the reformed rite in public. Yet the corollary was that many parts remained without ministers. It took time for the universities to train a graduate preaching ministry, as in England, and even with resident ministers the pace of reform was slow in the average Lowland parish of around 600 inhabitants. After 1567 many more readers were recruited, notably from the religious houses of the old church. In 1574 over three-quarters of all parishes were served by a reader rather than a minister. Over the country as a whole, there was one minister for every three or four parishes: it was another 30 years before most parishes had their own

2 Cowan, *Scottish Reformation*, pp. 159, 162, 170; Kirk, *Patterns of reform*, p. 130; Whyte, *Scotland before the industrial revolution*, p. 98.

ministers.[3] In the Highlands, however, progress was much slower. The General Assembly was informed in 1562 that 'the north country for the most part was destitute of ministers'; and despite steady advances thereafter, large parts of the western Highlands and Islands remained without ministers into the seventeenth century. The first appointments to Hebridean parishes were not until 1609.[4]

Even where the Reformation had early established a strong presence, however, many parts exhibited a tenacious loyalty to the old church. Very often the attitude of local landowners proved crucial. In parts of Ayrshire, for instance, the earls of Cassillis and Eglinton and the abbot of Crossraguel maintained the mass and protected Catholics, despite the reforming initiatives of the earl of Glencairn. In 1561, Cassillis attended preaching on Sunday and mass on Monday. Yet by 1564, the abbot had died after leasing Crossraguel to Cassillis who, on his marriage in 1566, undertook 'to reform his churches in Carrick'; and by 1567 four of Crossraguel's five kirks had Protestant services, as opposed to just one before the earl's reforms. The Catholic earls of Errol and Huntly likewise opposed reform in Aberdeenshire. In the 1560s, 85 out of 91 parishes in Aberdeenshire had reformed service, but in the 1580s Protestant incumbents faced physical violence in some parishes and Jesuit activity was widespread.[5] Even in Edinburgh, there were more Catholics than Protestants in 1565. In 1563 and again in 1569 many priests were prosecuted for saying mass. Saying mass became a capital offence in 1567, but apparently only two people were executed for this crime. In 1600 it was thought that around a third of the nobility and gentry were Catholics. Yet a distinction needs to be made between occasional illicit masses or private worship in noble households and more thoroughgoing attempts to revive Catholic worship. Of the latter, the only notable instance occurred in Ayrshire at Easter 1563 with the public celebration of mass at Kirkoswald and Maybole by Archbishop Hamilton, protected from disruption by an armed force led by local lairds.[6]

3 Donaldson, *Scottish Reformation*, pp. 85–6; Lynch, *Scotland*, pp. 198–9, 201; I.B. Cowan, *Regional aspects of the Scottish Reformation* (London, 1978), pp. 33–4; Goodare, *State and society in early modern Scotland*, p. 176; Whyte, *Scotland before the industrial revolution*, pp. 105, 107; John Knox, *The history of the reformation of religion within the realm of Scotland* (ed. C.J. Guthrie; Edinburgh, 1982), pp. 229, 235.

4 Kirk, *Patterns of reform*, pp. 130, 152–3; Lynch, *Scotland*, p. 198; Cowan, *Regional aspects of the Scottish Reformation*, pp. 33–4 (quotation, p. 34).

5 Cowan, *Regional aspects of the Scottish Reformation*, pp. 30, 35; Kirk, *Patterns of reform*, pp. 142, 153; Wormald, *Court, kirk and community*, p. 133.

6 Donaldson, *Scotland*, p. 153; Wormald, *Court, kirk and community*, p. 133; Whyte, *Scotland before the industrial revolution*, p. 104.

In more conservative regions, however, the situation was even less satisfactory. In Berwickshire throughout the 1560s mass was still being celebrated in a large number of parish churches, and the nominally-conforming incumbents were in 1569 summoned before the privy council. In Dumfriesshire and Kirkcudbrightshire, Lord Maxwell's influence prevented the introduction of a reformed ministry for many years. Systematic resistance was organised by the schoolmaster of Dumfries, who was minister at Caerlaverock, and by the abbot of New Abbey, where a high altar still stood and mass was regularly celebrated: in 1579 they were charged with 'enticing the people to papistry'. Exceptionally for the Lowlands, Catholicism lingered on in these conditions into the seventeenth century. The same was true in Aberdeenshire, under the patronage of the Huntly family.[7] Ironically, however, the advance of reform in more remote parts was powerfully assisted by the conformity of three pre-Reformation bishops there. Already in 1561, Bishop Alexander Gordon's efforts in Galloway had promoted a reformed ministry some 30 strong, and the Reformation quickly took root. In the Highlands, the kirk faced an even more uphill struggle, but in Orkney and Shetland, despite initial resistance, Bishop Adam Bothwell had by 1567 secured a Protestant incumbent for nearly every church in his diocese. And by that date too, Bishop Robert Stewart had established 11 ministers in Caithness.[8] Yet, as in Ireland, many chiefs saw the Reformation as a threat to their way of life, and there was also an acute shortage of Gaelic-speaking ministers. From the isles, pilgrimages were made to Irish shrines, and it was reported of the Clan Donald stronghold of Islay in 1615 'that the religion that the country people has here amongst them is popish'. The kirk was further hampered by a Jesuit mission, mounted from the late 1570s by the Scottish college at Douai, which revived Catholicism in certain parts. There was even, from 1619, an Irish Franciscan mission conducted from Louvain among the Catholic clans of the western Highlands. Intermittent missionary activity, Protestant as well as Catholic, was to determine the eventual outcome in these districts during the seventeenth and early eighteenth centuries. Yet Catholic missionaries were too few in numbers to affect the overall pattern of reform in Scotland.[9]

7 Cowan, *Regional aspects of the Scottish Reformation*, pp. 32, 35; Whyte, *Scotland before the industrial revolution*, p. 105.

8 Cowan, *Regional aspects of the Scottish Reformation*, pp. 33–4; Donaldson, *Scottish Reformation*, pp. 86–8; Kirk, *Patterns of reform*, pp. 153, 317.

9 Cowan, *Regional aspects of the Scottish Reformation*, pp. 33–4; Whyte, *Scotland before the industrial revolution*, p. 105; C. Giblin, *The Irish Franciscan mission to Scotland, 1619–1646* (Dublin, 1964).

[1 5 2]   Nonetheless, as the Reformation took hold in the parishes, a visibly different kirk developed from that south of the border, one in which liturgical
practice and church government were much more in tune with practice in
'the best reformed churches' of continental Europe. The key difference was
that, with no 'godly prince' at hand in Scotland to temper the pattern and
pace of reform, the new church enjoyed remarkable freedom to abandon as it
thought fit medieval accretions which, as was argued, had no firm foundation in scripture and to promote instead practices more attuned to the order
of the primitive church. Thus, ceremonies such as the celebration of saints'
days, the sign of the cross in baptism, episcopal confirmation of children,
funeral sermons, distinctive outdoor clerical attire and the white surplice and
cope, even the use of organs, were discontinued. Ministers wore only the
black teaching gown, parishioners sat for communion receiving ordinary
bread, and burials took place 'without all kinds of ceremony'.

The same, more radical approach was apparent in regard to church government where the traditional names and offices of archbishop, bishop,
archdeacon, dean, cathedral dignities – the superstructure of the medieval
church – were jettisoned in a bid to concentrate resources on the parish.
The 13 pre-Reformation dioceses were replaced by differently-configured
provinces assigned to superintendents – 10 were envisaged, but financial
exigencies meant that only 5 were ever appointed, and the 3 conforming
bishops were recognised as commissioners along with a number of other
ministers commissioned as overseers. Even so, the measures for oversight of
the 1,080 parishes in Scotland still compared favourably with the English
provision of only 26 sees for 10,000 parishes. Likewise, the legislative
activities of provincial councils and diocesan synods, with the episcopal and
archidiaconal courts, were superseded by a series of reformed courts (congregational kirk session, superintendent's court, provincial synod, general
assembly). Discipline was now maintained by elders and the graded series of
church courts, primarily through mutual censuring and fraternal correction,
instead of by bishops and archdeacons, with excommunication now a last
resort.[10] In consequence, not only was a clear distinction established in the
1560s between church and state, but the ecclesiastical authorities were able
to push ahead with 'a thorough and speedy reformation' in the parishes
'without tarrying for the magistrate' (as was objected of Elizabeth's efforts to
maintain a church with 'an English face' and the magistrate's discretionary
power in external forms of worship). Thus, the whole impetus for reform in

10   Kirk, *Patterns of reform*, pp. 334–46 (quotation, pp. 334, 338); Donaldson, *Scottish Reformation*,
      pp. 111–13.

Scotland was quite different from that in Elizabethan England: on the one hand, conservative landowners, sometimes supported by Catholic clergy, were able to obstruct the reform process in a way which Elizabeth as supreme governor would never have tolerated; but where the kirk could operate freely reform in the parishes was generally a speedier and more wholesale process.

Nevertheless, once James VI came of age in the mid-1580s, affording the prospect of a 'godly prince' in Scotland for the first time, the question of relations between church and state was necessarily revisited. Already in 1574, the regent had extracted an oath from the clergy acknowledging the king as 'supreme governor of the realm, as well in things temporal as in the conservation and purgation of religion'. This statement of royal power over the church was the signal for a prolonged dispute between the king and the Presbyterians over the 'polity', or structure, of the Scottish church. As a youth, James had had as tutor George Buchanan, a leading exponent of limited monarchy, and in particular the right of the 'people' (by which was meant the aristocracy) to depose wicked monarchs. James remained unconvinced, however. Nor was he much impressed when Andrew Melville argued that:

> There is Christ Jesus, the King, and his Kingdom the Kirk, whose subject King James the Sixth is, and of whose Kingdom not a King, nor a Lord, nor a Head, but a Member.

James disliked Presbyterian arguments for two reasons. First, their ministers claimed the right to correct the king not just in spiritual matters but in temporal too, on the grounds that the kingdom of God was superior to any earthly kingdom. Second, Presbyterian notions of a parity among ministers had much wider implications for the social hierarchy, extending even to the ousting of divine-right monarchy by a more democratic system of government. In the circumstances, James's preference was for an episcopal system of government, with ecclesiastical legislation in parliament (where he could control it) rather than an independent general assembly. To begin with, however, James was on the defensive, forced to make concessions, but leaving the way open for the introduction of something akin to an Elizabethan system of church government if opportunity served. In 1578 the General Assembly had adopted a programme aimed at replacing bishops by presbyteries. The king sanctioned the introduction of presbyteries in 1586, but only on condition that bishops were permanent moderators of presbyteries and synods. In 1592 this Presbyterian system received statutory recognition, by which time bishops had almost died out, although they were never abolished.[11]

11 Donaldson, *Scottish Reformation*, pp. 144 (quotation), 203–5, 216–19; idem, *Scotland*, pp. 148–50, 172, 187, 194–200; Wormald, *Court, kirk, and community*, pp. 128–30, 146–8.

For a long time, the dispute with the Presbyterians hung in the balance. In 1584, in the reaction following the defeat of the Ruthven raiders, the king seized his opportunity to pass the 'Black Acts' which asserted the power of the king over all persons and estates, denounced 'the new pretended presbyteries' and reaffirmed the authority of bishops. Despite renewed pressure, the king never conceded that ecclesiastical assemblies could meet without his authority (and so legislate), and the 1592 act allowed only one general assembly per annum – at a time and place to be nominated by the king. In 1596, he began to tamper with the assembly (convening it in conservative Perth, instead of Edinburgh where Melville's supporters would be in a majority), and the following year he got the assembly to agree that ministers should only be appointed to the chief towns with the king's consent. In 1604, he prorogued it for a year, and then indefinitely; and none at all met after 1618.[12]

The other way in which James hoped to extend his influence over the church was by the restoration of bishops. The question arose in regard to the church having a voice in parliament, by which the Presbyterians understood the intrusion of ecclesiastical commissioners, in place of the extinct lords spiritual, but James saw as an excuse for bishops: 'Busk him as bonnily as ye can', warned the Presbyterians, 'and bring him in as fairly as ye will, we see him well enough. We see the horns of his mitre.' Nonetheless, using powers which had not been exercised since the early Reformation period, James first convoked a convention of (well-picked) delegates of synods to secure approval, and then in 1600 he appointed by letters patent three titular bishops of Aberdeen, Ross and Caithness (in the conservative north). An act of 1606 'for the restitution of the estate of bishops' aimed to recover episcopal temporalities (finance). Initially, these 'parliamentary bishops', as they were called, had seats in parliament but no role in the church. The king soon moved to rectify this, however. In the north, the Presbyterian organisation was ineffective, so allowing the intrusion of bishops as commissioners of their dioceses without disruption. In 1606, a nominated assembly was intimidated into accepting 'constant moderators' of the presbyteries, viz. that the bishops should act as chairmen. In advance of this, Andrew Melville and seven other ministers were summoned to London for consultations and detained: Melville went to the Tower, and then into exile where he died in

---

12   Donaldson, *Scottish Reformation*, pp. 210–14; Donaldson, *Scotland*, pp. 181, 198–201, 204, 207; Wormald, *Court, kirk, and community*, pp. 128–30.

1622. Subsequently, the king had the minutes of the assembly rewritten so that it appeared to consent to constant moderators of synods as well, i.e. diocesan episcopacy. Finally, in 1610, episcopal consecration and an apostolic succession were restored by sending the three Scottish bishops to Westminster for ordination by English bishops. In this way, by gradually adding to episcopal functions in church and state, the king had recreated something closer to the Anglican system − a mixed polity, a combination of bishops with presbyteries jointly operating kirk sessions. In fact, most of the ministers regarded the new system as a restoration of early Reformation practice, and only a few doctrinaire Melvillians held out against compromise.[13]

Having restored diocesan episcopacy, James began a series of liturgical changes. In 1614 a royal proclamation ordered the celebration of holy communion at Easter, while in 1615 all colleges were ordered to use *The Book of Common Prayer* for certain parts of their services. The University of St Andrews was likewise ordered to observe the greater festivals of the Christian Year. Various other proposals then surfaced for a new liturgy, a book of canons, a confession of faith and catechism, and the observance of Easter, but the king encountered much opposition. In 1618, James pushed through the Five Articles of Perth in the teeth of opposition. These prescribed kneeling for communion, the observance of the Christian Year (holy days to be kept at Christmas, Good Friday, Easter, Ascension Day and Whit Sunday), and the restoration of private communion, private baptism and confirmation. There was widespread refusal to accept them and a dozen ministers were eventually deprived for non-conformity. James had planned to go even further, with the introduction of a new liturgy based on *The Book of Common Prayer*, but he realised that he had gone too far, and in return for the ratification by parliament of the Five Articles in 1621, he promised that there would be no more innovations, and he kept his word. As has recently been argued, what James aimed at was not a straight copy of the Anglican system but 'congruity', a mutual acceptance by the two churches respectively of the credentials of the other as a reformed church, with toleration of diversity on non-essentials.[14]

13   Donaldson, *Scotland*, pp. 201–7 (quotation, pp. 202, 205); idem, *Scottish Reformation*, pp. 220–25; Wormald, *Court, kirk, and community*, pp. 128–30; John Morrill, 'A British patriarchy? Ecclesiastical imperialism under the early Stuarts' in A.J. Fletcher and Peter Roberts (eds), *Religion, culture and society in early modern Britain: essays in honour of Patrick Collinson* (Cambridge, 1994), pp. 216–18.
14   Donaldson, *Scotland*, pp. 208–11; Morrill, 'A British patriarchy?', pp. 214–21.

Change and continuity in the Tudor church

Particularly in regard to the liturgy, King James's innovations in the Scottish church reflected his appreciation of the particular direction in which the Elizabethan church had since developed. In the event, the statutory phase of Tudor reform had come to an unexpected close with the enactment of the Elizabethan settlement in 1559. Apart from Elizabeth herself, almost no one had anticipated this. The settlement had pleased very few: most conservatives saw it as blatantly heretical, while reformers were irked by Elizabeth's retention of many ceremonies which they saw as inappropriate in a reformed church. For her part, Elizabeth's difficulty was that the religious middle ground which Henry VIII had adeptly exploited, and to which she was instinctively disposed, had since collapsed. Mary's English bishops had solidly opposed the settlement in the 1559 parliament, and subsequently refused to serve. To steer the bills through parliament, conservative amendments had been needed so as to detach the bishops' lay supporters. Yet for Protestants, the concessions then made had reduced the settlement to the absolute minimum which they could accept with a good conscience. Indeed, it was widely expected that the settlement would shortly collapse through its own inadequacies. Protestants argued for further reform, particularly in regard to the prayer book, so as to purge the church of the remaining dregs of popery: Catholics expected that strife and divisions in the reformed camp would soon lead to a restoration of the old faith.[15]

Yet statutory enactment was only the first stage in a wider programme to implement the changes and to secure popular assent at local level for the Elizabethan settlement. This enforcement of the Reformation in the parishes proved to be an extremely long-drawn-out affair which sapped the regime's energies in other directions for most of the reign. Moreover, although for almost 30 years the popular response to change had been a serious source of concern to successive Tudor monarchs, it was only under Elizabeth that the full dimensions of this problem became apparent. There were a number of reasons for this. In the first place, the earlier changes had been piecemeal. The reforms introduced by Henry VIII as Supreme Head had indeed sparked widespread unrest, notably the Pilgrimage of Grace which engulfed northern England in 1536–7. Yet the government had early on become aware of widespread and mounting concern among the lower orders and political nation alike at the direction of royal policy, and throughout the 1530s mounted a vigorous and generally effective campaign of propaganda –

15   Jones, *Faith by statute*, passim.

essentially the first such news management campaign in British history – so as to counteract popular unrest. This had aimed to convince different audiences with a range of pamphlets issued by the king's printer, Thomas Berthelet. Altogether, there were over a dozen, ranging from Bishop Stephen Gardiner's *De vera obedientia* (1535), for intellectuals both home and abroad; to the popular tract, *A little treatise against the muttering of some papists in corners* (1534); and *A remedy for sedition* (1536) which was written by Richard Morison specifically against the Pilgrimage of Grace. Conversely, dissidents who had hoped to exploit the press to publicise the case for Catholic orthodoxy found their efforts blocked. The English presses were simply unavailable. Queen Catherine's chaplain, Thomas Abell, had his pamphlet, *Invicta veritas* (1532) printed abroad and smuggled in; but this was the only anti-government pamphlet throughout the 1530s to escape the government's vigilance, and Abell was soon imprisoned in the Tower and attainted. These official pamphlets were also backed by proclamations informing the king's subjects of the government's view of recent developments and by circular letters to local officials exhorting them to vigilance and to report and arrest dissidents. The 1534 Treasons Act, moreover, extended the definition of treason to those who spoke out against the royal supremacy, and other related statutes with long justificatory preambles were also printed to ensure wider circulation.

Altogether, between 1532 and 1540 it has been calculated that 883 people in England and Wales were charged with treason for opposing the regime: and of these, 308 (or around 38 per cent) were eventually executed. It is going too far, however, to claim that the 1530s witnessed a 'reign of terror'. Most of the victims were executed in the aftermath of major rebellion (178 of them after the Pilgrimage of Grace and the Lincolnshire Rising), or were the victims of high dynastic politics. The policy failures which resulted in the principled stand and subsequent execution of leading Catholics, like Sir Thomas More and Bishop John Fisher, were very much the exception to the rule. Nonetheless, 63 people died a traitor's death at this time for speaking words against the royal supremacy.[16]

For the most part, however, men grumbled in private or, like most English humanists, chose to see in the king's eccentric behaviour an opportunity for long-needed reform of the church. And in any case, throughout Henry VIII's reign, Sunday by Sunday priests had continued to celebrate mass in Latin in their parish churches according to the established Sarum Use, and the traditional observances of the ritual year had also continued much as

---

16 G.R. Elton, *Policy and police: the enforcement of the Reformation in the age of Thomas Cromwell* (Cambridge, 1972).

before. More fundamental changes had begun under Edward VI, but again in a piecemeal and gradual manner. The introduction of the English prayer book in 1549 had once again sparked off insurrections, particularly the risings in Devon and Cornwall, with other rebellions in Oxfordshire and Buckinghamshire, and also in Yorkshire. But after that, things had quietened down. The government began a new round of changes, with the Edwardian Ordinal in 1550, and a revised prayer book in 1552. Moreover, outside Lowland England, where the administrative machinery was more formidable but popular support for reform was also stronger, actual enforcement of changes was tardy and partial: the minority regimes of Edward's reign were much less regarded than Henry VIII had been. Throughout Armagh diocese, for instance, mass and traditional ceremonies continued as before until at least August 1551 because of Archbishop Dowdall's blank refusal to implement any of the Edwardian reforms.[17] In any case, the most far-reaching and controversial changes were only sanctioned in Edward's final few months when the regime was distracted by more urgent issues.

It was, accordingly, relatively easy for the Marian authorities to secure the restoration of traditional Catholicism and full communion with Rome. However we interpret the evidence for Protestant activity in the mid-Tudor period (altogether the names of c.3,000 suspected Protestants are known for the period 1525–58), it is clear that on Mary's accession Protestants comprised only a small fraction of her subjects. Protestantism was strongest in some of the largest towns, notably London, Norwich, Ipswich, Bristol and Coventry, and in some smaller port or cloth towns, but it was concentrated in the south-east, in an arc from Norfolk round to Sussex, with a spur from London up the Thames valley. Its geographical distribution is apparent from the incidence of burnings for heresy under Mary. There were at least 282 (including 51 women), with 67 victims in London, 11 in Middlesex, 39 in Essex, 58 in Kent, 23 in Sussex, 18 in Suffolk and 14 in Norfolk. Apart from 10 victims burned in Gloucester, very few were burned in western England, only 1 throughout the north, just 3 in Wales, and none at all in Ireland.[18]

In some parts, the burnings excited popular sympathy for the victims, and they were clearly a political mistake, but no one would argue that in consequence Protestantism was any more entrenched on Elizabeth's accession than it had been on Edward's death. Thus Elizabeth's decision in 1559 to

17 Henry Jefferies, *Priests and people of Armagh in the age of Reformations, 1518–1558* (Dublin, 1997), pp. 158–9, 163.
18 Haigh, *English Reformations*, pp. 194–202, 230–4; Dickens, *English Reformation*, p. 295; Williams, *Recovery, reorientation and Reformation*, p. 303.

implement sweeping changes virtually overnight faced the government in a particularly acute form with a range of problems which had previously exercised it only intermittently. The government's basic difficulty stemmed from the nature of the settlement itself, together with the machinery available for its enforcement. In effect, the Elizabethan settlement prescribed a church which was doctrinally Protestant but liturgically Catholic. For the theologically learned, the Thirty-Nine Articles upheld such typically Protestant tenets as predestination, justification by faith and the sufficiency of holy scripture for salvation, and they rejected traditional Catholic teaching on transubstantiation, purgatory and the efficacy of good works. Yet, in other respects, things continued much as before: the Elizabethan prayer book was essentially an English translation of the Sarum Use of the pre-Reformation church in the English territories, albeit with small – though theologically significant – changes, particularly in the communion service, designed to prevent priests from 'counterfeiting' the mass. The church also continued to be governed through the traditional three-fold ministry (bishops, priests and deacons) and ecclesiastical structures, with bishops ruling dioceses (supported by archdeacons, deans and cathedral chapters), and rectors and vicars (financed chiefly by church tithes) in charge of parishes, assisted – particularly in the case of dependant chapels – by stipendiary curates. And the terms of this latest Elizabethan settlement continued to be enforced by the ponderous visitation machinery of the medieval church. Regular visitations were designed to detect infringements and shortcomings of all kinds: the clergy, churchwardens and parishioners were sworn to make presentments in response to sets of injunctions and articles of inquiry read by the visitors; and subsequently delinquents were hauled up before the traditional church courts, still administering medieval canon law, and threatened with suspension or excommunication for offences detected at visitation. Among the laity, those who failed to attend church on Sundays and holy days were to forfeit 12 pence per Sunday, to be levied by the churchwardens for the relief of the poor. Overall, in terms of its ministry, administrative structures and funding mechanism, the Elizabethan church exhibited a striking continuity with the institutions of the pre-Reformation church which was far removed from the practice of the best reformed churches.[19] And this conservatism

19   On the nature of the Elizabethan settlement, see for instance, Christopher Haigh, *English Reformations: religion, politics, and society under the Tudors* (Oxford, 1993), chs 14–16; Claire Cross, *The Royal Supremacy in the Elizabethan church* (London, 1969); W.P. Haugaard, *Elizabeth and the English Reformation: the struggle for a stable settlement of religion* (Cambridge, 1968); Norman Jones, *The birth of the Elizabethan age: England in the 1560s* (Oxford, 1993), ch. 3.

soon alienated the more radical Protestants who called for further changes to purify the church of the remaining dregs of popery: the preacher, John Field, for instance, denounced the Elizabethan settlement as 'a certain kind of religion, framed out of man's own brain and fantasy, far worse than that of popery (if worse may be), patched and pieced out of theirs and ours together'.[20]

At the same time, however, at local level the injunctions issued by Elizabeth in July 1559, and the subsequent royal visitation which enforced the new settlement, were designed to ensure quite radical change, both in terms of the physical appearance of parish churches, 'the scenic apparatus of worship', and in many other aspects of popular religion. Essentially, the Elizabethan settlement imposed a marked shift in the presentation of religion, from traditional Catholic spectacles like the miracle of the mass, processions, images and holy pictures, to a more austere, bibliocentric approach based on Bibles and sermons. Protestantism was a religion of the Word and generally proved more attractive in the towns, among merchants and artisans where levels of literacy were higher, than among rural dwellers. The Tudor south-east was indeed more urbanised, but most of the queen's subjects lived in the countryside, particularly in Wales and the Tudor north where illiterate peasants who had no understanding of the theological issues behind this shift were needlessly alienated.

The thoroughgoing nature of the changes at which the authorities aimed may be discerned both from the injunctions and articles of inquiry – designed for 'the suppression of superstition' and 'to plant true religion' – and also the prominence among the visitors of returned Marian exiles such as Horne, Jewel and Sandys who were shortly after appointed to the episcopal bench. The visitors were instructed to investigate the state of the clergy and to require their subscription to the royal supremacy, the prayer book and the injunctions. The injunctions and articles of inquiry were largely modelled on those of Edward VI's reign: they made provision for the removal of all shrines, abused images, monuments of superstition, holy pictures and paintings. Altars were to be dismantled and replaced by communion tables, and in each church there should be provided a pulpit, a Bible and a copy of Erasmus's *Paraphrases* in English. The Edwardian *Book of Homilies* was reissued, with a homily read every Sunday unless there were a sermon. Sermons were to be preached at least once a quarter which should purely and sincerely declare the Word of God, and discourage such superstitious practices as 'offering of money, candles or tapers to relics, or images, or

20   Patrick Collinson, *Elizabethans* (London, 2003), p. 238 (quotation).

kissing and licking of the same, praying upon beads', all of which were now
forbidden, as indeed were processions about the church and churchyard and
ringing or knolling of bells during the service.

Instead, the clergy were to ensure that their parishioners learned the
Lord's Prayer, Creed and Ten Commandments in English, and they were to
instruct the youth of the parish in these and in the catechism prescribed
by the prayer book. Likewise, instead of money bestowed 'upon pardons,
pilgrimages, trentals, decking of images, offering of candles, giving to friars
and upon other like blind devotions', the parishioners' oblation and alms
should be put in a strong chest, now to be provided by every parish for the
relief of their poor neighbours, as also all profits arising from fraternities,
guilds, church flocks and moneys which had previously supported obits and
dirges, 'and the finding of torches, lights, tapers and lamps', all of which were
now proscribed. Finally, the churchwardens were to supply the visitors with
inventories of 'vestments, copes or other ornaments, plate, books and specially of grails, couchers, legends, processionals, hymnals, manuals, portuals,
and such like' – now redundant following the establishment of true religion.[21]

Enforcing the Elizabethan settlement: the opening phase

Around London and the south-east, where there were already large numbers
of Protestants, where returning exiles quickly provided the backbone of a
committed preaching ministry, and where the government had the resources
to monitor closely the enforcement of the settlement, rapid progress towards
reform was possible – although even here, conservative resistance was quite
widespread. Yet in most parts of the Tudor state, the authorities might hope,
realistically, for no more than a gradual transformation in popular religious
practice, spreading outward from the towns – where churches were wealthier,
levels of literacy higher, and social control more easily imposed – to take in
eventually even poor illiterate peasants in the 'dark corners of the land'. Any
sharp and rigid enforcement of the settlement was beyond the government's
resources and perhaps counterproductive anyway. Lacking any alternative
pool of clergy, the government could only appeal to loyalty and rely on

21 Bray (ed.), *Documents of the English Reformation*, pp. 334–48 (quotations, pp. 335, 336, 341,
    344); Eamon Duffy, *The stripping of the altars: traditional religion in England 1400–1580* (New
    Haven, 1992), pp. 568–9.

general acquiescence by existing clergy: by weeding out the recalcitrant from key positions, by introducing committed Protestants, and by weaning conservative clerics away from traditional practices through close supervision and careful instruction, the authorities might hope to establish a basic level of conformity. Yet it was not until the 1570s, when the Elizabethan church began to receive significant numbers of graduate preaching ministers trained in Oxford and Cambridge, that the real work of evangelisation could begin.

The surviving *Act Book* of the northern province of York, together with extant churchwardens accounts from elsewhere, show that the visitors aimed at a strict enforcement of the injunctions. From the outset, however, the response to the visitations was equivocal: in the northern province, only 312 of the parish clergy subscribed to the supremacy, the prayer book and the injunctions out of perhaps 1,000, although some subscribed later. In the southern province, perhaps two-thirds of the clergy subscribed. Altogether, around 300 clergy lost their benefices in the first two years of the reign, but probably an even larger number of unbeneficed clergy simply withdrew and became domestic chaplains or schoolmasters. Clearly, the Elizabethan settlement evinced no great enthusiasm among the lower clergy, but there was also a reluctance to follow the principled example of the Marian bishops.[22] In Ireland and Wales, not even the bishops were able to maintain a united front: the aged Bishop Kitchen of Llandaff subscribed, as did many of the Irish bishops. About a dozen chiefly higher clergy refused the oath in Wales. About the same number did so in English Ireland – although a number of apparently voluntary withdrawals may conceal deprivations. There may also have been a decision by the authorities not to tender the oath to clergy living outside the main English districts.[23]

Yet subscription to the settlement did not mean firm support. Everywhere the church's ministry was heavily dependant on clergy trained originally as Catholic priests, most of whom had served under three different religious settlements over the previous dozen years. Even in 1576, 37 per cent of the clergy in three Lincoln archdeaconries had been ordained before Elizabeth's reign. Indeed, one impact of the Reformation had been a marked slump in the number of recruits coming forward for the ministry: in many dioceses, for instance, ordinations dropped to a trickle between 1548, when the Edwardian reforms got under way, and 1555, when full communion with

22   Haigh, *English Reformations*, pp. 243–4; C.J. Kitching (ed.), *The royal visitation of 1559: act book for the northern province* (Surtees Soc., clxxxvii; Gateshead, 1975).
23   Ellis, *Ireland in the age of the Tudors*, pp. 228–9; Glanmor Williams, *Welsh Reformation essays* (Cardiff, 1967), ch. 6.

Rome was restored. And at best, the numbers of Protestant clerics among the returning exiles of Mary's reign did no more than balance the deprivations of Marian clergy unwilling to subscribe to the settlement.[24] There had, for instance, been 172 priests working in south Lancashire in 1554, but by 1563 only 51 of them were still serving there and there were only 98 clergy altogether. At least 21 had since died, but seemingly many more had simply withdrawn.[25] Thus, the severe shortage of clergy meant that the early Elizabethan church had to accept almost anyone willing to serve, no matter how unsatisfactory. Not surprisingly, many clergy kept as close to the old order as they could, exploiting Elizabeth's liturgical concessions to the limit. They wore the traditional vestments and retained the traditional gestures; they mumbled the English services half audibly like the old Latin ones; and they illicitly elevated the host at communion, ignoring the new rubrics which were specifically designed to prevent such 'counterfeiting the mass'.

In Ireland, moreover, conservative clergy had even more latitude: 'forasmuch as in most places of this realm, there cannot be found English ministers to serve in the churches', a special clause in the Uniformity Act permitted clergy who did not know English to use a Latin version of the prayer book.[26] This *Liber precum publicarum*, issued in 1560 – but not generally authorised for public use in England – allowed for a requiem celebration of holy communion and its reservation for the sick, and its rubrics were also in many respects more conservative. Its use may have been quite widespread: following the union of the dioceses of Meath and Clonmacnois, Bishop Brady reported in 1576 that of the 224 parish churches, 105 were served only by curates, of whom only 18 spoke English, the rest having 'very little Latin, less learning and civility'. To the unlearned, these Latin services perhaps looked reassuringly like mass. Initially, moreover, no articles of religion, akin to the English Thirty-Nine Articles, were prescribed: in 1567, Lord Deputy Sidney and the Irish bishops issued the Twelve Articles, a bland statement of reformation principles based on the English Eleven Articles of 1561 (see above, p. 137) which offered little further definition of the church's theology but yet remained the only confession of faith until 1615. In any case, the Elizabethan settlement could only be fully enforced in the main English districts. Elsewhere, even senior clergy could maintain a foot in both camps: for instance, Archbishop Bodkin of Tuam, Kilmacduagh and Annaghdown

24 Haigh, *English Reformations*, pp. 215–16, 228, 244, 248.
25 Christopher Haigh, *Reformation and resistance in Tudor Lancashire* (Cambridge, 1975), pp. 215–16.
26 2 Eliz. I c. 2 (*Stat. Ire*, i, 284–90 (quotation, p. 290)).

[1 6 4]   nominally accepted each successive settlement, but could still put on a show in his cathedral for the visiting papal nuncio in 1563 who reported that 'mass is sung and said, and he himself is daily in the choir'.[27]

Yet it was not just the clergy who gave cause for concern. In London and parts of south-east England where Protestantism had deep roots, the bonfires of roods and images which accompanied the royal visitation had some popular support; and in many parishes sympathetic locals worked with the visitors to ensure prompt and full compliance.[28] Under Edward VI, there had been widespread concealment of Catholic ornaments and books: for instance, in St Canice's cathedral, Kilkenny, at the start of Mary's reign the clergy 'brought forth their copes, candlesticks, holy water stock, cross and censers', and then a few days later suddenly set up 'the altars and images' – to the disgust of the Edwardian bishop there, John Bale. In 1559, however, the visitors hoped to extinguish all hope of a restoration of the old order by insisting on the destruction of these externals of Catholic worship and also by making diligent inquiry as to who was secretly keeping images and ornaments. Episcopal visitations in 1560 and 1561 followed up this activity.[29] In Dublin, two large Bibles supplied by the archbishop of York were erected in the cathedrals of Christ Church and St Patrick and work on repainting the cathedral walls with scriptural texts 'instead of pictures & popish fancies' began on 25 May 1560.[30]

Yet, if the authorities now insisted on the destruction of Catholic books and ornaments, local congregations were also more keenly aware of the implications of this demand: the purchase of the necessary equipment for prayer book services under Edward VI and then for mass again under Mary had proved very expensive, and neither settlement had lasted. Most parishes thus hesitated to remove and destroy Catholic ornaments, vestments and other furniture, or even to purchase the more costly items for Protestant worship. At Leigh in Lancashire, when in 1564 Bishop Downham finally insisted on the removal of all images, altars and rood lofts, the churchwardens who removed the rood and images were abused and told that 'you were

27   Haugaard, *Elizabeth and the English Reformation*, pp. 112–17, 239–42; Ellis, *Ireland in the age of the Tudors*, pp. 226–7, 230 (quotation), 233 (quotation); Alan Ford, 'The Church of Ireland, 1558–1634: a puritan church?' in idem, James McGuire and Kenneth Milne (eds) *As by law established: the Church of Ireland since the Reformation* (Dublin, 1995), pp. 57, 236 n. 40; 'The Eleven Articles', printed, Bray (ed.), *Documents of the English Reformation*, pp. 349–51.

28   Haigh, *English Reformations*, pp. 242–3.

29   Kitching (ed.), *The royal visitation of 1559*; John Bale, *The vocacyon of Johan Bale*, pp. 62, 67; Duffy, *Stripping of the altars*, pp. 570–1.

30   N.B. White (ed.), 'The annals of Dudley Loftus' in *Anal. Hib.*, x (1941), p. 235.

best now to go and paint a black devil, and set him up and worship him, for that will serve well for your religion'.[31] In London in the mid-1550s the going rate for a rood with images of Mary and John was £7, plus another £4 for images of the patron saints.[32] Even a paten to replace the one confiscated in 1553 cost the parishioners of Morebath in Devon 7s. 11d.; and when the Elizabethan settlement took effect there the parishioners paid out 4s. 4d. for a copy of *The Book of Common Prayer* and 20s. for a Bible and a copy of Erasmus's *Paraphrases*.[33] Much more expensive to buy was the communion cup: few parishes could immediately raise the £3 19s. which it cost, and many parishes preferred in any case to hold on to their chalices for as long as possible so as to make the new communion services appear more like the old mass. Very often chalices were only exchanged for cups in the 1570s under episcopal pressure.[34] It is thus hard to tell whether reluctance to change reflected more religious conservatism or financial prudence.

In general, however, churches were fitted out for prayer book services quite quickly in 1559–60, because the basic equipment needed was less elaborate and less costly than for mass. Concurrently, however, Catholic equipment was illicitly conveyed away against another change in religion. Surviving churchwardens' accounts indicate that vestments, books, and other small and costly items like pyxes, censers and sanctus bells which were readily concealed were commonly kept for over a decade. In Morebath, Devon, for instance, the missal and chasuble were immediately entrusted to parishioners for safe keeping, but the rood-loft could not be concealed and had to come down in 1562.[35] In Christ Church Cathedral, Dublin, the rood-loft still survived in 1564 when the doom tympanum was replaced by the royal coat of arms. Yet the dismantling of rood-lofts was expensive, and in the Tudor north few were removed until the 1570s.[36] Altars, images and the roods themselves were an easier target: in most parts altars were quickly replaced by communion tables, roods and images were burned, but some

31 Haigh, *Reformation and resistance in Tudor Lancashire*, p. 220.

32 Haigh, *English Reformations*, p. 211.

33 Eamon Duffy, *The voices of Morebath: Reformation and rebellion in an English village* (New Haven, 2001), pp. 160, 170–1; Haigh, *English Reformations*, pp. 246–7.

34 Robert Whiting, *The blind devotion of the people: popular religion and the English Reformation* (Cambridge, 1989), pp. 159–60; Duffy, *The voices of Morebath*, p. 178; Haigh, *English Reformations*, p. 247.

35 Duffy, *The voices of Morebath*, pp. 171–2.

36 Raymond Gillespie (ed.), *The proctor's accounts of Peter Lewis 1564–1565* (Dublin, 1996), pp. 37, 39; Ronald Hutton, 'The local impact of the Tudor Reformations' in Christopher Haigh (ed.), *The English Reformation revised* (Cambridge, 1987), pp. 135–6; Haigh, *English Reformations*, pp. 245–6.

images were merely hidden. Altar stones (and also holy-water stoups) were very often buried: in the cathedral and parish churches around Durham they were quickly re-erected during the Northern Rising.[37] By spring 1566, growing fears in Lincoln diocese of wholesale evasion of aspects of the settlement prompted a detailed inquiry there as to the fate of every image, ornament or book used in Mary's reign. The extant returns for 180 parishes show that just 45 had complied promptly with the main requirements of the Elizabethan settlement by destroying altars, images and mass books; but at least 82 parishes had evaded full compliance for over 3 years in regard to particular images, books or vestments. In general, it took over 10 years of constant pressure by the authorities to ensure that parish churches through-out England were properly equipped and decorated as prescribed in the injunctions.[38]

Poverty and the Word in the pastoral uplands

Yet Lincoln diocese lay within the English Lowland zone in which Tudor government was at its most effective: in this region of market towns and nucleated villages, parishes were generally smaller and wealthier, and this in turn meant that ecclesiastical livings were more likely to attract able, graduate clergy. Conditions for reform were much more promising in a small Lowland parish of 50 households served by a resident graduate preach-ing minister and supported by substantial churchwardens than in a large and poor upland parish. Parishes in the Tudor north, Wales and parts of Ireland were predominantly of the latter sort, however: in England as a whole the average parish had 243 communicants in 1604, but in the diocese of Chester there were 696. The average Lancashire parish contained 350 households. A similar point can be made about the value of livings. A benefice worth £13 a year, it has been estimated, provided a comfortable income in the 1530s for a rector or vicar with his 'usual' expenses; but the *Valor Ecclesiasticus* shows that half the livings in England were then worth less than £10 a year, and unbeneficed clergy generally received much less. In Wales, however, the proportion of livings worth less than £10 annually rose to 70 per cent, and in English Ireland to 85 per cent. In fact, 23 per cent of livings in Wales were wretchedly poor, worth £5 a year or less; and in

37 Haigh, *English Reformations*, pp. 245–6; Duffy, *Stripping of the altars*, pp. 570, 583–4.
38 Duffy, *Stripping of the altars*, pp. 568–74; Haigh, *English Reformations*, pp. 246–7.

English Ireland 64 per cent lay in this category.[39] Even if the authorities could readily enforce reform in Lowland England, it was quite another story elsewhere. Among the poor and dispersed communities of the pastoral uplands, the pattern was of sprawling parishes of up to 1,000 communicants served by ill-educated, barely conformist rectors, sometimes assisted by one or more stipendiary curates staffing outlying chapels of ease.

The Protestant emphasis on vernacular services, in place of the traditional, culturally-neutral Latin, also presented other difficulties outside English-speaking regions. The reformers insisted that it was 'a thing plainly repugnant to the word of God, and the custom of the primitive church, to have public prayer in church, or to minister the sacraments, in a tongue not understanded of the people'.[40] Yet for the inhabitants of about half the British Isles this vernacular was one of the Celtic languages: sermons and services in English were unintelligible. Even in Cornwall, where the authorities ignored demands for a Cornish translation of the prayer book, prayers and sermons in Cornish had still to be provided for the dwindling number of monoglot Cornish speakers in west Cornwall.[41] And everywhere, there was a great shortage of preachers: Archbishop Whitgift reckoned, in 1585, that there were only 600 livings throughout the 9,000 parishes of England and Wales that could adequately support preaching ministers. A more urgent consideration initially was to find sufficient numbers of licensed preachers to meet the requirements for quarterly sermons in each parish. In 1561, the dioceses of Llandaff and St Asaph had 5 clerics apiece able to preach, Bangor just 2. St David's, the largest diocese in Wales, had 10 by 1570, and 14 by 1583. Only in the 1590s did this problem ease: in 1592, 54 out of 144 St Asaph clergy were able to preach, 43 out of 154 in Bangor, but still only 18 out of 155 in Llandaff. Not all were able to preach in Welsh, however.[42]

The evidence for Ireland is much slighter, but clearly conditions were even worse there. Dublin and Meath dioceses contained the richest livings. In 1604 Dublin had 26 preaching ministers, but Meath had only 8, of whom just 1 could preach in Gaelic, although 2 more clergy there were able to teach in Gaelic. As the returns for the Irish *Valor* show, Irish benefices were in

39   Ellis, *Ireland in the age of the Tudors*, pp. 201–3; Haigh, *Reformation and resistance in Tudor Lancashire*, p. 231.

40   'Articles of religion agreed upon by the archbishops and bishops of both provinces and the whole clergy . . . 1562', no. 24, printed, Bray (ed.), *Documents of the English Reformation*, pp. 284–311.

41   Mark Stoyle, *West Britons: Cornish identities and the early modern British state* (Exeter, 2002), p. 46.

42   Glanmor Williams, *Wales and the Reformation* (Cardiff, 1997), pp. 226, 231, 300–1, 391.

[1 6 8] any case miserably endowed, making it difficult to attract well-qualified clergy. In the 22 dioceses for which valuations were chiefly made between 1584 and 1630, for instance, only 19 benefices (9 of them bishoprics) were returned as worth £30 sterling or more per annum – the income considered necessary for a preaching minister. The Reformation had in fact exacerbated a long-standing problem, since the proscription of certain traditional sources of income (for such things as votive candles, obits and dirges) left the clergy even poorer. In the returns for the royal visitation of 1615 (which excluded all but 2 dioceses in Armagh province), just 161 resident preachers were recorded out of 651 clergy: Dublin and Meath dioceses had 21 and 31 resident preachers respectively, but throughout the whole province of Tuam there were just 11.[43] One reason for the impoverishment of Irish livings was the disturbed conditions which persisted in many parts throughout the Tudor period. For instance, the vicarage of Ardnurcher, in the extreme south-west marches of Co. Westmeath, was of no value in time of war, but worth £50 a year in peacetime. Likewise, livings north of Carlisle in the Anglo-Scottish border region, were worthless in wartime: Bishop Nicolson recorded that many churches there 'were burned down, and the miserable incumbents of others were under a necessity of deserting their cures, flying for their lives'. At Bewcastle in 1604 the curate was lodged in the castle but was accustomed 'to say service within the walls of the church in dry weather'.[44]

A more insidious and widespread cause of dilapidation was impropriation. In Ireland, a far higher proportion of rectories (60 per cent, as opposed to roughly 40 per cent in England) had been impropriated to suppressed abbeys and religious houses, and at the Reformation they passed into the hands of lay farmers. Bishop Brady's 1576 report on Meath and Clonmacnois indicated that 105 of the 224 parishes were impropriated and served only by curates living on the bare altarages: 'in many places the very walls of the churches [were] down, very few chancels covered, windows and doors ruined and spoiled'. A generation later, these impropriations were mostly farmed by Catholic recusants who paid the curates quite inadequate

---

43 Ellis, *Ireland in the age of the Tudors*, pp. 232–4; Alan Ford, *The Protestant Reformation in Ireland, 1590–1641* (2nd ed., Dublin, 1997), ch. 4.

44 J. Caley (ed.), *Valor Ecclesiasticus temp. Henr. VIII* (6 vols., Record Commision, 1810–34), v, 287; William Nicolson, *Leges marchiarum or border-laws* (London, 1705), pp. liv–v; R.P. Sanderson (ed.), *Survey of the debateable and border lands . . . 1604* (Alnwick, 1891), p. 36; S.G. Ellis, 'Economic problems of the church: why the Reformation failed in Ireland' in *Journal of Ecclesiastical History*, xli (1990), p. 251.

stipends and failed to maintain the chancels. In fact, the 1615 visitation revealed that no less than 133 (70.7 per cent) of the rectories were impropriate. One response to the poverty of livings was to permit incumbents to hold additional livings in plurality. Yet this was in turn a major cause of non-residence. By 1615, the Church of Ireland had only around 800 clergy altogether to serve 2,492 parishes.[45]

Even more essential for vernacular services was a reliable translation of the basic texts. In Wales, a start had been made during Edward VI's reign. *Yn a llyvyr hwn* (1547), sponsored by Sir John Pryce of Brecon, was the first book printed in Welsh, and contained translations of the Ten Commandments, the Lord's Prayer and the Creed. Salesbury's book then supplied translations of the Epistles and Gospels appointed for each Sunday and holy day.[46] An initial plea under Elizabeth to permit 'such Welsh or Cornish children as could speak no English to learn the catechism in the Welsh tongue or the Cornish language' was ignored, but during the 1560s these translations came into general use, particularly after Bishop Thomas Davies of St Asaph had in 1561 required that 'after the Epistle and Gospel in English, the same should also be read in Welsh', and likewise with the catechism. Moreover, Welsh enthusiasts like Salesbury and Bishop Richard Davies were almost certainly the impetus behind the private act passed by the English parliament in 1563 authorising Welsh translations of the Bible and prayer book. Parliamentary opposition to the use of Welsh in public worship prompted an amendment that English Bibles and prayer books be placed alongside the new Welsh versions so that the people, by conferring both together, 'might the sooner attain to the knowledge of the English tongue'. By 1567 translations of *The Book of Common Prayer*, the *Psalter* and the *New Testament* had been published. Finally, in 1588, the whole Bible appeared in Welsh.[47]

In Ireland, there was more reluctance among Tudor officials to concede Gaelic translations of the Bible and prayer book. The reformers' demand for vernacular services cut across traditional Tudor policy of promoting English culture as a means of training the wild Irish to 'civility'. Most recently, a statute of 1537 'for the English order, habit and language' had blamed the 'savage and wild kind and manner of living' by 'rude and ignorant people' there on the diversity of language and customs: it required them to conform

---

45 Ellis, *Ireland in the age of the Tudors*, pp. 232–4; Alan Ford, *The Protestant Reformation in Ireland, 1590–1641* (2nd ed., Dublin, 1997), ch. 4.

46 Philip Jenkins, 'The Anglican church and the unity of Britain: the Welsh experience, 1560–1714' in Ellis and Barber (ed.), *Conquest and Union*, p. 118.

47 Williams, *Wales and the Reformation*, pp. 236–47, 350–3.

in 'language, tongue, in manners, order and apparel, with them that be civil people, and do profess and knowledge Christ's religion' in the English Pale.[48] The concession of an official status within the Tudor kingdom of Ireland to a language which had long been branded by English officials as seditious and barbarous also appeared to undermine the kingdom's officially English identity. Thus, it was not until 1571 that the first Gaelic book appeared in Ireland. Queen Elizabeth had advanced money to the Irish bishops for type and a press for a Gaelic New Testament shortly after the Welsh prayer book and Bible had been authorised in 1563. In 1567, however, the publication of the Welsh prayer book and New Testament coincided with the printing in Edinburgh of *Foirrm na n-Urrnuidheadh*, a Gaelic translation by John Carswell, bishop of the Isles, of the Genevan-inspired *Book of Common Order* (1564). Written in classical common Gaelic, the standard literary language, 'especially for the men of Scotland and Ireland', Carswell's *Foirrm* was a serious embarrassment to the ecclesiastical authorities in Ireland. The queen angrily demanded to know what had happened to the Gaelic New Testament, threatening the bishops that, if it did not presently appear, she should be repaid her money. Four years later, a short book appeared, compiled by John Kearney: it included translations of the catechism in *The Book of Common Prayer*, of the Twelve Articles of Religion, and some prayers from Carswell's book. Yet it was not until 1603 that the promised Gaelic New Testament was finally printed, though reputedly completed in 1587. The Gaelic version of the prayer book was delayed even longer, only finally appearing in 1608.[49] For monoglot Gaelic speakers, therefore, the publication of the basic works for vernacular services came more than a generation after similar provision had been made for Welsh speakers, and at a time when religious divisions had hardened. This delay was to prove crucial to the fate of the Tudor Reformation in Ireland.

Tarrying for the magistrate

Everywhere, the enforcement of the Elizabethan settlement also depended in large measure on the attitude of local nobles and gentry who supplied the backbone of local government. Within each parish, the churchwardens were charged by the Act of Uniformity to levy the weekly fine of 12d. on those

48   Statute roll, 28–9 Henry VIII c. 26 (*Stat. Ire.*, i, 119–27 (quotations, p. 120)).
49   Ellis, *Ireland in the age of the Tudors*, pp. 235, 258 (quotation).

who failed to attend church on Sundays. Churchwardens were also supposed to present any shortcomings in the conduct of the clergy, in church attendance by the laity, or in the furniture of the churches.

In Dublin city, for instance, a proclamation by Lord Lieutenant Sussex in 1564 ordered strict enforcement by the churchwardens of the fine on householders 'that missed coming to church on Sundays'. Thereupon 'many came to church', but 'at first they would go to mass in the morning and to church in the afternoon'; and 'to prevent that, a roll of the housekeepers' names was called by the wardens of each parish'.[50] Yet the office was unpopular and churchwardens could easily be intimidated or bribed by the gentry. They were seen as 'weak persons' who were 'loth to offend their betters or neighbours' by presenting them for non-attendance or failure to receive communion. Accordingly, during visitations, presentments were usually required from incumbents and curates too; but humble parish clergy also feared reprisals, particularly if they owed their benefices to Catholic patrons. Before 1581, when in England and Wales it was raised to £20 a month, the recusancy fine was no great deterrent to wealthy parishioners: a parishioner of Ashhurst, Sussex, threatened with presentation by the churchwardens, replied that 'he cared not if they did present him, for it [is] but a matter of xijd. [12 pence].' Even if presented, it was not difficult to avoid correction simply by failing to appear in court, since excommunication was no longer the sanction that it had once been. Recusants in particular would usually ignore a summons, and they hardly minded being excommunicated for contumacy. In theory, the church could secure a writ *de excommunicato capiendo* requiring the sheriff to imprison excommunicates until they sought absolution, but it rarely did so because there was no way of enforcing the writ, particularly if the sheriff proved uncooperative.[51]

Above the traditional church courts were the ecclesiastical commissions through which Elizabeth chose to exercise her royal supremacy. There was the High Commission in London, with authority throughout England and Wales, its counterpart in Dublin for Ireland, a subordinate High Commission for the province of York, and various diocesan commissions. The commissions were mixed bodies of clerics and laymen with powers to imprison, to impose fines or bonds, or to order arrest by the sheriff. These commissions

50   White (ed.), 'Annals of Dudley Loftus', p. 237.
51   R.B. Manning, *Religion and society in Elizabethan Sussex: a study of the enforcement of the religious settlement 1558–1603* (Leicester, 1969), pp. 25–28 (quotation, p. 25), 131–4; Williams, *Wales and the Reformation*, p. 316 (quotation); Haigh, *Reformation and resistance in Tudor Lancashire*, pp. 18–19, 230–6.

were much more powerful bodies, but faced the same difficulties as the traditional church courts in forcing defendants to appear and in extorting its penalties. Fines for contumacy were regularly imposed on defendants for failure to appear, for instance by the Dublin and York High Commissions, but the commissions then relied on cooperation by the sheriff to secure collection. In fact, most of these fines remained unpaid. Moreover, not all the commissions were reliable. In 1568 the Chester commission had to be purged of three gentry who were 'suspected in religion', but two others also suspect were retained; and in the 1580s it was discovered that the registrar of the Dublin High Commission was warning Catholics that proceedings for recusancy had been initiated against them.[52]

Finally, much depended on the attitude of the sheriffs and justices of the peace (JPs), who were also closely involved in enforcing aspects of the settlement. The government was anxious to ensure that these key local officials were favourable in religion. Thus, in Hampshire, four Catholic JPs were replaced in 1561–2 at the behest of the energetic Bishop Horne, and three more in 1564.[53] A statute of 1563 required sheriffs, lawyers and JPs to subscribe to the supremacy. In practice, however, the oath was often evaded: initially at least the government could not generally afford to purge the peace commissions of Catholic sympathisers because this would have adversely affected other aspects of local government. In 1564 all the English bishops were required to certify the religious attitudes both of JPs and other important local gentry who might be added to the commissions. The returns suggest that, overall, around half the JPs supported the settlement, but that some 150 out of around 850 were committed Catholics. These figures are, however, somewhat misleading. The Protestant heartland of Lowland England, with its many small shires, often had larger peace commissions than the sprawling upland shires. Nonetheless, there were strong Catholic pockets in the dioceses of Winchester, Chichester, and Hereford. For instance, in Chichester Bishop Barlow thought that only 10 out of 22 JPs were reliable, and of the other gentry 10 favoured the settlement and 10 did not. During the 1560s, moreover, 5 of the sheriffs were also Catholics. Not

---

52 Haugaard, *Elizabeth and the English Reformation*, pp. 130–35; Haigh, *Reformation and resistance in Tudor Lancashire*, pp. 212–13, 233–4; Ellis, *Ireland in the age of the Tudors*, pp. 231–2; R.D. Edwards, *Church and state in Tudor Ireland: a history of the penal laws against Irish Catholics 1534–1603* (Dublin, 1935), pp. 247, 273–4.

53 R.H. Fritze, 'The role of the family and religion in the local politics of early Elizabethan England: the case of Hampshire in the 1560s' in *Historical Journal*, xxv (1982), pp. 278–9.

until late 1569 did the whole peace commission swear the supremacy.
The north presented a much more serious problem. Sir Ralph Sadler complained in 1569 that scarcely 10 gentry throughout the north supported the Elizabethan settlement. In Lancashire, only 6 of the 25 JPs were 'favourable', and all but one of the first 9 Elizabethan sheriffs were unsympathetic.[54] In fact, the failure of the Northern Rising of 1569 broke the power of the Catholic landed families in Durham and Northumberland, and Protestant gentry also took control in Norfolk and Suffolk after the fall of the duke of Norfolk in 1572, but it was not until 1587 that a generally reliable bench was secured in Lancashire.[55]

As for conditions elsewhere, the scanty evidence suggests that the response of local magistrates in Wales and Ireland was much the same as in the Tudor north. Bishop Scory of Hereford reported in 1564 that none of the Radnor JPs was 'counted favourers of this religion but the best of them is judged but a neuter'. Similarly, Archbishop Parker's return for the then vacant diocese of Llandaff was distinctly non-committal concerning the 11 JPs he listed.[56] In 1577, when the privy council requested the names of Catholic recusants in Wales, the bishops could find very few, probably because they were reliant on the churchwardens for information. Yet Bishop Bleddyn of Llandaff reported one JP for recusancy, complained that others harboured Catholic priests, and also criticised the sheriffs for slackness in arresting excommunicates. Later proceedings in Glamorgan and Monmouthshire were sabotaged by JPs who warned recusants in advance of impending arrests; and successive bishops of St David's likewise criticised the slackness of local officials in regard to recusancy.[57]

54 Mary Bateson, 'A collection of original letters from the bishops to the privy council, 1564' in *Camden Society Miscellanea*, ix (1895), pp. 1–84; Fletcher and MacCulloch, *Tudor rebellions*, doc. no. 23 (quotation). Cf. Jones, *The birth of the Elizabethan age*, pp. 74, 84–5; Manning, *Religion and society in Elizabethan Sussex*, pp. 241–8; Haigh, *Reformation and resistance in Tudor Lancashire*, p. 213.

55 Mervyn James, *Family, lineage and civil society: a study of society, politics, and mentality in the Durham region 1500–1640* (Oxford, 1974), pp. 67–70, 78–9, 147; S.J. Watts, *From border to middle shire: Northumberland 1586–1625* (Leicester, 1975), pp. 77–8, 95–7; Diarmaid MacCulloch, *Suffolk and the Tudors: politics and religion in an English county 1500–1600* (Oxford, 1986), pp. 95–104, 195–7; A.H. Smith, *County and court: government and politics in Norfolk, 1558–1603* (Oxford, 1974), pp. 48–53, 82–3, 207–8, 218; Haigh, *Reformation and resistance in Tudor Lancashire*, pp. 212–13, 285.

56 Jones, *Birth of the Elizabethan age*, p. 74 (quotation); Williams, *Wales and the Reformation*, p. 233.

57 Williams, *Wales and the Reformation*, pp. 233–4, 264, 266, 315–16; idem, *Welsh Reformation essays*, pp. 172, 176–7.

The situation was worse still in Ireland, where enforcement of the settlement was initially confined to the English heartland of the Pale, south Leinster, and some isolated outposts. Between 1561 and 1564 local commissions were issued to enforce the settlement in Westmeath, Armagh province, south Leinster, Munster, Connaught and Thomond. Finally, a High Commission was established in 1564. It imprisoned the deprived, but still active, Marian bishop of Meath, who had 'manifestly contemned and openly showed himself to be a misliker of all the Queen's Majesty's proceedings'; and it procured presentments from juries empanelled for every parish in the English Pale. These revealed 'many and great offences' against the settlement. Yet nothing had been presented against the most notorious contemners of religion, the lords and gentry. Examined individually, however, they confessed 'that the most part of them had continually, since the last parliament, frequented the mass . . . and that very few of them ever received the holy communion or used such kind of public prayer and service as is presently established'. Evidently, many were evading the settlement by maintaining Catholic priests as chaplains. Other reports noted that, initially at least, the ordinary people continued to attend their parish churches as before, most especially in the towns. The magistrates and judges, however, were singled out for their slackness in enforcing the settlement. Moreover, the supremacy oath was not enforced. When, in 1584, an attempt was first made to require all the JPs and town magistrates to subscribe the supremacy, there was a wholesale refusal to act among the Pale gentry named to the commission.[58]

Overall, the evidence indicates that, in the final analysis, effective enforcement of the settlement depended on the attitude of the local magistrates and clergy. Where the Reformation already enjoyed some support, where a well-educated preaching ministry was available, and where local nobles and gentry proved cooperative, full enforcement of the Elizabethan settlement followed fairly speedily: but that rarely happened outside the Home Counties. In other parts of the English Lowlands, change in the parishes was more gradual, taking a decade or more. In the Tudor north, Wales and some parts of Ireland, only a bare conformity had been imposed by the 1570s – on a population where clergy and laity remained largely Catholic in sympathy. Slow progress continued throughout the 1580s in the north and Wales until

58 Ellis, *Ireland in the age of the Tudors*, pp. 231–2; M.V. Ronan, *The Reformation in Ireland under Elizabeth, 1558–80* (London, 1930), pp. 139–40 (quotation); Edwards, *Church and state in Tudor Ireland*, pp. 198 (quotation), 236–8, 270–4.

full conformity was finally achieved. In most of Gaelic Ireland, however, not [175] even a bare conformity had been imposed. Subsequently, escalating opposition to the Tudor conquest throughout Ireland undermined enforcement of the settlement, with the result that by the 1590s attitudes among the indigenous elites were, with few exceptions, firmly fixed in recusancy.[59]

The Catholic threat

Essentially, opposition to the Elizabethan settlement took two radically different forms, which indeed played off each other. Among those who believed that reform had not gone far enough, there emerged the Puritan movement, whilst others who thought change had gone too far were eventually swept up into the Counter-Reformation movement. Particularly in the Tudor borderlands, the population's innate conservatism, the inadequacy of enforcement procedures, and the more tenacious survival of aspects of the pre-Reformation church was to provide more fertile ground for missionaries from continental Europe embracing the new militant form of Catholicism shaped by the Council of Trent.

One territory where Catholic missionaries had considerable success was in Ireland. In the more English parts at least, the early response to the Elizabethan settlement had mirrored that elsewhere in the Tudor borderlands. And as elsewhere, the official response to activities by church-papists and other conservative practices had until the mid-1570s been generally cautious, if not tolerant, in the expectation that Catholicism would gradually wither away as old priests died off. Then in 1573/4 the community of Catholic exiles established at Douai began to ordain and supply new priests for work among organised Catholic congregations in England and elsewhere. Between 1574 and 1603 about 600 seminary priests were supplied, of whom around 460 are known to have worked in England. Concurrently, seminary priests and Jesuits sought to stem the drift of church-papists towards conformity by demanding strict recusancy. The response of the authorities was to adopt a much tougher line with Catholics at home. In 1577 and 1578, 2 Douai priests were executed, and by 1585, 27 priests and 8 laymen had been executed. In 1580, moreover, the York High Commission conducted a drive against recusants, hundreds being bound

59   Ellis, *Ireland in the age of the Tudors*, pp. 237–41.

over to attend church, take communion and ensure the conformity of their families.[60]

In English Ireland, the shift among conservative lay folk from church-papism and occasional conformity to general recusancy had begun in the later 1570s. In 1574, the papal nuncio regretted that in towns everywhere Catholics attended communion and sermons by the bishops; but recusancy increased, presumably with the encouragement of priests and Jesuits, and was general by the mid-1580s in Dublin diocese and in the early 1590s in Munster. Initially, increased activity by the High Commission, which had been remodelled in 1577, dissuaded many. The first Jesuit was executed in Ireland as early as 1575, when 9 Franciscan clergy were also put to death; and by 1585 at least 49 Catholic clergy had been executed or killed out of hand.[61] Hitherto, Catholicism had been practiced openly in Gaelic parts and border areas, and secretly elsewhere: in 1574, for instance, the government knew of around 60 active religious houses in Connaught. Such activity, however, was overwhelmingly a continuation of pre-Reformation practice. The existence of independent Gaelic lordships did indeed present a different kind of problem from that faced by the government in other Tudor border-lands, but it was chiefly the towns and the English Pale which had the resources to support an alternative Catholic mission. Here, rich merchants and wealthy gentry could afford to employ Catholic chaplains, and the surprising failure of the government to confiscate chantry foundations in Ireland or to prevent Catholic patrons of benefices from appropriating parochial endowments meant that resources which should have been available to the Elizabethan church were diverted to maintain recusant priests.

In England, William Allen encouraged the most promising seminary priests to work with the gentry or in the towns, restricting the less able to 'uplandish places where there is no other better learned than themselves'. The result was that the most effective Catholic challenge was mounted in those parts where the established church was best able to meet it, rather than in Wales and the English north where it had most hope of success. Perhaps a similar strategy was adopted for Ireland: at any rate, it was in the English Pale and the towns that Jesuits and seminary priests first established themselves, whereas the Franciscans focused on Gaelic Ireland.[62]

---

60 Haigh, *English Reformations*, pp. 261–4.
61 Ford, *Protestant Reformation in Ireland*, pp. 35–40; Ellis, *Ireland in the age of the Tudors*, pp. 238–40; Edwards, *Church and state*, p. 247, app. i.
62 Colm Lennon, *Sixteenth-century Ireland: the incomplete conquest* (Dublin, 1994), pp. 316–24; Ellis, *Ireland in the age of the Tudors*, pp. 240–1; Haigh, *English Reformations*, p. 261 (quotation).

The Puritan threat

So far as Protestants were concerned, however, deprived Marian clergy, church-papists and seminary priests were simply different manifestations of an international Catholic conspiracy to overthrow true religion. And initially, faced with this Catholic threat, the overwhelming majority of Protestants were prepared to follow the government's lead. There was a general expectation that, once the Catholic threat had been exorcised and the Elizabethan settlement imposed, further reforms would follow to purify the church of the remaining dregs of popery. For instance, the new Ornaments Rubric – imposed by Elizabeth until 'other order' should be taken – required clergy to wear a cope or traditional mass vestments at holy communion and a surplice for other services. Edwin Sandys, future bishop of Worcester, believed 'that we shall not be forced to use them', but soon learned otherwise. And when, in October 1559, Elizabeth restored in the Chapel Royal a small silver cross and two lighted candles on the table 'standing altar-wise', this provoked a crisis in which some of the newly-appointed bishops considered resignation. Even so, moderate Protestants were generally content with Elizabeth's initial moves to banish superstition, and in 1563 she permitted Convocation to draw up a broadly Calvinist statement of faith, the Thirty-Nine Articles, and allowed a new *Book of Homilies*.[63]

The pressure for further reform increased during the 1560s as more Protestants lost faith in the queen's good intentions, but from the very outset there were those like Miles Coverdale, the Edwardian bishop of Exeter, William Whittingham, and John Foxe, the martyrologist, who refused posts in the Church of England because of their reservations about its reformed character. They toured the country preaching, or accepted private patronage (which did not require conformity), and later this led to the establishment of Puritan lectureships as in market towns (initially Coventry, Colchester, Ipswich and Leicester) the magistrates began to engage their own preachers. And because these salaried preaching appointments in parish churches were privately-funded, they were free from prayer book restraints. Initially, the Puritan movement generally took the form of a church within a church, as ministers tended to neglect the prescribed services in favour of sermons, psalm singing and, as discussed below, 'prophesyings'. Moreover, the government, preoccupied with the Catholic threat, was lax in enforcing

---

63 Haugaard, *Elizabeth and the English Reformation*, pp. 183–5, 273–6 (quotation, p. 184); Patrick Collinson, *The Elizabethan Puritan movement* (London, 1967), p. 65 (quotation).

conformity. Gradually, however, conformist Protestants came to distinguish Puritans by peculiarities of behaviour. They were especially keen on preaching, and frequently took the initiative in establishing 'exercises of prophesying'. These comprised conferences of preaching clergy devoted to systematic Biblical exposition, very often a regular weekday meeting, with a moderator in charge and a panel of preachers, three or four of whom preached on the one text before a large audience of godly laymen (often JPs) and other less learned clergy. By the early 1570s, the bishops were happy to license them as a means of educating less qualified clergy who were required to undertake Bible study, but there were no such exercises in Wales and in large parts of northern England they developed rather later.[64]

Gradually, however, a gulf opened up between those Protestants who allowed a greater role for the magistrate in regulating *adiaphora* (things indifferent) and Puritans who argued that the Bible or 'the whole course of scripture' was the sole authority in matters of religion. The concept of *adiaphora*, influential in German Lutheran churches, sought to distinguish between what was essential to salvation and lesser points which might be varied by the magistrate. These included such matters as surplices, wafer bread in communion, or the sign of the cross in baptism which Puritans believed were papistical and inappropriate in a reformed church. When the first Convocations met in 1563, proposals by members of the Lower House of Canterbury Convocation for important changes in the prayer book were only narrowly defeated — to discourage kneeling at communion, suppress 'all curious singing and playing of organs', and abolish saints' days, liturgical dress, the cross in baptism and baptism by midwives. It was these ceremonies, rather than the more fundamental questions of church discipline, which initially provoked dissent and prompted Puritans to argue that the Church of England was 'but halfly reformed'.

By 1565 Elizabeth was urging the bishops to crack down on nonconformity. In 1566 Archbishop Parker required ministers to wear the surplice: 110 London clergy were summoned before the archbishop and required to subscribe. Thirty-seven who refused were suspended. Most eventually conformed, but a few were deprived and the wearing of popish vestments also elicited a protest from the General Assembly of the Scottish kirk. Those deprived joined the ranks of itinerant unbeneficed preachers, such as the newly-ordained John Field, curate at the Minories without Aldgate, and Thomas Wilcox, who both preached among a group 'who

64 Collinson, *Elizabethan Puritan movement*, pp. 27–8, 51, 65–6, 71–2, 126–7, 168–79, 210–11.

called themselves puritans or unspotted lambs of the Lord' (the first recorded use of the term) in one of the earliest separatist chapels. Thus, the persecution of non-conforming ministers from 1566 onwards gradually prompted the establishment of conventicles, as during the Marian persecution. These congregations were separatists, with a form of covenant subscribed by members on their admission, they had elected officers, and used the Genevan prayer book. They also had to hand convenient models of reformed churches, the French and Dutch congregations in London, but particularly Scotland. Leading separatists told John Knox: 'We desire no other order than you hold.'[65]

Throughout the 1560s, however, there was widespread sympathy with the more moderate Puritan demands even among the bishops, some of whom lent discreet support to unsuccessful proposals in the 1563 convocation and the 1566 parliament (the alphabet bills). In the 1571 parliament, the alphabet bills were revived, with some support from the bishops. They included measures to impose a restricted and general subscription to the Thirty-Nine Articles, and to revive Cranmer's *Reformatio Legum Ecclesiasticarum* with the intention of introducing a reformed church discipline in lieu of the old system of church courts and canon law; but there was also a bill to purify the prayer book which annoyed the bishops. And the queen generally opposed these initiatives. Only the Thirty-Nine Articles were endorsed in parliament, but concurrently the bishops approved a set of canons in convocation which, *inter alia*, required the clergy to subscribe *all* the Articles. Subsequently, leading Puritans were required to subscribe the Articles, the prayer book and the surplice. In this way, Field (with others) was silenced and reduced to earning a living as a schoolmaster.

By this date, some of the Puritans were losing confidence in the bishops' good intentions. Mounting frustration at the Puritan leadership's failure to secure any concessions in the 1571 parliament persuaded more radical spirits like Field and Wilcox to resort to public polemic. This came in the guise of an *Admonition to the Parliament*, an outspoken tract which argued that Episcopal government was 'anti-Christian and devilish and contrary to the scriptures', surveyed the 'popish abuses yet remaining in the English church', and condemned the prayer book as 'an unperfect book, culled and picked out of that popish dunghill, the mass book'. Apart from the outspokenness of the *Admonition*, its attack on bishops struck a new note, one which was in

---

65   Collinson, *Elizabethan Puritan movement*, pp. 27, 59–91 (quotations, pp. 27, 65, 86, 91); Kirk, *Patterns of reform*, pp. 334–67 passim.

line with the developing Presbyterian movement in Scotland and the views of Calvin's successor in Geneva, Theodore Beza, but hardly likely to be acceptable to the queen and her bishops. The result was a campaign to stamp out Presbyterian tendencies. Field and Wilcox were sentenced to a year in prison, and there was a drive against other Puritan publications in London. Ministers were also required to subscribe articles defining church law on authority, and a number were suspended for refusing.[66]

By the mid-1570s, Elizabeth was also increasingly concerned about the prophesyings. She saw them as seditious, in part because the sermons increasingly took the form of divisive expositions of differences between biblical practices and papistical ceremonies retained in *The Book of Common Prayer*. For the Puritans, the sermon was the chief part of the service, whereas the queen's preference was for ministers who could 'read the scriptures and homilies well unto the people', with just three or four licensed preachers in each diocese. In 1576 she prohibited prophesyings throughout the province of Canterbury; and when Archbishop Grindal protested, he was suspended. Subsequently, however, a compromise was brokered, in which only the rowdiest exercises were suppressed and the laity excluded from the ministers' discussions.[67] Nonetheless, it was becoming clear by the late 1570s that Puritan efforts to pressurise the queen into allowing further reform would fail. Moderate Puritans had disapproved of the *Admonition*, seeing it as counterproductive; and recent appointments to the episcopal bench – John Aylmer, bishop of London, or John Whitgift, bishop of Worcester, for instance – were mostly unsympathetic to the movement. This left the Puritans to choose between reluctant conformity and separatism. Only the more radical took the latter step, and interestingly only in Lowland England. The radicals might score occasional propaganda victories, such as the Marprelate tracts in the late 1580s, but hopes increasingly rested on the prospect of better times under King James. In this, they were to be disappointed: in response to the now traditional Puritan demands, the king would

---

66 Peter Lake, *Anglicans and Puritans? Presbyterianism and English conformist thought from Whitgift to Hooker* (London, 1988), ch. 1; G.R. Elton, *The parliament of England, 1559–1581* (Cambridge, 1986), pp. 205–12; Collinson, *Elizabethan Puritan movement*, pp. 65–6, 116–20; Heal, *Reformation in Britain and Ireland*, pp. 372–8; Haugaard, *Elizabeth and the English Reformation*, pp. 205–32, 254–7.

67 Collinson, *Elizabethan Puritan movement*, pp. 191–221; Lake, *Anglicans and Puritans?*, ch. 2; W.T. MacCaffrey, *Queen Elizabeth and the making of policy, 1572–1588* (Princeton N.J., 1981), pp. 83–91; Christopher Haigh, *Elizabeth I* (London, 1988), pp. 40–1 (quotation, p. 41); idem, *English Reformations*, pp. 274–5.

only allow that a preaching ministry, as in Scotland, was one of the marks of a true church which the English church should have as far as possible.[68]

The basic reason, however, why the Elizabeth settlement took root, after two short-lived and conflicting religious settlements under Edward VI and Mary, was that Elizabeth reigned for 45 years. By the time she died in 1603, the prayer book was second nature to most of her subjects: few could remember anything else. And at a time when continental Europe was riven by religious wars, the Elizabethan settlement was increasingly seen as a golden mean between popery and fanaticism. In the longer term, too, the ecclesiastical reforms promoted by the Tudor state have come to exercise an enduring influence on the development of Christianity right up to the present, and not just within the Anglican communion. Initially, the Tudor Reformation had attracted comment and criticism chiefly for the evident breach which it constituted with the traditions of the medieval church. Yet already by 1600 the settlement's essentially conservative nature and continuity with a medieval past was beginning to attract attention. Within the Anglican tradition, the regular public recitation of the Offices of Morning and Evening Prayer (Matins and Evensong), alongside celebrations of the Eucharist, preserved the pre-Reformation tradition in parish churches of mass, matins and evensong. For instance, the quintessentially Anglican Collect for Purity ('Almighty God, unto whom all hearts be open, all desires known') with which the Eucharist opens is actually just an English translation of the medieval Sarum Use ('Deus, cui omne cor patet et omnis voluntas loquitur').[69] And this continuity is underlined not just by the physical buildings, cathedrals and parish churches, but also by such ancient customs as Rogationtide processions, Harvest Festivals, the office of churchwarden, the structure of episcopal governments, even the retention for beneficed clergy of such titles as rector and vicar, all of which hark back to a medieval past. More recently, the continuing influence of the Tudor Reformation has also been underlined by developments affecting the other main Christian traditions. For instance, with the reforms of Vatican II, vernacular services in English have finally ousted the *Sarum Use*'s Counter-Reformation successor, the Latin Tridentine rite, so that the celebrant now faces the congregation, addressing them in English where formerly, as Bishop Bale had unkindly

---

68 Collinson, *Elizabethan Puritan movement*, p. 201; Heal, *Reformation in Britain and Ireland*, pp. 471–5; D.H. Willson, *King James VI and I* (London, 1956), pp. 201–10; Morrill, 'A British patriarchy?', pp. 216–17.

69 Cf. F.H. Dickinson (ed.), *Missale ad usum insignis et praecularae ecclesiae Sarum* (Burntisland, 1861), p. 580.

described it, 'he turneth his back to the people and telleth a tale to the wall in a foreign language'.[70] And the precise wording in the new English *Missal* both of the Lord's Prayer and of much else besides ultimately reflects the influence of the royal injunctions and the Acts of Uniformity: there had been wide variations in the English wording of prayers in the pre-Reformation church.[71]

Before 1603, the Elizabethan settlement had in practice developed in somewhat different directions in different parts of the Tudor state. Thereafter, when the new British multiple monarchy faced the further problem of a markedly different religious settlement in Scotland, attempts were made to promote what has recently been described as a policy of 'congruity' between the English, Irish and Scottish churches. Even in Ireland, where reform had made least progress, the coincidence of the completion of the conquest with the so-called 'second Reformation' presented the authorities with new opportunities. And as a recent attempt to apply to Ireland the insights of the continental 'confessionalisation' paradigm has noted, it was predominantly after 1603 that the characteristic features of the process were most apparent.[72] That the particular implementation of 'congruity' should prove so disastrous for monarchical authority was quite unforeseen.

---

70 John Bale, *The vocacyon of Johan Bale*, eds Peter Happé and J.N. King (Binghamton, N.Y., 1990), p. 66.

71 For different English translations of the Lord's Prayer, see Duffy, *Stripping of the altars*, plates 37, 39.

72 Morrill, 'A British patriarchy?', pp. 209–37; Alan Ford, *The Protestant Reformation in Ireland, 1590–1641* (2nd ed., Dublin, 1997), pp. 7–47; Ute Lotz-Heumann, *Die doppelte Konfessionalisierung in Irland: Konflikt und Koexistenz im 16. und in der ersten Hälfte des 17. Jahrhunderts* (Tübingen, 2000), sect. B iv–v, C.

7

STATE INTERVENTION AND THE PROBLEMS OF SOCIETY

Throughout Reformation Europe, the outbreak of religious conflict prompted Renaissance princes to claim new powers to regulate the spiritual lives of their subjects. Yet, the Reformation crisis was not the only major catalyst at this time in the development of the early modern state. All over Europe, population levels were rising in the sixteenth century, following the decline of the fourteenth century and then a period of stability. So far as we can judge, this pattern also holds good for the British Isles. The resultant economic pressures led both to social distress and popular unrest. The British monarchies struggled to respond to these unfamiliar problems, as did other princes. But what was the remedy? The symptoms were clear for all to see, registered in what contemporaries described as a 'universal dearth' and the increase in 'masterless men', but the rudimentary economic theories of the period (which extolled the notion of 'the just price' and attributed inflation to human 'greed') simply failed to address the underlying economic trends.[1]

Population trends and 'the just price'

Only for England from c.1525 do we have reliable estimates of the population increase (thanks largely to the introduction of parish registers in 1538). These suggest that, whereas plague and famine had reduced England's population to perhaps 2 million in 1450, by 1500 it had begun to rise again. After 1520 this rise accelerated: between 1525 and 1541 population grew extremely quickly by 23 per cent from 2.26 million to 2.77 million before slackening off somewhat, especially after the mid-1580s. Although mortality from famine and plague hit particular regions hard from time to time, there

---

1   See, for instance, R.H. Tawney, *Religion and the rise of capitalism* (ed. London, 1990); Keith Wrightson, *Earthly necessities: economic lives in early modern Britain* (New Haven, 2000); Wood, *Riot, rebellion and popular politics*, pp. 95–100.

was only one general reversal in population growth, in the late 1550s, when famine and then an influenza epidemic briefly reduced population levels by more than 5 per cent. By 1601 population had increased to 4.1 million, and it reached a seventeenth-century peak of 5.25 million by 1651.[2] Estimates for Wales suggest a population of just 200,000 in 1500 and 230,000 in 1550, but rising quite steeply to 317,000 by 1601 and almost 400,000 by 1650.[3] Even less reliably, the population of Scotland, it is suggested, may have risen from 600,000 in 1500 to 690,000 by 1550, to 800,000 by 1600, and 1.23 million by 1691.[4] As regards Ireland, one 'guesstimate' puts the population of Ireland in 1470 at little more than 500,000, perhaps rising gradually in the early sixteenth century: but from 1550 increasing levels of violence may have prevented any significant overall increase until peace returned in 1603. By 1672 it was 1.7 million, but the 1650s in particular may have seen a drastic decline from a peak of 2.1 million in 1641.[5] If these figures are at all accurate, they suggest that the population of the British Isles as a whole may have risen from less than 3.5 million in 1450 to nearly 8.5 million two centuries later.

Population density in the archipelago varied considerably from region to region, however, from under 20 people per square mile around 1600 in parts of Ireland or the Anglo-Scottish border region, to four or five times that level in most of England and Wales. South-east England was the most urbanised and densely-populated part of Britain; and in Ireland the English Pale and the south were more densely populated; but the populations of Scotland and Wales were fairly evenly distributed. Even south-east England remained overwhelmingly rural, however. The best estimate of England's overall urban population indicates that in 1520 around 125,000 people (or 5 per cent of England's total population) lived in towns of 5,000 inhabitants or more,

2   E.A. Wrigley and R.S. Schofield, *The population history of England 1541–1871: a reconstruction* (London, 1981), pp. 207–10, 531–2; Robert Tittler and Norman Jones (eds), *A companion to Tudor Britain* (Oxford, 2004), p. 313; D.M. Palliser, *The age of Elizabeth: England under the later Tudors 1547–1603* (London, 1983), pp. 34–8, 53.

3   Wrigley and Schofield, *Population history of England*, pp. 528, 566; Jenkins, *Modern Wales*, pp. 17, 38; Joan Thirsk (ed.), *The agrarian history of England and Wales: Volume IV 1500–1640* (Cambridge, 1967), pp. 142–3.

4   I.D. Whyte, *Scotland before the Industrial Revolution: an economic and social history c.1050–c.1750* (London, 1995), pp. 112–13; Robert Tittler and Norman Jones (eds), *A companion to Tudor Britain* (Oxford, 2004), pp. 323–4. Only the figure for 1691 is in any way reliable: see Michael Flinn (ed.), *Scottish population history from the seventeenth century to the 1930s* (Cambridge, 1977), pt 3.

5   Ellis, *Ireland in the age of the Tudors*, pp. 39–40; Raymond Gillespie, *The transformation of the Irish economy 1550–1700* (Dundalk, 1991), pp. 12–13; L.M. Cullen, 'Population trends in seventeenth century Ireland' in *Economic and Social Review*, vi (174–5), pp. 149–65.

rising to 335,000 (around 8 per cent) by 1600; but in Wales only one town, Carmarthen, had even 2,000 inhabitants. A few Scottish towns expanded significantly during the sixteenth century, mainly after 1570: Edinburgh from 10,000 to 18,000 inhabitants, Aberdeen from 3,000 to 6,000, Dundee from 4,000 to 7,000, Glasgow from 4,000 to 8,000, and St Andrews from 4,000 to 14,000. By 1639, it has been calculated, around 12 per cent of Scotland's population lived in towns of over 2,000 inhabitants, whereas only 2½ per cent had done so in 1560. These growth rates outstripped those of English provincial centres although in England population growth had begun rather earlier, in the 1530s: Norwich from 12,000 to 15,000 inhabitants, Bristol from 10,000 to 12,000, York from 8,000 to 12,000, and Exeter from 8,000 to 9,000. One reason for this difference may be the astonishing growth of London, rising from 60,000 to over 200,000 inhabitants as it became one of the four largest cities in Europe and also acted as a magnet in terms of the direction and volume of population flow. In Ireland, urban growth began only with the advent of more peaceful conditions after 1603. In 1540 the largest Irish town, Dublin, had a population of around 8,000; Waterford was not that much smaller; and Limerick impressed an English observer as 'a wondrous proper city' which 'may be called little London for the situation and the plenty'. Yet the population of major Irish towns apparently declined during the later sixteenth century: Dublin had only around 6,000 inhabitants in 1600, Galway around 4,000, Limerick 3,000, and Waterford and Cork only 2,400 inhabitants each. Thereafter, the major Irish seaport towns of Galway, Limerick and Waterford all grew significantly: Dublin's population reached 45,000 by 1685, with Cork's numbering almost 5,500 by 1641.[6]

This population expansion created an increased demand for food, particularly corn for bread. The towns in particular were dependent on the market for their food. It has been calculated that the proportion of England's population engaged in non-agricultural pursuits, and so dependent on the market, was already 24 per cent by 1520 and that by 1600 this had increased to 30 per cent.[7] The trends were no doubt similar elsewhere in the British Isles.

---

6 Tittler and Jones (eds), *Tudor Britain*, pp. 297, 313, 364–6; Collinson (ed.), *The Sixteenth Century*, p. 33; Palliser, *Age of Elizabeth*, pp. 202–4; Jenkins, *Modern Wales*, pp. 11, 34–5; Thirsk (ed.), *Agrarian history of England and Wales*, pp. 144–6; Whyte, *Scotland before the Industrial Revolution*, ch. 10; Gillespie, *Transformation of the Irish economy*, pp. 28–9; Ellis, *Ireland in the age of the Tudors*, pp. 36–8, 50 (quotation, p. 37); T.W. Moody, F.X. Martin and F.J. Byrne (eds), *A new history of Ireland. III Early modern Ireland 1534–1691* (Oxford, 1976), pp. 390–1.

7 Tittler and Jones (eds), *Tudor Britain*, p. 313.

The problem was most acute in England. Some areas such as the Fens and the Somerset Levels were drained, but by and large there were no major technological innovations which could produce more food from a fixed amount of land. The available food supply remained fairly inelastic, and so led to an alarming increase in the price of food (particularly grain for bread) and rents on tenancies, which greatly outstripped wage rates. Broadly, grain prices increased sixfold during the sixteenth century, but wage rates only doubled, so causing distress among the poor. In the half-century after 1600, grain prices rose more slowly, but wage rates also rose.[8] Historians have constructed various indices to illustrate the impact of the Tudor price rise, notably the Phelps Brown and Hopkins index, which measures the price of a composite 'basket of consumables' and the equivalent wage rate of a building craftsman in southern England.[9] Table 1 opposite outlines the overall trends, expressed in decennial averages.

The table suggests that prices remained fairly stable until around 1520, but then doubled within 30 years, had tripled by 1570, and continued to rise rather less sharply into the 1630s, by which time they were six times higher than a century before. Meanwhile, the wages both of a building craftsman and an agricultural labourer simply failed to keep pace with prices: the indices show that the real value of these wages dropped by over 40 per cent between 1500 and 1550, then declined more slowly to 1600 – by which time they had dropped by more than half – when they finally stabilised at the lower level. In the case of an agricultural labourer, the initial decline was less steep – probably because he benefited from payments in kind and could secure higher rates of pay for seasonal work related to the harvest – but the eventual result was much the same.

These were the overall trends, but in fact prices fluctuated considerably from year to year. Since harvest failure also drove up the price of grain, initially at least the upward overall trends would not have been discernible to contemporaries. The indices of the price of a composite 'basket of consumables' and of a building craftsman's wages (the wage index following in brackets, when available) show nothing unusual until 1513 at the earliest, when the price index rose to 120 (83), with a further rise to 167 (60) in 1521 following a run of three bad harvests, another peak of 248 (46) in

8 On all this, see the tables in the Statistical Appendix to Thirsk (ed.), *Agrarian history of England and Wales*, pp. 814–65 (esp. tables I, XV, XVI).

9 E.H. Phelps Brown and S.V. Hopkins, 'Seven centuries of the prices of consumables, compared with builders' wage rates', reprinted in P.H. Ramsey (ed.), *The Price Revolution in sixteenth-century England* (London, 1971), pp. 18–41.

Table 1 Wage rates in southern England[10]

Decade	(Index 1451–75 = 100) (1)	(Index 1451–75 = 100) (2)	Agricultural labourer (Index 1450–99 = 100) (3)	Building craftsman (Index 1450–99 = 100) (3)
1450–59	101	96	105	104
1460–69	101	101	100	100
1470–79	101	97	104	103
1480–89	95	111	86	93
1490–99	101	97	104	103
1500–09	101	104	97	96
1510–19	101	114	89	88
1520–29	106	133	80	76
1530–39	110	138	80	68
1540–49	118	167	71	70
1550–59	160	271	59	51
1560–69	177	269	66	62
1570–79	207	298	69	64
1580–89	203	354	57	57
1590–99	219	443	49	47
1600–09	219	439	50	46
1610–19	228	514	44	39
1620–29	253	511	50	39
1630–39	287	609	47	–
1640–49	304	609	50	49

(1) Money wage rate (wages index), (2) cost of living (prices index), (3) purchasing power of wage rate

1546, and then one of 409 (37) in 1557, when prices were four times their early Tudor level. After each peak, prices fell back, usually with the onset of better harvests. It was not until 1587, when the price index stood at 491 (41) that the 1557 peak was exceeded, but with the run of four bad harvests in 1594–7 the index rose to 685 (29) in 1597. The equivalent wage rate of 29 for that year was quite literally a starvation wage and the worst ever recorded in seven centuries of English history. Thereafter things improved somewhat, in that wages kept pace with prices, but there were further peaks in 1638 when the price index stood at 707 (36) and in 1650 when it measured 839 (34). Of course, the impact of inflation was by no means uniform

10   This table is based on Thirsk (ed.), *Agrarian history of England and Wales* (Cambridge, 1967), p. 865 (table XVI).

for the entire labour force, but the various indices do at least illustrate the increasing severity of the Tudor economic climate for the English poor. These long-term trends caused by demographic growth were also exacerbated in the 1540s by high government expenditure in wartime and by the coinage debasement. War in the 1540s cost the Tudor regime £3.5 million, and the debasement also swelled the size of the circulating medium temporarily: it more than doubled from £1.23 million in 1542 to £2.66 million in 1551, before falling back to £1.45 million with the recoinage. Following years of bad harvest the peasantry and urban poor starved. Bad harvests in 1519–21, 1527–9, 1544–5, 1549–51, 1554–6, 1586–7 and 1594–7 caused higher rates of mortality, but the worst years of the century were 1555–7 (when dearth coincided with an influenza epidemic) and 1596–8. Plague also hit London hard in the 1520s and 1592–3 and Devon in 1546–7 and 1589–93, while a viral disease called 'the sweat' caused many deaths at least once a decade.[11]

In Scotland, population growth began rather later than in England, particularly from the 1570s onwards, but it likewise led to price inflation. General prices, it has been calculated, increased fourfold between 1550 and 1625, and some agricultural prices, such as the price of barley, rose ninefold in the century to c.1635. Harvest failure led to widespread mortality. In 1623, Dumfries lost over a tenth of its inhabitants, Dunfermline perhaps a quarter, and Kelso a third. Some of these crises were regional or local, but many were general and often corresponded with crises in England, such as that of 1594–8. Sometimes, outbreaks of plague in the aftermath also increased mortality, as in 1597–9. As in England, inflation was exacerbated by the deliberate debasement of the coinage by the crown, particularly between 1560 and 1600 when the ratio between the Scots pound and the pound sterling fell from 4:1 to 12:1.[12] The evidence for Ireland is largely impressionistic. Initially at least, land values in English Ireland were quite buoyant: rents rose on the estates of the earls of Kildare to 1534, for instance. On a particular stretch of marchland in north Co. Kilkenny rents rose eightfold between 1495 and 1537, but then stagnated until 1600 before

11 Phelps Brown and Hopkins, 'Seven centuries of prices', pp. 38–41; Wrigley and Schofield, *Population history of England*, pp. 638–85; Hoskins, *Age of plunder*, pp. 85–8; Palliser, *Age of Elizabeth*, pp. 46–54, 386–7; C.E. Challis, *The Tudor coinage* (Manchester, 1978), pp. 238–47; Hoyle, 'War and public finance', p. 90.
12 R.A. Houston, 'The population history of Britain and Ireland, 1500–1750' in Michael Anderson (ed.), *British population history from the Black Death to the present day* (Cambridge, 1996), p. 120; Lynch, *Scotland*, pp. 183–4; Whyte, *Scotland before the industrial revolution*, pp. 77, 111–31, 274–6; Wrightson, *Earthly necessities*, pp. 130–1, 198.

quadrupling within ten years with the onset of more peaceful conditions.[13]
In Dublin the price of wheat seems to have mirrored that in England: in
famine years it rose from 10s. (50p) a peck in 1497 to 20s. (£1) a peck in
1561, although 13s. 4d. (67p) a bushel (4 pecks) was more normal by the
latter date.[14] Maximum wages in Dublin were fixed by the city in 1555 at
15d. per day Irish (10d. sterling) for master craftsmen and 7½d. Irish (5d.
sterling) for labourers, without meat and drink; or 6d. and 3d. respectively
with meat and drink. These rates marked a substantial advance on those
prescribed by the English statutes of 1351 and 1388 which had also been
applied to Ireland in 1388, but they still look low by comparison with
English rates of the time. In 1564–5 Christ Church Cathedral, Dublin was
paying its labourers 7d. Irish per day, without meat and drink. There was
apparently little movement in local Irish prices in the late sixteenth century,
perhaps because population levels were static, and contemporaries commented favourably on their low level. Once population began to rise after
1603, however, prices soon followed: the price of land rose from 8 or
9 years' purchase in the 1620s to 20 years' purchase in the late 1630s, but
land values then collapsed during the crises of the 1640s and 1650s.[15]

If the poor had simply died quietly in the streets, the government might
not have been too disposed to interfere with such manifestations of God's
will. Unfortunately, however, they did not: riots and disturbances ensued.
In part, this unrest was fuelled by traditional assumptions about prices,
unemployment and the social hierarchy which increasingly conflicted with
the realities of socio-economic change. Medieval theologians, such as
Thomas Aquinas, had believed that all commodities had a 'just price', fixed
by God, so that the price of a loaf of bread, for instance, reflected corn prices
as dictated by the harvest, the amount of labour to make and bake the loaf,
and an honest reward for the baker reflecting his skill and craftsmanship.
Experience, moreover, had hitherto seemed to confirm the theory: prices had
remained stable for longer than anyone could remember, since the 1380s in
fact. Reformers like Martin Luther, in his *Tract on Trade and Usury* (1524),

---

13 David Edwards, *The Ormond lordship in County Kilkenny 1515–1642* (Dublin, 2003), pp. 22–5;
    Ellis, *Tudor frontiers*, ch. 4.
14 British Library, Add. MS 4791, f. 135v; Ciaran Brady, *The chief governors: the rise and fall of
    reform government in Tudor Ireland, 1536–1588* (Cambridge, 1994), p. 228; Edwards, *Ormond
    lordship*, p. 37.
15 Gillespie, *Transformation of the Irish economy*, pp. 9–10, 59; J.T. Gilbert (ed.), *Calendar of ancient
    records of Dublin*, I (Dublin, 1889), pp. 452–3; H.F. Berry (ed.), *Statutes and ordinances, and acts
    of the parliament of Ireland, King John to Henry V* (Dublin, 1907), pp. 488–90; Raymond
    Gillespie (ed.), *The proctor's accounts of Peter Lewis 1564–1565* (Dublin, 1996), *passim*.

required the seller to adhere to prices 'fixed by public authority' or 'the price of common estimation', but otherwise to 'consider the income needed to maintain him in his station in life, his labour, and his risk', and not to 'take advantage of scarcity', nor to 'corner the market' so as to raise prices. Once prices began to rise, therefore, the initial response was to try to fix them – as the Tudor government did by statute and proclamation from the 1530s.

Broadly, the theory of the 'just price' held sway until Jean Bodin published an alternative theory of prices in 1568. Those who sought to sell their wares above the usual price were castigated as greedy and avaricious: such merchants, so John Wycliffe argued, must be wicked, 'for now been they poor, and now full rich, for wrongs that they doen'.[16] Conversely, in all the statutes and regulations of the late medieval and early Tudor periods it was assumed that those at the bottom of the social scale, the poor, could be divided into two simple moral categories – that the 'impotent poor' (the aged, maimed soldiers, and the handicapped), those who were physically incapable of work and deserving of help, could be distinguished from the 'sturdy beggars' and 'vagabonds' who preferred idleness and crime to honest toil. The same was true in Scotland. Thus, legislation aimed to deter the able-bodied from idleness by punishment, on the assumption that work was available for the willing and able: they were forbidden to wander at will through the country-side.[17] And when rising population led to increased unemployment, the government's response was to prescribe harsher punishments so as to encourage 'sturdy beggars' to find work.

Finally, as was expounded by the theory of 'the great chain of being', men and women were all taught to know their particular place in society: they had been ordained by God to their station in life. Contemporary accounts of life under the English and Scottish monarchs had described a society of orders which was essentially static, in which everyone knew their place, and in which social status broadly reflected land and wealth. There were of course certain anomalies such as the wealthy merchant families of cities like Dublin, Edinburgh, York and, of course, London (although many merchants bought up land and sought to establish themselves as landed gentry); there was Thomas Wolsey, the butcher's son, who rose to be lord chancellor and a cardinal; and there was, by contrast, Henry Grey, half-brother and heir of the third earl of Kent (*d.* 1523), who never assumed the title 'by reason of his

16 Tawney, *Religion and the rise of capitalism*, pp. 52–3, 103–4, 289 (quotations, pp. 104, 289); Palliser, *Age of Elizabeth*, pp. 139–50; Williams, *Tudor regime*, p. 192.
17 Williams, *Tudor regime*, p. 196; Whyte, *Scotland before the Industrial Revolution*, pp. 167–8.

slender estate'.[18] As population levels began to rise after 1500, so conven- tional ideas about the bonds of society, order and hierarchy, and provision for the poor came under strain. Tensions rose between town and country and between landlord and tenant. Inflation netted vast profits for producers at the expense of those on fixed incomes and rents or those dependant on the market for their food. Those peasants who had a freehold or secure lease of their holding prospered, since their produce commanded higher prices on the market: landlords, by contrast, sought to raise rents, to alter lease condi- tions, or to introduce new dues and obligations on their tenants so as to maintain their incomes. Thus inflation created great tensions in society and also appeared to undermine the social hierarchy by holding out the prospect of those of low degree becoming wealthier than their betters.

Riot and rebellion

As tensions between landlords and tenants rose, these changes were mani- fested in an increased number of riots and other disturbances, particularly enclosure riots. Enclosure riots were the most typical and widespread mani- festation of agrarian protest in early-modern England, but were less common in Wales, and unknown in Ireland and Scotland. Most commonly, they took the form of throwing down hedges and were especially prevalent in the English midlands. Enclosure was an ambiguous term which denoted the fencing of land, engrossing or consolidation of arable strips, hedging and cultivation of waste ground, and the division of common pasture. Some forms of enclosure were obviously beneficial; but what fuelled popular dis- content and attracted official condemnation was enclosure which led to the extinction of common rights over a piece of land or to depopulation and unemployment as lords converted land from tillage to pasture: in both cases, it drove peasants off the land and diminished the supply of corn. According to one modern study of English enclosure riots, in the period 1509–53 there was a fourfold increase in such riots after c.1530.[19]

Elsewhere, however, economic conditions were different, and so this type of enclosure dispute was infrequent or non-existent. In Wales, for instance,

18   J.R. Lander, *Crown and nobility 1450–1509* (London, 1976), p. 291; Peter Gwyn, *The King's Cardinal: the rise and fall of Thomas Wolsey* (London, 1990), p. 1.
19   R.B. Manning, *Village revolts: social protest and popular disturbances in England, 1509–1640* (Oxford, 1988), pp. 32–3, 38–9, 322; Wood, *Riot, rebellion and popular politics*, pp. 82–9; Williams, *Tudor regime*, pp. 180–1; Wrightson, *Earthly necessities*, pp. 102–4.

enclosure itself was pervasive in many southern Lowland manors by 1640: but enclosures in Wales did not give rise to anything like the same number of disputes as in England because they were most frequently geared to arable cultivation and so did not lead to evictions and depopulation. Moreover, the nearby uplands also included large stretches of unenclosed waste. Between 1558 and 1625, there is evidence of only two enclosure disputes from west Wales before the English central courts.[20] In Scotland the absence of rural unrest and enclosure riots before the eighteenth century has been noted by historians: the lack of agricultural innovation, the close personal ties between lords and tenants, and the preponderance of short-term leases have been adduced as explanations.[21] Almost certainly, similar reasons could be offered for the absence of rural protest in Ireland. In the more English parts of the east and south and around the larger cities, there was enclosure on a significant scale by the late fifteenth century. In 1598 Co. Kilkenny was described as having 'the most show of civility' of the border counties, partly in respect of 'the English manner of enclosure of their grounds'. In most parts, however, the land was unenclosed. In Munster, for instance, enclosure only became a significant feature of the countryside with the onset of planta-tion. Gaelic Ireland did not, in any case, possess a peasantry in the accepted European sense of the term: the bottom stratum of Gaelic society were mere share-cropping labourers, entirely dependent on their landlords for stock and, though claimed as subjects by the chief and bound to remain within the lordship, wandering from place to place and master to master. Only with the extension to Gaelic Ireland of English rule and English forms of land tenure in the seventeenth century did the peasantry begin to be integrated into the state and forms of popular resistance develop, notably in the 1641 rising.[22]

Apart from the allegedly deleterious effects of enclosure, officials grew increasingly concerned at the threat to public order, because gatherings of 20 or 30 men to throw down the hedges of an unpopular landowner could quickly develop into something much more serious. The events which led to the 'rebellions of Commonwealth' in 1549, and particularly Kett's rebellion,

20 Williams, *Recovery, reorientation and Reformation*, pp. 386–8; Manning, *Village revolts*, pp. 325, 327.

21 Wormald, *Court, kirk and community*, pp. 50–2; Houston and Whyte (eds), *Scottish society*, p. 25.

22 Michael MacCarthy-Morrogh, *The Munster plantation: English migration to southern Ireland 1583–1641* (Oxford, 1986), pp. 228–30; Art Cosgrove (ed.), *A new history of Ireland. II Medieval Ireland 1169–1534* (Oxford, 1987), p. 477; Moody, Martin and Byrne (eds), *New history of Ireland*, iii, 36, 149–50 (quotation, p. 149); S.G. Ellis, 'Communal autonomy and peasant resistance: commentary from a British perspective' in Peter Blickle (ed.), *Resistance, representation and community* (Oxford, 1997), pp. 60–4.

illustrate what might happen if the government lost control of the situation.
This explosion of unrest which affected large parts of England in 1549 had
in many ways been building for much of Henry VIII's reign. The government of Protector Somerset, under a boy-king, was however much less
regarded, and eventually the commons took things into their own hands. By
the late 1540s, food prices were consistently double their level 30 years
before, whereas wages had risen by only 20 per cent. The rise in population
prompted increased land use, rackrenting (exhorbitant increases in rents)
and different forms of enclosure by landlords, so creating tensions between
landlords and tenants, riots and complaints. Preachers very often took up
these complaints, arguing, as William Forest did, that the greediness of rackrenting landlords was causing depopulation and unemployment. Actually,
the harvests were good in 1547 and 1548 and grain prices low, but inflation
nonetheless accelerated both because of the currency debasement and also
heavy military expenditure on war with France and Scotland. Somerset also
raised popular expectations that the government would crack down on
greedy landlords. He issued a proclamation for a 'view or inquiry' into the
extent to which the existing legislation on enclosure was being enforced,
explaining that this was in response to the desire of the industrious poor for
work and the 'pitiful complaints' of the king's poor subjects. A week earlier,
on Whitsunday, there had been a serious riot in the Hertfordshire village
of Northaw, where the lord, Sir William Cavendish, auditor of the court of
Augmentations, had procured a royal commission to enclose the very extensive common land in the area. There had been a previous confrontation
about the commons in 1544, and this time the rioters proceeded to set up a
camp on the disputed commons, thus anticipating the events of the following year. Several other riots followed in summer and autumn, around the
same time as a commission chaired by John Hales investigated conditions in
seven Midland counties. The commission discovered that the laws concerning enclosure had not been enforced, Hales arguing that the commons were
'greatly decayed through the greediness of a few men'. He sponsored two
bills in parliament to control tillage and regrating during winter 1548–9:
these were rejected. During May 1549, there were numerous further enclosure riots in south-eastern counties, followed by the more serious explosion
in June in Devon and Cornwall. Somerset responded by issuing pardons
to the rioters, and then in July a second enclosure commission. At this
point, however, the government was overwhelmed by popular risings
which soon involved 27 counties – in effect all of Lowland England as far
north as Seamer in the North Riding of Yorkshire, except for London – and

described by contemporaries in their immediate aftermath as the 'rebellions of Commonwealth'.[23]

At the same time, the government's ecclesiastical policies were also fuelling popular unrest. Many of the revolts were directed principally against religious reforms, most notably the revolt in Devon and Cornwall, but also in Buckinghamshire and Oxfordshire, and around Seamer in Yorkshire. In many parts, however, there was widespread enclosure rioting as part of a movement which began in 1548 and continued until 1552. Much the most serious was Kett's rebellion which began in late June as a riot against landlords who were enclosing common land.[24] The commons threw down the hedges of an enclosure made by Robert Kett, a substantial Norfolk landowner, who then, surprisingly, agreed to stand by the rioters (notwithstanding his own economic interests in the enclosure conflict) until they had obtained their rights. He led them in a march on Norwich, and the rebels, 16,000 strong, then set up camp on Mousehold Heath on 12 July. Here too, there was a religious dimension to the movement, but it was quite Protestant in tone. The rebels ostentatiously used the new prayer book and loudly proclaimed the Gospel as a means of legitimating socio-economic grievances. Thomas Conyers, a Norwich incumbent, daily held services under the Oak of Reformation at the main rebel camp, and a succession of evangelical preachers also officiated there, including Dr. John Barrett and Archbishop Cranmer's servant, Robert Watson. Elsewhere in the south-east, there had been what the earl of Arundel in Surrey described as 'a quavering quiet', but many of the local gentry were away in London or Windsor to where the government had summoned them with a view to raising an army against the

---

23   M.L. Bush, *The government policy of Protector Somerset* (London, 1975), pp. 42–51, 63–4, 74–5; Jennifer Loach, *Edward VI* (New Haven, 1999), pp. 58–69 (quotation, p. 64); Fletcher and MacCulloch (ed.), *Tudor rebellions*, pp. 65–7; MacCulloch, *Thomas Cranmer*, p. 429.

24   The best contemporary account of the revolt is Nicholas Sotherton's narrative, *The Commoyson in Norfolk 1549* (ed. Susan Yaxley, Stibbard, 1987). The rebel articles are published in Fletcher and MacCulloch (eds), *Tudor rebellions*, pp. 156–9; and new material concerning Somerset's role in Ethan Shagan, 'Protector Somerset and the 1549 rebellions' in *English Historical Review*, cxiv (1999), pp. 34–63. Fletcher and MacCulloch (eds), *Tudor rebellions*, chs 6, 10 and Wood, *Riot, rebellion and popular politics*, pp. 62–71 offer short up-to-date summaries, incorporating the conclusions of the important doctoral dissertation by Amanda Jones ('"Commotion time": the English risings of 1549', University of Warwick PhD thesis, 2003). Perhaps the best modern account is Diarmaid MacCulloch, 'Kett's rebellion in context' in *Past & Present*, no. 84 (1979), pp. 36–59; but particularly on the wider context, see also B.L. Beer, *Rebellion and riot: popular disorder in England during the reign of Edward VI* (Kent State, 1982); Julian Cornwall, *Revolt of the peasantry* (London, 1977). Bush, *Government policy of Protector Somerset*, ch. 4 remains useful, and on the agrarian background, Manning, *Village revolts*.

rebels in Devon and Cornwall. In their absence, rebel camps were suddenly [195] established at three other places in Norfolk, three in Suffolk, and eleven else-where. (There was trouble in adjoining counties – Cambridge, Essex, Surrey, Sussex, Lincoln and Kent.) The revolts were coordinated and planned, and the remaining gentry were unable to contain the movements. Writing at the height of the disturbances, on 7 July, William Paget held Somerset person-ally responsible for the unrest: 'and what is the cause? Your own levity, your softness, your opinion to be good to the poor.'[25]

To judge from the rebel articles subscribed by representatives from Norfolk, Suffolk and Norwich city, the revolt was essentially a threefold protest. Almost half the articles related to agrarian grievances: articles demanded the restoration of traditional rents for land (articles 5, 6, 14), and outlined complaints against enclosures and about the use of the commons (1, 3, 11, 13, 29) and about new levies and charges by lords (2, 17, 19, 21). Another group of articles protested against bad government and failures of law enforcement (articles 12, 18, 27, 28), notably a demand to enforce 'good laws, statutes, proclamations' made for the people but concealed by JPs and other officials (27). Finally, there were articles for reform of religion (articles 4, 8, 15, 20, 22). Some of these were distinctly anti-clerical, demanding that priests should not purchase land (article 4) and should mit-igate their tithe demands (22). The demand that clergy 'not able to preach and set forth the word of God' should be dismissed 'and the parishioners there to choose another' recalled articles of the German Peasants' War of 1525, as did article 16: 'We pray that all bond men may be made free, for God made all free with his precious blood shedding.' This demand reflected the survival of serfdom on the estates of the disgraced duke of Norfolk: Norfolk was perceived as a hard grasping landlord who was attempting to revive serfdom on his East Anglian estates. Paget at least saw the similarity between the troubles in summer 1549 and events in Germany in 1525, and urged repression rather than appeasement.

A feature of popular revolts, found also in 1549, was the willingness of the commons to be led by gentry, like Kett and his brother, where they could find them. In both town and countryside, those who assumed leadership of the revolt were those just outside the governing classes. Kett thought that the government in London was on his side and that the leading gentry had

25 Fletcher and MacCulloch (eds), *Tudor rebellions*, pp. 67–70, 160 (quotations, pp. 67, 160); Wood, *Riot, rebellion and popular politics*, pp. 62–6; MacCulloch, 'Kett's rebellion', p. 40; Shagan, 'Protector Somerset and the 1549 rebellions', pp. 34–63.

failed, as JPs, to enforce the law. Norwich was a city riven by social and religious conflicts and divided between a wealthy merchant class and a poor commonalty. The latter ('the scum of the city') joined the rebels, and the city authorities led by the mayor, Thomas Cod, were initially so overawed by the rebels' strength that they cooperated with them to avoid bloodshed: but on 30 July when the marquis of Northampton arrived with an army (including – to the rebels' fury – 1,000 'gorgeously apparelled' Italian mercenaries) they declared for the king. Elsewhere in the south-east, Somerset persuaded the rebel camps to disperse without much bloodshed, but Northampton mishandled the situation. The rebels attacked the city, and following a bloody battle in which over 40 were slain, the marquis retired in disarray. The local gentry panicked and 'fled in their doublets and hosen'. Eventually, the earl of Warwick was put in charge of a new army of 12,000 men (including many mercenaries) and found, on arrival at Norwich, that the rebel camp had shifted to Dussindale, making it much easier to deploy his cavalry against them. The rebels were routed on 27 August, with allegedly 3,000 killed. Kett and his brother were tried for treason on 26 November; Kett was hanged at Norwich castle and his brother from the steeple of Wymondham church. Nevertheless, Somerset's fellow-councillors thought that the duke was indirectly responsible for the widespread disorders through his excessive leniency to the poor, and he was ousted in a *coup d'état* in October.[26]

The kind of widespread popular movement which had engulfed Lowland England in 1549 was not destined to be repeated. In part this was because later monarchs took more care to read and respond to signs of popular discontent. Nonetheless, the underlying tensions between landlords and tenants grew worse in the late sixteenth century, and from about 1586 to 1608 there was a sequence of harvest failures, dearth and food riots, along with a marked increase in the frequency of enclosure riots. There were also minor revolts centred on Oxfordshire in 1596 and on Northamptonshire in 1607 (the Midland Revolt) and the forest riots known as the Western Rising of 1626–32, but only the Midland Revolt resulted in a battle. There were food riots again in 1622 and 1629–31. The proliferation of enclosure disputes eased in the 1610s, however, perhaps in part because wealthier farmers now often came to collective agreements with one another or their lord: enclosures were conducted 'with the agreement of the most part of the better

---

26 Fletcher and MacCulloch (eds), *Tudor rebellions*, pp. 73–89, 156–9; Wood, *Riot, rebellion and popular politics*, pp. 62–71 (quotation, p. 63); Sotherton, *Commoyson in Norfolk*, pp. 21–9 (quotations, pp. 23, 28–9).

sort', with the poor sometimes offered compensation. In other words, the [1 9 7]
community of interest which had previously sustained traditions of popular
protest was increasingly eroded after 1549 by social change which produced
a new class of farmers – 'the better sort' of villagers on the margins of the
gentry – who dominated local office holding and excluded the poor. By
comparison with earlier disputes the geographical distribution of enclosure
disputes also shifted: over 40 per cent of those disputes reaching the central
courts between 1558 and 1625 originated in the English west midlands or
the Welsh border counties, whereas the bulk of earlier disputes had originated in counties to the east and south.[27] Long before the popular revolts of
the late 1540s, however, the authorities had also begun to assume greater
powers in a bid to regulate the economy and to relieve social distress. The
result was a marked extension in the competence and area of activities of the
state, with new officials, new structures, and new legislation, most notably
the Elizabethan Poor Law.

Regulating the economy

The early modern era was not the first in which British monarchs had intervened in the economic activities of their subjects. Medieval governments had
concerned themselves with the issue of coinage, supervising the quality of
cloth, controlling foreign trade, and so on. Nonetheless, the volume, range
and complexity of Tudor regulations outstripped the ambitions of previous
kings. Much of the initiative for this regulation of the economy came from
unofficial, not governmental quarters: local or regional interests were important in this, but perhaps more surprisingly, so also was popular pressure.
Despite its centralised form and the aristocratic domination of key offices in
central and local government, the English state proved responsive to a much
wider group of subjects, particularly in regard to socio-economic problems.
This sensitivity was a key influence in the extension of state power in the
sixteenth century and its channelling in directions which accorded more
with the interests of 'the middling sort' below the ranks of the gentry. From

---

27 Manning, *Village revolts*, pp. 3, 58, 79, 82, 157, 220–52, 314, 323, 325, 327; Wood, *Riot,
    rebellion and popular politics*, pp. 82–9, 95–100 (quotation, p. 83); Buchanan Sharp, *In contempt
    of all authority: rural artisans and riot in the west of England, 1586–1660* (Berkeley, 1980),
    chs 4–5.

1381 to 1644, for instance, direct taxation normally affected only a small minority. Successive efforts to broaden the tax base by introducing some form of poll tax foundered on popular opposition, expressed or implied, even when the government secured the consent to such measures of the commons' representatives in parliament – as it did in the events leading to the Peasants' Revolt of 1381 and the Taxpayers' Strike of 1525.[28] Attempts to introduce a more effective system of taxation also led to localised unrest or resistance in 1489, 1513 and 1523 in Yorkshire, and in 1497 in Cornwall.[29] Not until the introduction of excise duty during the Wars of the Three Kingdoms were the lower classes subject to taxation, and then in very different circumstances. And without the necessary financial resources, English kings were unable to develop the bureaucratic and military base which underpinned royal absolutism in continental Europe.[30]

A similar fate had befallen the efforts of landlords to use parliament to maintain villeinage, restrict the mobility of labour, and keep down wages in the aftermath of the Black Death. In the short term, the labour laws established by reactionary measures like the Statute of Labourers (1351) and the Statute of Cambridge (1388) had been vigorously enforced and partially successful. Yet growing unrest culminated in the revolt of 1381. Passive resistance and more localised trouble continued into the fifteenth century, but gradually the labour laws ceased to be enforced, wages rose, and conditions of villeinage were relaxed.[31] In the late middle ages, therefore, parliament effectively failed to shore up royal and seigneurial power when economic conditions favoured the lower orders. In the sixteenth century, however, when socio-economic trends again became unfavourable to peasants and artisans, the threat or actuality of unrest prompted the government to intervene more extensively and in novel ways to try to regulate the economy. This

28 R.B. Dobson, *The Peasants' Revolt of 1381* (2nd ed., London, 1983), pt. 2; Bernard, *War, taxation and rebellion*, ch. 5; Diarmaid MacCulloch, *Suffolk and the Tudors: politics and religion in an English county, 1500–1600* (Oxford, 1986), ch. 10.

29 Goodman, *Wars of the Roses*, pp. 107–16; M.E. James, 'The murder at Cocklodge' in *Durham University Journal*, lvii (1965), pp. 80–9; Guy, *Tudor England*, pp. 60–1; Fletcher and MacCulloch (eds), *Tudor rebellions*, ch. 3.

30 M.J. Braddick, 'Popular politics and public policy: the excise riot at Smithfield in February 1647 and its aftermath' in *Historical Journal*, xxxiv (1991), pp. 597–626; C.S.L. Davies, 'Peasant revolt in France and England: a comparison' in *Agricultural History Review*, xxi (1973), pp. 122–34; Ellis, 'Crown, community and government', pp. 187–204.

31 John Bellamy, *Crime and public order in England in the later middle ages* (London, 1973), pp. 33–6, 159–61; Rodney Hilton, *Bond men made free: medieval peasant movements and the English rising of 1381* (London, 1973), pp. 110, 151–5, 231–2; M. McKisack, *The fourteenth century* (Oxford, 1959), pp. 334–41.

led to the establishment of new administrative structures as the government tried to mitigate the worst effects of these changes on the poor.

From 1489, the government attempted by statute to limit enclosure, engrossing of farms, and the conversion of arable land to pasture so as to reduce unemployment and to increase the supply of corn. Like many other aspects of Tudor socio-economic policy, the campaign gradually became more sophisticated: it sought to distinguish between different farming regions in which arable or pasture farming predominated and in particular between tolerable and prejudicial forms of enclosure (see above, p. 191). The latter were castigated as sins against the commonwealth, depopulating the land, creating unemployment and reducing the corn supply.[32] The procedures for enforcement were also gradually improved. The statute of 1489 was a general act against the throwing-down of houses and depopulation but, since enforcement lay with manorial lords, it proved ineffective. It was confirmed by statutes in 1514 and 1515 which forbade new enclosures and ordered demolished buildings to be reconstructed and land restored to tillage which had been converted to pasture since 1485. A statute of 1536 made prosecution by the crown possible. A statute of 1533 limited the number of sheep to be kept by any one man, and forbade the engrossing of farms. Later statutes of 1549 and 1555 also discouraged the keeping of sheep in the hope of turning land back to the plough. Between 1517 and 1607, five commissions of inquiry were issued to investigate illegal enclosures and stimulate prosecution.[33] Probably the most determined was Cardinal Wolsey's inquiry of 1517–18. Proceedings were commenced against 264 landlords (including 9 peers, 3 bishops, 32 knights and 51 heads of religious houses): 74 defendants immediately pleaded guilty and undertook to rebuild farmhouses or convert pasture back to cultivation; and altogether 188 cases ended in clear verdicts by the courts – a very high proportion for Tudor legislation. The inquiries resulted in 97 houses and 2 barns being rebuilt and 3,260 acres of land being returned to tillage.[34] Yet this activity was not totally effective, partly because enclosure had been practiced for centuries before 1485 (the date limiting prosecution), partly because much enclosure was done by agreement between lords and tenants, and partly

32   P.H. Ramsay, *Tudor economic problems* (London, 1963), pp. 19–22.

33   Williams, *Tudor regime*, pp. 180–3; Joan Thirsk, *The rural economy of England* (London, 1984), ch. 6.

34   J.J. Scarisbrick, 'Cardinal Wolsey and the common weal' in E.W. Ives *et al.*, (eds), *Wealth and power in Tudor England: essays presented to S.T. Bindoff* (London, 1978), pp. 45–67; Williams, *Tudor regime*, pp. 180–5.

because many farmhouses had decayed in the fifteenth century when the country's population was low and lords had been forced to concentrate on pasture for lack of tenants.

Government action did, however, bring to light many alleged offences against the statutes. There were 583 actions brought in the court of exchequer 1518–68, most of them in the years 1518–30 and 1539–56, but the great majority (70 per cent) concerned minor offences where only one house had been destroyed. Enclosure was a particularly sensitive issue, for the commons often saw in the practice the root of all social ills. Regulation of enclosure thus played well with this segment of the population, and the government's consistent enforcement of the statutes seems to have deterred landlords from evicting tenants and converting their lands to pasture. By 1593 a great abundance of both labour and grain was recorded throughout the realm and parliament felt sufficiently confident to repeal the major enclosure statutes.[35] The next four years, however, witnessed a series of bad harvests, causing widespread famine. Though statutes limiting enclosure were hastily re-enacted in 1597, it was too late: in late 1596 George Abbot, the theologian and future archbishop of Canterbury, described the extent of the devastation:

> Behold what a famine [God] hath brought into our land . . . One year there hath been hunger; the second year there was a dearth, and a third, which is this year, there is great cleanness of teeth . . . our years are turned upside down; our summers are no summers; our harvests are no harvests; our seed-times are no seed-times.[36]

There were complaints about enclosures in Oxfordshire in late 1596, and the Midland Revolt of 1607 and subsequent inquiry revealed much enclosing activity from 1593 onwards. This suggests that government action and attitudes had acted as some restraint on landlords before 1593, but in the seventeenth century, as conditions improved, the legislation gradually fell into disuse.[37]

Despite these measures, however, rising population put increasing pressure on the available food supply. The government therefore moved to regulate

35 Williams, *Tudor regime*, pp. 180–5; Thirsk (ed.), *Agrarian history of England and Wales*, ch. 4; Palliser, *The age of Elizabeth*, pp. 178–85.
36 Palliser, *The age of Elizabeth*, pp. 49 (quotation), 184.
37 Thirsk (ed.), *Agrarian history of England and Wales*, pp. 227–34; E.F. Gay, 'The Midland Revolt and the inquisitions of depopulation of 1607' in *Transactions of the Royal Historical Society*, 2nd ser., xviii (1904), 195–244; Wrightson, *Earthly necessities*, pp. 209–12; Ramsay, *Tudor economic problems*, p. 27; Williams, *Tudor regime*, p. 184.

the supply and availability of food, especially of corn and bread, so as to alleviate shortages in time of famine. Its mechanism was a combination of proclamations prohibiting exports, council orders requiring the distribution of grain, commissions regulating grain sales and hoarding, plus licences to individuals to export. The whole mechanism was underpinned by statutes regulating trade and prices, but in practice the government's approach was marked by flexibility: statutes were increasingly modified by royal proclamations, individual merchants were granted privy council licences to export corn in times of plenty and town authorities were frequently charged with overseeing food supply and distribution. More overt intervention was called for when in 1586 a harsh winter and a poor harvest caused dearth in many parts. In response, the government ordered JPs in Wiltshire to allow corn to be sent to the badly affected city of Bristol, while the justices of Hampshire and Sussex received a similar order to supply London.[38] By and large, the government aimed to protect the interests of the consumer without making things so difficult for producers that they simply switched out of food-producing altogether. And overall, the evidence suggests that the privy council went to considerable trouble to be well-informed both about the state of the food-supply in the provinces and regional variations on the national picture, and equally that it descended into minute detail in shaping an effective policy and seeing it enforced. This policy had a substantial impact on the overall situation even though it was far from being fully successful. The crown's interest in the food supply was not of course confined to the relief of the rural and urban poor so as to prevent disorders: supplies for garrisons, overseas possessions, and military and naval expeditions had to be provided. Broadly, the crown sought to prevent the export of grain overseas in time of shortage, to encourage its import in time of dearth, to ensure that home-grown corn should be brought to the market and sold at a fair price, and to redistribute corn from well-supplied regions of the realm to those in need. It was assisted by local initiatives, such as credit, private charity, and subsidised grain for poor neighbours. Moreover, although governments could not prevent dearth, these interventions did address popular explanations of the phenomenon, which attributed it to God's punishment for sin, evil practices, greedy middlemen, and enclosures. In regulating the market in this way, the government relied heavily on the royal prerogative to stimulate

38   Williams, *The Tudor regime*, pp. 185–93; Wood, *Riot, rebellion and popular politics*, pp. 95–100; Braddick, *State formation*, pp. 118–20.

activity by its local officials, issuing a series of council orders which increased in frequency and complexity as the century progressed. Only the broad outline and main developments can be traced here.[39]

Export of corn was controlled by statute, modified increasingly by proclamation and licences. Until 1534, between 1555 and 1571, and from 1593 onwards, the export of grain was governed by a fifteenth-century statute. This forbade export overseas unless the price fell below a certain threshold, originally 6s. 8d. (£0.33) a quarter for wheat and lesser sums for other grains, rising to 20s. (£1) a quarter from 1593. In practice, however, proclamations and licences for export of specified amounts were sometimes issued, notwithstanding the statute; and more often the privy council prohibited exports even when prices fell below the threshold. Yet smuggling was common, partly because grain could legally be exported to Ireland or (until 1558) Calais, and customs officials were corrupt. From 1534 to 1555, all export was forbidden by statute, except with a royal licence; and from 1571 to 1593 a new statute allowed export in English ships after proclamation if the council were certified by local men of an abundance of corn. The corn-badgers who acted as links between growers and consumers were frequently made scapegoats for scarcity and high prices: thus statutes of 1552 and 1563 required badgers to be licensed by JPs and regulated their activities.[40]

Originally, the council relied on the normal officers of local government to execute its orders concerning the increasingly detailed regulation of the grain trade. In 1565, however, special commissioners for the restraint of the grain trade were appointed. They were authorised to stop shipments of corn and to license exports, and from 1576 they became a regular part of the machinery of local government. Similarly, the council also required local government officials to ensure that corn reached the markets at a reasonable price for consumers. It attempted to ensure that grain was moved from well-supplied regions of the realm to those in need, ordering JPs in counties which normally supplied London or major towns to permit the corn to be sent despite shortages. It also worked with town authorities who had long

39 John Walter and Keith Wrightson, 'Dearth and the social order in early modern England' in *Past & Present*, lxxi (1976), pp. 22–42; John Walter, 'The social economy of dearth in early modern England' in idem et Roger Schofield (eds), *Famine, disease and the social order in early modern society* (Cambridge, 1989), pp. 75–128; Williams, *Tudor regime*, pp. 185–8.

40 N.S.B. Gras, *The evolution of the English corn market* (Cambridge Mass., 1926); V.R. Ponko, 'N.S.B. Gras and Elizabethan corn policy: a re-examination of the problem' in *Economic History Review*, xvii (1964–5), pp. 24–42; Thirsk (ed.), *Agrarian history of England and Wales*, ch. 8.

enforced a system of regulations to control the price of bread and to pre-vent the most common offences against marketing food – 'engrossing', 'forestalling' and 'regrating'. In 1536, for example, Henry VIII rebuked the town of Galway for allowing its merchants to forestall the market there and also for attracting merchants strangers from Limerick to Galway. Some borough corporations also tried to build up stocks of corn against periods of dearth. The government aimed to extend these mechanisms over producers, traders and consumers outside the towns too.

Conciliar interventions usually coincided with periods of dearth. Beginning in 1527, and again in 1544 and 1545, special commissioners were appointed during years of bad harvest to search all barns, compile a survey of available grain, and compel its owners to take it to market for sale. By mid-century, however, JPs were being charged with these tasks. During the hard winter of 1586–7 the privy council introduced standing orders to JPs for supplying the markets in time of need. This *Book of Orders* (and later *Books of Orders* issued in dearth years down to 1631) codified and supervised the traditional system for regulating the market, and to ensure a controlled distribution. Its regulations held the price mechanism in check, requiring corn to be sold openly each week at a fair price; and it became the model for the working of the internal market in grain for the next two centuries. In times of dearth, the crown encouraged imports of grain, exceptionally by direct action itself, in 1546 for instance, but more usually by encouraging towns and individual merchants to import supplies. England was self-sufficient in years of good harvest. Mediocre or bad harvests brought short-ages, although the promotion of imports did not play a major role in the government's strategy. It also forbade the use of grain for making starch, or feeding sheep on peas which were the best stand-by for the poor when corn was scarce; and it even went so far as to order and encourage the clergy to preach sermons on the virtues of abstinence among the wealthy and patience among the hungry. Finally, from the 1530s the government tried to regulate the price of meat, beer, wine, sugar, and later butter, cheese and (on one occasion) grain under Edward VI by statute and proclamation: the strategy failed because of the underlying flawed concept of the 'just price' and because of regional variations in supply and demand. After 1558 national price fixing was abandoned in favour of a more localised system which took account of these regional variations. Overall, the privy council certainly pursued its objectives energetically. It issued detailed orders and required frequent reports by local commissioners: by the standards of the time, it was well informed about supplies of corn in times of dearth. There is some evidence of evasion – hoarding and illegal exports – but on the whole the system was enforced, and the prosecution of offenders was not uncommon.[41] The system seems to have alleviated the worst shortages and distress, so that food riots and rebellion were unusual. There was certainly smuggling and evasion, reluctance to sell at less high prices, and profiteering; but the system did mitigate the rigours of a totally free-market economy, which was perhaps the best an early-modern government could do.

If prices rose, what about wages, and conditions of employment? Here the basis of government activity was the statute of 1388 (re-enacted under Henry VIII) which imposed national maxima for wages and empowered JPs to assess actual rates within these limits. Likewise, boroughs set maximum wages for their inhabitants, but some went a stage further and also set minimum wages for textile workers to try to protect them against exploitation. Yet, the legislation probably did little to help the poor because the 1388 statute had been conceived at a time of declining population and shortage of labour, as a means of holding wages down, whereas in the sixteenth century with inflation and unemployment driving real wage costs lower, there was a need to raise wages so that they kept pace with the cost of food. Nonetheless, JPs were concerned to fix wage maxima at points which ensured an adequate supply of labour – which drove wages up – while also resisting demands for excessive wages. For instance, the grand jury of Worcestershire echoed a common view when it complained that 'we find the unreasonableness of servants' wages a great grievance, so that servants are grown proud and idle'. Such problems were not effectively tackled until 1563. An increasing recognition that England was subject to regional variations moved the government to pass the Statute of Artificers which, *inter alia*, instructed JPs to assess maximum wages in each county. After 1563 the government occasionally intervened in specific areas where workers were thought to be especially vulnerable to exploitation. In 1595, for instance, the privy council ordered clothiers to raise the wages of textile workers to insulate them from the worst effects of high prices. While these measures no doubt went some way toward redressing regional imbalances and instances of exploitation in certain sectors, wages in the late sixteenth century simply did not match soaring prices: it is estimated that between 1570 and 1600 wages in Chester rose by 40 per cent while prices increased by more than

41 Paul Slack, *Poverty and policy in Tudor and Stuart England* (London, 1988), chs 6–7; Wood, *Riot, rebellion and popular politics*, pp. 97–8; Williams, *Tudor regime*, pp. 189–95; *S.P. Hen. VIII*, ii, 309–11.

100 per cent. In Rutland, prices doubled in roughly the same period while assessed wages remained predominantly static.[42]

The poor law

Most important of the innovations were the poor laws which aimed to regulate begging and to encourage the poor to work. Ironically, in the early sixteenth century, the legal basis of the poor laws remained three statutes which had been passed in the years following the Peasant Revolt, in a very different economic climate. Yet the Tudor response to increasing unemployment was initially to revive and tinker with the existing statutory controls rather than directly to tackle the problem. Until 1576, it was presumed that only those poor who were physically incapable of working (the aged and 'impotent') should be unemployed and therefore deserving of relief, although this was increasingly not the case: it licensed them to beg in the towns in which they dwelt or to return to their birthplace. In Dublin, for instance, a bye-law of 1558 permitted beggars to beg only within the ward in which they dwelled; those found begging in other wards were to be set in the stocks for 24 hours; and 'strange beggars' were not to beg within the city at all. Similarly in Scotland, a statute of 1535 established the principle that every parish should be responsible for its own poor. In England, all those capable of work (sturdy beggars, vagrants and vagabonds) were to be imprisoned until dealt with by the justices of gaol delivery or, if they had left their masters without licence, they were to be set in the stocks. Statutes of 1495 and 1531 devised new punishments for sturdy beggars. The 1495 statute ordered that vagabonds be set in the stocks for three days and then sent home, and that an impotent beggar be allowed to beg only in the hundred where he had previously dwelled or been born. A proclamation of 1530 which was confirmed by statute in 1531 ordered that vagabonds be whipped before putting them in the stocks, because the idleness of the poor is 'the mother and root of all vices'. Concurrently, the 1531 statute instructed JPs to give licences to beg to the impotent poor. They likewise had traditionally not been allowed to wander the countryside, but should beg in the town in which they then were or, if they could not be maintained there, should go elsewhere or return to their birthplaces. Thus, the main difference was that impotent poor were

---

42   Williams, *Tudor regime*, pp. 177–80 (quotation, p. 180); Palliser, *The age of Elizabeth*, pp. 19, 150–2, 156–9, 317–18, 323–4; Wrightson, *Earthly necessities*, pp. 146–7.

not punished for begging, provided they begged at home or in their usual townland: no state relief was available. Moreover, the general aims remained the same – to deter the able-bodied from idleness by punishment, and to keep both categories of poor immobile so that they did not wander at will through the countryside.[43]

From the mid-1530s, however, there was increasing recognition that the able-bodied poor might be unemployed through no fault of their own, and gradually the machinery was established to support them and to provide them with work. An ambitious official bill of 1536 proposed a national scheme for the relief both of the impotent and the able-bodied poor. Those able to work were to be employed on 'certain common works' – such as making roads, repairing harbours, and scouring watercourses. All this was to be financed by a special tax on income and capital, while the impotent poor were to be relieved in their parishes by voluntary alms collected by 'censors or overseers of poverty and correctors of idleness' supervised by JPs. The casual distribution of alms was forbidden. The bill was presented personally by Henry VIII himself in the Commons, but it failed, probably because it attempted to levy a compulsory income tax. It was replaced by a much more conservative statute to last only until the next parliament (in fact, later in 1536). This committed the government to intervention in principle for the first time, and acknowledged that the able-bodied poor should be found work, but it provided no special machinery for doing so. Nonetheless, some of the proposals of the 1536 bill were subsequently taken up by individual town corporations which erected similar machinery for poor relief by means of bye-laws.[44] Within their several jurisdictions, schemes for compulsory poor relief were thus introduced by London in 1547, Norwich in 1549, York in 1550, Cambridge and Ipswich in 1557, and Exeter in 1560. In turn, these schemes eventually prompted parliament under Elizabeth I to sanction an effective national scheme.[45] For instance, Exeter instructed its burgesses in 1562 to introduce a bill in parliament to amend the national poor relief laws

43 Williams, *Tudor regime*, pp. 196–201 (quotation, p. 197); Slack, *Poverty and policy*, pp. 113–19; Ramsay, *Tudor economic problems*, p. 159; Gilbert, *Calendar of ancient records of Dublin*, I, 479; Smout, *History of the Scottish people*, p. 84.

44 G.R. Elton, *Studies in Tudor and Stuart politics and government*, ii (Cambridge, 1974), pp. 137–54 (quotations, pp. 141, 145); idem, *Reform and renewal: Thomas Cromwell and the common weal* (Cambridge, 1973), pp. 73–4, 123–6.

45 Palliser, *Age of Elizabeth*, pp. 124–8; J.A. Youings, *Sixteenth-century England* (London, 1984), p. 262; Slack, *Poverty and policy*, pp. 119–26; John Pound, *Poverty and vagrancy in Tudor England* (London, 1971), ch. 5.

to give JPs power to use coercion against those who refused to contribute. Although the bill failed, it anticipated the national statutory scheme of 1572 for compulsory poor relief. The Elizabethan system was to last, with modifications, down to 1834.[46]

Following moves in 1552 and 1563 towards a system of compulsory contributions, the statute of 1572 instituted an effective and ongoing scheme of national taxation for poor relief (somewhat surprisingly in view of the crown's inability to secure consent to an effective system of royal taxation). JPs were to list the poor in each parish, assess the money needed to maintain them, and appoint overseers for taxing parishioners. A statute of 1598 reduced the JPs' role to a supervisory one, with the actual work now falling squarely on the parochial overseers of the poor and the churchwardens. By the 1650s the system was operational in perhaps a third of England's 10,000 parishes. Similar moves towards the provision of work culminated in an act of 1576, which ordered the provision of raw materials – wool, flax, hemp or iron – on which the able-bodied poor could be set to work, and which grudgingly admitted that unemployment could arise as a result of misfortune as well as idleness. Houses of correction were to be established in every shire and corporate town. Thus, along with the statutes of 1598 and 1601 which codified and clarified the body of existing legislation, the poor laws were reorganised on new principles, operating under the direction of the privy council. Work had to be provided for those who could not find it; begging was wrong and the helpless should be a charge on the community; the parish was to be the organisation responsible for the task, and JPs should supervise the parochial overseers in the discharge of this duty. By the early seventeenth century, we find parish vestries regulating the collection and distribution of poor rates and devising schemes to provide poor children with board and clothing or to bind them as apprentices to learn useful trades. Assistance, however, was discretionary and conditional upon conformity to the behavourial expectations of the parish officers. In this way, the wealthier and more fortunate members of society were brought to provide for the poor. Thus, after 1576, a sophisticated system of poor-relief was established, and the once amorphous poor masses emerged into three distinct categories: sturdy beggars or vagabonds, the aged or 'impotent', and the deserving unemployed. But the government's acknowledgement of the existence of the

---

46   W.T. MacCaffrey, *Exeter, 1540–1640: the growth of an English county town* (2nd ed. Cambridge Mass., 1975), p. 227; Paul Slack, *The English poor law, 1531–1782* (London, 1990).

latter variety of poor did little to change its perception of the poor as a potentially dangerous segment of society, one that had to be controlled to ensure public order. From 1572, all able-bodied poor were registered and expected to carry valid papers; all those remaining were deemed to be vagabonds – broadly, any person unemployed but physically capable of work. Punishment for such idleness consisted of whipping and boring of an ear for the first offence; subsequent offences made the vagabond a felon, a distinction that carried with it the possibility of execution.[47]

Interestingly, in Scotland a scheme for compulsory poor relief and the provision of work was enacted by parliament within three years of the 1572 statute. Its provisions were much the same, and followed a similar history of repressive legislation 'for the staunching of masterful idle beggars'. Yet, like earlier, more limited statutes of 1425, 1535 and 1552, it proved entirely ineffectual. In other respects, the Scottish response anticipated English measures: as early as the 1570s Regent Moray's government granted provost-marshals (see below, pp. 211–12) wide powers to control the 'great number of rascal people' impersonating soldiers. After 1581, new commissions were introduced to address petty crimes, to tackle certain social abuses and regulate prices in times of dearth.[48] In Scotland, however, royal authority and central government remained much less powerful than in England and its response to socio-economic problems was, accordingly, less comprehensive. The unprecedented burden of the long war with Spain (1585–1604; see below, pp. 255–65), moreover, which in England had served to focus Tudor efforts to extend its controls to all corners of the realm, was not felt in the northern kingdom. Scotland was not at war. Thus many of the laws originating at the centre were unenforceable in the localities where the instruments

47 Pound, *Poverty and vagrancy in Tudor England*, ch. 4; Slack, *Poverty and policy*, pp. 122–31; Williams, *Tudor regime*, pp. 196, 200–2; M.J. Braddick, *State formation in early modern England, c.1550–1700* (Cambridge, 2000), pp. 108–12; Wrightson, *Earthly necessities*, pp. 215–21; Steve Hindle, *The state and social change in early modern England, c.1550–1640* (London, 2000), pp. 162–3, 220–23; idem, 'Exclusion crises: poverty, migration and parochial responsibility in English rural communities, c.1560–1660' in *Rural History*, vii (1996), pp. 125–49. And see now, more generally, Hindle, *On the parish? The micro-politics of poor relief in rural England, c.1550–1750* (Oxford, 2004).

48 T. Thomson and C. Innes (eds), *The acts of the parliaments of Scotland* (vols ii and iii, Edinburgh, 1815), ii, 347, iii, 86–9, 576; R. Mitchison, 'The making of the old Scottish poor law' in *Past & Present*, lxiii (1974), pp. 58–93; Lindsay Boynton, 'The Tudor provost-marshal', in *English Historical Review*, lxxviii (1962), pp. 441–2 (quotation, p. 442); Ellis, 'The commons and the state', p. 143; Jenny Wormald, *Court, kirk and community: Scotland, 1470–1625* (Edinburgh, 1981), p. 162; Wrightson, *Earthly necessities*, p. 217.

of central government were few and noble power continued to predominate. Another difficulty was the pervasiveness of private jurisdictions in Scotland, particularly the regalities, which severely limited royal justice.

The Scottish church also took an interest in poor relief: in 1560, the *Book of Discipline* proposed to use tithe income for this purpose, called on land-lords to cease oppressing their tenants, and threatened those oppressing the poor with ecclesiastical discipline. It was a long time, however, before the reformed church got its hands on this income, and the support of the lairds, merchants, and tradesmen was so important to the kirk that no action was taken about their exploitation of the poor. A statute of 1597 transferred to the kirk session the duty of supervising poor relief; and following the Union of the Crowns, King James tried to strengthen royal justice by introducing English-style local officers. By 1613 the system of justices, and below them constables, was operating in most of Scotland, and a statute of 1617 gave the local justices and constables the duty of assessing parishes and punishing vagrants. Even so, when the harvest failed in 1623 and famine loomed, the privy council commanded the justices to levy only a temporary poor rate, recognising that a permanent one was impossible. Yet even this encountered resistance: the justices of East Lothian, for instance, flatly refused to levy the rate – which 'is odious and smells of an taxation'. Edinburgh had instituted a regular poor rate in the 1580s, and gradually almshouses and houses of correction were established in all the major burghs. Further developments occurred in the 1650s, as the Cromwellian regime tried to strengthen its control of local government. Yet efforts to build up an English-style system of poor relief failed because of the different structures of power at local level. Only very slowly during the seventeenth century did a voluntary system of poor relief become effective, mainly through the burghs and by church col-lections instituted by the kirk, but even this was absent from the highlands. The basic difference was that in Scotland the less powerful central executive proved unable to enforce the law against the vested interests of landowners who resisted rates.[49]

In Ireland things were even worse. It was reported in 1623 that the island 'swarms with more vagrant persons and beggars' than elsewhere, and these were 'not restrained within the parishes where they were born' but 'suffered

49 T.C. Smout (ed.), *A history of the Scottish people, 1560–1830* (London, 1972), pp. 84–7; Goodare, *State and society in early modern Scotland*, p. 65; Whyte, *Scotland before the industrial revo-lution*, pp. 165–9, 203, 259; F.D. Dow, *Cromwellian Scotland, 1651–1660* (Edinburgh, 1979), pp. 162–4, 178–81.

to range where they please'. A rudimentary system of voluntary relief sustained by the corporations and private benefactors, with almshouses and hospitals, had grown up. The Cromwellian regime was particularly alarmed at the numbers of poor in Dublin and made determined efforts to remove them. In 1652, the corporation authorised a monthly levy for poor relief. Elsewhere, however, there were still 'great multitudes of poor swarming in all parts'. Some were rounded up and shipped to the West Indies and the state also provided some money to support local initiatives elsewhere in Ireland. Essentially, however, an effective Irish poor law was not a priority for government. Despite the 'great trains of loose and vagrant persons' – a reflection in part of the more militarised character of Irish society – the threat to security was in Ireland contained by the existence of a standing army.[50]

Inhibiting vagrancy

In England, no doubt partly as a sop to the political nation, the gradual establishment of an effective system of poor relief was accompanied by increasingly stern measures against vagrancy. The vagrancy act of 1495 ordered special searches for vagrants in all the towns and villages of the realm, and its provisions were enforced and tightened by later statutes and proclamations which placed the onus for this on the parish constables supervised by JPs. For instance, during two national campaigns in 1569–72 and 1631–9 the privy council received reports of 742 arrests for vagrancy for an 8-month period during the first campaign, and of 24,867 arrests in 8 years during the second.[51] The Statute of Cambridge had in 1388 instituted licences as a means of restricting labour mobility and holding down wages in response to the labour shortages. Tudor and early Stuart governments retained and extended the system for reasons of public order, so that by 1572 all able-bodied transient poor were expected to have valid papers. The poor law of 1563 also required licensed beggars to wear badges or tokens. The range of punishments meted out to vagrants was also extended, from

---

50 George O'Brien (ed.), *Advertisements for Ireland* (Dublin, 1923), p. 44; T.C. Barnard, *Cromwellian Ireland: English government and reform in Ireland, 1649–1660* (Oxford, 1975), pp. 74–5 (quotation, p. 74).

51 A.L. Beier, *Masterless men: the vagrancy problem in England, 1560–1640* (London, 1985), pp. 14–16, 148–9, 155–6; Palliser, *Age of Elizabeth*, pp. 121–2.

stocks and imprisonment, to whipping (by statute of 1531), flogging and boring ears (1572 statute), branding (1604 statute), and also at times hair-polling, the pillory, the ducking-stool and ear-cropping. Vagrancy was also made a felony for repeated offences in six separate statutes passed between 1536 and 1604. For example, between 1603 and 1638 Wiltshire constables reported the punishing of 982 vagrants by whipping, while 143 more were sent to gaol to await gaol delivery: of the latter, 64 were committed for trial as felons. Increasingly under Elizabeth the prospect of imprisonment and trial for felony was used to encourage vagrants to enlist for military service overseas, although in theory recruitment was voluntary. The same also theoretically applied in the case of transportation – transportation to the colonies, especially Virginia, began in 1607 – although the Vagrancy Act of 1597 offered some statutory authority by providing that dangerous rogues should be banished overseas. Finally, whereas houses of correction had originally been established to employ the willing poor and correct the unwilling, they were increasingly used as common gaols. Yet the original idea retained some currency until the establishment of workhouses in the later seventeenth century.[52]

As the scale of the problem increased during the sixteenth century, the common law traditions of trial by jury and oral testimony, on which government had earlier relied, were increasingly eroded by statutes (outlined above) which enjoined summary justice. Constables and JPs were empowered to proceed by examination and punishment, without trial. Nevertheless, these extensions of summary justice worried both legal theorists and members of parliament who suggested that they were contrary to Magna Carta because they oppressed the 'free subject'. Undoubtedly, they constituted a significant extension of state authority, although of course the status of the victims, and the apparent threat to order and society which they posed, eased acceptance. Moreover, as the 1495 statute noted, the act of 1383 involved 'great charges ... to [the king's subjects] for bringing of vagabonds to the gaols'; and Tudor England had not enough gaols to contain those apprehended. The most novel extension of these powers, however, was the use of provost-marshals proceeding by martial law.[53]

Provost-marshals were military in origin, possibly replicas of the French *prévôts*, and were appointed from Henry VIII's reign to discipline the armed

---

52 Beier, *Masterless men*, pp. 154–64; Slack, *Poverty and policy*, pp. 49–76.
53 Beier, *Masterless men*, pp. 156–7 (quotation, p. 157); Slack, *Poverty and policy*, pp. 94–8; Hindle, *The state and social change*, pp. 162–6; Williams, *Tudor regime*, pp. 202–4.

forces. In the aftermath of major risings in 1536, 1549 and 1569, however, the office was occasionally used against civilians, especially beggars; and in 1556 in the more turbulent conditions of Ireland the marshal of the army was ordered to proceed against suspects, vagabonds, and all idle and master-less folk.[54] During the war years from 1585, the office of provost-marshal became a paramilitary force with wide powers, and even during the long period of peace from 1604 the government continued to use martial law against civilians. From the 1590s, there were provost-marshals in every shire and major town. Originally their duties had been chiefly to control dis-charged soldiers, but increasingly they rounded up vagrants. And unlike constables and JPs they were full-time and well paid, each accompanied by 6 to 10 well-armed and mounted attendants. Not surprisingly, they were also more effective. In two Hertfordshire hundreds in 1633, 136 vagrants were taken, 95 by the marshals and 41 by the parish officers.[55]

Closely related in origins to the office of provost-marshal was that of lord-lieutenant, which was also a Tudor development. Lieutenants had tradi-tionally been appointed for limited periods to lead royal armies during periods of war and rebellion and had power of martial law which was exer-cised under the Tudors by the appointment of a provost-marshal. During the widespread rebellions of 1549, numbers of lieutenants were appointed to raise troops and quell the rebels. In the aftermath, however, with discontent still simmering, the government seems to have realised the potential of the office for policing the shires; and by 1551 the country was divided into areas each with a lieutenant, whose commission was renewed annually, performing military and peace-keeping duties. The lieutenant had overall responsibility for maintaining order and security and was given charge of the newly-revived militia. From 1585, the lords-lieutenants' commissions regularly authorised them to appoint provost marshals. In the case of the lieutenancy, however, the office was unpaid and normally filled by a leading noble of the region, with the county gentry acting as his deputies.[56]

How should these changes be assessed? Clearly, they were the product of many different political and socio-economic influences. The interests of

54   L. Boynton, 'The Tudor provost-marshal' in *English Historical Review*, lxxvii (1962), pp. 437–55; Hindle, *The state and social change*, pp. 162–6.
55   Boynton, 'Tudor provost-marshal', pp. 437–55; Beier, *Masterless men*, pp. 152–3.
56   G. Scott-Thomson, *Lords lieutenant in the sixteenth century: a study in Tudor local administration* (London, 1923); Bush, *Government policy of Protector Somerset*, p. 127; Boynton, 'Tudor provost-marshal', p. 441; idem, *The Elizabethan militia 1558–1638* (London, 1967), pp. 7–12, 145; MacCulloch, *Suffolk and the Tudors*, pp. 77–8.

producers and consumers, of nobles and peasants, and of crown and community were not always easy to reconcile. Yet equally clearly agitation and unrest by the lower orders had a significant impact on the development of the English state, particularly in the sixteenth century. Only rarely were these changes a direct response to popular insurrections, but under the threat of disorder, Tudor governments began to assume a much more active role in regulating the economy and society. These new responsibilities in turn prompted the creation of new offices – provost-marshals, parochial overseers of the poor, and county lieutenants – while also leading to an extension in the powers of existing officials like the JPs and constables. Much of the new machinery was repressive in aim, intended like the fourteenth-century labour laws to consolidate aristocratic power over the commons. Yet remarkably in a political society dominated by landlords dependent in large part on rents from corn-growing tenants, the government consistently put the interests of consumers before those of producers in framing its policy. Within the towns, too, the ruling elite was persuaded to sanction and enforce policies which ran against its own economic advantage in the interests of public order. The result was the creation of a comparatively enlightened system of poor relief and a mechanism for regulating the economy for the good of the community as a whole.

Undoubtedly, the new structures were less efficient in practice than had been intended, and much depended on private charity and local initiatives. Yet they were broadly successful, at least from the government's viewpoint. Some people did die of starvation, nonetheless. Exceptionally in 1623, 161 people were buried in the churchyard at Greystoke, Cumberland, four times the normal number, and 62 of these deaths occurred in the 3 months from September. The church register there records some of these deaths as caused by starvation: 'a poor fellow destitute of succour', 'a poor, hungerstarved beggar boy', a 'child died for very want of food and maintenance to live', a 'woman died for want of means to live'. England and Wales were not generally as vulnerable to famine as Scotland. (In the same year, the parish gravemaster at Burntisland in Fife paid for 329 burials between April and November, perhaps a third of the population.) As a result of a combination of rising population and inflation, the wages of urban and rural labourers had fallen by the 1590s, in terms of their real purchasing power, to less than half the average for the later fifteenth century. Yet, even in the years 1595–8 which saw a crisis of subsistence and major revolts in many parts of Europe, the dramatic inflation of prices and disastrous drop in wages with consequent starvation in upland, pastoral regions, produced nothing worse than a village rising in Oxfordshire.[57] This must surely reflect in some measure the relatively enlightened system of poor relief.

Equally importantly, the response to the problems of poverty and unrest led to a substantial increase in the power of the state, apparent both in the creation of new offices and an extension in the normal range of government activities. The overall effect was no doubt to consolidate and stabilise the existing social hierarchy. Yet perhaps there was also a price to pay in terms of the wider diffusion of power within the state. One of the effects of sixteenth-century inflation was to accelerate the stratification of peasant society which had been continuing since the mid-fourteenth century, so that the peasantry were increasingly divided into comparatively prosperous freeholders and farmers and relatively landless labourers. With regard to public order, however, the interests of the wealthier peasants were substantially the same as the gentry; and it was these leading villagers who were increasingly involved in local government as constables, overseers of the poor, and as jurors serving on the increasing numbers of inquests. Thus in some measure this extension of government was effected by the further integration of the 'middling sort' into the early modern state.[58] Yet Lowland England's predominantly dispersed patterns of landholding, its 'civil' society, and its structures of power were not replicated in Ireland and Scotland where landlords and lineages were stronger, society more militarised, and the power of central government much weaker. Arguably the critical difference was the relative diffusion of political influence and, in the countryside, the landed rights of the peasantry: in England, the state was increasingly dependent on the 'middling sort' to maintain order and, negatively, the traditions of rural protest acted as a check on autocratic tendencies. In Scotland and Ireland, however, efforts to impose English-style local officials and legislation on regions with different power structures were initially unsuccessful.

---

57 John Walter, 'A "rising of the people"? The Oxfordshire rising of 1596' in *Past & Present*, cvii (1985), pp. 90–143; A.B. Appleby, *Famine in Tudor and Stuart England* (Liverpool, 1978); Walter and Schofield (ed.), *Famine, disease and the social order*, ch. 1; Peter Laslett, *The world we have lost* (London, 1965), ch. 5 (quotations, pp. 121–2); Wrightson, *Earthly necessities*, pp. 198–9; Palliser, *Age of Elizabeth*, pp. 140–2, 156–60.

58 J.S. Morrill and J.D. Walter, 'Order and disorder in the English Revolution' in Anthony Fletcher and John Stevenson (eds), *Order and disorder in early modern England* (Cambridge, 1985), pp. 150–3; Wood, *Riot, rebellion and popular politics*, pp. 110–11.

THE EMERGENCE OF A BRITISH
STATE SYSTEM, 1560–84

The 20 months from the accession of Queen Elizabeth to the treaty of Edinburgh and the Scottish Reformation Parliament saw the establishment of Protestant regimes in both British monarchies. With the increasing confessionalisation (i.e. restructuring on confessional lines) of European politics, this meant that, for the first time, ministers in Edinburgh and London looked upon their counterparts in the other British monarchy as natural allies. Conversely, religious differences gradually undermined traditional ties both between England and Spain and between Scotland and France, so erecting an ideological barrier between the British kingdoms and the leading monarchies of continental Europe. In 1560, however, the two British regimes were in a very weak position, and not just because the throne of both kingdoms was now occupied by a woman: in both countries Protestants saw themselves as an embattled minority threatened both at home and abroad by the satanic forces of the papal Antichrist. In Scotland, there was no legally-constituted government: in 1559–60 the Protestant Lords of the Congregation had illegally deposed Queen Mary's regent and established themselves as 'the Great Council of the Realm', while Mary remained in France, pawn of the Guise interest.[1] Yet, the role of the northern kingdom in European politics had traditionally been distinctly marginal: the confessional edge to Scottish politics was now more overt, but weak regencies in the name of monarchs who were under age or absentees were nothing very new in Scotland. The English monarchy, however, had traditionally carried more weight in European politics. Henry VIII in particular had had a clear strategy of dynastic aggrandisement through war and aggressive diplomacy aimed at recovering the erstwhile English territories in continental Europe. The policy was perhaps unrealistic, and in its impact on royal finances and

---

1   Dawson, *Politics of religion in the age of Mary, queen of Scots*, ch. 3; Wormald, *Mary queen of Scots*, pp. 95–109 (quotation, p. 102); R.B. Wernham, *Before the Armada: the growth of English foreign policy 1485–1588* (London, 1966), ch. 19.

[2 1 6] the English economy, ultimately disastrous; but no one was left in any doubt about the king's determination to cut a figure on the European stage.[2]

Not until the reign of Elizabeth did an English monarch again have the opportunity and the resources to shape a forward policy. 'She seems to me', wrote Philip II's ambassador, 'incomparably more feared than her sister, and gives orders and has her way as absolutely as her father did.' Yet Elizabeth had no such vision of dynastic or imperial greatness. She simply dealt with the various problems which beset her rule as they arose. Initially, of course, these problems were unremitting, but later, from the 1570s, when the regime was fully established, the queen still had no strategic plans concerning England's position on the margins of Europe. Specifically, should the English monarchy aim, through war and diplomacy, to play a major role in the European state system, as under her father? Or should the monarchy focus more on the British Isles, where recent events in both Ireland and Scotland had underlined the weaknesses of English power? Both options had their merits and shortcomings, as particular developments under Edward VI and Mary had shown. Yet Elizabeth's failure to dictate policy meant that the initiative passed to her ministers, most notably Cecil, and even to the political nation at large, in a way which Henry VIII would never have allowed. Elizabeth remained true to her motto, *semper eadem* (always the same), but the price was a constant struggle to stand still; and of course in the end she failed.[3]

Until 20 years ago, traditional nationalist perspectives on Elizabeth's reign seemed to imply that the queen had a split personality in regard to her two kingdoms. The queen of England inherited chaos and division and imposed unity and concord: the queen of Ireland, by contrast, reduced many of her subjects to starvation and large areas of her kingdom to ashes. How could a monarch who ruled England so skilfully and successfully get things so badly wrong in Ireland?[4] Recent writings point towards the development of a more holistic interpretation of the reign, in which a long period of comparatively effective and successful rule throughout the Tudor state (especially in Lowland England, less so in Wales and the north, even less in

2 Susan Doran, *England and Europe in the sixteenth century* (Basingstoke, 1999), pp. 1–26.
3 Susan Doran, *Elizabeth I and foreign policy, 1558–1603* (London, 2000), passim; Christopher Haigh, *Elizabeth I* (2nd ed. London, 1998), passim; J.E. Neale, *Queen Elizabeth I* (ed. London, 1960), p. 72 (quotation).
4 Although other opinions were already being voiced, the contrasting interpretations of Elizabeth were neatly expressed in the titles to the conclusions of Williams, *Tudor regime*, ch. 14 ('The Tudor achievement') and my *Tudor Ireland: crown, community and the conflict of cultures 1470–1603* (London, 1985), pp. 314–20 ('The Tudor failure').

Ireland) was followed by a shorter period (beginning in 1579 in Ireland, but only after 1588 in England) of growing inertia and disillusionment.[5] As regards lasting achievements, moreover, the political unification of the British Isles and the creation of a British multiple monarchy had, in retrospect, appeared to constitute Elizabeth's legacy to her British successors. In March 1603, the surrender of the rebel earl of Tyrone to Elizabeth's last viceroy marked the completion of the Tudor conquest of Ireland, and six days earlier King James VI of Scotland had quietly succeeded to the English throne on the death of Elizabeth herself. The Anglo-Scottish dynastic union had long been the major goal of King James's foreign policy, and the conquest of Ireland was of course a traditional ambition of English monarchs, though hardly an urgent priority. As recent research has increasingly shown, however, in both cases the circumstances which had brought about these momentous developments owed little to far-sighted planning on Elizabeth's part, although perhaps rather more to the manoeuvrings of her ministers.[6]

Centre and periphery under Elizabeth

The closing months of 1560 found Elizabeth and her ministers still grappling with fundamental problems concerning the establishment of the regime. These included the question of Elizabeth's marriage and the succession, the financial crisis, and the wider political and ideological implications of the religious settlement. From the outset, Elizabeth's preference for a Protestant settlement had shaped her choice of ministers, household officials and privy council. The leading councillors and members of the household were almost all identified with reform, either the queen's Boleyn and Howard relatives, or other members of her household under Mary, or members of Edward VI's government. Her first privy council of 20 included two Marians, Archbishop Heath and Sir Thomas Cheyney, who soon disappeared, and nine nobles. Two-thirds of Mary's councillors were dismissed,

---

5 In the reaction to English romantic nationalist presentations of Elizabeth, I think the decisive contribution was Haigh, *Elizabeth I* (1st ed., London, 1988; 2nd ed., London, 1998). References here to this work are to the second edition.

6 See, for instance, Brendan Bradshaw and John Morrill (eds), *The British problem, c.1534–1707: state formation in the Atlantic archipelago* (Basingstoke, 1996), chs 1–6; Stephen Alford, *The early Elizabethan polity: William Cecil and the British succession crisis, 1558–1569* (Cambridge, 1998); J.E.A. Dawson, 'Anglo-Scottish relations: security and succession' in Robert Tittler and Norman Jones (eds), *A companion to Tudor Britain* (Oxford, 2004), ch. 10.

although some of the more moderate bureaucrats, such as Lord Treasurer Winchester and Sir John Mason, treasurer of the chamber, and some regional magnates, the earls of Arundel, Derby, Pembroke and Shrewsbury, provided continuity. The inclusion of six regional magnates was a conscious attempt by Elizabeth to associate them with the regime, but in practice the magnates were mainly absentees, ruling their regions, leaving trusted officers and relatives to do most of the work. The exclusion of religious conservatives and the subsequent decline of the magnate element thus left a ruling group of committed Protestants, with a common political and ideological outlook.[7] Yet, this council was quite unrepresentative of the political nation as a whole.

By 1561, the main changes implicit in the transition from Catholic forms of worship to the Elizabethan religious settlement had been imposed in the parishes, but no one was under any illusion concerning popular support for the settlement. Unrest might explode into rebellion at any time, and Elizabeth's religious preferences had also exacerbated the regime's other difficulties. In particular, such support as the Reformation yet enjoyed was largely confined to the more urbanised English Lowlands, so compounding long-standing difficulties of government in the Tudor borderlands. The scarcity of reliable, reform-minded nobles and gentry available to serve in local government in these regions underlined the weakness of central control. Tudor administrative reform initiated by Henry VIII had broken up traditional power structures in the borderlands, but only in Wales had Tudor reform won general acceptance among the local elites. Mary, in particular, had opted to rehabilitate fallen magnate families who were victims of Henry VIII's policies – the Percies, Dacres and Fitzgeralds, for instance – in the hope that this would strengthen Tudor rule in the provinces. Elizabeth could continue this strategy, and hope that office and loyalty would override religious conservatism, or she could bring in more trusted outsiders who might lack regional authority. In practice, she opted for the latter. She was in any case very sparing in the creation of new peerages: the increase in population and the expansion of the gentry notwithstanding, there were only 55 English peers when she died, although there had been 57 at her accession. Moreover, despite the extension of Tudor rule throughout Ireland, the number of Irish peers also remained more or less static: she created the MacCarthy More earl of Clancare in 1565, and Hugh O'Neill was eventually allowed

7   Haigh, Elizabeth I, pp. 10–11, 41, 70–2; Williams, *Tudor regime*, pp. 425–8, 452–6; Wallace MacCaffrey, *Elizabeth I* (London, 1993), ch. 3.

to succeed his grandfather as earl of Tyrone, but the earldom of Desmond disappeared after the fourteenth earl's attainder.[8]

Yet this conservatism underlined the status of the nobility, which she reinforced in other ways too. At least in central and southern England, Elizabeth actively courted the nobles. She involved them in local and national government, appointed them to the council and on embassies abroad, visited them on summer progresses and encouraged their regular attendance at court. Royal progresses kept mainly to the Home Counties, however, and never penetrated west of Bristol or north of Stafford. And court attendance was much more difficult for the Irish nobility, who had also to defend their estates. Her kinsman, Thomas Butler, eleventh earl of Ormond ('Black Tom'), spent much time at court (to the detriment of his local influence), and was briefly the queen's favourite in 1566, but other Irish peers visited mainly under duress, upon receipt of a summons to answer for misconduct.[9] Elizabeth's distrust of the marcher lords in turn impacted on the conduct of government in these regions.

For its part, the government of Wales caused few problems. As president of the council there, Elizabeth appointed Sir Henry Sidney. Moreover, other nobles and gentry with Welsh estates, such as Robert Dudley (earl of Leicester from 1564) in north Wales, William Herbert, earl of Pembroke, in Glamorgan, William Somerset, earl of Worcester, in Gower and Monmouthshire, and Sir James Croft in Herefordshire were also closely connected to the regime, even if not above advancing their own interests at the expense of law and order. Very few Welshmen were appointed to the council, but they included leading landowners like Sir John Perrot, and 13 of Elizabeth's 16 Welsh bishops were also local men.[10] Elsewhere, however, the situation was much more difficult. In Ireland, Elizabeth's decision to continue as governor the inexperienced but ambitious Thomas Radcliffe, earl of Sussex, did little to mend fences with the nobles and gentry of the English Pale and the

8 Williams, *Tudor regime*, pp. 421–56; Haigh, *Elizabeth I*, chs 2–3. There is as yet no detailed study of the Irish peerage, but see the remarks in Victor Treadwell, 'The Irish parliament of 1569–71' in *Proc. R.I.A.*, lxv (1966), sect. C, pp. 55–89; idem, 'Sir John Perrot and the Irish parliament of 1585–6' ibid., lxxxv (1985), sect. C, pp. 259–308; *Handbook of British Chronology* (3rd ed., London, 1986), pp. 490–7.

9 Haigh, *Elizabeth I*, pp. 51–69, 152–3; Ellis, *Ireland in the age of the Tudors*, pp. 286, 298–9, 304; idem, 'Centre and periphery in the Tudor state', in Robert Tittler and Norman Jones (eds), *A companion to Tudor Britain* (Oxford, 2004), pp. 136–7; Edwards, *Ormond lordship*, pp. 98–100, 180–200.

10 Williams, *Wales*, pp. 307, 336–7; J.G. Jones, *Wales and the Tudor state: government, religious change and the social order 1534–1603* (Cardiff, 1989), pp. 53–4.

leading earls, Desmond and Kildare, who were alienated by Sussex's coercive policies, or with Shane O'Neill and the expropriated midland Irish, who were its main targets. Promoted lord lieutenant on his return to Ireland in mid-1560, Sussex continued where he had left off, but was hamstrung by the reduction in the size of the army to 1,500 men and by Elizabeth's injunctions to economy. Renewed political instability and the sharp deterioration in Anglo-Gaelic relations brought about by military adventures in the Gaelic midlands and Ulster heightened fears concerning the Pale's defence. They also seemed to threaten a new Geraldine League surrounding the earl of Kildare who was disappointed of the governorship. The new-found amity with Edinburgh had prompted the most powerful Scottish magnate, the earl of Argyll, to volunteer his services in Ulster, where the MacDonalds of Antrim and Calvagh O'Donnell of Tyrconnell were his clients. Cecil appreciated the value of Argyll's political influence and military support against Shane O'Neill. His enthusiastic support for a Gaelic Reformation would also have assisted the queen's efforts to persuade the Irish chiefs to accept her religious policies. A scheme was devised whereby the MacDonalds of Antrim (who were subjects of the Scottish crown, and so 'strangers' in Ireland) would become English subjects, and O'Donnell a 'faithful and true subject', in return for Argyll's assistance against O'Neill. Yet Sussex saw the Ulster situation in exclusively Irish terms, was anxious to keep out the Scots, and so ignored Argyll's offers of support, with the result that, from an English perspective, affairs in Ulster steadily deteriorated.

In 1561 and 1563, Sussex mounted expeditions against O'Neill, who promptly went to ground, and in between Elizabeth listened to other counsels, notably the earl of Kildare. She even received the chief at court, upon a safe-conduct. Yet, without Argyll's support, the lieutenant lacked the troops and money to impose a military solution in Ulster. O'Neill gradually extended his grip on the province, capturing Argyll's client chiefs, first O'Donnell in 1561 and then James and Sorley Boy in 1565 when he defeated the Antrim MacDonalds at the battle of Glentaisie. Thereupon, Argyll reversed his strategy, opening negotiations with O'Neill just as Elizabeth despatched a new governor, Sir Henry Sidney, to address the situation. In 1567, O'Neill was defeated at Farsetmore by the O'Donnells while trying to restore his position in Tyrconnell and then killed by the MacDonalds with whom he was negotiating Sorley Boy's release. O'Neill's murder initially raised English hopes, but in the aftermath, Argyll swiftly restored his influence, creating through marriage alliances a coalition of the three major Ulster chiefs. Turlough Luineach O'Neill, Shane's successor, married Lady Agnes, widow of James MacDonald; and their daughter, Finola (*Iníon Dubh*, 'the dark-haired daughter'), married the young Tyrconnell chief, Hugh O'Donnell. Their dowries came in the form of redshanks: in August 1569 O'Neill and O'Donnell received their brides on Rathlin as also 32 galleys with 4,000 men despatched from Islay. This revolutionary realignment of Ulster politics both stabilised the North Channel area and also paved the way for the province's successful resistance to Tudor expansion down to 1603. Instead of the peaceful assimilation of Ulster in terms of politics and religion, the stage was set for the bloody struggle which culminated in the Nine Years' War.[11]

In the midlands, Sussex's efforts to control the Leix-Offaly plantation through his brother cut across the earl of Kildare's traditional role in defending the English Pale and his hegemony over the border chiefs. Kildare's supporters boasted 'that 'tis the earl and not the English power that preserveth the [Pale] from burnings and other mischiefs', and even those unsympathetic to Kildare's pretensions thought that Sussex's defence arrangements were inadequate and excessively onerous. Moreover, with the Irish nobility barely conformist or staunchly Catholic, almost the only leading Irish magnate on whom Elizabeth relied absolutely was her kinsman and courtier, Black Tom Butler of Ormond. In the ongoing feud between Ormond and his less able and educated rival, Gerald Fitzgerald, fourteenth earl of Desmond, she took stern measures against Desmond, but frequently turned a blind eye to Ormond's misconduct. Yet not even Ormond was ever appointed governor.[12]

Affairs were not much better in the Tudor north, save that the establishment of a more anglophile, Protestant regime in Scotland reduced the traditional problems of border defence to one of controlling the border surnames and other disruptive elements in marcher society. As president of the council there, Elizabeth had initially continued the fifth earl of Shrewsbury. Shrewsbury's marriage alliances with the leading northern magnates, the

11   Dawson, *Politics of religion in the age of Mary, queen of Scots*, pp. 104–10, 126–37, 155–65; Ellis, *Ireland in the age of the Tudors*, pp. 276–9; Ciaran Brady, 'Shane O'Neill departs from the court of Elizabeth: Irish, English, Scottish perspectives and the paralysis of policy, July 1559 to April 1562' in S.J. Connolly (ed.), *Kingdoms United? Great Britain and Ireland since 1500: integration and diversity* (Dublin, 1999), pp. 13–28.

12   Ellis, *Ireland in the age of the Tudors*, pp. 271–8 (quotation, p. 276); V.P. Carey, *Surviving the Tudors: the 'wizard' earl of Kildare and English rule in Ireland, 1537–1586* (Dublin, 2002), ch. 4; Edwards, *Ormond lordship*, pp. 98–100, 180–200; Ciaran Brady, 'Faction and the origins of the Desmond rebellion of 1579' in *Irish Historical Studies*, xxvii (1980–1), pp. 289–312. For Desmond, see now, Anthony McCormack, *The earldom of Desmond: the decline and crisis of a feudal lordship, 1463–1583* (Dublin, 2005).

earls of Northumberland, Cumberland, and Lord Dacre, had helped to heal their disputes and rivalries, although Cumberland and Dacre remained at odds with the *arriviste*, Thomas, Lord Wharton, ennobled by Henry VIII. After Shrewsbury's death in 1560, a succession of reliable outsiders held the presidency, the earl of Rutland (1561–3), Archbishop Young of York (1564–8), the earl of Sussex (1568–72), and finally the queen's cousin, the earl of Huntingdon (1572–95). Yet the basic difficulty was the same: Elizabeth distrusted the northern nobles, who were solidly Catholic, and she opted to pack the administration with southerners and lesser men. In 1559, the two wardens, Northumberland and Dacre, were suspected of hindering the English effort in Scotland on religious grounds. Northumberland was replaced in the east marches by an old soldier, Lord Grey, then by the reliable southerner, the earl of Bedford, and finally by the queen's cousin, Lord Hunsdon (1569–96); and a local rival of the Percies, the lax but conformist Sir John Forster, served as warden of the middle marches (1560–95). Dacre remained warden until his death in 1563, but was kept at court, and thereafter the obedient Henry, Lord Scrope of Bolton, ruled the west marches until his death in 1592. Thus, even earlier than was the case in Ireland, distaste for the Elizabethan religious settlement and exclusion from office helped to reunite the northern magnates into a coherent Catholic block, and so formed the background to the Northern Rising of 1569–70.[13]

Elizabethan finance

Reliance on outsiders to rule the borders also compounded the government's difficulties in regard to a second basic problem surrounding the stability of the regime, financial solvency. Lacking the local *manraed* of the great magnates, these outsiders required larger garrisons for border defence. Larger garrisons not only cost more but exacerbated logistical problems because these borderlands were not self-sufficient in regard to food. In the early 1560s, Irish military expenditure was running at around IR£45,000 per annum, which was more than ten times the queen's revenues there, so requiring an annual subvention of over £23,000 from England. The upkeep of the

13   R.W. Hoyle, 'Faction, feud and reconciliation amongst the northern English nobility' in *History*, lxxxiv (1999), pp. 590–613; Haigh, *Elizabeth I*, pp. 56–7, 65; R.R. Reid, *The king's council in the north* (London, 1921), pp. 187–210; S.J. Watts, *From border to middle shire: Northumberland 1586–1625* (Leicester, 1975), pp. 95–116.

garrison town of Berwick normally cost £15,000 a year, but the rebuilding of the fortifications in the 1560s, and the concurrent increase in personnel, raised this to £40,000 annually. Carlisle on the opposite march was a further expense, although the loss of Calais saved £25,000. In 1562 Elizabeth, recalling the successful Scottish intervention two years earlier, saw an opportunity in the French civil wars to recover Calais. She would subsidise the Huguenots to the tune of £40,000 in return for Newhaven (Le Havre), to be exchanged for Calais when the war was over. Within months, however, the Huguenots and Catholics made peace, and the English garrison occupying Newhaven was soon forced by the French and an outbreak of plague to withdraw. Elizabeth became more cautious than ever in regard to the risks and expense of foreign campaigns.[14]

Perhaps the major achievement of Elizabeth's financial policy was the recoinage, already projected in 1556, which was accomplished in 1560–1. Base money, £560,000, was withdrawn from circulation and converted into fine coin, and the skilfully-managed operation even netted the queen a small profit. Yet even here, Elizabeth's differing priorities were underlined by further issues for Ireland in 1559 of a wretchedly debased coinage, minted from old debased English coins. In fact, this coinage was never recalled and during the crisis years of 1601–3, it was even augmented by a new issue which was less than 3oz fine.[15] For the most part, like much else about Elizabeth, her financial policies were extremely conservative. Initially, her ordinary revenues averaged less than £200,000 a year, and she also inherited debts of £300,000 from Mary. Military operations in France and Scotland in 1559–60 and in 1562–3 (including the navy, ordnance, and refortifying Berwick) cost a further £750,000. Until 1574, she was forced to borrow abroad at interest, but thereafter she was able to manage short-term deficits by exacting forced loans from wealthy subjects or by borrowing from London corporation, generally without paying interest. The measures needed to balance the budget, however, had mostly been initiated under Mary, or even by the Northumberland regime. Lord Treasurer Winchester, who remained in office until his death in 1572, had already improved the

---

14 Anthony Sheehan, 'Irish revenues and English subventions, 1559–1622' in *Proceedings of the Royal Irish Academy*, xc (1990), sect. C, pp. 35–65; Ellis, *Ireland in the age of the Tudors*, pp. 183–5, 345; C.G. Cruickshank, *Elizabeth's army* (Oxford, 1966), pp. 207–12, 283; M.C. Fissel, *English warfare 1511–1642* (London, 2001), pp. 37–40; Williams, *Tudor regime*, p. 70; Wallace MacCaffrey, 'The Newhaven expedition, 1562–1563' in *Historical Journal*, xl (1997), pp. 1–21.

15 Challis, *Tudor coinage*, pp. 126–7, 258, 263–5, 268–74.

management of crown estates, and had also secured a significant increase in customs revenue through Mary's revision of the *Book of Rates*. Thus, net income from crown estates was initially £66,448 per annum, but rose only to £88,767 annually by 1603, in part because rents were not increased to match inflation, and also because at both the start and end of the reign there were massive sales of land, worth in all £25,000 a year, as Elizabeth struggled to balance the books. Worse still, customs revenue which, thanks to Mary's reforms, had yielded £89,000 in 1558/59 slumped to £60,000 a year by the mid-1570s. They recovered to £91,000 per annum during Elizabeth's last five years, but should have been worth far more had the *Book of Rates* been revised in line with inflation. Revenue from feudal dues, worth around £14,000 a year, also stagnated until 1598.[16]

In the circumstances, Elizabeth's discharge of her inherited debts and the accumulation of a credit balance of £300,000 by 1584 seems quite surprising. In part, it was done by rigid economies. At court, salaries were frozen and, partly by reducing bouge of court/food allowances, household expenses were restricted to £40,000 per annum. Courtiers and officials were rewarded mainly by grants of wardships and monopolies rather than by gifts of money and land. The cost of building projects under Elizabeth also averaged less than 10 per cent of her father's lavish expenditure on buildings: she even disposed of 7 superfluous palaces.[17] More importantly, from 1564 to 1585 a long period of peace allowed the reduction of military expenses to a minimum. Yet, during that period, Elizabeth sought and was granted taxation in every session of parliament, save that in 1572. Initially, subsidies were justified quite traditionally by the expense of actual war with France (1559) and the Newhaven expedition (1562–3), but thereafter the justification for Elizabeth's exceptional levy of subsidies in peacetime was the need to meet 'extra-ordinary' charges incurred by the threat of war. Between 1559 and 1571 grants of lay taxation yielded £690,000, with further grants from the clergy.

Essentially, therefore, Elizabeth became increasingly reliant on parliamentary taxation, but earlier attempts to justify taxation on grounds of good rule, necessity, or the increasing costs of government were abandoned. Perhaps one reason why Elizabeth's demands encountered so little opposition was the declining yield of parliamentary subsidies, from £140,000 in 1559 to £80,000 by 1601 – in a period of rising prices and growing prosperity for the political nation. The nobility's self-assessments were only a fraction of

16 Williams, *Tudor regime*, pp. 70–3; Guy, *Tudor England*, pp. 240, 380, 382.
17 Williams, *Tudor regime*, p. 73; Guy, *Tudor England*, pp. 380–1.

their real wealth: Lord Burghley's real income was perhaps £4,000 a year, but he continued to assess himself at 200 marks. Other wealthy subjects were similarly underassessed by the subsidy commissioners in their books; but below the ranks of the gentry, assessments approximated more closely to taxpayers' true worth. In part, however, this failure was offset by an escalation in the incidence of local taxation – especially to meet the rising costs of poor relief, and military preparedness from the mid-1580s.[18]

Overall, therefore, Elizabeth's initial attempts to achieve financial solvency were heavily reliant on measures already put in place under Mary, and thereafter she allowed the revenues to stagnate until the growing cost of war after 1585 prompted sporadic corrective measures. This pattern was largely repeated in microcosm in regard to the Irish revenues, save that there were no Marian reforms to help balance the books initially, and corrective measures had to be taken rather earlier, from 1579, in response to growing unrest and rebellion.[19] Perhaps one reason for Elizabeth's lacklustre record on finance was the regime's initially very narrow base of support. Traditionally, the revenues of English monarchs had accrued overwhelmingly from southern and central England, the monarchy's core territory. With the notable exception of Henry VIII, moreover, successive monarchs since Edward IV had maintained financial solvency chiefly by maximising existing sources of revenue (and limiting expenses), rather than by acquiring new ones. Yet the marked extension from the 1530s onwards of royal power and central control in the Tudor borderlands produced no comparable expansion in the crown's income from these areas which, as we have seen (ch. 5), also posed the greatest challenge to the government's religious policies. For much of Elizabeth's reign the government was perhaps too worried about religious dissent there to risk further alienating the local elites by new fiscal initiatives, and during the war years it was too preoccupied with other problems.

Royal marriages, the Tudor succession and Scottish civil war

The third major difficulty still facing the regime in 1560 was the question of the queen's marriage and the succession. It was widely believed that rule by a

18   G.R. Elton, *The parliament of England 1559–1581* (Cambridge, 1986), pp. 151–74; Williams, *Tudor regime*, pp. 70–5; Guy, *Tudor England*, pp. 381–4.
19   Ellis, *Ireland in the age of the Tudors*, pp. 183–4, 345.

woman was a punishment visited by God on the kingdom, and the antithesis of proper order: this allegedly explained the disasters of Mary's reign. Yet all the arguments against female rule advanced under Mary also applied to Elizabeth. John Knox now decided that in Elizabeth's case God might make an exception and allow the regiment of women so that she could restore the Gospel, but few were persuaded that a Protestant queen was any better than a Catholic queen. Elizabeth was perhaps fortunate that, notwithstanding her claim to the throne under Henry VIII's third Act of Succession 1544, there was no credible male claimant. By the terms of Henry VIII's will, resting on this statute, Lady Catherine Grey, descended from Henry VIII's younger sister, Mary, and sister of the ill-fated Lady Jane, was Elizabeth's next heir. Henry's will had specifically excluded the Stewart line, now represented by the Scottish queen, Mary Stewart, granddaughter of his elder sister, Margaret, but in Catholic eyes, Elizabeth was illegitimate. Thus, Mary Stewart was not only the Catholic claimant to the English throne, she also had a strong claim to be Elizabeth's next heir. Discussion therefore quickly shifted to the question of Elizabeth's marriage and the succession. In the English parliament of 1559, for instance, the House of Commons petitioned the queen to marry and produce an heir; and Elizabeth also answered succeeding parliaments in 1563, 1566 and 1576 that, although of herself she preferred to remain single, she would nonetheless marry for the sake of her subjects. The purpose of marriage, however, was to settle the succession by producing an heir, not to supply a king consort who could rule in Elizabeth's stead. Any doubts about Elizabeth's ability to rule were quickly dispelled; and when marriage to a foreign prince was discussed, the English negotiating position was Mary's 1553 marriage treaty which had excluded Philip of Spain from rule. Yet, so long as Elizabeth remained unmarried, the discussion returned, sooner or later, to the question of the Scottish succession.[20]

On the death of Mary Tudor, Mary queen of Scots had quartered the English arms on her armorial bearings, so publicly asserting her title to the English throne. She refused to ratify the treaty of Edinburgh, because the French had agreed to the English demand that she should no longer use the arms of England, and she refused to ratify the acts of the Scottish Reformation parliament; but otherwise she did nothing. After the death of her husband, Francis II, in December 1560, she sought another continental marriage. Only in mid-August 1561, and with considerable reluctance, did she return to Scotland. The French court and Mary's Catholic subjects led by the

20   Haigh, *Elizabeth I*, pp. 10–15; Wallace MacCaffrey, *Elizabeth I* (London, 1993), pp. 70–1.

influential George Gordon, earl of Huntly, hoped that Mary would then spearhead a Catholic revival. Instead, she agreed to an arrangement suggested by her half-brother, Lord James Stewart, whereby she herself could hear mass in her private chapel at Holyrood in return for her acceptance of the existing Protestant settlement and English alliance. As Dr. Jenny Wormald has argued, the only plausible explanation for this decision is that, by abandoning her claim to the English throne, she hoped instead to harness Protestant support for her claim to be recognised as Elizabeth's heir.[21]

From an English perspective, this was indeed good news. Elizabeth simply dangled this prize in front of Mary, as a means of dissuading her from marrying into the Habsburg or Valois royal families. She advised Mary to marry an English nobleman or a Protestant prince, finally making it clear in August 1563 that marriage against her advice would incur English enmity, and throwing in the sop that continued friendship would eventually bring her to inquire into Mary's right to succeed her. Initially, there was no shortage of suitors for Elizabeth's hand, both princes such as Eric XIV of Sweden, the Archduke of Austria, and the dukes of Holstein and Saxony, and also her own subjects, such as the earl of Arundel, Sir William Pickering and Robert Dudley. The most serious flirtation – and the most disreputable – was with Dudley, whose wife was apparently dying: she then died, and Dudley was accused of poisoning her; and a second rumour about a Dudley marriage involved a restoration of Catholicism in return for Philip II's support in overcoming conciliar opposition. Within a few years, however, Elizabeth had apparently determined to remain single: perhaps in 1564, she told a Scottish emissary that 'I am resolved never to marry, if I be not thereto necessitated by the queen my sister's harsh behaviour toward me'. Thus, although the marriage issue was kept open, this was chiefly as a political weapon, to tame claimants to the throne.[22]

Until the mid-1560s, therefore, Elizabeth was in the unusual but fortunate position of wielding considerable influence in Scottish affairs without offering very much in return. For Elizabeth to recognise the Catholic claimant while remaining unmarried and childless might endanger her own position; and if she married, any child she had would have a prior claim anyway. For Mary, however, the English alliance also involved a difficult balancing act: in England, she needed to court the support of the Catholic magnates, while remaining on good terms with Elizabeth. In Scotland, she maintained a

21 Wormald, *Mary queen of Scots*, pp. 102–7, 146–7.
22 Haigh, *Elizabeth I*, pp. 15–18 (quotation, p. 18).

Catholic household, while surrounding herself politically with Protestants. A shrewder politician than Mary might at least have kept open the option of the Auld Alliance and a Catholic restoration as a means of extracting concessions from Elizabeth. In terms of government, moreover, the contrast with Elizabeth's choice of ministers and nomination to her first privy council is very plain. She nominated to her privy council in September 1561 the leading Protestants of 1559–60, and also retained the existing officers of state, led by the secretary, William Maitland of Lethington. Her council numbered 16, of whom 10 were earls, but there were only 4 Catholics (the earls of Huntly, Erroll, Atholl and Montrose – the bishops were all excluded). Then, in 1562, she alienated the leading Catholic magnate, the highly influential Huntly, dispossessing him of the northern earldom of Moray, which he had held since 1549, in order to confer the earldom on Lord James Stewart. When Mary came north on progress, Huntly's captain refused to admit her to Inverness castle and trouble soon escalated into a pitched battle in which Huntly was killed: he was posthumously forfeited, and one of his sons executed, although his heir, Lord Gordon, remained in prison. Mary's dismal record in council also underlined her sheer lack of interest in Scottish affairs of state. Apart from the earl of Atholl, the regular attenders were all Protestants. The Scottish monarchy was less institutionalised, more intimately personal, than its English counterpart, but even in the first 16 months after her return from France Mary herself attended less than a third of the meetings for which the attendance is recorded, and only 5 out of 50 meetings in 1564, whereas 30 years later her son, James VI, regularly attended council meetings, appearing, for instance, at 37 out of 47 recorded meetings in 1596. Moreover, between 1561 and 1565, the amount of business conducted by her council was very limited.[23]

In other respects, however, Mary manoeuvred quite skilfully in holding to the difficult strategy she had set herself, at least initially. It was far from inevitable that a Catholic monarch in a Protestant kingdom would lead to the breakdown which occurred in 1567. Mary was no Catholic zealot, but a politique or even crypto-Protestant. Far from trying to overthrow the Scottish Reformation, she worked to create a viable settlement, trying to ensure that the 1562 compromise concerning thirds of benefices (see above, p. 145) was implemented, and frequently reissuing a proclamation which forbad any alteration in the existing religious settlement. On foot of this, several priests were prosecuted for saying mass. Of course the thirds of benefices compromise also proved a lucrative source of income to Mary, [2 2 9] eventually netting SC£32,000 a year by 1565; and since her jointure as dowager queen of France also realised SC£30,000, Mary's financial position was unusually sound for a Stewart monarch. Moreover, for the first time since 1542, Scotland again had a glittering Renaissance court, reassuring the nobles with the cult of honour and fostering a new sense of patriotism, with Mary the patron of poets and inspirer of poetry – yet one which cost the nobles very little. This eased the nobles' acceptance of her, particularly since, following the death of her husband, Mary no longer represented the French connection. Administratively too, Scotland remained a very devolved kingdom with a lineage society in which kinship still counted for more than religious differences – despite hotheads like John Knox who denounced her as a wicked and ungodly idolatress. From 1562 to 1565 Mary also spent unwontedly lengthy periods of time on progress showing herself to her subjects in different parts of her kingdom. Finally, Protestant control of the privy council and the great offices of state was not threatened, and the Catholics were leaderless.[24]

Yet Mary ran into trouble over her marriage. Ironically, her personal preferences in this regard and the provision of an heir accorded far more closely with the expectations of the age than Elizabeth's unconventional posture. Her eventual choice was Henry Stewart, Lord Darnley, grandson of Margaret Tudor, and son of the 'assured', or unionist, earl of Lennox, forfeited in 1544. In theory, Darnley was an admirable choice because he stood next to Mary in succession to the English throne and had also been raised in England. Yet the marriage alienated both Elizabeth and also key members of Mary's government, James, earl of Moray, and the staunchly Protestant earls of Argyll and Glencairn. Argyll, the queen's brother-in-law, enjoyed a close friendship with Mary, but for many Scottish nobles loyalty to the crown was conditional on duty to the commonweal and, in Argyll's case, to religion too. In fact, foreign suitors had shown far more interest in Elizabeth than Mary. In October 1562, Elizabeth had very nearly died from smallpox: in the crisis, her council showed itself solidly against the prospect of Mary's succession; and after she had recovered, Elizabeth still refused to nominate a successor. Thus, in 1563 Mary actively courted a match with a Habsburg or Valois prince, probably hoping to coerce Elizabeth to nominate her as her successor. The most likely match was Philip II's mad son, Don Carlos, but

---

24   Wormald, *Mary queen of Scots*, pp. 114–16, 151–2; Lynch, *Scotland*, pp. 210–13.

these various advances were politely rejected: Philip II, in particular, was not convinced that Mary's religious commitment was such that she could even deliver a Catholic Scotland, let alone a Catholic England. By this stage too, Mary's intimate associations with a French poet and an English captain were undermining her prestige even in Scotland. In 1564 Elizabeth responded (almost insultingly) by offering her reputed lover, Robert Dudley, as a suitable husband, creating him earl of Leicester in the presence of the Scottish ambassador, Sir James Melville, so as to enhance his status. Yet her refusal, in March 1565, to include an acknowledgement of Mary as her heir marked the failure of this unwelcome suggestion. Instead, Mary took up another, apparently light-hearted and unintended, suggestion made by Elizabeth to Melville – of 'yonder long lad', Lord Darnley. The match was approved in Catholic circles (notably, the French and Spanish courts), and a papal dispensation sought for this marriage between cousins. Elizabeth withheld approval, but too late: Darnley had been allowed to leave England in February 1565. Mary created Darnley earl of Ross in May, then duke of Albany in July, then without waiting for the dispensation, she married him. Although the marriage was celebrated according to Catholic rites, Darnley, a nominal Protestant, refused to attend the nuptial mass, and he continued thereafter to attend St Giles church and listen to John Knox's sermons. Moreover, the day before the wedding, entirely on her own authority, Mary had declared him king of Scotland.[25]

Within a few months, relations had broken down between Mary and Darnley, who proved immature and irresponsible, but not before she had become pregnant. Nonetheless, the marriage spelled the end of Moray's pro-English policy, the collapse of the Protestant alliance, and a political realignment by which the disappointed Moray, together with the staunch Protestant earls of Argyll, Glencairn and Rothes and others, drew closer to ecclesiastical hard-liners like Knox, while other Protestants, most notably Lethington and the earls of Morton and Cassillis, and the Catholics remained with the queen. Mary courted noble support, restoring the imprisoned Lord Gordon as earl of Huntly, advancing Lord Erskine to the earldom of Mar, and favouring not only Darnley's Lennox relatives but also James Hepburn, earl of Bothwell, recently returned from France. Encouraged by Elizabeth's offers of support, in August Moray and Argyll rebelled, alleging the danger to the Protestant settlement. The aptly-named Chase-about Raid saw their

25 Wormald, *Mary queen of Scots*, pp. 132–50 (quotation, p. 147); Donaldson, *Scotland*, pp. 115–18; Dawson, *Politics of religion in the age of Mary, queen of Scots*, pp. 35–47.

army and the queen's chase ineffectually about southern Scotland over the next few weeks, but this time Elizabeth refused military assistance, and most Scottish Protestants held aloof. Moray fled to England in October, and Argyll withdrew to the Highlands out of Mary's reach. Nonetheless, Mary now had nothing to gain from a pro-English, Protestant stance: in the revolt's aftermath Protestants lost influence with her, so alienating some who had hitherto remained loyal; a few Catholics were admitted to the council, and Mary tried to persuade individual nobles to attend mass. Darnley went to mass on Christmas Day, but by then Mary's relationship with her French secretary, David Rizzio, promoted from musician in 1564, was causing scandal; and when Mary summoned the earls of Moray, Argyll, Glencairn and their supporters to stand trial at the forthcoming parliament in March, they managed to suborn Darnley, promising him the crown matrimonial in parliament. Rizzio was abducted from Holyrood and stabbed to death, followed shortly by the return of Moray from England. Over 120 people were involved in the murder.

Mary quickly detached Darnley from the conspirators, enabling their escape from Holyrood to Bothwell's castle of Dunbar, and a political compromise was patched up. Thereafter, for over a year, the queen's government consisted of an uneasy coalition of Moray, Argyll and Glencairn, restored to favour and political power (so improving relations with Elizabeth), and the earls of Huntly, Atholl and Bothwell (later, her lover) with, from September, Lethington. In June, Mary was delivered of a son, James, so provoking Elizabeth's famous outburst, 'the queen of Scots is lighter of a bonny son, and I am but barren stock'. Yet Darnley remained a liability, from whom Mary was now totally estranged. His subsequent denial that he knew of the Rizzio plot also alienated him from his co-conspirators. Leading councillors urged a divorce, but Mary was afraid that this might bastardise Prince James. The final straw was Darnley's failure in December, despite being present in Stirling castle, to attend Prince James's christening there (by Archbishop Hamilton, according to Catholic rites), so casting doubts on the prince's legitimacy. In February, the house where he was staying was blown up by gunpowder: realising what was afoot, Darnley escaped before the explosion, but he was finished off in the garden, perhaps by a different group of conspirators, by strangulation. Bothwell was widely thought responsible for the murder, but Mary was then pregnant by him. Accordingly, he was found not guilty at his trial, and was divorced from his countess on grounds of adultery. He then abducted Mary and, having been promoted duke of Orkney, he married her in May in accordance with the reformed rite. Yet these developments alienated all shades of public opinion, and in June a powerful group of 12 earls and 10 lords captured Mary. She was imprisoned at Lochleven, where she miscarried of twins, and was forced to abdicate in favour of her son. King James VI was crowned and anointed at Stirling on 29 July 1567 by Adam Bothwell, reformed bishop of Orkney, with John Knox preaching the sermon. On 22 August, Moray was proclaimed regent.[26]

Initially, Mary's supporters, notably Argyll and the Hamiltons, had little option but to acknowledge the young king, notwithstanding their distrust of Moray. Yet in May 1568 Mary escaped from Lochleven, precipitating civil war as the Queen's Party fought to restore her to the throne. Following her crushing defeat at Langside, however, Mary fled to England, a disastrous error of judgement since it meant that, without a queen to restore, the Queen's Party had no hope of long-term success. Mary's arrival in England caused immense problems there, but the continuance of civil war in Scotland over the next five years also greatly increased Elizabeth's leverage in Scottish affairs. Initially, the King's Party controlled the national institutions as well as the boy king, but with Huntly holding out in the north and Argyll's Highland base virtually impregnable, a stalemate ensued. Then in January 1570, Moray was assassinated. The Queen's Party gained momentum, with the earl of Huntly now running his own administration in the north, but Elizabeth sent English troops into southern Scotland and even had the earl of Lennox nominated regent. Lennox was killed the following year, and his successor, the earl of Mar, died in October 1572, after which the staunchly Protestant and anglophile earl of Morton became regent. A low point for the King's Party came in May 1571 with the 'creeping parliament' held in the Canongate when, in order to avoid fire from the castle held by the Queen's Party, members assumed undignified postures. The following month, the Queen's Party held their own parliament in the tollbooth of Edinburgh, the normal location. Yet the former was better attended, and with the defection of Argyll and lords of the south-west in August 1571, the Queen's Party began to break up. The capture of Edinburgh castle with English assistance in May 1573 finally ended the civil war. Meanwhile, however, the Anglo-Scottish alliance of 1560 based on common religious and political interests had been replaced by a very different kind of relationship between London and Edinburgh, with Scotland reduced to little more than a Tudor

---

26 Guy, 'My heart is my own': the life of Mary queen of Scots, pp. 244–352; Wormald, Mary queen of Scots, pp. 150–66; Donaldson, Scotland, pp. 114–31; Lynch, Scotland, pp. 212–18; Dawson, Politics of religion in the age of Mary, queen of Scots, pp. 122–6, 144–55.

client state and English interests maintained by the distribution of pensions to leading nobles like Argyll.[27] [2 3 3]

Mary, the Norfolk marriage scheme, and rebellion

In England, Elizabeth faced a major dilemma about what to do with Mary. Mary herself naively expected that her good cousin Elizabeth would assist in the recovery of her throne, and until 1570 Elizabeth toyed with the idea of restoration under strict conditions and restraints. Initially, however, she played for time, calling a conference at York in October, continued at Westminster between November and January 1569, to decide whether Mary was innocent or guilty of the murder of Darnley and so whether she might be restored. Attempts to portray proceedings as a kind of 'trial' also supported traditional English claims to imperial rights over Scotland, as Cecil in particular appreciated. Mary was represented by commissioners, but Moray attended in person and eventually produced the celebrated 'casket letters', allegedly (and, for the most part, probably) written by Mary to Bothwell, but doctored so as to implicate her in the plot to murder Darnley. Thereupon, Elizabeth ruled, illogically, that there was no reason to doubt the honour of either party, so permitting her politically very sensible decision to maintain the status quo. Mary was held prisoner at the earl of Shrewsbury's castle of Tutbury while Moray returned to Scotland. Thereby, she ensured an amenable government in Scotland without appearing to condone rebellion against lawful authority. By 1571 English politicians were ignoring Mary's claim to the Scottish throne and concentrating on the danger she posed to Elizabeth and English security. In all this, Elizabeth's approach – the secure confinement of an awkward domestic rival – seemed to be vindicated by the events surrounding the Norfolk marriage scheme and then the Ridolfi plot.[28]

Notwithstanding her imprisonment, Mary's claim to the English succession remained and some courtiers, including Leicester, worried both about their own position should Elizabeth die and also the threat of a Catholic

27 Dawson, *Politics of religion in the age of Mary, queen of Scots*, pp. 48–56, 153–5, 191–9; Donaldson, *Scotland*, pp. 162–6; Wormald, *Mary queen of Scots*, pp. 172–80.

28 Wormald, *Mary queen of Scots*, pp. 174–8; Guy, *'My heart is my own': the life of Mary queen of Scots*, pp. 396–436; Dawson, *Politics of religion in the age of Mary, queen of Scots*, pp. 171–3, 192–9; Penry Williams, *The later Tudors: England 1547–1603* (Oxford, 1995), pp. 254–6.

restoration. They saw their best hope in securing, as a prelude to Mary's restoration to the Scottish throne, undertakings from her to a Protestant establishment, an anglophile policy, and marriage to some English magnate who would then control her. The duke of Norfolk, England's premier peer and recently widowed, seemed the best bet. Yet these schemes were compromised by the activities of a Florentine banker, Roberto Ridolfi, a papal agent, who hatched a plot to restore Catholicism and also became privy to the courtiers' plans. Norfolk himself was conformist, but Catholics had hopes of his conversion. Both Ridolfi and the Spanish ambassador, Guerau de Spes, were in touch with a group of ardent Catholics, northern gentry clustered around the earl of Northumberland, who had hoped to secure Mary's release when she was first held at Carlisle or Bolton, but were less enthusiastic about the Norfolk marriage. Among these was Leonard Dacre, senior member of the leading border family and Northumberland's cousin, but now Norfolk's bitter enemy following a dispute between them over the Dacre inheritance. Gradually, however, two parallel conspiracies took shape: the one reflected policy disputes in council and sought the dismissal of Cecil (with Leicester's support) as a prelude to a palace revolution backed by Norfolk and conservative peers to restore Catholicism; the other (which even Cecil eventually came to hear about) was to use Norfolk to precisely the opposite end, the preservation of the Protestant settlement in both kingdoms. There was also a third group of malcontents, in Ireland, who identified with the Norfolk faction and hoped to secure the recall of Sir Henry Sidney, Elizabeth's abrasive governor there. Yet when, in September 1569, Elizabeth got to hear of the marriage proposal and angrily forbade it, Norfolk's Protestant support evaporated, leaving only the Catholic plot. The duke departed from court for East Anglia without leave, but when summoned back, he obeyed the queen's command and was lodged in the Tower. Three court allies, Arundel, Pembroke and Lumley, were also briefly detained.[29]

By then, rebellion had already been sparked in Ireland, chiefly by Sidney's drive to extend central control and curb traditional rights and immunities, but also by the threat to Old English land titles from the activities of adventurers like Sir Peter Carew and Sir Richard Grenville. In the absence of the earls of Ormond and Desmond, a shadowy convention of Munster lords held in spring 1569 had sent an offer of the crown of Ireland to Philip II,

---

29   W.T. MacCaffrey, *The shaping of the Elizabethan regime: Elizabethan politics, 1558–1572* (Princeton, 1968), chs 10, 12; Nicholas Canny, *The Elizabethan conquest of Ireland: a pattern established 1565–1576* (Hassocks, 1976), pp. 142–52.

and Spanish agents also approached Ormond, then at court. In June, simultaneous risings were launched by Ormond's younger brothers led by Sir Edmund Butler, and by Sir James Fitzmaurice, cousin to the earl of Desmond, who had been arrested in 1567 and incarcerated in the Tower. Fitzmaurice and the earl of Clancare descended on Kerrycurrihy, overthrew the recently-established English colony there, and chased the survivors into Cork, which stood siege rather than surrender them. Fitzmaurice issued a proclamation that, instead of 'the Catholic faith by God unto His church given', the queen intended to impose 'another newly invented kind of religion', he urged the citizens to expel 'all therein that be Huguenots', and he declared that Spanish aid was coming. His stand attracted some (predominantly neo-feudal) support, but the towns remained loyal, as did most major landowners. By contrast, Butler refused to meddle in matters of religion. Claiming that Ormond and the queen had been murdered in England, he attacked English colonists around Ormond, destroying Carew's settlement in Idrone. Initially, this strategy won him considerable support, but the truth soon emerged. The suspicions of the Ormond gentry were further raised by Fitzmaurice's arrival with Clancare to aid Butler in besieging Kilkenny and his announcement that 'the Butlers are become friends to the Geraldines'. At court, Ormond was seriously embarrassed, but when in August the earl arrived home to restore order, his brothers quickly submitted. On Ormond's orders 165 rebels were killed outright or were executed after surrender, but his brothers were eventually pardoned, although attainted by parliament.[30]

Meanwhile, Sidney's arrival in Desmond with 600 troops broke rebel control of the countryside, and in September he appointed Sir Humphrey Gilbert as colonel to complete the province's pacification. Gilbert's ruthless campaigning quickly reduced Fitzmaurice's support. Within six weeks he had captured 23 castles without artillery, slaughtering the occupants, man, woman and child, of any that resisted. By December, Clancare and most Geraldines had submitted, though Fitzmaurice remained at large, sheltering (like 'a silly wood-kerne') in the glen of Aherlow. At this point, a provincial council was established for Connaught; but the misplaced zeal of the new president, Sir Edward Fitton, in proscribing Gaelic customs and purging the province of popery before he had the means to promote civility and true religion, quickly fuelled opposition there, particularly from the sons of the earl

---

30 Canny, *The Elizabethan conquest of Ireland*, pp. 142–52 (quotations, pp. 145, 147); David Edwards, 'The Butler revolt of 1569' in *Irish Historical Studies*, xxviii (1992–3), pp. 228–55; idem, *Ormond lordship*, pp. 196–211; Ellis, *Ireland in the age of the Tudors*, pp. 288–300.

of Clanrickard: the garrison was increased and martial law imposed. Briefly, the earl of Thomond also rebelled: he arrested Fitton's new sheriff of Clare and declared 'that he would do nothing with the lord deputy nor lord president but as the duke of Norfolk would say'. Soon after, however, he submitted to his cousin, the earl of Ormond. Munster remained under martial law until the appointment in February 1571 of a provincial council for Munster. Over the next two years the president, Sir John Perrot, despatched an estimated 800 traitors by common or martial law before Fitzmaurice's final submission in April 1573. How far the Irish rebellions of 1569–70 were – notwithstanding the predominance of local issues – also linked to the court intrigues of 1569 is difficult to say. Initially, Ormond had hoped with Norfolk's support to replace Sidney as governor of Ireland. A garbled version of the court manoeuvrings was reported to Sidney by Sir Edmund Butler: that his enemy, 'the earl of Leicester . . . should marry the queen and be king of England' and that Sidney 'should be king of Ireland'. With Norfolk's arrest, however, these hopes collapsed. Ormond focused on saving his brothers, and attention switched to events in the English north.[31]

Within the circles of the northern earls, it was believed that, following the queen's refusal of her consent to the Norfolk marriage, the duke had little option but to launch a rising. This, supposedly, would favour northern plans both for reformation of religion and the naming of Mary as Elizabeth's successor, for which the general support of the nobility was expected, and hopefully also Spanish assistance. Yet, instead of the anticipated signal to rise, fixed for 6 October, Norfolk sent the earl of Westmorland, his brother-in-law, a brief message: he and Northumberland were not to move, otherwise his head was forfeit. For some weeks, the earls agonised over what now to do while rumours of a rising swept the north. Hearing the rumours, Lord President Sussex summoned the earls to York, where they acknowledged having heard the rumours but protested their loyalty. As the government examined Norfolk and his associates, however, Elizabeth refused to accept Sussex's assurances that all was now quiet. She demanded more information, commanding him to order the earls to court. Sussex protested that this would frighten them into revolt and vainly urged the queen either to desist or to send an army to compel them. By mid-November the earls were in open revolt: on the fourteenth they marched to Durham Cathedral, pulled

31 Canny, *The Elizabethan conquest of Ireland*, pp. 142–52 (quotations, pp. 149–50); Edwards, 'Butler revolt', pp. 228–55; Ellis, *Ireland in the age of the Tudors*, pp. 290–300 (quotations, pp. 297, 298).

down the communion table, destroyed the English Bible and prayer books, and celebrated mass.[32]

Northumberland and Westmorland had taken this step with great reluctance. They were discontented by Elizabeth's intrusion of others – particularly members of her Protestant courtier circle – into offices they considered rightfully theirs: her cousin, Lord Hunsdon, had charge of Berwick and the east march, and Northumberland's rival, Sir John Forster, was warden of the middle marches. They were also alienated by Bishop Pilkington of Durham, an enthusiastic former exile, and his Protestant senior clergy, whose aggressive assault on traditional religious imagery and church furniture aroused fierce local resentment in a region which was still overwhelmingly Catholic. Both earls were surrounded by Catholic advisers, who urged action, and Northumberland had been formally reconciled to the Catholic faith in 1567. Despite these grievances, however, the earls realised that, without Norfolk, the chances of a successful revolt were slim. When approached, the response of the Spanish ambassador, de Spes, was discouraging, as also was Philip II's governor of the Netherlands, the duke of Alva. Left to themselves, the earls would probably not have stirred; but their countesses were made of sterner stuff: Lady Westmorland, Norfolk's sister, rallied the earls, exclaiming that 'we and our country were shamed for ever, that now in the end we should seek holes to creep into', and the countess of Northumberland rode with the rebel army through Yorkshire. The main agitators for the rising were all enthusiastic Catholics – Westmorland's uncle, Christopher Neville; Richard Norton, the 81-year-old sheriff of Yorkshire, who had been out in the Pilgrimage of Grace; Thomas Markenfeld, Norton's son-in-law; and Dr. Nicholas Morton, ex-canon of Canterbury cathedral. The last two were religious exiles who had returned in 1568. The earls were also persuaded that if they did not rebel, they would have to flee because they were already under suspicion.[33]

The earls had no clear strategy and very little money, however. Issuing proclamations that 'diverse new set up nobles about the queen' went about 'to overthrow and put down the ancient nobility of this realm' and 'to set up and maintain a new found religion and heresy, contrary to God's word', they

---

32 MacCaffrey, *The shaping of the Elizabethan regime*, ch. 13; Cuthbert Sharp (ed.), *Memorials of the rebellion of 1569* (1840), repr. ed. Robert Wood (Shotton, 1975), pp. 5–47; Fletcher and MacCulloch, *Tudor rebellions*, pp. 104–5.

33 Sharp (ed.), *Memorials of the rebellion of 1569*, pp. 5–47 (quotation, p. 199); Fletcher and MacCulloch, *Tudor rebellions*, ch. 8, docs 22–4; Norman Jones, *The birth of the Elizabethan age: England in the 1560s* (Oxford, 1993), pp. 80–4; MacCaffrey, *Shaping of the Elizabethan regime*, ch. 13.

marched slowly south from Brancepeth towards Tutbury (15–22 November), raising troops as they went, with the intention of rescuing Mary. Tenurial bonds between the lords and their men were no doubt weaker than 50 years before, particularly following the long interregnum on the Percy estates, but Northumberland had no opportunity to raise his tenantry. At the start of the rising, the Neville tenants flocked in eagerly enough to Westmorland's castle at Brancepeth, and large numbers joined from Richmondshire, Durham and Kirby Moorside. The earls' religious aims were also generally popular. Sir Ralph Sadler asserted that there were 'not ten gentlemen in all this country that favour [the queen's] proceedings in the cause of religion'. But among the gentry trimming was a typical response: 'if the father be on this side, the son is on the other; and one brother with us, and the other with the rebels'. And as the earls moved south appeals to traditional loyalties and the old faith evoked less response among the commonalty than money and coercion. Sir George Bowes observed how 'mass was yesterday at Darnton; and John Swinburn with a staff drove before him the poor folks to hasten them to hear the same'. The earls also lacked the money to pay many foot soldiers. By the time they halted on Bramham Moor near Tadcaster (22–24 November), the rebel army had only 3,800 footmen but 1,600 horsemen – mainly 'gentlemen and their household servants and tenants and the head husbandmen', so reported Bowes, then besieged in Barnard Castle. With these they controlled all the country east of the Pennines. Sussex's commissions to raise troops secured little response from the local gentry, and with only 400 horsemen, he dared not leave York to confront the earls. Yet the key centres, York, Newcastle, Berwick and Carlisle, remained in loyal hands, and the earls' expectations of support from other conservative northern peers like Cumberland, Derby and Wharton were disappointed. Elsewhere, Regent Moray forbade Scottish participation, Lord Hunsdon moved cautiously south from Berwick, Mary was removed from Tutbury to Coventry to forestall a rescue, and an army of 10,000 was now advancing north against the rebels. The queen was also very lucky in the timing of the revolt: Leonard Dacre, who was Cumberland's brother-in-law and whose hopes had risen with Norfolk's fall, was then at court; and just after the rising had collapsed Pope Pius V responded by issuing the famous bull, *Regnans in Excelsis*, in which he excommunicated and deposed Elizabeth and absolved her subjects from their allegiance to her.

The decision of the earls, on 24 November, to turn back to Knaresborough was, in effect, an admission of failure. By 30 November they were back at Brancepeth. Rebel forces took Barnard Castle when Bowes's men deserted, and also Hartlepool, hoping for a landing there by Spanish troops; but on 16 December, with the royal army approaching, the earls fled, first to Hexham, then to the Dacre stronghold of Naworth, and finally into Scotland. Dacre had meanwhile returned home, made contact with the earls, and gathered a force of 3,000 men at Naworth on the pretence of resisting rebellion. On Elizabeth's orders, Lord Hunsdon advanced with 1,500 men to arrest him. In the only real battle of the campaign, Dacre encountered Hunsdon's arquebuses early on 20 February: 'his footmen gave the proudest charge upon my shot that ever I saw', so Hunsdon reported, but they were scattered by Hunsdon's cavalry. Dacre fled into Scotland, leaving 300 of his men dead on the field.[34]

With no one left to fight, the queen's army simply pillaged the region. Against Sussex's orders, they drove off 'all the cattle of the country, and ransomed the people in such miserable sort, and made such open and common spoil, as the like, I think, was never heard of, putting no difference between the good and the bad'. A few leaders were tried and executed at Tyburn in 1570. In Scotland, Northumberland was betrayed to Moray, and was eventually surrendered to Hunsdon in 1572: he was beheaded at York. Yet Westmorland, Northumberland's countess, Dacre, Norton and Markenfeld eventually escaped to the Netherlands, and two rebels joined Fitzmaurice in Ireland. Elizabeth ordered the execution of 700 of the rank and file by martial law, a savage reprisal which anticipated the savagery of her officers in Ireland. It also contrasted sharply both with the rebels' moderate treatment of their victims and her father's retribution after the more serious and widespread Pilgrimage of Grace. Yet leading officers like Sussex and Bowes had no taste for this kind of severity: the actual number of executions was probably no more than 450, and many gentry were allowed to purchase their lives by surrendering their lands and goods to the crown.

The consequences of the rising for the north were drastic. Elizabeth's policies had alienated key members of a lineage society of marcher lords and their gentry followers who could still hope to command their tenantries to challenge the crown. Northumberland, at least, had initially shown evidence of religious conformity; but just as her policies were to do in Ireland ten years later, Elizabeth's replacement of less reliable local rulers by safe southerners had an effect quite opposite to her intentions. It had come close by

34 Sharp (ed.), *Memorials of the rebellion of 1569*, pp. 42–3, 45, 130–44, 214–24 (quotations, pp. 42, 45, 219); MacCaffrey, *Shaping of the Elizabethan regime*, ch. 13; Fletcher and MacCulloch, *Tudor rebellions*, ch. 8 (quotations, pp. 98, 151); Jones, *Birth of the Elizabethan age*, pp. 82–3, 260–1; James, *Society, politics and culture*, pp. 293–5.

1569 to creating a solid block of Catholic nobles, united by a common distaste for 'true religion'. After 1570, Cecil and the Protestant court circle were never seriously challenged in government again, but the crisis did nothing to broaden the narrow basis of support for the regime and there was a further price to pay in terms of the good rule of the region. Of the four great northern families, only the Cliffords survived. The Percies soon recovered their title, to which the seventh earl of Northumberland's brother succeeded, but they became a southern family, forbidden to reside in the north. The Dacre and Neville estates were confiscated, although southern nobles like Lord William Howard picked up some of these lands. Sussex urged the opportunity 'not only to settle all these parts in surety but to frame good government along the whole borders'. In fact, the borders were greatly weakened by the destruction of their traditional lords, so accelerating the phenomenon known as 'the decay of the borders'. Yet, by then, increased cooperation between London and Edinburgh meant that the rule and defence of the far north was far less of a priority for the regime. And as regards the events of 1569–70, the death of the principals and a policy of reorientating the religion of their heirs gradually smoothed over the region's political alienation from the centre.[35]

In the aftermath of the revolt, Sussex was ordered to invade Scotland to capture the rebels sheltering there and punish those who were protecting them. This powerful English intervention was directed against the Marians and enabled the King's Party to regain control. Eventually, Norfolk was released from the Tower in August 1570, having signed a submission. In spring 1571, however, Ridolfi, the Florentine banker, who had also been released and had gone abroad, devised a scheme for an invasion of England by the duke of Alva with papal backing. Concurrently, Mary's English supporters were to organise a rising to assist the invasion. Alva was unenthusiastic, but ordered to cooperate by King Philip, and by the time the government got wind of the scheme in May 1571, Norfolk was also involved: he had agreed to lead a rising if Alva invaded with 10,000 troops. Norfolk went to the Tower in September; the Spanish ambassador, de Spes, was expelled; and

---

35 Sharp (ed.), *Memorials of the rebellion of 1569*, pp. 130–44, 214–24 (quotation, p. 130); MacCaffrey, *Shaping of the Elizabethan regime*, ch. 13; Fletcher and MacCulloch, *Tudor rebellions*, ch. 8 (quotation, p. 103); R.W. Hoyle, 'Faction, feud and reconciliation amongst the northern English nobility, 1525–1569' in *History*, lxxxiv (1999), pp. 590–613; Robert Newton, 'The decay of the borders' in C.W. Chalklin and M.A. Havindon (eds), *Rural change and urban growth 1500–1800* (London, 1974), pp. 2–31; Watts, *From border to middle shire*, p. 57; Ellis, *Ireland in the age of the Tudors*, p. 297.

the duke was convicted in January following a trial which was also intended [2 4 1]
to destroy Mary's reputation. Elizabeth agonised over his execution, but the
duke finally went to the scaffold. She resisted pressure in parliament to put
Mary on trial, but thereafter support for her cause gradually subsided.[36]

Anglo-Scottish relations, frontier defence and Catholic intrigues

By 1573, therefore, there was an air of increased security about the newly-
created British state system, based on continuing good relations between the
two British monarchies, confessional congruity between two established
churches, and increasing political stability in the British archipelago. The
Scottish civil war had ended, and in England the resolution of the crisis
surrounding Mary, the Norfolk conspiracy, and the northern rising had
reduced the chances of a successful coup against the Elizabethan regime. All
the same, this remained a fragile accord between two weak regimes which
were constantly threatened by events in continental Europe. Analysing the
situation from an English perspective, Sir Francis Knollys observed: 'The
avoiding of Her Majesty's danger doth consist in the preventing of the conquest of the Low Countries betimes; secondly, in the preventing of the revolt
of Scotland from Her Majesty's devotion; . . . and thirdly, in the timely
preventing of contemptuous growing of the disobedient papists here in
England.'[37] Only in regard to this third danger did the remedy rest in the
government's own hands. In Scotland, the regent, Morton, cultivated the
English alliance. A 'Catholic interest' had survived among the northern
earls, but it was powerless without the support of the continental powers:
and for the present the alternating phases of the French wars of religion
precluded attempts by France to re-establish the Auld Alliance. What might
happen when King James began his personal rule was another matter. In
France the Huguenots and the Queen Mother had since 1570 favoured a
marriage alliance between Elizabeth and Henry, duke of Anjou, heir to the
throne. Elizabeth entertained such proposals, in part with the aim of supporting the Protestant princes against the Catholic Guises, but without much

36 MacCaffrey, *Shaping of the Elizabethan regime*, ch. 15; R.B. Wernham, *Before the Armada: the growth of English foreign policy 1485–1588* (London, 1966), pp. 312–15; Donaldson, *Scotland*, pp. 163–4.
37 Quoted, Patrick Collinson, *Archbishop Grindal, 1519–1583: the struggle for a reformed church* (London, 1979), p. 57.

enthusiasm. Religion proved an insuperable barrier to the marriage, since Elizabeth refused any public concession of Catholic worship. Yet the growing power of Spain prompted the two sides to agree a defensive alliance in April 1572. By the treaty of Blois, each country promised to come to the aid of the other if attacked.

In any case, if and when the French resumed a forward policy, a more likely target was the Netherlands where the Dutch Sea Beggars – nobles exiled after the revolt there in 1566 – had captured the port of Brille and begun to oust Spanish troops from the northern provinces. English interests lay in preserving local liberties under Spanish sovereignty, so keeping the French out and Spanish troops tied down, and preventing Philip II from consolidating his position in the Netherlands or supporting a Catholic 'enterprise' against England. It was unlikely, however, that the Dutch rebels could survive without foreign support. Elizabeth was extremely uncomfortable with the idea of supporting rebels against their lawful prince. Yet if the French, encouraged by Dutch appeals for assistance, aimed at annexing the Low Countries, the outcome might be even worse. On the other hand, the two Catholic monarchies were far stronger than England, and if Elizabeth openly sent military assistance to the Dutch rebels, not only would such a strategy place a serious strain on England's modest financial and military resources, but King Philip might retaliate by mounting the very enterprise against England which this strategy was designed to prevent. It was hard to know what to do, and the privy council was divided between those such as Leicester and Sir Francis Walsingham, appointed secretary of state in 1573, who urged open support for the Dutch, whose cause was godly; and those like the more cautious Burghley who was even prepared to support Alva against the French. In response, Elizabeth blew hot and cold, but in practice did very little.[38]

Meanwhile, a heavy price was paid elsewhere in the British Isles for Elizabeth's policies. In Scotland, the victory of the King's Party had in part been achieved by English subsidies, but Elizabeth then refused to support Morton – as both the regent himself pleaded and her own ambassador, Henry Killigrew, advised – by distributing pensions to those peers (12 to 15 out of a total of 53) who were 'well affected'. Argyll, for instance, told Killigrew that he would rather have £200 from Elizabeth than 2,000 crowns from France. This decision saved the queen all of £2,000 a year, but

---

38   Donaldson, *Scotland*, pp. 166–72; Wallace MacCaffrey, *Queen Elizabeth and the making of policy, 1572–1588* (Princeton, N.J., 1981), p. 168; Williams, *The later Tudors*, pp. 271–5.

the resultant tension reinforced traditional perceptions among the Scots of the English reputation for meanness and, conversely, English perceptions of the Scots as poor, venal and greedy. Killigrew predicted a revival of French fortunes in Scotland, with a consequent increase in the cost of border defence. And by 1577, the growing French threat was indeed prompting a reconsideration. The need to strengthen English influence was further underlined in January 1578 by the defeat of the Dutch at Gembloux by the Spanish commander, Don John of Austria. Thomas Randolph was hastily despatched to shore up Morton's position with the assurance that 'Her Majesty will not stick at money': £2,000 arrived. Yet the *coup d'état* in the spring – the first of many over the next eight years – which saw the earls of Atholl and Argyll seize control of the 12-year-old King James, was inspired entirely by Scottish domestic politics. Nonetheless, Morton's fall seriously jeopardised English influence in Scotland. Fortunately for Elizabeth, he regained control of the king as a result of a compromise agreement worked out over the summer, but the queen then withdrew her subsidies. The folly of this was soon demonstrated when Esmé Stewart, seigneur d'Aubigny, first cousin to Lord Darnley, returned from France in September 1579 and quickly established a hold on the young king. Thus, Elizabeth's interventions in Scotland down to 1579 eventually convinced the Scots that her Scottish policy simply reflected the perceived needs of English security – to deny the continental powers any foothold within the British Isles – but that otherwise she remained quite indifferent to the particular configurations of Scottish politics.[39]

Her rule of the Tudor borderlands was hardly more satisfactory. In the far north, Sir Ralph Sadler had reported after the Scottish war of 1557–9 that never in 20 years had he known the borders 'in such disorder': 'for now the officer spoileth the thief' without bringing him to trial, 'the thief robbeth the true man', and true men paid blackmail to thieves. English borderers had even paid blackmail to Scots, so he asserted, a development 'which I never heard of before'. Moreover, during 'the long peace' which followed, the border surnames had little option but to turn their hand to other pursuits, notably reiving and robbery in the Northumberland and Durham Lowlands. And particularly after the customary restraints on their activities had been removed in 1569–70 with the fall of the great northern magnates, they now

39   K.M. Brown, 'The price of friendship: the 'well affected' and English economic clientage in Scotland before 1603' in R.A. Mason (ed.), *Scotland and England 1286–1815* (Edinburgh, 1987), pp. 139–62 (quotation, p. 145); Donaldson, *Scotland*, pp. 171–3; Dawson, *Politics of religion in the age of Mary, queen of Scots*, pp. 198–9, 211–12.

[2 4 4]   became virtually uncontrollable. Yet, with the continuing weakness of the English borders, even the English surnames eventually lost out in the traditional cross-border reiving: for instance, the number of horsemen which the Tynedale surnames could muster dwindled from 391 in 1538 to 134 by 1580 and to only 21 by 1595. Another indication of this military collapse were the successive surveys recording the decay of border service: the 1584 returns, for instance, showed that of 1,522 Northumberland tenancies which had owed border service in 1535/6, only 200 were still furnished for service 50 years later. And at a time of rising population, increasing stretches of the march were waste.[40]

Yet, shorn of their international dimension, the activities of the border surnames were of far less concern to the London government. By the later sixteenth century, the defence of God's elect nation against popery was replacing the debate about civility and savagery in the rhetoric of Englishness: in the north, this shift was epitomised by the appointment and long rule as lord president of the energetic Puritan earl of Huntingdon (1572–95). In 1586, William Harrison even alleged that the inhabitants of Tynedale and Redesdale had by the annual visits by the famous Puritan preacher, Bernard Gilpin, 'been called to some obedience and zeal unto the word' so that 'at this present their former savage demeanour is very much abated, and their barbarous wildness and fierceness so much qualified that there is hope left of their reduction unto civility'. Thus, for Harrison at least, civility was another word for Protestantism. In the far north at least, however, the increase of 'true religion' under Elizabeth came at the expense of a much more traditional duty of monarchy, the maintenance of justice and good rule and the defence of the queen's subjects against enemies and rebels.[41]

Much the same could be said about the conduct of government in Tudor Ireland. Even before Munster had been fully pacified, Lord Deputy Sidney had in 1571 been recalled. He was sharply reprimanded for meddling in common-law matters and the excessive costs of his administration. 'Rash dealings' by adventurers 'in matters of land' were henceforth to be restricted

---

40 S.G. Ellis, 'Integration, identities and frontiers in the British Isles: a European perspective' in Harald Gustafsson and Hanne Sanders (eds), *Vid Gränsen: Integration och identitet i det förnationella Norden* (Gothenburg, 2006), pp. 19–45; idem, *Tudor frontiers*, p. 120; S.J. Watts, *From border to middle shire: Northumberland 1586–1625* (Leicester, 1976), pp. 25–30.

41 John Hodgson, *A history of Northumberland* (3 pts in 7 vols, Newcastle, 1820–25), II, i, p. 75 (quotation); Watts, *From border to middle shire*, pp. 77–8.

to 'mere Irish' parts like Ulster. His eventual replacement, Sir William Fitzwilliam, Sussex's client, was ordered to economise, but was hamstrung by the army's reduction to 1,300 troops and the summons of Ormond, his chief supporter, to court. Fitzwilliam executed his brief by focusing on the English Pale. Lords President Fitton and Perrot, left to their own devices, soon resigned and, particularly with Desmond's release from detention, provincial government in Connaught and Munster was again entrusted to the local earls. In Ulster, meanwhile, two plantation projects – Sir Thomas Smith's private colony in the Ards peninsula (1572–3) and the more ambitious scheme by Walter Devereux, earl of Essex, to conquer and colonise Antrim (1573–5) – had not only antagonised Turlough Luineach O'Neill and Clan Donald but also alienated more tractable chiefs like Sir Brian O'Neill of Clandeboye, driving them to make common cause. Both projects proved expensive failures, with a sad record of atrocities.

At this point, the Leicester faction recovered the deputyship with the reappointment of Sidney, who rashly promised to make Ireland self-sufficient within three years at a cost of IR£60,000 and with a garrison of only 1,100 men. Sidney likewise had to manage without a leading local supporter, the earl of Kildare, whom Fitzwilliam had recently had arrested at a council meeting on a trumped-up charge of inciting Gaelic resistance to the midlands plantation and who spent the next three years in the Tower. Sidney's return inaugurated a new round of interventionist government, with presidents and councils now financed by appropriating the quasi-Gaelic rights of coign (free quartering on the country) and livery by which local lords had hitherto maintained their private armies of kerne and gallo-glass. These rights would then be commuted for fixed payments by a series of 'compositions', so making the councils financially self-sufficient and undermining the ability of regional magnates to oppose them. Essentially, this strategy was an extension to the provinces of a scheme initially proposed for the English Pale, where Sidney proposed that the governor's various rights to purveyance, militia and labour services should all be commuted for a composition rent of IR£5 per ploughland. Yet in pressing composition the governor's need for money forced him to exceed the bounds of political discretion so exacerbating the distrust between the Elizabethan military and Ireland's local Englishry. In Connaught and Munster composition was eventually imposed and the councils re-established (1575–8). Proclamations of martial law threatened with summary execution the erstwhile swordsmen and armed retainers of the magnates, forcing them into a grudging conformity. Desmond's cousin, Fitzmaurice, and other retainers fled to France to intrigue for foreign intervention. Yet, despite mounting opposition, a repetition of the major revolts of 1569–73 was – just! – avoided.

In the English Pale, however, Sidney's proposal and exorbitant demands for purveyance (cess) – designed to force a composition – reignited an earlier dispute about the burden of these exactions, fuelling the Palesmen's fears that the government's real purpose was to establish a new form of military taxation which could be imposed without the consent of parliament. Many landowners simply refused to pay, leading lords like Baltinglass, Delvin and Howth actively organised resistance, and three Pale lawyers arrived at court to petition the privy council. The queen's intervention eventually produced a compromise, but shortfalls on composition and military expenses meant that Sidney's administration was proving far more expensive than envisaged and his abrasive style of government was also alienating traditionally loyal sections of the local Englishry. By Michaelmas 1577 the deputy had exceeded his estimates (by IR£14,000), and he finally left Ireland under official disapproval the following September. The Munster president, Sir William Drury, was Sidney's temporary replacement in Dublin, so leaving the province unguarded just as Fitzmaurice's long-threatened invasion was at last materialising with papal support.[42]

By 1578, with leading magnates antagonised and traditional supporters exasperated by the recent conduct of government, the Dublin government was sitting on a powder keg. At this point, an expedition to Ireland financed by Pope Gregory XIII and led by the renegade Elizabethan, Captain Thomas Stukeley, reached Lisbon but was then diverted to Morocco. Fitzmaurice secured the remnants of this force and, with King Philip's connivance, set sail from Spain with some 60 Italian and Spanish soldiers and landed at Smerwick (17 July 1579). His company included the eminent English exile, Dr. Nicholas Sander, who now issued proclamations calling on the people of Ireland to rally to the papal standard. Initially, the response was discouraging: Desmond immediately informed Lord Justice Drury and began preparations to crush the invaders, but the earl dared not trust his retainers against Fitzmaurice and without reinforcements he began to waiver. The mounting distrust between New English officials and the province's local Englishry eventually led in November to Desmond's proclamation as a traitor. Shrewdly, Elizabeth appointed Ormond general of Munster, but not until

---

42   Ellis, *Ireland in the age of the Tudors*, pp. 300–10; V.P. Carey, *Surviving the Tudors: the 'Wizard' earl of Kildare and English rule in Ireland, 1537–1586* (Dublin, 2002), ch. 7; McCormack, *Earldom of Desmond*, chs 4–6.

February did she send the troops needed to back his diplomacy by force and so the revolt dragged on. Then in July, with the revolt almost over, a new, and quite separate, rebellion broke out quite unexpectedly in Leinster. Its nominal leader was James Eustace, Viscount Baltinglass, a zealous young Old English noble, recently returned from Rome, who bluntly informed Ormond that 'a woman uncapax of all holy orders' could not be supreme governor of the church, and that under Elizabeth Ireland had suffered 'more oppressing of poor subjects under pretence of justice' than ever before. Although Baltinglass was soon joined by the fugitive Sander and Desmond's brother, the revolt quickly collapsed. Its military backbone proved to be the disaffected Gaelic chief, Feagh MacHugh O'Byrne. In rocky, thickly-wooded Glenmalure, O'Byrne inflicted an embarrassing defeat on Arthur Lord Grey de Wilton, the newly-appointed governor of Ireland, when the latter, against expert advice, advanced into the Wicklow mountains with fresh reinforcements. This reverse encouraged minor risings elsewhere, but the Pale remained unsympathetic: Kildare, for instance, described Baltinglass as 'a very simple man without wisdom, manhood, or any other quality meet to embrace such an enterprise'. Then, just as the government seemed to recover control, came another emergency.[43]

In September 1580, one of Stukeley's captains, Bastiano di San Giuseppi, landed with 600 Italian and Spanish troops and reoccupied Fitzmaurice's fort at Smerwick. With further reinforcements – Grey had 6,437 troops by mid-October – the deputy easily contained the situation, and when, in November, the invaders surrendered in the expectation of mercy, he massacred the entire garrison. Politically, however, these events were disastrous for crown–community relations. Rebellion was anathema to the vast majority of the Palesmen, and elsewhere in the Englishry Fitzmaurice had attracted little support. Yet by 1580 the abrasive conduct of New English officials was driving different groups of malcontents to make common cause. The 'chief original' of unrest in the Pale, as even ministers admitted, was 'cess and the oppression of the soldier'; but many of those involved in the earlier cess controversy were fervently Catholic lawyers who now joined the marcher

43   Ellis, *Ireland in the age of the Tudors*, pp. 311–15; Carey, *Surviving the Tudors*, ch. 8 (quotation, p. 209); Lennon, *Sixteenth-century Ireland*, pp. 202–5; Edwards, *Ormond lordship*, pp. 228–37; Ciaran Brady, 'Conservative subversives: the community of the Pale and the Dublin adminis-tration, 1556–86' in P.J. Corish (ed.), *Radicals, rebels and establishments: Historical Studies XV* (Belfast, 1985), pp. 26–8; H.C. Walshe, 'The rebellion of William Nugent, 1581' in R.V. Comerford *et al.* (eds), *Religion, conflict and coexistence: essays presented to Monsignor Patrick J. Corish* (Dublin, 1990), pp. 26–52; Christopher Maginn, *'Civilizing' Gaelic Leinster: the expan-sion of Tudor rule in the O'Byrne and O'Toole lordships* (Dublin, 2005), ch. 5.

gentry and disgruntled Leinster Irish, while two leading Dublin merchants, William FitzSimon and Alderman Walter Sedgrave, supplied Baltinglass with weapons and powder. The government's overreaction to the hazy plotting of hot-headed idealists bent on holy war triggered the very reaction which Elizabeth had striven to avoid.

In December, the arrest in council of Delvin and the recently-released Kildare, both implicated in Baltinglass's original plans, precipitated the so-called Nugent conspiracy. Led by Delvin's brother, the poet William Nugent, who was alienated by the growing New English hold on government, and by John Cusack of Ellistonrede, who championed 'the cause of religion', some minor Pale gentry planned a combined raid with Ulster chiefs to release them. The Irish council's initial response to these various disturbances about the Pale was moderate: 9 gentry executed for their part in the Baltinglass revolt, others of 'mean calling' despatched by martial law; 25 gentlemen later arrested for the Nugent conspiracy, 7 mostly unrepentant Catholics executed. But then, in January 1582, Cusack turned queen's evidence in return for a pardon, implicating others, including important men like Chief Justice Nicholas Nugent and Lord Dunsany. Lord Grey now became convinced, quite wrongly, of a widespread Catholic conspiracy in the Pale, and believed that severity alone would achieve results. A fresh wave of arrests and trials of gentry and lawyers followed, including Chief Justice Nugent, executed after a show trial. By the time the privy council intervened in April to halt the executions, 17 gentry had suffered, besides lesser fry summarily executed; but William Nugent and others escaped by flight, and 45 gentry paid fines. Nonetheless, this evidence of widespread collusion between Gaelic clansmen and Old English landowners in a seemingly general Catholic conspiracy provided New English officials with an excellent opportunity to discredit the entire Old English political community. Urging Elizabeth to 'use a sharp and a severe course', reproving the 'arrogant zeal to popish government' of local politicians, they argued that she should rely solely on Englishmen and not 'leave the Irish to tumble to their own sensual government'.[44]

Nonetheless, the revolt in Munster dragged on. Ormond's conduct as general of Munster was bitterly attacked by New English officials who thought him too lenient. Ormond in turn hindered Grey's grants of traitors'

---

44 Walshe, 'The rebellion of William Nugent', pp. 26–52; Richard Bagwell, *Ireland under the Tudors* (3 vols., London, 1885–90), iii, 82, 88, 89 (quotations); Ellis, *Ireland under the Tudors*, pp. 314–16; Lennon, *Sixteenth-century Ireland*, pp. 202–5; Brady, 'Conservative subversives', pp. 26–8.

lands to deserving servitors like Captain Walter Ralegh, the executioner
at Smerwick. Eventually, Elizabeth revoked Ormond's commission (May
1581), but chiefly to save money, and she also discharged 4,600 troops over
the next nine months. The result was that the army now lacked the manpower to carry out effectively the systematic destruction decreed by Grey in
a bid to starve the rebels into submission. Even so, Sir William St Leger
reported that in Cork between 20 and 70 died daily of starvation, and Grey's
secretary, the poet Edmund Spenser, described how from

> woods and glens [the people] came creeping forth upon their hands, for their
> legs could not bear them. They looked anatomies of death, they spake like
> ghosts crying out of their graves, they did eat of the dead carrions . . . yea and
> one another soon after in so much as the very carcasses they spared not to scrape
> out of their graves.

In March 1582 St Leger thought that 30,000 people had starved to death in
Munster during the previous 6 months. According to one modern estimate,
almost 9,000 were killed in the fighting and nearly 40,000 died from famine
and disease – in other words, over 30 per cent of the province's population.
A 'most populous and plentiful country [was] suddenly left void of man or
beast'. Yet without the manpower to hunt down the ringleaders, the army's
conduct simply drove previously loyal landowners into revolt to replace
those caught. In April 1581 Dr. Sander died of dysentery; and Baltinglass
fled to the continent in November. Yet Elizabeth grew increasingly impatient
at the apparently fruitless expense, and in spring 1582 she recalled Grey.
Even New English officials were disturbed at his unsparing repression:
Spenser called him 'a bloody man who regarded not the life of Her Majesty's
subjects no more than dogs, but had wasted and consumed all so as now she
had nothing almost left but to reign in their ashes'. On his own admission,
Grey had executed as governor almost 1,500 'chief men and gentlemen' by
martial law, besides 'killing of churls, which were innumerable'.

To New English dismay, however, Elizabeth reappointed Ormond in
December as governor of Munster, with 1,000 troops and power to pardon
all rebels except Desmond himself. Unhindered this time by other counsels,
Ormond soon cleared the rebels out of Tipperary and Waterford, forcing
Desmond back into Kerry. By May 1583, 206 gentry had been killed,
but 921 had been pardoned after submission, including Lord Lixnaw and
Desmond's countess. Penned into west Cork and Kerry with a small fugitive
band, the rebel earl refused unconditional surrender: he was hunted down
and killed near Tralee in November, and his head sent to adorn London

Bridge. The final act in the tragedy had taken place amid renewed intrigues by New English officials to have Ormond recalled on financial grounds: they now feared that the earl would be appointed deputy and seek to discredit them. In fact, Elizabeth's choice as deputy fell on Sir John Perrot, a personal favourite and a protégé of Leicester with previous experience of Irish service as president of Munster. Yet the intrigues against Ormond reflected the almost complete breakdown of trust between New and Old English in Ireland and the polarisation of loyalist political opinion. Old English attitudes to crown government were fundamentally altered by the experience of recent events. Hitherto, the Old English leadership had rested with men who remembered the more optimistic political climate of St Leger's days. Yet Grey's unprecedentedly oppressive administration seemed to confirm the view of younger men that English government was necessarily hostile to the local community. These younger politicians, moreover, included a disproportionate number of committed Catholic lawyers whose victimisation during Grey's repression had also served to enhance their status. In the 1560s, Elizabeth's policies in the far north of England had subordinated good rule and defence to ideology and come close to creating a solid block of Catholic nobles. In Ireland these mistakes were repeated on a much larger scale, and with long-term consequences in terms of political and religious alienation which were to prove even more disastrous.[45]

Given its proximity to Ireland and its position as a likely entry point for raiding and invasion, Wales was also a continuing concern for Elizabeth's government, particularly as the threat of war with Spain loomed. It was feared that feuds among the gentry (for instance in Glamorgan between rival factions led by the Mansells and Stradlings in the 1570s) might lead to open war. The Denbighshire gentry were likewise split in the 1580s into western and eastern factions. These rivalries also showed a tendency to mirror court factions because the gentry of individual shires divided for and against leading nobles and courtiers, for instance in Glamorgan gentry linked to the earls of Pembroke, Sir James Croft and Sir Henry Sidney respectively. In 1576 Dr. David Lewis thought that the 'great disorders in Wales, especially in south Wales, have grown much of late days', and he criticised in particular the evil practices of *cymortha* (illegal exactions) and retaining by the gentry. A

---

45 Anthony McCormack, 'The social and economic consequences of the Desmond rebellion of 1579–83' in *Irish Historical Studies*, xxxiv (2004–5), pp. 1–15; Bagwell, *Ireland under the Tudors*, iii, pp. 97–9; Ellis, *Ireland in the age of the Tudors*, pp. 316–18 (quotations, p. 317); Edmund Spenser, *A view of the present state of Ireland*, ed. W.L. Renwick (Oxford), 1970, p. 106 (quotation); Edwards, *Ormond lordship*, pp. 228–37.

particular concern to the government was the apparent link between disaffected gentry and Catholic recusancy. At Plas Du in Llŷn, for example, a
Catholic circle of reputedly 80 surrounded the local squire, Thomas Owen,
whose brother, Hugh, a seminary priest, had been involved in the Ridolfi
plot in 1571. And opposition to Sir John Perrot in west Wales was led by
alleged Catholics like William Phillips of Picton.

In the 1570s, a Catholic exile, Morys Clynnog, hatched an elaborate plan
for a rising and invasion, with a landing at Menai. The government feared
that Catholic resistance in Wales was exceptionally strong, but the evidence
suggests rather that closer supervision which in the late 1570s replaced
the government's previously more relaxed attitude simply uncovered more
breaches of the law. The first appearance of Catholic missionaries, in 1577,
prompted the privy council to demand reports from the bishops of the
number of recusants in their dioceses: the Welsh bishops reported very few
recusants in 1577 (13 in Llandaff, 2 elsewhere), but by 1603, 800 active
recusants were recorded. And in Glamorgan, the number of recusants
presented at Great Sessions rose steeply from 4 in 1584 to 77 in 1587. The
first Welsh Catholic martyr, the schoolmaster, Richard Gwyn, was executed
at Wrexham in 1584. Altogether, in the period of harshest persecution
(1577–1618), there were 10 known Welsh martyrs out of a total for
England and Wales of 209. Overall, gentry feuds and residual Catholic loyalties were of themselves no more of a threat than in England, but perhaps
because of the exposed location of Wales things appeared otherwise to the
government.[46]

Also giving cause for concern at this critical juncture were events in
Scotland. Elizabeth's failure in the 1570s to cement good Anglo-Scottish
relations by entering into a formal defensive league or by subsidising the
Morton administration eventually allowed the establishment there of a pro-
French administration headed by Esmé Stewart, created duke of Lennox in
1581. Of itself, this development was not disastrous for Elizabeth, since
she then enjoyed good relations with France. Yet, many ministers of the kirk
refused to cooperate with Lennox, denouncing him as an agent of the
Counter-Reformation. He was eventually overthrown by radical Presbyterians,
the Ruthven Raiders, in a palace revolution in August 1582 which took the

46   Philip Jenkins, *A history of modern Wales 1536–1990* (London, 1992), pp. 86–9, 97–101,
     111–15; J.G. Jones, *Wales and the Tudor state: government, religious change and the social order
     1534–1603* (Cardiff, 1989), pp. 102–3, 200–2 (quotation, p. 200); W.J. Tighe, 'Elizabethan
     Herefordshire: Sir James Croft, his friends and his foes' in *Historical Journal*, xxxii (1989),
     pp. 257–79; Williams, *Recovery, reorientation and Reformation*, pp. 316–20.

shape of the seizure of the king's person. Elizabeth had encouraged the Ruthven Raid, but the Ruthven administration, although pro-English, then received no practical English assistance. Its critics naturally looked elsewhere for support. In June 1583 King James was rescued by a coalition of predominantly northern peers – Catholics, Marians and *politiques* – led by the earl of Huntly. The Ruthven regime collapsed. The new administration was led by James Stewart, earl of Arran. Initial alarmist reports reaching England had suggested another French Catholic regime: King James was even writing to the pope and the duke of Guise at this time. Yet following the failure in April 1584 of the Stirling Raid – an attempt by anglophile Protestants, encouraged by English diplomats, to repeat the Ruthven Raid – Elizabeth and Arran came to an understanding.[47] In 1584, therefore, on the eve of the king's majority, the political situation in Scotland stood very much in the balance. For King James, his security had twice recently been threatened by the Anglo-Protestant faction. His Catholic subjects, however, had shown themselves loyal supporters of monarchy. It was far from clear, therefore, that in the ensuing Anglo-Spanish war the young king's best option was a pro-English policy. To date, he had indeed very little to be grateful to Elizabeth for and everything to gain from keeping open the option of playing the Catholic card. A more considered and sensitive approach by Elizabeth to relations with the northern kingdom might not only have smoothed much of the instability of Scottish politics since 1578 but also have secured her a more reliable ally.

By the end of 1584, events were moving quickly towards confrontation between England and Spain. The Elizabethan regime was now increasingly preoccupied with the Dutch crisis and the necessity of an English expedition to the Netherlands. It was, however, singularly ill-prepared for this major confrontation with Europe's most powerful, and militantly Catholic, monarchy which, in the event, was to last for the rest of the reign. Elizabeth had now reigned for 26 years, but in many ways the government's position was now weaker than it had been after the first 13. This was clearly the case in Ireland where the government's mishandling of Gaelic chiefs and Old English magnates and gentry had driven political and religious dissidents to make common cause. In the north, the borders were in a very weak state and the queen's officers failed to maintain justice and good rule, at a time when the attitude of the Scots under their young king remained unclear. The

47 Donaldson, *Scotland*, pp. 172–83; Julian Goodare and Michael Lynch (eds), *The reign of James VI* (East Linton, 2000), pp. 35–7, 96–7, 112–13.

defence of Wales against a Spanish landing also gave cause for concern. Only [253] in Lowland England did the situation seem less unsatisfactory; but even here the government's grip on events seemed weak: the revenues were stagnating, the yield from taxation declining, and the privy council was dangerously narrow and unrepresentative of the political nation at large. In short, Elizabeth had squandered the opportunities of the last decade to consolidate royal authority in the Tudor borderlands. And, whereas in her first two decades Elizabeth's character – her innate conservatism and indecisiveness, combined with a fierce determination to hold the strings of policy – had frequently worked in her favour, during the war years, when commanders needed to make spot decisions, Elizabeth's personality was much less of an asset.

THE TESTING-TIME OF THE PROTESTANT STATE SYSTEM, 1584–1603

James VI celebrated his eighteenth birthday in June 1584, so becoming the first Scottish king to enter on his personal rule since James V in 1528. In James lay the future not only of his peripheral Scottish kingdom, but also the future of the British Isles. For, as Elizabeth's reign wore on, it had become increasingly clear that the 'virgin queen' would remain so, making her the last Tudor occupant of the English throne. Though Elizabeth would not tolerate discussion of the succession, the queen was steadily grooming James, her godson – through a heady mixture of bullying and the dispensation of maternal advice (clothed in lectures on princely responsibilities) – as her most likely successor. Distrusted by both Elizabeth and her ministers, James was far from an ideal candidate; but the presence of an adult male of the Protestant persuasion seated on the Scottish throne, whose dynastic claim to the English crown could not easily be overlooked, demanded a much closer relationship with the northern kingdom.[1]

In 1584, however, the prospect of the regal union eagerly longed for by James and only reluctantly accepted as a possibility by many in England remained purely academic. In Scotland, the adult king, even with English support, could only muster the most precarious of grips on a decentralised kingdom still dominated by an intractable nobility (a significant rump of whom remained Catholic) and a fiercely independent kirk. This internal uncertainty, coupled with James's recurrent flirtations with continental powers, made Scotland an unreliable, and potentially dangerous, neighbour. Elizabeth, on the other hand, was riding a wave of two successive decades of relative peace and prosperity: the queen was stronger than she had ever been. The last years of the sixteenth century were to remain Elizabeth's even as a deteriorating socio-economic climate brought fresh challenges for Tudor administrative structures and events in Europe and Ireland forced the queen

---

1   W.T. MacCaffrey, *Queen Elizabeth and the making of policy, 1572–1588* (Princeton, 1981), pp. 425–7.

to lead her country through a period of prolonged instability and war. In [255] the intervening years, James VI had no recourse but to consolidate his position within his own kingdom, waiting patiently to enter into the uncharted dynastic and political territory that would follow upon Elizabeth's death. James's patience and largely consistent cooperation with England ensured that the seventeenth century would belong to the Stuarts and that they would inherit a British state without borderlands and based on multiple kingdoms.

England's long war with Spain

With the signing in August 1585 of the treaty of Nonsuch, open intervention in the Low Countries replaced more than a decade of goodwill and less conspicuous English military and financial support for the Dutch rebels. The die had been cast, but only reluctantly so: Elizabeth committed to send an expeditionary force of 6,400 infantry and 1,000 horse and to provide the rebels with an annual sum of £126,000. Yet she still held out hope of reaching a separate accommodation with the duke of Parma.[2] Nevertheless, Nonsuch marked the official beginning of England's war with Spain and put paid to the queen's efforts to remain somehow outside, or indeed above, the fray of a Europe bitterly divided over religion. It also altered the traditional diplomatic scene. With only two Protestant states – Holland and Zeeland – evading Parma's inexorable advance in the Low Counties, and faced with what was perceived to be the overwhelming military might and unlimited financial reserves of Catholic Spain, the queen was moved to lend increasingly generous financial assistance to the embattled Henry of Navarre, the Protestant heir to the French throne.

Closer to home, war with Spain compelled Elizabeth to redouble her efforts to reach a more permanent accommodation with Scotland. The result was the treaty concluded at Berwick in July 1586. The treaty – which pledged England and Scotland to armed assistance of the other in the event of an attack by a third party – lent much-needed diplomatic weight to the informal alliance that had gradually developed between the two kingdoms during Elizabeth's reign. And though Berwick fell short of actually naming James

---

2   Charles Wilson, *Queen Elizabeth and the revolt of the Netherlands* (London, 1970); MacCaffrey, *Queen Elizabeth, 1572–1588*, pp. 348, 398; D.M. Palliser, *The age of Elizabeth: England under the later Tudors, 1547–1603* (New York, 1983), p. 26.

as Elizabeth's successor, its formal acknowledgement of a military alliance underpinned by the Protestant faith helped to strengthen the king's still uncertain government against both the vestiges of regency government and rogue elements within the Scottish nobility. Above all, however, this 'straighter friendship' tied Scotland firmly to what was emerging as England's wider struggle against the Catholic alliance led by the Pope and Philip II and backed by Guise.[3]

English intervention in the Low Countries also influenced Tudor policy in relation to Ireland where Sir John Perrot, the former president of Munster, had been appointed deputy in January 1584. Ostensibly, Perrot's deputyship augured well. As discussed above (ch. 8), the revolts in Munster and Leinster had been suppressed without provoking a more widespread rebellion and, at his installation speech, the energetic new deputy spoke optimistically of how the queen regarded her subjects of Ireland and of England equally. Perrot, moreover, unveiled a comprehensive programme, promising both to reform areas subject to royal government and to extend Tudor rule into the remaining semi-autonomous Gaelic regions. In theory, Perrot's approach to the government of Ireland was greatly influenced by the successful, and largely peaceful, integration of Wales into the Tudor state; in practice the deputy's strategy strongly resembled the earlier bouts of programmatic government pioneered by Sussex and Sidney. And, like his predecessors, Perrot's programme identified specific problem areas and earmarked them for special attention. But some of those same areas of concern highlighted by Sussex and Sidney – most notably the inability of Tudor government to penetrate parts of Gaelic Ulster and the continued infiltration of that province by Scots – remained; and to these were added Perrot's determination to launch an extensive plantation in Munster on the earl of Desmond's attainted lands, to extend composition for cess throughout Ireland based on a uniform unit of assessment, and to commence a campaign to promote religious conformity. Perrot was also faced with a growing divide between the kingdom's New English and Old English communities, and his experience in Ireland had shown him the potential for either of these interests to undermine a deputy's ability to introduce policy. He thus hoped to secure local consensus, and legislative support for his ambitious programme, through parliament.[4]

3   MacCaffrey, *Queen Elizabeth, 1572–1588*, p. 424; S.J. Watts, *From border to middle shire: Northumberland, 1586–1625* (Leicester, 1975), p. 17 (quotation).
4   Ellis, *Ireland in the age of the Tudors*, pp. 318–22; Ciarán Brady, *The chief governors: the rise and fall of reform government in Tudor Ireland, 1536–1588* (Cambridge, 1994), pp. 291–300.

But the threat of war with Spain and, ultimately, actual war in the Netherlands immediately undercut the lord deputy's far-reaching programme. The
crown instructed Perrot to cut costs and, above all, to avoid unnecessary confrontation so that money and soldiers could be directed to the Netherlands.
The affects of Tudor involvement on the continent were first felt in Ulster
where the deputy had, shortly after his arrival, attempted to end infiltration
by Scots and to integrate the province into his programme through the
imposition of a general (and onerous) composition on its Gaelic chiefs.
Perrot initially envisaged the erection of fortified towns, backed by a garrison of 2,400 English soldiers, to ensure the successful implementation of his
'settlement' of Ulster. The division of the O'Neill heartland of Tyrone and
the expulsion of Sorley Boy MacDonald and the other Scots would follow.
But his ambitious strategy was everywhere undermined amid fears of a
Spanish invasion. The queen baulked at the proposed outlay of additional
men and money, and the existing English troops there – which in the meanwhile had been left under the command of local chiefs – were steadily transferred to the Netherlands. The privy council also determined to leave Tyrone
intact and in the hands of the O'Neill chief, Turlough Luineach, for life,
while Hugh O'Neill, baron of Dungannon, was created second earl of Tyrone
with a view to the Anglophile earl becoming the crown's principal agent
in Ulster. Perrot, moreover, was commanded to reach an accommodation
with the Scots: MacDonald was eventually denizened in 1586 and, much to
Perrot's chagrin, was granted lands in north-east Ulster.[5]

Yet, despite his setbacks in Ulster, Perrot was determined to implement
the remainder of his programme, and he summoned parliament to secure
the local political and financial support which was now essential for his
programme to proceed. Parliament, the first convened in Ireland in over a
decade, opened in April 1585; and the extent to which Tudor government
had penetrated Ireland was clear: an unprecedented number of Gaelic lords
and delegations attended and, since 1560, the parliamentary franchise had
been extended to seven new boroughs and cities while an equal number of
new counties were represented.[6] From the outset, however, a well-organised
opposition – chiefly Catholic Old English Palesmen – frustrated Perrot's
initiatives. Their opposition was focused primarily on the composition bill,

5 Ellis, *Ireland in the age of the Tudors*, pp. 318–22; Hiram Morgan, *Tyrone's rebellion: the outbreak of
    the Nine Years' War in Tudor Ireland* (London, 1993), pp. 29–54.
6 Victor Treadwell, 'Sir John Perrot and the Irish parliament of 1585–6', in *Proceedings of the
    Royal Irish Academy*, lxxxv (1985), sect. C, pp. 282–306; Ellis, *Ireland in the age of the Tudors*,
    pp. 318–22.

supposedly leading to the imposition of a permanent tax, and a bill extending the English parliament's anti-Catholic legislation to Ireland. These bills, the opposition argued, amounted to a twin assault on the constitutional liberties and the freedom of conscience of the queen's Irish subjects. Controlling both houses, this now galvanised Old English bloc forced the deputy, in late May, briefly to prorogue parliament having accomplished little. Perrot then changed tack, appealing to the queen to break the impasse; but, as in Ulster, Elizabeth was not prepared to press her Irish subjects too hard while conflict loomed in the Netherlands. Perrot was forced to abandon the composition and anti-Catholic bills. When in April 1586 parliament was reconvened, 5 of the government's 16 bills were defeated, 2 were heavily amended and another withdrawn; other than the attainders of Baltinglass and Desmond, and some commonwealth bills of lesser import, the government had little to show after two sessions of parliament. Perrot's programme lay in tatters.[7]

With hindsight it is tempting to view the shortcomings of Perrot's deputyship – particularly his difficulties in Ulster – as a prelude to the violent upheaval that engulfed Ireland in the 1590s; but from the contemporary perspective of an English state facing into war with Catholic Europe, Perrot's administration admirably served its intended purpose: the maintenance of the *status quo*. This, of course, was not Perrot's intention, but he nevertheless avoided a repeat of the revolts of the early 1580s, which were estimated to have cost the crown £215,201 16s.[8] – an unacceptable expenditure at this juncture. Perrot also strengthened Tudor government in Connaught and Munster, the provinces most vulnerable to Spanish invasion. Indeed it was in Connaught that Perrot's programme enjoyed its most notable success. Here, he improved upon earlier efforts at composition by negotiating a settlement acceptable to local lords, including the powerful earls of Clanrickard and Thomond, converting feudal exactions due to them into fixed rents. This Composition of Connaught, as it was known, laid the foundations for English government in the province, so creating after 1585 a solid base of English support which was to last well into the seventeenth century.[9] In Munster, Perrot oversaw the private plantation on the earl of Desmond's

---

7   Ibid.

8   Christopher Maginn, 'The Baltinglass rebellion, 1580: English dissent or a Gaelic uprising?', in *Historical Journal*, xlvii (2004), p. 231.

9   Bernadette Cunningham, 'Political and social change in the lordships of Clanricard and Thomond, 1569–1641', (unpublished MA thesis, NUI, Galway, 1979), pp. 31–5; Ellis, *Ireland in the age of the Tudors*, pp. 322–5.

attainted lands. Though the carefully planned endeavour was fraught with problems arising primarily from inaccurate land surveys, and compounded by a fundamental misunderstanding of the feudal complexities of land-holding which had prevailed under the Desmonds, the plantation gradually proceeded: by 1589 several dozen English undertakers, albeit a far smaller number than the 8,500 settlers originally envisaged, were in possession of nearly 300,000 acres.[10] Thus, at a time when more pressing events had forced the English crown to assign a low order of priority to its Irish kingdom, Perrot's deputyship, at the very least, ensured that Ireland did not emerge as an additional area of concern. It is clear that the existence of a Gaelic polity, which had yet to be fully integrated into the Tudor state, highly organised constitutional opposition in the English Pale, and the prevalence of recus-ancy throughout Ireland, should have cast doubt over the future of the English presence in the kingdom – indeed in these difficulties can be seen the fundamental challenges posed by multiple monarchy – but, by the time of Perrot's recall in 1588, the likelihood of a Spanish invasion of southern England dominated Tudor thinking, so ensuring that the lessons implicit in the setbacks of his deputyship were ignored.

Thus far in its war against Spain the Tudor regime had cast an outward appearance of strength and unity. The presence in the Netherlands after 1585 of a sizeable English expeditionary force had, despite the earl of Leicester's many shortcomings as commander-in-chief, proved sufficient to tilt the balance of the conflict in favour of the Dutch rebels, at once stalling Parma's advance and distracting Philip II.[11] That Leicester's forces – comprised primarily of English volunteers and conscripts – were augmented by the earl's tenants from the barony of Denbigh in north Wales, several hundred Gaelic troops from Leinster and, briefly, by more than 2,000 Scottish soldiers, reinforced the image of a British Isles united in its opposi-tion to Spanish power.[12] Meanwhile, the ease with which Sir Francis Drake criss-crossed the Atlantic harrying Spanish ports from the West Indies to Cadiz reflected the growing confidence and reach of English sea power.

---

10   Michael McCarthy-Morrogh, *The Munster plantation: English migration to southern Ireland* (Oxford, 1986), chs 1–4; Nicholas Canny, *Making Ireland British, 1580–1650* (Oxford, 2001), ch. 3.

11   Palliser, *The age of Elizabeth*, p. 26. For a more critical assessment of English intervention in the Netherlands, see Wilson, *Queen Elizabeth and the revolt of the Netherlands*, pp. 123–36.

12   Peter Roberts, 'The English crown, the principality of Wales and the council in the Marches, 1534–1641', in John Morrill and Brendan Bradshaw (eds), *The British problem, c.1534–1707: state formation in the Atlantic archipelago* (London, 1996), p. 133; Public Record Office, State Papers 12/233/85 (i); MacCaffrey, *Queen Elizabeth, 1572–1588*, p. 361.

Within England, the discovery in August 1586 of yet another murky plot to assassinate Elizabeth involving Mary Stewart finally led to the execution in February 1587 of the ageing Scottish queen. Though this most recent conspiracy, the so-called Babington plot – like the Throckmorton plot to murder Elizabeth which had been thwarted in late 1583 – stood little real chance of success, both contained shadowy links with Catholic English exiles and were designed to place Mary on the throne in anticipation of an amphibious Spanish landing on English shores.[13]

With the assassination of William 'the Silent', prince of Orange, still fresh in the minds of many, these conspiracies touched a nerve in a country whose childless Protestant monarch had yet to designate a successor and prompted, in late 1584, the drafting of a Bond of Association. The thousands of Protestant (and Catholic) gentlemen who flocked to sign this Bond pledged to hunt down and kill anyone adjudged to have made an attempt on Elizabeth's life. Yet there was more to the Bond than the signatories' devotion to their queen: it also debarred from the succession any person in whose name the assassination attempt was committed and, extraordinarily, made provision for an interim government in the event the queen was killed. Burghley who, together with Walsingham, had spearheaded the drafting of the Bond proudly saw it as an example of a Protestant nation united in a 'fellowship and society'; but its appeal to mob violence and conception of English government without a sovereign, however temporary, alarmed Elizabeth.[14] The Bond, moreover, while implicitly directed at Mary, around whom conspiracy gathered like moths to a flame, cast doubt as to whether her issue would also be excluded from the succession. The following year the Bond was amended by the Queen's Safety Act, which exempted the descendents of anyone found complicit in a plot to murder the queen and, at the queen's insistence, dashed the radical plans for the establishment of a provisional government in the event of Elizabeth's death. Nevertheless, the Queen's Safety Act, and its antecedent the Bond of Association, reflects the degree of support within England for Elizabeth and the rejection of any return to a Catholic monarchy. Thus, when after the discovery of the Babington plot Elizabeth was faced with the overwhelming desire of her subjects to see Mary removed, once and for all, as a threat to both the English succession and to the safety of England itself, the queen had little

---

13   J.A. Bossy, *Under the molehill: an Elizabethan spy story* (New Haven and London, 2001).

14   Mark Nicholls, *A history of the modern British Isles, 1529–1603: the two kingdoms* (Oxford, 1999), pp. 257–8 (quotation, p. 257).

choice but to sanction the death of another sovereign. The puritan M.P.,
Job Throckmorton, spoke for many in England when he contemptuously
referred to the queen of Scots as 'the daughter of sedition, the mother
of rebellion, the nurse of impiety, the handmaid of iniquity, the sister of
unshamefastness'.[15] Mary's execution demonstrated the strength and unity
of England under Elizabeth and extinguished any faint hope that remained
of England returning to Catholic rule. Only the reaction of the Scottish king
remained to be seen; and when it became clear that the English throne (and
his annual receipt of an English pension worth £4,000) was of more value
to James VI than avenging the death of the mother he had never known
and 'whose existence was an obstacle to his position and prospects', the
Elizabethan regime was assured of its security within Britain.[16]

Yet widespread domestic support for Elizabeth, peace with Scotland and
relative stability in Ireland could not protect the Tudor regime from the massive Spanish frontal assault rumoured to be imminent by 1588. Indeed, the
threat of invasion reversed the traditional political geography and military
certainties of the British Isles. Historically, Ireland, Wales and Scotland had
marked the frontiers of English influence, and it was in these peripheral areas
where threats to English power had been most likely to materialise. But the
prospect of an expansionist Spanish state willing to commit tens of thousands of men to an invasion of southern England transformed what had been
the centre of English power into an exposed frontier.

The remarkable defeat of the dreaded Spanish Armada in high summer
1588 – more a triumph of superior English naval technology and seaman-
ship than a 'Protestant wind' – did little to alter this new reality, for England
lacked the military capacity either to eradicate the bulk of the scattered
Spanish fleet which had survived the engagement, or to deliver to Spanish
shores a decisive counter-invasion capable of bringing Philip II to his
knees.[17] Nor did the Armada's failure dampen the Spanish monarch's enthusiasm for a sea-borne invasion of England: Spanish fleets again set sail in
1596 and 1597 with the intention of making landfall in England. With a
population estimated at, in the late sixteenth century, a mere 3,500,000 (less
than half that of Spain) and still without a standing army on a par with other
major European states, the Elizabethan government could not dictate the

---

15   Quoted in, J.E. Neale, *Elizabeth I and her parliaments, 1584–1601* (London, 1957), p. 110.
16   Gordon Donaldson, *Scotland: James V to James VII* (Edinburgh, 1965), p. 184 (quotation);
     MacCaffrey, *Queen Elizabeth and the making of policy*, pp. 424–5.
17   For the Armada, see Colin Martin and Geoffrey Parker, *The Spanish Amada* (London, 1988).

course of what was emerging as a prolonged struggle against a state whose monarch was bent on the regime's destruction.[18] The government thus had little choice other than to adopt a strong defensive posture militarily, exploiting England's physical separation from mainland Europe. One of the keys to this evolving strategy, as we have seen, was continued Tudor dominance over Scotland and in Ireland, so as to present a unified chain of British resistance. Equally important, however, was the Tudor government's sensitivity to the problems facing its English subjects. The hardships brought on the lower levels of English society by such 'invisible' socio-economic trends as rising population, spiralling inflation and the expansion of urban centres were exacerbated, after 1585, by the added burden of war and, in 1586–7 and between 1593 and 1597, by harvest failure. As previously outlined (ch. 5), the Tudor government responded to this potentially dangerous combination of forces – which threatened to spark widespread domestic unrest – by assuming a greater role in regulating the economy and creating new administrative structures to maintain control of the commons. In the long term, the effectiveness of the Tudor response to the related problems arising from nearly two decades of war, demographic change and an economic downturn increased the power of the state in England.[19]

Many of the socio-economic problems confronting the English state late in Elizabeth's reign were all too familiar. Faced with the interlocking problems of inflation, unemployment and regional depopulation, dearth and the threat of starvation, and poverty, the crown's overriding concern had always been to prevent unrest and the disruption of the social order. In this Elizabeth's objective was little different. But the unprecedented demands of war and the more extreme versions of traditional socio-economic phenomena, which gradually revealed themselves as the queen's reign progressed, stretched longstanding administrative structures to the limit.

The Elizabethan government was forced to intervene more frequently, and extensively, refining earlier Tudor responses still further and, in certain instances, conceiving wholly new methods of governing. Yet this response did not, at any stage in Elizabeth's reign, amount to a coherent policy or an

18 G.R. Elton, *England under the Tudors* (3rd ed., London, 1991), p. 359; Cf. Palliser, *The age of Elizabeth*, ch. 2.
19 S.G. Ellis, 'The commons and the state: representation, influence, and the legislative process: England', in Peter Blickle (ed.), *Resistance, representation, and community* (Oxford, 1997), p. 138; M.J. Braddick, *State formation in early modern England, c.1550–1700* (Cambridge, 2000), pp. 103–72.

overarching programme of government. Rather it was characterised by a [263] series of *ad hoc* innovations designed to address specific areas of concern.[20] As discussed above, the desire to prevent social unrest was the driving force behind the crown's efforts to meet these socio-economic challenges. For it was recognised, by Elizabeth's reign, that if prices consistently outstripped wages, if work was not provided for the unemployed, and if the realm was not fed, then a substantial segment of society was liable to sink into poverty, and in the swelled poor masses, it was thought, lay a threat to order and security. This recognition was a significant departure from traditional attitudes toward the poor, which held that only those poor who were physically unable to work, the aged and the 'impotent', should be unemployed, and thus deserving of relief. During the war years from 1585, vagrants were frequently encouraged to enlist in the military and the Vagrancy Act of 1597 ordered that exceptionally dangerous vagabonds be transported overseas or placed permanently in galley-service.[21] It was in these uncertain years that the repression of vagrancy and the military defence of the realm became virtually indistinguishable tasks. The steady influx of hordes of disbanded soldiers returned from the wars everywhere strained the government's measures to regulate the economy, provide poor-relief, suppress vagrancy and organise England's defence. Particularly in the coastal shires, fears of unruly soldiers and sailors congregating and causing disturbances was just as much a concern to the government as the threat of Spanish invasion. JPs, constables and parish churchwardens, the traditional instruments of local government, were no longer sufficient to meet the challenges arising from increasing levels of vagrancy and an expanding unemployed soldiery. In the face of war, these instruments had to be supplemented, and the government responded by relying more heavily on its regional representatives. The position of lord lieutenant – normally a leading regional magnate who had, since the late medieval period, been appointed in an *ad hoc* capacity to raise military forces in the counties – became an appointment of longer duration and added importance. In Wales, after 1585, the lord president assumed the more military title of lord lieutenant and was similarly charged with supervising defences in conjunction with local sheriffs and JPs.[22] It was through

---

20 Ellis, 'The commons and the state', pp. 138–9; Penry Williams, *The Tudor regime* (Oxford, 1979), pp. 175–7, 187, 215.

21 A.L. Beier, *Masterless men: the vagrancy problem in England, 1560–1640* (London, 1985), pp. 152–70.

22 J.G. Jones, *Early modern Wales, c. 1525–1640* (London, 1994), p. 95.

these increasingly powerful regional officers that the government experimented with provost-marshals a new officer authorised to proceed by martial law against civilians.

The prospect of foreign invasion in 1588, coupled with the return in the following year of the English fleet from Portugal, however, prompted the government to allow its lords lieutenant to appoint provost-marshals in each shire, and most major towns, to maintain order and to prevent unrest. Though controlling disbanded soldiers were the provosts' primary concern, they were also authorised, under the auspices of martial law, to execute both vagrants – many of whom were thought to be masquerading as soldiers and thus adding to the general confusion – and even those merely suspected of vagrancy. JPs and constables were similarly empowered by martial law at this time, but the office of provost-marshal proved more efficient. When in 1595 rioting erupted in London, it was a provost-marshal who was appointed with authority 'to apprehend all such as shall not be readily reformed & corrected by the ordinary officers of justice, and them without delay to execute upon the gallows, by order of martial law'.[23] Despite experiments in Ireland in the mid-1550s, their introduction in England was truly a radical departure from Tudor norms, and the crown was careful to stress that such measures were temporary. Yet as the war continued so too did the work of the lords lieutenant and, with them, the provost-marshal. Indeed, the once temporary position of county lieutenant had developed into a lifelong appointment as the crown's principal local administrative official, while the provost-marshal was rapidly assuming jurisdiction over civil order: what had been the provosts' secondary function, dealing with civilians, became their primary purpose. Thus, by the close of Elizabeth's reign, traditional Tudor points of contact between central and local government – JPs and constables (and more so sheriffs in Wales and Ireland) – had been augmented by the introduction of lords lieutenant and provost-marshals.

The Elizabethan government's efforts to regulate the economy and oversee the provision and distribution of food throughout the realm, its introduction of a national scheme for poor relief and measures to control the commons and soldiery did much to prevent widespread domestic unrest at a time when such a development would have had serious implications for England's war with Spain. But this multi-faceted response to socio-economic

23 Lindsay Boynton, 'The Tudor provost-marshal', in *English Historical Review*, lxxviii (1962), pp. 437–48, 451 (quotation, p. 451).

problems exacerbated by war also led to a striking extension of the power [265] of the state. For, in order to lend substance to its national initiatives in the localities, the state had come to rely more heavily on, and strengthen its ties with, local government. Indeed, many of the state-sponsored innovations introduced at this time either emulated or worked in tandem with local initiatives, particularly in regard to the distribution of food and poor relief. With more regular links between central and local government thus established, the state's authority was allowed entry to areas of English society that had hitherto been beyond its reach. Yet such an elaborate diffusion of political power within the state also served to involve a greater proportion of the commons in local government, with leading villagers supplying the growing number of constables, overseers of the poor and jurors needed to keep the bureaucracy functioning.[24] At the same time, the continued threat of foreign invasion forced the commons to assume a more prominent role in contributing to the defence of their English state: in addition to serving in the wars in unprecedented numbers, taxpayers granted the queen subsidies in six wartime parliaments between 1585 and 1601 with relatively little hesitation.[25] In late Elizabethan England, the related phenomena of expanding state power and continued war combined to strengthen royal authority and integrate the commons more firmly into the early modern English state.

The reassertion of royal authority in Scotland

In Scotland, things were otherwise. The entrance of James on his personal rule, and the fall of the earl of Arran's regime in November 1585, had done much to bolster royal authority in the kingdom. Indeed, James VI was, as one historian has described him, an 'unchallenged Protestant king of an undoubted Protestant country', whose monarchy stood as a symbol of unity for all Scots.[26] But an unchallenged and universally accepted king though he was, James still reigned over what was a devolved and deeply fragmented kingdom. The reconstitution of royal authority in James, therefore, merely added an additional dimension to a Scottish political scene already divided

---

24 Ellis, 'The commons and the state', p. 146. Cf. Hindle, *State and social change in early modern England*, pp. 171–3.
25 Elton, *England under the Tudors*, p. 363.
26 Wormald, *Court, kirk and community*, p. 149.

between the two great pillars of Scottish society: the nobility and the kirk.[27] The assertion of royal authority over an overmighty nobility and an influential church – which had for long conspired to retard the extension of the state's power – had to be achieved before James could realise his goal of a centralised monarchy along the lines of what had emerged under the Tudors.

James believed in autocracy and the pre-eminence of his own kingship, but he did so only in an academic sense. In practice, he was a shrewd and flexible politician willing to negotiate or compromise when circumstances demanded. He was fully aware that if he embarked on an aggressive promotion of royal authority in Scotland, then he would risk alienating either the nobility or the church, or both; and lacking a standing army, and anything approaching the elaborate instruments of government found in Elizabethan England, James needed these powerful institutions to maintain effective control of government.[28] His intention to build consensus had been made clear as early as 1583, when the king proposed to 'draw his nobility to unity and concord and to be known to be a universal king'.[29] This was given substance when he assembled his privy council in the wake of the collapse of Arran's regime. The king's council was, in effect, a broad coalition of interests, which included members of the ultra-Protestant Ruthven faction (the earls of Angus, Mar and the Master of Glamis) former members of Arran's more moderate administration (the Master of Gray and John Maitland) and the conservative Catholic magnates (the earls of Huntly, Montrose, Crawford and Marischal). John Maitland of Thirlestane had been the chief architect of the coalition and emerged both as James's chief minister and the guiding hand behind Scottish policy for the next decade. The central thrust of Maitland's ministry was to ensure that the king maintained strong links with the two forces which he held to be of paramount importance: England and the kirk.[30] But Maitland's humble ancestry and leanings toward Presbyterianism, together with James's own innate conservatism, compelled the king to involve his nobility more closely in central government. Yet the territoriality and feuding, which permeated Scottish noble culture and undermined royal authority, was an obstacle which had first to be addressed. Thus, on the occasion of his twenty-first birthday in June 1587, James invited the leading lights of the nobility to Edinburgh where bitter enemies

27   Julian Goodare, *State and society in early modern Scotland* (Oxford, 1999), pp. 73–5.
28   Nicholls, *A history of the modern British Isles*, pp. 302–3.
29   Donaldson, *Scotland: James V to James VII*, p. 187.
30   Ibid.

were made to walk before him hand in hand. This scene is eerily reminiscent of the procession to St Paul's Cathedral that took place in 1458 at the beginning of a period of prolonged noble discord in England. In this instance, Henry VI had attempted to reconcile the feuds of his English nobility in a 'love-day' by marching pairs of enemies before him through the streets of London. The effects of James's intercession to end noble feuding, like that of Henry's, endured for little more than the day itself. What is striking, however, is that the late sixteenth century witnessed in Scotland a dangerous tug-of-war between noble factions and the monarchy similar to that which had occurred in England nearly 150 years earlier. And, as in mid-fifteenth century England, the private wars of the Scottish nobility still maintained the capacity to throw the entire kingdom into upheaval.

What began as a local dispute in the remote north-eastern corner of Scotland between George Gordon, sixth earl of Huntly, and James Stewart, second earl of Moray, set the stage for a major confrontation between the Scottish nobility and the crown in 1594. The earl of Huntly was an 'over-mighty' subject of the highest order. His far-reaching feudal connection and unrivalled dominance in the highlands, coupled with his influence at court and in the royal chamber, positioned him second only to the king in terms of power and prestige. Huntly, however, was also the leading Catholic noble in Scotland whose overt links with Spain had earned him, and the cadre of other Catholic northern earls, the enmity of the Protestant nobility and the kirk. Yet the king was not prepared to press the Catholic interest too far, lest he upset the precarious balance of power in place since 1585 and risk handing the advantage to the kirk. James, moreover, relied on Huntly's military muscle to see off the growing threat posed by his capricious cousin, Francis Stewart, earl of Bothwell. A leading Protestant noble and a kinsman of Moray, Bothwell had, in April 1591, been accused of witchcraft and conspiring against the king. But Bothwell escaped to his earldom near the border shires and from there launched a series of hit and run attacks on the king's person. In desperation, the king granted Huntly wide-ranging powers to suppress Bothwell. Huntly, however, used the opportunity to settle his feud with the earl of Moray. Huntly's sensational murder of the 'bonnie Earl of Moray' in February 1592, and the discovery the following year of a Catholic conspiracy and blank letters – the so-called 'Spanish blanks' – bound for Spain signed by Huntly and several northern earls, frightened the Protestant polity and turned public opinion in Scotland and England against the government. An incensed clergy voiced their support for Moray and Bothwell, whom they felt were victims of a Catholic conspiracy, and pressed

[268]   the king to march against Huntly. Queen Elizabeth, meanwhile, expressed her displeasure with James by lowering his annual pension and despatching ambassadors armed with stinging letters.[31]

The concerns of a panicky Scottish kirk, meanwhile, weighed heavily on the king in these years. An unexpected denunciation of Scottish Presbyterianism in a fiery sermon delivered at Paul's Cross by the future archbishop of Canterbury, Richard Bancroft, in early 1589 had sparked an international incident which highlighted the many contentious issues in English and Scottish ecclesiastical politics. Bancroft had not only accused Scottish Presbyterianism of corrupting Englishmen, he had gone so far as to proclaim that James VI planned to strengthen episcopacy in Scotland. An incensed group of ministers, calling themselves the 'Ministry of God's word in Scotland, presently assembled in Edinburgh', responded by composing a supplication to Elizabeth, which instructed the queen to reprimand Bancroft and to reform the abuses rife within the English church. The supplication was never sent, so it fell to the king to defend the honour of the Scottish kirk.[32] James prevailed upon Burghley to force Bancroft to make a public apology, but Burghley was slow to act and, in the end, Bancroft's published submission fell well short of a full apology.[33] The uncertainties in both kingdoms surrounding church governance and the power of the monarch *vis à vis* the church, at a time when it appeared that resurgent Catholicism posed the greatest threat, became manifest in aggressive polemic, or 'ecclesiastical vitriol'.[34]

Bancroft's untimely intervention into the delicately balanced world of Scottish ecclesiastical politics had the unintended effect of pushing the king and the Presbyterians closer together. At the General Assembly in August 1590 James Melville, nephew of the leading radical Presbyterian minister Andrew Melville, condemned the so-called 'Black Acts', which had strengthened episcopacy and subjected the kirk to royal authority in 1584, and poured scorn on 'these Amaziahs, the belly-god bishops in England,

---

31   Keith Brown, *Bloodfeud in Scotland, 1573–1625: violence, justice and politics in an early modern society* (Edinburgh, 1986), ch. 6; Donaldson, *Scotland: James V–James VII*, pp. 189–91; W.T. MacCaffrey, *Elizabeth I: war and politics, 1588–1603* (Princeton, 1992), pp. 307–13.

32   Felicity Heal, *Reformation in Britain and Ireland* (Oxford, 2003), pp. 412–15; Jenny Wormald, 'Ecclesiastical vitriol: the kirk, the puritans and the future king of England', in J. Guy (ed.) *The reign of Elizabeth I: court and culture in the last decade* (Cambridge, 1995), pp. 171–91.

33   O. Chadwick, 'Richard Bancroft's submission', in *Journal of Ecclesiastical History*, iii (1952), 58–73.

34   Heal, *Reformation in Britain and Ireland*, p. 412. Cf. Wormald, 'Ecclesiastical vitriol'; Patrick Collinson, 'Ecclesiastical vitriol: religious satire in the 1590s and the invention of Puritanism', in Guy (ed.) *The reign of Elizabeth I*, pp. 150–70.

[who] . . . were seeking conformity of our kirk with theirs, as did Achaz and Urias with the altar of Damascus'. In keeping with the mood of the Assembly James declared 'As for our neighbour kirk in England, it is an evil said mass in English, wanting nothing but the liftings. I charge you, my good people . . . to stand to your purity, and to exhort the people to do the same; and I, forsooth, as long as I brook my life and crown, shall maintain the same.' The king's address brought down the house.[35]

Yet James still had to act decisively to resolve what had the potential to develop into a fully-fledged crisis of royal authority. In an effort to garner the full support of the clergy, the king reluctantly consented in the 1592 parliament to 'The Ratification of the Liberty of the True Kirk', which recognised the kirk's Presbyterian constitution. The 'Golden Acts', as they became known, superseded the 'Black Acts' of 1584.[36] In the same parliament, the king also secured the forfeiture of the earl of Bothwell's estates, so isolating the earl from his Protestant supporters.[37] James reluctantly marched against the northern earls in early 1593 and made repeated attempts to root out Bothwell; but Huntly did not give battle, preferring instead to withdraw to the highlands, while Bothwell remained elusive. Substantial areas of the kingdom thus remained beyond the king's reach, and it seemed that the situation would settle into a stalemate with James's authority extending to only half of his subjects.

But, in 1594, the king came under renewed pressure from the clergy, and from England, to campaign against the northern earls and declare their lands forfeit. This provoked an unlikely alliance between Huntly and Bothwell, both of whom cast aside their differences and entered into concerted rebellion. Despite their defeat of a royal force under Argyll at Glenlivet in October, the king quickly gained the upper hand, and the hastily assembled rebel coalition dissolved. Following a brief exile, the northern earls were reconciled with the king and, eventually, the established church. In 1599 Huntly was created a marquis; Bothwell went into exile in 1595 never to return.[38] The rebellion was to be the last great show of noble resistance to crown authority in James's reign. While noble power in the localities remained largely intact, the king had, with the suppression of Huntly and

---

35 Heal, *Reformation in Britain and Ireland*, pp. 412–15; Wormald, 'Ecclesiastical vitriol', pp. 176–7 (quotations, p. 177).

36 Goodare, *State and society in early modern Scotland*, pp. 195–6; Heal, *Reformation in Britain and Ireland*, p. 414.

37 Donaldson, *Scotland: James V–James VII*, p. 193.

38 Brown, *Bloodfeud in Scotland*, pp. 160, 167–73.

Bothwell, humbled the nobility and established the crown's pre-eminence in the kingdom.

Since the passing of the 'Golden Acts' in 1592, however, the already out-spoken Scottish clergy had grown increasingly bold, regularly interfering in affairs of state. In 1593, for instance, the General Assembly had attempted to persuade the convention of royal burghs to suspend trade with Catholic Spain. By 1596, neither the king of Scotland, nor the queen of England was safe from the kirk's criticism: James was widely admonished for 'banning and swearing', while David Black, the minister of St Andrews, preached that 'all kings are devil's children', and that Elizabeth was no more than an atheist; the pertinacious Andrew Melville was so bold as to declare to the king's face that he was 'but God's silly vassal'. In this time of Presbyterian ascendancy the clergy had clearly over-played its hand, and following a riot sparked by unfounded rumours of a papist conspiracy in Edinburgh in December 1596, the government moved against the General Assembly, reviving an act which prohibited speech against the king and privy council and declaring their powers illegal.[39] James summoned his own convention of ministers at Perth in February and then a full General Assembly at Dundee in May, so as to encourage the attendance of more moderate ministers from the north and northeast. Maitland's death in 1595 had lost the kirk its most ardent supporter in government and the king now assumed a more central role in the state's administrative and ecclesiastical affairs.

James's thoughts on monarchy, made manifest in his political writings *Basilikon Doron* and the *Trew Law of Free Monarchies*, were greatly influenced by the events of 1596–7. In the former, an advice book to his son, he dis-cussed the consequences of popular reformation: 'some fiery spirited men in the ministry . . . finding the gust of government sweet, they began to fantasy to themselves, a democratic form of government'. The king noted that the doctrine of ministerial parity was 'the mother of confusion and enemy to unity'.[40] The king of Scotland's taste for episcopacy, and its intrinsic links to royal authority, was becoming apparent.

Thus James had, by 1597, at last asserted a measure of royal control over the nobility and kirk within his kingdom. This new authority enjoyed by the Scottish crown contributed to a more direct relationship between central and local government which had been developing (with only occasional

39   Maurice Lee, 'James VI and the revival of episcopacy in Scotland, 1596–1600', in Maurice Lee (ed.), *The 'inevitable' union and other essays on early modern Scotland* (East Linton, 2003), pp. 82–7; Donaldson, *Scotland: James V–James VII*, pp. 194–5 (quotations).
40   Heal, *Reformation in Britain and Ireland*, pp. 415–16 (quotations, p. 416).

interruptions) from the 1580s. A centralised state structure had emerged, its steady imposition of higher levels of taxation, its implementation of new laws and increased custom duties and frequent intervention in noble feuds permeated all levels of society. In many ways, however, Scotland remained a feudal society where ties of kinship still counted for more than loyalty to the state or respect for its laws. The kirk, too, continued to wield enormous influence in Scottish society and stubbornly resisted James's Erastian (the church placed entirely under the control of the state) measures. Thus, at the turn of the century, an emergent centralised and bureaucratic Scotland – governed by the king, his bishops, and a rising tide of burgesses, lairds and lawyers – existed side by side with the old feudal and Presbyterian Scotland, governed by nobles and ministers.[41] The problems which gave rise to these differing representations of Scotland were clearly deep-rooted, but James did little to address Scotland's underlying division: as he had earlier remarked to Elizabeth, it would take three reigns to accomplish the work needed to be done in Scotland.[42] His thoughts turned increasingly to the English succession which, he believed, would solve the inherent problems of his own kingdom through its incorporation into a larger entity, a united Britain.

The struggle for Britain and Ireland's Gaelic district

Anglo-Scottish relations improved apace with James's reassertion of royal authority. Though the Tudor government was ever watchful of its northern neighbour, and was prepared to countenance even the wildest rumour of Papist or Spanish sympathies either there, or within the exiled Scottish community abroad, its suspicions in the main proved groundless. The border, too, could occasionally throw up a diplomatic row – as in 1596 when raiders crossed into England to rescue the imprisoned border laird, Willie Armstrong, from Carlisle castle. But incidents of serious disorder on both sides of the frontier steadily decreased.[43] There was, however, one area that continued to be a point of contention between the two kingdoms. The Gaelic district, which stretched from Ulster to the Western Isles and adjoining Scottish mainland, remained beyond the effective control of either the

41 Lynch, *Scotland*, pp. 236–8.
42 MacCaffrey, *Elizabeth I: war and politics*, p. 307.
43 Ibid., pp. 318–22.

English queen or the Scottish king. From the mid-1580s, James had made some effort toward reducing the more recalcitrant island chiefs to obedience. In 1589 he intervened in the most recent bout of the bloody MacLean-MacDonald feud, inducing two principal chiefs of the Clan Donald and the MacLean chief to travel, on the pretence of royal arbitration, to Edinburgh whereupon they were imprisoned. But short of money, the king determined in 1591 to release the trio in return for their payment of substantial fines and an undertaking to pay crown rents on their lands in future.[44] The return of the MacLean and MacDonald chiefs scarcely improved the crown's revenues or authority in the district, and though royal expeditions to the Isles were discussed in 1592, 1596 and 1600, none progressed beyond the planning stage. Royal authority in the Western highlands and Isles thus remained sporadic and generally weak. James's attitude to Scotland's Gaelic regions, both strategically and ideologically, was not unlike that adopted by earlier Tudor monarchs to Ireland. The king was content to rely on the power of regional magnates, such as the earls of Argyll and Huntly, to govern his kingdom's periphery. The existence of a substantial Gaelic population in the Western highlands and Isles, moreover, was not easily reconciled with James's developing sense of a British identity based on what were, in essence, English notions of 'civility'. In *Basilikon Doron*, James's manual for king-craft written in 1598, the king distinguished between those 'that dwelleth in our mainland, that are barbarous for the most part, and, yet mixed with some show of civility; the other, that dwelleth in the Isles, are utterly barbarous, without any sort or show of civility'.[45] Because the region had not posed a serious threat to the Scottish monarch's authority since the collapse of the Lordship of the Isles in the fifteenth century, James could afford to assign this backward part of his kingdom a low priority.

Elizabeth, however, could not as easily dismiss this Gaelic district as peripheral. Remote though it was, the nature of England's war at sea with Spain had rendered even the most inaccessible regions vulnerable to amphibious landings. The Armada had inadvertently demonstrated this when its surviving crews had struggled ashore in western Scotland and Ulster, finding no quarter in some areas, but succour in others. The queen, moreover, was faced with a rapidly deteriorating situation in Ireland as the century drew to a close. Hugh O'Neill, second earl of Tyrone, had been

---

44 Donald Gregory, *The history of the western highlands and isles of Scotland, 1493–1625* (Edinburgh, 1881), pp. 240–2.
45 Lynch, *Scotland*, p. 241.

proclaimed a traitor in June 1595 and Gaelic Ulster was in open rebellion. For nearly a decade royal authority in the province had come increasingly to rely on the talent, influence and loyalty of Tyrone; but these years also saw the earl struggle both to establish his authority over rival contenders for the Gaelic rights due to an O'Neill chief and to prevent the incursion into his lordship of the growing number of English captains and minor officials who hoped to benefit from an Ulster governed in a way more reminiscent of Tudor government at it existed elsewhere in Ireland. Yet Tyrone proved remarkably successful in both, so much so that in 1592 the acknowledged O'Neill chief, Turlough Luineach, abdicated in his favour and Sir Henry Bagenal, the marshal of the army and the chief proponent of extending Tudor rule further into Ulster, was directed by the privy council not to inter-fere in Tyrone. Hugh O'Neill's success rested on his ability to function simul-taneously as the leader of Gaelic Ulster's emerging generation of disaffected chiefs and a loyal English earl backed by the government and key players at court. These dual roles, however, had become strained as several of Tyrone's Gaelic allies violently rejected the local Tudor structures of government which had, by the early 1590s, crept into their lordships. Tyrone had faced such delicate situations before, but with his old allies at court all dead, and new men gathered around Elizabeth, Tyrone thought his position particu-larly vulnerable. In May 1595 he besieged the royal garrison at Monaghan and personally led the attack which mauled a relief-force at Clontibret, com-manded by Marshal Bagenal.[46]

The Irish military historian G.A. Hayes-McCoy remarked that 'no chief, great or small, attempted a revolt in Ireland in the latter sixteenth century without soliciting mercenary aid in the Isles'.[47] Known as redshanks, these landless Scots mercenaries had become a staple of warfare throughout Ulster and northern Connaught at this time, enabling chiefs with greater access to the Isles, most notably the young Hugh Roe O'Donnell whose mother Finola was the daughter of James MacDonald and Lady Agnes Campbell, to emerge as major powers. Through O'Donnell, Tyrone earnestly sought to harness the manpower of the Isles to supplement his already considerable military strength. Elizabeth had repeatedly attempted to put pressure on

---

46 For the origins of the Nine Years' War, see now Nicholas Canny, 'Taking sides in early modern Ireland: the case of Hugh O'Neill, earl of Tyrone', in Vincent Carey and Ute Lotz-Heumann (eds), *Taking sides? Colonial and confessional mentalités in early modern Ireland* (Dublin, 2003), pp. 94–105; Morgan, *Tyrone's rebellion*, pp. 167–92; Ellis, *Ireland in the age of the Tudors*, pp. 334–9.

47 G.A. Hayes-McCoy, *Scots mercenary forces in Ireland, 1565–1603* (Dublin, 1937), p. 205.

James to address the mercenary trade in the Western Highlands and Isles. As we have seen, James's authority in the region was feeble at best, but the king preferred to use the Isles as a negotiating tool with Elizabeth, allowing the queen to believe that the flow of men from Gaelic Scotland was like a valve which he could switch on or off at will. Occasionally, as in late 1593, James responded to English pressure ordering Argyll, his lieutenant in the west, to halt the mercenary trade with Ireland; the queen subsequently wrote to the king thanking him for 'the staying of any resort to our realm of Ireland by any subjects of yours who usually frequent the company and actions of diverse barbarous rebels in the northern provinces of our kingdom'.[48] In the main, however, the Scottish king winked at the mercenary service and, by the time of his rebellion, Tyrone was not only hiring redshanks, but also importing ammunition, arms and equipment from Lowland Scotland.[49]

English forces in Ireland were ill-prepared to respond to a challenge of this magnitude. In addition to hired mercenaries, Tyrone had brought to the field at Clontibret a disciplined army armed with muskets and formed in companies after the English fashion. That the vast preponderance of this army were volunteers, and had been raised by proclamation from within Ulster, was a significant departure from traditional Gaelic forms of warfare. Decades of carefully grooming O'Neill to be an effective English military commander had suddenly backfired. With little more than a thousand troops available to him outside Munster and Connaught, the recently appointed Irish deputy, Sir William Russell, requested reinforcements and the immediate despatch of a senior military commander.[50] Fortunately for the crown, its military commitment on the continent began to diminish in the years preceding Tyrone's rebellion. Thousands of English troops had been sent to northern France in 1589, 1591–2 and 1593 to aid the Protestant King Henry IV; but following the war-weary king's conversion to Catholicism in July 1593 (and with his commitment to tolerate Protestantism within his kingdom assured) English involvement in France was ended. From 1594, moreover, English financial and military commitments in the Netherlands were greatly reduced as a sovereign Protestant state confidently emerged. All that remained of the English military presence on the continent was 2,000 soldiers stationed in Brittany to prevent the Spanish army, which in 1590 had invaded the region, from establishing a bridgehead on the Channel. In

---

48   Ibid., p. 217.
49   Morgan, *Tyrone's rebellion*, p. 182; Cyril Falls, *Elizabeth's Irish wars* (London, 1950), p. 83.
50   Ellis, *Ireland in the age of the Tudors*, pp. 337–9.

1595, however, the Spanish were driven out of Brittany and the Channel [275] was once again made safe. England's war at sea with Spain dragged on, but from 1595 the crown was free to devote greater attention to its troubled Irish kingdom, which was to dominate English politics for the remainder of Elizabeth's reign.[51]

In May 1595, 1,600 veterans from Brittany under the command of the former president of Munster, John Norris, arrived in Ireland together with other reinforcements, increasing the strength of the English army there to some 7,000 men. Tyrone remained master in Ulster, but as a former soldier in the royal army he also understood that his existing forces were no match for the vast resources of the Tudor state. He thus sought to explore (and to exploit) every diplomatic avenue available to him in an effort to equalise this imbalance.[52] The first card that O'Neill played, though somewhat reluctantly, was the Catholic card. In order to enlist the support of Philip II, O'Neill had to depict his rebellion as a war to preserve Catholicism in Ireland. O'Neill now openly endorsed the petitions which O'Donnell and several other chiefs had made to the Spanish king, requesting an army of 6,000 or 7,000 men and offering the kingdom of Ireland to Archduke Albert, the governor of the Spanish Netherlands and the Spanish king's nephew. This appeal to Catholicism was also designed to broaden the allure of the rebellion to include the confederates' coreligionists, the Old English community who, crucially, controlled the towns and, as seen during Perrot's deputyship, continued to wield considerable influence in the Tudor administration in Ireland.[53] The second card played by O'Neill was the Gaelic one. When Turlough Luineach O'Neill died in September 1595 Tyrone was chosen by the O'Neill clansmen to succeeded him as the ruling O'Neill. This symbolic nod to Ireland's Gaelic past coincided with O'Neill's efforts to foment anti-English sentiment among the remnants of the Gaelic polity outside Ulster. O'Neill also sought assistance from the kingdom of Scotland beyond that traditionally offered by its Gaelic regions and appealed to the earl of Argyll and James VI to intervene on his behalf. Throughout, however, O'Neill continued to negotiate with the government recognising the queen's reluctance to commit large numbers of troops in Ulster while at war with Spain.[54]

51 R.B. Wernham, *After the Armada: Elizabethan England and the struggle for western Europe, 1588–1595* (Oxford, 1984), ch. 22; p. 552; MacCaffrey, *Elizabeth I: war and politics*, pts 3 & 4; Nicholls, *A history of the modern British Isles*, pp. 279–83.
52 Canny, 'Taking sides in early modern Ireland', p. 105.
53 Morgan, *Tyrone's rebellion*, ch. 9; Ellis, *Ireland in the age of the Tudors*, pp. 340–2.
54 Canny, 'Taking sides in early modern Ireland', pp. 104–6.

This multi-faceted strategy yielded mixed results. The ageing Philip II, eager to avenge the sack of Cadiz, was prepared to offer military assistance; but following the dispersal in October 1596 of two Spanish fleets – one bound for the south-west of England and another destined for Ireland – Spain could offer little more than monetary assistance and goodwill. The innately conservative Old English, meanwhile, ignored O'Neill's call to arms in the name of Catholicism, believing it to be an elaborate ploy to extend his own Gaelic over-lordship throughout Ireland. O'Neill's appeals to Gaelic chiefs outside Ulster met with greater success: O'Donnell drove deep into Connaught, exploiting Gaelic discontent with the presidency of Sir Richard Bingham, and Feagh MacHugh O'Byrne once again came out in rebellion in close proximity to Dublin city, so forcing the lord deputy to divert troops from Ulster. Neither the earl of Argyll nor James VI, however, appear seriously to have entertained O'Neill's overtures, and a combination of English pressure on the Scottish king, and internal disorder in the Western Highlands and Isles, conspired to prevent much greater numbers of red-shanks from drifting into Ulster. Ironically, O'Neill enjoyed his most con-sistent success negotiating with the government. Following the expiry of a truce in early 1596, O'Neill was pardoned in May as part of a settlement: the queen would agree to withdraw English garrisons from Ulster and recognise both the indivisibility of Tyrone and Armagh and O'Neill's control over traditional O'Neill vassal-chiefs, in return for the immediate submission of the confederates, their acceptance of Tudor sovereignty in Ireland, and the establishment of Tudor governing structures within the province. The settlement, however, was immediately undermined when Spanish emissaries arrived in Ulster announcing that a sizeable Spanish invasion force had already been assembled, and that it was prepared to embark for Ireland once O'Neill resumed hostilities. With the promise of substantial Spanish military assistance, hopes of a peaceful settlement with the Tudor state were aban-doned. Of all the diplomatic avenues explored by O'Neill, it had, by late 1596, become clear to him that an alliance with Spain was his best hope of winning a major war against the Tudor state. Faith had thus emerged as the force that would unify and drive O'Neill's rebellion.[55]

A period of intermittent war between the confederates and the govern-ment was ended when, in August 1598, O'Neill ambushed a force of 4,000 foot and 300 horse sent to relieve the beleaguered garrison at Blackwater Fort. It was the greatest military defeat suffered by English forces in Tudor

---

55 Ellis, *Ireland in the age of the Tudors*, pp. 339–42.

Ireland: Marshal Bagenal, and nearly 1,000 of his troops, lay dead on the field north of Armagh known as the Yellow Ford. O'Neill's victory instantly transformed the military situation in Ireland. The government was for the first time thrown on the defensive as the rebellion spread throughout the country. Tudor rule in those Gaelic areas conquered during the sixteenth century unravelled with surprising rapidity as disaffected chiefs recaptured their lands with O'Neill's military assistance. By October, the Munster plantation had been completely overthrown and the confederates were threatening Leinster, the seat of Tudor government. The speedy despatch of more than 6,000 English troops, 1,500 of whom were Netherlands veterans, allowed the earl of Ormond – lately appointed lord lieutenant of the queen's forces in Ireland – to prevent the rebellion from entering Leinster; but with the exception of the walled towns, parts of the earldoms of Ormond, Clanrickard and Thomond and the traditional Pale area, Ireland was under confederate control. In these areas Tudor rule amounted to little more than military occupation, and when its military authority collapsed so too did royal control.[56]

Tudor government, however, was more firmly imbedded among the Old English community in the towns. Despite the fact that it was they who bore the brunt of the war in Ireland, quartering an increasing number of unruly English soldiers, and they who suffered most acutely from the spiralling prices and harvest failures experienced throughout the British Isles in the mid-1590s, the Old English remained steadfast in their allegiance to the crown.[57] O'Neill's efforts to depict his rebellion as a religious crusade had not convinced his coreligionists to join him and, lacking heavy artillery, he could not forcibly enter the towns. Thus, after his victory at the Yellow Ford, O'Neill attempted to broaden the appeal of his war still further through the creation of a new patriot ideology based not only on faith, but also on loyalty to one's country or fatherland. In 1599 O'Neill issued a proclamation, promising to any who would join him:

> I will imploy myself to the utmost of my power in their defence and for the
> extirpation of heresy, the planting of the Catholic religion, the delivery of
> our country of infinite murders, wicked and detestable policies by which this
> kingdom was hitherto governed, nourished in obscurity and ignorance,

---

56 Canny, 'Taking sides in early modern Ireland', pp. 106–7; Ellis, *Ireland in the age of the Tudors*, pp. 345–6.
57 Colm Lennon, *Sixteenth-century Ireland: the incomplete conquest* (Dublin, 1994), p. 295.

maintained in barbarity and incivility and consequently of infinite evils which were too lamentable to be rehearsed.[58]

This, and other written expressions of O'Neill's political ideology which followed, were designed to assure the Old English that both their position in society and their possessions would be respected in a Gaelic-dominated Ireland. Through O'Neill's efforts long-held ethnic distinctions between *Gaedhil* and *Gaill* were suddenly replaced in the Gaelic mind by the principals of a shared faith and fatherland. This is not to say that the Gaelic past was dismissed – indeed Gaelic poetry was composed for O'Neill at this time linking him and his ancestors with Ireland's ancient Gaelic heroes – but O'Neill was moving away from traditional Gaelic propaganda based on ethnicity and locality in an effort to win over his fellow 'Irishmen'.[59] The Old English community's disdain for O'Neill and his rebellion, however, remained unchanged. Yet, even without the support of the Old English, the notion of a Catholic kingdom emerging in the British Isles, dominated by O'Neill, and backed by Spain was a doomsday scenario for the Tudor state, and Elizabeth was forced to take drastic action to re-establish English dominance in Ireland.

In April 1599 Robert Devereux, second earl of Essex, arrived in Ireland with 17,300 men – the largest army to leave England during the reign. The once peripheral Irish kingdom had gradually emerged as the crucial theatre in the Tudor state's wider military struggle against Spain and now demanded the leadership of England's most powerful noble. Essex was the queen's handsome young favourite and the highest ranking military-man in the realm: the stepson to the queen's beloved earl of Leicester, an influential privy councillor and the hero of the Cadiz expedition, the earl's popularity throughout the realm had moved the poet Edmund Spenser to laud him as 'England's glory and the wide world's wonder'.[60] There was, however, more at stake than the Irish kingdom's future attachment to the English crown when Essex arrived in Dublin as lord lieutenant. The grand expedition was an extension of an increasingly bitter struggle for power at the very centre of Tudor government. The deaths from 1588 of the earls of Leicester and Warwick, Sir James Croft, comptroller of the household, Sir Walter Mildmay, the chancellor of the exchequer, Secretary Walsingham, Lord

58   Hiram Morgan, 'Hugh O'Neill and the Nine Years' War in Tudor Ireland', in *Historical Journal*, xlvi, p. 25.

59   Canny, 'Taking sides in early modern Ireland', p. 106; Morgan, 'Hugh O'Neill and the Nine Years' War', p. 27.

60   W.T. MacCaffrey, *Elizabeth I* (New York, 1993), p. 404.

Chancellor Christopher Hatton and, in 1598, of Burghley had robbed [2 7 9] Elizabeth of both her trusted inner circle of advisors and her old friends. The fiercely conservative queen, her sense of security shaken, did her best to maintain the appearance of continuity by appointing, one by one, younger sons to key positions in government which their fathers had held; but this could not change the fact that the ageing queen was, by the late 1590s, surrounded by a new and less familiar generation of courtiers whose thoughts naturally turned to a time after her death. Essex saw himself as the rightful leader of this new generation and aggressively sought, through an elaborate network of patronage, stretching from Essex to North Wales and including covert correspondence with James VI, to dominate Tudor government in the queen's declining years, thereby ensuring pride of place for himself and his supporters under Elizabeth's still unnamed successor.

Yet Burghley had groomed his son, Robert Cecil, as his political heir, and during Essex's absence at Cadiz the queen had appointed the young Cecil as principal secretary.[61] Thereafter, the earl's efforts to marginalise the Cecil interest and monopolise patronage and power gave rise to a phenomenon hitherto absent from the Elizabethan court: 'factionalism' or political conflict. Throughout Elizabeth's reign policy differences and personal disputes at court had created animosities and rivalries – most notably those between Cecil and Leicester and between Sussex and Leicester – but these had not evolved into the aggressive factional alliances which had characterised the Henrician or Edwardian courts. Elizabeth's firm grip on government, and a genuine devotion to the queen on the part of privy councillors and courtiers alike, had ensured that rivalries were never placed before the interests of the state.[62] After Cadiz, however, Essex believed his popularity among both the commons and the greatly expanded officer corps to rival that of the queen. In his biography of Elizabeth, Wallace MacCaffrey pointedly remarked, 'there could no more be two suns in the political sky than in the heavens'. By the late 1590s, Essex had lost sight of this most basic axiom. He frequently clashed with Elizabeth and everywhere sought military glory to overshadow

---

61   Ibid., pp. 399, 401–3.

62   Simon Adams, 'Eliza enthroned? The court and its politics', in Chris Haigh (ed.), *The reign of Elizabeth I* (London, 1984), pp. 67–8; Paul Hammer, 'Patronage at court, faction and the earl of Essex', in John Guy (ed.), *The reign of Elizabeth I: court and culture in the last decade* (Cambridge, 1995), pp. 65–71; M.A.R. Graves, *Burghley: William Cecil, lord Burghley* (London, 1998), pp. 120–2; Phillip Edwards, *The making of the modern English state, 1460–1660* (London, 2001), pp. 211–13. For a different perspective, see Christopher Haigh, *Elizabeth I* (London, 1988), pp. 99–101.

the fact that he owed his position more to the queen's desire to live vicari-
ously through a son she never had than to his own experience in the field.
When, in July 1598, the question arose as to who should succeed to the
vacant Irish governorship the queen favoured Cecil's suggestion that Sir
William Knollys, Essex's uncle and chief ally, accept the appointment. Essex
strenuously objected and – aware that only political ruin awaited the man
who accepted the poisoned chalice that was the Irish deputyship – put
forward a member of the Cecil faction as a candidate. When Elizabeth
rejected the proposal the earl flew into a rage in which he reputedly went to
unsheathe his sword in response to the queen boxing his ears. Essex stormed
off to his estates to brood over his treatment while Elizabeth retreated to her
chambers to do the same. The stand-off between queen and favourite lasted
several months, but in the aftermath of the disaster at the Yellow Ford the
earl reluctantly yielded and returned to a grim court. In this moment of
national crisis, Essex, 'England's glory', had no choice but to accept the Irish
command. Prior to his departure he ruefully noted, 'the queen had irrevoc-
ably decreed it; the council do passionately urge it; and I am tied by my own
reputation to use no tergiversation'.[63]

While Essex's enemies may have delighted at the immense task confronting the earl in Ireland, many others were concerned that in a reckless fit
of resentment he might turn his army against the queen. These fears were
lent some substance when it was learned that Essex contemplated sailing for
Wales with part of his army in an effort to link up with his affinity there.
Unlike the earl of Huntly or, indeed, O'Neill, the earl of Essex was not a
powerful frontier magnate possessed of a numerous and warlike tenantry.
His support in north Wales, among such local gentry families as the Trefors
of Trefalum and the Salusburys of Rug, did not produce the sort of battle-
hardened fighting men necessary to mount a real challenge to government.[64]
Rather Essex was that new breed of Elizabethan noble that owed power and
position to the queen and was thus almost entirely reliant on the royal army
to provide his military strength. Ultimately, Essex's allies in England coun-
selled against using the royal army in such a manner and the earl remained in
Dublin placing half of his forces in garrisons. But, instead of marching
against O'Neill as the queen had directed, the earl embarked on an eight-
week progress through Munster and south Leinster. Elizabeth and Essex,
meanwhile, exchanged angry letters – the former ordering her lieutenant

63   MacCaffrey, *Elizabeth I*, pp. 404–11.
64   Jones, *Early modern Wales*, pp. 190–1.

north to engage O'Neill, the latter obsessed over his loss of royal favour and the words and actions of his enemies at court. When, in September 1599, the earl finally marched toward Ulster he parleyed with O'Neill – suspiciously conversing in private with him for 30 minutes. The outcome was a humiliating 6-week truce renewable the following spring. The queen was incandescent with rage. Without licence, Essex returned to London to defend his position, leaving behind a caretaker administration and a demoralised army depleted both by desertion and disease. The expedition was a spectacular failure: by 1600 O'Neill marched the length of Ireland unopposed, collecting submissions as far south as Cork and, at court, the Essex faction was in disgrace.[65]

In January Charles Blount, lord Mountjoy, was appointed as Essex's successor in Ireland. Though without previous experience of high command, Mountjoy was a unifying figure, popular with both the Cecilian and Essex factions. He was the queen's more tractable and levelheaded favourite. Essex, meanwhile, wallowed in country exile stripped of his lucrative crown offices and cut off from his court connections. The earl's relationship with Elizabeth – the key to his meteoric rise to wealth and prominence – had never recovered from his foolhardy outburst of July 1598. The spell which Essex had cast over the queen was broken and after his failure in Ireland Essex was, for the first time in his career, powerless. In Mountjoy's appointment, however, the disgraced earl saw an opportunity to reassert his position at court through force. Essex secretly urged Mountjoy to employ his Irish army against the queen's councillors. Though Mountjoy had looked after Essex's estates during the earl's confinement, and was briefly involved in Essex's earlier scheme to force Elizabeth formally to acknowledge James VI as her successor, he was not prepared to move against the queen. Instead, Mountjoy prevaricated and, the following month, hastily departed for Ireland leaving Essex and his intrigues behind.[66]

Denied Mountjoy's military assistance, the earl planned to gather his adherents at his London residence and, from there, storm the court and seize the queen. His popularity among the city's masses, he assumed, would make up for what he lacked in military strength. Essex was self-destructing. By February 1601, rumours of the earl's intentions had reached the privy council and Essex was summoned to court for interrogation. He refused and, with 200 gentlemen, launched his desperate coup. The commons, however, did

65   Ibid., pp. 412–13; Falls, *Elizabeth's Irish wars*, pp. 225–47.
66   *Oxford DNB*, s.v. Charles Blount.

not rally to the earl. His hare-brained uprising collapsed. The queen could not afford to hesitate in exacting vengeance, lest it be construed as royal weakness in the face of noble ambition. Thus, with uncharacteristic speed, Essex was executed. But, more typically of Elizabeth, the majority of the earl's supporters were spared.

Nevertheless, the way was now clear for Robert Cecil to dominate the council and to steer the reign to its fast approaching conclusion. For the queen's indispensable secretary, three matters now assumed precedence. The first was the tentative peace negotiations with Spain, underway since 1598. With the hawkish Essex gone, Cecil could press for the accommodation with Spain longed for by his father. The second was to ensure that the necessary diplomatic channels were in place to transfer power to the Scottish king upon the queen's death. Finally, there was the war raging in Ireland, the outcome of which held the other two matters in the balance. Mountjoy's decisive victory over O'Neill was essential to enable England to negotiate from a strong position in Europe, and English dominance in Ireland was necessary to preserve the balance of power in the British Isles at the critical juncture when a Scottish king acceded to the English throne.[67]

The direction of the campaign in Ireland had been decided prior to Mountjoy's arrival in February 1600. The new deputy was to oversee the reform of the demoralised and unruly army left by his predecessor and open up new fronts against the confederates through the plantation of strongly-defended garrisons deep within rebel-held areas. Central to this strategy was the establishment of two garrisons supported by sea 'behind' O'Neill. Military control, formerly concentrated in the deputy, was to be decentralised so as to avoid a scenario in which one lumbering English army might be outmanoeuvred or counterattacked by smaller Irish contingents. By September Mountjoy's cautious and calculated implementation of his military objectives had taken their toll on the confederates: government authority had been recovered in Munster and the landing of a substantial English expeditionary force on Lough Foyle had forced O'Neill to fight on two fronts.[68] In an effort to undermine O'Neill's economic base, moreover, Mountjoy ravaged the countryside unsparingly, a tactic which he employed, 'to its utmost limits with an intentness and fixity of purpose that amounted to almost blind automatism'.[69] O'Neill understood that he could not

---

67 MacCaffrey, *Elizabeth I*, pp. 292–3, 415–16.
68 *Oxford DNB, s.v.* Charles Blount.
69 F.M. Jones, *Mountjoy, 1563–1606* (Dublin, 1958), p. 78.

confront such a purposeful and well-resourced commander as Mountjoy without military assistance. He appealed to Ireland's Old English population, emphasising a common faith and fatherland – in April he had informed the pope that he was fighting '*pro Romano et libertate patria*' – but the Catholic Old English were unconvinced: the concept of England as a foreign power interfering in Irish affairs remained anathema.[70] Spain was O'Neill's only hope of defeating Mountjoy's army – roughly 13,000 strong – and, in early 1601, Philip III finally agreed to commit 6,000 troops to further the confederate struggle against Elizabeth.

Yet, the Spanish invasion force that disembarked in the extreme south of Ireland, at Kinsale, in September 1601 numbered just under 3,500 and was almost immediately besieged by Mountjoy. With his allies pinned in the small coastal town, O'Neill had no choice but to abandon the relative safety of Ulster and lead his forces on a long and dangerous winter march to Kinsale. The confederate army, numbering some 6,500, was divided between O'Neill and O'Donnell and took separate routes to Kinsale, the former travelling through the Pale, the latter via Connaught. In this way, the confederate armies avoided any confrontation with crown forces before successfully regrouping outside Kinsale in late December. O'Neill, however, remained reluctant to meet Mountjoy in direct military confrontation. He hoped instead to avoid battle long enough for disease, hunger and exposure to force the deputy to abandon the siege of Kinsale and withdraw for the winter. But, under pressure from O'Donnell and the Spanish to engage the enemy, and aware that crown forces had to be defeated in the field if the war was to be won, O'Neill risked all and attacked the exhausted royal army early on Christmas Eve.[71]

The royal army had been reduced by sickness and desertion to 6,600 able-bodied men. The army, moreover, comprised both English soldiers and Irishmen led by the loyalist earls of Thomond and Clanrickard. O'Neill hoped that a substantial number of these Irishmen in crown service would defect to the confederates as he deployed his army at dawn into three 'battles' organised like Spanish *tercios*. Mountjoy, however, launched a swift counterattack with heavy English cavalry. O'Neill's forces, inexperienced in formal field combat, broke and the Irish attempt at the *tercio* formation collapsed. The besieged Spaniards failed to sally forth and the confederate

70   Morgan, 'Hugh O'Neill and the Nine Years' War', p. 23.
71   Canny, 'Taking sides in early modern Ireland', pp. 108–9; G.A. Hayes-McCoy, *Irish battles* (London, 1969), pp. 144–73.

army was routed. Kinsale was the military defeat which O'Neill had feared. It marked the effective end of O'Neill's Gaelic confederacy. The Spaniards surrendered and were permitted to return to Spain. In sharp contrast, Mountjoy offered the confederates no quarter and doggedly pursued them as they limped back to Ulster. In September 1602 the deputy entered the heart of Tyrone and destroyed the O'Neill inauguration stone, so symbolising the Tudor overthrow of both O'Neill and the Gaelic order.[72]

Yet the Tudor state's military victory in Ireland had come at a cost. Since 1596, the war in Ireland had been the greatest expense in its wider military conflict with Spain. For the period 1591–5 England's annual Irish military expenditure amounted to £28,987, but between 1595–9 payments from England peaked at £103,776 per annum. Before its final conclusion in 1603, the war in Ireland had cost the crown £2 million. In human terms, 30,592 soldiers from 36 English counties were sent to Ireland between 1594–1602; 6,611 soldiers from 13 Welsh counties fought for the English crown in Ireland in the same period. A further 3,000 English troops stationed in the Netherlands were redeployed in the Irish theatre and nearly 2,000 horse bands were raised, thus making the total number of troops sent to Ireland more than 42,500, approximately 19 per cent of the available manpower in England and Wales. In marked contrast to the conflict in the Netherlands, which saw a number of Englishmen volunteer to fight on behalf of their fellow Protestants, Ireland was a much less attractive destination and many sought to avoid recruitment. This, coupled with the demands for such large levies by the late 1590s, provided some local authorities with an opportunity to disburden their area of vagabonds and the impotent. A well-known report of a levy assembled at Bristol prior to its departure for Ireland noted:

> There was never beheld such strange creatures brought to any muster . . . they are most of them either lame, diseased boys, or common rogues. [Their] small weak starved bodies taken up in fairs, markets and highways to supply the places of better men kept at home.[73]

As discussed above, such a high proportion of men leaving and then returning from the wars effected profound social changes in the Tudor state and forced the government to act in increasingly novel ways to maintain law and order. In addition to the emergence of such offices as the provost-marshal

---

72 *Oxford DNB, s.v.* Charles Blount.
73 John McGurk, *The Elizabethan conquest of Ireland: the 1590s crisis* (Manchester, 1997), pp. 32–5, 99–102 (quotation, p. 33); Ellis, *Ireland in the age of the Tudors*, pp. 343–5.

as an instrument of government to control returned soldiers, statutes were [285] enacted in 1593, 1597 and 1601 whereby a system of compulsory relief was established for disabled soldiers. But, by 1602, the long war in Ireland had pushed Elizabeth to the brink of bankruptcy and the commons grumbled under the weight of years of high national taxation. For though Mountjoy had won the decisive battle at Kinsale and re-established royal control over most of Ireland, his failure to capture or kill O'Neill meant that English military expenditure in Ireland could not be substantially reduced. Exhausted, the queen authorised Mountjoy in February 1603 to offer a beaten O'Neill a pardon on terms.[74]

The last years of the last Tudor

Even in the last months of Elizabeth's reign there remained an official silence concerning the matter of the succession. But the now 69-year-old queen's insistence that the inevitable be quietly ignored had become a liability. While Elizabeth remained popular, nearly two decades of war and heavy taxation had caused the majority of English people to welcome the advent of a new reign and the changes which it promised. The execution of Essex, moreover, had proved a most unpopular decision: the commons continued to lionise the earl as 'England's glory'. Though Robert Cecil, Elizabeth's hunchbacked secretary, was cast as the villain in the tragedy of Essex, the queen, too, saw her popularity dented by the incident. For the first time in her long reign Elizabeth was out of step with her subjects, and her stubborn refusal to name James Stewart as her successor only served to heighten the kingdom's impatience with its ageing sovereign.[75]

The publication in early 1594 of *A Conference About the Next Succession to the Crowne of Ingland* had shown the danger inherent to the regime's unwillingness to settle the succession. Written by the English Jesuit Robert Persons, under the pseudonym 'R. Doleman', and smuggled into England from the Low Countries, the treatise opened with the argument that the monarch's power derived from the people and that the 'commonwealth' was thus empowered to overthrow the monarch or to resist the accession of his heir. The remainder of the work purported to offer a detached examination of rival rights and claims to the throne, but Persons' Spanish sympathies were

74   McGurk, *The Elizabethan conquest of Ireland*, pp. 99–102, 119, 262–4.
75   MacCaffrey, *Elizabeth I*, pp. 443–5.

[286] unmistakeable and the claim of the Spanish infanta emerged as superior to that of James VI.[76] The exiled Persons had badly misjudged the mood of his countrymen: English Protestants, and the preponderance of English Catholics, recoiled from his theory of political resistance and the possibility of a Spanish succession. Catholic criticism of the *Conference*, in the form of printed tracts and petitions in support of James VI, steadily increased in number and intensity in the last years of Elizabeth's reign, making a mockery of the government's silence regarding the succession.[77] But, while the privy council and court outwardly respected the queen's wishes, the covert lines of communication established with Holyroodhouse during the later 1590s grew more formal. Not surprisingly, Robert Cecil emerged as the Scottish king's principal ally in the English government – in short, the man who would guide James on his journey to the throne. Others, however, most notably Sir Walter Ralegh, Sir Henry Cobham and Henry Percy, earl of Northumberland, also opened correspondence with the Scottish king independently of Cecil.[78]

Elizabeth was surely aware of the subtle shift in English attentions to the Scottish court. The queen herself had long anticipated James as her successor. Who else was suitable for the English throne? Elizabeth's long reign had seen the emergence of an insular British identity based on England and Scotland's similar laws and administrative structures and, most crucially, their shared adherence to the Protestant faith, an identity which was further strengthened by continued war and the threat of foreign invasion in the closing decades of her reign. The possibility of a continental monarch acceding to the English throne was, for the vast majority of the English, simply unthinkable. James, for his part, desired above all else the English crown and showed himself a committed Protestant and, aside from occasional lapses, a consistent ally of the Tudor state. That his succession would deliver to England its first adult king since Henry VIII's death in 1547 also had its attractions. James's marriage to Anne of Denmark, moreover, the daughter of the suitably Protestant and politically innocuous Frederick II of Denmark

---

76 Robert Persons [Parsons], *A conference about the next succession to the crowne of Ingland. where unto is added a genealogie* (Antwerp, 1594); Peter Holmes, 'The authorship and early reception of *A conference about the next succession to the crown of England*', in *Historical Journal*, 23 (1980), pp. 415–29.

77 Holmes, 'The authorship and early reception', pp. 424–5.

78 MacCaffrey, *Elizabeth I*, pp. 443–5. Cf. Joel Hurstfield, 'The succession struggle in late Elizabethan England', in *Elizabethan government and society*, S.T. Bindoff, J. Hurstfield and C.H. Williams (eds) (London, 1961), pp. 369–96. For a more critical interpretation of the queen in her last years, see Haigh, *Elizabeth I*, pp. 170–3.

and Norway, had already produced two sons, Henry and Charles, and thus [287] held the promise of future dynastic stability, a phenomenon unknown in England since Henry VII's reign. For Elizabeth, James's succession was in the best interest of her kingdom and, though their relationship remained, to the end, that of two independent sovereigns, the queen did nothing to hinder his advancement.

In March 1603 Elizabeth died and the crown passed peacefully to James VI of Scotland, who thereby became James I of England. This union of the crowns was made possible through the marital union engineered a century earlier by Henry VII between his daughter Margaret and James IV of Scotland. With O'Neill's surrender to Mountjoy coming within a week of the regal union in Britain, the political unification of the British Isles was complete. For the first time, the same monarch ruled England, Scotland and Ireland. In this way, the political framework emerging in the British Isles in 1603 was not unlike the examples of dynastic union and multiple, or composite, monarchy common elsewhere in early modern Europe. Thus, it seemed, the Tudor legacy to England's first Stuart king was the political union of the archipelago's three kingdoms. The Tudor record in achieving this end was indeed impressive, particularly in the outlying regions where, through a policy of political centralisation, administrative uniformity and cultural imperialism, Wales, the north of England and, finally, Ireland had been integrated into the Tudor state. Regal union now removed the only remaining military frontier in the British Isles, moving James to declare that the borders between the contiguous kingdoms were now the 'middle shires'. Yet the Tudor success was not confined to the integration of the periphery. James also inherited a highly centralised English kingdom confident in its Protestantism and a rising political and commercial force in Europe. Indeed in Elizabeth's final decades, England had stood resolute against the military and economic might of Spain, so that by 1603 all that was left for James to do was to conclude the peace with an exhausted enemy.[79]

A more thoughtful examination of the Tudor legacy, however, reveals that it had intrinsic failings and created an entirely new array of problems for its Stuart successors. In their inexorable drive to impose centralised administrative structures and the cultural norms of Lowland England on what had been

79 B.P. Levack, *The formation of the British state: England, Scotland and the union, 1603–1707* (Oxford, 1987), pp. 2–3; S.G. Ellis, 'Tudor state formation and the shaping of the British Isles', in S.G. Ellis and Sarah Barber (eds), *Conquest and Union: fashioning a British state, 1485–1725* (London, 1995), pp. 61–2; J.H. Elliott, 'A world of composite monarchies', in *Past and Present*, 133 (1992), pp. 48–71; Williams, *The Tudor regime*, pp. 457–67.

semi-autonomous border regions, the Tudors had strained the relationship between the court and local political communities. Former border regions such as Wales and the north of England, for example, which had been incorporated into the Tudor state with relative ease, became politically marginalised within the developing English nation-state. In the 1601 parliament, where the House of Commons had swelled to 462 Members, Wales returned only 29 MPs, while the north of England returned a mere 16 MPs. Yet nowhere was the tension between the court and the local community more acute than in the Irish kingdom. Here the pattern of integrating outlying regions into the Tudor state had gone awry, provoking widespread disaffection and, ultimately, full-scale war between Gaelic confederates and England. Ireland was a kingdom won, and retained, through overwhelming military force, a protracted and brutal act which left a legacy of religious and racial animosity. The unity of the British Isles implied by dynastic union in 1603, moreover, only went so far. England and Scotland remained separate kingdoms and retained separate laws, political institutions and churches. Though James was perhaps the most avid proponent of effecting a more 'perfect union' of the kingdoms – even issuing upon his arrival in London a 'proclamation for the uniting of England and Scotland' – he met resistance, in both kingdoms, and was forced to reconsider his plans for the immediate creation of a united British state. Thus, in practice, dynastic union was tantamount to dual monarchy: the governance of England and Scotland, two sovereign and unified states with a dependent kingdom, Ireland, attached to the former. Nevertheless, composite monarchy – the legacy of Tudor state formation – was unprecedented in the British Isles and the task of making this new political dynamic work fell to James VI and I.[80]

---

80 Ellis, 'Tudor state formation and the shaping of the British Isles', pp. 62–3; Levack, *The formation of the British state*, pp. 1–8.

10

BRITISH MULTIPLE MONARCHY, 1603–37

English historians have traditionally viewed the 22-year reign of James I as a failure. It was, they argued, a period in which a decadent and morally bankrupt king with absolutist ambitions repeatedly clashed with resilient English parliaments, so giving rise to the political and social divisions which ultimately led to what was commonly referred to as the English Civil War.[1] By contrast, most Scottish historians have commented favourably on James VI's reign, highlighting the king's role as a unifying force for the Scottish kingdom and his success in tackling the English problems bequeathed to him by Elizabeth.[2] Historians of Ireland, meanwhile, have tended to concentrate more heavily on the colonial aspects of James's reign and the enduring legacy of colonisation and plantation in Ireland.[3] Reconciling these differing interpretations of James's reign, however, has been made easier through recent scholarship, which suggests that James was the victim of hostile contemporary descriptions of his rule which tarnished his image among English historians for generations. It is now widely accepted that James acted as a stabilising influence in both Scotland and England and that to see in his reign the general crisis of the 1640s is to read history backwards.[4] With regard to Ireland, no attempt can be made to divorce James from the comprehensive crown-sponsored plantation schemes introduced in his reign, but increasingly Irish historians have come to view royal policy

---

1   Laurence Stone, *The causes of the English revolution, 1529–1642* (London, 1972).

2   Jenny Wormald, 'James VI and I: two kings or one?' in *History*, lxviii (1983), pp. 187–209.

3   See, for instance, T.W. Moody, *The Londonderry plantation, 1609–41: the city of London and the plantation in Ulster* (Belfast, 1939); Michael Perceval-Maxwell, *The Scottish migration to Ulster in the reign of James I* (London, 1973); Raymond Gillespie, *Colonial Ulster: the settlement of east Ulster, 1600–41* (Cork, 1985).

4   See, for instance, Conrad Russell, 'Parliamentary history in perspective, 1604–29', *History*, lxi (1976), pp. 1–27; idem, *Unrevolutionary England, 1603–42* (London, 1990); Maurice Lee, *Great Britain's Solomon: King James VI and I in his three kingdoms* (Urbana, 1990); David Smith, *A history of the modern British Isles, 1603–1707: the double crown* (Oxford, 1998), pp. 29–31. See now also, Ronald Asch, *Jakob I (1566–1625) König von England und Schottland; Herrscher des Friedens im Zeitalter der Religionskriege* (Stuttgard, 2005).

in Ireland in terms of the king's broader strategy to integrate Gaelic districts of Ireland and the Isles into a greater Britain.[5] Thus, far from being a period characterised by frustrated absolutism or the crown's avaricious pursuit of Irish land, the reign of James VI and I is emerging as more than two decades of stability, when many of the inherent difficulties of multiple monarchy presented themselves but were defused by a moderate king.

James VI and I's perfect union

The key to the governance of multiple kingdoms, James reasoned, was the creation of a united kingdom. Ireland, still under the governance of Mountjoy in 1603, was temporarily set aside as the king attempted to achieve the perfect union of the kingdoms of England and Scotland. The king immediately established the pursuit of this goal as the central theme of the early part of his reign.[6] In March 1604 James told his first English parliament:

> I am the Husband, and all the whole Isle is my lawful Wife; I am the Head, and it is my Body; I am the Shepherd, and it is my flock: I hope therefore no man will be so unreasonable as to think that I that am a Christian King under the Gospel, should be a Polygamist and husband to two wives; that I being the Head, should have a divided and monstrous Body.[7]

The king's forthright assertion of his position, however, wrong-footed a parliament deeply suspicious of all things Scottish and a commission was hastily assembled to explore the viability of union. The following month, parliamentary debate on the union commenced and English hostility to union was made clear. Yet James requested the enactment of a statute altering the royal style from 'King of England, Scotland, France and Ireland' to 'King of Great Britain'. The king badly misjudged the depth of hostility to union in England, and the Commons voiced its opposition to any change in style: the statute was not passed. His initial efforts thus frustrated, the king decided to adopt a more gradual programme for union, embarking on a series of largely symbolic measures to promote if not the union then the image of

---

5   Jane Ohlmeyer, '"Civilizing of those rude parts": colonization within Britain and Ireland, 1580s–1640s' in Nicholas Canny (ed.), *The Oxford history of the British Empire* (Oxford, 1998), i, pp. 124–47; Canny, *Making Ireland British*, pp. 194–200.

6   For this, see Bruce Galloway, *The union of England and Scotland, 1603–1608* (Edinburgh, 1986).

7   Neil Rhodes, Jennifer Richards and Joseph Marshall (eds), *James VI and I: selected writings* (Ashgate, 1988), p. 297 (quotation).

Britishness. In October 1604 James assumed, by royal proclamation, the royal style which parliament would not grant him and returned to the theme of union, declaring that the inhabitants of Britain shared 'a community of Language, the principal means of Civil society, and unity of Religion, the chiefest band of hearty Union, and the surest knot of lasting peace'. He also introduced a common coinage and oversaw the design of a single flag, the Union flag, for his two kingdoms. When the English parliament was reconvened in late 1606, the commissioners appointed two years earlier recommended the removal of trade barriers and the abolition of mutually hostile laws between the two kingdoms. To this was added the king's desire to extend legal rights to any person born in England or Scotland after his accession to the English throne and to naturalise those born in either kingdom before his accession.[8]

The vast majority of English parliamentarians, however, revealed themselves to be fiercely opposed to union in any form. For, while James may have intended for his reforms to address specific areas where union would be mutually beneficial, each raised more fundamental questions concerning the relationship between the English and Scottish kingdoms. The naturalisation of those born in the northern kingdom, for instance, touched a nerve among many Englishmen who feared that such an act would inevitably lead to England being overrun by beggarly Scots. Nicholas Fuller gave expression to what he saw as England's position:

> One man is owner of two pastures, with one hedge to divide them; the one pasture bare, the other fertile and good. A wise owner will not pull down the hedge quite, but make gates, and let them in and out . . . If he do, the cattle will rush in multitudes, and much against their will return.[9]

Parliament, moreover, was loath to support any proposal which might extend England's cherished common law tradition, and its 'ancient constitution', to anyone other than 'natural subjects'. Indeed, Sir Edwin Sandys, the English parliament's most outspoken critic of the union, encapsulated parliamentary feeling when he remarked that the Scots 'are better than aliens, but not equal with natural subjects'.[10] The removal of trade barriers, too, raised difficult questions concerning the discrepancy in wealth between the two kingdoms. What was to be gained, many parliamentarians wondered, from economic

8   Galloway, *The union of England and Scotland*, pp. 96–108; W.B. Patterson, *King James VI and I and the reunion of Christendom* (Cambridge, 1997) (quotation, p. 31).

9   Smith, *A history of the modern British Isles*, p. 25.

10   T.K. Rabb, *Jacobean gentleman: Sir Edwin Sandys, 1561–1629* (Princeton, 1998), p. 126.

union with a kingdom so poor as Scotland? But the king's response – ambiguous calls for 'a uniting of both laws and parliaments of both nations' – did little to answer these questions or assuage English fears.

The tables were then suddenly turned on the king when Sandys outlined an alternative vision of union – a so-called incorporative union – in which Scotland would be ruled by English laws and institutions.[11] The Scots had long feared that union with England would see their kingdom assume a subordinate role: like their southern neighbours, the Scots were equally keen to preserve the integrity of their kingdom's sovereignty and national institutions. Sandys's proposal produced the desired affect: the king was forced to abandon many of his proposals for union amid a storm of opposition in both kingdoms. By 1608, only the smallest steps had been taken toward effecting a more 'perfect union': in May 1607 all laws limiting trade and communication between England and Scotland were (for a trial period) repealed and, in the following year, English legal rights were granted to Scots born after James's accession to the English throne (the *post nati*). Thus James's various efforts to unite his British kingdoms had been soundly defeated: only the king himself clung to the belief that the union of the crowns had effected anything other than one king ruling two independent kingdoms. Speaking to parliament in May 1607 James declared:

> [The Union] is no more perfect, as now it is projected, than a child, that is born without a beard . . . The Union is perfect in me; that is, it is a Union in my blood and title; yet but *in embrione* perfect. Upon the late Queen's death, the child was first brought to light; but to make it a perfect man, to bring it to an accomplished Union, it must have time and means; and if it be not at the first, blame not me; blame time; blame the order of nature.

But James came to accept that while he was ready for union the political establishments in both his kingdoms were not and the king never again raised the matter in parliament.[12]

Yet the defeat of the proposed union should not detract from the king's overall success in governing his two British kingdoms. From the outset, James was careful to maintain the support of the body politic in Scotland and England and so constructed a system of government that struck a balance between the demands of the two kingdoms. With the king and court relocated to London after April 1603, the administration of Scotland was entrusted to the Scottish privy council. Made up of a reduced number of

11   Ibid., pp. 127–8.
12   Smith, *A history of the modern British Isles*, pp. 25–7 (quotation, p. 27).

trusted royal officials, the council kept the king fully abreast of developments in Scotland and governed it with such efficiency that in a speech delivered to the 1607 parliament James declared: 'This I must say for Scotland, and may truly vaunt it . . . here I sit and govern Scotland now, which others could not do by the sword'.[13] It was the governance of his English kingdom, however, which presented the greater challenge. To offset the shock of the new, James retained Robert Cecil and his supporters as the most prominent force in a privy council which nearly doubled in size, from 13 seats upon Elizabeth's death to 25 under the new king. Though James made sure that his council contained a broad assortment of English political interests, he packed his inner entourage, the Gentlemen of the Bedchamber, almost exclusively with his own countrymen. This latter action, coupled with the king's proclivity to bestow gifts and pensions disproportionately on Scots, alarmed many English observers who (not without a touch of xenophobia) feared that a Scottish faction would soon dominate the court. For an absentee monarch, however, these were necessary measures to maintain the support of the otherwise distant Scottish nobility and, generally, James's English servants also benefited from his largesse. The new king thus cut a very different figure from his niggardly predecessor, reintroducing extravagance and spectacle to the royal court. In the first four months of his reign, he spent £64,000 on jewellery and created 906 knights. Elizabeth, by contrast, had created a mere 878 knights in her entire reign. In this way, James established the royal court in London as the centre of the political world in his two kingdoms. But real political power in England continued to be concentrated in Cecil, ennobled earl of Salisbury in 1605, the king's chief advisor and the man who managed the day-to-day affairs of the kingdom's government. His dominance, combined with the king's lavish spending and wide distribution of patronage, precluded the emergence of a rival political faction and ensured that in the decade after 1603 England and Scotland experienced a period of stability and prosperity not witnessed in nearly 20 years.[14]

Dual kingship also afforded James the political leverage to address certain areas which had hitherto been beyond the jurisdiction of an English or a Scottish monarch. The first matter to be addressed was England's ongoing war with Spain. As a Scottish king, with no direct quarrel with Philip III, James was able to assume an almost neutral position at the negotiating table

13 Maurice Lee, 'James VI's government of Scotland after 1603', in *The 'inevitable' union*, p. 133 (quotation); Goodare, *State and society in early modern Scotland*, pp. 286–7.
14 Smith, *A history of the modern British Isles*, pp. 39–40, 46–7; Edwards, *The making of the modern British state*, pp. 262–3, 265–6.

and, with Cecil's assistance, successfully concluded the treaty of London in August 1604 which formally ended two decades of hostility between England and Spain. Thereafter, military expenditure was greatly reduced and, in conjunction with a commercial treaty with France, trade between Britain and the continent flourished.[15] Control of London and Edinburgh also allowed James to tackle the problem posed by the borders from a position of unprecedented strength. As we have seen, the transformation of the troublesome border region into what the king preferred to call the 'middle shires' was central to his plans to effect closer union between his two kingdoms. The region's continued potential for disorder was revealed in the 'busy week', beginning in late March 1603, during which the Grahams, Elliots, Armstrongs and other border surnames caused serious disturbances in the Cumberland borders. In April, James announced, by proclamation, his intention to replace march law with the laws and courts of England and Scotland and, the following month, he outlined his ultimate goal for the borders:

> Utterly to extinguish as well the name as substance of the borders, I mean the difference between them and other parts of the kingdom. For doing thereof it is necessary that all quarrels amongst them be reconciled and all strangeness between the nations removed.[16]

In 1605, the crown established a joint border commission – comprised of 5 English and 5 Scots – to root out lawless elements. In its first year the commission's mounted border guard executed 140 'thieves'. When in 1606–7, the commission sought to rid Cumberland of the unruly (and numerous) Grahams, it was decided to transport the entire lineage, including women and children, to Ireland, where it was thought that the English Grahams, despite their recalcitrance, would make better tenants than the native Irish. By 1621, the commission was so successful that the border guard was disbanded.[17] However, it was in the outlying regions of Scotland and Ireland that the impact of the crown's enhanced jurisdiction was most strongly felt. As we have seen, in the 1590s James had begun to take tentative steps toward strengthening royal influence in the Western Highlands and Isles, but the upheaval caused by O'Neill's rebellion, followed by the succession and then

15 Smith, *A history of the modern British Isles*, p. 31.

16 Galloway, *The union of England and Scotland*, p. 16 (Quotation); Watts, *From border to middle shire*, pp. 27–8.

17 Donaldson, *Scotland: James V–James VII*, p. 227; S.G. Ellis, *The Pale and the far north: government and society in two early Tudor borderlands* (Galway, 1986), p. 27.

the king's efforts to achieve the union, had prevented the completion of this [2 9 5]
task. It was not until late 1607 when a series of unrelated events began to
unfold which presented the crown with an opportunity to stamp its authority on the region.

King James and his Gaelic subjects

In 1608 Andrew Stewart, Lord Ochiltree – with English and Irish logistical
assistance – made an expedition to the Isles where he lured a number of
island chiefs aboard his ship and transported them to Edinburgh. The chiefs
were detained for ten months and, during this time, government officials
were placed in control of their affairs and charged with 'civilising' the western seaboard. Following a second expedition to the Isles in autumn 1609 led
by Andrew Knox, bishop of the Isles, the chiefs were compelled to abide by a
series of legislative reforms known as the Statutes of Iona which, *inter alia*,
required that individual chiefs assume responsibility for the conduct of their
clansmen and appear annually before the council. This policy of delegating
authority to chiefs was pursued in tandem with the tried and tested method
of charging the governance of the Highlands and Isles to regional magnates.
The earl of Argyll and Kenneth Mackenzie, ennobled Lord Kintail in 1609,
spearheaded an aggressive extension of royal authority in the south-west and
the north-western Highlands respectively after 1607.[18] Central to James's
efforts to extend royal control in the region, however, was the colonisation
of the Irish lands confiscated by the crown following the sudden withdrawal
from Ulster of the earls of Tyrone and Tyrconnell. To the astonishment of
Irish officials, Hugh O'Neill and Rory O'Donnell, together with a host of
followers, had departed from Ireland in September 1607 never to return.
Since his surrender and subsequent pardon in 1603, Tyrone had steadily
reasserted his authority in Ulster, but his lordship was devastated and –
following Mountjoy's replacement as deputy by the more aggressive Sir
Arthur Chichester in 1605 – the earl found his position threatened by former vassal chiefs and government officials who saw his continued political
survival as an obstacle to their advancement. In desperation, Tyrone abandoned his earldom and followed O'Donnell into exile on the continent.
Known in Irish historiography as the 'Flight of the earls', the departure of

18 A.I. Macinnes, 'Crown, clans and fine: the "civilizing" of Scottish Gaeldom, 1587–1638', in
Northern Scotland, xiii (1993), pp. 34–8.

O'Neill and O'Donnell left Gaelic Ulster exposed, and the crown responded in 1609 by supporting a radical plan to resettle their lands with settlers from England and Scotland.[19]

The origins of the crown's strategy in Ulster can be discerned in James's earlier policy toward the Isles and Highlands. In 1597, the king had encouraged the 'plantation' of 'answerable inlands [Lowland Scots] subjects' and the establishment of burghs among the 'utterly barbarous' Gaelic islanders: shortly thereafter, adventurers from Fife established a small colony on the island of Lewis.[20] Similarly, in the transplantation of the Grahams to Ireland in 1606–7 can be seen the crown's willingness to settle what it deemed to be a more 'civilised' people in an 'uncivilised' environment. After 1603, James regarded the culture of south-east England as the epitome of 'civility', placing Lowland Scottish culture below it and Gaelic culture at the bottom of what Jenny Wormald has described as a 'three-tiered system'.[21] Thus Scots lowlanders and border surnames, though less 'civil' than Lowland Englishmen, were still possessed of a higher degree of 'civility' than were Gaelic peoples. What the crown attempted in Ireland in 1609, however, was unprecedented in terms of its scale and ambition. Influenced by the thinking of Sir John Davies, Ireland's solicitor-general – who advocated the total extirpation of Gaelic law and custom – the crown granted lands in six of the nine counties in the province of Ulster to English and (Lowland) Scots planters (known as undertakers) civil and military servants of the crown in Ireland (known as servitors) and the so-called 'deserving Irish' – natives who had during Tyrone's rebellion remained loyal to the crown. Each group received estates ranging in size from 1,000 to 2,000 acres, but the undertakers received the largest proportion of lands and were required both to introduce English and Scots settlers onto their estates and to oversee the construction of towns. The Ulster plantation, as it was called, was intended, in one fell swoop, to sever Gaelic Ulster's links with Gaelic Scotland and to establish a loyal British colony in what had traditionally been Ireland's most recalcitrant region.[22] And, in the short term, this policy was a success. Within several years Ulster was a land ethnically, economically and physically transformed, and a permanent wedge had been driven between those Gaelic areas of Ulster and Scotland which had survived the king's assertion of royal authority.

19   Canny, 'Taking sides in early modern Ireland', pp. 110–14.
20   Donaldson, Scotland: James V–James VII, pp. 228–31.
21   Wormald, Court, kirk and community, pp. 192–3.
22   Philip Robinson, The plantation of Ulster: British settlement in an Irish landscape, 1600–1670 (Belfast, 1994).

James thus seemed justified in regarding his Irish policy as one of his [2 9 7] 'masterpieces'.[23]

It is ironic that James resorted to such a hostile policy toward his Gaelic subjects at time when Gaelic ideology in Ireland was moving toward an acceptance of his kingship. For centuries, a recurring theme in the writings of the hereditary Gaelic learned classes had been the restoration of an ethnically Gaelic king to rule over all of Ireland. Thus, the Gaelic literati had disregarded the parliamentary act declaring Henry VIII king of Ireland in 1541 because he was not a *Gaedhil*. But in the intervening years Ireland's Gaelic polity had repeatedly risen against the Tudor state and, in so doing, had developed a more pronounced sense of national identity based on a distinctly Gaelic political culture and a common belief in Catholicism. The military triumph of England over O'Neill had stripped Gaelic Ireland of its political manifestation, while the steady advance of the Reformation in parts of Scottish Gaeldom – among the Campbells in particular – further contributed to a distinct sense of Catholic Irish Gaeldom.[24] Indeed these developments moved the highly conservative Gaelic poetic class to adjust its traditional outlook of the surrounding world. In a reflection of the widening gulf between Irish and Scottish Gaeldom, the term *Albanaigh* was increasingly employed to describe the *Gaedhil* and the *Gaill* of the kingdom of Scotland; Ireland's Catholic population, meanwhile, once rigidly distinguished as *Gaedhil* and *Gaill*, were now subsumed by the term *Éireannaigh*.[25] The accession of James VI to the English throne, however, presented the Gaelic learned classes with an opportunity to reconcile Gaelic Ireland's political situation with its confession in a British context. As a king of Scotland, Gaelic genealogists were able to construct impeccable pedigrees linking James to the medieval kings of Ireland who gave Scotland its first Gaelic king. The ability of the learned classes to portray James as a Gaelic king, combined with the establishment in Ireland of a new church policy which permitted Catholics to give their allegiance in matters temporal to a non-Catholic monarch, allowed Gaelic Ireland to accept the new English king as king of Ireland as well. This profound shift in Gaelic ideology is

23   Smith, *A history of the modern British Isles*, p. 46.
24   Jane Dawson, 'Calvinism and the Gaidhealtachd in Scotland' in Andrew Pettegree, Alastair Duke and Gillian Lewis (eds), *Calvinism in Europe, 1540–1620* (Cambridge, 1994), pp. 231–53; S.G. Ellis, 'The collapse of the Gaelic world, 1450–1650', in *Irish Historical Studies*, 31 (1999), pp. 464–69.
25   Ellis, 'The collapse of the Gaelic world', p. 466; Breandán Ó Buachalla, 'Poetry and politics in early modern Ireland', in *Eighteenth-century Ireland*, vii (1992), pp. 160–1.

most clearly evident in the poetry composed for James upon his accession. An Ulster poet wrote that 'three crowns . . . shall be placed on James's head' and, in an effort to bestow on the new king the ultimate seal of legitimacy in the Gaelic world, cast James as 'Ireland's spouse':

> The Saxons' land has been long – 'tis well known – prophesied for thee; so likewise is Ireland due to thee, thou are her spouse by all the signs.[26]

As royal policy in Ulster and the Western Highlands and Isles had demonstrated, however, King James saw no place for Gaelic culture in his kingdoms and cared little that Ireland's Gaelic elite had now redefined themselves as royalists.

Religious 'congruity' and fiscal crisis

Yet, with regard to religion, James showed himself to be a ruler willing to accommodate diversity. Indeed, the crown's ecclesiastical policy after 1603 attempted to appeal to the wide religious spectrum that existed in its three kingdoms. This was no easy task, for upon his accession James was expected to be all things to all men in matters of religion. Catholics had high hopes that the new king, on account of his mother's much-vaunted Catholicism, would be tolerant of their faith. Old English Catholics in many southern Irish towns were so confident of this that on learning of James's accession they defiantly re-established Catholic worship, expelled Protestants and reconsecrated churches. English Puritans expected that James would go further in reforming the church than his predecessor and (wasting little time) presented him on his journey south in 1603 with the 'Millenary Petition' which outlined their aspirations. The Scottish kirk, meanwhile, hoped that the king's absence would allow it to pursue a Presbyterian agenda, while English clergy expected James's presence would maintain the power of the episcopate in England.[27]

Alive to the impossibility of pleasing all of these interests, James sought to win the support of the moderate majorities within each. The king

26 Breandán Ó Buachalla, '"James our true king": the ideology of Irish royalism in the seventeenth century', in D.G. Boyce (ed.), *Political thought in Ireland since the seventeenth century* (London, 1993), pp. 7–13 (quotations, p. 10).
27 Smith, *A history of the modern British Isles*, pp. 36–7.

determined not to attempt to convert his Catholic subjects. But he demanded their outward conformity. Thus, in summer 1603, Mountjoy marched south into Munster with 5,000 troops, quickly disabusing Ireland's Old English community of its expectation that the new monarch would tolerate public expressions of Catholicism. When the citizens of Waterford produced a medieval municipal charter which, they claimed, empowered them to refuse the deputy entry, the lord deputy reportedly threatened to 'cut King John's charter in pieces with King James's sword' and quickly restored the government's authority in the towns.[28] By contrast, the vast preponderance of English Catholics were prepared to exhibit outward conformity in return for the king's willingness to respect their liberty of conscience. But a band of extremists, led by the Catholic-convert Guy Fawkes, devised an audacious plan to blow the king, the prince and parliament to smithereens in November 1605 by exploding kegs of gunpowder secretly placed in the cellars of Westminster. Yet, even in the anti-Catholic hysteria surrounding the discovery of the 'Gunpowder plot', government sanctions against recusants were mild: so long as Catholics swore an oath denying papal authority over kings, they might continue to worship in private. To promote dialogue between the different shades of English Protestants, James assembled leading Puritans and selected bishops at a three-day conference at Hampton Court in early 1604. Though the king expressed his firm commitment to episcopacy at the conference – famously declaring 'No bishop, no king' – he agreed to several of the reformers' major requests, which included revisions to *The Book of Common Prayer*, the introduction of measures to limit pluralism and to promote a preaching ministry, and a new translation of the Bible (eventually published in 1611).[29] In return, James expected their conformity to the established church. In Scotland, the crown embarked on a more thoroughgoing policy of reform which reasserted royal authority over the Scottish kirk. In 1606, the Scottish parliament acknowledged James to be supreme governor of the church and, in 1612, the General Assembly recognised the episcopal authority of bishops. These seemingly drastic changes in church government, however, were made palatable by the crown's decision to leave the distinctly Scottish Presbyterian structures of the lower church untouched. In this way, the king brought a certain 'congruity' to the divergent English

---

28 *Oxford DNB, s.v.* Charles Blount (quotation).
29 Patrick Collinson, 'The Jacobean religious settlement: the Hampton Court conference', in Howard Tomlinson (ed.), *Before the English Civil War* (London, 1983), pp. 27–51 (quotation, p. 40).

and Scottish churches without undermining the structural integrity or upsetting the ecclesiastical principles of either. The king had thus created in his kingdoms a broad religious middle ground in which moderates of all shades might live, prosper and worship in exchange for their outward recognition of the established church.[30]

Yet, for all of James's success in tackling the finer points of governing multiple kingdoms, the basic task of financing the monarchy continued to confound the king. James's personal extravagance and maintenance of a lavish court, combined with his need to provide separate households for himself, Queen Anna and Prince Henry, had come at a cost: by 1606 the royal debt stood at a towering £816,000.[31] But prodigious royal expenditure was only partly to blame for the crown's fiscal woes. At the heart of the problem lay the antiquated method of financing the monarchy. Like his medieval predecessors, the king was expected to 'live of his own', that is to be financially self-sufficient. This meant that the crown continued to rely on traditional sources of royal revenue: income from crown estates and the exploitation of feudal rights, namely wardship, marriage, purveyance and custom duties.[32] Because the king's income from Scotland amounted to a paltry two per cent of the crown's overall wealth, and Ireland had yet to be rendered profitable, it was to his English kingdom that James looked for the vast preponderance of this revenue.[33] Elizabeth, however, had sold many royal estates to pay for the war against Spain. Inflation, meanwhile, steadily diminished the value of the remaining crown estates. The exploitation of feudal rights thus continued to be the crown's most lucrative source of income. But the king's recourse to ancient custom to keep the monarchy afloat was widely resented, and strained the crown's relationship with the English parliament. In 1604 the Commons objected to the legality of purveyance (the monarch's right to purchase goods for the court at reduced prices) and rejected a proposal by the Lords to grant an annual tax in its stead.[34]

---

30 John Morrill, 'A British patriarchy? Ecclesiastical imperialism under the early Stuarts', in Anthony Fletcher and Peter Roberts (eds), *Religion, culture and society in early modern Britain: essays in honour of Patrick Collinson* (Cambridge, 1994), pp. 209–37; Smith, *A history of the modern British Isles*, pp. 36–9, 48–9; Keith Brown, *Kingdom or province? Scotland and the regal union, 1603–1715* (London, 1992), pp. 90–1.

31 David Thomas, 'Financial and administrative developments', in Tomlinson (ed.), *Before the English Civil War*, pp. 104–5.

32 Edwards, *The making of the modern English state*, pp. 266–7.

33 Keith Brown, 'Reformation to union, 1560–1707', in R.A. Houston and W.W.J. Knox (eds), *The New Penguin history of Scotland: from earliest times to the present day* (London, 2001), p. 238.

34 Smith, *A history of the modern British Isles*, p. 33.

The controversy surrounding the crown's feudal dues resurfaced in 1606 when a merchant, John Bate, was sued in the court of exchequer for refusing to pay impositions (additional custom tariffs imposed by royal prerogative) on imported currants. Though Bate argued that the imposition on currants was illegal because it had not received parliamentary consent, the judges found for the king, their decision resting on the principle that the right to levy impositions was within the king's 'absolute' prerogative. Sensing an opportunity to use the verdict to tackle the royal finances, Salisbury (appointed treasurer in May 1608) updated the *Book of Rates* to account for inflation and extended impositions to include 1,400 items. Salisbury's policy netted the crown an additional £70,000 annually.[35] Yet this additional income was not sufficient to cover the royal debt. Nor would it meet the monarchy's long-term financial needs. Thus, in 1610, Salisbury presented to parliament a bold plan, known as the 'Great Contract', whereby the king would surrender his feudal dues in return for a single payment of £600,000 and an annual payment of £200,000 thereafter. The Contract, however, proved too radical a departure from the existing system of finance: the king was loath to part with his feudal incomes, while MPs shrank from the notion of seeking £200,000 a year from their constituencies. Parliament, moreover, feared that it might fade into irrelevance if the king was assured of an annual income.[36] By early 1611, discussions had reached an impasse and both sides abandoned the Contract. The failure of the Contract was a lost opportunity and a major blow to Salisbury who had envisaged the resolution of the crown's financial difficulties as his legacy. The crown, meanwhile, still faced with rising debts, had begun to sell knighthoods to augment its income. In 1611 it established the order of baronets which sold baronetages for £1,095 each.[37] But the sale of honours to as many as could afford its purchase quickly devalued the honour itself, creating resentment among the nobility. Despite the efforts of Lionel Cranfield, appointed lord treasurer in 1622, to address royal expenditure, the remainder of James's reign was plagued by problems arising from the royal finances. When the king died in 1625 the methods of financing the monarchy had little changed and the royal debt stood at £1,000,000.[38]

35 Thomas, 'Financial and administrative developments', p. 106.
36 Edwards, *The making of the modern English state*, p. 269.
37 Smith, *A history of the modern British Isles*, pp. 34–5.
38 Thomas, 'Financial and administrative developments', pp. 108–9; Edwards, *The making of the modern English state*, p. 266.

[302] Faction, favourites and the drift towards war

In the last years of his reign, James found it increasingly difficult to maintain the delicate balance of power which he had created within and between his three kingdoms. In England, the death in 1612 of Salisbury marked the beginning of a prolonged period of bitter factional division, scandal and administrative corruption which brought the court into disrepute and worsened the crown's already dismal financial situation. James called parliament in April 1614 so as to obtain a subsidy to help offset his colossal debt. But court politics had poisoned the king's relationship with parliament: the so-called 'Addled Parliament' sat for only eight weeks and was dissolved in acrimony without enacting any legislation. Only the meteoric rise in the king's affections of the English courtier, George Villiers, eclipsed the main political factions which had emerged following Salisbury's death. After 1619, however, factional division gave way to the domination of king and court by one man. Villiers was not the first handsome young courtier to capture James's affections; but his arrival on the political scene at a time when the ageing king was subject to a range of new pressures at home and abroad allowed him to assume a central role in English government. James heaped honours upon his favourite: he was appointed lord admiral in 1617, ennobled as duke of Buckingham in 1623 and, with no further heights to reach, rumours abounded in late 1624 that he was to be created 'Prince of Tipperary in Ireland, with the high command of Lord High Lieutenant of that Kingdom'. That Villiers also maintained a close friendship with Prince Charles (James's heir following Prince Henry's untimely death in 1612) further enhanced his influence and ensured his political survival in the next reign.[39] Indeed, after 1623, Buckingham grew ever closer to the future king and together they assumed a greater control of government as the king's health deteriorated.

In these years the old king's natural distaste for war had led him to champion an alliance with Catholic Spain, so as to prevent his three kingdoms from being dragged into the religious conflict which had erupted on the continent following the usurpation of the Bohemian throne by Frederick, Elector Palatine and husband of James's daughter Elizabeth. But an alliance with the hated Spanish, which centred on Prince Charles marrying the Spanish infanta, proved most unpopular in England. Spain had occupied the

39 Roger Lockyer, *Buckingham: the life and political career of George Villiers, first duke of Buckingham, 1592–1628* (London, 1981), pp. 25–50, 154–6 (quotation, p. 215).

Palatinate in response to Frederick's actions, exiling him and Elizabeth.[40] Charles and Buckingham – in the wake of their impetuous excursion to Madrid to conclude the marriage treaty in person – emerged as the chief proponents of war with Spain and their influence was sufficient to convince the king to summon parliament in 1624 for the purpose of financing the war which he had strived to avoid. The kingdom was united in its opposition to Spain and Charles and Buckingham worked to ensure that parliament passed an impressive array of both foreign and domestic legislation. Parliament voted for £300,000 in taxes to finance a war against Spain – on the provision that a war council accountable to parliament dispensed the money and negotiations with Spain were ended – and passed 73 statutes of domestic import in less than 4 months.[41] With England on a war footing and a new government forming around Prince Charles and Buckingham, James died in March 1625.

In 1603 James had promised his Scottish subjects that he would return to his northern kingdom every three years. Yet, by the time of his death, the king had only set foot in Scotland again on one occasion. The demands of governing his English kingdom militated against more frequent visits and generally after 1612 James sought to maintain the *status quo* there. When in summer 1617 he returned to Scotland, however, the king was taken aback by the simple ceremonial of the kirk. James, who had grown accustomed to the formality of the English church, forced the General Assembly which met at Perth in 1618 to pass a series of liturgical reforms known as the Five Articles of Perth. For many Scots the Articles – which included provisions for kneeling at communion and the observation of holy days – smacked of popery and were thus ignored. But James was adamant that the reforms be observed and, in 1621, he flexed his royal muscles and convinced a hostile parliament to lend the contentious Articles statutory authority. Yet the king's insistence on introducing major liturgical reforms to the kirk was more than just another statement of royal authority over the church, rather it was a symptom of over a decade of absentee monarchy. Immersed in the affairs of English government, drawn to the spectacle of English worship, and sporting an English favourite who concentrated the majority of his patronage on Englishmen, James had lost touch with his Scottish kingdom. The furore

---

40   J.R. Jones, *Britain and Europe in the seventeenth century* (London, 1966), pp. 18–21.
41   Simon Adams, 'Foreign policy and the parliaments of 1621 and 1624', in Kevin Sharpe (ed.), *Faction & parliament: essays on early Stuart history* (London, 1978), pp. 168–71; Conrad Russell, *Parliaments and English politics, 1621–1629* (Oxford, 1979), pp. 145–203; Smith, *A history of the modern British Isles*, pp. 62–3.

surrounding the Articles had pushed the Scottish polity to the brink of outright opposition to the state and support for radical Presbyterianism increased. James, however, was still possessed of the political acumen to realise that any further tinkering with the kirk would provoke a more serious backlash and, wisely, he made no effort to see the strict enforcement of the statutes.[42]

Ironically, Ireland – that kingdom which had caused his predecessor such difficulty – presented James with no major challenges in his last years. Following the success of the Ulster plantation, the New English officials in control of the Dublin administration established smaller plantations between 1618–20 in counties Wexford, Leitrim and Longford, and in several baronies in King's and Queen's counties and in county Tipperary. This influx of Protestant British settlers had already begun to tilt the balance of power in Ireland against the Catholic Old English community: the Irish parliament of 1613–15 saw, for the first time, the emergence of a sizeable Protestant majority in both houses. The Old English, however, were not prepared simply to relinquish power. In parliament, they had once again shown themselves capable of mounting effective opposition to the government and fought to safeguard both their political influence and religion. The issue of whether further plantations should be sanctioned, and thereby a further diminution of Old English power effected, was to dominate Irish politics until 1625.[43]

The 22 year rule of the kingdoms of England, Scotland and Ireland by one king had demonstrated that multiple monarchy supplied a political framework within which the British Isles might successfully be governed. Indeed the political stability and increased economic prosperity which characterised the reign of James VI and I stands in marked contrast to the decades of uncertainty and turmoil which plagued the three kingdoms in the latter half of the sixteenth century. Much of his success in these years can of course be attributed to his Tudor predecessors. Upon Elizabeth's death James was handed without contention an efficient and highly centralised kingdom, England's long war with Spain was all but over and the conquest of Ireland had, at last, been completed. Yet the task of making the British manifestation of composite monarchy work fell exclusively to James. In this the king showed himself to be a competent ruler whose flexibility and

---

42 Brown, *Kingdom or province?*, pp. 96–9; Smith, *A history of the modern British Isles*, p. 49.

43 Aidan Clark with R.D. Edwards, 'Pacification, plantation, and the Catholic question, 1603–23', in *A new history of Ireland*, iii, 210–19.

willingness to compromise allowed him to create a middle ground of sufficient breadth to attract moderates of all cultural, political and religious shades. But maintaining the integrity of the moderates in three divergent kingdoms was a delicate and ongoing balancing act. James's long-term solution to this problem was total union – the implementation in his kingdoms of one law, one political establishment and one religion. Yet, with the possibility of the unification of England and Scotland dashed early in his reign, the king was denied the most straightforward method of achieving this end. Thereafter, James sought gradually to align both the cultures and the political and religious institutions of his three kingdoms squarely behind the monarchy. In doing so, however, James placed the future of multiple monarchy in the British Isles solely on the ability of his successor, Charles I.

At James's extravagant funeral held in Westminster Abbey Bishop John Williams, James' chaplain, finished his sermon – the contents of which were later published as *Great Britain's Solomon* – by turning to the new king. He reassured the mourners: 'Though his father be dead, yet is he, as though he were not dead, for he hath left one behind him most like himself.'[44] Yet Charles I was a different man from his father and would prove an altogether different king. Where James had been erudite and engaged by intellectual debate, and frequently moved to express his innermost thoughts and ideas either in print, or to his councillors, or before parliament, Charles was aloof and reticent; where the former king had been gregarious and lavish in his expenditure on his family and his court, the new king was diffident and austere; and where James had repeatedly shown his willingness to sacrifice rigid definitions of contentious constitutional and religious issues to achieve compromise, Charles displayed signs of inflexibility and an aversion for ambiguity.[45] In an age of personal monarchy – when the sovereign's personality was inseparable from his government – and as ruler of three divergent kingdoms, these character traits carried in them the potential for danger. At the time of his accession, however, Charles's personality remained an unknown quantity to all those outside his innermost circle – and even to them it remained something of a mystery. To his subjects he was the jilted hero of the marriage negotiations in Madrid, the popular leader of the 'Prince's party' in the 1624 parliament and the youthful embodiment of all the excitement and anticipation associated with a new reign. But, above all,

---

44   P. Gregg, *King Charles I* (London, 1981), p. 112 (quotation).
45   L.J. Reeve, *Charles I and the road to personal rule* (Cambridge, 1989) Chapter 6; Conrad Russell, *The causes of the English civil war* (Oxford, 1990); Smith, *A history of the modern British Isles*, pp. 65–6.

Charles was the son whom 'Britain's Solomon' had left behind 'most like himself'.

Finance and religion: Charles I's war and his English kingdom

The apparent similarities between the two monarchs were further enhanced by the fact that Charles saw his own reign not as the beginning of a new era but as a continuation of his father's.[46] Aside from his initial moves to introduce a greater degree of propriety to the court and to dispense with some of its more decadent aspects, the new king made a deliberate effort to replicate James's rule. Charles confirmed 28 of James's 30 privy councillors in office, retained all of James's old servants in the privy chamber and bedchamber – many of them Scots – and replaced his lord chamberlain of more than a decade with William Herbert, earl of Pembroke, his father's trusted friend and chamberlain.[47] Like his father, Charles saw England as his principal kingdom and made London his home. In the kingdom of his birth, he continued Sir Thomas Hamilton, earl of Melrose, as his Scottish secretary. In Ireland, Henry Carey, viscount Falkland, was retained as lord deputy.[48] But the most important link to the previous reign was the continued presence and influence of James's beloved duke of Buckingham at the centre of government. Much to the astonishment of the court, and to the general dismay of his rivals, Buckingham carried both his position as the king's favourite and his virtual dominance of royal patronage perfectly intact into the new reign.[49] The naturally untrusting Charles had come to regard his father's favourite as a surrogate older sibling as members of his own immediate family were one by one taken from him either through death or marriage. In the four years since Charles entered on his majority, moreover, his relationship

---

46 *Oxford DNB, s.v.* Charles I; G.E. Aylmer, *The king's servants: the civil service of Charles I, 1625–1642* (London, 1974), pp. 257, 344–5.

47 S.R. Gardiner, *A history of England under the duke of Buckingham and Charles I, 1624–28* (2 vols, London, 1875) ii, pp. 167–8; K. Sharpe, 'The image of virtue: the court and household of Charles I, 1625–42', in *Politics and ideas in early Stuart England: essays and studies* (London, 1989), pp. 148–9; K.M. Brown, 'The Scottish aristocracy, Anglicization and the court, 1603–38', in *Historical Journal*, 36, 3 (1993), p. 554.

48 *Handbook of British chronology* (eds) E.B. Fryde *et al.* (Cambridge, 1986), p. 194; *A new history of Ireland*, ix, p. 488.

49 *Oxford DNB, s.v.* George Villiers.

with Buckingham had developed into a close personal friendship, one which [307]
assumed definite political connotations following their journey to Madrid
and their determination, upon their celebrated return to London, to gather
parliamentary support for war against Spain.[50] Thus, with his father dead,
Buckingham was all that remained of Charles's family and the new king,
more so perhaps than James himself, placed the duke's counsels and well-
being above all else.

It is ironic that in his desire to emulate his father's reign Charles had as the
centrepiece of his own an impending war with Spain. This was precisely the
inheritance that James had sought so strenuously to avoid bequeathing to his
successor, but through the combined efforts of Charles and Buckingham,
James was persuaded in the last months of his reign to dissolve the treaties
with Spain and to enter into a marriage treaty with France. It was Buckingham's
intention that a French match would form the foundation of a grand alliance
of Protestant and Catholic powers to combat Habsburg hegemony.[51]
Charles, for his part, saw in a French alliance the means by which he might
redeem the personal humiliation he had suffered in Madrid and recover
the Palatinate for his sister and brother-in-law. However, the focus on far-
reaching political strategy and personal vindication instead of on present-
centred and dispassionate diplomacy gave the French the upper hand in the
marriage negotiations, and Louis XIII's minister, Cardinal Richelieu, easily
wrung a string of concessions from James and Charles, who countersigned
the treaty in late 1624. Under its terms, Charles was to wed the French king's
15-year-old sister, Henrietta Maria. It was agreed that the future queen,
and her entourage, would enjoy the freedom to practise Catholicism and to
raise her children as Catholics until the age of 13. The treaty, however, also
contained an appendage committing James (and Charles after him) to the
suspension of penal laws against Catholics. With this they had secretly consented to religious concessions as extensive as those Spain had demanded –
and this despite Charles's pledge to the 1624 parliament that if he married
a Catholic, freedom of religion would not extend beyond his wife. France,
however, was the only country capable of counterbalancing Habsburg power
and was central to Buckingham's immediate plans for war.[52]

During the marriage negotiations, the duke had procured verbal assurances from Louis that France would commit to recovering the Palatinate

50   K. Sharpe, *The personal rule of Charles I* (Yale, 1992), p. 5.
51   Lockyer, *Buckingham*, p. 225.
52   Lockyer, *Buckingham*, pp. 199–201, 205, 208–9; Russell, *Parliaments and English politics*,
      p. 209.

through its support of a joint military expedition – then being assembled in England under the command of the German mercenary, Count Mansfeld. But Louis and Richelieu were loath to provoke the Habsburgs prematurely and, following a Huguenot rebellion at La Rochelle, all offers of French assistance, including the expedition's freedom to land in French territory, were withdrawn. James, moreover, determined to the last to avoid war with Spain, had forbidden Mansfeld to cross Spanish territory. Lacking adequate money and supplies, and now denied an overland passage to the Palatinate, Mansfeld's raw English conscripts embarked from Dover in January only to languish off the coast of Flushing, where most of them succumbed to starvation and disease. In an effort to resuscitate the faltering military alliance, meanwhile, Buckingham agreed to loan English ships to the French, so as to expedite the suppression of the Huguenots and thereby refocus Louis on his commitment to regaining the Palatinate. English Protestants, however, were horrified at the use of the king's ships against their coreligionists and the Huguenot rebellion only intensified in the face of government persecution. Nevertheless the three Stuart kingdoms were now committed to a French alliance and war with Spain seemed inevitable: in May 1625 Charles married Henrietta Maria by proxy outside Notre Dame and interred his father, the last restraint on a Spanish war, in Westminster. The following month Charles convened parliament determined to obtain the funds necessary to begin in earnest the war that he (and Buckingham) had so actively sought to inherit.[53]

Charles saw his first parliament as a continuation of his father's last. In his abrupt opening address, the king reminded both Houses of their part in the decision to go to war and of the financial responsibilities that this entailed:

> I hope that you do remember that you were pleased to employ me to advise my father to break both those treaties that were then on foot, so that I cannot say that I come hither a free, unengaged man. It is true that I came into this business willingly, freely, like a young man, and consequently rashly; but it was by your entreaties, your engagement . . . I pray you remember that this being my first action, and begun by your advice and entreaty, what a great dishonour it were both to you and me if this action so begun should fail for that assistance you are able to give me.[54]

Thus, for Charles, the purpose of the 1625 parliament was abundantly clear: to honour its commitment of the previous year by granting him the supply necessary to wage war against Spain and liberate the Palatinate. The only other

53   Lockyer, *Buckingham*, pp. 230–1.
54   Gardiner, *History of England*, i, p. 190 (quotation).

matter of business was the life grant of tonnage and poundage[55] customarily made to all new kings since Henry VI. The grant had become a significant component of ordinary royal revenue and was essential to a king facing the massive expenditure of an offensive war.[56]

The 1625 parliament, however, did not proceed according to the king's design. Gone was the spirit of cooperation and unity of purpose so evident just 13 months earlier. Sir Robert Phelips voiced the concern of many in the Commons when he took issue with the king's argument that parliament was engaged to support a war. 'There is no engagement', he claimed, 'the promises and declarations of the last parliament were in respect of a war: we know yet of no war nor of any enemy.'[57] Parliament learned that the subsidies voted in 1624 – intended to fund a naval campaign against Spain – had been spent in a number of other areas, including Mansfeld's failed expedition. Indeed, £37,000 had gone to finance a navy and, by May, preparations were underway to press 10,000 men to accompany the small fleet docked at Portsmouth; but the only activity at sea in evidence was France's use of English ships against the Huguenots. Reluctant to return to their already burdened constituencies seeking additional money when they were unsure of how it would be used, the Commons agreed to grant the king two subsidies – approximately £140,000 – until war with Spain was commenced. A restive Commons then took the unusual step of voting Charles tonnage and poundage for one year, with the hope that this would give the Commons leverage on other levies on imports, particularly on customs and impositions, and would provide the king with a timeframe in which to employ the money received from tonnage and poundage to its original purpose: ridding the seas of pirates, which were then menacing the areas off Cornwall and Wales. Hoping to postpone a decision on this radical break with tradition, the Lords quietly allowed the bill to lie dormant.[58]

On the king's behalf, Sir John Coke laid bare the financial burdens that a modern European war placed on the crown, indicating that two subsidies were insufficient to wage war for a year.[59] He prevailed upon the Commons to vote additional subsidies. Unfortunately for the crown, the contentious

---

55 Duties imposed on every ton of wine imported, and every pound's worth of goods that was either imported or exported.

56 Russell, *Parliaments and English politics*, pp. 204–37.

57 Russell, *Parliaments and English politics*, p. 226 (quotation).

58 Ibid., 229; Glanmor Williams, *Renewal and reformation: Wales, c.1415–1642* (Oxford, 1993), pp. 374, 379.

59 Ibid., p. 236.

matter of supply was, from the start, intertwined with religion and, in the summer of 1625, religion was inseparable from what some interpreted as a tangible manifestation of God's displeasure: plague. The worst outbreak of plague yet witnessed in the seventeenth century descended on London as Members gathered there in May.[60] The opening of parliament was then delayed for a month while Charles awaited the final component of the Anglo-French marriage treaty: the arrival in England of Henrietta Maria. Rumours of religious concessions – spawned by the delayed arrival of a Catholic queen replete with 28 priests and the 'scandal' of English ships at La Rochelle – and fears of foreign invasion, mingled with fear of the plague to create an extraordinarily tense atmosphere.[61] In these circumstances the thoughts of many in the Commons turned to religion. One member warned of tolerating recusants, declaring that there was 'more cause to fear the plague of our souls, than our bodies.'[62] Another, John Pym, availed of the heightened religious sensitivity to return to an issue which had provoked outrage in the 1624 parliament. The controversial writings of Richard Montagu – most notably his *A Gagg for the New Gospell? No: a New Gagg for an Old Goose* – had been severely criticised for what many members saw as Montagu's attack on the Calvinist doctrine of predestination and his leniency toward certain forms of Catholic worship. Montagu had made it clear that the purpose of his writings was to defend the Church of England against enemies on both sides: 'to stand in the gap against Puritanism and Popery, the Scilla and Charbodis of ancient piety'. But in the nervous atmosphere of 1625 Pym argued that Montagu's writings 'tended to the disturbance of church and state'. That Montagu was supported by a cadre of theologians, including William Laud, bishop of St David's, who sought to restore reverence and decorum to the Church of England, branded him an 'Arminian'.[63] In his defence, Montagu wrote that he had been accused of being a Papist and an Arminian, but that he 'flatly defied and opposed the One; and God in Heaven knoweth that [he] never so much as yet read word in the other'.[64] Unconvinced, the Commons intended to make an example of

60   P. Slack, *The Impact of plague in Tudor and Stuart England* (Oxford, 1990), pp. 216–17, 237; P. Clark and P. Slack, *English towns in transition, 1500–1700* (Oxford, 1976), p. 89.

61   Russell, *Parliaments and English politics*, pp. 211–16.

62   Russell, *Parliaments and English politics*, pp. 229–30.

63   An 'Arminian' was, literally, a follower of the Dutch theologian Jacobus Arminius, but more practically the term is used to describe anti-Calvinist bishops and clergy who stressed the role of free will in achieving salvation.

64   *Oxford DNB*, *s.v.* Richard Mountague (quotations); *s.v.* Durham House Group. Cf. N. Tyacke, *Anti-Calvinists: the rise of English Arminianism, c.1590–1640* (Oxford, 1987).

Montagu and had him taken into custody; but in early July the king unexpectedly interceded on Montagu's behalf, appointing him a royal chaplain-
in-ordinary. Having thus extended royal protection to Montagu, Charles
abruptly commanded the Commons to drop the matter and, shortly thereafter, adjourned parliament to Oxford. But the second session produced no
further grant of supply and Charles had no recourse but to dissolve his first
parliament having been voted just two subsidies.[65]

Finance and religion, the two most intractable issues of the 1625 parliament, were to dominate the early years of Charles's reign. The crown's par-
simony and reliance on parliament to share the costs of war was nothing
new of course. Nor were doctrinal differences and ambiguities within the
Church of England a recent phenomenon. War, however, had magnified the
importance of these issues and lent them a sense of urgency which they
lacked hitherto. The scale and complexity of the war which Charles and
Buckingham had entered into, moreover, was unlike any previously experienced. In Elizabeth's reign, Spain's attempted invasion of south-east England
and intervention in Ireland had aligned the kingdom firmly behind the
crown's 'blue water' naval campaign against an expansionist Catholic empire.
After 1625, however, the identity of the enemy was less clear and the task of
motivating a population, which had known peace for a generation, to fight
and finance an offensive land war was more difficult.

Thus, in an attempt to garner immediate popular and parliamentary
support for war, Buckingham organised a naval assault against the Spanish
treasure fleet in autumn 1625. The expedition, however – a ham-handed
attempt to recreate Ralegh's celebrated attack on Cadiz – was a complete
failure, resulting in the loss of nearly half the English fleet. It was a clear
demonstration that England's war effort was crippled without greater support from parliament. In dire financial straits the king, already reduced to
collecting tonnage and poundage without parliamentary consent, was again
forced to seek supply from parliament. When, in early 1626, parliament
assembled Coke, now secretary of state, revealed that Charles's commitments
arising from the war amounted to over £1,000,000. But the Commons was
unmoved by the crown's financial predicament and made the grant of subsidies conditional upon the redress of grievances.[66] Chief among these grievances was Buckingham. As lord admiral – and the king's widely-resented
favourite – the duke bore the blame for the débâcle at Cadiz and endured

65 Russell, *Parliaments and English politics*, pp. 238–59.
66 Russell, *Parliaments and English politics*, pp. 260–70.

blistering attacks on his conduct. The king, however, made no distinction between criticism of Buckingham and criticism of himself and, by association, of his father. Charles warned the Commons: 'Remember that Parliaments are altogether in my power for the calling, sitting and continuance of them, therefore as I find the fruits of them either good or evil, they are to continue or not to be.'[67] Yet the assault on the duke only intensified. Sir John Eliot spearheaded the attack. He railed against Buckingham's 'excesses' and asked:

> [W]hat are they but the visible evidences of an express exhausting of the state, a chronicle of the immensity of his waste of the revenues of the crown! No wonder, then, our king is now in want, this man abounding so. And as long as he abounds the king must still be wanting.

Eliot then went so far as to compare the duke with Sejanus – the infamous favourite of the Roman tyrant Tiberius – and asked rhetorically: '[D]oes not this kingdom, does not Scotland, does not Ireland speak it?' In May the Commons voted articles for Buckingham's impeachment.[68] When after a month it became apparent that no supply could be obtained without sacrificing his favourite, Charles angrily dissolved his second parliament and took the leading role in persuading his privy council to seek a compulsory, or forced, loan from the English and Welsh counties on the grounds that 'the emergency cannot endure so long a time as the calling of a parliament'.[69]

Simmering religious tension had exacerbated the crown's difficulties in the 1626 parliament. Montagu's case had shown that the issue of Arminianism divided the court and the bench of bishops, and pointed to a worrying doctrinal split within the Church of England.[70] The extension of royal protection to Montagu was, for Arminians, a signal that the king was sympathetic to their anti-Calvinist stance. Buckingham's failure to condemn Arminianism after presiding over a religious conference held at his London residence in February, moreover, was proof enough for Calvinists of the duke's Arminian leanings.[71] Coinciding as it did with the opening of parliament this conference was conducted at a most inauspicious time. For in addition to the plethora of charges levelled against Buckingham in parliament was added the ire of devout Calvinists, one of whom accused the duke

---

67 Russell, *Parliaments and English politics*, p. 292 (quotation).
68 Gardiner, *History of England*, ii, pp. 53–5 (quotations); Smith, *A history of the modern British Isles*, p. 70.
69 R. Cust, 'Charles I, the privy council, and the forced loan', *Journal of British Studies*, xxiv (1985), pp. 208–33 (quotation, p. 219); Russell, *Parliaments and English politics*, p. 301.
70 Russell, *Parliaments and English politics*, p. 232.
71 Lockyer, *Buckingham*, pp. 306–7.

of being 'the principal patron and supporter of a semi-pelagian, semi-popish faction, dangerous to the church and state, lately set on foot among us'.[72] Religious tension of a different sort, meanwhile, threatened to undermine the crown's alliance with France. Charles's decision to honour his promise to the 1625 parliament and enforce penal laws against Catholics was in breach of the Anglo-French marriage treaty. Thereafter, diplomatic relations with the French steadily deteriorated. Buckingham, moreover, correctly identified the queen's household as being in league with many of his opponents in parliament and sought to infiltrate this single faction at court outside his control. The independence of Henrietta Maria's swollen household, however, which the French intended to establish as a Catholic oasis at the heart of Protestant Britain, was protected under the marriage treaty and was intertwined with the matter of religion.[73] Charles was thus made to choose between his favourite and his wife. The king chose the former, to the cost of his marriage and the Anglo-French alliance, and in August 1626 expelled most of the queen's entourage from Britain. The diplomatic breakdown with France was complete: France had, in the spring, made peace with Spain, and Charles espoused the cause of international Protestantism and prepared for war with two great powers.[74]

By summer 1627 the forced loan had brought in £264,000, the equivalent of nearly five parliamentary subsidies. This money allowed the crown to sustain the war at a time when Catholic forces were threatening to overrun Protestant-held territories on the continent. It also provided the financial basis for a major naval expedition to relieve the Huguenots in July. The expedition, however, an amphibious assault (led personally by Buckingham) on Île de Rhé off La Rochelle, was a dismal failure, one which was compounded over the following 15 months as men, money and resources were poured into La Rochelle in an ultimately futile attempt to sustain Huguenot resistance. The loan, moreover, bred widespread resentment and placed unprecedented strain on county communities already burdened with high taxation.[75]

It was to the institution of lieutenancy – and to the deputy lieutenants in particular – that the crown looked both to supervise the machinery for collecting the forced loan and to provide the troops for its overseas war.

---

72 Russell, *Parliaments and English politics*, p. 298.
73 Russell, *Parliaments and English politics*, pp. 263–7.
74 Lockyer, *Buckingham*, pp. 293–6, 334–8.
75 Cf. R.W. Stewart, 'Arms and expeditions: the ordnance office and the assaults on Cadiz (1625) and the Isle of Rhé (1627)', in M.C. Fissel (ed.) *War and government in Britain, 1598–1650* (Manchester, 1991), pp. 112–32.

[3 1 4]   Collecting the unpopular loan was a precarious undertaking for the eight to
ten deputy lieutenants per county whose authority rested on their popularity
and reputation in the localities. Opposition to the loan steadily increased –
especially in light of the refusal of the royal judges to give an unqualified
sanction to its legality – and dozens of prominent leaders of county society
were imprisoned for non-payment and obstructing collection.[76] The deputies
were thus placed in the difficult position of having to choose between
loyalty to king and loyalty to community. Under pressure from above, most
deputy lieutenants supervised the loan's collection, though some – notably
Thomas Wentworth in Yorkshire and John Hampden in Buckinghamshire –
were imprisoned for their refusal to do so. Yet, while the loan would have
long-term constitutional implications, it was an immediate fiscal success.
This was due in no small part to the central government's continued ability
to exercise authority in the shires through the institution of the lieutenancy.
Indeed, so important was the lieutenancy to the crown that recalcitrant
deputies, like Wentworth and Hampden, were continued in office during
their imprisonment.[77]

It was the concurrent burden of an offensive war, however, which tested
the lieutenancy as it had not been subsequent to assuming its final form in
Elizabeth's reign. Since late 1624, when 14,000 troops were demanded for
Mansfeld's expedition, the lieutenants had raised and billeted soldiers,
secured their coat and conduct money, outfitted the levies and conveyed
them to their port of departure. Initially, the 'soldiers' raised were in fact men
pressed into service and, as in Elizabeth's time, were drawn from the lower
ranks of society. The available number of vagrants, unemployed labourers
and marginal cottagers, however, was soon exhausted and constables were
forced to undertake the more difficult assignment of seeking out 'able bodied
men fit for the wars' among those substantial householders who were not
already enrolled in the trained bands. In the absence of regular funding from
the government, moreover, deputy lieutenants had no recourse other than to
raise coat and conduct money in the localities and billet soldiers in private
households. As Professor Barnes has written, these expedients led to abuses
and corruption: 'pressed men buying exemption from service, abusive pressing by officers for the purposes of extortion or to settle personal and political
scores, exorbitant levying of coat and conduct money, heavy-handed and
even illegal suppression of resistance to levying men and money, embezzle-

76   M. Kishlansky, *A monarchy transformed: Britain, 1603–1714* (London, 1996), p. 109.
77   Russell, *Parliaments and English politics*, pp. 76, 333.

ment of money and equipment, and some plain brutality'.[78] And as the war [3 1 5]
dragged on – and produced a succession of military failures – the task of
receiving, billeting and preserving order among a steady stream of demoralised, ill-disciplined and defeated soldiers also fell to the lieutenancy.
Geared principally toward defence – and accustomed to providing much
smaller numbers of troops mainly for service in Ireland – the lieutenancy
was, without greater financial support from the crown, unequal to these
multifarious tasks: it remained an amateur and unpaid instrument of central
authority in the shires, which could neither produce the number nor the
calibre of soldiers required to wage a successful war against professional
continental armies. The combined burden of collecting the forced loan and
supervising the war effort had brought the institution of lieutenancy into
disrepute and thereby strained this vital link between central and local
government to breaking point. On a deeper level, however, the difficulties
experienced by the lieutenancy in these years are symptomatic of the early
modern British state's continued reliance upon local cooperation in the
absence of a more developed centralised bureaucracy and a standing army.[79]

Charles I's interventions in Ireland and Scotland: a pattern established

With the English kingdom and its traditional forms of government buckling
under the weight of war, it is significant that the king did not receive greater
assistance from his other kingdoms. Charles had in fact, from the outset of
his reign, sought to elicit financial and military assistance from Ireland and
Scotland, but longstanding religious and cultural divisions in the former and
underdeveloped political structures in the latter conspired to undermine the
king's efforts to distribute the burdens of war more evenly among his three
kingdoms. Where the unprecedented demands of an offensive war had
shown government in England to be antiquated, they were to reveal government in Ireland and Scotland to be anachronistic.

More than two decades after the completion of the Tudor conquest,
Ireland remained the least stable of the Stuart kingdoms. The Jacobean

---

78 T.G. Barnes, 'Deputies not principals, lieutenants not captains: the institutional failure of
lieutenancy in the 1620s', in *War and government in Britain*, pp. 58–83 (quotations, p. 61).
79 V. Stater, 'War and the structure of politics: lieutenancy and the campaign of 1628', in *War
and government in Britain*, pp. 87–9.

policy of plantation had settled thousands of British colonists in formerly contumacious Gaelic areas – most extensively in Ulster and Munster – greatly strengthening both royal government in Ireland and the Protestant New English community which had come to dominate the Irish administration. But Ireland's army of nearly 4,000 men – the only standing army in the British Isles – belied its peaceful façade. Ireland's defeated Gaelic community did not simply disappear, nor was a substantial proportion of it assimilated into the new social and political order. Rather the majority of the Gaelic community remained as disadvantaged under-tenants whose numerical superiority and close links with Catholic Europe fuelled Protestant fears of rebellion. The rapid increase in British political power and influence, moreover, had come at the expense of the steadfastly loyal Old English community and plans for further plantation mooted by land-hungry British servitors threatened to alienate this still powerful and wealthy political grouping. Unlike their politically inarticulate Gaelic coreligionists, however, the Old English were intimately familiar with English law and government. In 1613 they had mounted an effective defence of their position in the Irish parliament, resulting in the government's withdrawal of anti-Catholic bills and the reduction of the British majority in the Commons – a majority gained through the king's constitution of dozens of borough seats in planted areas. But successful Old English opposition in the Irish parliament offered only temporary respite: the British parliamentary majority was permanent and the crown, which continued to regard the Old English as but 'half-subjects' by virtue of their commitment to Catholicism, was prepared to countenance radical suggestions, emerging from the Irish administration and involving leading English and Scottish courtiers, that the policy of plantation be extended to any area where crown title to land was discovered. The onset of war in 1625, however, provided the Old English with an opportunity to offer Charles something which advocates of potentially disruptive plantation schemes could not: the immediate promise of money.[80] The king's desperate need for money thus led him to effect an immediate change in Irish policy and to offer Catholics in Ireland the chance to demonstrate through their actions what Gaelic poets and Old English clerics, such as Peter Lombard, the primate of Ireland, had already worked out ideologically: that separate religious and secular loyalties posed no threat to the crown.[81]

---

80 Canny, *Reformation to restoration*, pp. 184–5; idem, *Making Ireland British*, pp. 261–6.
81 A. Ford, '"Firm Catholics" or "loyal subjects"? Religious and political allegiance in early seventeenth-century Ireland', in D.G. Boyce (ed.) *Political discourse in seventeenth and eighteenth-century Ireland* (Basingstoke, 2001), p. 13.

Discussions in England between the Old English representative, the [3 1 7]
Pale landowner, Sir John Bath, and a high-ranking member of the English
government produced in late 1625 a new framework for the crown's Irish
policy. Bath proposed that were the oath of supremacy, which prohibited
Catholics from holding official positions and inheriting estates, to be
replaced by an oath 'touching their temporal subjection and obedience
only', then Old English leaders might assume greater military responsibility
in Ireland, so helping to make the kingdom secure both from invasion and
from 'the tumults of the malcontent mere Irish'. A central feature of this
military responsibility, Bath acknowledged, would be for Irish landowners
to adopt English military practice by replacing the feudal custom of 'risings
out' with English-style trained bands. It was also understood that the Old
English would make an unspecified monetary contribution to offset the
costs of the standing army. Eager to secure Ireland from internal and external
threats at such small cost, the English privy council agreed in principle to
show favour 'to the Irish of English race' and to begin the military experiment in the Pale.[82] The failure of the Cadiz expedition, and the landing on
Ireland's southern and western shores of more than 1,000 of its survivors –
'fleet soldiers' as they were called – made the king's financial and military
needs more acute and thus strengthened the hand of the Old English. In
October, Lord Deputy Falkland was instructed to discontinue the enforcement of recusancy fines and, the following month, an assembly of mostly
Old English peers and Palesmen reported that the Pale could muster 3,000
men to be organised in trained bands. The Pale, moreover, granted a
IR£3,000 benevolence to the king, giving rise to suggestions that similar
contributions be made throughout Ireland.[83]

Yet Falkland and the Irish administration were not prepared to hand
Old English Catholics the political advantage implicit in the trained bands
scheme 'for thereby we should have put arms into their hands of whose
hearts we rest not well assured'.[84] Denied British support, the scheme to
introduce trained bands proved unworkable and was abandoned. The alternative to organising non-professional forces to support the army was to
enlarge the standing army, but Old English and British alike baulked at the
king's suggestion that they should pay for the projected military increase.

82   A. Clarke, *The Old English in Ireland, 1625–42* (Dublin, 2000), pp. 28–34 (quotations, pp. 32–3).

83   A. Clarke, 'The army and politics in Ireland, 1625–30', in *Studia Hibernica*, iv (1964), pp. 34–6.

84   Ibid., p. 37.

The billeting on the population of 'fleet soldiers' and a force of some 2,200 largely Catholic volunteers – organised to reinforce Buckingham's expedition to Rhé – had already prompted widespread complaints that to quarter, or 'cess', troops in private households outside Ulster contravened a long-standing agreement with the crown.[85] At a time when he faced war with France as well as Spain, Charles could not allow the impasse over Ireland's defence to continue indefinitely and summoned representatives from the Old English and British communities to England for negotiations.

Concluded in May 1628, the negotiations produced an elaborate compromise: the king promised his Irish subjects a series of concessions – known as the Graces – in return for their undertaking to make a substantial contribution toward the upkeep of the army, which was to be placed in garrison, and to pay an immediate subsidy of £40,000 and further subsidies amounting to £80,000 over the next two years. The Graces, which were to receive statutory authority in the next Irish parliament, addressed a wide range of grievances across Ireland's communal divide. On balance, however, the Old English had negotiated a deal better suited to their long-term interests. For the Graces promised to introduce legislation whereby the king would renounce all royal claims to land held by undisputed title for 60 years; separate legislation, meanwhile, was promised for Connaught, where comparatively recent landowners – many of whom were Gaelic proprietors who had either defaulted on loans, or owed substantial sums, to Old English creditors – would be guaranteed security of tenure. Though the British were assured that full toleration of Catholics would not be granted, the Graces did promise to abolish the oath of supremacy as a prerequisite for heirs taking formal possession of estates and to replace it with an oath of allegiance, not unlike Bath's earlier suggestion.[86] Thus, by making what was a modest financial contribution to the king's floundering war effort, it appeared that the Old English had outmanoeuvred the British interest and achieved in the Graces both security of their title to lands in perpetuity and *de facto* toleration for Catholicism.

The Old English had been assured that the Irish parliament would convene in November 1628, so as to ratify the Graces; but when, in the previous summer, Falkland had issued writs for parliamentary elections he did so in

85 Treadwell, *Buckingham and Ireland*, p. 282; Clarke, 'The army and politics in Ireland', pp. 42–4; idem, *Old English in Ireland*, p. 37.
86 Clarke, *The Old English in Ireland*, pp. 46–59; idem, 'The army and politics in Ireland', pp. 44–7; Canny, *Reformation to restoration*, pp. 186–7; idem, *Making Ireland British*, p. 265.

contravention of Poynings's law – which stated that an Irish parliament could not be summoned until all projected legislative measures had been approved by the English privy council. The English judges ordered that the lengthy process be repeated from the beginning in accordance with Poynings's law. By then, however, the circumstances that had precipitated the Graces had changed. The war was drawing to a close and, no longer beholden to Old English financial and military support, Charles neglected to initiate the process which would give statutory authority to his Graces. A combination of New English pressure and the death of Falkland's patron (Buckingham), moreover, had led in 1629 to the deputy's recall and the formation of an interim government dominated by the New English interest and bent on undermining the Old English position. The Old English felt that they had been betrayed and pressured Charles to honour his Graces. The king eventually responded in 1632 by appointing a new deputy whom both communities hoped would uphold their interests.[87]

A less likely target for Spanish invasion, and possessed of a more uniform polity, Charles expected his Scottish kingdom to contribute to the war effort as well. James's long and peaceful reign had introduced an unprecedented level of political stability to Scotland. The benefits of more settled conditions were particularly evident in the Lowlands where favourable weather conditions and general economic prosperity had prompted a marked increase in population. Two decades of regal union, moreover, had done much to curb lawlessness in the once dangerous border shires. Cattle from Galloway and linen from Glasgow could now safely travel overland to the lucrative London market and the production of wool in the southern shires steadily increased.[88] The benefits of political stability were less obvious in the Highlands, but the success of the Ulster plantation had ended the centuries-old relationship between Gaelic Scotland and Ireland, whereby the former provided thousands of mercenaries for the escalating wars of autonomous Irish chiefs. The colonisation of Ulster with preponderantly Lowland Scots had created a ready market for Scottish goods and ensured that future Scottish migration to Ireland would be driven by economic rather than military expedients.[89]

87   Clarke, *The Old English in Ireland*, pp. 54–74; Canny, *Reformation to restoration*, p. 187.
88   T.C. Smout, *A history of the Scottish people, 1560–1830* (London, 1985), pp. 101–4.
89   A.I. Macinnes, *Charles I and the making of the covenanting movement, 1625–41* (Edinburgh, 1991), p. 32. Cf. M. Perceval-Maxwell, *The Scottish migration to Ulster in the reign of James I* (London, 1973).

Yet, for all the political and economic improvements wrought during James's reign, Scotland remained a highly decentralised kingdom whose disparity in wealth with England was everywhere apparent. By 1625 the king could appoint a mere eight sheriffs in his northern kingdom. Heritable jurisdictions thus continued to predominate in regional and local government to the exclusion of royal authority. Scotland's essentially feudal system of landholding, moreover, survived largely untouched into the new reign.[90] Nowhere was the economic difference between the British kingdoms more evident than in government expenditure: in the financial year 1624 the Scottish administration's total expenditure was approximately £13,000; annual English expenditure, meanwhile, had exceeded £1,000,000 by the end of James's reign.[91] Charles thus inherited in Scotland a relatively poor kingdom with an underdeveloped central administration, which was incapable of shouldering the burden of war in any substantive way.

Charles, however, was unprepared to accept such obstructions to his royal authority (and, by extension, to his foreign policy) in his native kingdom. In late 1625 he summoned a convention of estates – an attenuated parliament with the right to tax – where his need for financial support, not only to run the Scottish administration but 'likewise such designs as we have in hand both at home and abroad for the weal of our kingdoms' was made clear. The king offered to forego taxation if the expenses of his Scottish coronation were met and 2,000 troops were raised and supplied to defend against invasion. The Scottish estates chose the former alternative and, in marked contrast to his first English parliament, quietly voted the king £50,000 over the next four years.[92] The introduction of trained bands to Scotland was authorised by the king early the following year with a view to creating an inexpensive standing army, but any immediate hopes of the scheme coming to fruition were dashed when, in March 1627, the proposed muster master Alexander Lindsay, Lord Spynie, received a royal commission to raise 3,000 soldiers to aid Charles's ally the king of Denmark. It subsequently proved impossible for the crown to levy the additional taxes necessary to support a standing army without greater cooperation in the localities and the scheme was temporarily abandoned.[93]

90 Brown, *Kingdom or province*, p. 103; A.I. Macinnes, *The British revolution, 1629–1660* (London, 2005), pp. 86–7.
91 Macinnes, *Charles I and the making of the covenanting movement*, p. 41.
92 Ibid., p. 43 (quotation).
93 Ibid., p. 141; *Oxford DNB, s.v.* Alexander Lindsay.

Charles, meanwhile, was biding his time until the convention was dissolved, and its financial contribution toward the war assured, to unveil his plans for a royal revocation. It was not uncommon for Scottish monarchs to revoke all crown gifts made during their minority – the most recent example was James's 1587 revocation. Charles, however, had no minority and the final form of the revocation was unprecedented in its complexity, scope and ambition: a general revocation of all crown grants of royal and secularised kirk property with a retrospective timeframe stretching back, in most instances, to 1455. The proclaimed intention of the revocation scheme was to abolish the worst aspects of Scotland's feudal system of landholding – in particular the liberation of heritors, or gentry, from dependence on the nobles – and to provide income for the kirk through the crown's redistribution of land and landed revenue. But the crown's unilateral actions raised constitutional apprehensions and, of more immediate concern to most, undermined the security of titles to land. The revocation prompted broad-based opposition from across the Scottish political nation against what was perceived to be a brazen effort on the part of the crown to restructure Scottish society, so as to extract more revenue. The refusal of the nobility and landowners to surrender their estates and the crown's manifest inability to enforce the terms of its revocation in the localities led, by 1630, to the scheme's effective abandonment.[94]

That Charles was prepared to implement the revocation scheme against the protests of the political nation and the advice of his Scottish privy councillors – many of whom he replaced in the late 1620s and early 1630s as part of a deliberate policy of restructuring Scottish government and sub-ordinating Scottish officials to court-based officials – and without consulting the Scottish parliament reveals much about the king's personality and his attitude toward his northern kingdom.[95] Between 1628 and 1633 Charles relied on the earl of Mentieth, lord president of the Scottish privy council, who divided his time between Edinburgh and London, to keep him abreast of developments in Scotland.[96] A Scottish king had not seen Scotland since 1617 and it was not until 1633 that Charles returned to the kingdom of his birth to convene parliament and to be crowned. But here too the king showed himself to be oblivious to Scottish sensitivities: parliament was forced to give statutory authority to the revocation scheme, the Act of

94 Macinnes, *Charles I and the making of the covenanting movement*, pp. 49–72; Brown, *Kingdom or province*, pp. 101–4; Smith, *A history of the modern British Isles*, p. 101.
95 Macinnes, *Charles I and the making of the covenanting movement*, pp. 50–1.
96 Ibid., pp. 82–6.

Revocation as it became known, and the coronation ceremony, held in the abbey kirk of Holyrood, rather than the traditional venues of Scone or Stirling, was borrowed almost entirely from the English ceremony. The occasion, moreover, saw Charles crowned before an ornate crucifix woven into a splendid tapestry, which to most Scots was not only alien, but also, as John Spalding commented, 'bred great fear of inbringing of popery'.[97] The crown's estrangement from the Scottish political nation mirrored the latter's diminishing confidence in absentee kingship. These twin phenomena had become apparent in the later years of James's reign; but it was Charles's efforts to effect sweeping changes from above before even setting foot in Scotland which created an atmosphere of distrust. That such radical change was attempted at a time when deteriorating weather conditions caused food production to falter and the demands of war meant higher taxation, the impressment of soldiers and a disruption in international trade, turned distrust into outright defiance of royal authority.

Yet there was more to Charles's experience in Scotland than the actions of an absentee king woefully out of touch with the will of his subjects. His seemingly arbitrary exercise of the royal prerogative fits a pattern of a king experimenting with authoritarian measures in the face of unprecedented financial and military pressures arising from war. Similar experimentations can be seen in Ireland with the promise of the Graces and in England with the billeting of troops in private households and the levying of the forced loan. But for all Charles's experimentation, it was clear that the English parliament remained the only institution in the three kingdoms capable of financing the war and, as was made clear in his opening speech to his next parliament, the king preferred to obtain supply in the traditional manner: '[T]his way of Parliament', he declared, 'is the most ancient way and the way I like best'.[98] Yet it was also in the English parliament where opposition to Charles's authoritarian style of government was most effective. Ironically it was to be Charles's repeated recourse to parliament and the continued success of English parliamentary opposition to royal authority that conspired to move the king to abandon the institution of parliament in England and to rely on the royal prerogative to rule his three kingdoms.[99]

97 J. Morrill, 'The National Covenant in its British context', in J. Morrill (ed.) *The Scottish National Covenant in its British context, 1638–51* (Edinburgh, 1990), p. 3 (quotation); Smith, *A history of the modern British Isles*, p. 101.
98 R. Lockyer, *Tudor and Stuart Britain*, p. 303 (quotation).
99 Macinnes, *The British revolution*, pp. 74–5.

English constitutional opposition

The continuation of war into 1628 left Charles with a stark choice: to call another English parliament, so as to obtain supply, or to withdraw immediately from the war. Convinced that to follow the latter course would be to sunder his martial reputation and to besmirch his honour, the king convened his third parliament. However, the goodwill which the crown had hoped to create through the timely release of the more than 70 gentlemen imprisoned for their refusal to pay the forced loan was lost when it was alleged (falsely) that Sir Robert Heath, the attorney general, had under instruction from Charles doctored judicial records to show that five of the imprisoned gentlemen – the so-called Five Knights who, in late 1627, had attempted to sue *habeas corpus* – had received judgment against them when in fact judgment in their case had been postponed pending a further hearing.[100] Thus when, in March 1628, Members assembled they did so amid mounting fears that in prosecuting the war the crown had violated fundamental English liberties. Extra-parliamentary taxation, the billeting of soldiers on civilians, the imposition of martial law and arbitrary imprisonment emerged as the four principal concerns – the 'murdering grievances' as Phelips called them – and the Commons resolved, with a unity of purpose unknown in recent sittings, that no subsidies should be voted until these liberties were confirmed. A measure of the mistrust which the crown's actions had engendered in the political nation was the Commons' decision to frame the four grievances in an unambiguous legal document – a Petition of Right – and to seek, with the Lords' support, the king's assurances that the Petition would receive the full force of law. In return, the Commons offered five subsidies. Charles interpreted the Petition – particularly its denial of a king's right to imprison on command – as an assault upon his royal prerogative, and responded with an equivocal answer that in no way diminished his powers. The Commons would vote no subsidies in return for such an answer. In desperate need of money to resupply his troops at La Rochelle, the king reluctantly accepted the Petition of Right in early June, but ordered that his first answer be printed

---

100 It has been shown that Heath did not tamper with records of the court: M. Kishlansky, 'Tyranny denied: Charles I, attorney general Heath, and the Five Knights' Case' in *Historical Journal*, 42 (1999), pp. 53–83. For the old view, see J. Guy, 'The origins of the petition of right reconsidered', in *Historical Journal*, 25 (1982), pp. 289–312.

alongside it.[101] The king now saw no reason why parliamentary business should not proceed smoothly and warned: 'I have done my part, wherefore if this Parliament have not a happy conclusion the sin is yours: I am free of it.'[102] But the Commons presented the king with a remonstrance, which named Buckingham as 'the principal cause' of the 'evils and dangers' confronting the kingdom. That the Commons had passed the subsidy bill concurrent to the preparation of the remonstrance did little to assuage Charles's anger. He interpreted the remonstrance as an attack on both his friend and his right to appoint ministers.[103] Facing a second remonstrance reproaching him for collecting tonnage and poundage 'contrary to Your Majesty's royal answer to their late Petition of Right', Charles prorogued parliament.[104]

The five subsidies voted – anticipated at approximately £276,000 – provided the crown with only a quarter of the money needed to repay existing debts and continue the war.[105] Throughout England, but especially in the south-eastern coastal counties, demoralised and unpaid soldiers menaced county society: whether it was the Irish troops which rioted in Essex, the Scots regiment which ran amok on the Isle of Wight, or simply the Gloucestershire men billeted in Devon, the sheer number of unruly strangers billeted in private households moved many communities to refuse to accept any further troops. The mood in the counties mirrored events in parliament: criticism in the Commons of billeting and the government's failure to pay billeters stiffened resistance to the government in the counties.[106] Charles and Buckingham, however, were content to leave the preservation of domestic order to the already overburdened deputy lieutenants. Their chief concern rested with the launch of another expedition to La Rochelle. Yet this expedition was to be a component of Buckingham's wider initiative to negotiate the war's end. The duke had come to accept that peace was the

---

101   Russell, *Parliaments and English politics*, pp. 323–89. Cf. J. Guy, 'The origins of the Petition of Right reconsidered', in *Historical Journal*, 25, 2 (1982), pp. 289–312; M.B. Young, 'The origins of the Petition of Right reconsidered further' in *Historical Journal*, 27, 2 (1984), pp. 449–52.

102   Smith, *A modern history of the British Isles*, p. 73; Russell, *Parliaments and English politics*, p. 383 (quotation).

103   Russell, *Parliaments and English politics*, pp. 377–85; Sharpe, *The personal rule of Charles I*, p. 41.

104   Gardiner, *History of England*, ii, p. 307 (quotation).

105   Russell, *Parliaments and politics*, pp. 334, 347.

106   Stater, 'War and the structure of politics', pp. 89–97; R. Ashton, *The English Civil War: conservatism and revolution, 1603–1649* (2nd ed. London, 1989), p. 58. Cf. P. Christianson, 'Arguments on billeting and martial law in the parliament of 1628', in *Historical Journal*, 37 (1994), pp. 539–67.

only way to restore the crown's finances; and a final expedition, whether it succeeded or failed, would both fulfil Charles's obligations to the Huguenots and allow him an honourable exit from the war.[107]

In August 1628, the duke travelled to Portsmouth to oversee the fleet's final preparations. Buckingham was aware of his unpopularity and was intimately familiar with the problems caused by demobbed and disgruntled soldiers: his coach had twice been attacked in 1626 by angry sailors; in Februrary 1628 there had been a mutiny in front of his London residence and, as recently as June, a mob had killed his astrologer because of his association with the duke. But Buckingham had reacted to his unpopularity and threats to his person with indignation. It is thus not without a hint of irony that Buckingham was murdered by an embittered and unpaid soldier while preparing a fleet which was to serve as a prelude to peace. His murderer, John Felton, claimed that it was through reading parliament's remonstrance that he decided to 'do his country a great service' and kill the duke.[108] The general public greeted Buckingham's death with satisfaction; many saw heroism in Felton's actions and rejoiced. Charles retreated to his chamber where he grieved alone. Neither Charles nor his subjects had known his kingship without Buckingham's counsels and it remained to be seen whether the king would emerge a different ruler with changed policies.

In the short term, however, some of Charles's privy councillors saw in Buckingham's death an opportunity to rebuild the relationship between crown and subject. In an effort to recreate the success of the 1624 'patriot party', a coalition emerged which sought to give the next session of parliament specific assurances regarding personal liberties and the defence of Calvinism along with a commitment to resume the more popular (and less expensive) 'blue water' policy in return for supply. The political momentum generated by the coalition won over even those councillors wary of summoning another parliament: the earl of Dorset, for instance, now hoped that the next session would become 'a day of jubilee by striking a covenant between sovereign and subject'. Charles, too, was stirred from his torpor by the growing optimism and looked forward to a successful parliament.[109] But

---

107   R. Cust, 'Was there an alternative to the personal rule? Charles I, the privy council and the parliament of 1629', in *History*, 299 (2005), pp. 334–5.

108   Lockyer, *Buckingham*, pp. 342–3, 362, 453–8 (quotation, p. 458); Treadwell, *Buckingham and Ireland*, pp. 294–5.

109   Cust, 'Was there an alternative to the personal rule?', pp. 330–52 (quotaton, p. 340). For what had become the standard interpretation, see Russell, *Parliaments and English politics*, pp. 390–6.

[326] the crown's commitment to the liberties enshrined in the Petition of Right was almost immediately called into question when it emerged that after the prorogation of parliament Charles had had the Petition printed with his original answer. The recent promotion of William Laud, archbishop of Canterbury, and other 'Arminian' bishops, moreover, had betrayed the king's high-church leanings and a Commons subcommittee implored the king to 'confer bishoprics and other ecclesiastical preferments ... upon learned, pious and orthodox men'.[110] For many in parliament, Arminianism was more than a religious matter: it was a conspiracy – a 'Trojan horse ... ready to open the gates, to Romish tyranny and Spanish monarchy' – whose leaders were opposed to parliaments because they feared persecution. In this explosive environment the bill for tonnage and poundage, a matter inseparable from the dispute about the rights of the subject and religion, stood little chance of success and the king adjourned parliament to defuse the crisis. But when the Houses reassembled the tensions that beset the 1629 parliament boiled over: fearing that Charles intended to dissolve or prorogue parliament, John Eliot and several adherents prevented the session from ending by holding the speaker in his chair and locking the chamber's doors until resolutions were passed declaring that supporters of Arminianism and anyone who collected, or paid, tonnage and poundage was an enemy of the 'kingdom and commonwealth'. The attempt to strike a 'covenant between sovereign and subject' had failed: the 1629 parliament was the last English parliament to sit for 11 years.[111]

Authoritarian rule in three kingdoms

The peace treaties concluded with France and Spain in 1629 and 1630 respectively, afforded Charles his first opportunity to rule his three kingdoms without the extraordinary burdens and privations of war. It was Buckingham, rather than the king, moreover, whom public opinion held responsible for the inglorious handling of the war; and it was the duke who took this ignominy with him to the grave. Charles chose no new favourite – a sign

---

110 Smith, *A history of the modern British Isles*, pp. 73–4 (quotation, p. 74).
111 Russell, *Parliaments and English politics*, pp. 401–16 (quotation, p. 407); Reeve, *Charles I and the road to personal rule*, pp. 84–7. Cf. L.S. Popofsky, 'The crisis over tonnage and poundage in parliament in 1629', in *Past & Present*, 126 (1990), pp. 44–75.

widely believed to herald a return to Elizabethan-style politics, where the sovereign mediated the recommendations of carefully balanced factions at court and in council.[112] The king's relationship with his queen was also much improved after Buckingham's demise and in 1630 and 1633 she gave birth to Princes Charles and James. The 1630s augured well and seemed to offer a second beginning to Charles's reign. Indeed, by 1638, the Stuart kingdoms were prosperous and at peace, and the crown was fiscally sound. The ostensible stability of the 1630s, however, disguised mounting disaffection throughout Britain and Ireland caused by the king's vigorous efforts to effect major reforms in the areas of central and local government, royal finance and religion. This is not to imply that Charles sought to unite the institutions of his three kingdoms, rather that his policies in the 1630s reflected a desire to impose order and to assert his authoritarian style of government in each kingdom.[113] Indeed it was the very failure to achieve closer union under James which allowed Charles to manipulate the separate institutions in the three kingdoms in his favour. But shorn of a dominant favourite, of the advice of the English parliament and of the fog of war, it became increasingly clear that it was Charles alone who was the driving force behind royal policy and that the crown's authoritarian policies mirrored his own temperament.

The English privy council lay at the heart of Caroline government in the 1630s. In the years of non-parliamentary rule the importance and efficiency of the council increased dramatically: between 1629 and 1640 it met on more than 1,000 occasions and handled a broad sweep of government business. Standing committees – each charged with advising on a specialist subject, such as trade, foreign policy or Ireland – grew out of the council, and subcommittees were sprung from the former to advise on more specific subjects.[114] Charles showed an interest in the minutiae of government unseen since Henry VII. He was a regular feature at meetings of both the council and the committees and saw the body as the principal means of centralising royal authority. JPs were required to report to the privy council more regularly following the introduction in early 1631 of a new *Book of Orders*, which regulated, *inter alia*, the apprehension of vagrants, the maintenance of highways and poor relief. Similar regulations were issued to JPs in Scotland in 1634, so as to enhance royal authority in the localities. Nobility and gentry,

---

112   Cust, 'Was there an alternative to the personal rule?', p. 336.
113   Smith, *A history of the modern British Isles*, p. 100; *Oxford DNB*, *s.v.* Charles I.
114   Smith, *A history of the modern British Isles*, pp. 86–7; Aylmer, *The king's servants*, pp. 21–2.

moreover, were ordered to remain in the shires where they could attend to the work set out for them by the council. Those who resided in London, and who did not procure a special dispensation from the attorney general, risked a summons before Star Chamber, where the privy council functioned as a law court. Through the council, Charles also sought to overhaul the inadequate trained bands. The military obligations of lords lieutenants and their deputies were more rigidly defined and muster masters were appointed in each county to oversee the creation of a modernised 'exact militia'. The creation of a muster master was first mooted in Scotland when, in 1626, Lord Spynie was appointed royal muster master. In 1634 Charles sought to reactivate Spynie's patent in an effort to extend the 'exact militia' scheme to his northern kingdom.[115]

Within the privy council the king relied on only a handful of trusted and like-minded councillors, most notably Laud, appointed archbishop of Canterbury in 1633, and Lord Treasurer Weston, to advise him on critical matters of state. The emergence of a council within a council was not lost on excluded councillors, one of whom in 1637 bemoaned that public affairs were 'not divulged to us that are of the Common not the Cabinet Council'.[116] In Scotland and Ireland there emerged regional extensions of this 'Cabinet Council'. In the 1630s the Scottish privy council was reduced to little more than a rubber stamp as its English counterpart assumed a greater role in formulating Scottish policy. Charles's appointment in 1632 of Thomas Wentworth as lord deputy of Ireland, meanwhile, marked another extension of the council's authority. A former critic of Buckingham and a keen supporter of the Petition of Right, Wentworth reinvented himself as an unswerving advocate of royal policy and became a rising star of the privy council following his appointment in 1628 as president of the Council of the North. In Ireland, he erected an authoritarian regime, not unlike that which emerged in England, whose central goal was the advancement of crown interests – particularly with regard to finance – irrespective of vested local interests. Indeed a central feature of Wentworth's government was his ability to play on the fear of Ireland's communities of one another. In this way, he prevented the emergence of broad-based opposition to his far-reaching programme of political, financial and ecclesiastical reform, known

---

115 Macinnes, *Charles I and the making of the covenanting movement*, p. 141; idem, *The British revolution*, p. 97; J. Morrill, *Revolt in the provinces: the people of England and the tragedies of war, 1638–1648* (London, 1999), p. 35.

116 Smith, *A history of the British Isles*, pp. 86–8 (quotation, p. 87).

collectively as 'thorough'.[117] Aspects of 'thorough' were anticipated in the revocation scheme in Scotland. The widespread opposition provoked by the revocation – what a contemporary historian called 'the groundstone of all the mischief that followed after' – should have sounded a note of caution; but Charles was as steadfast in his support of Wentworth in Ireland as he was of the continued attempts to implement the revocation scheme in Scotland.[118]

Central to the reform of government was the reform of royal finances. The war years had generated debt of nearly £2,000,000 and Charles worked closely with his council (Weston in particular) to limit expenditure and revive crown finances. Caroline fiscal policy was to exploit crown rights wherever possible: pensions were reduced, fines on recusants were enforced, new monopolies were sold to the highest bidder and – following the introduction in 1635 of a new *Book of Rates* – custom duties were raised. Medieval sources of income were also resurrected: fines were imposed on freeholders, who owned land worth £40 or more and who had not come forward to be knighted at Charles's coronation or at the birth of his children, and on landowners whose estates overlapped medieval boundaries of royal forests and, in 1635, the fourteenth-century levy for naval support paid in emergencies by coastal towns and counties – known as Ship Money – was extended throughout England and Wales. The equivalent of three parliamentary subsidies, Ship Money was the most lucrative of Caroline fiscal expedients and was levied annually between 1635 and 1639.[119] The result of these measures was that by 1637 the crown's annual income was 50 per cent higher than it had been in 1625.

Yet efforts to increase royal revenue were not confined to England and Wales. A central feature of 'thorough' was to render Ireland financially independent of the English exchequer and to seek out additional crown revenues. Wentworth achieved the former by farming the Irish customs, exploiting the court of wards and by imposing unprecedented fiscal burdens on the British community, who, he reasoned, had profited most by the peaceful decades

117   A. Clark, 'The government of Wentworth, 1632–40', in T.W. Moody, F.X. Martin and F.J. Byrne (eds) *A new history of Ireland, vol. iii. Early modern Ireland, 1534–1691* (Oxford, 1976), pp. 243–69; *Oxford DNB, s.v.* Thomas Wentworth; Cf. H. Kearney, *Strafford in Ireland, 1633–41: a study in absolutism* (Manchester, 1959).

118   Macinnes, *The British revolution*, pp. 78–9, 97–8; Brown, *Kingdom or province*, pp. 100–1; Smith, *A history of the modern British Isles*, p. 101 (quotation).

119   Williams, *Renewal and reformation*, pp. 480–1; A. Thrush, 'Naval finance and the origins and development of ship money', in Fissell (ed.) *War and government in Britain*, pp. 133–62. Cf. S.P. Salt, 'Sir Simon D'Ewes and the levying of Ship Money, 1635–1640', in *Historical Journal*, 37 (1994), pp. 253–87.

since the completion of the conquest and were thus the least likely to risk their gains through rebellion. Royal revenues would be augmented primarily through renewed plantation and, in the long-awaited Irish parliament of 1634, Wentworth secured six subsidies before flatly rejecting the Graces. In 1630 the king also launched a scheme for a common fishing in the waters surrounding his kingdoms. His principal intention was to deny foreign fisherman access to the North Sea off Scotland and a confederation of provincial fishing associations drawn from all three kingdoms and regulated by a council of English, Irish and Scottish adventurers was established.[120] English interests dominated the common fishing from the start, however, and it was Scottish as much as foreign fishermen who suffered from the scheme. English interests were placed ahead of Scottish interests throughout the 1630s: customs on bulk exports from Scotland, most notably coal, were doubled in 1634 to make English exports more attractive and in 1636 Scotland's silver coin was devalued twice to arrest the circulation of foreign currency.[121]

For Charles, religious reform was inseparable from the reforms which were pursued in government and finance. The king shared the 'ceremonialist' religious views of Laud – who later wrote that ceremonies were 'the hedge that fence the substance of religion from all the indignities which profaneness and sacrilege too commonly put upon it' – and together they set out to rebuild the power and wealth of the church and clergy. As Laud explained to Charles, 'if it [the church] had more power, the King might have more both obedience and service'.[122] Thus, under the crown's ecclesiastical policy, 'Laudian' bishops came to dominate not only senior church offices, but an ever-increasing number of clergy were appointed to secular offices as well: parish clergy served as JPs, a bishop was appointed Lord Treasurer – the first since the fifteenth century – and Laud himself sat on both the English and Scottish privy councils. Another, more visible, manifestation of the new ecclesiastical policy was the heightened importance attached to ritual and to the sacraments, and hence to the communion table, or 'altar' as it was increasingly called, in public worship. Laud recommended that all altars be situated in the east end of churches, where they should be railed in. Resistance to the 'altar policy' was widespread, but because of regular episcopal visitations and the king's unswerving commitment to the policy,

---

120   Macinnes, *Charles I and the making of the covenanting movement*, pp. 108–13.

121   Idem., *The British revolution*, pp. 105–7.

122   *Oxford DNB*, *s.v.* William Laud.

by 1640 approximately 80 per cent of English parishes had railed-in altars [3 3 1]
standing against the chancel's east wall.[123] In Ireland Wentworth, too,
worked closely with Laud to bring the Church of Ireland into accord with
ecclesiastical reforms in England.[124] Wentworth deployed all the prerogative
institutions at his disposal, including the newly established Court of High
Commission, to enforce ecclesiastical reforms and to reclaim secularised
church property. Church estates reclaimed from Protestant and Catholic
laymen served as a means of enticing English clergy to Ireland – chief among
them was John Bramhall whom Wentworth appointed bishop of Derry and
charged with overseeing the ecclesiastical reforms – and would additionally
provide a solid foundation for future plantations.[125] The authorisation, by
royal prerogative, of liturgical innovations in the form of a Scottish book
of canons (1636) and a Scottish prayer book (1637) was designed to bring
the Scottish kirk into conformity with the other Stuart kingdoms. The
new liturgy, carefully edited by Laud, sought to wean Scots away from the
preaching ministry and to introduce ceremony into reformed Scottish
tradition. It also required that all clergy and laity acknowledge the royal
supremacy in matters ecclesiastical.[126]

The king's authoritarian reforms in state and church produced an
undercurrent of disaffection that belied the calm of England and Wales in
the 1630s. The introduction of a new *Book of Orders*, military reforms and
requirements that nobility and gentry regularly reside in the shires were
widely seen as examples of central (outside) interference in the day-to-day
affairs of the localities. The reforms enjoyed greater success nearer to
London, but by and large all the shires acquiesced in the crown's bid to
centralise royal authority.[127] Caroline fiscal expedients – particularly revived
feudal exactions – provoked deeper resentment and raised uncomfortable
questions regarding the extent of the king's prerogative power. In 1637 John
Hampden, a land-locked Buckinghamshire gentleman, refused to pay Ship
Money and his subsequent trial turned on whether the king could levy what
had become a regular tax without parliamentary consent. By a narrow
majority, the judges ruled in favour of the king's right to levy Ship Money on

123   Smith, *A history of the modern British Isles*, pp. 92–3.
124   N. Tyacke, *Anti-Calvinists: the rise of English Arminianism, c.1590–1640* (Oxford, 1987),
      pp. 181–244.
125   Canny, *Making Ireland British*, pp. 276–7. Cf. J. McCafferty, 'John Bramhall and the church
      of Ireland in the 1630s', in A. Ford, J. McGuire and K. Milne, *'As by law established': the church
      of Ireland since the reformation* (Dublin, 1995), pp. 100–11.
126   Macinnes, *The British revolution*, pp. 109–12; Brown, *Kingdom or province*, pp. 110–11.
127   Morrill, *Revolt in the provinces*, p. 35.

the grounds that it was a form of conscription rather than a tax. This high-profile case, however, brought the dispute over the royal prerogative into the public domain and divided opinion throughout the kingdom. Laud's radical ecclesiastical reforms – which many believed to be inching the Church of England ever closer to Rome – provoked even more rancorous debate; but public dissent fell silent following a series of high-profile trials in 1637 and 1638 in which critics of Laud were convicted of libel in Star Chamber and then fined, imprisoned and mutilated. Disaffection from the crown's authoritarian policies, however, did not coalesce to form a coherent opposition.[128] In England and Wales, where the institutions of government were most firmly entrenched and ethnic and religious uniformity was greatest, resistance was always unlikely and the reforms introduced in the 1630s were grudgingly accepted.

128   Smith, *A history of the modern British Isles*, pp. 86–98.

11

THE DESTRUCTION AND RESTORATION OF MULTIPLE MONARCHY, 1637–60

Few of the inhabitants of Britain or Ireland could have imagined when, in March 1625, Charles Stuart peacefully succeeded his father, James VI and I, as king of England, Scotland and Ireland that during his reign internal upheaval and bouts of internecine warfare would threaten the very existence of the Stuart monarchy. Still fewer could have conceived that a result of these conflicts would be the king's trial, his public execution and the abolition of royal government, the House of Lords and the Established Church in Britain and Ireland. Indeed, the vast majority of the Stuarts' former subjects, living by late 1651 as citizens of the 'Commonwealth of England, Scotland and Ireland', were scarcely more able to comprehend that the deeply revered and centuries-old institution of the monarchy was in fact no more.

Yet there was precious little time for them to reflect upon the constitutional, institutional and politico-religious revolutions that had occurred over the preceding decade. The unsteady 'Commonwealth' government quickly gave way to a republican regime in which Oliver Cromwell – the providentialist leader of the parliamentarian armies which had steadily triumphed in each of the three kingdoms over forces loyal to the Stuarts – exercised authority from 1653 until his death nearly five years later as 'Lord Protector of England, Scotland and Ireland'. The Cromwellian Protectorate, however, failed to unite a sufficient proportion of the deeply-scarred political nation of England and Wales behind the notion of republican government; Ireland and Scotland, meanwhile, had been bludgeoned into compliance by Cromwell's New Model Army, and continued republican government demanded the military occupation of both. Cromwell's bold reconfiguration of the three former kingdoms into a single polity, led by the godly and governed by a single parliament seated at Westminster, appealed to too narrow a segment of the population; and the existence of a 'lord protector' only served to provide a focal point around which disaffection with the new regime might gather. Thus, when in 1658, Cromwell's less capable son, Richard, succeeded him as head of state, the Protectorate collapsed with startling rapidity, leaving political chaos in its wake. Republican government in Britain and Ireland had proved unworkable and in 1660, riding a wave of nostalgia for the House of Stuart – and the comparatively stable and prosperous decades prior to the 1640s with which it was associated – the English and Scottish parliaments, respectively, restored Charles I's son as king of England and Ireland and king of Scotland without incident.

With the restoration of three independent kingdoms united in the person of Charles II, a more familiar pattern of state formation, which had begun more than two centuries earlier, was resumed in the British Isles. That the restoration of the monarchy was attempted at all following the bloodiest series of wars and the worst social and political unrest that Britain and Ireland had yet known, attests to the solid foundations for government and society laid by the Tudors and early Stuarts. However, it also reveals something of the nature of the conflicts that had erupted in the 1640s. Far from pushing England, Wales, Scotland and Ireland further apart, the war (or wars) of the three kingdoms, as some historians have come to refer to them, and the religious, political and constitutional matrices out of which these wars emerged, conspired to draw each nation more closely together.[1] Indeed this period's most radical and seemingly its most disruptive act – the elimination of the monarchy, which had long served as the central and binding force in government and society in Britain and Ireland – failed to arrest the established process of state formation. Rather the regicide merely caused the redefinition of the relationship between the nations, presenting alternative models for state formation – aspects of which, like the establishment in London of a single parliament for the British Isles, were realised a century and a half later, while others, such as republican government for Britain and Ireland, were unique to the mid-seventeenth century. Thus, while the future form of the religious, political and constitutional relationship within and between England, Scotland and Ireland was uncertain and fiercely contested there was seldom any question as to whether there would (and should) be a relationship between them. With James VI and I's accession in 1603 the notion of any one of these nations establishing a wholly independent political identity outside of a linked polity was unlikely, but by 1660 it was unimaginable.[2]

1   J. Morrill, 'The wars(s) of the three kingdoms', in G. Burgess (ed.) *The new British history: founding a modern state, 1603–1715* (London, 1999), pp. 65–91.

2   J. Morrill, 'The fashioning of Britain', in S.G. Ellis and S. Barber (eds), *Conquest and union: fashioning a British state, 1485–1725* (London, 1995), p. 38.

Challenge to authoritarian rule: the Scottish National Covenant [335]

Reaction in the other Stuart kingdoms to Charles I's authoritarian reforms was far less passive than in England. In Scotland, the crown's attempts in 1634 to relaunch the commissions of the peace with the new *Book of Orders* and to establish a national militia were, like the revocation scheme, soundly defeated. Such authoritarian reforms lived or died depending on the cooperation of nobility and gentry, and in Scotland the crown enjoyed too little support in the localities to see them implemented. But the subordination of the Scottish privy council to its English counterpart and Charles's introduction of economic expedients, which favoured his English kingdom, could not be thwarted so easily. This left many Scots feeling as though their self-determination was being steadily eroded and that the kingdom had been relegated to an English province.[3] It was the public outcry that greeted the introduction of the canons and prayer book, however, which transformed feelings of disaffection into widespread resistance. There were protests and riots across Scotland in summer 1637 and, by November, a committee-based provisional government, later known as the Tables, had been erected in Edinburgh. Royal government in Scotland had collapsed. In February 1638, a cross-section of the Scottish political nation set out their position in a National Covenant, a public band encompassing God, crown and people, 'for the maintenance of religion and the King's Majesty's authority, and for the preservation of the laws and liberties of the kingdom'. Rebellion was not the intention of the opposition's leaders, but because the Covenant placed 'true religion' – Protestantism as defined in the Negative Confession[4] – before the subject's loyalty to the king and entitled God's chosen people (the Scots) to resist the king if he failed to uphold the religion, laws and liberties of the kingdom, their movement was implicitly revolutionary. An evangelical campaign in the localities, moreover, popularised the Covenant among the masses and established it as the touchstone of a crusade to preserve the kirk from popish innovations conceived in London and implemented by its bishops.[5] Charles appointed James, marquis of Hamilton – the pre-eminent courtier of the 1630s and Anglophile heir to

---

3 Brown, *Kingdom or province*, pp. 110–11.
4 The Negative Confession, or King's Confession, was an anti-Roman Catholic document signed in January 1581 by James VI.
5 Macinnes, *Charles I and the making of the covenanting movement*, pp. 155–77 (quotations, pp. 173, 176); Brown, *Kingdom or province*, pp. 112–15; P. Donald, 'The Scottish national covenant and British politics, 1638–1640', in *The Scottish National Covenant in its British context*, pp. 90–105.

Scotland's leading noble family – to negotiate with the Covenanters, so 'to win time', the king claimed, 'until I be ready to suppress them'.[6] Hamilton told the king that 'it shall never be my advice if your Majesty can clearly see how you can effect your end without the hazarding of your three crowns'. Yet, for the king, the Covenant was a direct challenge to his authority and its signatories were rebels. Charles, however, underestimated the strength and cohesion of what had fast become a national movement. Negotiations collapsed when, in late 1638, the General Assembly baldly proclaimed episcopacy abolished in Scotland. Charles intensified his efforts to reduce the Scots, whom he firmly believed had merely been led astray by a small number of radicals, through force.[7]

A contributing factor in the developing crisis was the flight of radical Presbyterian ministers and a growing number of Scottish settlers from Ulster to Lowland Scotland. Wentworth's far-reaching reforms had alienated all sections of Irish society from the government, but it was the Scottish settlers who had imported covert praying societies, known as conventicles, and religious revivalism to Ulster in the 1620s that found the deputy's ecclesiastical reforms and his intolerance of nonconforming Presbyterianism unbearable. The arrival in Scotland of religious refugees coincided with the introduction of the crown's liturgical innovations and stiffened their kinsmen's resistance to the canons and prayer book.[8] Concerned that the Covenanting movement might spread to Ulster, and at the instigation of the majority of Scottish settlers who wished to demonstrate their loyalty, Wentworth required in May 1639 that all Scots in Ulster swear an oath that they would remain loyal to the king and not enter into contrary 'oaths, covenants and bonds'. Most swore the 'black oath', as the Scots remembered it, but others fled to Scotland to avoid its application.[9]

For Wentworth, his ability to administer the 'black oath' and his success in preventing the Covenanting movement from spreading to Ireland were demonstrations of the power that he had built up in the kingdom since 1632. Though disaffection from the government surmounted Ireland's religious and ethnic divisions, so long as Wentworth's enemies remained disunited

6   Smith, *A history of the modern British Isles*, p. 110 (quotation).
7   J. Scally, 'Counsel in crisis: James, third marquis of Hamilton and the Bishops' Wars, 1638–1640' in J.R. Young (ed.) *Celtic dimensions of the British civil wars* (Edinburgh, 1997), pp. 18–34 (quotation, p. 22).
8   Macinnes, *Charles I and the making of the covenanting movement*, pp. 155–7.
9   Clarke, 'The government of Wentworth', *NHI*, iii, p. 268 (quotation).

and the king remained supportive, the deputy was invincible. Wentworth's abilities were not lost on Charles who had ordered his deputy to mobilise troops in Ireland for use against the Scots. The Irish army, commanded by Randal MacDonnell, the Catholic earl of Antrim, whose influence straddled east Ulster and the western highlands and isles, would attack Scotland from the west, while another army, led by Hamilton, would land in the royalist north-east; a large English army would form the crucial third prong to the attack and invade from the south. The king thus intended to deploy the resources of his three kingdoms to crush the Covenanters.[10] Charles, however, encountered difficulties in raising an English army. Several critics of the king's authoritarian rule had established secret contacts with the Covenanters. It was observed, moreover, that 'the people through[out] all England are generally so discontented . . . I think there is reason to fear that a great part of them will be readier to join with the Scots than to draw their swords in the King's service'.[11] That the king raised his army from the militias and without parliamentary subsidies compounded his difficulties. The English conscripts that confronted the Covenanters outside Berwick were poorly trained, inadequately funded and wholly insufficient to engage in battle; the Irish army, meanwhile, had failed to materialise and Hamilton's amphibious landing in the highlands had proved ineffective. Fortunately for Charles, the nobility present on both sides sought compromise and a fragile truce was brokered at Berwick in June 1639 before the royal army could be tested. But the First Bishops' War, as it was called, had exposed the crown's weaknesses and its inability to mobilise effectively the military resources of the three kingdoms. The following month Wentworth assured his master that:

if the distempers of Scotland had either continued, or shall kindle again, I am most confident we might and shall propound a way to make this kingdom considerably active to enforce those gainsayers to due obedience, and settle the public peace of all your kingdoms.

10 Brown, *Kingdom or province*, pp. 118–19; Cf. J. Ohlmeyer, *Civil war and restoration in the three Stuart kingdoms: the career of Randal Mac Donnell, Marquis of Antrim, 1609–83* (Cambridge, 1993).

11 C. Russell, *The fall of the British monarchies, 1637–1642* (Oxford, 1991), pp. 60–4, 68–70, 151–3; P. Donald, *An uncounselled king: Charles I and the Scottish troubles, 1637–1641* (Cambridge, 1990), pp. 135–6, 184–5, 244–7; idem, 'New light on the Anglo-Scottish contacts of 1640', in *Historical Research*, 62 (1989), pp. 221–9; Lockyer, *Tudor and Stuart Britain*, p. 323 (quotation).

Determined to recommence hostilities, Charles accepted Wentworth's offer and summoned him to England where he joined Charles's closest advisors sitting on a war council.[12]

When in 1640 Wentworth returned to Ireland as lord lieutenant and earl of Strafford he appeared at the pinnacle of his power and was determined to use Ireland's resources to assist the crown. While in England, he had convinced Charles that Scotland should be conquered and then ruled as a dependency of the English crown – not unlike England's relationship with Ireland. The support of the English parliament, Wentworth contended, was vital in the pursuit of this end and Charles resolved to convene parliament in April. In the meantime, however, Strafford intended to establish his management of the Irish parliament as a model to be emulated in England. Through his careful management of parliamentary elections – and the desire of New and Old English interests to demonstrate their loyalty to Charles in his moment of crisis – Strafford secured subsidies worth nearly £150,000 to be used to raise a new Irish army of 9,000 men. Troops numbering 1,000, mainly Protestants, were drawn from the standing army to form the backbone of this army, but the preponderance of the remaining soldiers were recruited from the Catholic population.[13] His work in Ireland complete, Strafford left the kingdom's government in the hands of a deputy and returned to England to support his king in parliament. Yet the English parliament did not follow the Irish example as Strafford had hoped. Eleven years of authoritarian rule had done nothing to redress the grievances expressed by the Commons in the 1620s; indeed the far-reaching reforms in government, finance and religion that characterised the period had given rise to an array of new grievances, most notably the annual exaction of Ship Money. Thus, despite the threat which the Covenanters posed to England, parliament resolved that the redress of grievances must precede supply. Indeed some parliamentary leaders hoped to make common cause with the Covenanters, so as to undo the crown's ecclesiastical reforms. Charles, however, was unwilling to make concessions and, at Strafford's instigation, dissolved what became known as the Short Parliament after just three weeks.[14]

---

12 M.C. Fissell, *The Bishops' Wars: Charles I's campaigns against Scotland, 1638–40* (Cambridge, 1994), pp. 3–38; Smith, *A history of the modern British Isles*, pp. 110–11; Clarke, 'The government of Wentworth', in *NHI*, iii, pp. 268–9 (quotation).

13 Canny, *From Reformation to restoration*, pp. 202–3; *Oxford DNB, s.v.* Thomas Wentworth; Clarke, *The Old English in Ireland*, pp. 125–8, 131–2.

14 Russell, *The fall of the British monarchies*, pp. 90–123; Smith, *A history of the modern British Isles*, pp. 110–12.

Thereafter Charles's prerogative rule in his three kingdoms became impossible to maintain. The king hoped to relaunch in summer 1640 the same
elaborate military assault on Scotland that had failed him the previous year.
It produced the identical result; only this time it provoked a Covenanter
army to invade England in August, so beginning the Second Bishops' War.
The king's ill-equipped and demoralised army was routed at Newburn and
nearly 20,000 Scottish troops occupied north-eastern England, determined
to effect in England the same changes they had brought to Scotland. The
day of the defeat at Newburn, moreover, twelve English peers, led by Francis
Russell, earl of Bedford, and in regular (and treasonous) communication
with Covenanter leaders, submitted a petition to Charles requesting that a
parliament be summoned to negotiate a settlement with the Scots and
address grievances as a prelude to the 'uniting of both your realms against
the common enemies of the reformed religion'.[15] In Ireland, meanwhile, an
unprecedented inter-religious partnership had developed in parliament,
whose third session reconvened in Strafford's absence. Strafford's deputy,
Sir Christopher Wandesford, was powerless in face of united British and
Old English opposition, which sought to destroy Strafford's domination of
the Irish government. This opposition proved vital in the accumulation of
evidence against Strafford, which was presented in the next English parliament. In a letter written to the speaker of the Commons in England, the Irish
Commons asked that he remember:

> the near links and great ties of blood and affinity betwixt the people of this
> kingdom and the famous people of England from whose loins they are
> descended . . . being therefore flesh of their flesh and bone of their bone
> subjects to one gracious sovereign and governed by the same laws.[16]

Authoritarian rule had collapsed in the Stuart kingdoms and the king had no
recourse but to conclude a humiliating truce with the Scots and to summon
the English parliament.

The wars of the Stuart kingdoms

The strength of the Covenanting movement cast a long shadow over parliament as it assembled in November 1640. Since late 1637 Scotland had

---

15   Russell, *The fall of the British monarchies*, pp. 123–51 (quotation, p. 150); Donald, 'The
     Scottish national covenant and British politics', pp. 99–103; *Oxford DNB, s.v.* Charles I.
16   Clarke, *The Old English in Ireland*, pp. 129–36 (quotation, p. 136).

undergone a revolutionary transformation in church and state. The abolition of episcopacy was upheld in August 1639 by a General Assembly in Edinburgh and Presbyterian clergy inexorably tightened their grip in the localities. Representatives drawn from Scotland's four estates, or Tables – the nobles, gentry, burgesses and clergy – formed themselves into an executive or fifth Table, which led the Covenanters' provisional government. The need to raise and mobilise an army to defend the Covenant provided the fifth Table with the impetus to formalise the movement's relationship with the localities. Working closely with the gentry, committees of war – each with their own convener – were established in the shires to recruit troops, collect the first national tax levied by the Covenanters in March 1640 and maintain support for the movement. The fifth Table was eventually reconstituted as a Committee of Estates, which introduced radical constitutional changes: the gentry had their vote doubled in parliament, subscription to the National Covenant was made mandatory for all public office holders and a Triennial Act ensured that parliament would be convened at least once every three years. Integral to this restructuring of central and local government was the successful mobilisation of a standing army. Veterans returned from the continental wars, most notably Alexander Leslie, brought with them their knowledge of the latest innovations in military strategy and technology to form the nucleus of a Covenanter army, which proved itself capable not only of keeping order within the movement, but also of decisively defeating the crown's forces in the Bishops' Wars. Thus the Covenanters had, with the active support of the clergy and through the creation of a professional standing army, achieved within several years what decades of Stuart rule could not: the destruction of noble power and the concentration of power in a centralised government, what Allan Macinnes has called 'the triumph of oligarchic centralism'.[17]

The strength of the Covenanter movement was such that it influenced both the tone and the course of the English parliament. The security offered by the Covenanter army allowed a decade of resentment against Charles's non-parliamentary rule to rise to the surface. The king was powerless: the Houses lashed out at recent royal policies in church and state and sought the removal and punishment of his 'evil counsellors'. Within a week articles of impeachment were prepared against the reviled Strafford. Strafford's

17   Macinnes, *The British revolution*, pp. 123–30; E.M. Furgol, 'Scotland turned Sweden: the Scottish Covenanters and the military revolution, 1638–1651', in *The Scottish National Covenant in its British context*, pp. 134–55; Macinnes, *Charles I and the making of the covenanting movement*, pp. 183–206.

enemies in Ireland joined with those in England and among the Covenanters to accuse him of 'endeavouring to subvert the ancient and fundamental laws and government of England and Ireland' and of provoking war against the Scots. When it became clear, however, that Strafford had acted at Charles's behest, and that he could not be convicted without impugning the king, an act of attainder[18] was passed. With angry mobs gathering outside Whitehall baying for Strafford's blood, Charles had no alternative but to consent to the execution of his closest advisor in May 1641. By the time of Strafford's death, Laud and the judges who had found against Hampden in the Ship Money case had been impeached and more than half of Charles's privy council had been either exiled, gaoled or disgraced.[19]

Yet the influence of the Covenanters went beyond affording disaffected members of parliament the opportunity to attack royal policy. The constitutional changes undertaken by the Covenanters in Scotland also provided the English parliament with a model for the establishment of constitutional checks on the monarch. Though he declared before parliament in early 1641 his desire to 'reduce all matters of religion and government to what they were in the purest times of Queen Elizabeth's days', Charles was no longer trusted. In February the king reluctantly accepted a Triennial Act, identical to that enacted in Scotland, and in May he assented to a bill which forbade him from dissolving the current parliament without the consent of both Houses. These major reforms were followed by a number of smaller reforms designed to dismantle the institutions of prerogative rule: the collection of tonnage and poundage without parliamentary consent was declared illegal, the courts of High Commission and Star Chamber were abolished – and with them the Council of the North and the criminal jurisdiction of the Council in the Marches – and the recent feudal exactions, such as Ship Money, were outlawed. But, while parliament was unified in its support for political, legal and constitutional reforms, divisions were soon apparent regarding ecclesiastical reform. The Scots were pressing for the abolition of episcopacy in England and Wales and this view was popular both in parliament, where a petition and subsequently a bill for the abolishment of episcopacy was hotly debated, and in the counties, where riots and popular iconoclasm threatened law and order. It was initially Bedford in the Lords and Pym in the Commons who led this grouping which sought radical

18   A bill of parliament, passed by Commons, Lords and King, depriving a felon of rights to inherit or transmit an estate and the forfeiture of an estate as the consequence of outlawry.

19   Macinnes, *The British revolution*, pp. 129–30; Smith, *A history of the modern British Isles*, pp. 113–14 (quotation, p. 114).

[3 4 2] reforms in church and state. Others, however, most notably Dorset in the Lords and Edward Hyde in the Commons, wished to reform bishops and saw a correlation between the preservation of episcopacy and the preservation of the existing social, political and constitutional order.[20]

It was as the natural leader of this latter interest that Charles began to reconstruct his power-base. So long as the Scots remained on English soil, however, the king's ability to arrest constitutional change and defend episcopacy was limited. In August, Charles and the Lords negotiated a settlement with the Scots – the treaty of London – whereby the crown paid the Covenanters' war-costs and accepted in their entirety the recent reforms in church and state in Scotland. The Covenanters, however, had also sought to strengthen Scotland's relationship with England and to establish a unified church. They proposed that war should not be declared within the three kingdoms without the approval of both parliaments and that neither Scotland nor England should wage war against a foreign power without the consent of the two parliaments. The English parliament agreed to the proposals, but reserved the right to determine the form of the English church. In return, the Scots withdrew from England, having negotiated a new confederal relationship in Britain that, for them, exorcised any remaining spectres of provincialism. The treaty, together with a subsequent meeting of the Scottish estates, which both ratified the treaty and imposed further restrictions on the royal prerogative, had reduced Charles to little more than a figurehead in Scotland. But, with the departure of the Scots from England, the immediate crisis that had forced Charles to summon parliament into existence had passed and the king could reasonably hope that the Long Parliament, as it became known, would now dissolve itself.[21]

Then came insurrection in Ireland – an unforeseen consequence of the Covenanters' humbling of the king and his subsequent prostration before the Long Parliament. A mixture of fear of the Covenanting movement and a desire to emulate its success in negotiating terms with an enfeebled crown moved a group of indebted Catholic gentry of Gaelic extraction, led by Sir Phelim O'Neill – JP, MP and lawyer – to seize key fortifications in Ulster

20 Smith, *A history of the modern British Isles*, pp. 113–19 (quotation, p. 119); Macinnes, *The British revolution*, pp. 135–7; Roberts, 'The English crown, the principality of Wales and the council in the marches', in Bradshaw and Morrill (eds) *The British problem*, p. 145; J.S. Morrill, 'Order and disorder in the English revolution, in A. Fletcher and J. Stevenson (eds) *Order and disorder in early modern England* (Cambridge, 1985), pp. 137–42.
21 A. Macinnes, 'The Scottish constitution, 1638–51: the rise and fall of oligarchic centralism', in Morrill (ed.) *The Scottish national covenant in its British context*, pp. 117–18.

in late October 1641.[22] O'Neill was reputed to have explained that he had [343] entered into insurrection:

> with the lords and gentry of this kingdom for the preservation of his Majesty's prerogative and their own religion and liberties against the Puritan faction in England, Scotland and Ireland who intended . . . to enact such laws whereby the inhabitants of Ireland should conform in religion to the Church of England otherwise to be deprived of life, liberty and estates.

Another conspirator, Hugh Oge MacMahon, insisted on the insurgents' loyalty to the king 'but that they did this for the tyrannical government was over them, and to imitate the Scots who got a privilege by that course'.[23] Theirs was thus an insurrection which sought neither to uproot the Ulster plantation, nor to resurrect the deposed Gaelic order, but instead to force Charles to address the present religious and economic grievances of his Irish Catholic subjects. The leaders of the insurrection, however, overestimated their ability to control the insurrection outside their power-base of central Ulster and underestimated the depth of the animosity and resentment which many Ulster Catholics felt for their socially and economically superior Protestant neighbours. Widespread unemployment arising from an economic downturn in the previous decade, moreover, and the presence in Ulster of large numbers of disbanded soldiers who had formerly served in Strafford's army provided a ready supply of men prepared to avail of the breakdown of authority to commit depredations. What resulted was a spontaneous popular onslaught against the province's Protestant farming community. An estimated 3,000 British Protestants were killed in Ulster and thousands more were cast off their lands, fleeing either to the safety of walled towns or to England.[24] By mid-1642, the insurrection had spread piecemeal to Connaught, Leinster and Munster: only a handful of walled towns, including Dublin and its immediate hinterland, remained under government control.

The Irish insurgency immediately transformed the king's political fortunes. Rumours swept London, where the Long Parliament had reassembled in

---

22 *Oxford DNB, s.v.* Phelim O'Neill.
23 Canny, *Making Ireland British*, pp. 461–550 (quotations, p. 471); N. Canny, 'What really happened in Ireland in 1641?', in J. Ohlmeyer (ed.) *Ireland from independence to occupation, 1641–1660* (Cambridge, 1995), pp. 24–42; M. Perceval-Maxwell, *The outbreak of the Irish rebellion of 1641* (Dublin, 1991).
24 Canny, 'What really happened in Ireland in 1641?', in *Ireland from independence to occupation,* pp. 30–1; idem., *Making Ireland British*, pp. 473–4; R. Gillespie, 'The end of an era: Ulster and the outbreak of the 1641 rising', in C. Brady and R. Gillespie (eds) *Natives and newcomers: the making of Irish colonial society, 1534–1641* (Dublin, 1986), pp. 191–213.

[3 4 4] October, that some 20,000 Protestants had been massacred in Ireland and that O'Neill had bandied about a royal commission authorising the insurrection. Though the actual number of Protestants killed was far fewer and the commission was one of a number of forgeries employed by the insurgents, Pym and his associates in parliament, who had been losing ground to the king, seized upon these horrifying reports and offered them as proof of the king's involvement in a popish conspiracy. Charles had hoped to procure an army to suppress the rebellion: his initial reaction was to request assistance from the Covenanters. But, despite their concern for their kindred in Ireland, the Scots were loath to violate the treaty of London and offered 10,000 troops to the English parliament if it consented to military action. Pym feared that if given an army the king would turn it, and the Irish insurgents, against his opponents in England.[25] Pym thus resolved to present to the Commons a comprehensive indictment of Charles's government that he and his allies had been preparing since the opening of the Long Parliament. Later known as the Grand Remonstrance, this document rehearsed the litany of grievances that had arisen since Charles's accession and contrasted them with the beneficial reforms of the Long Parliament. The intention of the Remonstrance was to win greater support in parliament for further reforms, namely that royal advisors should have the confidence of parliament and that 'a general synod of the most grave, pious, learned and judicious divines' be convened to 'consider of all things necessary for the peace and good government of the church'. The Grand Remonstrance provoked heated debate within a parliament that was heading in two different directions. The Remonstrance, however, was passed, by eleven votes, in late November 1641.[26]

Remembered by many as a turning point, the Remonstrance split parliament into two opposing camps. Charles's rejection of the Remonstrance sharpened this division. Yet it was the events stemming from his attempt in early 1642 to impeach one member of the Lords and five of the Commons, including Pym, of high treason that made compromise virtually impossible. Following the Lords' failure to give the order to arrest the accused, Charles led an armed band to Westminster to apprehend them. This was a flagrant breach of parliamentary privilege and further proof for those who would cast Charles in the role of a traitor that the king was untrustworthy and

25 Canny, *Making Ireland British*, p. 537; Macinnes, *The British revolution*, pp. 141–2; Brown, *Kingdom or province*, pp. 123–4; Russell, *The fall of the British monarchies*, pp. 418–22.
26 Russell, *The fall of the British monarchies*, pp. 424–9; Smith, *A history of the modern British Isles*, pp. 120–3; Lockyer, *Tudor and Stuart Britain*, pp. 334–5 (quotation, p. 335).

prepared to use force against his opponents. The accused, moreover, were nowhere to be found: they had been alerted to the king's intentions and secreted away among sympathisers in London. Charles travelled to London and demanded that its governing body, the Common Council, hand over the fugitives, but his actions had alienated most Londoners and angry crowds aroused by economic hardship and political uncertainty swarmed the king's carriage.[27] Charles's inability to arrest the parliamentary leaders signalled the failure of his bid to reclaim control of government by force, but it was his subsequent decision to abandon the capital that handed his enemies their greatest advantage. Pym and his associates were returned to Westminster in triumph and set about gaining control of England's military apparatus. Following Charles's refusal in February to relinquish control over the armed forces, the Houses enacted the Militia Ordnance, empowering parliament to appoint lords lieutenant and leaders of the trained bands. In legislating without royal assent parliament had entered uncharted constitutional waters. The Houses, however, claimed that in 'this time of imminent danger' they were entitled to do so. The king responded in April by attempting to commandeer the munitions stored at Hull; but the town's governor, under instruction from parliament, denied the king access.[28] Charles's appearance before Hull was difficult to misinterpret: amid reports that the queen was pawning the crown jewels to raise troops on the continent and the Irish insurgency had assumed the form of a nationwide Catholic confederacy, the prospect of armed conflict between king and parliament came into view.

The possibility of a compromise between king and parliament was more apparent than real when in June the latter recast its demands in the form of the Nineteen Propositions. Charles responded in deed and in word: he countermanded the Militia Ordinance by resurrecting the royal Commission of Array to raise troops and through his published answer to the Propositions he portrayed parliamentary demands as threatening to 'the fundamental laws and [the] excellent constitution of this kingdom'. Caught between parliamentarian and royalist propaganda and their countervailing orders to establish military support in the localities was the majority of Englishmen who hoped to stay out of the developing conflict. Leading gentry in 22 counties sought to adopt formal neutrality pacts; others refused to answer the call of either the Militia Ordinance or the Commission of Array. That a

27   Russell, *The fall of the British monarchies*, pp. 447–53.
28   Smith, *A history of the modern British Isles*, pp. 124–5 (quotation, p. 125); Kishlansky, *A monarchy transformed*, pp. 149–50.

majority resisted choosing a side in the face of the deteriorating political situation is a measure of the stability and the instinctual localism of English society.[29] The difficulty of both sides in raising troops from among their supporters, moreover, points to how demilitarised the kingdom had become. Gone were the days when nobles could harness their hard-bitten tenants to wage war and threaten the political establishment.[30]

Yet it was becoming increasingly difficult for the moderate majority to avoid choosing a side. In August parliament declared Charles's supporters 'traitors' and the king assumed a warlike posture against parliamentarian 'rebels'. That both sides were committed to defend the same thing, namely the church and constitution of England, did not make their choice any easier. However, there existed a hardcore minority of committed parliamentarians and royalists who firmly believed the other side to be part of a conspiracy to subvert the church and constitution of England. Generally speaking, parliamentarians were distinguishable by their desire to effect further reforms in the church and a belief that there existed a popish conspiracy to destroy the kingdom. Royalists, on the other hand, sought to uphold episcopacy and believed religious fanatics and radicals to be engaged in a conspiracy from within to overturn the existing social order and the rule of law. It was the activism and tenacity of this minority of extremists which ultimately drove the unorganised moderates to choose a side. When fighting engulfed the kingdom in late autumn 1642 it divided (almost equally) all social classes between two seemingly irreconcilable ideological causes. But the fighting of the next 18 months produced only stalemate and both sides sought to involve their allies in Scotland and Ireland to vanquish the other. By 1644 the subjects of all three Stuart kingdoms were at war with one another. It was a war that would send as many as one in three of all of Charles's subjects who bore arms to fight in a kingdom other than the one of their birth.[31]

At a meeting of Catholic lay and clerical leaders in June 1642 a provisional executive was nominated to act on behalf of a confederation of Irish Catholics until a representative assembly was convened. The emergence of the confederation was made possible through the alliance in late 1641 of

29 Morrill, *The revolt in the provinces*, pp. 52–9, 64; Smith, *A history of the modern British Isles*, pp. 126–8 (quotation, p. 126); Kishlansky, *A monarchy transformed*, pp. 153–5.

30 Russell, *The fall of the British monarchies*, pp. 455–6. John Morrill has argued that it was the lack of will not the absence of a capacity to fight that delayed civil war in England: J. Morrill, 'The British problem, *c.*1534–1707', in B. Bradshaw and J. Morrill (eds) *The British problem, c.1534–1707: state formation in the Atlantic archipelago* (London, 1996), p. 29.

31 Morrill, 'The war(s) of the three kingdoms', in Burgess (ed.) *The new British history*, p. 65.

the original, mostly Gaelic, insurgents and the Old English.[32] Since James's accession most Gaelic poets had ceased to distinguish between Ireland's inhabitants along ethnic lines. For the Gaelic elite, a common commitment to Catholicism and the Stuarts now united *Gaedhil* and *Gaill*, that is the Gaelic and Old English communities. The Old English were slow to appropriate this ideology, but in *c.*1634 the Old English priest-poet Geoffrey Keating articulated in his influential and widely circulated manuscript *Foras Feasa ar Éirinn* that the Irish and Old English had merged into a single Catholic nation and employed the designation *Éireannaigh*, or Irishmen, to describe them. The Irish Catholic nation was not conceived as a separate political entity; rather it was depicted as occupying a prominent place within a kingdom that enjoyed the same constitutional relationship with the Stuarts as England and Scotland. This view of Ireland as an independent kingdom became central to Confederate thinking in the 1640s and was employed to legitimise the confederacy as a political vehicle to secure for Irish Catholics the same rights as Charles's other subjects. Thus, in June 1642, the Confederates swore an oath 'to bear true faith and allegiance' to Charles 'by the grace of God, king of Great Britain, France and Ireland' but also pledged to 'defend, uphold, and maintain all his and their just prerogatives, estates and rights, the power and privilege of the parliament of this realm, the fundamental laws of Ireland, the free exercise of the Roman Catholic faith and religion throughout this land'.[33]

Ostensibly, the Catholic Confederates shared many similarities with the Scottish Covenanters. The Irish Catholics sought to dictate terms to the crown through a popular show of force and, like the Covenanters, swore an oath of association. The arrival back in Ireland of Owen Roe O'Neill and other veterans in Spanish service, moreover, transformed Ulster's Gaelic insurgents into a professional army – an echo of Leslie's return to Scotland from the continental wars. The Confederates then erected their own government: in October 1642 a general assembly met in Kilkenny and appointed a supreme council, not unlike the committee of estates, to administer areas under confederate control.[34] Yet, despite these similarities with the

32 M. Ó Siochrú, *Confederate Ireland, 1642–9: a constitutional and political analysis* (Dublin, 1999), pp. 27–54.

33 Macinnes, *The British revolution*, pp. 17–19; B. Ó Buachalla, *Foras feasa ar Éirinn, history of Ireland: foreward* (Dublin, 1987), pp. 1–8; B. Cunningham, *The world of Geoffrey Keating* (Dublin, 2000), pp. 31–40, 83–101; P.J. Corish, 'The rising of 1641 and the confederacy, 1641–5', in *NHI*, iii, p. 298 (quotation).

34 Macinnes, *The British revolution*, p. 145; Ó Siochrú, *Confederate Ireland*, pp. 49–54. Cf. J.I. Casway, *Owen Roe O'Neill and the struggle for Catholic Ireland* (Philadelphia, 1984).

Covenanting movement, the Catholic Confederacy was a fundamentally different entity, facing a range of different circumstances. An obvious difference was the Confederates' inability to secure control of the kingdom. Notwithstanding O'Neill's return, there were in Ireland by 1644 four armies: a Scottish army, under the command of Major-General Robert Monro and funded by the English parliament, based in Antrim; a mixture of English and Scots forces loyal to the English parliament in Ulster and Munster; troops loyal to the king under James Butler, the earl of Ormond, stationed in Dublin; and the Confederate armies placed under separate provincial commands in Ulster, Leinster and Munster.[35] The Confederacy, moreover, failed to develop institutions of government to match the efficiency and centralisation of those in Scotland. Its supreme council, comprised of six members from each of Ireland's four provinces, was unable to exercise effective control of government when the unicameral assembly, which met on nine occasions between 1642 and 1648, was not in session. Local interests and residual ethnic tensions thus dominated the chronically underfunded and bureaucratic Confederate government.[36] But perhaps the most striking difference between the Confederates and the Covenanters was the association in the minds of British Protestants of Irish Catholics with 'massacres' and with Charles. Reports of Irish massacres of Protestants had assumed fantastic proportions – it was later claimed that, by March 1642, 154,000 Protestants had been killed – and, though no formal alliance existed between the king and the Confederates until 1649, the two sides were in frequent negotiations and concluded a truce in September 1643. For the king's enemies, Charles and the Confederates were different aspects of the same popish conspiracy.

Less than a fortnight after the conclusion of the truce between the royalists and the Confederates, the English parliament entered into a Solemn League and Covenant with the Scots. Negotiated by the radical wing of the Covenanters and the hawkish group in the Long Parliament, the Solemn League and Covenant secured Scottish military intervention on behalf of the parliamentarians. But the Solemn League was more than a military alliance. In return for their military assistance, the Covenanters sought to build on the treaty of London by establishing a closer political relationship with England

---

35 S. Wheeler, 'Four Armies in Ireland', in Ohlmeyer (ed.) *Ireland from independence to occupation,* pp. 43–65.

36 Macinnes, *The British revolution,* p. 145; Ó Siochrú, *Confederate Ireland,* pp. 205–36. Cf. D.F. Cregan, 'The Confederate Catholics of Ireland: the personnel of the confederation, 1642–9', in *Irish Historical Studies,* 29 (1995), pp. 490–512.

and by spreading Presbyterianism to England and Ireland. The former was [349] achieved in February 1644 when a new executive, comprised of English and Scots representatives, known as the Committee of Both Kingdoms, was established to coordinate the British war effort in England and Ireland. Most Englishmen, however, recoiled from Scottish Presbyterianism and the notion of the Scots dictating the form of the English church. Pym had been the driving force behind the Long Parliament's negotiations with the Covenanters, but following his death in late 1643 negotiations with the Scots fell to a radical grouping ascendant in the Commons led by Sir Henry Vane junior and the hitherto obscure Huntingdon gentleman, Oliver Cromwell. Both men were opposed to Presbyterianism and Vane brokered a compromise whereby both sides agreed to pursue religious uniformity in the three kingdoms according to the 'word of God and the example of the best reformed churches.'[37] The benefits of a British military alliance were realised when a Covenanter army under the command of Leslie, now earl of Leven, crossed into the north of England. The king's army was forced to confront the combined Scots/parliamentarian army amassing outside the royalist stronghold of York. Aided by a stunning cavalry charge commanded by Cromwell, the royalists were routed at Marston Moor in early July and soon after York surrendered. But the Scots/parliamentarian forces were unable to deliver the *coup de grâce*. Recrimination among the parliamentarian military leadership, between Cromwell and Edward Montagu, earl of Manchester, in particular, allowed royalist forces to regroup in the West Country and Wales.[38] The Scots' commitment in England, moreover, was shaken when a royalist rebellion began in the highlands, which threatened to overturn the Covenanting government.

Not all Scots were content with the direction of the Covenanting movement. In August 1640 a group of nobles, led by James Graham, earl of Montrose, had secretly signed the Cumbernauld Band in protest of the Covenanters' invasion of England. The signatories felt excluded from the oligarchic committee of estates and resented the growing influence of Archibald Campbell, earl of Argyll, and his adherents in government. They also wished to preserve a greater measure of royal authority, but Montrose's inability to mobilise the considerable reservoir of sympathy for the king that still existed in Scotland, especially in the highlands, ensured that the Band

---

37 Brown, *Kingdom or province*, pp. 126–7; Smith, *A history of the modern British Isles*, pp. 141–2 (quotation, p. 141).

38 J. Kenyon and J. Ohlmeyer (eds) *The civil wars: a military history of England, Scotland and Ireland, 1638–1660* (Oxford, 1998), pp. 138–41.

came to nothing.[39] The departure of the Covenanter army for England in summer 1644, however, presented Montrose with an ideal opportunity to strike in the king's name. Montrose envisaged a three-pronged assault against the Covenanters: rebellion would be raised in the north and east, an Irish force would attack from the west and the main royalist army would strike from the south. It was a strategy reminiscent of that twice pursued unsuccessfully by Charles in the Bishops' Wars, only this time the Irish invasion had already been effected. In July, Gaelic troops raised by Antrim, with the assistance of the Irish Confederacy, and commanded by Alastair MacColla MacDonald had landed in the western isles, thereby driving a wedge between Scotland and the Covenanting army in Ulster. The suppression of a rebellion in the north-east and the royalist defeat at Marston Moor undid Montrose's grand strategy, but after linking up with MacColla's Gaelic forces, Montrose won a string of victories including his defeat of Argyll's army at Inverlochy in February and his defeat of a Covenanting army at Kilsyth in August 1645. The highland clans – hostile to the centralising influence of the Covenanting government and opposed to the imposition of Presbyterianism – flocked to Montrose's standard, providing the royalist campaign in Scotland with a cohesion and a momentum absent from the royalist war-effort in England. The overtly Gaelic and Catholic composition of the campaign, however, repelled moderate Scots who might otherwise have joined the royalist cause. And as the campaign moved further away from the highlands Montrose's Gaelic support dwindled apace. Montrose resolved to march what remained of his forces south to join the king, but he was surprised and routed by Covenanter troops at the border. Any hope of securing Scotland for the king was lost.[40]

The infighting among parliamentarian commanders that followed the failure to build upon the victory at Marston Moor exposed the growing divisions within the Long Parliament. Oliver Cromwell, the hero of Marston Moor, was prominent in the war group in parliament. Closely associated with the Independents – so-called because of their opposition to a national church structure and distrust of Scottish Presbyterianism – the war group

39 Macinnes, *The British revolution*, p. 137; Brown, *Kingdom or province*, p. 122; E.J. Cowan, *Montrose: for covenant and king* (London, 1977), pp. 96–101.

40 Macinnes, *The British revolution*, pp. 173–4, 176–7; idem, 'Scottish Gaeldom, 1638–1651: the vernacular response to the Covenanting movement dynamic', in J. Dwyer, R.A. Mason, A. Murdoch (eds) *New perspectives on the politics and culture of early modern Scotland* (Edinburgh, 1982), pp. 59–90; D. Stevenson, *Alasdair MacColla and the highland problem in the seventeenth century* (Edinburgh, 1980), pp. 69–70, 73, 99–101; idem, *Scottish Covenanters and Irish Confederates* (Belfast, 1981), pp. 139–63; Brown, *Kingdom or province*, pp. 128–9.

urged that the parliamentarian armies be overhauled. Cromwell saw Manchester's failures in the field as an outgrowth of his reluctance to vanquish the king. The moderates in parliament, or Presbyterians, as they became known, because of their preference for Presbyterian church structures and a continued alliance with the Scots, still hoped to negotiate a settlement with Charles.[41] But following Charles's rejection of the Uxbridge Proposition proffered by the moderates in January 1645, the war party gained the upper hand. They introduced a Self-Denying Ordinance, whereby all members of parliament would relinquish their military commands and civil offices. The Ordinance, passed in April 1645, thus prevented the aristocracy from filling military positions and thereby shattered the local and regional influence of peers who had served as lords lieutenant. This cleared the way for the formation of a New Model Army – an amalgamation of parliament's existing regional armies into a single national army. The New Model was controlled from Westminster and financed by parliament through an onerous monthly assessment levied on each county. The veteran soldier, Sir Thomas Fairfax, who held no seat in parliament, was appointed its first commander. Cromwell received a temporary exemption from the Self-Denying Ordinance and was appointed commander of the cavalry – in April 1645 he was permanently exempted. The New Model scored its first victory over royalist forces at Naseby in June, which Cromwell attributed to 'none other but the hand of God'.[42] In the New Model Army parliament had found the means not only to defeat Charles's forces, but also to release the Long Parliament from its reliance on Scots military assistance.

Charles had attempted to enlist military support from Ireland through his despatch of Edward Somerset, earl of Glamorgan, as his personal envoy to the Confederates in 1645. The Confederacy, however, had yet to defeat either the Scots or the parliamentarian armies in Ireland; and royalist forces, commanded by the earl of Ormond, still held Dublin. The Confederacy, moreover, was riven with internal disagreements. The Confederate leaders, many of whom were Old English and based in Leinster, distrusted Owen Roe O'Neill and his predominantly Gaelic Ulster army. Catholic landowners were also at odds with influential Catholic clerics, such as Bishop Nicholas French, who were not prepared to accept a settlement unless it included the

41   Smith, *A history of the modern British Isles*, pp. 143, 153.
42   M. Kishlansky, 'The case of the army truly stated: the creation of the new model army', in *Past & Present*, 81 (1978), pp. 51–74; Smith, *A history of the modern British Isles*, p. 144 (quotation). Cf. I. Gentles, 'The choosing of officers for the new model army', in *Historical Research*, 67 (1994), pp. 264–85.

[3 5 2] freedom to practice Catholicism openly and free from the state's interference. That some of the more radical clerics insisted that all church lands
secularised since the Reformation be restored to the church did little to
draw landowning Catholic moderates and the clergy together. In August
Glamorgan negotiated a secret agreement with the Confederates, which
promised freedom of worship and the appointment of a Catholic lord lieutenant in return for 10,000 troops to aid the king. But news of the treaty
outraged Charles's enemies in Britain and the king distanced himself from
Glamorgan and the concessions he had promised in his name.[43]

The arrival in October 1645 of Archbishop Rinuccini, the papal nuncio
to the Confederacy, strengthened the hand of the militant religious faction
within the Confederacy. Returned soldiers like O'Neill, the nephew of the
exiled Hugh O'Neill, earl of Tyrone, no longer held claim to lands in Ireland
and wished to see at least some of the plantations undone. O'Neill, the
natural leader of Ireland's disadvantaged and dispossessed Gaelic population, found common ground with those religious, now led by Rinuccini,
who advocated a radical religious settlement with the king. Rinuccini
rejected the treaty concluded between the moderate Confederates and
Ormond in March 1646 and excommunicated anyone who adhered to it. An
anonymous Gaelic poet later added: 'My curse will fall on those members of
the clergy and on their company, until judgement day . . . who brought
shame on Ireland and were in opposition to the Gaelic nobles upon whom
fell the late nuncio's interdict.' Charles, however, could never agree to the
demands that Rinuccini and O'Neill sought and remain king of England and
Scotland.[44] Thus, having failed to secure Irish military support and with the
New Model Army advancing into the West Country, Charles surrendered
himself to the Scots at Newark in May 1646; royalist forces at Oxford capit-
ulated the following month, so ending what became known as the first
English Civil War. But O'Neill's decisive victory over the Scots army at
Benburb, county Tyrone, in June ensured that any settlement to the wars of

43 Wheeler, 'Four armies in Ireland', in Ohlmeyer (ed.) *Ireland from independence to occupation*,
    pp. 44–54; T. Ó hAnnracháin, 'Rebels and confederates: the stance of the Irish clergy in
    the 1640s', in Young (ed.) *Celtic dimensions*, pp. 96–115; Jason McHugh, '"Soldier of Christ":
    the political and ecclesiastical career of Nicholas French, Catholic bishop of Ferns (1603–
    1678)', (unpublished PhD Thesis, NUI, Galway 2005).
44 Canny, *Making Ireland British*, pp. 564–6; T. Ó hAnnracháin, *Catholic reformation in Ireland:
    the mission of Rinuccini, 1645–1649* (Oxford, 2002); M. O Riordan, '"Political" poems in the
    mid-seventeenth-century Irish crisis', in Ohlmeyer (ed.) *Ireland from independence to occupation*,
    pp. 116–17.

the three kingdoms would have to take into account the continued existence of the Catholic Confederacy in Ireland.[45]

There could be no government in the British Isles without the king. On this point the English parliament, the Covenanting government and the Irish Confederates were agreed. But the Confederacy's commitment to the royalist cause, the increasingly militant position of its leadership and O'Neill's inability to build on his success at Benburb had left the Confederates politically isolated, militarily vulnerable and on a collision course with the Protestant kingdoms of Britain. The task of finding a lasting settlement that would restore the king to power in Britain and Ireland thus fell exclusively to the victorious English and Scots. English parliamentarians and Scottish Covenanters, however, disagreed fundamentally on how negotiations were to proceed. Charles was all too aware of the growing tensions between the allies and his surrender to the Covenanters was intended to make the British parliaments 'irreconcilable enemies'. In general, the parliamentarians – the Independents in particular – sought to exclude the Scots from proposals on Ireland and regarded the king's future as an English, rather than a British, matter. The Scots, meanwhile, insisted that the English parliamentarians approach Ireland in accordance with the Solemn League and Covenant and that Charles swear the Covenant as a prelude to the establishment of Presbyterianism in England. In July 1646 the Presbyterian majority in parliament, led by Denzil Holles, presented Charles with peace proposals at Newcastle. The Newcastle Propositions, as they were known, required the king to swear the Covenant and to establish a Presbyterian church in England, to cede control of the military to parliament for two decades and to exclude from pardon 58 prominent royalists. Charles delayed his response in the hope that the Scots would offer more favourable terms. But the Scots were not prepared to compromise on religion and began negotiations with Holles and the Presbyterians that would see the king handed over to parliament. Charles rejected the Newcastle Propositions in December and the following month the Scots delivered the king to the parliamentarians and withdrew their army from England, in exchange for £400,000.[46]

With the war won, the Scots gone and the king secure, the majority Presbyterians sought to restore stability to England and confirm their hold on power. In waging the war parliament had resorted to fiscal and legal

45 Wheeler, 'Four armies in Ireland', in Ohlmeyer (ed.) *Ireland from independence to occupation*, pp. 54–5; G.A. Hayes-McCoy, *Irish battles* (London, 1969), pp. 174–99.
46 Macinnes, *The British revolution*, pp. 171–3; *Oxford DNB, s.v.* Charles I; Kishlansky, *A monarchy transformed*, pp. 169–71.

expedients more radical than those employed by the king. A weekly assessment and a land tax – equal to a parliamentary subsidy every two weeks – were introduced as well as an excise duty on most basic goods. Martial law and conscription were imposed and other basic rights of the subject, such as *habeas corpus* and trial by jury were ignored. Thus, by 1647, resentment of parliament was widespread and Holles and his allies were eager to relieve the population of what they believed to be an unnecessary burden: the army. By 1647, however, the New Model numbered 22,000 men; parliament retained an additional 40,000 men in its provincial armies. Holles planned to reduce the entire army to less than 7,000 and send a detachment to reinforce parliamentarian forces in Ireland. The remainder, Holles assumed, would simply go home. But with payment in arrears and concern among the soldiery mounting about acts committed during the war the majority of the New Model Army resisted disbandment. The army began to organise and appealed to the Independents and senior army officers in parliament, like Oliver Cromwell, for support. In June the army mutinied and agents of the regiments, or 'agitators', took a Solemn Engagement not to disband before their grievances were addressed. The army's demands were then raised to an entirely new level when a junior army officer took possession of the king.[47]

Yet Charles was a willing prisoner. He saw in the army a possible vehicle for his own interests, another means by which to divide and rule his opponents. The army established a General Council to represent its soldiers and officers and articulate their grievances. The Army Council then issued a declaration, which announced it as a political entity: 'We are not a mere mercenary army', the declaration proclaimed, 'hired to serve any arbitrary power of state but called forth . . . by . . . Parliament to the defence of their own and the people's just rights and liberties.'[48] Fearing that the army would mount a coup, Holles encouraged a London mob to enter Westminster as a show of solidarity with the Presbyterian leadership. The Independents in the Commons subsequently abandoned London and sought refuge among the New Model at St Albans. In August the Independents returned to London at the head of the New Model Army and thereby gained control of parliament. Just as Charles had hoped, the Army Council in conjunction with the Independents had, in late July, offered him a new settlement, the so-called Heads of the Proposals. The stage was now set for a permanent settlement

47 John Morrill, *The nature of the English revolution: essays by John Morrill* (London), pp. 307–31; Smith, *A history of the modern British Isles*, pp. 147–50; 153–4; A. Woolrych, *Britain in revolution, 1625–1660* (Oxford, 2002), pp. 369–70.
48 Lockyer, *Tudor and Stuart Britain*, p. 351 (quotation).

between the king and the Independents, with the backing of the army. The Proposals were a reflection of the belief in the army that parliament had in its prosecution of the war become despotic. They called for the redistribution of seats in the Commons to make the lower house 'an equal representative of the whole' and the establishment of biennial parliaments. Under this settlement, control of the military and the power to appoint to major offices would return to the crown after ten years. The Covenant and the erection of Presbyterian church structures, moreover, were to be abandoned in favour of an episcopacy stripped of its 'coercive power, authority and jurisdiction'.[49]

Charles, however, refused to accept the Heads of the Proposals. Instead he played for time in the firm belief that he could attain an even more favourable settlement. He was alive to the people of England's disaffection from parliament and to the divisions that were emerging within the army. Charles also saw opportunity in Ireland where parliament's appointment of the prominent Independent Philip Sidney, Viscount Lisle, as lord lieutenant had raised apprehensions that an English conquest was imminent. Lisle's regime was openly hostile to Catholic and Protestant Irish alike and, in spring 1648, the Protestant parliamentarian, Murrough O'Brien, Lord Inchiquin and president of Munster, opened negotiations with the Confederates, which led to his defection to the royalist coalition that had emerged around Ormond. In Scotland, moreover, James Hamilton and an alliance of moderate Covenanters and royalists had won control of the Committee of Estates from the hard line Covenanter government. Hamilton also feared that the Independents had sent Lisle to conquer Ireland, but saw this as part of a bid to re-establish English hegemony in the British Isles and, perhaps, as a prelude to the conquest of Scotland. From these disparate strands of disaffected in Britain and Ireland, Charles stitched together a grand alliance to defeat the Independents and restore royal authority.[50]

At the heart of this elaborate three-kingdom stratagem was the secret Engagement concluded between the king and the Scots in December 1647. In return for military aid, Charles agreed to establish Presbyterianism in England for a three-year trial period and to 'endeavour a complete union of the kingdoms', that is to promote an incorporating union similar to that envisaged by his father. Yet, such was the Scots' eagerness to reach a settlement with Charles, they did not require him to swear the Covenant and

49 Smith, *A history of the modern British Isles*, pp. 154–5 (quotations, p. 155).
50 J. Adamson, 'Strafford's ghost: the British context of viscount Lisle's lieutenancy of Ireland', in Ohlmeyer (ed.) *Ireland from independence to occupation*, pp. 128–59; *Oxford DNB*, s.v. Charles I.

guaranteed both his military authority and his right to appoint advisors.[51] The following spring and summer there were royalist uprisings in South Wales, East Anglia, Kent and Yorkshire. In July, Hamilton invaded England with 10,000 soldiers. Michael Jones, the parliamentarian governor of Dublin, wrote to the Speaker of the Commons:

> Ormond and Inchiquin are confederate, as with the Irish, so with the now rising party in Scotland, and with some Scots in Ulster, and that there have letters lately arrived in Munster sent from Scotland by an express, which have been communicated by Inchiquin to the Rebels' Council at Kilkenny.[52]

The so-called Second Civil War had begun. But Charles's attempt to mobilise the military potential of royalist elements within his three kingdoms failed utterly. The New Model had already suppressed most of the uncoordinated royalist uprisings by the time Hamilton's Engagers crossed the border. In August, Cromwell routed Hamilton's army at Preston, triggering an anti-Engagers backlash in Scotland which saw Argyll returned to power with Cromwell's support. Inchiquin had concluded a truce with the Confederates in May, but this only exacerbated religious and ethnic divisions within the Confederacy. Irish aid never materialised and Charles was left at the mercy of parliament.[53]

In April 1648 the Commons had voted that the 'fundamental government of the kingdom by King, Lords, and Commons' should not be altered. The Second Civil War had not changed this most fundamental principle of government and society in the British Isles and in September parliamentary commissioners prevailed upon the king to accept the Newport Propositions – a diluted version of the terms offered at Newcastle. True to form, Charles accepted some of the terms, rejected others and all the while made it known that he was entering into a 'mock treaty', which he would repudiate at his earliest opportunity.[54] To the army this was unacceptable and in November they presented parliament with a Remonstrance. Drafted by Henry Ireton, Cromwell's son-in-law, the Remonstrance demanded an immediate end to negotiations at Newport, the dissolution of the Long Parliament, which was to be replaced by annual or biennial parliaments chosen on a reformed

51 Macinnes, *The British revolution*, pp. 186–7; Smith, *A history of the modern British Isles*, pp. 157–8 (quotation, p. 157).

52 Adamson, 'Strafford's ghost', in Ohlmeyer (ed.) *Ireland from independence to occupation*, p. 158 (quotation).

53 Macinnes, *The British revolution*, pp. 186–7; Morrill, *Revolt in the provinces*, pp. 173–6.

54 Kishlansky, *A monarchy transformed*, pp. 180–1 (quotation).

franchise and with the power to elect a new king, and a trial for Charles. [357]
Unlike the majority in parliament, the experience of the Second Civil War
had changed fundamentally the army's relationship with the king. It was
Charles, they argued, who had betrayed them and it was Charles who again
plunged them into war. As the army officers faced into renewed hostilities in
April 1648 they gathered at a prayer meeting. There they concluded 'that it
was our duty, if ever the Lord brought us back again in peace, to call Charles
Stuart, that man of blood, to an account for that blood he had shed, and
mischief he had done . . . against the Lord's cause and people in these poor
nations'. For the army, their victory represented divine providence – the
triumph of good over the evil spawned by the sacrilege committed by
'Charles Stuart'.[55] Thus, when parliament set the Remonstrance aside in a
final attempt to conclude a treaty with Charles and thereby defuse the situation, radical elements within the army lost patience and took matters into
their own hands. In December, troops led by Colonel Thomas Pride entered
the Commons and purged the house of those members who were unwilling
to bring Charles to trial. What remained following 'Pride's Purge' was the
'Rump' of the Long Parliament of approximately 150 members willing to
support the army and the Independents.[56]

This new regime did not consider itself bound by the axiom that England
should be governed, 'by King, Lords, and Commons'. In January, the
Commons acted unilaterally, declaring that 'the Commons of England in
Parliament assembled, being chosen by and representing the people, have
the supreme power in this nation'. The Rump then used its new constitutional powers to set up a High Court of Justice to try the king.[57] Since being
brought to London from the Isle of Wight in December, Charles had refused
any settlement. He believed that the army would lose its nerve, or that military assistance was forthcoming either from Ireland, or from his wife and
family on the continent. But Charles underestimated the commitment to
regicide of a determined minority of Independents and army officers in
whose eyes the monarchy had long since been demystified. Charles stood
accused of making war against his people, of being 'a tyrant, traitor and
murderer, and a public and implacable enemy to the Commonwealth of
England'. Ironically, Charles's finest hours of his disastrous reign came in his

55   Patricia Crawford, 'Charles Stuart, that man of blood', *Journal of British Studies*, 16 (1977),
     pp. 41–61 (quotation, p. 54).
56   Smith, *Constitutional royalism and the search for a settlement*, pp. 138–40, 196–7; David
     Underdown, *Pride's Purge: politics in the Puritan Revolution* (Oxford, 1971).
57   Smith, *A history of the modern British Isles*, p. 161 (quotation).

refutation of the charges levelled against him.[58] He refused to enter a plea because, he argued, the court had no authority to try a king, and if the army could try the king then, he claimed, 'I do not know what subject . . . can be sure of his life or anything that he calls his own'. Defendants who refused to plead were guilty of treason and Charles was sentenced to death.[59] Charles I accepted his fate with dignity and was beheaded at Whitehall on 30th January 1649. In death Charles was to become more popular than ever he was in life.

Commonwealth *vs.* multiple monarchy

The regicide made it impossible for the Rump Parliament to draw back from the revolution which it had set in motion. A return to monarchical rule was unthinkable, but there existed no preconceived structure of government to erect in its stead. The Rump thus proceeded piecemeal: in February government was entrusted to an executive Council of State, under the presidency of Cromwell; the following month acts were passed abolishing the monarchy and the House of Lords. It was not until May that England was declared a 'Commonwealth and Free State', in which the existing unicameral parliament retained its 'supreme authority' and the Council of State retained its executive function. The vast preponderance of English and Welsh watched in astonishment as the Independents, with the backing of the army, completed their revolution.[60]

The establishment of the English Commonwealth transformed England's relationship with Scotland and Ireland. From an English perspective, it was the crown that formed the link between England and Scotland and the abolition of the monarchy had ended that regal union. Ireland, meanwhile, was seen as a dependent state, just as it had been seen as a dependent kingdom. The Scots, however, had prior to parliament's abolition of the monarchy proclaimed the prince of Wales, then in exile on the continent, Charles II, king of Great Britain and Ireland. The Scots were horrified by their king's execution. Yet their provocative decision to style Charles II as king of all

---

58   J.S.A. Adamson, 'The frightened Junto: perception of Ireland, and the last attempts at settlement with Charles I', in J. Peacey (ed.) *The regicides and the execution of Charles I* (Basingstoke, 2001), pp. 36–93; *Oxford DNB, s.v.* Charles I; Smith, *A history of the modern British Isles,* pp. 161–4 (quotation, p. 161).

59   Lockyer, *Tudor and Stuart Britain,* p. 357 (quotation).

60   Blair Worden, *The Rump Parliament, 1648–53* (Cambridge, 1974).

Britain, rather than king of Scots, was motivated by more than a simple desire for revenge. The Scots government hoped to establish a covenanted monarchy with the new king and was not prepared to allow a small group of sectarian republicans to demolish the confederal union with England and the possibility of extending the Covenant throughout the archipelago. Charles's trial and execution also caused a major realignment of forces in Ireland. In January Ormond and the royalists concluded the so-called 'Second Ormond Peace' with the Confederates. The Confederation was dissolved and it was agreed that the former Confederate forces would combine with Inchiquin's Protestant troops and Ormond's royalists to form an 18,000 strong Irish army to be despatched to England. In March 1649 Cromwell told the Council of State:

> I had rather be over-run with a Cavalierish interest than a Scotch interest; I had rather be over-run with a Scotch interest than an Irish interest; and I think of all, this is most dangerous. If they shall be able to carry on their work, they will make this the most miserable people in the earth, for all the world knows their barbarism – not of any religion, almost any of them, but in a manner as bad as Papists.

Perceived as the more immediate threat, and as a dependent state of the English Commonwealth, Ireland was to be dealt with first.[61]

For a brief moment it seemed that Ireland's divided polity had buried their ethnic and religious differences to combat a common enemy. Upon learning of Charles's execution, the ministers of the Presbyterian church in Ulster issued a 'Necessary Representation', a blistering attack on the 'sectarian party in England'. The Ulster Scots rose up and forced George Monck and his parliamentarian forces to retreat to Dundalk. Hoping to support these efforts, Ormond sent a royalist force to the north which seemed to mirror the new political dispensation in Ireland: two regiments of Catholic Irish troops from Leinster and Connaught, together with a contingent of Scottish highlanders, drove into the heart of Protestant Ulster. The presence of Catholic troops in Ulster, however, proved too much for the Ulster Scots and coordinated action quickly ceased. The influential O'Neill/Rinuccini faction within the Confederacy, moreover, had rejected the 'Second Ormond Peace'. Rinuccini returned to Italy in February and O'Neill, and his army,

---

61 Corish, 'Ormond, Rinuccini and the Confederates, 1645–9', in *NHI*, iii, pp. 316–35; D. Stevenson, 'Cromwell, Scotland and Ireland' in J. Morrill (ed.), *Oliver Cromwell and the English Revolution* (London, 1990), pp. 149–79; W.C. Abbott (ed.), *The writings and speeches of Oliver Cromwell* (4 vols, Cambridge Mass. 1937–47), ii, p. 38 (quotation).

became fugitives from their former allies. In desperation, O'Neill opened negotiations with parliamentary commanders in Ulster.[62] The royalist cause in Ireland was thus already unravelling by the time parliamentarian reinforcements arrived in summer 1649. The parliamentarian victory over Ormond outside Dublin in August denied royalists the capital and paved the way for Cromwell's campaign which began shortly thereafter.[63]

Cromwell's first objective in Ireland was to remove the military threat posed by royalists, thereby depriving Charles II of a possible bridgehead from which to invade England. Following their defeat in August, the royalists adopted a defensive strategy and fell back on the towns and castles in their control. This reluctance to challenge the New Model Army in the field dictated that Cromwell's campaign would be one of siege warfare. In all, Cromwell occupied 25 fortified towns and castles in a counter-clockwise sweep, which stretched from north Leinster to west Munster and lasted 9 months; however it was the sieges of Drogheda and Wexford in September and October respectively which are most remembered. More than 5,000 civilians were massacred at these sieges, which Cromwell thought to be 'a righteous judgment of God upon these barbarous wretches who have imbrued their hands in so much innocent blood; and that it will tend to prevent the effusion of blood for the future'. Cromwell had avenged the massacres of Protestants in 1641 – that Drogheda was never a Confederate town and that its inhabitants were predominantly English did not matter. For Cromwell the conquest of Ireland was more than a military necessity, it represented an opportunity for England to wipe away its past mistakes and begin the civilising process anew. By May 1650 royalist resistance was waning and Cromwell returned to England. The military conquest of Ireland that Cromwell had begun, however, continued for another two years and paved the way for the English parliament's revolutionary reform of its Irish dependency in 1652.[64]

Charles II's return to Scotland and his acceptance of the Covenant in June 1650 represented a clear threat to the English Commonwealth. Cromwell had assumed command of the Commonwealth's land forces upon his arrival

---

62 K. Forkan, 'The south Ulster borderland as a political frontier in the 1640s', in *Breifne*, xl (2004), pp. 284–5 (quotation, p. 284); Ó hAnnracháin, *Catholic reformation in Ireland*, pp. 198–231.

63 Hayes-McCoy, *Irish battles*, pp. 200–13.

64 *Oxford DNB*, *s.v.* Oliver Cromwell; T.C. Barnard, *Cromwellian Ireland: English government and reform in Ireland, 1649–1660* (Oxford, 1975); Thomas Carlyle (ed.), *Oliver Cromwell's letters and speeches with elucidations* (4 vols, NY, reprint 1974), ii, p. 60 (quotation).

back in England and, in July, launched a pre-emptive campaign against the Scots. Cromwell's tactical brilliance was again shown in his decisive defeat of Leslie's numerically superior army at Dunbar in September. Cromwell, however, attributed his victory to 'the great hand of the Lord'.[65] The defeat allowed Cromwell control of south-east Scotland, so destabilising Argyll's radical covenanter government, which had assumed control of the General Assembly in the months following Hamilton's defeat at Preston. Argyll's government had sponsored a comprehensive programme of reform, confirmed in the Act of Classes passed by the Scottish Estates in January 1649, which stripped Engagers and other former royalists of their civil and military offices and gave the kirk a veto over office holders. But this programme alienated the nobility and created political divisions within the Covenanting movement. The disaster at Dunbar, moreover, led radical Covenanters in the south-west to issue a Remonstrance denouncing the government's support for Charles II. Cromwell's exploitation of these divisions coupled with his military superiority enabled him to occupy the south-west by December, breaking the influence of the Remonstrants. The collapse of the Remonstrants and the presence, and increasing power, of Charles moved the Covenanters to put aside their differences and a coalition formed dedicated to defending the kingdom and the covenant. In January 1651 Charles was crowned King of Great Britain and Ireland at Scone, but was reminded that he 'hath not absolute power to do what he pleaseth' for 'total government is not upon a king'; the Act of Classes was subsequently suspended to allow former royalists to partake in the newly constituted Committee for Managing the Affairs of the Army. After Dunbar, Cromwell had hoped to avoid conquering Scotland; but the British pretensions of the Scots made conquest and, eventually, closer union inevitable. His campaign continued until September when the king was lured into an invasion of England. Despite the dislike of many Englishmen for the Commonwealth, the English were war-weary and withheld their support from their putative sovereign. The Scottish army was routed at Worcester in September – Charles made a harrowing escape to the continent. Though fighting dragged on for another year, Scotland, like Ireland, had been brought under the effective control of England.[66] In October 1651 the Rump declared that Scotland was to be 'incorporated into, and become one Commonwealth with this of England'.[67]

65 *Oxford DNB*, *s.v.* Oliver Cromwell (quotation).
66 Brown, *Kingdom or province*, pp. 133–6; Macinnes, *The British revolution*, pp. 188–92; Stevenson, *Revolution and counter-revolution*, pp. 193–210 (quotation, p. 197).
67 Smith, *A history of the modern British Isles*, p. 178 (quotation).

[362] Cromwell's Commonwealth

Cromwell's subjugation of Ireland and Scotland removed any remaining military threats to the English Commonwealth from within the archipelago. Peace allowed the leaders of the army the freedom to contemplate a long-term political settlement to the wars of the three kingdoms. Since 1649, the unicameral Rump Parliament had maintained stability in England and financed the war effort. The latter was managed through the continuation of the unpopular excise and onerous monthly assessments, while the former was sustained by the Rump's innate social conservatism. Following the regicide, there were few changes in English government or society: property rights were upheld, most institutions of government – Exchequer, Chancery, Assizes, Commissions of the Peace – were retained and, despite the abolition of bishops, the parish structure, including the payment of tithes, was left untouched. Power within these structures, moreover, continued in the hands of the gentry.[68] The Rump itself, dominated by conservative lawyers and intellectual republican theorists, displayed an aversion to any further constitutional change. Attendance at parliament was steadily decreasing and the number of committees dwindled. The Rump's lethargy is revealed in its legislative record: in 1649 it passed 125 acts; by 1652 the number of acts passed had fallen to 44. To Cromwell and the army officers the Rump Parliament had failed to produce a godly Commonwealth. Its members, they argued, had become more concerned about their own welfare than England's, and nowhere was their selfishness more evident than in the Rump's unwillingness to dissolve itself and hold new elections on a broad franchise. New elections, however, had been avoided for a reason, namely that they would return a majority of royalists and Presbyterians, so exposing the narrow support base of the revolution. Cromwell had hoped that the government would broaden its appeal by offering a general amnesty to royalists, but in order to help offset the costs of war the Rump had sold off the estates of 780 former royalists. The most obvious political settlement was a military government, but Cromwell was reluctant to accept civil authority. In April 1653 a compromise was reached whereby the Rump would dissolve itself and power would be transferred to an interim council of MPs. The army would then oversee elections to ensure that candidates were suitably pious and faithful to the nascent Commonwealth. But when Cromwell

68   J. Morrill, 'Politics in an age of revolution, 1630–1690', in J. Morrill (ed.) *Oxford's illustrated history of Tudor and Stuart Britain* (Oxford, 1996), pp. 377–9.

THE DESTRUCTION AND RESTORATION

learned that parliament was planning to proceed with elections without the army's supervision he led a contingent of musketeers into Westminster and dissolved the last remnant of the Long Parliament.[69]

As lord general of the highly politicised army, it was Cromwell who held the true power in the British Isles. This was formally acknowledged in December 1653 when the Army Council voted to adopt the Instrument of Government, whereby Cromwell was installed as Lord Protector. Until his death, Cromwell was to exercise 'the chief magistracy and the administration of the government over [the Commonwealth of England, Scotland and Ireland and the dominions thereunto belonging] and the people thereof'. Yet Cromwell was slow to assume the role that only he could play. As one historian has recently indicated, he 'reiterated that he saw it as a duty laid upon him by God and not as something he sought and enjoyed'.[70] Following the Rump's dissolution, he had experimented with a parliament of the godly, inspired by one of a number of millenarian sects to emerge after the regicide and chosen by the Army Council. But, like the Rump, this Nominated Assembly, 'The Parliament of Saints', foundered on the unwill-ingness of a majority to upset the existing social order and, after just five months, its conservative members voted 'to deliver up unto the Lord General Cromwell the powers which they received from him'.[71] Cromwell again refused to contemplate an extended period of military rule. Instead, he turned to the device for government conceived by Major-General John Lambert, and based on the Heads of the Proposals, that thrust political power upon him.

The Instrument of Government, a written constitution, envisaged a mixed government comprised of an elected monarch, a powerful council of state, a parliament and a standing army of 30,000 men. Cromwell would not accept the title of king, so the title Lord Protector was chosen. The council, num-bering between 13 and 21 lifetime members, advised the Protector on civil and military matters and was given the responsibility of choosing future lord protectors. The Instrument established a unicameral parliament comprised of 400 English and Welsh members and an additional 30 Irish and 30 Scottish members. Though the number of county members increased, the franchise

69   J.S.A. Adamson, 'Oliver Cromwell and the Long Parliament' in Morrill (ed.), *Oliver Cromwell and the English Revolution*, pp. 83–5; Kishlansky, *A monarchy transformed*, pp. 187–204; *Oxford DNB*, *s.v.* Oliver Cromwell.
70   *Oxford DNB*, *s.v.* Oliver Cromwell (quotations).
71   A. Woolrych, *Commonwealth to protectorate* (Oxford, 1986), pp. 56–75, 278–333; Smith, *A history of the modern British Isles*, pp. 183–4 (quotation, p. 184).

was reserved for those who held property or goods worth £200, thereby narrowing the electorate. Parliaments were to meet triennially and had the power to enact and amend law; bills that passed parliament but were not signed by the Protector became law after 20 days. The first parliament was set for September 1654 – in the meanwhile, the Protector was empowered to issue ordinances that carried the full force of law. A national church was also established, but religious toleration was guaranteed only for the minority who were not Episcopalians or Catholics.[72] The Instrument was thus a conservative document, which at once re-established a traditional pattern of government in England and wedded Cromwell, and the army with him, to the political settlement.

The first parliament in which English, Irish and Scottish representatives sat together convened in September 1654. In just four years Cromwell's armies had achieved what centuries of kings and queens could not (or would not): comprehensive political union in the British Isles. Cromwell told members that the 'great end' of the parliament should be 'healing and settling'. But the assembly of parliament quickly revealed that the Protectorate enjoyed little popular support. The majority of English and Welsh members returned were Presbyterian and, as in former parliaments, drawn from the propertied gentry. These members refused to ratify the Instrument of Government because, they believed, it circumscribed the authority of parliament. The government also faced opposition from committed republican members, who argued that the Instrument was the product of a small group of army officers and regarded Cromwell's acceptance of the Protectorate as a betrayal. Cromwell and his council responded by requiring members to accept the principle of government by a single person and parliament. One hundred members subsequently withdrew from parliament in protest and those who remained subjected the government to sustained criticism over religion and the military establishment. Only by dissolving parliament in January 1655 did Cromwell avoid a more serious clash between the government and parliament.[73]

Yet opposition to the Protectorate was not confined to parliament. Royalists planned a general rebellion for March, but the arrest of prominent rebel leaders thwarted their efforts. In Wiltshire, however, several hundred rebels proclaimed Charles II and wrought havoc throughout the West Country. Though the rebellion was easily suppressed, the failure of the population to

72 Kishlansky, *A monarchy transformed*, pp. 206–7.
73 Smith, *A history of the modern British Isles*, pp. 185–7 (quotation, p. 187).

oppose the rebels reflected a general unwillingness to support the regime in any positive way. Cromwell's division of England and Wales into eleven military districts, each governed by a major-general to counter the royalist threat, did little to garner support for the regime in the localities. Unlike deputy lieutenants, whose power had rested on their familiarity in the localities, the major-generals were outsiders granted sweeping powers to raise regional militias and tax former royalists, so as to root out 'dangerous persons'. They were also responsible for the promotion of 'godliness and virtue', hence bear-baiting, cock-fights, stage plays and other activities deemed ungodly, were banned. The government imprisoned without trial those whose actions 'tended to the disturbance of the peace of the nation', a necessity which Cromwell himself condoned: '[I]f nothing should be done but what is according to law,' he remarked, 'the throat of the nation may be cut, till we send for some to make a law'. But, despite the unpopularity of the government among the general population, few were prepared to resort to violence to overthrow it – the rising in Wiltshire had shown the futility of armed rebellion. Thus, for change to occur, an accommodation had to be found within the existing constitutional framework.[74]

Support for the Commonwealth in Ireland and Scotland, meanwhile, was entirely dependent on the threat of overwhelming military force. The scale of the Commonwealth's military commitment was in reasonable proportion to the settlements that it imposed: nearly 30,000 troops were required to maintain peace in Ireland; 18,000 troops were required to control Scotland. In August 1652, the Rump passed the Act for the Settlement of Ireland which effected the greatest transfer of land yet witnessed in Ireland's history. In one stroke, Old English and Gaelic landowners were stripped of their medieval distinctions and dispossessed as Irish Catholics. Their lands were to form the economic basis for a new English landowning class in Ireland. In 1642 the English parliament had earmarked 2,500,000 acres of Irish land for those who would loan or 'adventure' money to help re-establish the government's authority. Thus 600 Protestant 'Adventurers' were granted vast amounts of land and a further 12,000 English soldiers received Irish land as payment for their military services. It was proposed, moreover, that the native population, excluding the 100,000 or so liable for execution under the Act, should receive lands west of the river Shannon, on the banks of

74 C. Durston, *Cromwell's major-generals: godly government during the English revolution* (Manchester, 2001); Anthony Fletcher, 'Oliver Cromwell and the localities' in D.L. Smith (ed.), *Cromwell and the Interregnum* (Oxford, 2003), pp. 123–40; Abbott, *Writing and speeches*, iv, p. 275 (quotation).

which colonies of soldiers would be placed to prevent their interaction with the English population. In this way, Protestant settlers could transform the remaining three-quarters of Ireland into a prosperous and civil English entity without fear of being contaminated by Catholicism, or of the natives procuring military support from England's enemies. Though the scheme proved far too great a logistical undertaking for the Commonwealth or Protectorate governments to effect – only a few hundred were executed and the transplantation of Irish Catholics was generally limited to prominent Catholic leaders – the proportion of land held by Catholics plummeted from 59 per cent in 1641 to 22 per cent in 1660. The ground had been laid for a minority 'Cromwellian' English elite who dominated the civil and military establishment for the remainder of the decade. Ulster Presbyterians and the New English (or Old Protestants as they were now known) were viewed with suspicion and were marginalised in the new regime.[75]

As a free and Protestant nation, Scotland was not subjected to the large-scale dispossession and colonisation witnessed in Ireland. The settlement imposed in Scotland, however, was no less far-reaching in its intent. The Scots were given a nominal right to consent to Scotland's incorporation into the Commonwealth announced by the Rump in late 1651. Commissioners were despatched to Scotland and instructed the shires and burghs to elect two deputies to come to Dalkeith to assent to incorporative union. There was little support for incorporation into the Commonwealth, but the deputies were representative of a conquered nation and given little choice. In April 1654 the union of Scotland and Ireland with England was affirmed by an ordinance issued by the Lord Protector and council. Civil government in Scotland was initially entrusted to eight parliamentary commissioners before being replaced in April 1652 by the Commission for the Administration of Justice. Under the Protectorate, power was devolved to a Scottish Council. Though a small Scottish presence was evident on both the Commission and the Council, overall participation in government was slight. The government actively sought to break the power of the Scottish landed elite: the confiscation of lands of all those in arms against parliament were to serve as a prelude to a systematic assault on the power of landlords. 'It is', as an English army officer remarked, 'in the interest of the Commonwealth of England to break the interest of the great men of Scotland, and

---

75 K. Bottingheimer, *English money and Irish land: the 'Adventurers' in the Cromwellian settlement of Ireland* (Oxford, 1971), pp. 30–53; J.R. Mac Cormack, 'The Irish adventurers and the English civil war', in *Irish Historical Studies*, 10 (1956), pp. 21–58; Barnard, *Cromwellian Ireland*.

to settle the interests of the common people upon a different foot from the interests of their lords and masters.' With little more to lose, William Cunningham, earl of Glencairn, raised rebellion in 1653. The rebellion, however, was confined to the highlands, which both prolonged its duration and limited its impact. By 1655, resistance had been crushed.[76]

In Scotland, as in Ireland, the settlements imposed under the Common-wealth and inherited by the Protectorate were sustained through military occupation. Disaffection from the regime was widespread, but by the later 1650s there was a growing sense of sullen acceptance of the government. This was due in part to Cromwell's understanding that military occupation could not be sustained indefinitely. The appointment in 1655 of Cromwell's son Henry as Major-General of the army in Ireland marked a departure from the aggressive policies implemented in the wake of the conquest. Henry Cromwell relaxed persecution of Catholics and Presbyterians and healed divisions between 'Cromwellian' settlers and Old Protestants. Though Cromwell could do little to prevent the emergence of a society in which the majority Catholic population was controlled by a minority of land-owning English Protestants, he managed by 1657 to reduce the number of English troops serving in Ireland to 9,000. In Scotland, the Scottish Council, under the direction of Lord Broghill, the former lord president of Munster, achieved some success in its efforts to eliminate heritable jurisdictions and feudal dependencies and strengthen commissions of the peace. Less successful were the government's attempts to introduce religious toleration. Remonstrants and former royalists, known as Resolutioners, were united in their adherence to strict Presbyterianism. Nevertheless, by 1657, there was a growing accep-tance of the regime and the number of English troops in Scotland – under the command of the former commander of parliamentarian forces in Ireland, Lieutenant-General George Monck since 1651 – was reduced to 10,500. Thus neither the Irish nor the Scots were supportive of the Protectorate, but there existed neither a military, nor a constitutional solution to their grievances. The 60 Irish and Scottish MPs were carefully screened to ensure their support for the Protectorate and, in any event, represented less than 20 percent of the overall Commons.[77]

---

76 Frances Dow, *Cromwellian Scotland, 1651–1660* (Edinburgh, 2000); Macinnes, *The British revolu-tion*, pp. 200–3; Smith, *A history of the modern British Isles*, pp. 178–80 (quotation, p. 179).

77 J.R. Young, *The Scottish parliament, 1639–1661: a political and constitutional analysis* (Edinburgh, 1996), pp. 297–303; Smith, *A history of the modern British Isles*, pp. 176–80; Macinnes, *The British revolution*, pp. 202–3.

In early 1657 a group of English MPs offered Cromwell the crown of the three kingdoms as the central component of a new written constitution, which became known as The Humble Petition and Advice. It was hoped that Cromwell's acceptance of a 'known' form of government accountable to a strengthened parliament would at once limit the government's reliance on the army and lend the constitutional settlement permanency. Cromwell accepted that military rule could not be sustained indefinitely – he was forced to abandon his experiment with government through major-generals in January – and wished to see the dominance of civil government reasserted. The Humble Petition proposed the restoration of an upper house, here called the 'Other House', of between 40 and 70 lifetime peers appointed by the king and council. Parliament was to be given the power to appoint and dismiss councillors and pledged £1,000,000 annually to maintain the army and £300,000 to support the civil administration. Cromwell accepted the new constitution in May 1657, but he refused the kingship, preferring instead to remain Lord Protector. The coronation of King Oliver would have been an affront to the army and Cromwell himself, who remarked, 'I would not seek to set up that, that providence hath destroyed and laid in the dust; and I would not build Jericho again'. Cromwell, however, was king in all but name: under the new constitution he was empowered to nominate his own successor and his second installation as Lord Protector in June 1657 had all the trappings of a royal coronation.[78]

Yet parliament refused to ratify the Humble Petition. Members roundly criticised Cromwell's appointments to the Other House, while republicans attacked its very existence. A petition was circulated in London, meanwhile, calling for the Protectorate's abolition and the restoration of a single chamber parliament. With the army grumbling over mounting arrears of pay, Cromwell feared that these interests might coalesce to form a coherent threat to the Protectorate and dissolved parliament in February 1658.[79] A permanent constitutional settlement thus continued to elude Cromwell. Though he had established a balance between the army and the civilian government, it was a temporary arrangement wholly dependent on the force of Cromwell's personality. His efforts to reconcile the two interests had failed. So too did his efforts to establish freedom of religious expression and promote godliness: Ireland remained an overwhelmingly Catholic nation, Scotland clung to its Presbyterianism and much of England continued to use

78   Woolrych, *Britain in revolution*, pp. 638–63; Abbott, *Writing and speeches*, iv, p. 473 (quotation).
79   Lockyer, *Tudor and Stuart Britain*, p. 374.

the old prayer book and rejected the so-called 'reformation of manners'. In the longer term, however, the inability to win the support of a majority of the population anywhere in the British Isles was Cromwell's greatest failure. In the course of 1658 his health steadily deteriorated and, in early September, he died. Cromwell's elaborate funeral was modelled on that of King James whose beloved son Cromwell had sentenced to death nearly a decade earlier.

The collapse of republican government

Before his death Cromwell nominated his eldest son Richard to succeed him as Lord Protector. Neither a soldier, nor a statesman, Richard Cromwell was nevertheless thrust into the treacherous middle ground occupied by his father between the army and the politicians. His already precarious position was further complicated by the financial crisis that he inherited: the annual English deficit was a manageable £30,500, but the military occupation of Scotland and Ireland created annual deficits of £163,619 and £138,690 respectively. Pay for the army was six months in arrears and by April 1659 the Protectorate's total debt stood at over £2,000,000.[80] In January 1659 Cromwell summoned parliament to procure the supply necessary to pay the increasingly restless army, but the Commons had a different agenda. Republicans refused even to recognise Cromwell as Protector and debate focused on asserting control over the army and rolling back religious tolera-tion, rather than on supply. In April General Charles Fleetwood, the com-mander of the army in England and Richard Cromwell's brother-in-law, intervened and forced Cromwell to dissolve parliament and to recall the Rump. Cromwell's power had ceased to exist: he formally resigned as Lord Protector in May. The Rump, however, proved equally unsatisfactory in advancing the interests of the army and in October the army forcibly dis-solved the Rump, establishing outright military rule in its stead.[81]

Failed royalist risings in Cheshire and Lancashire in summer 1659 reflected continued royalist impotence in the face of the army. Even as the army split into opposing factions and military rule collapsed in December leaving no government whatsoever for more than a week, the royalists were unable

---

80   Macinnes, *The British revolution*, p. 224.
81   Woolrych, *Britain in revolution*, pp. 707–26; R. Hutton, *The restoration: political & religious history of England and Wales, 1658–1667* (Oxford, 1985), pp. 42–67.

organise. Order was only restored when George Monck, who had initially fought for Charles I, marched his army south from Scotland and occupied London in February 1660. Monck had rejected the military rule of his colleagues and feared the influence of religious radicals within the army. Before leaving Scotland, he had appealed to the Scottish nobles to maintain order in his absence – the royalist earl of Glencairn featured prominently – and was joined on his march south by disaffected Scots. In Ireland, the Old Protestant interest led by Sir Charles Coote and other army officers had seized Dublin and assumed power in December.[82] Monck restored those royalist parliamentarians whom Pride had purged in December 1648. At Monck's instigation the reborn Long Parliament subsequently established a national Presbyterian church, appointed him Lord General and set a date for free elections before dissolving itself in March 1660. Monck had concurrently established lines of communication with Charles's exiled court in the Netherlands. In April Charles issued the Declaration of Breda, in which he offered a general pardon to all his subjects (though not the regicides), promised to pay in full the army's arrears and to resolve disputed titles to lands, and expressed his hope that 'those wounds which have so many years together been kept bleeding may be bound up'. In all of this, and in all other matters, Charles pledged to collaborate with and be advised by a free parliament. The elections produced a Convention – so-called because there existed no legal authority to summon it – overwhelmingly receptive to Charles's declaration. Monck allowed events to unfold. In May the Convention, together with a restored House of Lords, restored the Stuart monarchy in England and Ireland amid a surge in support for Charles II. The same month the Scottish parliament proclaimed Charles king of Great Britain and Ireland and, in Dublin, Charles was proclaimed king of Ireland.[83]

In 1660 England, Scotland and Ireland again divided into three separate kingdoms linked by a single crown. Ostensibly, then, Charles II acceded to a multiple monarchy identical to that inherited by his father in 1625. But the unprecedented interaction of Britain and Ireland's four nations in the intervening 35 years had transformed the relationships between the peoples in the archipelago. The political, religious and social upheavals and wars caused by Charles I's efforts to assert authoritarian government in each of his three

82 Macinnes, *The British revolution*, pp. 225–6; Brown, *Kingdom or province*, 140–2; A. Clarke, '1659 and the road to restoration', in Ohlmeyer (ed.) *Ireland from independence to occupation*, pp. 241–64.

83 Lockyer, *Tudor and Stuart Britain*, pp. 375–8 (quotation, p. 377); Smith, *A history of the modern British Isles*, pp. 193–6.

kingdoms upset the delicate balance of power in the British Isles on which
his father had based his reign. Yet the upheaval and war that characterised
Charles's reign had the combined effect of drawing England, Scotland and
Ireland closer together and ultimately produced new political and constitutional relationships between them which were capable of functioning in the
absence of the crown. That these alternative vehicles for state formation
failed to put down lasting roots should not obscure the fact that the inhabitants of the British Isles in the seventeenth century were unable or unwilling
to erect their nations into independent political entities. The Interregnum
had shown that the political future of the archipelago lay in an English-
dominated multiple monarchy, a vehicle for state formation which Charles II
found to be much sturdier than his predecessors.

CONCLUSION

With the restoration of the monarchy in 1660, the political instability which had characterised the British state over the previous two decades was not destined to disappear immediately. For one thing, Charles II could not govern as his father had, for three main reasons. First, the reforming legislation of 1641 had swept away both the prerogative courts, prerogative forms of revenue, such as Ship Money, and also traditional feudal revenues, which were replaced by fixed excises and a hearth tax. Second, although the king himself sought to bring into government the so-called Presbyterians, as well as old royalists, and even Cromwellians, no such policy of comprehension operated in regard to the church. Pressure from the gentry in the English Cavalier parliament forced a restoration of the narrow conformity to the words and rubrics of the Elizabethan church. Thus, a comprehensive political settlement was yoked to a narrow Anglican religious settlement. The third continuing source of instability was the problem of multiple monarchy itself. After the early Stuart moves towards integrative union, and the ruthless imposition of incorporative union in the 1650s, Charles II abandoned any attempt to integrate his three kingdoms. He devolved Scottish government on Scots and Irish government chiefly on the Protestant communities of Ireland. In Scotland, however, the religious settlement (effectively that bequeathed by James VI in 1625) was bitterly contested by hardline Covenanters, prompting a series of rebellions and so an enlarged standing army there. And in Ireland, not only was the religious settlement unworkable (since the overwhelming majority of the population was Catholic, whose services were illegal), but only the small Church of Ireland minority (some 10 per cent of the population) was eligible for public office. Moreover, the Irish land settlement left almost everyone discontented, from Catholics (who felt they had got back far too little land) to Cromwellians (who felt they had surrendered far too much).

Overall, therefore, the Restoration settlement settled very little. It left crown and communities to work out a new political *modus vivendi* both in all three kingdoms and also in regard to the wider problems of multiple monarchy. It also left Anglicans and Scottish Episcopalians on the one hand and Catholic and Protestant non-conformists on the other to reach a workable compromise in regard to religious comprehension and toleration. Thus, further conflict and change, such as the Revolution and the War of the Two Kings in 1688–91 or the Anglo-Scottish parliamentary union of 1707, were quite foreseeable, although not inevitable.[1]

Nonetheless, the pattern of state formation which is apparent in the British Isles from the mid-fifteenth century to the mid-seventeenth century was not untypical of other parts of Europe where, likewise, the early modern period saw a transition from disparate groups of territories dynastically linked to multiple monarchies (or dynastic agglomerates). And elsewhere, too, this pattern of state formation saw periods of tension and conflict between the constituent parts (core and periphery) of the new conglomerate states alternate with periods of retrenchment, even contraction, and also with other periods in which state power and authority advanced in a relatively peaceful manner.

Reading history backwards, there is a tendency among historians to assume that progress towards a united kingdom coterminous with the British Isles was somehow inevitable, a kind of British 'manifest destiny'. But what is clear from the untidy pattern of conflict and change over two centuries is that the apparently felicitous process of building an 'island kingdom' which modern British politicians have perceived and extolled, as opposed to the supposedly less fortunate experiences of the continentals, was as much a product of failure as of far-sighted planning and achievement. Traditional Anglo-Scottish hostilities did not simply fade away, and the very location of the British multiple monarchy's capital city – in the extreme south-east of the larger island, closest to the continent – epitomises this failure. It reflected the ambition of successive English monarchs to consolidate or recover their continental possessions, rather than to build an archipelagic kingdom. And even after such ambitions had been shown to be quite unrealistic, from the later sixteenth century, the horizons of English politicians in regard to the problems of multiple monarchy were generally lower than those of Scottish or Irish politicians. (The same might also have been said, at least until recently, about the interests of modern historians.) Thus, the British state developed the way it did in large part because English monarchs

---

1 A good summary of the Restoration is John Morrill, 'Politics in an age of revolution, 1630–90' in idem (ed.), *Oxford illustrated history of Tudor and Stuart Britain*, pp. 381–8.

lost out in the struggle with their French rivals in regard to territories in northern and western France. The only territorial acquisitions they made – some wild sparsely-inhabited countries in Ireland – were seen as very poor compensation, and scarcely worth the trouble of conquering, if there had been any other way of preventing foreign intrigues.

From the perspective of the northern kingdom, moreover, Scotland's Auld Alliance with France was a necessary protection against English aggression. Briefly in the 1550s, it was even conceivable that Britain would be reduced to the status of a disputed military outpost, or borderland, in the wider Habsburg–Valois struggle for European hegemony. It was only the growing weakness of England in the European state system, and more especially the late and unexpected Scottish Reformation, which created for the first time a community of interest between two very vulnerable Protestant regimes and chivvied them in the direction of a defensive alliance. Even then, things would have turned out differently if Elizabeth had married and had children, or if the 1543 Succession Act and Henry VIII's last will and testament excluding the Stuart line had been observed. Only a series of quite unexpected coincidences created the British multiple monarchy of the seventeenth century.

Nevertheless, within the parameters described by this unanticipated trajectory of political and religious developments in the British Isles, there was a pattern of state formation which may be described as British. It was in many ways akin to what happened elsewhere in early modern Europe, as we have seen, but there were also some aspects which were peculiar to the British archipelago. Many of the particular underlying pressures which promoted closer integration in a British context were noted in King James's proclamation of 1604 styling himself King of Great Britain – a community of language and religion, geographical contiguity on the one island, similar systems of law, administration and land tenure, with sheriffs, coroners, writs and juries. There was also, at times, a conscious attempt to systematise and centralise, with such developments as the sweeping extensions of English common law and local government structures in Wales and Ireland from the 1530s, the attempts to plant 'civility' in parts of the Western Isles and Ireland, and the introduction of a common coinage and a union flag.[2] Perhaps the most fundamental way, however, in which the pattern of state

2   Galloway, *The union of England and Scotland*, pp. 58–62; Patterson, *King James VI and I and the reunion of Christendom*, p. 31; Asch, *Jakob I.*, pp. 62–85.

formation reshaped political relationships within the British Isles was in regard to issues of culture and identity.

Within the British archipelago, the traditional organising principle for broad surveys is nation-centred, with separate grand narratives focusing on the rise of four nations, the consolidation of their respective national territories, and their senses of identity *vis-à-vis* other nations. Yet this practice tends to obscure the extent to which the four nations, and even to an extent their national cultures, were themselves influenced by the British pattern of state formation. Of course the same four nations inhabiting the British Isles in 1450 (some accounts would add the Cornish) still inhabited the same parts of the islands in 1660. In that sense there was continuity, but in the intervening two centuries the image, self-representation and cultural stereotypes of these nations had changed quite radically, as also had the actual population groups comprehended in each nominal nation. If we take the wealthiest and militarily most dominant nation, an Englishman in 1450 might be defined as an English subject born within the territories under the allegiance of the English crown and 'of English blood and condition'. Only about half the British Isles then spoke varieties of English, which was also steadily ousting Latin and 'law French' as the language of government. Yet, the English nation then included the English communities of Ireland, Wales and also Calais (which was parcel of Henry VI's crown of England, not France), although perhaps excluding those Cornish people who spoke only Cornish, since English culture (language, custom and dress) was of the essence of English identity. A second characteristic of Englishness was the coupling of national identity to what we might now describe as rights of citizenship: free subjects of the English crown (as opposed to the 'mere Welsh' or 'mere Irish', whose status equated to that of serfs) were *ipso facto* English. They alone were free at law. As late as the 1540s, the process of surrender and regrant aimed to transform Gaelic chiefs and clans (hitherto 'Irish enemies') into 'English subjects'.[3] By the late sixteenth century, however, only those subjects born within the realm of England were now accounted English, and increasingly Englishness was also identified with Protestantism. The Catholic Old English of Ireland, for instance, were clearly excluded on grounds of religion.

3 *Cal. Carew MSS 1515–74*, no. 171; Maginn, *'Civilizing' Gaelic Leinster*, ch. 3, and pp. 115–17. On the problem of citizenship more generally, see now S.G. Ellis, 'Citizenship in the English state during the Renaissance' in idem, Guðmundur Hálfdanarson and A.K. Isaacs (eds), *Citizenship in historical perspective* (Pisa, 2006), pp. 85–96. On language, see especially, G. Price, *The languages of Britain* (London, 1984); G. Price (ed.), *The Celtic connection* (Gerrards Cross, 1992); G. Williams, *Religion, language and nationality in Wales* (Cardiff, 1979).

In regard to Welsh identity, the statutes of 1536 and 1543 (the so-called Welsh Act of Union) had not only redrawn the administrative boundary between England and Wales but had also established a unity of jurisdiction and administration for Wales in place of its late medieval fragmentation. For the first time, too, the rights of free-born English subjects had been conferred on non-English peoples, the 'mere Welsh', so removing the legal distinctions between the two peoples. The Union thus had a fundamental impact in shaping Welsh senses of identity, since it promoted the idea of a single territorial entity called Wales, just as it downgraded the status of Welsh, hitherto the most potent symbol of Welshness, as the language of government. Differences of culture (language and custom) remained import-ant as indicators of nationality: indeed, the Welsh language, which became the normal vernacular of church services in Wales, showed remarkable resilience. (In Cornwall, and also in Caithness, Orkney and Shetland where Norn was spoken, the failure to provide prayer books and Bibles in Cornish and Norn hastened the collapse of these languages.) Yet, religious differences between English and Welsh did not emerge at this time as a significant ingredient in Welsh identity, in contrast to Ireland. And in the longer term, as acculturation between English and Welsh continued apace in Wales, the inhabitants of Wales, whether native or settler, were increasingly seen Welsh.

In many ways, the British pattern of state formation prompted the same kind of developments in the reshaping of Irish identity during this period. The Irish in 1450 were the *Gaedhil*, the peoples of Gaelic speech and culture living in Ireland or Scotland. The main catalyst for change in Ireland, however, was not union but the erection of Ireland into a separate Tudor kingdom, with the 'wild Irish' after *c.*1540 increasingly accorded the rights of English subjects. Culturally, however, the incorporation of Gaelic Ireland into the Tudor state exerted strong anglicising pressures, with measures to promote 'English civility', and English was also the language of law and government. And following the (nominal) abolition of legal distinctions between Irish and English, acculturation also eroded other traditional distinctions between native and settler there. In Ireland, however, a crucial difference was the role of religion in moulding a sense of Irishness, in opposition to a new wave of English (and later, Scots) settlers. By the early seventeenth century, the Irish were the *Éireannaigh*, a new term which denoted the Catholic people of Ireland (whether *Gaedhil* or *Gaill*, viz. English by descent). The term *Gaill* was now reserved for the real foreigners, the New English and Scots Protestants, the British settlers. Remarkably, the Gaelic learned classes were able, despite the Tudor conquest, to construct a new sense of Irishness based on faith and fatherland, in opposition to English attempts to transform Ireland into a *Saxa nua* (a new England).[4] This new sense of Irishness, however, was set firmly within a British context: there was no separatist tradition of independence from the Stuart dynasty or the other Stuart kingdoms. In the longer term, however, the failure of the Church of Ireland to develop a vibrant Gaelic tradition (akin to the church in Wales) militated against the development of a Gaelic print culture in Ireland, since Catholic prayer books (and indeed services) were chiefly in Latin. Thus, the Irish nation now comprised the Catholic inhabitants of Ireland, including descendants of the medieval Englishry who were English by speech and culture; but the Gaelic tradition – formerly of the essence of Irish identity – was by the eighteenth century increasingly the preserve of the illiterate Catholic peasantry. There was also an enduring resentment of all things English, a legacy of the Tudor and Cromwellian conquests.

Religion was likewise important in Scotland in moulding a common sense of Scottishness among a population with roughly the same ethnic mix of *Gaedhil* and *Gaill* (in effect, Highlanders/Islanders and Lowlanders), but crucially Scotland was on the other side of the sectarian divide from Ireland. The advance of the Reformation in Scottish Gaeldom meant that, with the exception perhaps of clans like the MacDonalds of Clanranald which remained Catholic, traditional ties with Irish Gaeldom declined and the *Gaedhil* of Scotland were increasingly seen as 'Scots', not 'Irish'. Already before the Reformation, the Stewart monarchy had been consolidating its hold over Scottish Gaeldom, and from the late sixteenth century there were also attempts to plant 'civility' among the *Gaedhil* and to proscribe particular Gaelic customs. In Scots Gaelic, the term *Albanuidh* (the people of Scotland) came into vogue to describe collectively the *Gaedhil* and *Gaill* of Scotland. Residual senses of a pan-Gaelic identity lingered among Catholic clans like Clanranald, but by 1660 even the standard literary language of medieval Gaeldom, classical common Gaelic, had collapsed, together with the traditional bardic schools which had sustained it. The earliest printed materials in Gaelic, Bishop Carswell's translation of *The Book of Common Order* or, for the Church of Ireland, Kearney's catechism, were in the literary language, but by the later seventeenth century writings in Gaelic were invariably in the various regional dialects. For instance, in 1688 when 'Irish' Bibles were reprinted for use in Scotland, extensive revisions were needed to make the language intelligible for Scots Gaelic speakers. Even so, a stronger Gaelic

4   Ellis, 'Collapse of the Gaelic world', pp. 467–9.

literary tradition had developed in Scotland, where the Highlands remained predominantly Gaelic-speaking, but even here, English was increasingly understood.[5]

Finally, there were also attempts, particularly by King James after 1603, to promote a sense of Britishness among the subjects of the new multiple monarchy, but in the short term at least attempts to unite four separate nations into a single supranational British identity were far too ambitious. James assumed the title of King of Great Britain, introduced a common coinage and a union flag, and tried to rename England as South Britain and Scotland as North Britain, with the erstwhile border region restyled the Middle Shires. Thereupon, the English, Scots and Welsh were invited to consider themselves as Britons. Many of the latter two were indeed so willing, describing themselves as Britons as well as Scots and Welsh, the English rather less so. Thereafter, however, Britishness enjoyed a distinctly chequered history. Efforts to promote this British identity languished under Charles I. They were resurrected in a different guise during the British republic of the 1650s, but following the Restoration their association with the failed republic rendered any such initiatives unusable for at least a generation.

Despite this failure, however, the untidy pattern of state formation in the British Isles over two centuries had left an indelible mark on the culture and identity of its different population groups. By 1660, Anglicisation (or rather the promotion of Lowland values) was increasingly bringing even the landowning elites of 'the Celtic fringe' within the parameters of what had previously passed for 'English civility'. Everywhere 'English' forms of law and administration had ousted indigenous Celtic ones. English was the language of government and, with some exceptions, of the church too. The position of English as the predominant literary language of the British Isles was thus assured, and even in the traditional Celtic heartlands spoken English was also increasingly familiar. There was, at one level, a very familiar ring to the three kingdoms and four nations over which King Charles II was restored as ruler in 1660, but the preceding two centuries had also brought about an increasing congruity of culture, political ideas and senses of identity among the inhabitants of the British Isles.

5 Ibid.; S.G. Ellis, 'Languages 1500–1800' in Barry Cunliffe, Robert Bartlett, John Morrill, Asa Briggs, and Joanna Bourke (eds), *The Penguin Atlas of British and Irish History* (London, 2001), pp. 152–3.

BIBLIOGRAPHY

Abbott, W.C. (ed.) (1937–47), *The writings and speeches of Oliver Cromwell* (4 vols, Cambridge, Mass.).

Adams, Simon (1978), 'Foreign policy and the parliaments of 1621 and 1624' in Sharpe, K. (ed.), *Faction & parliament*.

Adams, Simon (1984), 'Eliza enthroned? The court and its politics' in Haigh, C. (ed.), *The reign of Elizabeth I*.

Adams, Simon (2002), 'Britain, Europe and the world' in Collinson, P. (ed.) *The short Oxford history of the British Isles*.

Adamson, J.S.A. (1990), 'Oliver Cromwell and the Long Parliament' in Morrill, J. (ed.), *Oliver Cromwell and the English Revolution*.

Adamson, J.S.A. (1995), 'Strafford's ghost: the British context of viscount Lisle's lieutenancy of Ireland' in Ohlmeyer, J. (ed.), *Ireland from independence to occupation*.

Adamson, J.S.A. (2001), 'The frightened Junto: perception of Ireland, and the last attempts at settlement with Charles I' in Peacey, J. (ed.), *The regicides and the execution of Charles I*.

Alford, Stephen (1998), *The early Elizabethan polity: William Cecil and the British succession crisis, 1558–1569* (Cambridge).

Anderson, Michael (ed.) (1996), *British population history from the Black Death to the present day* (Cambridge).

Appleby, A.B. (1978), *Famine in Tudor and Stuart England* (Liverpool).

Arthurson, Ian (1994), *The Perkin Warbeck conspiracy 1491–1499* (Stroud).

Asch, Ronald (2004), 'Thomas Wentworth' in Matthew and Harrison (eds), *Oxford Dictionary of National Biography*.

Asch, Ronald (2005), *Jakob I. (1566–1625) König von England und Schottland; Herrscher des Friedens im Zeitalter der Religionskriege* (Stuttgart).

Ashton, R. (1989), *The English Civil War: conservatism and revolution, 1603–1649* (2nd ed., London).

Aston, M. (1984), *Lollards and reformers: images and literacy in late medieval religion* (London).

Atlas of Ireland (Royal Irish Academy, Dublin, 1979).

Aylmer, G.E. (1974), *The king's servants: the civil service of Charles I, 1625–1642* (London).

Bale, John (1990), *The vocacyon of Johan Bale* (eds) Happé, Peter and King, J.N. (Binghamton).

Bagwell, Richard (1885–90), *Ireland in the age of the Tudors* (3 vols) (London).

[3 8 0]

Barnard, T.C. (1975), *Cromwellian Ireland: English government and reform in Ireland, 1649–1660* (Oxford).

Barnes, T.G. (1991), 'Deputies not principals, lieutenants not captains: the institutional failure of lieutenancy in the 1620s' in Fissel, M.C. (ed.), *War and government in Britain*.

Bartlett, Robert and MacKay, Angus (eds) (1989), *Medieval frontier societies* (Oxford).

Bateson, Mary (1895), 'A collection of original letters from the bishops to the privy council, 1564' in *Camden Society Miscellanea*, ix.

Bean, J.M.W. (1958), *The estates of the Percy family, 1416–1537* (Oxford).

Beer, B.L. (1982), *Rebellion and riot: popular disorder in England during the reign of Edward VI* (Kent State).

Beier, A.L. (1985), *Masterless men: the vagrancy problem in England, 1560–1640* (London).

Bellamy, John (1973), *Crime and public order in England in the later middle ages* (London).

Bennett, Michael (1987), *Lambert Simnel and the battle of Stoke* (Gloucester).

Bennett, Michael (1990), 'Henry VII and the Northern Rising of 1489' in *English Historical Review*, cv.

Bernard, G.W. (1986), *War, taxation and rebellion in early Tudor England: Henry VIII, Wolsey and the Amicable Grant of 1525* (Brighton).

Bernard, G.W. (2005), *The King's Reformation: Henry VIII and the remaking of the English church* (New Haven).

Berry, H.F. (ed.) (1907), *Statutes and ordinances, and acts of the parliament of Ireland, King John to Henry V* (Dublin).

Berry, H.F. (ed.) (1910), *Statute rolls of the parliament of Ireland, reign of King Henry VI* (Dublin).

Bindoff, S.T., Hurstfield, J. and Williams, C.H. (eds) (1961), *Elizabethan government and society* (London).

Blickle, Peter (ed.) (1997), *Resistance, representation, and community* (Oxford).

Bonner, Elizabeth (1996), 'The recovery of St Andrews castle in 1547: French naval policy and diplomacy in the British Isles' in *English Historical Review*, cxi.

Bonner, Elizabeth (1997), 'The genesis of Henry VIII's "rough wooing" of the Scots' in *Northern History*, xxxiii.

Bonner, Elizabeth (1999), 'Scotland's "Auld Alliance" with France, 1295–1560' in *History*, lxxxiv.

Bossy, J.A. (2001), *Under the molehill: an Elizabethan spy story* (Newhaven and London).

Bottingheimer, Karl (1971), *English money and Irish land: the 'Adventurers' in the Cromwellian settlement of Ireland* (Oxford).

Boyce, D.G., Eccleshall, R. and Geoghegan, V. (eds) (1993), *Political thought in Ireland since the seventeenth century* (London).

Boyce, D.G. (ed.) (2001), *Political discourse in seventeenth and eighteenth-century Ireland* (Basingstoke).

Boynton, Lindsay (1962), 'The Tudor provost-marshal' in *English Historical Review*, lxxviii.

Boynton, Lindsay (1967), *The Elizabethan militia, 1558–1638* (London).

Braddick, M.J. (1991), 'Popular politics and public policy: the excise riot at Smithfield in February 1647 and its aftermath' in *Historical Journal*, xxxiv.

Braddick, M.J. (2000), *State formation in early modern England, c.1550–1700* (Cambridge).

Bradshaw, Brendan (1970), 'George Browne, first Reformation archbishop of Dublin' in *Journal of Ecclesiastical History*, xxi.

Bradshaw, Brendan (1974), *The dissolution of the religious orders in Ireland under Henry VIII* (Cambridge).

Bradshaw, Brendan (1979), *The Irish constitutional revolution of the sixteenth century* (Cambridge).

Bradshaw, Brendan and Morrill, John (eds) (1996), *The British problem c.1534–1707: state formation in the Atlantic archipelago* (Basingstoke).

Bradshaw, Brendan and Roberts, Peter (eds) (1998), *British consciousness and identity: the making of Britain, 1533–1707* (Cambridge).

Brady, Ciarán (1980–1), 'Faction and the origins of the Desmond rebellion of 1579' in *Irish Historical Studies*, xxvii.

Brady, Ciarán (1985), 'Conservative subversives: the community of the Pale and the Dublin administration, 1556–86' in Corish, P.J. (ed.), *Radicals, rebels and establishments*.

Brady, Ciarán and Gillespie, Raymond (eds) (1986), *Natives and newcomers: the making of Irish colonial society, 1534–1641* (Dublin).

Brady, Ciarán (1991), 'The decline of the Irish kingdom' in Greengrass, M. (ed.) *Conquest and coalescence*.

Brady, Ciarán (1994), *The chief governors: the rise and fall of reform government in Tudor Ireland, 1536–1588* (Cambridge).

Brady, Ciarán (1999), 'Shane O'Neill departs from the court of Elizabeth: Irish, English, Scottish perspectives and the paralysis of policy, July 1559 to April 1562' in Connolly, S.J. (ed.), *Kingdoms United?*

Bray, Gerald (ed.) (1994), *Documents of the English Reformation* (Cambridge).

Brown, Keith (1986), *Bloodfeud in Scotland, 1573–1625: violence, justice and politics in early modern Scotland* (Edinburgh).

Brown, Keith (1987), 'The price of friendship: the "well affected" and English economic clientage in Scotland before 1603' in Mason, R.A. (ed.), *Scotland and England*.

Brown, Keith (1992), *Kingdom or province? Scotland and regal union, 1603–1715* (Basingstoke).

Brown, Keith (1993), 'The Scottish aristocracy, Anglicization and the court, 1603–38' in *Historical Journal*, xxxvi.

Brown, Keith (2001), 'Reformation to union, 1560–1707' in Houston, R.A. and Knox, W.W.J. (eds), *The new Penguin history of Scotland*.

Burgess, Glenn (ed.) (1999), *The new British history: founding a modern state, 1603–1715* (London).

Bush, Michael (1967), *The Elizabethan militia, 1558–1638* (London).

Bush, Michael (1971), 'The problem of the far north: a study of the crisis of 1537 and its consequences' in *Northern History*, vi.

Bush, Michael (1975), *The government policy of Protector Somerset* (London).

Bush, Michael (1996), *The Pilgrimage of Grace: a study of the rebel armies of October 1536* (Manchester).

Bush, Michael and Bownes, David (1999), *The defeat of the Pilgrimage of Grace* (Hull).

[382]

Calendar of the Carew manuscripts preserved in the archiepiscopal library at Lambeth, 1515–74 [etc.] (1867–73) (6 vols, London).

Calendar of inquisitions post mortem, Henry VII (1898–1955) (3 vols, London).

Caley, J. (ed.) (1810–34), *Valor Ecclesiasticus temp. Henr. VIII* (6 vols, Record Commission).

Cameron, J.K. (ed.) (1972), *The first Book of Discipline* (Edinburgh).

Cameron, James (1998), *James V: the personal rule, 1528–1542* (East Linton).

Campbell, W. (1873), *Materials for a history of the reign of Henry VII* (2 vols, London).

Canny, Nicholas (1976), *The Elizabethan conquest of Ireland: a pattern established, 1565–1576* (Hassocks).

Canny, Nicholas (1987), *From Reformation to Restoration: Ireland, 1534–1660* (Dublin).

Canny, Nicholas (1995), 'What really happened in Ireland in 1641?' in Ohlmeyer, J. (ed.), *Ireland from independence to occupation.*

Canny, Nicholas (ed.) (1998), *The Oxford history of the British Empire, i: the origins of Empire to 1689* (Oxford).

Canny, Nicholas (2001), *Making Ireland British, 1580–1650* (Oxford).

Canny, Nicholas (2003), 'Taking sides in early modern Ireland: the case of Hugh O'Neill, earl of Tyrone' in Carey, Vincent and Lotz-Heumann, Ute (eds), *Taking sides?*

Carey, Vincent (2002), *Surviving the Tudors: the 'wizard' earl of Kildare and English rule in Ireland* (Dublin).

Carey, Vincent and Lotz-Heumann, Ute (eds) (2003), *Taking sides? Colonial and confessional mentalités in early modern Ireland* (Dublin).

Casway, J.I. (1984), *Owen Roe O'Neill and the struggle for Catholic Ireland* (Philadelphia).

Casway, J.I. (2004), 'Phelim O'Neill' in Matthew and Harrison (eds), *Oxford Dictionary of National Biography.*

Cavendish, George (1959), *The life and death of Cardinal Wolsey* (Early English Texts Society, Oxford).

Chadwick, O. (1952), 'Richard Bancroft's submission' in *Journal of Ecclesiastical History*, iii.

Chalkin, C.W. and Havindon, M.A. (eds) (1974), *Rural change and urban growth, 1500–1800* (London).

Challis, C.E. (1978), *The Tudor coinage* (Manchester).

Chrimes, S.B. (1972), *Henry VII* (London).

Chrimes, S.B., Ross, C.D. and Griffiths, R.A. (eds) (1972), *Fifteenth-century England 1399–1509: studies in politics and society* (Manchester).

Christianson, P. (1994), 'Arguments on billeting and martial law in the parliament of 1628' in *Historical Journal*, xxxvii.

Clarke, Aidan (1964), 'The army and politics in Ireland, 1625–30' in *Studia Hibernica*, iv.

Clark, Aidan with Edwards, R.D. (1976), 'Pacification, plantation, and the Catholic question, 1603–23' in Moody, T.W. *et al.* (eds), *A new history of Ireland.*

Clarke, Aidan (1976), 'The government of Wentworth, 1632–40' in Moody, T.W. *et al.* (eds), *A new history of Ireland.*

Clarke, Aidan (1995), '1659 and the road to restoration' in Ohlmeyer, J. (ed.), *Ireland from independence to occupation.*

Clarke, Aidan (2000), *The Old English in Ireland, 1625–42* (2nd ed., Dublin).

Clarke, P. and Slack, P. (1976), *English towns in transition, 1500–1700* (Oxford).

Coburn-Walshe, Helen (1990), 'The rebellion of William Nugent, 1581' in Comerford, R.V. *et al.* (eds), *Religion, conflict and coexistence.*

Collinson, Patrick (1967), *The Elizabethan Puritan movement* (London).

Collinson, Patrick (1979), *Archbishop Grindal, 1519–1583: the struggle for a reformed church* (London).

Collinson, Patrick (1983), 'The Jacobean religious settlement: the Hampton Court conference' in Tomlinson, Howard (ed.), *Before the English Civil War.*

Collinson, Patrick (1995), 'Ecclesiastical vitriol: religious satire in the 1590s and the invention of Puritanism' in Guy, J. (ed.), *The reign of Elizabeth I.*

Collinson, Patrick (ed.) (2002), *The short Oxford history of the British Isles: the sixteenth century* (Oxford).

Collinson, Patrick (2003), *Elizabethans* (London).

Comerford, R.V., Cullen, M., Hill, J.R. and Lennon, Colm (eds) (1990), *Religion, conflict and coexistence: essays presented to Monsignor Patrick J. Corish* (Dublin).

Condon, Margaret (1979), 'Ruling elites in the reign of Henry VII' in Ross, Charles (ed.), *Patronage, pedigree and power.*

Connolly, S.J. (ed.) (1999), *Kingdoms United? Great Britain and Ireland since 1500: integration and diversity* (Dublin).

Corish, P.J. (1976), 'The rising of 1641 and the confederacy, 1641–5' in Moody, T.W. *et al.* (eds), *A new history of Ireland,* iii.

Corish, P.J. (1976), 'Ormond, Rinuccini and the Confederates, 1645–9' in Moody, T.W. *et al.* (eds), *A new history of Ireland,* iii.

Corish, P.J. (ed.) (1985), *Radicals, rebels and establishments: Historical Studies XV* (Belfast).

Cornwall, Julian (1977), *Revolt of the peasantry* (London).

Cosgrove, Art (ed.) (1987), *A new history of Ireland. II. Medieval Ireland, 1169–1534* (Oxford).

Coss, P.R. (1989), 'Bastard feudalism revised' in *Past & Present,* no. 125.

Cowan, E.J. (1977), *Montrose: for covenant and king* (London).

Cowan, I.B. (1978), *Regional aspects of the Scottish Reformation* (London).

Cowan, I.B. (1982), *The Scottish Reformation* (London).

Crawford, P. (1977), 'Charles Stuart, that man of blood' in *Journal of British Studies,* 16.

Cregan, D.F. (1995), 'The Confederate Catholics of Ireland: the personnel of the confederation, 1642–9' in *Irish Historical Studies,* xxix.

Cross, Claire (1969), *The royal supremacy in the Elizabethan church* (London).

Cross, Claire, Loades, David and Scarisbrick, J.J. (eds) (1988), *Law and government under the Tudors: essays presented to Sir Geoffrey Elton on his retirement* (Cambridge).

Cruickshank, C.G. (1966), *Elizabeth's army* (Oxford).

Cruickshank, C.G. (1971), *The English occupation of Tournai* (Oxford).

Cruickshank, C.G. (1990), *Henry VIII and the invasion of France* (Stroud).

Cunningham, Bernadette (1979), 'Political and social change in the lordships of Clanricard and Thomond, 1569–1641' (unpublished MA thesis, National University of Ireland, Galway).

Cunningham, Bernadette (2000), *The world of Geoffrey Keating* (Dublin).

Curry, Anne (1979), 'The first English standing army? Military organisation in Lancastrian Normandy, 1420–1450' in Ross, Charles (ed.), *Patronage pedigree and power in later medieval England.*

Curtis, Edmund (ed.) (1932–43), *Calendar of Ormond deeds, 1172–1350* [etc.] (6 vols, Dublin).

Cust, R. (1985), 'Charles I, the privy council, and the forced loan' in *Journal of British Studies*, xxiv.

Cust, R. (2005), 'Was there an alternative to the personal rule? Charles I, the privy council and the parliament of 1629' in *History*, 299.

Davies, C.S.L. (1973), 'Peasant revolt in France and England: a comparison' in *Agricultural History Review*, xxi.

Davies, Rees (1966), 'The twilight of Welsh law, 1284–1536' in *History*, li.

Davies, Rees (1978), *Lordship and society in the March of Wales 1282–1400* (Oxford).

Davies, Rees (ed.) (1988), *The British Isles 1100–1500: comparisons, contrasts and connections* (Edinburgh).

Davies, Rees (1989), 'Frontier arrangements in fragmented societies: Ireland and Wales' in Bartlett and MacKay (eds), *Medieval frontier societies* (Oxford, 1989).

Davies, Rees (1991), *The age of conquest: Wales 1063–1415* (Oxford).

Davies, Rees (1994), 'The peoples of Britain and Ireland 1100–1400 I. Identities' in *Transactions of the Royal Historical Society*, 6th ser., iv.

Davis, Norman (ed.) (1976), *Paston letters and papers of the fifteenth century*, ii (Oxford).

Davis, J.F. (1983), *Heresy and Reformation in the south-east of England, 1520–1559* (London).

Dawson, J.E.A. (1987), 'Two kingdoms or three?: Ireland in Anglo-Scottish relations in the middle of the sixteenth century' in Mason, R.A. (ed.), *Scotland and England.*

Dawson, J.E.A. (1989), 'William Cecil and the British dimension of early Elizabethan foreign policy' in *History*, lxxiv.

Dawson, J.E.A. (1994), 'Calvinism and the Gaidhealtachd in Scotland' in Andrew Pettegree, A. *et al.* (eds), *Calvinism in Europe.*

Dawson, J.E.A. (2002), *The politics of religion in the age of Mary, queen of Scots: the earl of Argyll and the struggle for Britain and Ireland* (Cambridge).

Dawson, J.E.A. (2004), 'Anglo-Scottish relations: security and succession' in Tittler and Jones (eds), *A companion to Tudor Britain.*

Dickens, A.G. (1989), *The English Reformation* (2nd ed., London).

Dickinson, F.H. (ed.) (1861), *Missale ad usum insignis et praecularae ecclesiae Sarum* (Burntisland).

Dobson, R.B. (1983), *The Peasants' Revolt of 1381* (2nd ed., London).

Dockray, Keith (ed.) (1988), *Three chronicles of the reign of Edward IV* (Gloucester).

Donald, P. (1989), 'New light on the Anglo-Scottish contacts of 1640' in *Historical Research*, lxii.

Donald, P. (1990), *An uncounselled king: Charles I and the Scottish troubles, 1637–1641* (Cambridge).

Donald, P. (1990), 'The Scottish national covenant and British politics, 1638–1640' in Morrill, J.S. (ed.), *The Scottish national covenant.*

Donaldson, Gordon (1960), *The Scottish Reformation* (Cambridge).

Donaldson, Gordon (1965), *Scotland, James V–James VII* (Edinburgh).   [3 8 5]

Donaldson, Gordon (ed.) (1974), *Scottish historical documents* (Edinburgh).

Doran, Susan (1999), *England and Europe in the sixteenth century* (Basingstoke).

Doran, Susan (2000), *Elizabeth I and foreign policy, 1558–1603* (London).

Dow, Frances (2000), *Cromwellian Scotland, 1651–1660* (Edinburgh, 2000).

Duffy, Eamon (1992), *The stripping of the altars: traditional religion in England c.1400–c.1580* (New Haven).

Duffy, Eamon (2001), *The voices of Morebath: Reformation and rebellion in an English village* (New Haven).

Durston, C. (2001), *Cromwell's major-generals: godly government during the English revolution* (Manchester).

Dwyer, John, Mason, R.A. and Murdoch, Alexander (eds) (1982), *New perspectives on the politics and culture of early modern Scotland* (Edinburgh).

Eaves, R.G. (1971), *Henry VIII's Scottish diplomacy 1513–1524: England's relations with the regency government of James V* (New York).

Edwards, David (1992–3), 'The Butler revolt of 1569' in *Irish Historical Studies*, xxviii.

Edwards, David (2003), *The Ormond lordship in county Kilkenny, 1515–1642: the rise and fall of Butler feudal power* (Dublin).

Edwards, Phillip (2001), *The making of the modern English state, 1460–1660* (London).

Edwards, R.D. (1935), *Church and state in Tudor Ireland: a history of the penal laws against Irish Catholics 1534–1603* (Dublin).

Elliott, J.H. (1992), 'A world of composite monarchies' in *Past & Present*, no. 133.

Ellis, S.G. (1976–7), 'Tudor policy and the Kildare ascendancy in the lordship of Ireland, 1496–1534' in *Irish Historical Studies*, xx.

Ellis, S.G. (1980), 'Thomas Cromwell and Ireland, 1532–1540' in *Historical Journal*, xxiii.

Ellis, S.G. (1981), 'Henry VIII, rebellion and the rule of law' in *Historical Journal*, xxiv.

Ellis, S.G. (1985), *Tudor Ireland: crown, community and the conflict of cultures, 1470–1603* (London).

Ellis, S.G. (1986), 'Crown, community and government in the English territories, 1450–1575' in *History*, lxxi.

Ellis, S.G. (1986), *The Pale and the far north: government and society in two early Tudor borderlands* (Galway).

Ellis, S.G. (1986), *Reform and revival: English government in Ireland, 1470–1534* (London).

Ellis, S.G. (1990), 'Economic problems of the church: why the Reformation failed in Ireland' in *Journal of Ecclesiastical History*, xli.

Ellis, S.G. (1995), *Tudor frontiers and noble power: the making of the British state* (Oxford).

Ellis, S.G. (1995), 'Tudor state formation and the shaping of the British Isles' in Ellis and Barber (eds), *Conquest and union*.

Ellis, S.G. and Barber, S. (eds) (1995), *Conquest and union: fashioning a British state, 1485–1725* (London).

Ellis, S.G. (1997), 'The commons and the state: representation, influence, and the legislative process: England' in Blickle, P. (ed.), *Resistance, representation, and community*.

Ellis, S.G. (1997), 'Communal autonomy and peasant resistance: commentary from a British perspective' in Blickle, P. (ed.), *Resistance, representation and community*.

Ellis, S.G. (1998), *Ireland in the age of the Tudors: English expansion and the end of Gaelic rule, 1447–1603* (London).

Ellis, S.G. (1998–9), 'The collapse of the Gaelic world, 1450–1650' in *Irish Historical Studies*, xxxi.

Ellis, S.G. (1999), 'Civilizing Northumberland: representations of Englishness in the Tudor state' in *Journal of Historical Sociology*, xii.

Ellis, S.G. (1999), 'The English state and its frontiers in the British Isles, 1300–1600' in Power and Standen (eds), *Frontiers in question.*

Ellis, S.G. (2001), 'Languages 1500–1800' in Barry Cunliffe, Robert Bartlett, John Morrill, Asa Briggs and Joanna Bourke (eds), *The Penguin atlas of British and Irish History* (London).

Ellis, S.G. (2002), 'From dual monarchy to multiple kingdoms: unions and the English state, 1422–1607' in Macinnes and Ohlmeyer (eds), *The Stuart kingdoms in the seventeenth century* (Dublin).

Ellis, S.G. (2002), 'The limits of power: the English crown and the British Isles' in Collinson, P. (ed.), *The Short Oxford History of the British Isles.*

Ellis, S.G. (2003), 'An English gentleman and his community: Sir William Darcy of Platten' in Carey and Lotz-Heumann (eds), *Taking sides?*

Ellis, S.G. (2004), 'Butler, John, sixth earl of Ormond' in Matthew and Harrison (eds), *Oxford Dictionary of National Biography.*

Ellis, S.G. (2004), 'Centre and periphery in the Tudor state' in Tittler and Jones (eds), *A companion to Tudor Britain.*

Ellis, S.G. (2004), 'Fitzgerald, Thomas, seventh earl of Desmond' in Matthew and Harrison (eds), *Oxford Dictionary of National Biography.*

Ellis, S.G. (2006), 'Citizenship in the English state during the Renaissance' in idem, Guðmundur Hálfdanarson and A.K. Isaacs (eds), *Citizenship in historical perspective* (Pisa).

Ellis, S.G. (2006), 'Integration, identities and frontiers in the British Isles: a European perspective' in Gustafsson and Sanders (eds), *Vid gränsen.*

Elton, G.R. (1972), *Policy and police: the enforcement of the Reformation in the age of Thomas Cromwell* (Cambridge, 1972).

Elton, G.R. (1973), *Reform and renewal: Thomas Cromwell and the common weal* (Cambridge).

Elton, G.R. (1974), *Studies in Tudor and Stuart politics and government* ii, (Cambridge).

Elton, G.R. (1977), *Reform and Reformation: England, 1509–1558* (London).

Elton, G.R. (1982), *The Tudor constitution* (2nd ed., Cambridge).

Elton, G.R. (1986), *The parliament of England, 1559–1581* (Cambridge).

Elton, G.R. (1991), *England under the Tudors* (3rd ed., London).

Falls, Cyril (1950), *Elizabeth's Irish wars* (London).

Fissel, M.C. (1991), *War and government in Britain, 1598–1650* (Manchester).

Fissel, M.C. (1994), *The Bishops' Wars: Charles I's campaigns against Scotland, 1638–1640* (Cambridge).

Fissel, M.C. (2001), *English warfare 1511–1642* (London).

Fletcher, A.J. and Stevenson, J. (eds) (1985), *Order and disorder in early modern England* (Cambridge).

Fletcher, A.J. and Roberts, P. (eds) (1994), *Religion, culture and society in early modern Britain: essays in honour of Patrick Collinson* (Cambridge).

Fletcher, A.J. (2003), 'Oliver Cromwell and the localities' in Smith, D.L. (ed.), *Cromwell and the Interregnum*.

Fletcher, A.J. and MacCulloch, D. (2004), *Tudor rebellions* (5th ed., London).

Flinn, Michael (ed.) (1977), *Scottish population history from the 17th century to the 1930s* (Cambridge).

Ford, Alan, McGuire, J. and Milne, K. (eds) (1995), *As by law established: the Church of Ireland since the Reformation* (Dublin).

Ford, Alan (1995), 'The Church of Ireland, 1558–1634: a puritan church?' in Ford, *et al.* (eds), *As by law established*.

Ford, Alan (1997), *The Protestant Reformation in Ireland, 1590–1641* (2nd ed., Dublin).

Ford, Alan (2001), ' "Firm Catholics" or "loyal subjects"? Religious and political allegiance in early seventeenth-century Ireland' in Boyce, D.G. (ed.), *Political discourse in seventeenth and eighteenth-century Ireland*.

Forkan, Kevin (2004), 'The south Ulster borderland as a political frontier in the 1640s' in *Breifne*, xl (x).

Foster, Andrew (2004), 'Durham House Group' in Matthew and Harrison (eds), *Oxford Dictionary of National Biography*.

Frame, Robin (1977), 'Power and society in the lordship of Ireland, 1272–1377' in *Past and Present*, no. 76.

Frame, Robin (1982), *English lordship in Ireland 1318–1361* (Oxford).

Fritze, R.H. (1982), 'The role of the family and religion in the local politics of early Elizabethan England: the case of Hampshire in the 1560s' in *Historical Journal*, xxv.

Fryde, E.B., Greenway, D.E., Porter, S. and Roy, I. (eds) (1986), *Handbook of British chronology* (3rd ed., London).

Furgol, E.M. (1990), 'Scotland turned Sweden: the Scottish Covenanters and the military revolution, 1638–1651' in Morrill, J.S. (ed.), *The Scottish National Covenant*.

Furgol, E.M. (2004), 'Alexander Lindsay' in Matthew and Harrison (eds), *Oxford Dictionary of National Biography*.

Galloway, Bruce (1986), *The union of England and Scotland, 1603–1608* (Edinburgh).

Gardiner, S.R. (ed.) (1872), *Paston letters*, I (London).

Gardiner, S.R. (1875), *A history of England under the duke of Buckingham and Charles I, 1624–28* (2 vols, London).

Gay, E.F. (1904), 'The Midland Revolt and the inquisitions of depopulation of 1607' in *Transactions of the Royal Historical Society*, 2nd ser., xviii.

Gentles, I. (1994), 'The choosing of officers for the new model army' in *Historical Research*, 67.

Giblin, C. (1964), *The Irish Franciscan mission to Scotland, 1619–1646* (Dublin).

Gilbert, J.T. (ed.) (1889–1944), *Calendar of ancient records of Dublin* (19 vols, Dublin).

Gillespie, Raymond (1985), *Colonial Ulster: the settlement of east Ulster, 1600–41* (Cork).

Gillespie, Raymond (1986), 'The end of an era: Ulster and the outbreak of the 1641 rising' in Brady, C. and Gillespie, R. (eds), *Natives and newcomers*.

Gillespie, Raymond (1991), *The transformation of the Irish economy, 1550–1700* (Dundalk).

[3 8 8]   Gillespie, Raymond (ed.) (1996), *The proctor's accounts of Peter Lewis 1564–1565* (Dublin).

Gillingham, John (1981), *The Wars of the Roses* (London).

Gillingham, John (1995), 'Foundations of a disunited kingdom' in Grant and Stringer (eds), *Uniting the Kingdom?*

Goodare, Julian (1999), *State and society in early modern Scotland* (Oxford).

Goodare, Julian (ed.) (2000), *The reign of James VI* (East Linton).

Goodman, Anthony (1981), *The Wars of the Roses: military activity and English society, 1452–97* (London).

Goring, Jeremy (1971), 'The general proscription of 1522' in *English Historical Review*, lxxxvi.

Grant, Alexander (1984), *Independence and nationhood: Scotland 1306–1469* (London).

Grant, Alexander (1988), 'Scotland's "Celtic fringe" in the late middle ages: the MacDonald lords of the Isles and the kingdom of Scotland' in Davies, R. (ed.), *The British Isles 1100–1500*.

Grant, Alexander and Stringer, Keith (eds) (1995), *Uniting the Kingdom? The making of British history* (London, 1995).

Gras, N.S.B. (1926), *The evolution of the English corn market* (Cambridge Mass.).

Graves, M.A.R. (1998), *Burghley: William Cecil, lord Burghley* (London).

Graves, M.A.R. (2003), *Henry VIII: a study of kingship* (London).

Greengrass, Mark (ed.) (1991), *Conquest and coalescence: the shaping of the state in early modern Europe* (London).

Gregg, P. (1981), *King Charles I* (London).

Gregory, Donald (1881), *The history of the western highlands and isles of Scotland, 1493–1625* (Edinburgh).

Griffith, M.C. (1940–41), 'The Talbot-Ormond struggle for control of the Anglo-Irish government' in *Irish Historical Studies*, ii.

Griffiths, R.A. (1981), *The reign of Henry VI* (London).

Griffiths, R.A. (1986), 'The English realm and dominions and the king's subjects in the later middle ages' in Rowe, J. (ed.), *Aspects of government and society in later medieval England*.

Gunn, S.J. (1991), 'The accession of Henry VIII' in *Historical Research*, lxiv.

Gunn, S.J. (1995), *Early Tudor government, 1485–1558* (Basingstoke).

Gustafsson, Harald (2002), 'The conglomerate state: a perspective on state formation in early modern Europe' in *Scandinavian Journal of History*, xxiii.

Gustafsson, Harald and Sanders, Hanne (eds) (2006), *Vid gränsen: Integration och identitet i det förnationella Norden* (Gothenburg).

Guth, D.J. and McKenna, J.W. (eds) (1982), *Tudor rule and revolution* (Cambridge).

Guy, J. (1982), 'The origins of the petition of right reconsidered' in *Historical Journal*, xxv.

Guy, J. (1988), *Tudor England* (Oxford).

Guy, J. (1995), 'Thomas Wolsey, Thomas Cromwell and the reform of Henrician government' in MacCulloch, D. (ed.), *The reign of Henry VIII*.

Guy, J. (ed.) (1995), *The reign of Elizabeth I: court and culture in the last decade* (Cambridge).

Guy, J. (2004), *'My heart is my own': the life of Mary queen of Scots* (London).

Gwyn, Peter (1990), *The king's cardinal: the rise and fall of Thomas Wolsey* (London).

Hadfield, Andrew and McVeagh, John (eds) (1994), *Strangers to that land: British perceptions of Ireland from the Reformation to the famine* (Gerrards Cross, Bucks.).

Haigh, Christopher (1975), *Reformation and resistance in Tudor Lancashire* (Cambridge).

Haigh, Christopher (ed.) (1984), *The reign of Elizabeth I* (London).

Haigh, Christopher (ed.) (1987), *The English Reformation revised* (Cambridge).

Haigh, Christopher (1993), *English Reformations: religion, politics, and society under the Tudors* (Oxford).

Haigh, Christopher (1998), *Elizabeth I* (2nd ed. London).

Halliwell, J.O. (ed.) (1839), *Warkworth's Chronicle* (Camden Soc., London).

Hammer, Paul (1995), 'Patronage at court, faction and the earl of Essex' in Guy, J. (ed.), *The reign of Elizabeth I*.

Haugaard, W.P. (1968), *Elizabeth and the English Reformation: the struggle for a stable settlement of religion* (Cambridge).

Hay, Denys (ed.) (1950), *Anglica Historia* (London).

Hay, Denys (1966), *Europe in the fourteenth and fifteenth centuries* (London).

Hayes-McCoy, G.A. (1937), *Scots mercenary forces in Ireland, 1563–1603* (Dublin).

Hayes-McCoy, G.A. (1969), *Irish battles* (London).

Haynes, Samuel (ed.) (1740), *A collection of state papers relating to affairs in the reigns of King Henry VIII . . . Queen Elizabeth from the year 1542 to 1570* (London).

Heal, Felicity (2003), *Reformation in Britain and Ireland* (Oxford).

Hicks, M.A. (1980), *False, fleeting, perjur'd Clarence: George duke of Clarence, 1449–78* (Gloucester).

Hicks, M.A. (1986), 'The Yorkshire rebellion of 1489 reconsidered' in *Northern History*, xxii.

Hilton, Rodney (1973), *Bond men made free: medieval peasant movements and the English rising of 1381* (London).

Hindle, Steve (1996), 'Exclusion crises: poverty, migration and parochial responsibility in English rural communities, c.1560–1660' in *Rural History*, vii.

Hindle, Steve (2000), *The state and social change in early modern England, c.1550–1640* (Basingstoke).

Hindle, Steve (2004), *On the parish? The micro-politics of poor relief in rural England, c.1550–1750* (Oxford).

Hodgson, John (1820–5), *A history of Northumberland* (3 pts in 7 vols, Newcastle).

Holmes, P. (1980), 'The authorship and early reception of "A conference about the next succession to the Crown of England"' in *Historical Journal*, xxiii.

Horrox, Rosemary (1989), *Richard III: a study of service* (Cambridge).

Hoskins, W.G. (1976), *The age of plunder: the England of Henry VIII, 1500–1547* (London).

Hotle, C.P. (1996), *Thorns and thisles: diplomacy between Henry VIII and James V 1528–1542* (Lanham).

Houston, R.A. (1996), 'The population history of Britain and Ireland, 1500–1700' in Anderson, Michael (ed.), *British population history*.

Houston, R.A. and Knox, W.W.J. (eds) (2001), *The new Penguin history of Scotland: from earliest times to the present day* (London).

[3 9 0]   Houston, R.A. and Whyte, I.D. (eds) (2005), *Scottish Society, 1500–1800* (Cambridge).

Hoyle, R.W. (1995), 'War and public finance' in MacCulloch, D. (ed.), *The Reign of Henry VIII*.

Hoyle, R.W. (1999), 'Faction, feud and reconciliation amongst the northern nobility' in *History*, lxxxiv.

Hoyle, R.W. (2001), *The Pilgrimage of Grace and the politics of the 1530s* (Oxford).

Hudson, A. (1988), *The premature Reformation: Wycliffite texts and Lollard history* (Oxford).

Hudson, W.S. (1980), *The Cambridge connection and the Elizabethan settlement of 1559* (Durham, NC).

Hurstfield, Joel (1961), 'The succession struggle in late Elizabethan England' in Bindoff, S.T. *et al.* (eds), *Elizabethan government and society*.

Hutton, Ronald (1985), *The restoration: political & religious history of England and Wales, 1658–1667* (Oxford).

Hutton, Ronald (1987), 'The local impact of the Tudor Reformations' in Haigh, C. (ed.), *The English Reformation revised*.

Hutton, Ronald (1994), *The rise and fall of merry England* (Oxford).

Hutton, Ronald (1996), *The stations of the sun* (Oxford).

Inquisitions and assessments relating to Feudal Aids ... 1284–1431 (1899–1906) (4 vols, London).

Ives, E.W., Knecht, R.J. and Scarisbrick, J.J. (eds) (1978), *Wealth and power in Tudor England: essays presented to S.T. Bindoff* (London).

James, M.E. (1965), 'The murder at Cocklodge' in *Durham University Journal*, lvii.

James, Mervyn (1986), *Society, politics and culture: studies in early modern England* (Cambridge).

Jefferies, Henry (1988–9), 'The Irish parliament of 1560: the Anglican reforms authorised' in *Irish Historical Studies*, xxvi.

Jefferies, Henry (1997), *Priests and people of Armagh in the age of Reformations, 1518–1558* (Dublin).

Jenkins, Philips (1992), *A history of Modern Wales, 1536–1990* (London).

Jenkins, Philip (1995), 'The Anglican church and the unity of Britain: the Welsh experience, 1560–1714 in Ellis and Barber (eds), *Conquest and union*.

Jones, Amanda (2003), '"Commotion time": the English risings of 1549' (unpublished PhD thesis, University of Warwick).

Jones, F.M. (1958), *Mountjoy, 1563–1606* (Dublin).

Jones, J.G. (1989), *Wales and the Tudor state: government, religious change and the social order 1534–1603* (Cardiff).

Jones, J.G. (1994), *Early modern Wales, c.1525–1640* (London).

Jones, J.R. (1966), *Britain and Europe in the seventeenth century* (London).

Jones, N.L. (1982), *Faith by statute: parliament and the settlement of religion* (London).

Jones, Norman (1993), *The birth of the Elizabethan age: England in the 1560s* (Oxford).

Kearney, H.F. (1959), *Strafford in Ireland, 1633–41: a study in absolutism* (Manchester).

Kempe, A.J. (ed.) (1835), *The Losely manuscripts* (London).

Kenyon, J. and Ohlmeyer, J. (eds) (1998), *The civil wars: a military history of England, Scotland and Ireland, 1638–1660* (Oxford).

Kingston, Simon (2004), *Ulster and the Isles in the fifteenth century: the lordship of Clann Domhnaill of Antrim* (Dublin).

Kirk, J. (1989), *Patterns of reform: continuity and change in the Reformation kirk* (Edinburgh).

Kishlansky, Mark (1978), 'The case of the army truly stated: the creation of the new model army' in *Past & Present*, no. 81.

Kishlansky, Mark (1996), *A monarchy transformed: Britain, 1603–1714* (London).

Kishlansky, Mark (1999), 'Tyranny denied: Charles I, attorney general Heath, and the Five Knights' Case' in *Historical Journal*, xlii.

Kishlansky, Mark (2004), 'Charles I' in Matthew and Harrison (eds), *Oxford Dictionary of National Biography*.

Kitching, C.J. (ed.) (1975), *The royal visitation of 1559: Act Book for the northern province* (Surtees Soc., clxxxvii; Gateshead).

Knecht, R.J. (1982), *Francis I* (Cambridge).

Knox, John *The history of the reformation of religion within the realm of Scotland* (ed.) Guthrie, C.J. (Edinburgh, 1982).

Lake, Peter (1988), *Anglicans and Puritans? Presbyterianism and English conformist thought from Whitgift to Hooker* (London).

Lander, J.R. (1976), *Crown and nobility 1450–1509* (London).

Lander, J.R. (1980), *Government and community: England, 1450–1509* (London).

Laslett, Peter (1965), *The world we have lost* (London).

Lee, Maurice (1990), *Great Britain's Solomon: King James VI and I in his three kingdoms* (Urbana, Il.).

Lee, Maurice (ed.) (2003), *The 'inevitable' union and other essays on early modern Scotland* (East Linton).

Lee, Maurice (2003), 'James VI and the revival of episcopacy in Scotland, 1596–1600' in Lee, M. (ed.), *The 'inevitable' union*.

Lennon, Colm (2005), *Sixteenth-century Ireland: the incomplete conquest* (2nd ed., Dublin).

Letters and papers, foreign and domestic, Henry VIII (21 vols) (London, 1862–1932).

Levack, B.P. (1987), *The formation of the British state: England, Scotland and the union, 1603–1707* (Oxford).

Loach, Jennifer (1999), *Edward VI* (New Haven).

Loades, D.M. (1979), *The reign of Mary Tudor: politics, government and religion in England, 1553–1558* (London).

Lockyer, Roger (1981), *Buckingham: the life and political career of George Villiers, first duke of Buckingham, 1592–1628* (Harlow).

Lockyer, Roger (2004), 'George Villiers' in Matthew and Harrison (eds), *Oxford Dictionary of National Biography*.

Lockyer, Roger (2004), *Tudor and Stuart Britain, 1471–1714* (3rd ed., London).

Lynch, Michael (1981), *Edinburgh and the Reformation* (Edinburgh).

Lynch, Michael (1991), *Scotland: a new history* (London).

MacBain, Alexander and Kennedy, John (eds) (1892–4), *Reliquiae Celticae: texts, papers, and studies in Gaelic literature and philosophy* (2 vols, Inverness).

MacCaffrey, Wallace (1968), *The shaping of the Elizabethan regime: Elizabethan politics, 1558–1572* (Princeton).

[3 9 2]   MacCaffrey, Wallace (1975), *Exeter, 1540–1640: the growth of an English county town* (2nd ed., Cambridge, Mass.).

MacCaffrey, Wallace (1981), *Queen Elizabeth and the making of policy, 1572–1588* (Princeton).

MacCaffrey, Wallace (1992), *Elizabeth I, war and politics, 1588–1603* (Princeton).

MacCaffrey, Wallace (1993), *Elizabeth I* (London).

MacCaffrey, Wallace (1997), 'The Newhaven expedition, 1562–1563' in *Historical Journal*, xl.

MacCarthy-Morrogh, Michael (1986), *The Munster plantation: English migration to southern Ireland, 1583–1641* (Oxford).

Macauley, J.S. (2004), 'Richard Montague' in Matthew and Harrison (eds), *Oxford Dictionary of National Biography*.

MacCormack, J.R. (1956), 'The Irish adventurers and the English civil war' in *Irish Historical Studies*, x.

MacCulloch, Diarmaid (1979), 'Kett's rebellion in context' in *Past & Present*, no. 84.

MacCulloch, Diarmaid (1986), *Suffolk and the Tudors: politics and religion in an English county 1500–1600* (Oxford).

MacCulloch, Diarmaid (1988), 'Bondmen under the Tudors' in Cross, C. *et al.* (eds), *Law and government under the Tudors*.

MacCulloch, Diarmaid (ed.) (1995), *The reign of Henry VIII: politics, policy and piety* (Basingstoke).

MacCulloch, Diarmaid (1996), *Thomas Cranmer: a life* (New Haven and London).

MacCulloch, Diarmaid (1999), *Tudor church militant: Edward VI and the Protestant Reformation* (London).

MacDonald, A.M. (ed.) (1911), *The MacDonald collection of Gaelic poetry* (Inverness).

MacDougall, Norman (1982), *James III, a political study* (Edinburgh).

MacDougall, Norman (1989), *James IV* (Edinburgh).

Macinnes, A.I. (1990), 'The Scottish constitution, 1638–51: the rise and fall of oligarchic centralism' in Morrill, J.S. (ed.), *The Scottish national covenant in its British context*.

Macinnes, A.I. (1991), *Charles I and the making of the Covenanting movement, 1625–1641* (Edinburgh).

Macinnes, A.I. (1993), 'Crown, clans and fine: the "civilizing" of Scottish Gaeldom, 1587–1638' in *Northern Scotland*, xiii.

Macinnes, A.I. (1996), *Clanship, commerce and the house of Stuart, 1603–1788* (East Linton).

Macinnes, A.I. and Ohlmeyer, Jane (eds) (2002), *The Stuart kingdoms in the seventeenth century: awkward neighbours* (Dublin).

Macinnes, A.I. (2004), *The British revolution, 1629–60* (London).

Mac Niocaill, Gearóid (ed.) (1992), *Crown surveys of lands 1540–41 with the Kildare rental begun in 1518* (Dublin).

Maginn, Christopher (2004), 'The English marcher lineages in Co. Dublin in the later middle ages' in *Irish Historical Studies*, xxxiv.

Maginn, Christopher (2004), 'Charles Blount' in Matthew and Harrison (eds), *Oxford Dictionary of National Biography*.

Maginn, Christopher (2004), 'The Baltinglass rebellion, 1580: English dissent or a Gaelic uprising?' in *Historical Journal*, xlvii.

Maginn, Christopher (2005) *'Civilizing' Gaelic Leinster: the extension of Tudor rule in the O'Byrne and O'Toole lordships* (Dublin).

Manning, R.B. (1969), *Religion and society in Elizabethan Sussex: a study of the enforcement of the religious settlement 1558–1603* (Leicester).

Manning, R.B. (1988), *Village revolts: social protest and popular disturbances in England, 1509–1640* (Oxford).

Martin, Colin and Parker, Geoffrey (1988), *The Spanish Armada* (London).

Mason, R.A. (ed.) (1987), *Scotland and England 1286–1815* (Edinburgh).

Massey, Robert (1984), 'The land settlement in Lancastrian Normandy' in Pollard, A.J. (ed.), *Property and politics*.

Matthew, H.G.C. and Harrison, Brian (eds) (2004), *Oxford Dictionary of National Biography* (Oxford).

McCafferty, John (1995), 'John Bramhall and the church of Ireland in the 1630s' in Ford, Alan *et al.* (eds), *'As by law established'*.

McCormack, Anthony (2004), 'The social and economic consequences of the Desmond rebellion of 1579–83' in *Irish Historical Studies*, xxxiv.

McCormack, Anthony (2005), *The earldom of Desmond, 1463–1583: the decline and crisis of a feudal lordship* (Dublin).

McGurk, J. (1997), *The Elizabethan conquest of Ireland: the 1590s crisis* (Manchester).

McHugh, Jason (2005), '"Soldier of Christ": the political and ecclesiastical career of Nicholas French, Catholic bishop of Ferns (1603–1678)', (unpublished PhD thesis, NUI, Galway).

McKenna, J.W. (1982), 'How God became an Englishman' in Guth and McKenna (eds), *Tudor rule and revolution*.

McKisack, M. (1959), *The fourteenth century* (Oxford).

McNeill, Charles (ed.) (1950), *Calendar of Archbishop Alen's register, c.1172–1534* (Dublin).

Merriman, Marcus (2000), *The rough wooings: Mary queen of Scots, 1542–1551* (East Linton).

Milton, Anthony (2004), 'William Laud' in Matthew and Harrison (eds), *Oxford Dictionary of National Biography*.

Mitchison, R. (1974), 'The making of the old Scottish poor law' in *Past & Present*, no. 63.

Moody, T.W. (1939), *The Londonderry plantation, 1609–41: the city of London and the plantation in Ulster* (Belfast).

Moody, T.W., Martin, F.X. and Byrne, F.J. (eds) (1976), *A new history of Ireland*, iii: *early modern Ireland* (Oxford).

Moody, T.W., Martin, F.X. and Byrne, F.J. (eds) (1976), *A new history of Ireland*, ix. *Maps, genealogies, lists* (Oxford).

Morgan, Hiram (1993), 'Hugh O'Neill and the Nine Years' War in Tudor Ireland' in *Historical Journal*, xxxvi.

Morgan, Hiram (1993), *Tyrone's rebellion: the outbreak of the Nine Years' War in Tudor Ireland* (London).

[3 9 4]   Morgan, P.T.J. (1966), 'The government of Calais 1485–1558' (unpublished D.Phil. thesis, Oxford University).

Morrill, J.S. and Walter, J.D. (1985), 'Order and disorder in the English revolution' in Fletcher, A. and Stevenson, J. (eds), *Order and disorder.*

Morrill, J.S. (1990), *Oliver Cromwell and the English Revolution* (London, 1990).

Morrill, J.S. (ed.) (1990), *The Scottish national covenant in its British context, 1638–51* (Edinburgh).

Morrill, J.S. (1990), 'The National Covenant in its British context' in Morrill, J.S. (ed.), *The Scottish National Covenant.*

Morrill, J.S. (1993), *The nature of the English Revolution: essays by John Morrill* (London).

Morrill, J.S. (1994), 'A British patriarchy? Ecclesiastical imperialism under the early Stuarts' in Fletcher, A.J. and Roberts, P. (eds) *Religion, culture and society.*

Morrill, J.S. (1995), 'The fashioning of Britain' in Ellis, S.G. and Barber, S. (eds), *Conquest and union.*

Morrill, J.S. (1996), 'The British problem, c.1534–1707' in Bradshaw, B. and Morrill, J.S. (eds), *The British problem.*

Morrill, J.S. (ed.) (1996), *The Oxford illustrated history of Tudor and Stuart Britain* (Oxford).

Morrill, J.S. (1996), 'Politics in an age of revolution' in Morrill, J.S. (ed.), *The Oxford illustrated history of Tudor and Stuart Britain.*

Morrill, J.S. (1999), *Revolt in the provinces: the people of England and the tragedies of war, 1638–1648* (2nd ed., London).

Morrill, J.S. (1999), 'The war(s) of the three kingdoms' in Burgess (ed.), *The new British history.*

Morrill, J.S. (2004), 'Oliver Cromwell' in Matthew and Harrison (eds), *Oxford Dictionary of National Biography.*

Murphy, Virginia (1995), 'The literature and propaganda of Henry VIII's first divorce' in MacCulloch, D. (ed.), *The reign of Henry VIII.*

Neale, J.E. (1953–7), *Elizabeth I and her parliaments* (2 vols, London).

Neale, J.E. (1960), *Queen Elizabeth I* (London).

Newton, Robert (1974), 'The decay of the borders' in Chalkin and Havindon (eds), *Rural change and urban growth.*

Newton, Michael (2000), *A handbook of the Scottish Gaelic world* (Dublin).

Nicholls, K.W. (2003), *Gaelic and Gaelicised Ireland in the later middle ages* (2nd ed., Dublin).

Nicholls, Mark (1999), *A history of the modern British Isles, 1529–1603: the two kingdoms* (Oxford).

Nicholson, Ranald (1974), *Scotland: the later middle ages* (Edinburgh).

Nicholson, William (1705), *Leges marchiarum or border-laws* (London).

Northumberland County History Committee (ed.) (1905–40), *A history of Northumberland,* (15 vols, Newcastle-upon-Tyne).

O'Brien, George (ed.) (1923), *Advertisements for Ireland* (Dublin).

Ó Buachalla, Breandán (1987), *Foras feasa ar Éirinn, history of Ireland: foreword* (Dublin).

Ó Buachalla, Breandán (1992), 'Poetry and politics in early modern Ireland' in *Eighteenth-century Ireland: Iris an dá chultúr,* vii.

Ó Buachalla, Breandán (1993), '"James Our True King": the ideology of Irish royalism in the seventeenth century' in Boyce, D.G., *et al.* (eds), *Political thought in Ireland since the seventeenth century.*

Ó Buachalla, Breandán (1996), *Aisling Ghéar: na Stíobhartaigh an t-aos léinn* (Dublin).

Ó hAnnracháin, Tadhg (1997), 'Rebels and confederates: the stance of the Irish clergy in the 1640s' in Young, J.R. (ed.), *Celtic dimensions.*

Ó hAnnracháin, Tadhg (2002), *Catholic reformation in Ireland: the mission of Rinuccini, 1645–1649* (Oxford).

Ohlmeyer, Jane (1993), *Civil war and restoration in three kingdoms: the career of Randall MacDonnell, marquis of Antrim, 1609–1683* (Cambridge).

Ohlmeyer, Jane (ed.) (1995), *Ireland from independence to occupation, 1641–1660* (Cambridge).

Ohlmeyer, Jane (1998), '"Civilizing of those rude parts": colonization within Britain and Ireland, 1580s–1640s' in Canny, N. (ed.), *The Oxford history of the British Empire.*

O Riordan, Michelle (1995), 'Political poems in the mid-seventeenth-century Irish crisis' in Ohlmeyer, J. (ed.), *Ireland from independence to occupation.*

Ó Siochrú, Mícheál (1999), *Confederate Ireland, 1642–9: a constitutional and political analysis* (Dublin).

Otway-Ruthven, A.J. (1980), *A history of medieval Ireland* (2nd ed., London).

Palliser, D.M. (1983), *The age of Elizabeth: England under the later Tudors, 1547–1603* (London).

Patterson, W.B. (1997), *King James VI and I and the reunion of Christendom* (Cambridge).

Peacey, Jason (ed.) (2001), *The regicides and the execution of Charles I* (Basingstoke).

Perceval-Maxwell, M. (1973), *The Scottish migration to Ulster in the reign of James I* (London).

Perceval-Maxwell, M. (1991), *The outbreak of the Irish rebellion of 1641* (Dublin).

Persons [Parsons], Robert (1594), *A conference about the next succession to the crowne of Ingland. Where unto is added a genealogie* (Antwerp).

Pettegree, Andrew, Duke, Alastair and Lewis, Gillian (eds) (1994), *Calvinism in Europe, 1540–1620* (Cambridge).

Phelps Brown, E.H. and Hopkins, S.V. (1971), 'Seven centuries of the prices of consumables, compared with builders' wage rates' in Ramsey, P.H. (ed.), *The Price Revolution.*

Pollard, A.J. (ed.) (1984), *Property and politics: essays in later medieval English history* (Gloucester).

Pollard, A.J. (1988), *The Wars of the Roses* (London).

Pollard, A.J. (1990), *North-eastern England during the Wars of the Roses* (Oxford).

Ponko, V.R. (1964–5), 'N.S.B. Gras and Elizabethan corn policy: a re-examination of the problem' in *Economic History Review*, xvii.

Popofsky, L.S. (1990), 'The crisis over tonnage and poundage in parliament in 1629' in *Past & Present*, no. 126.

Potter, David (1993), *War and government in the French provinces: Picardy 1470–1560* (Cambridge).

Potter, David (1995), 'Foreign policy' in MacCulloch, D. (ed.), *The reign of Henry VIII.*

Pound, John (1971), *Poverty and vagrancy in Tudor England* (London).

[3 9 6]   Power, Daniel and Standen, Naomi (eds) (1999), *Frontiers in question: Eurasian borderlands, 700–1700* (Basingstoke).

Price, G. (1984), *The languages of Britain* (London, 1984).

Price, G. (ed.) (1992), *The Celtic connection* (Gerrards Cross).

Pronay, Nicholas and Cox, John (eds) (1986), *The Crowland Chronicle Continuations: 1459–1486* (London).

Pugh, T.B. (1972), 'The magnates, knights and gentry' in Chrimes, S.B. *et al.* (eds), *Fifteenth-century England.*

Quinn, D.B. and Nicholls, K.W. (1976), 'Ireland in 1534' in Moody, T.W. *et al.* (eds), *A new history of Ireland*, iii.

Rabb, T.K. (1998), *Jacobean gentleman: Sir Edwin Sandys, 1561–1629* (Princeton).

Ramsay, P.H. (1963), *Tudor economic problems* (London).

Ramsay, P.H. (ed.) (1971), *The Price Revolution in sixteenth-century England* (London).

Reeve, L.J. (1989), *Charles I and the road to personal rule* (Cambridge).

The register of Richard Fox, lord bishop of Durham, 1494–1501 (Surtees Soc., Durham, 1932).

Reid, R.R. (1921), *The king's council in the north* (London).

Rhodes, Neil, Richards, Jennifer, and Marshall, Joseph (eds) (1988), *James VI and I: selected writings* (Basingstoke).

Ridley, N.T. (ed.) (1854), *Ingulph's Chronicles* (London).

Roberts, Peter (1996), 'The English crown, the principality of Wales and the council in the marches, 1534–1641' in Bradshaw and Morrill (eds), *The British problem.*

Roberts, Peter (1998), 'Tudor Wales, national identity and the British inheritance' in Bradshaw and Roberts (eds), *British consciousness and identity.*

Robinson, Philip (1994), *The plantation of Ulster: British settlement in an Irish landscape, 1600–1670* (Belfast).

Robson, Ralph (1989), *The rise and fall of the English highland clans: Tudor responses to a mediaeval problem* (Edinburgh).

Ronan, M.V. (1930), *The Reformation in Ireland under Elizabeth, 1558–80* (London).

Ross, Charles (1972), 'The reign of Edward IV' in Chrimes, S.B. *et al.* (eds), *Fifteenth-century England.*

Ross, Charles (1974), *Edward IV* (London).

Ross, Charles (ed.) (1979), *Patronage, pedigree and power in later medieval England* (Gloucester).

Ross, Charles (1981), *Richard III* (London).

Rowe, John (ed.) (1986), *Aspects of government and society in later medieval England: essays in honour of J.R. Lander* (Toronto).

Russell, Conrad (1976), 'Parliamentary history in perspective, 1604–1629', in *History*, lxi.

Russell, Conrad (1979), *Parliaments and English politics, 1621–1629* (Oxford).

Russell, Conrad (1990), *The causes of the English civil wars. The Ford Lectures delivered in the University of Oxford* (Oxford).

Russell, Conrad (1990), *Unrevolutionary England, 1603–1642* (London).

Russell, Conrad (1991), *The fall of the British monarchies, 1637–1642* (Oxford).

Sahlins, Peter (1989), *Boundaries: the making of France and Spain in the Pyrenees* (Berkeley).

Salt, S.P. (1994), 'Sir Simon D'Ewes and the levying of Ship Money, 1635–1640' in [3 9 7]
    Historical Journal, xxxvii.

Samman, Neil (1995), 'The progresses of Henry VIII, 1509–1529' in MacCulloch, D.
    (ed.), *The reign of Henry VIII*.

Sanderson, R.P. (ed.) (1891), *Survey of the debateable and border lands . . . 1604* (Alnwick).

Saul, Nigel (ed.) (1994), *England in Europe 1066–1453* (London).

Scally, J. (1997), 'Counsel in crisis: James, third marquis of Hamilton and the Bishops'
    Wars, 1638–1640' in Young, J.R. (ed.), *Celtic dimensions*.

Scarisbrick, J.J. (1978), 'Cardinal Wolsey and the common weal' in Ives, E.W. *et al.*,
    (eds), *Wealth and power in Tudor England*.

Scarisbrick, J.J. (1984), *The Reformation and the English people* (Oxford).

Scarisbrick, J.J. (1997), *Henry VIII* (2nd ed., London).

Scattergood, John (ed.) (1983), *John Skelton: the complete English poems* (London).

Schofield, Roger (1988), 'Taxation and the political limits of the Tudor state' in Cross,
    C. *et al.* (eds), *Law and government under the Tudors*.

Scott, Brendan (2006), *Religion and Reformation in the Tudor diocese of Meath* (Dublin).

Scott-Thomson, G. (1923), *Lords lieutenant in the sixteenth century: a study in Tudor local
    administration* (London).

Shagan, Ethan (1999), 'Protector Somerset and the 1549 rebellions' in *English Historical
    Review*, cxiv.

Sharp, Buchanan (1980), *In contempt of all authority: rural artisans and riot in the west of
    England, 1586–1660* (Berkeley).

Sharp, Cuthbert (ed.) (1975), *Memorials of the rebellion of 1569* (1840), repr. ed. Robert
    Wood (Shotton).

Sharpe, Kevin (ed.) (1978), *Faction & parliament: essays on early Stuart history* (London).

Sharpe, Kevin (1989), 'The image of virtue: the court and household of Charles I,
    1625–42' in Sharpe, K., *Politics and ideas in early Stuart England: essays and studies*
    (London).

Sharpe, Kevin (1992), *The personal rule of Charles I* (New Haven and London).

Sheehan, Anthony (1990), 'Irish revenues and English subventions, 1559–1622' in
    Proceedings of the Royal Irish Academy, xc, sect. C.

Simms, Katharine (1987), *From kings to warlords: the changing political structure of Gaelic
    Ireland in the later middle ages* (Woodbridge).

Skene, W.F. (ed.) (1871–2), *J. de Fordun, Cronica Gentis Scotorum* (Edinburgh).

Slack, Paul (1988), *Poverty and policy in Tudor and Stuart England* (London).

Slack, Paul (1990), *The English poor law, 1531–1782* (London).

Slack, Paul (1990), *The impact of plague in Tudor and Stuart England* (Oxford).

Smith, A.H. (1974), *County and court: government and politics in Norfolk, 1558–1603*
    (Oxford).

Smith, D.L. (1994), *Constitutional royalism and the search for settlement, c.1640–1649*
    (Cambridge).

Smith, D.L. (1998), *A history of the modern British Isles, 1603–1707: the double crown*
    (Oxford).

Smith, D.L. (ed.) (2003), *Cromwell and the Interregnum* (Oxford).

[3 9 8]   Smout, T.C. (1985), *A history of the Scottish people, 1560–1830* (London).

Sotherton, Nicholas (1987), *The Commoyson in Norfolk 1549*, Yaxley, Susan (ed.) (Stibbard).

Spence, R.T. (1977), 'The pacification of the Cumberland borders, 1593–1628' in *Northern History*, xiii.

Spenser, Edmund (1970), *A view of the present state of Ireland* (ed.), Renwick, W.L. (Oxford).

Spreight, Helen (1996), 'Local government and the south-western rebellion of 1549' in *Southern History*, xviii.

Starkey, David (1985), *The reign of Henry VIII: personalities and politics* (London).

Starkey, David (ed.) (1987), *The English court from the Wars of the Roses to the Civil War* (London).

State Papers, Henry VIII (11 vols) (London, 1830–52).

Stater, V. (1991), 'War and the structure of politics: lieutenancy and the campaign of 1628' in Fissel, M.C. (ed.), *War and government in Britain*.

The statutes at large passed in the parliaments held in Ireland (20 vols) (Dublin, 1786–1801).

Stevenson, David (1977), *Revolution and counter-revolution in Scotland, 1644–5* (London).

Stevenson, David (1980), *Alasdair MacColla and the highland problem in the seventeenth century* (Edinburgh).

Stevenson, David (1981), *Scottish covenanters and Irish confederates* (Belfast).

Stevenson, David (1990), 'Cromwell, Scotland and Ireland' in Morrill, J. (ed.), *Oliver Cromwell and the English Revolution*.

Stewart, R.W. (1991), 'Arms and expeditions: the ordnance office and the assaults on Cadiz (1625) and the Isle of Rhé (1627)' in Fissel, M.C. (ed.), *War and government in Britain*.

Stone, Laurence (1972), *The causes of the English revolution, 1529–1642* (London).

Storey, R.L. (1968), *The reign of Henry VII* (London).

Storey, R.L. (1986), *The end of the house of Lancaster* (2nd ed., Gloucester).

Stoyle, Mark (2002), *West Britons: Cornish identities and the early modern British state* (Exeter).

Tawney, R.H. (1990), *Religion and the rise of capitalism* (London).

Thirsk, Joan (ed.) (1967), *The agrarian history of England and Wales Volume IV 1500–1640* (Cambridge).

Thirsk, Joan (1984), *The rural economy of England* (London).

Thomas, David (1983), 'Financial and administrative developments' in Tomlinson, H. (ed.), *Before the English Civil War*.

Thompson, J.A.F. (1965), *The later Lollards, 1414–1520* (Oxford).

Thomson, T. and Innes, C. (eds) (1814–72), *The acts of the parliaments of Scotland* (12 vols) (Edinburgh).

Thrush, A. (1991), 'Naval finance and the origins and development of ship money' in Fissel, M.C. (ed.), *War and government in Britain*.

Tighe, W.J. (1989), 'Elizabethan Herefordshire: Sir James Croft, his friends and his foes' in *Historical Journal*, xxxii.

Tittler, Robert and Jones, Norman (eds) (2004), *A companion to Tudor Britain* (Oxford).

Tomlinson, Howard (ed.) (1983), *Before the English Civil War* (London).

Treadwell, Victor (1966), 'The Irish parliament of 1569–71' in *Proceedings of the Royal Irish Academy*, lxv, sect. C.

Treadwell, Victor (1985), 'Sir John Perrot and the Irish parliament of 1585–6' in *Proceedings of the Royal Irish Academy*, lxxxv, sect. C.

Treadwell, Victor (1998), *Buckingham and Ireland, 1616–1628: a study in Anglo-Irish politics* (Dublin).

Tyacke, N. (1987), *Anti-Calvinists: the rise of English Arminianism, c. 1590–1640* (Oxford).

Underdown, David (1971), *Pride's Purge: politics in the Puritan revolution* (Oxford).

Walter, John and Wrightson, Keith (1976), 'Dearth and the social order in early modern England' in *Past & Present*, no. 72.

Walter, John (1985), 'A "rising of the people"? The Oxfordshire rising of 1596' in *Past & Present*, no. 107.

Walter, John and Schofield, Roger (eds) (1989), *Famine, disease and the social order in early modern society* (Cambridge).

Walter, John (1989), 'The social economy of dearth in early modern England' in Walter and Schofield (eds), *Famine, disease and the social order*.

Watts, John (1996), *Henry VI and the politics of kingship* (Cambridge).

Watts, S.J. (1975), *From border to middle shire: Northumberland, 1586–1625* (Leicester).

Wernham, R.B. (1966), *Before the Armada: the growth of English foreign policy, 1485–1588* (London).

Wernham, R.B. (1984), *After the Armada: Elizabethan England and the struggle for western Europe, 1588–1595* (Oxford).

Wheeler, S. (1995), 'Four armies in Ireland' in Ohlmeyer, J. (ed.), *Ireland from independence to occupation*.

White, N.B. (ed.) (1941), 'The annals of Dudley Loftus' in *Analecta Hibernica*, x.

White, N.B. (ed.) (1943), *Extents of Irish monastic possessions, 1540–1541* (Dublin).

Whiting, Robert (1989), *The blind devotion of the people: popular religion and the English Reformation* (Cambridge).

Whyte, I.D. (1995), *Scotland before the industrial revolution: an economic and social history c. 1050–c. 1750* (London).

Wilkinson, B. (1964), *Constitutional history of England in the fifteenth century* (London).

Williams, C.H. (ed.) (1967), *English Historical Documents, V: 1485–1558* (London).

Williams, Glanmor (1967), *Welsh Reformation essays* (Cardiff).

Williams, Glanmor (1979), *Religion, language and nationality in Wales* (Cardiff).

Williams, Glanmor (1987), *Recovery, reorientation and reform: Wales 1415–1642* (Oxford).

Williams, Glanmor (1992), *Wales and the Act of Union* (Bangor).

Williams, Glanmor (1993), *Renewal and Reformation: Wales c. 1415–1642* (Oxford).

Williams, Glanmor (1997), *Wales and the Reformation* (Cardiff).

Williams, Penry (1979), *The Tudor regime* (London).

Williams, Penry (1995), *The later Tudors: England, 1547–1603* (Oxford).

Williamson, A.H. (1982), 'Scotland, Antichrist and the invention of Great Britain' in Dwyer, J. *et al.* (eds), *New perspectives on the politics and culture of early modern Scotland*.

Wilson, Charles (1970), *Queen Elizabeth and the revolt of the Netherlands* (London).

Wolffe, B.P. (1964), 'Henry VII's land revenues and chamber finance' in *English Historical Review*, lxxix.

Wolffe, B.P. (1970), *The crown lands 1461–1536* (London).

Wolffe, B.P. (1972), 'The personal rule of Henry VI' in Chrimes, S.B. *et al.* (eds), *Fifteenth-century England*.

Wood, Andy (2002), *Riot, rebellion and popular politics in early modern England* (Basingstoke).

Woolrych, Austin (1986), *Commonwealth to Protectorate* (Oxford).

Woolrych, Austin (2002), *Britain in revolution, 1625–1660* (Oxford).

Worden, Blair (1974), *The Rump Parliament, 1648–53* (Cambridge).

Wormald, Jenny (1981), *Court, kirk and community: Scotland, 1470–1625* (London).

Wormald, Jenny (1983), 'James VI and I: two kings or one?' in *History*, lxviii.

Wormald, Jenny (1985), *Lords and men in Scotland: bonds of manrent, 1442–1603* (Edinburgh).

Wormald, Jenny (1991), *Mary queen of Scots, a study in failure* (London).

Wormald, Jenny (ed.) (1991), *Scotland revisited* (London).

Wormald, Jenny (1991), 'The house of Stewart and its realm' in Wormald, J. (ed.), *Scotland revisited*.

Wormald, Jenny (1995), 'Ecclesiastical vitriol: the kirk, the puritans and the future king of England' in Guy, J. (ed.) *The reign of Elizabeth I*.

Wrightson, Keith (2000), *Earthly necessities: economic lives in early modern Britain* (New Haven).

Wrigley, E.A. and Schofield, R.S. (1981), *The population history of England 1541–1871: a reconstruction* (London).

Youings, J.A. (1971), *The dissolution of the monasteries* (London).

Youings, J.A. (1979), 'The south-western rebellion of 1549' in *Southern History*, i.

Youings, J.A. (1984), *Sixteenth-century England* (London).

Young, J.R. (ed.) (1997), *Celtic dimensions of the British civil wars* (Edinburgh).

Young, M.B. (1984), 'The origins of the Petition of Right reconsidered further' in *Historical Journal*, xxvii.

INDEX